PROCESSING PEOPLE

cases in organizational behaviour

CONTRIBUTING AUTHORS

Arlene Kaplan Daniels
  Scientific Analysis Corporation, San Francisco, USA

Anthony J. Elger
  University of Warwick, England

Robert Fryer
  University of Warwick, England

Anne R. Edwards
  Monash University, Australia

Richard Hyman
  University of Warwick, England

John B. McKinlay
  Boston University, Mass., USA

Peter W. Musgrave
  Monash University, Australia

David Silverman
  Goldsmith's College, London, England

Kenneth A. Thompson
  The Open University, England

PROCESSING PEOPLE

cases in organizational behaviour

edited by

JOHN B. McKINLAY
Department of Sociology
Boston University

HOLT, RINEHART AND WINSTON
London · New York · Sydney · Toronto

Printed in Great Britain
by Unwin Brothers Limited
Old Woking, Surrey

CONTENTS

PREFACE

There can be little doubt that the growth and spread of complex formal organizations is one of the characteristics which distinguishes modern industrial society from earlier forms of social life. Various researchers have viewed this development with alarm, have cautioned against the "bureaucratic society" and have hailed the entrance of the "organizational revolution". Others have warned that if present trends continue, we will all be organizational creatures.

Of course, formal or complex organizations, total institutions, bureaucracies—call them what you will—are not new. The church, the military, government, etc., have, for countless ages, operated on more or less bureaucratic lines. While granting that organizations of some sort have been with us for a relatively long time, some observers suggest that in present times the characteristic form of organizations has changed somewhat, so that they pervade our lives in new ways. Today, in Western societies, most individuals are born within organizations, are raised and educated in them, spend the majority of their years employed by them, spend leisure time within them and, more often than not, die in them.

It appears that in post-industrial societies, key areas of social activity have been or are being taken over by bureaucracies and professional organizations. Moreover, increasingly, legal sanctions are being implemented to support the activity of organizations in areas of social life, which previously were not regarded as their legitimate domain. Prosecutions result if children do not attend schools, hospitalization if signs of "psychiatric disturbances" are displayed, and imprisonment for certain categories of social "deviance". Punitive legislation has been suggested as one way to cope with school truants or "drop outs", army "deserters" and even the chronically unemployed. Notice, in most cases, sanctions are applied or suggested for behavior which runs contrary to certain organizational practices (schools, army, welfare, etc.). Charismatic and traditional organizations, almost by definition, did not enjoy the support of such a body of law.

The idea for this symposium was first formulated after a request to the editor for some informal reaction to another text on formal organizations. While this latter text was a valuable source book at a general theoretical level, it lacked specificity with regard to particular organizations and issues. This book, in contrast, concerns itself with a fairly wide range of organizations which shape many important areas of our social life. The particular organizations considered include, among others, factories, churches, trade unions, universities, and prisons. In addition, two concluding chapters deal with the burgeoning literature on professionals in organizations, and clients in relation to organizations. The organizations selected for this volume are not intended to be representative of the range of possible organizations which daily impinge on our social lives. Clearly, if this was the aim, a much larger work would have to be commissioned so as to include, for example, hospitals, public welfare agencies, department stores, rehabilitation units, and the military. Of these, hospitals were considered for inclusion by the editor and publishers, and considerable effort was made to include a chapter on this subject. However, the absence of a separate chapter on this important organization is to a large extent compensated for by several contributions which employ and discuss findings from studies of hospitals.

Because there are so many books on, or related to, organizational theory, and because this volume differs in several important ways from almost all those presently available, some indication of the points of divergence should be given.

Most works on formal organizations share one or more of the following features. *First*, most traditional texts attempt a comprehensive coverage of the theoretical literature on all organizations or suggest that certain concepts and theories may be applicable to any organization. From such texts students often gain only a perfunctory acquaintance with a whole range of topics, little appreciation of certain theoretical and methodological subleties and the false impression that more order and coherence exist than is actually the case.

Rather than attempt to superficially cover a "representative" range of theoretical concerns, whose applicability to different organizational settings is undemonstrated, an attempt has been made in this book to introduce the reader to a variety of theoretical concerns *in relation to* a range of different organizations. No contributor has attempted to cover every aspect of the particular organization or area of activity under scrutiny, but each chapter has two main objectives: first, to introduce students to selected problems related to their area of concern; and, second, to intensify and deepen the grasp of certain core theoretical and empirical issues, especially as the editor felt that there were a number of theoretical concerns, which could be best discussed in relation to specific organizations. In this regard certain contributors were requested to direct particular attention to these issues.

In the *second* place, there are few volumes available which give separate and yet fairly detailed attention to the particular problems of different organizations. There are, of course, many independent case studies of factories, prisons, hospitals, mines, ships, etc. With each of these, however, the student of comparative organizations is typically faced with much reading and often considerable expense. By bringing together under one cover, a set of different theoretical perspectives on a range of quite different types of formal organizations, some progress should be made in bridging this gap.

Thirdly, most of the texts to date on formal organizations utilize data drawn from and employ concepts developed in the United States, and are prepared with a view to marketing primarily in that country. As a consequence, one is never quite sure whether the theories and concepts developed in these texts are applicable only to organizations in the United States, or may be generalized to other cultural settings. It is hoped that this symposium may fulfill a need for the discussion of organizations outside the United States; and with this in mind most contributors gave preference, wherever possible, to pertinent British literature. It is evident, from much of what follows, that this emphasis on British work was not always possible, but the material presented reflects fairly accurately the state of theory and research on both sides of the Atlantic. Hopefully, this text will acquaint those in the United States, interested in the study of comparative, organizational analysis, with some of the work being undertaken in Great Britain.

Fourthly, many texts on formal organizations are *either* written by one or sometimes two authors, *or* are collections of already published papers. In the editor's view, a symposium has certain advantages over both of these alternatives. On the one hand, it allows established authorities, or those actively researching in particular areas, to give a more definitive and up-to-date treatment than is usually possible when one person attempts an overview. On the other hand, it protects the student from having to read a series of warmed-up papers which were originally prepared for purposes other than student instruction. Of course, symposia have their disadvantages, principal among them being the difficulty of having to create conceptual unity and order material so that a sense of logic flows from one chapter to the next, and so that the reader is able to feel some satisfaction that he has read a book.

With this difficulty in mind, a word or two on the method of procedure for this volume may indicate how the editor attempted to resolve this problem. Before any chapter was drafted, I sent a letter to each contributor, describing the overall objectives and orientation of the symposium, outlining the contents and listing the other possible contributors. Each of the authors selected—some with international reputations—have a close acquaintance with the literature and the particular conceptual and empirical problems associated with the organization on which they were invited to contribute. On receipt of a firm commitment, detailed working notes were sent out with a view to ensuring thorough coverage and minimal repetitiveness and redundancy. Each contributor was also encouraged to espouse his or her own theoretical orientation. Hopefully, this strategy has suceeded in avoiding the erroneous conception that there is more order and agreement in the area of formal organizations than is actually the case.

The preparation of this text has been an education for the editor (and perhaps for the contributors), providing a unique opportunity for sharing common interests with colleagues whose specialist concerns sometimes varied widely. As each chapter really represents an individual foray into particular organizations or issues, the editor's primary task was to integrate and order the contributions into a coherent whole and to soften, as far as possible, any obtrusive stylistic differences. It should be emphasized, of course, that while responsibility for the organizations selected for this symposium rests solely with the editor, responsibility for the individual chapters must lie with the contributors.

It should be kept in mind that any text on a growing area of professional concern—and interest in formal organizations continues to increase—is in the nature of a report of work in progress and the state of the field. Hopefully, this symposium achieves some kind of balance between established concepts and theories, and areas in which there is still considerable uncertainty and debate.

Department of Sociology   John B. McKinlay
Boston University
Boston, Massachusetts 02215

KENNETH A. THOMPSON

RELIGIOUS ORGANIZATIONS

Kenneth A. Thompson *read sociology at Leicester University and subsequently received a doctorate from Oxford University. After teaching sociology at Rutgers University in New Jersey and Smith College, Massachusetts, he moved to the Open University in England where he is presently senior lecturer in Sociology. His main publications include:* Bureaucracy and Church Reform *(1970);* Sociological Perspectives *(edited with J. Tunstall, 1971);* People and Organizations *(edited with G. Salaman, 1973); as well as a translation from the French of Georges Gurvitch's* The Social Frameworks of Knowledge *(with M. A. Thompson, 1971). His research interests are in the fields of the sociology of religion and organizations. He is Chairman of a team of academics and BBC producers engaged in the production of a course on organizations for the Open University and is also co-director of a research project on the organization of international news agencies.*

All science proceeds by classifying and measuring the components of the phenomenon that it is studying, and by accounting for the development of similarities and dissimilarities between different examples of that phenomenon. When these basic procedures have been successfully standardized it then becomes possible to develop and test general theories which cover all cases that possess a set of shared characteristics.

In the field of organization studies a general theory would only be possible once these preliminaries had been accomplished. As things stand at present, despite some piece-meal progress, these preliminary stages have not yet been negotiated. Much work remains to be done on definitions, classification and measurement of the components of complex organizations in general, and in differentiating the various families or types of organization. What we have are: (a) individual case studies and comparisons of a small number of roughly similar organizations (inevitably dependent, therefore, on relatively crude methodologies, such as typologizing and dichotomizing), which have the advantage of providing at least a partial, empirical explanation of a real entity; and (b) broad-ranging and poorly substantiated "theories" about organizations in general, which make up for their lack of empirical data by their imagination and brilliance.

Perhaps more than most substantive areas in the field of organization studies, the study of religious organizations has suffered from these limitations. Most of the empirical research has taken the form of individual case studies, or rough comparisons, utilizing the methods of typologizing and dichotomizing.[1] In the absence of standardized sociological data on the structure and functioning of

religious organizations, theorizing has depended more on insight than information.

Despite the paucity of precise, quantitative studies of church organization, it is a field that has much to offer students of organizational behaviour. Most studies of other organizations have tended to develop formal models of organizational *functioning*, which is understandable (if not altogether satisfactory) in view of the fact that the majority of those organizations are predominantly "instrumental" or "utilitarian" in character. Business firms, armies, government departments, even hospitals and schools, are largely concerned with attaining a limited number of explicit goals in the most efficient manner. Organization theory, as a result, has tended to concentrate on such topics as processes of decision-making over a limited period, or else in explaining systems of communication, authority structures, and other formal characteristics. What is less evident in such studies is an interest in the *organic* evolution of an organization (the historical or developmental perspective), the value system and symbolic-meaning system of an organization (the "anthropological"[2] or cultural perspective), and the struggles for power, status and control within and between groups (the political dimension).

The sociology of religion has made some significant contributions to the study of these latter topics in recent years. The reasons for its strength in these areas are not hard to find. Firstly, the historical and developmental perspective comes naturally to students of religious organization because of the long life of most major religious bodies in contrast to that of other organizations such as business firms, and also the abundant historical data on religious groups. Secondly, perhaps more than most organizations, religious bodies have a strong ideological commitment and concern that extends to the point where even the rationality, according to which they evaluate their organization, may stress criteria of symbolic-appropriateness rather than of calculable efficiency. Finally, the strong ideological concern with the promulgation and propagation of certain values has produced a superabundance of conflict within and between religious groups. Struggles for power and status have been a prominent feature of religious hierarchies, and as one of the oldest professions the clergy provide rich material for the study of professionalization in its interaction with bureaucratization.

The developmental perspective

What has been referred to as the "organic" evolution of an organization needs to be viewed within a developmental and comparative framework. It involves research into historical origins of organizations, the tracing of growth stages, and the comparison of different types of organizations with regard to these factors. We will see later that investigation of the developmental process can be fruitfully combined with the study of the ideology and symbolic-meaning systems of organizations. In this way we may arrive at an understanding of the basic nature of a particular organization and its capacity for adaptation. This would furnish us with the data necessary to construct theories that can predict the most likely future developments. The purpose of the comparative approach is to make the theory more general in its scope, and this entails making precise comparisons between different types of organizations and plotting their typical responses to various types of circumstances.

The relevance of the developmental perspective for organization studies was underlined in a comment of Selznick, who noted that:

> The study of institutions is in some ways comparable to the clinical study of personality. It requires a genetic and developmental approach, an emphasis on historical origins and growth stages. There is a need to see the enterprise as a whole and to see how it is transformed as new ways of dealing with a changing environment evolve. As in the case of personality, effective diagnosis depends upon locating the special problems that go along with a particular character structure; and we can understand the character better when we see it as the product of self-preserving efforts to deal with inner impulses and external demands. In both personality and institutions "self-preservation" means more than bare organic or material survival. Self-preservation has to do with the maintenance of basic identity, with the integrity of a personal or institutional "self".
>
> Our problem is to discover the characteristic ways in which *types* of institutions respond to *types* of circumstances.[3]

To take one example of this developmental perspective, a study that the author undertook of long-term developments in the Church of England's organization hypothesized that throughout the process of organizational change there was an overriding concern with "pattern maintenance"—in the last resort highest priority was given to preserving a particular amalgam of characteristics that could be said to constitute the organization's basic identity. Consequently, the study paid greater attention to the symbolic-meaning system and self-perception of the organization than is normally the case in organization studies. But the hypothesis also specified that, whilst the final result at each stage would receive the impress of the basic institutional character and identity of the Church, it would be distilled through the various thought forms and modes of organization prevalent in the larger society in each historical period, and it would be affected by the outcome of struggles for power, status and control within and between groups, and so reflect the relative strengths of different interest groups at the same time.[4]

The basic organizational character of the Church of England was taken to be that of an Established Church or *ecclesia* type of religious body. This leads one into one of the best charted territories in the field of the sociology of religion—the use of typologies to classify and compare religious organizations and to suggest typical sequences of development. To characterize the Church of England as an *ecclesia* is to rank it on a continuum of types of religious body: cult, sect, institutionalized (or established) sect, denomination, *ecclesia*, world church. This is an elaboration of the pioneer distinction made by Weber, and popularized by Troeltsch, between church and sect. Troeltsch stated the dichotomy as follows:

> The Church is that type of organization which is overwhelmingly conservative, which to a certain extent accepts the secular order, and dominates the masses; in principle, therefore, it is universal, i.e. it desires to cover the whole life of humanity. The sects, on the other hand, are comparatively small groups; they aspire after personal inward perfection, and they aim at a direct personal fellowship between members of each group. From the very beginning, therefore, they are forced to organize themselves in small groups, and to renounce the idea of dominating the world.[5]

An interesting feature of this important typology is that it combines both internal structural features and a corresponding stance towards the external environment of the organization. Although, as we will see, the typology itself has been criticized and elaborated, its ambitious and imaginative attempt to embrace these two sets of features has a great deal to contribute to modern organization studies.

Yinger was one of the more recent sociologists to criticize the typology on the grounds that a simple dichotomy was inadequate to describe the full range of reality and consequently he produced the previously mentioned six-step classification based on two criteria—the degree of inclusiveness of the members of the society, and the degree of attention paid to the function of social integration as contrasted with the function of satisfying personal needs.[6] Thus, for example, the world church is the type of religious body which is relatively successful in supporting the integration of society, whilst at the same time satisfying, by its pattern of beliefs and observances, many of the personal needs of individuals on all levels of society, and so it is able to combine church tendencies with many of those that are often satisfied by sects. However, in heterogeneous societies this balance is likely to be achieved only very rarely and is not likely to be maintained for very long. The best example of the criteria of a world church being fulfilled, in Yinger's estimation, occurred in the thirteenth-century Roman Catholic Church. The *ecclesia*, like the world church, reaches out to the boundaries of the society, and seeks to include all classes, but it lacks the supra-nationality of the world church which can put itself above the classes of any one society. The *ecclesia* is less successful than the universal church in incorporating sect tendencies. It becomes so well adjusted to the dominant elements of a society that the needs of many of its adherents, particularly from the lower classes, are frustrated. It is more successful in reinforcing the personality needs of individuals of all classes. The denomination is a larger body than a sect; it has accommodated to most of the standards of the secular culture, and is organized as a body independent of the State, and living in a competitive relationship with other similar bodies, whilst respecting their freedom.

One typical developmental sequence suggested by studies using one version or other of the church–sect typology is that there is a tendency for sects, which begin as small, exclusive groups of the elect, standing in opposition to the accepted values of the wider society, to develop into denominations.[7]

Many scholars have taken this to be the typical life cycle of religious bodies—a process by which cults originate, develop into sects, and then change into denominations, sometimes emerging from the process as churches. This was Niebuhr's theory according to which sects develop educational and disciplinary agencies in order to make the children of first generation sect members conform to its beliefs and customs. The second generation holds its convictions less fervently than the founders whose beliefs were forged in the heat of conflict. The sect's administration tends to become more like that of the denominations, with more formalized leadership functions replacing the personalized control of charismatic leadership. Niebuhr's conclusion was that sectarian organization can endure in pure form for only one generation.

Moberg has provided the best summary of the claims made for this theory of a natural life cycle of religious bodies:

> Christianity originated as a despised Jewish cult, grew into a persecuted sect, developed into a somewhat tolerated denomination, and suddenly at the time of Emperor Constantine I emerged as a victorious church. Perhaps each major Christian body is destined to follow a similar sequence of development with repeated splintering of smaller sects aimed at reform.[8]

The classical illustration of this process is that of Methodism. Early Methodism stipulated that an experience of salvation was necessary for membership; primary group relations predominated with extensive practice of mutual aid; lay leadership was organized along sectarian lines.[9] However, even Methodism cannot be taken as a pure case of development along the sect–church continuum as it possessed some church-like features from the beginning due to its particular origins within the Church of England. For example, the conference of preachers was bureaucratically organized along lines similar to those of the Church of England, especially in the Wesleyan branch and particularly in America. A more obviously deviant case of development along the continuum from sect to church was that of Mormonism. It began with many sectarian traits, basing its membership on exclusiveness and voluntary election. Its early charismatic leadership became institutionalized in a set of offices which, because of the circumstances of its migration to a large expanse of western land and the nature of its doctrines, resulted in an authoritarian structure of central government. But Mormonism cannot be defined as sect, denomination or church. It has been suggested that in fact it is a mixture of all three, and that, because it has developed as a subculture with its own homeland within the larger nation, it has moved from being a sect to what might be called an *incipient nationality*.[10]

Despite these difficulties with regard to the thesis of a common life history of religious movements based on a movement along the sect–church continuum, it still offers many insights into religious organization. One aspect that the thesis illuminates is that of the differences that exist in degree of flexibility of church and sect forms of organization. Wilson has pointed out that, whilst all religious movements are affected in their organization by a special quality of religious ideology—its absoluteness—sects experience this more than denominations or churches. Sects are singularly lacking in the capacity for adaptability and flexibility of organization. Even sects which were clearly dying, such as the Shakers and the Girlingites, had few possibilities for action to prevent the process.[11] In order for a sect to survive more than one generation it has to move some distance along the sect–church continuum, if only to the extent of attaining some of the church-like capacity for adaptation of organization on the grounds of efficiency or economy.

Most distinctively sociological insights into religious organization have come from the study of sects and the thesis of a typical "sect to denomination" process of development. A great deal of light is thrown on the interaction of religious ideology and organization by determining just what factors in the organization and circumstances of sects promote or retard development towards a denominationed structure. Wilson has delineated certain subtypes of sect and has identified crucial elements in sect organization which are focal points of tension.[12] His hypothesis is that sects experience different types of tension which vary according to their own constellation of values, as well as to the circumstances of their origin. He shows that it is in responses to such tensions and attempts to manage them that we can expect to find the genesis of processes which cause some sects to develop into denominations, others to wither, some to be exterminated, some to fragment, and some to remain, over several generations, as sects. What he terms "conversionist" sects seem most subject to the denominationalizing tendency, whilst the "adventist" and "introversionist" types appear to be best protected from this development. The "gnostic" sect is less clearly protected, "but its distinctive ideology performs in some measure the functions which social insulating mechanisms perform for other types".[13]

Sect organization contains the same basic components as denominations and churches, although those components are less developed at the supra-local levels. Any autonomous religious organization includes procedures for the following activities:

1. agencies which arrange meetings or disseminate teachings;
2. persons invested with the right to call meetings, to supervise and control them;
3. decision-making processes with regard to instrumental concerns such as the ownership or hire of property, and the maintenance of premises;
4. agencies charged with maintaining essential agreement of belief and practice, however minimal;
5. arrangements for accepting new members;
6. procedures for determining the worthiness of new entrants and for maintaining discipline;
7. socialization of new members;
8. regulation of the sect's external relations with other bodies.[14]

The shift in a sect's organization towards a denomination type occurs when one or more of these components undergoes elaboration and formalization. Thus conversionist sects, such as those of orthodox fundamentalism or pentecostalism, centre their activity on evangelism and tend to develop a hierarchy of offices in which some officials direct campaigns of recruitment and others are concerned with the socialization and maintenance of the converted. They are distrustful of denominational organization, and yet, of all the sects, they are the most susceptible to this type of organization. Adventist sects, such as Jehovah's Witnesses and Christadelphians tend to discount organization because of the imminence of the advent which will overturn the present order. Weakness in organization often leads to the dissipation of such sects or, as among the Christadelphians, to schism. Where elaborate organization does evolve, as with the Jehovah's Witnesses, it is specialized in one function only—that of publishing the message—while other religious groups are regarded with hostility or suspicion. Introversionist sects are typified by reliance on inner illumination; little evangelism is undertaken, and organization is considered unnecessary. Frequently, however, informal power structures develop, as in the Quakers, the Exclusive Brethren and the Amana

Society. Gnostic sects, emphasizing some special body of knowledge of an esoteric kind (as in Christian Science and New Thought sects), are likely to adopt structures more in keeping with modern rationally ordered enterprises than with traditional ecclesiastical patterns. Thus Christian Science has a mixed pattern of secular and religious organization, including a board of directors.

Although most modern sects tend to develop some sort of centralized organization, however minimal, this does not automatically transform them into denominations. Indeed, central control may be effectively employed to prevent such trends, as with Jehovah's Witnesses.[15] The crucial question is whether the elite is specially trained for an institutionally differentiated role—that is, whether its function becomes that of a professional ministry.

It is clear, however, that movement from the sect end of the continuum towards that of denomination and church is not the only developmental sequence, and that there can also be a development in the opposite direction along the continuum.[16] Fürstenberg showed that there had been such a developmental sequence in Germany. Corresponding to the world church was the *Bruderschafts-kirche*, the original type of church organization of pre-Reformation days; for the *ecclesia* he used the terms *Volkskirche* and *Staatskirche*, the kind of religious body that emerged after the Reformation and which was dependent on the State; the equivalent of the denomination was the *Verbandskirche*, a voluntary association, politically independent and institutionalized around its own doctrinal and ecclesiological position. The development had been in the direction of the *Verbandskirche* as the Church's relationship with the State was called into question and as society became increasingly pluralistic.[17]

Parsons has maintained that this process is the predictable, organizational response to the modern pluralist society in which the religious and secular aspects of life are differentiated although not necessarily separated.[18] Other writers on religious organizations, such as Gustafson and Lee, have gone on to suggest that in spite of differences in formal polity, denominations tend to assume the same organizational shape.[19] Further research, however, is tending to disclose variations in the organization of bodies which have come from different ends of the church–sect continuum and which still contain some elements of their former position.[20] Thus charismatic leadership may be more prevalent in a sect-originated denomination, and traditional leadership in church- (*or ecclesia-*) originated denominations. In a sect, theology presses immediately on polity, either to minimize the degree of formal polity, or to closely regulate its nature. Consequently, its organization has few or no bureaucratic characteristics. In the sect-originated denomination, the correspondence between theology and polity is greatest at the congregational level, but less at the extra-parochial levels. National organization tends to grow up in a vacuum to meet pressing instrumental needs, hence the only authority at the national level is of the rational-pragmatic type described by Harrison in his study of the development of denominational organization in the American Baptist Convention.[21]

In a religious body that holds to an *ecclesia*-like self-identity, such as the Church of England, although it may take on many of the characteristics of a denomination, there remain substantial elements of its traditional inclusive aspirations and structures (as, for example, the territorial parish system). It also tends to maintain a relatively heterogeneous membership, and a more complex mixture of theological and ecclesiological principles than denominations of the sect-originated type. Consequently, its most persistent problem is often that of balancing differing groups or parties. Because the spectrum of doctrinal and organizational principles is wider within such a body, there is a tendency to resist systematic rationalization both in theology and in organization. Accumulation of power and authority in any one section would be dangerous because it could easily lead to the exclusion of other sections or principles and so disrupt the broad coalition on which its cherished identity rests.

This discussion of different sequences of development along the church–sect continuum could be useful in suggesting relevant hypotheses as to the typical problems that face religious organizations of various types. One should also caution against assuming that because most large religious bodies in modern societies are tending to develop the characteristics of the denominational type of religious organization, they must all be facing the same set of problems (and requiring the same solutions). In fact, careful comparisons between religious organizations developing in different directions along the church–sect continuum reveal some quite different sets of problems, as well as some that are shared. Thus in a sect-originated denomination the main problems revolve around the dichotomy between a theological and political commitment to congregational and even individual autonomy, and the need for efficient regional and national organization. In the case of an *ecclesia*, traditionally supported in various ways by the State, when state administrative and financial aid is withdrawn, there is a painful readjustment in the course of which it develops its organization increasingly in the direction of greater autonomy. This innovation in structure affects most immediately the norms of operation of the organization, but it also leads to a reassessment of the values which those norms embody, and of the belief system which makes those values viable and rational. Structural reform in an *ecclesia*, therefore, gives rise to acute theological party conflict, especially if the new structure is influenced by the methods and patterns of organization employed in secular government and commerce, where a prime requirement is for explicit definition of goals. The result is that party divisions are exacerbated for a time and the former compromise, on which the balance of power rested, is upset. Authority is denied the new patterns of organization on the grounds that they symbolize values inappropriate for a religious body, and the criticisms carry greater weight than usual in a period when some church parties are likely to be concentrating their efforts on reaffirming the institution's autonomous values as it adjusts to its new position in society.[22]

Nevertheless, despite these often neglected differences between the sect-originated and *ecclesia*-originated denominations, it is possible to suggest a set of hypotheses and theories as to the lines of development common to both. Harrison has summarized some of these developments in American denominations in thirty-four hypotheses and five theories, of which the following are a sample:

Hypothesis 1 One of the basic objectives of the official polities of all the major American Protestant denominations seems to be to minimize the authority of ecclesiastical officers.

Hypothesis 2 At the functional level there is no discernable difference between episcopal and non-episcopal denominations as regards democratic or authoritarian tendencies.

Harrison maintains that this hypothesis is supported by a developed sociological theory.

Theory 1 "Every institution, religious or secular, requires effective organization and leadership with sufficient formal authority or informal power to propel the institution towards its goal achievement. Therefore, if the formal polity of a religious group does not provide its leaders with sufficient authority to fulfill their assigned responsibilities the leaders will be forced to ignore the limitations of their system of polity and obtain the informal power to gain their legitimated goals."[23]

Hypothesis 3 Because goal achievement in modern technological society is achieved through bureaucratic organization with rationally defined lines of authority, and since most Protestant denominations are not traditionally oriented in this fashion, all the denominations are finding it necessary to redefine their formal polity. The formerly congregationally organized groups are the most drastically affected.

Hypothesis 4 The episcopal type of polity offers the most highly rationalized structure, in that it can most effectively attain organization goals that depend on specialized technical knowledge, swift and informed decisions, and leaders who can act with prompt and effective authority. On the basis of this, it can be further hypothesized that this will be the type of structure favoured in church reunion schemes.

Theory 2 All denominations are developing in the direction of a similar polity.

A concluding hypothesis is that, as systems of power and authority in the denominations come to resemble each other, differences of opinion in the realm of organizations are more likely to be generated by a preference for different symbols, traditional terminologies, and interpretative formulae rather than by any significant operational or functional differences.[24] Harrison points out that symbols are formative and determinative forces that are no less powerful than the operational forces, and that functional analysis fails in its task when it is claimed that beliefs and symbols obtain no functional significance. This brings us to the second area, mentioned above, in which the sociology of religion has much to contribute to organizational studies, that of symbolic-meaning systems.

The cultural perspective

What is here loosely termed the "cultural perspective" includes within its purview the symbols and the types of rationality employed by religious bodies in evaluating their organizations. Obviously these factors are important in any organization, and organizational theory neglects them at its peril, but they are of particular importance in the case of religious organizations for three reasons. *Firstly*, they are important because religious bodies have a strong ideological character in that they are concerned with the promulgation and propagation of certain values. *Secondly*, a religious group is always fundamentally a cultural organization in the sense that the end is achieved, at least in part, in the *process* of meeting with others, while in a utilitarian or instrumental association it is the *product* that is directly significant.[25] *Thirdly*, religious groups are probably unique in the extent to which their basic character causes them to favour the rationality of symbolic-appropriateness over one of a logico-experimental type. This last point requires some further elucidation before examining some examples of sociology of religion research that have explored the relationship and correspondence between religious symbols and models of organization.

Parson's discussion of different criteria of logical action provides some indication as to why religious groups tend to favour the criterion of symbolic-appropriateness over logico-experimental criteria. He points out that the ultimate ends of intrinsic means–end chains of reasoning must have an empirical location, because if the end is transcendental it cannot be said that the means employed are ineffective, but only that there is no criterion for determining logico-experimentally, whether the means are effective or not.[26] Logico-experimental criteria can only be applied on the intermediate, temporal level below that of any point of transcendental reference. In religious organizations, however, especially in those of the *ecclesia* and denomination types, extensive accommodation of such intermediate goals and values is always occurring and inviting the charge of "compromising" with the secular, from dissatisfied groups appealing to transcendental goals and values.

In examining the correspondences between religious symbols and the models of organization favoured by different religious groups, it is useful to bear in mind this discussion of the relation of transcendental ends to means, and especially to the means–end chain of reasoning. As Parsons explains:

> There seem to be two logical possibilities. First, a given transcendental end, like eternal salvation, may be held by the actor to imply one or more ultimate empirical ends as a necessary means to it . . . [But] the "theory" cannot be entirely logico-experimental, since one element at least, the transcendental end itself, is not observable even after the action. Hence not only, as in the case of an ultimate empirical end, is the end itself given, but the link between the last empirical link in the means–end chain and the ultimate transcendental end is nonlogical, since a scientifically verifiable theory can establish an intrinsic relation only between entities both of which are observable.[27]

Thus the setting of a compromise, temporal and empirical goal by church executives facilitates the adoption of formally rational organization, and can be tested by logico-experimental criteria.[28] But the empirical goal itself cannot be evaluated in its relation to the transcendental goals by a similar means–end chain of reasoning. However, Parsons does suggest a second logical possibility for relating transcendental ends to means:

Secondly, a transcendental end may be pursued directly without the intervention of an empirical end and an intrinsic means–end chain leading up to it. In so far the means–end relation cannot by definition be intrinsically rational. The question then arises whether it is merely arbitrary or there is a selective standard of the choice of means involved . . . there is at least one alternative selective standard, what has been called the symbolic. The term the "symbolic means–end relationship" will be used whenever the relation of means and ends can conveniently be interpreted by the observer as involving a standard of selection of means according to "symbolic appropriateness" that is, a standard of the order of the relation of symbol and meaning, not of cause and effect.[29]

There are two possibilities, therefore, for logically evaluating the relation between transcendental ends and the means employed in a religious organization. They are illustrated in the criticisms which church members often level at their religious organizations for becoming "bureaucratic" (in the derogatory sense). On the one hand, they are often criticisms of the empirical goals that have been adopted, and on the other hand they can be a sweeping condemnation of the symbolic-inappropriateness of the organizational form as judged by particular theological ideals about organization.

An example of these two sources of evaluation—the interposed empirical goal and symbolic-appropriateness—can be found in a discussion by Dillistone of the reasons for the preference that many modern Christians have for the "organic" model of organization:

Thus at a time when there is much dissatisfaction with over-specialization it is natural for men to turn back nostalgically to the middle ages when society seems to have been remarkably integrated and when every section seems to have found its own particular function to fulfil within the life of the unified whole. To these two attractions of a general kind must be added the particular fascination which this view holds for the Christian because of its relation to the New Testament conception of the Body, Divinely originated and sustained, then organic structures and categories must be of peculiar importance to Christian theologians and sociologists.[30]

There has been little empirical research in the sociology of religion that has dealt explicitly with the correspondences between certain religious symbols and the models of organization favoured by religious groups. However, it is possible to make some theoretical connections between the two sets of data that do exist— that on religious symbols and theology, and that on models and theories of organization. Two typologies of a symbolic type have been offered by Paul S. Minear and H. Richard Niebuhr. Minear has provided a selection of the main images of the Church in the New Testament, each of which emphasize a particular dimension that has been favoured by a religious group at some time. They are: (1) the People of God (stressing the historical dimension); (2) the New Creation (stress on the cosmic dimension); (3) the Fellowship in the Faith (emphasizing the personal factor); (4) the Body of Christ (which favours the corporate dimension, as we have seen).[31] A second typology can be derived from Neibuhr's discussion of different perceptions of the mission of Christ in the World. These are: (a) Christ against culture; (b) Christ the fulfilment of culture; (c) Christ above culture; (d) Christ and culture coexist; (e) Christ the transformer of culture.[32]

Peter Rudge, an Australian priest and student of ecclesiastical administration, is one of the few practitioners in the field of the sociology of religious organizations to attempt to systematically relate such typologies to a corresponding set of theories and models of organization.[33] Rudge maintains that it is possible to transpose some of the main points of sociological theories and models of organization into their theological counterparts. For example, conception of the organization would correspond to theology of the church, function of the leader to theology of the ministry, estimate of man to theology of man, and relation of the organization to the environment corresponds to theology of the church in society.

A typology of five major theories of leadership and organization can be constructed from current literature on the subject. They are: the Traditional, Charismatic, Classical (bureaucratic or mechanistic), Human Relations, and Systemic (or organic). The typology is a conflation of two sets of theories. The traditional, charismatic and classical positions are basically those developed by Max Weber in his discussion of the typical forms of administration that accompany the three main types of legitimate authority—traditional, charismatic, and rational-legal. The human relations and systemic theories have been largely developed in industrial management theory (which has also further developed Weber's classical bureaucratic theory).[34]

The *traditional* theory rests on Weber's definition, according to which a system of imperative authority is called "traditional" if legitimacy is claimed for it and believed, on the basis of the sanctity of the order and the attendant powers of control as they have been handed down from the past, and have always existed.[35] He distinguished three subtypes of administration: gerontocracy, patriarchalism and patrimonialism. The characteristics of this type of organization that have significance for organization studies are its methods of recruitment—loyalty to a chief, favouritism and depotism; and its methods of remuneration—maintenance within the household, allowance in kind, the right to use resources in return for services, appropriation of specific incomes or fees and the granting of benefices.

The *charismatic* type of authority derives from "a certain quality of an individual personality by virtue of which he is set apart from ordinary men and treated as endowed with supernatural, superhuman, or at least specifically exceptional powers or qualities".[36] The form of organization that attaches to such an authority is best typified by the band of disciples. The charismatic leader seems to be engaged in pursuing an intuition, and operates independently of any constituted office. There is a certain degree of randomness and unpredictability compared with the stability of traditional organization.

The *classical* theory of organization derives from Weber's description of the process by which charismatic and traditional sources of authority were steadily giving way to rational-legal authority in the modern world. He believed that modern Western organization could be characterized as possessing legal authority with a bureaucratic administration; it involved the exercise of control by the occupants of legally sanctioned offices on the basis of factual knowledge, which gave it the dual nature of rational-legal authority.[37] An organization administered on such lines is committed to striving for technical efficiency, precision of operation, control of experts, speed, continuity of policy, and an optimal return for the labour and money expended.

Human relations theory emphasizes the personal element in organizations over against the rather mechanistic picture of organizations suggested by classical theory. It also focuses on informal relations rather than the formal structure of organization. Its instigator was Mayo and the Hawthorne Experiments of the 1930s.[38] It directed attention to small group relationships, informal norms and sanctions, participative decision-making, and group dynamics in general. In some aspects it represents the influence of democratic theory on administration.

In terms of relationships between superior and subordinate, the classical and human relations theories may be regarded either as dichotomous, or simply as representing opposite ends of a continuum.[39] Warren G. Bennis has characterized the two extremes as "organizations without people" and "people without organizations".[40] As far as proponents of systemic theory are concerned, both classical and human relations theories go astray in focusing their attention on the internal relationship between superior and subordinate as the major determinant of organizational health. The systemic theory concentrates on adaptation of an organization to a fast-changing environment. Whereas classical theory produces a model of organization designed for mass, homogeneous and stable conditions, systemic theory lies at the other end of the continuum, favouring complete flexibility and innovation.[41]

Despite its derivation from the organic analogy, systemic theory owes its present popularity to the influence of cybernetics on modern thought. In the computer system there is a built-in self-regulating device (a "homeostat") by means of which the appropriate interaction with the environment is achieved in relation to the goals that are set. The computer makes the decision; but it cannot itself provide the goals nor acquire the information about the outside world. Transposed into managerial terms, the system within which the decisions are made is the organization; the task of management is to interpret the environment to the organization and to set its goals, and then to facilitate the decision-making process within the whole system so that there is a continuing and instantaneous rapport with the external world and a consistent focus on the purpose of the organization.[42]

Rudge suggests that correspondences can be found between these theories and models of organization and the symbols and models of theology. Thus, Minear's selection of images of the Church in the New Testament seems to correspond at some points with at least four of the theories of organization. The image of the People of God corresponds to the traditional theory of organization; the image of the New Creation corresponds to the charismatic theory; the image of the Fellowship in the Faith corresponds to human relations theory; the image of the Body of Christ corresponds to the systemic theory. It is interesting to note that no New Testament image corresponds to the classical theory with its emphasis on formal rationality, specialized division of labour, and relationships based on observance of written rules.[43] We will see later that this has important repercussions on clergy attitudes towards certain developments in denominational organization, especially where a bureaucratic definition of their role fails to correspond to any theology of ministry that is symbolically-appropriate by reason of its congruence with one of these images of the Church.

These suggestions for a systematic analysis of the different modes of perceiving and evaluating religious organizations (the cultural perspective) could eventually be combined with insights gained from the developmental perspective and the political dimension to provide a general theory of religious organization. Thus developmental sequences along the church–sect continuum might correspond to changes in the mode of perceiving and evaluating the organization in some determinate way. A likely hypothesis which could be deduced is that the charismatic type of organization would most closely fit the cult. Some sects would also fit this type of organization, although "established" sects,[44] especially, might begin to combine elements of the human relations model (particularly those with a largely middle class membership).

The denomination increasingly takes on the characteristics found in the classical bureaucratic type of organization, although the sect-originated, and the denomination with a more democratic (or congregationalist) ecclesiology, are more likely to include elements of the theory and practice of the human relations type. The *ecclesia* will tend to exhibit a traditional type of organization. The systemic, or organic, type of organization is largely a theoretical ideal in that it seeks to transcend such dichotomies as arise between the human relations approach to organization (maximum involvement of all members in decision-making) and the other three approaches (which represent different attempts to specialize decision-making), and the theological dichotomies between parity of all believers and specialized ministries. Despite its idealist nature, however, it plays an important role in many religious reform movements.[45]

Most sociologists who have studied religious organizations have concentrated on tracing developments along a simplified version of this typology. They have used Ferdinand Tönnies' distinction between *Gemeinschaft* and *Gesellschaft* types of organization.[46] These correspond roughly to the traditional and classical bureaucratic types respectively. The former refers to the natural community based on personal and diffuse ties; the latter is a rationally constructed organization based on contractual relationships. Francis has examined the development of religious orders in terms of this typology and showed that the familial, *Gemeinschaft* character of early monasticism had gradually given way to highly rationalized orders of a *Gessellschaft* type.[47] A Catholic sociologist, Greeley, has summarized recent developments in that Church as a movement from *Gemeinschaft* to *Gesellschaft*, and contends that just as the Catholic Church is getting something of a late start in its transition into the modern world, it will travel the road much more quickly than most other institutions. According to Greeley, it will tend to evolve much more quickly the post-*Gesellschaft* forms which modern man seeks in order to maintain some of the advantages and supports of *Gemeinschaft* society in a *Gesellschaft* world. Greeley seems to be predicting that the modern Church will quickly move beyond the rigidities of the classical bureaucratic type of organization so typical of other modern organizations, and eventually combine the best of both the human relations and systemic models. It is his belief that modern man looks to the Church to provide the advantages of both *Gemeinschaft* and *Gesellschaft*:

> He wishes to enjoy warm, intimate support of *Gemeinschaft* at the same time as he enjoys the freedom, and rationality, and the technological flexibility of a *Gesellschaft* world. Modern man wishes to put aside irrelevant myths and the obsolescent sacred symbols of the past but only so he might devise relevant and exciting new sacred symbols. Modern man wishes to put aside the primary groups in which his grandfathers were imprisoned and replace them with primary groups which enable him to enjoy even greater personal development and freedom. Modern man wants Community in the midst of his Associations.[48]

Although this statement comes from a sociologist, nothing could better illustrate our earlier observation that symbols are formative and determinative forces no less powerful than the operational forces in religious organizations. Although we need more studies of the structure and functioning of religious organizations along the lines laid down by the various organization theories, we should also pay more attention to the fact that organizations are judged not only for their efficiency, but also for their symbolic-appropriateness. Such considerations are essential for making sense of the bitter conflict that often seems to accompany attempts to change even quite minor parts of a religious organization. To take one example, the century of bitter party strife that ensued when the Church of England began reforming its organization in the 1830s is only explicable when it is shown that reforms were evaluated not just in efficiency terms, but also for their symbolic-appropriateness. It soon becomes clear that the symbols employed by the different church parties reflected their concern for different system problems (such as coexistence with the State to preserve the Establishment, or restoration of autonomous theological principles), and so it was not surprising that their evaluations of the reforms differed so widely.[49]

The political dimension

Just what is meant by the political dimension in organization studies is best brought out by discussing the differences between a cultural system (the subject of the last section) and a social system, and by listing some of the more relevant topics included in that dimension.

Amitai Etzioni has pointed out that many of the models of organization which are employed focus mainly on the attainment of goals, and that this is quite natural because the goals give organizational activity its orientation and legitimation. However, goals, as norms, or sets of meanings depicting target states, are cultural entities, while organizations, as systems of coordinated activities of more than one actor, are social systems. There is a tendency for cultural systems to be more consistent than social systems. Whereas cultural systems themselves simply depend on an internal logic for their consistency, in order for cultural images to be *realized* they require the investment of scarce means. The scarcity of means guarantees that social systems are always less perfect than their cultural anticipations. Also, social systems cannot devote all their means directly to goal activities because some of them are required for other functions, such as the production and recruitment of further means to the goal and the maintenance and servicing of those units that are performing goal activities. The structural position of managers and politicians leads them to realize the need to compromise, but holders of other positions are less likely to do so. Groups who are directly responsible for goal activities, such as professionals, are especially likely to develop a segmental perspective, and since their interests and subsystem values come closest to those of the organization as a whole, they find it easier to justify their bias. The significance of this for professional organizations such as hospitals and universities (even more so for religious organizations) is that:

> In systems in which managers are the group most committed to goal activities (e.g. in profit-making organizations), this tendency is at least partially balanced by the managers' other commitments (e.g. to system integration). But in organizations in which another personnel group is the major carrier of goal activities, the ordinary intergroup differences of interests and structural perspectives becomes intensified. In some cases it develops into a conflict between the idealists and the compromisers (if not traitors). In professional organizations such as mental hospitals and universities, the major carriers of goal activities are professionals rather than administrators.[50]

In religious organizations the congregationally-based clergy carry the main goal activities, therefore their viewpoint tends to devalue the contribution of other groups such as denominational executives, who are largely engaged in servicing or integrating the organization. The latter are sometimes painted as compromisers or even traitors, because their orientation to tasks not directly related to goal activities makes them seem less idealistic.

The distinction between cultural systems and social systems has been suggested as an important factor to be taken into consideration in studies of the parish as a unit of organization. According to Young and Hughes, parish analysis is complicated by the fact that the reality of the parish involves an interaction between the ideal religious cultural system, which structures the parish toward purely religious objectives, and the social system which allows the processes necessary for its continued existence to take place.[51] As a result, system activities which are directed toward material and operational ends may be accorded a religious or normative sanction which they do not necessarily require. Or, liturgical activities intimately connected with the achievement of religious ends may be controlled and carried on in a generally social and technical manner, with the result that the religious component gets submerged beneath an operationalistic emphasis.

> The eternal problem confronting complex organizations of this type is the tendency for normative controls relevant to the cultural system to be applied to social system activities and vice versa. This may lead to a competition of control structures with a resulting confusion as to the reference of a particular activity. As a result, religious sentiment may be allocated to operational procedures while religious activities may be viewed from an almost purely operational perspective.[52]

Not only are there different structural perspectives from one group to another within an organization, but there are also differences of interests. Paul, whose investigation into clergy attitudes and working conditions in the Church of England provides one of the best available sources of insights on large-scale religious organization, directed attention to this political dimension with the comment that:

> What it is important to see is yet another aspect of religious systems: in addition to their cultural and sacred character they are political systems: they are the instruments, the organizations, by which power is exercised. [53]

The Paul Report was in favour of rationalizing the organization of the Church of England and urged policies which would make possible the proper maintenance and pastoral care of the ordained ministry. "Yet without any particular theoretical intention of doing so, it raised the dangerous question of the role of the clergy as the guardian elite of the institutional church."[54] He concluded that, as in other institutions, the prestige and status of the elite had become bound up with the forms of the institution. Anything thought to threaten the elite—even a shift in the balance of power within the institution—was felt as a threat to the institution itself. The elite therefore tends to be conservative in the face of all changes which do not directly increase its own power and status. In the case of the Paul Report, the recommendation that seemed to threaten the clergy most was his suggestion that the parson's freehold should be abolished. According to Paul, the reason for the violent reaction from the clergy was they identified that freehold with the Church, and thought there could be no Church of England without it. They could not make an objective consideration of the church's overall requirements because "their emotional identification with the existing institution was too great: subconsciously it was all a power problem".[55]

As we saw in the last section, such objections to changes in a religious organization depend to a large extent on the seeming symbolic-inappropriateness of the new model or organization. But it is clear that political factors also play a part. The political dimension includes all those factors which involve the allocation of scarce resources, such as power, status and freedom, and which can result in conflict and the formation of interest groups. Among the topics frequently examined by the sociologists of religion which can be included in the political dimension are: roles and statuses; leadership and authority; and compliance structures.

Roles and Statuses

The Paul Report's recommendations for rationalizing the system of payment and deployment of the Church of England clergy were typical of a general trend in most large-scale religious bodies. An American sociologist, Scherer, has carried out extensive studies of American Protestant clergy, their backgrounds, recruitment, and career patterns, and finds a general trend from a patrimonial-patronage type of office and payment to a bureaucratic type. He lists their characteristics as follows:[56]

Like all changes in organization, this trend has met with some opposition, and limitations have been exposed. One source of objection has already been dis-

Patrimonial-patronage	*Bureaucratic*
Personal	Impersonal
Particular	Universal
Locally controlled	Centralized
Multiple sources of income	Single salary source
Non-standardized, sporadic	Regularized, scaled
Tradition, ceremonial	Purposefully rational
Fusion of public and private spheres of life	Separation of public and private

cussed in the context of the Paul Report's reception—that is, the essential conservatism of an elite in the face of changes that do not directly increase its own power and status. However, Neal, in a study of reactions to change in the Roman Catholic Archdiocese of Boston, found that priests could be divided into four types. She devised a fourfold typology based on two sets of variables: a general orientation to change or non-change, and to values or interests:[57]

	Changed oriented	Non-change oriented
Value oriented	The "Prophet"	The "Priest"
Interest oriented	The "Cosmopolitan Organization Man"	The "Local Organization Man"

Opposition or support for reforms that affect the clergy's role and status does not stem solely from the character of the individual clergyman, however, nor even from the particular position that he holds and the concomitant system problems with which he is mainly concerned (e.g. pattern-maintenance, integration, adaptation or goal attainment, as suggested by Neal). To some extent reforms succeed or fail according to the degree in which they allow for the various heterogeneous components of the clergy role. The fact of the matter is that the clergy role is a unique mixture of amateur and professional, standardizable and unstandardizable, elements. Some of this complexity was laid bare in a highly instructive public exchange of views on the Paul Report between the author and Wilson.[58]

Wilson criticized the assumption underlying the report that the clergy could be beneficially subjected to the same process of increasing rationalization and "professionalization" as had occurred in most of the other occupations of industrial society. His main objection to this assumption was that the role of priest is diffuse rather than specific. Of all social roles the priest's calls for the widest use of his purely *untrained* capacities, and calls into play, more than any other profession, his personality dispositions. Although a specialist, because of his theological training, his role requires the greatest use of amateur abilities. The successful priest is such less because of his specific training than because he has "developed a lively sympathy, acquired a sense of toleration, and because he is culturally informed and humanly committed". The inherent diffuseness of the clergy role means that there is a large element in it which is not susceptible to precise formulation and rationalization. Leslie Paul claimed, in reply, that whatever the diffuseness of operation of the ministry it was trained in theology, doctrine, liturgics, the scriptures, and so forth, and it was also marked out as a profession by its autonomy and authority over the Church.

But according to Wilson it was not the professional status of the clergy that was in dispute. The point was that the expertise on which the status depended was now less well regarded in society than it once was, whereas reliance on the completely non-professional skills which did bring a clergyman success would be reduced by the Paul Report proposals in order to increase the professionalism of the clergy and to make them more easily deployable. They would also be deployed by a new "bureaucracy" which would reduce their professional autonomy and authority over the church.

The Jesuit sociologist, Fichter, has also drawn attention to the unique mixture of organizational principles which affect the role of the religious professional. In his study, *Religion as an Occupation*, he stated that the central problem of analysis appeared to grow out of the fact that the group life of ecclesiastical personnel was not structured according to any clear-cut and exclusive organizational principle. The Roman Catholic priests, Brothers or Sisters who lived together could not be defined in a technical sense as a family, a community, a bureaucratic or a professional occupation, although their group life was touched by all of these structural types. The familial-communal mode of organization guided the cultural patterns of their daily domestic experiences. The system of authority under which they lived seemed to be derived mainly from the bureaucratic mode of organization. Their productive work was mostly affected by the professional principle of organization. The Roman Catholic religious functionary, more than most others, had to operate simultaneously on two levels: that of the primary local group, and that of the secondary association. The diocese and religious province are secondary associations, while the numerous rectories and local communities are primary groups.[59] To some extent this is the basic problem of all religious functionaries: religious organizations are ideologically committed to the notion of being quasi-primary groups whilst at the same time facing the necessity of operating as a secondary association. Fichter throws some light on the different implications for the religious functionary role of the two sets of principles—the bureaucratic and the professional. He lists their characteristics as:[60]

Bureaucratic mode	Professional mode
1. Centralized leadership	1. Leadership of expertness
2. Emphasis on procedures	2. Variability of procedures
3. Simplification of tasks	3. Totality of task
4. Little initiative	4. Broad initiative
5. Corporate responsibility	5. Personal responsibility
6. Impersonal relations	6. Close colleague relations
7. Ascribed status	7. Achieved status
8. Service to system	8. Service to client

One dysfunction of increased professionalization and specialization that Fichter found was that it loosened the dependence of the religious functionary on local church organization and caused him to identify more closely with like-minded professionals who perform the same tasks in other groups. Their performance of such specialized tasks could only be effectively evaluated by other members of that profession (e.g. social workers, psychiatrists, teachers, etc.) and not by their colleagues and superiors in the local religious organization. The movement within the Roman Catholic Church to develop new and more specialized ministries has, therefore, resulted in conflict between the traditional structure of diocese and religious order on the one hand, and the expectations of high professional competence on the other.

Rankin, who carried out research on the professionalization of the Methodist ministry in America, concluded that in some ways the Roman Catholic Church dealt more effectively with the dilemmas of the clergyman's role.[61] Methodist ministers had always emphasized the importance of the "secret Call", but at the same time they had become increasingly professional as clergymen in a large-scale organization. This posed an occupational dilemma: as a "spiritual calling" the ministry is expected to provide altruistic service; as an occupation within an increasingly bureaucratic structure it is expected to exhibit rational expertise.

Professionalization of the calling is intended to hold the balance between these two sets of demands. Professionalization stresses altruistic service irrespective of reward. According to Parsons, business occupations institutionalize acquisitiveness and self-interest in contrast to the altruistic disinterestness of the professions.[62] The professional person is not necessarily more altruistic by nature than the business man. He fulfils his obligation to service only when there is adequate institutional support for his professional role. In Parsons' terms his altruism is not so much motivational as institutional. Rankin shows that the Methodist ministry has become more professional in such things as training, certification, control of entry to the ministry, and professional ethics, all of which are in the hands of an autonomous body of ministers. However, it has also become more bureaucratic. Rankin found that the appointment process was centralized in the hands of the bishop and his cabinet, and that when a minister's name came up for consideration he was con-

sidered eligible for a given church appointment on the basis of his current salary level. His salary level was an initial measure of occupational achievement, and he could be promoted from smaller to larger churches, with appropriate increases in salary and fringe benefits, if he achieved measurable success in increasing congregations, making improvements in budget or buildings, and administering the church effectively.

The function of the professional stance, which includes ideological commitment to the calling along with rational efficiency, professional expertise and objectivity, is to maintain effective institutional support for both these aspects of the modern ministry. But if the church, in striving to maintain itself in a changing urban society, develops an institutional support for one aspect of professional life (rationality, expertise and universalism) more adequately than the other (altruistic disinterestedness), there is a tendency for the minister to deviate from the professional ideal and to overemphasize careerism. Rankin found evidence that the Methodist Church tended to oversupport the measurable achievements and undersupport the more subtle achievements of the minister. There was apprehension in the Methodist Church over the loss of the personal touch in the ministry, and a desire to see the minister relate to persons with particularity. At the same time the organizational structure was developing bureaucratic impersonality and professional detachment.

Donovan, in a study which dealt with similar role dilemmas in the Catholic priesthood, concluded that the Catholic Church had resolved the particularistic universalistic dilemma by institutionalizing the "total status" of the priest. The priest could be universalistic in his official functions as at confession, and yet he could also act in a more particularistic fashion as "Father" to the church family. He could thus be detached in some functions and yet thought of as a man personally devoted to his people. There was institutional support for both functions.[63] This contrasts with Rankin's finding that the Methodist minister got only verbal support for his role as devoted pastor, but institutional demands put a premium upon effectiveness in administering an efficient church and proving himself in terms of the career pattern of advancement. Blizzard came to similar conclusions about the Protestant minister's role dilemmas. Most of the ministers surveyed by him desired most to be the preacher-pastor in accordance with the seminary image, yet they spent an overwhelming block of their time on administration and organizational tasks along with a multitude of community responsibilities.[64] The problems are then exacerbated by the fact that church members have a quite different perception of how ministers spend their time, and also quite different priorities with respect to that allocation.[65]

The result of these different institutional pressures on the clergyman and the many-faceted nature of his occupational role means that he experiences problems in establishing self-indentification.[66] Blizzard suggests that clergy seek to overcome the conflicts between their many practitioner roles, such as preacher, teacher, priest, pastor, administrator, and organizer, by developing a self-conception based on some kind of integrative role, which provides a frame of reference. Typical integrative roles are those based on the father-shepherd image, specialist in interpersonal relations, the promotor, the community problem solver, the believer-saint and the evangelist.[67]

The nature and degree of role conflict seems to vary between denominations which have moved from different ends of the church–sect continuum. On the whole the Roman Catholic Church, although it has the standing of a denomination in the pluralistic religious situation of most democratic societies, has been most successful in minimizing the role dilemmas of its clergy. At the other end of the spectrum are the sects and sect-originated denominations, where there is a lack of consensus as to the basic role and status of the ministry. For instance, Pentecostal bodies retain the ideal of a non-professional, charismatic ministry, whilst at the same time requiring institutionalized leadership in order to exist. This disparity combines with a low social status to accentuate the role conflicts and status insecurity of their clergy.[68]

Underlying all these specific conflicts and insecurities, however, there is probably a basic uncertainty stemming from the fact that clergymen are unclear about the relationship between their institutional and their personal identities. A clinical psychologist who spent two hundred hours with a group of American Presbyterian clergymen over five years found that:

> . . . putting aside the myriad defences employed, a more persistent and prevalent problem of each man seemed to be low self-esteem and underestimation of the significance of himself and his role. The vastness of the minister's task would imply that a part of his feeling of inadequacy is warranted. Yet realistic doubt seemed greatly overshadowed by the unrealistic doubt and insecurity which each felt. It was difficult for these men to realize their actual significance as symbolic father figures and keepers of the ancient symbols.[69]

It has been suggested that the realistic doubts refer to the basic dilemmas of institutionalization which are ineradicable, but that the unrealistic doubts refer to the clergyman's confusion of his personal identity problems with the primary symbolic role of father or pastor of the religious group, which he tends to under-value.[70] Certainly clergymen give the appearance of being confused about their role performance. A recent study by Ashbrook of ministers' evaluation of their performance, their "task satisfactions", and their performance as perceived by members of the congregation, concluded that "the minister is a pretty poor evaluator of his own performance", and that "ministers and members failed to see church organization in the same way".[71]

A study by Douglas on predicting ministerial effectiveness theorized that effectiveness in the parish seems to be the result of the minister achieving the proper balance between the "able" and the "good" orientations.[72] That is, the minister, according to Douglas, must not only exhibit and possess the sincere, religious faith and practice of the good man, but must also have a drive to be successful and motivation for status, hard work, and reliable performance. Douglas suggests that ability to tolerate and resolve the conflict between "able" and "good" is similar to Chester Barnard's conclusion in *The Functions of the Executive*, that executives must be able to tolerate and overcome conflicting behaviour codes. Code conflict is particularly acute in ministerial practice because the self-promotion implicit in the "able" orientation contradicts the self-effacement and service motifs of the "good" orientation. This is what O'Dea terms "the dilemma of mixed motives". All religious organizations face this problem of motivating individuals to participate in such a way both as to contribute to organizational effectiveness as such and to internalize and uphold the religious culture of the collectivity. As Robertson points out:

> While religious denominations, like sects, are indeed primarily normative in modern societies, they frequently tend towards the utilitarian type, involving the exercise of, in the broadest sense, remunerative power: the manipulation of rewards and sanctions, including not only money but also status and prestige.[73]

It has been suggested that the current decline in the status of the minister of religion has been partly responsible for the motivation of church and denomination leaders to engage in ecumenical ventures, so as to restore some of their lost prestige in the wider society.[74]

Leadership and authority

In his study of the dilemma of authority and power in the American Baptist Convention, Harrison pointed out that the dilemma was not peculiar to that denomination, nor was it confined to religious organizations. He maintained that every voluntary and non-authoritarian association became involved in the problem of authority and power of its leadership. The issue could be more specifically defined and analysed in the Free Churches simply because of the explicit allocation of authority to the local unit and their refusal to grant legal authority to their ministerial and administrative leaders.

Weber's basic theory, and his typology of authority with regard to leadership, derived from his conviction that the key to understanding the authority relations of any social system was to be found in the basis of legitimacy for the persons in authority. Legitimacy could be rooted in tradition, law, or the charismatic qualities of the leader himself. Sect-originated denominations which do not have a tradition or a legal basis on which to legitimate their newly developed central leadership, offer only a rational-pragmatic authority to their leaders. The leaders have authority only as long as they produce results that are valued by the major groups in the denomination; they are never obeyed simply because they hold office, as in the case of legally legitimated authority.[75]

In *ecclesia*- or church-originated denominations the basis of legitimacy for persons in authority rests on an even more mixed set of principles. Firstly, there is usually a traditional elite which can claim authority, and, far from disappearing as the denomination develops a rational-legal bureaucracy, the existence of the elite may become even more important in a time of rapid change. Thus, Ross P. Scherer, in a study of ministers in the Missouri Synod of the Lutheran Church in America, stressed the importance of Weber's category of elite "carriers of culture", and suggested that ecclesiastical bodies like the Lutheran organization are especially compatible with a kind of "familistic self-perpetuation".[76]

Scherer found strong evidence to support his hypothesis that organizational requirements for continuity and change would demand the emergence of "birth" and "educational" elites which are characterized by tendencies, not only to ration-legal discrimination and judgement, but also to charismatic innovation and non-conformity as well. Non-elite groups in the ministry (ministers who were not descended from clergy families, and had not gone to the top seminary) were passed over by the organization because they lacked the background, disposition, and suitedness to serve as overall guides and "carriers of culture". The needs of the organization for continuity as well as change gave rise, therefore, to the ensuing career patterns in which the perpetuation of an elite within the ministry was guaranteed.[77]

The investigations by Morgan into the social and educational backgrounds of Anglican bishops provide further evidence of the important role played by elite "carriers of culture" in religious bodies of this type.[78] Morgan also showed that the character of the elite may change as the Establishment status of an *ecclesia* gives way to that more akin to the denominations, as the religious institution is subjected to the general process of institutional differentiation in modern society. In family backgrounds he found an unbroken decline in landed and peerage connections, and in terms of parental occupation there was a shift from the old landed ruling class to a more professional background. Especially worthy of note was the increase in the number of bishops whose fathers were themselves clergymen in the Church of England. In general there was a shift from a situation where the episcopacy was part of a broader social elite to one where it was a more narrowly defined ecclesiastical elite. There had also been an increase in the number of bishops who had attended "public school" and who had gone to the top four theological colleges. Morgan makes the important point that where authority is wholly or partially traditional, the central problem of recruitment to the elite is to discover those who are particularly responsible to traditional values. The desired characteristics cannot be guaranteed by any subsequent formal training; there has to be a degree of socialization prior to the occupation of the office and a degree that is greater than that expected of an office holder in a purely bureau-cratic system.

If one of the key indicators of effective leadership is the ability to satisfy the organization's requirements for both continuity and change, then success is likely to depend as much on the setting in which leadership is exercised as it does on the background and socialization of the leaders. Research by James O. Gibbs into the external adaptation of religious organizations tends to bear out this observation about the importance of contextual variables.[79]

Gibbs placed his study of religious organizations in the theoretical context of systems theory, according to which organizations may be viewed as one class of open systems, thus emphasizing the necessary dependence of any organization upon its environment. On the assumption that one mode of church adaptation to the external environment involves dealing with community-relevant social issues, he then explored several variables as predictors of this type of church adaptation to the external environment. The selected predictors ranged from community size and membership size to the educational composition of the membership and the experience of the pastor. A major theme of the research, which was carried out on local churches of the Northwest Annual Conference of the United Methodist Church of America, was that these variables are primarily indicators of key personnel and leadership resources. Both community size and membership size were found to be related to church response to issues, although membership size largely mediated the effects of community size. For example, if urban churches were more constrained to deal with social issues, it was through the operation of factors associated with larger membership (e.g. larger paid staffs) that these churches evinced greater response to issues. The authors suggested that the greater personnel resources that characterized the larger churches partially explained the relationship between membership size and response to issues. This can be related to the organizational research findings summarized by Starbuck which indicate that size correlates with organizational success, adaptation and survival.[80] Starbuck reported that large organizations in addition to employing more experienced personnel and spending disproportionately more money on research and development, tended to be older and to have accumulated more problem-solving knowledge.[81]

Another variable, percentage of members who had attended college, predicted some of the variation in response to issues, independent of membership size. A better-educated membership was interpreted as meaning (1) greater lay leadership resources, (2) increased awareness of the external environment, and (3) an attitudinal climate more conducive to dealing with social issues. A significant factor with regard to the relation between the background of leaders and the organization's adaptability, was that member education and response to issues was particularly strong in churches marked by more turnover on the board of trustees. High turnover at this level would tend to increase the variety and amount of information about community issues available to the leadership, and also provide greater involvement and participation of members in decision-making.

Vallier's studies of change in the Roman Catholic Church also adopted as a research strategy a focus on lay involvement and a fairly local unit of organization (in this case the diocese) as a basis for making comparisons.[82] By this method he was able to draw inferences about the factors that bear most directly on leadership and structural change. He used several levels of analysis in his comparisons of dioceses—three each in France, Chile and the United States; e.g. holding national culture constant and varying situational factors; holding situational factors constant (economic, political, demographic, etc.) and varying episcopal orientations; or holding episcopal orientations constant and varying the internal complexity of the dioceses or the diocese's location and importance in the national Church system.

Vallier used two concepts to help explain the general factors that might account for variations in the status and role of the laity in different dioceses. The first organizational concept was that of "relational infrastructure", which refers to the level of organizational solidity in the diocese and the degree of interstitial activity. The second concept was that of "episcopal autonomy", which refers to the bishop's freedom to take initiatives without being met by blocking counter-measures from other power groups.

When the two variables are put together there are four logical possibilities:[83]

		Level of "relational infrastructure"	
		High	Low
Degree of "episcopal autonomy"	High	1	2
	Low	3	4

Each combination is shown to have major implications for leadership and change:

Cell 1 (high–high) appears to be the most favourable for structural change because episcopal autonomy allows initiatives to be taken and the high level of relational infrastructure provides the structural basis on which these initiatives and decisions can be mobilized, channelled and implemented.

Cell 2 (high–low) allows episcopal initiatives, but there is little organization in the diocese, beyond that of the parishes and conventional formal programmes, to facilitate change and mobilization.

Cell 3 (low–high) is potentially frustrating because whilst the infrastructure for mobilization and reform exists, the episcopate is hemmed in by other power groups and routine administrative responsibilities.

Cell 4 (low–low) is the typical static, underdeveloped diocese, with neither episcopal autonomy nor relational infrastructure.

Vallier states that in all cases the ideological persuasion of the bishop is a critical factor, but when the level of episcopal progressiveness is controlled, the other two factors become extremely important.

Another comparative study that explored the political dimension of religious organizations was carried out by Benne.[84] It is a particularly significant piece of work because it compared three very different large-scale religious organizations within the same religious communion, Lutheranism. Once again the focus was on the regional level and compared the Illinois Synod of the Lutheran Church in America (LCA), the Northern Illinois District of the Lutheran Church—Missouri Synod (MS), and the Illinois District of the American Lutheran Church (ALC). The hypotheses tested, the results, and the models of political processes employed, constitute one of the most comprehensive pieces of research on religious organization, and deserve to be discussed in some detail.

Several hypotheses, drawn up for the overall project, were tested:

1. Religious structures have followed a pattern of organizational centralization that approximates the "American pattern".

2. There is a growing inconsistency between belief systems and organizational imperatives.

3. Associational values and standards of a universal, rational character will conflict with the pastoral, particularistic values of local units.

4. Cooperative planning and comity emerging from large organizational activity will tend to homogenize the denominations in terms of social class participation and basic values.

5. There will be a rise in interdepartmental competition as organizations diversify to meet the multiple needs of metropolitan life.

6. Growth in the churches has shifted the leadership from the lay control of the early period to professionals who resemble the managers of large industry.

7. The complexity of urban environments and the increasing size of the religious organizations will lead to decreasing representativeness of decision-making processes with a tendency to less formal procedures in setting policy.

8. Increasing organizational size and obligations will lead to decreasing engagement in social and public issues which might embarrass the executive personnel.

Findings

Hypothesis 1   All three Lutheran bodies were found to be highly centralized, but in different ways. The LCA had centralized at both the national and the regional level, so that the national centralization had been somewhat mitigated by strengthening the regional level. The MS had been so successful in securing uniformity of doctrine and general goals, and inculcating these at all levels, that the practical means of achieving the goals could be left to the districts, and so the organization had not become even more centralized in recent years. The ALC had experienced drastic centralization (especially by merger with another body, as in the case of the LCA) and had not preserved strong intermediate levels of authority and power. This led Benne to suggest that the two variables, increasing organization and increasing centralization, should be kept separate; centralization only occurs as a result of increasing formal organization when there is a failure to strengthen intermediate levels of organization at the same time as central organization is developed.

Hypothesis 2   Inconsistency between belief systems and organizational imperatives was found to exist in all three regional organizations. All believed that they were democratic in their decision-making processes and that they had preserved local autonomy. Benne comments:

> The avid belief in democratic procedure and local autonomy is an interesting phenomenon in the Lutheran churches. Lutheran theology of the church certainly does not prescribe these beliefs but nevertheless most executives and pastors feel they need to affirm them. This is probably part of the "American Way of Life" ideology that pervades American church life. But at any rate, the conflict between these ideas and the actual power structure is a real problem for the Lutheran churches.[85]

In the ALC, where the discrepancy was most acute, informal popular power structures had sprung up at the local level to combat the formal organization;

tension arose because these splinter groups, informed by belief in "democracy" and "local autonomy", were in conflict with a legal structure that was incompatible with their beliefs.

Hypothesis 3   The conflict between "cosmopolitan-universalistic" values and "local-particularistic" values was experienced most strongly in the ALC, where demands and standards of the national church "fell" from above without mediation or persuasion. In the LCA the conflict was strongest where an area of concern was under national auspices (e.g. the missions programme), but it was softened in its impact by involvement of regional executives in the national work, thus preserving an intermediate decision-influencing body that was accessible to the local units. In the MS the conflict was minimized by the overall solidarity of this body and the tight network of contacts that it encouraged at all levels of power, so that persuasion of the local units to accept the universal values was more successful.

Benne suggests that the lesson would seem to be that conflict over values as a result of organizational growth can be mitigated either by developing strong intermediate organization, or maintaining a solidarity based on homogeneity of membership (the Missouri Synod is overwhelmingly German in its origins and ethos).

Hypothesis 4   No generalization could be stated unequivocally about homogenization of the denominations in terms of social class and values as a result of cooperative planning and comity emerging from large organizational activity. However, cooperation on social action did seem to lower values to the lowest common denominator—it became less prophetic.

Hypothesis 5   No conclusion was offered.

Hypothesis 6   The tendency for leadership to shift to professionals who resemble business executives was evident in two of the denominations (LCA and ALC), and in the case of the LCA this also involved a trend from the traditional Lutheran pattern of clerical control to lay executive control (although they were not greatly different from the specialist executives in the ALC, who happened to be clergy). In the Missouri Synod control rested firmly in the hands of traditional-minded pastors.

Hypothesis 7   The trend towards unrepresentative decision-making processes and informal procedures in setting policies was evident in all three denominations, although in the case of the Missouri Synod this did not represent anything new as it had always used informal power structures and representativeness was not a problem where there was such a high value consensus.

Hypothesis 8   The denominations varied in their social involvement, with the LCA becoming heavily involved due to liberal leadership, and the Missouri

Synod and the ALC much less involved, the former simply abiding by its tradition of non-involvement, and the latter because it was too much interested in growth among the suburban middle classes to become involved in controversial issues. Where the denominations had developed cooperating agencies they were also becoming less involved, because of the need to reach a consensus between the official supporting bodies, which was impossible on controversial issues.

Benne concluded his analysis by drawing parallels between the three religious organizations and Kornhauser's typology of political systems. It is Benne's contention that religious organizations can be classified, described and understood by comparing them with different types of societies and the different kinds of political mechanisms by which these societies are governed. He took the models from Kornhauser's *The Politics of Mass Society*, where four types of society are distinguished (mass, totalitarian, communal and pluralistic). Benne suggested that the LCA approximates a pluralistic, Lockean-type democracy; that the MS conforms to a communal society; and that the ALC is similar to a mass society.

The types are distinguished on the basis of six characteristics: access to elites, availability of non-elites, intermediate groups, standards and values, psychological type of member and the political mechanism. Thus the LCA approximated a pluralistic system in the following ways:

1 *Access to elites* was relatively open and easy.
2 *Availability of non-elites* was such that they were not easily available for manipulation by a centralized power, but adequate machinery existed for non-elites to provide information and support, necessary to form opinions and patterns of response of their own, e.g. the existence of strong local synods functioned as a buttress between local units and the national will, because they possessed sufficient resources and power to run their own programmes.
3 *Intermediate groups*, such as the synods were not strong enough to protect the local units, but they also protected the national leaders from mass movements by providing a channel for expression of dissident opinions, and promoting effective church action by filtering the national will down through intervening levels of participation.
4 *Standards and values* in a pluralistic society are fluid and differentiated. Benne maintains that whilst a church cannot easily have a fluid and differentiated faith, it is possible to discern a greater degree of theological flexibility and modernity in a denomination like the LCA than in some other denominations.
5 *Psychological types*. The typical man in a pluralistic society is self-oriented and self-related, and is more likely to have selected his own value system. In the case of church executives, the contrast seemed, to Benne, to lie along the lines of greater sophistication and critical ability, as between, for example, the executives of the LCA and those of the MS.
6 The *political mechanism* in a pluralistic system is orderly, clearly delineated and representational. Thus the whole structure of the LCA from the national constitution down to the local constitution was legally outlined, and operated as a Lockean-type representative democracy.

According to Benne the MS, in contrast to the LCA, was more of a communal society, in the following respects:

1 *Access to elites* was limited to pastors with a particular kind of background (especially the right college background), and there was little opportunity to change leaders, who were traditionally re-elected as long as they maintained a strong doctrinal status quo.

2 *Availability of non-elites* for mobilization by the elite is relatively low because community tradition and status largely determine what men think, and the non-elites are also protected by time-worn customs and procedures. Benne suggests that an example of this in the MS was the immunity of local pastors to interference from the elite executives.

3 *Intermediate groups.* In the MS the districts were strong and relatively in-dependent with several close-fitting networks filtering the prescriptions of the church down to the local level and channelling sentiments upwards, so that the multiplicity of proximate groups stabilized and expedited church action.

4 *Standards and values* in the MS, as in any communal society, were standardized and traditional. Top executives saw one of their main functions as conservation of pure doctrine. Even cultural standards were strongly traditional, so that the German ethos and pattern of piety were maintained.

5 *Psychological types.* The traditional man of a communal society, like the MS, is group-oriented.

6 The *political mechanism* is based on continuity and custom rather than the individual leader or adaptation to social change. Church executives in the MS tended to be loyal, stable and efficient functionaries.

The ALC, with a strong, centralized national body and atomized local units resembled a mass society in its characteristics:

1 *Access to elites.* In a mass society the non-elites have direct access to the elites and they intervene directly and in an unrestrained manner; there is little inter-mediate organization which can fulfil the non-elites need for meaningful parti-cipation. In the ALC, as described by Benne, because the district organization was weak, annual conventions tended to be tense affairs, with all groups seeking to utilize that one opportunity to impose their will.

2 *Availability of non-elites.* In the absence of any machinery to mitigate national action the atomized local units were directly pressured by the national agencies on everything from stewardship to evangelism, and yet were isolated from responsible participation in the higher power structure.

3 *Intermediate groups* were weak in the ALC and so the prescriptions of the national organization were not effectively represented at the local level, and, because the district organization was powerless, it tended to become myopic and introspective.

4 *Standards and values* in a mass society are uniform and fluid, and apparently the ALC showed the greatest tendency to conform to the prevailing standards of

the outside world. As Benne comments, "Only the ALC would put out a chart showing 'The Soul-Potential of Refinancing', with graphs showing how many souls, churches, and benevolences can be obtained by using refinancing techniques. At the bottom of the chart a statement reminds the reader that 'savings and credit can be converted into souls won for Christ' ."[86]

5 The *psychological types*. Mass man is self-oriented, self-alienated, and very suggestible. Many of the pastors of the ALC were found to be isolated, with no real support from, or participation in, the district and national organizations, consequently they easily lost their loyalty to the church and were available to mass movements on the local level.

6 *Political mechanism*. As in a mass society, decision-making in the ALC varied from arbitrary national power to volatile mass democracy. Between conventions power rested in the national organization, but at convention time the national officers were directly subjected to the demands, not of responsible districts, but of "grass-roots" movements.

No doubt, like all typologies and analogies, Benne's comparison of church organizations and political systems can be misleading if taken too far, but he has shown that it can be most effective in the appropriate context of comparing the political processes of religious bodies.

Compliance structures

The previous discussion of roles and status, and authority, can only be analytically distinguished from the subject of compliance structures. In practice they are all inextricably woven together. Etzioni provided an invaluable contribution to the study of organizations in his notable work, *A Comparative Analysis of Complex Organizations*, published in 1961, when he devised a typology by which all organizations could be classified according to his criterion of "compliance"—the relationship of the leader and the led. According to the typology, organizations range from the authoritarian (involving extreme coercion by the leader with great resistance from members) to the utilitarian (moderate degrees of direction and cooperation) to the normative (little direction but complete commitment by the members). Etzioni classified religious bodies as belonging to the normative type of organization because they depended largely on full and free participation by their members.

Unfortunately, like all typologies (hence the cautionary words at the beginning of this paper about the limitations of this method), the ease of classification according to an *a priori* principle has given rise to neglect of the possible exceptions and variations.[87] Leaving aside all extreme cases of sects and even churches that become authoritarian, it is possible to find many cases where large areas of religious organization operate according to utilitarian principles. And in practice, rather than theory, almost all religious organizations carry within themselves interest groups and power relations that involve utilitarian considerations to a great degree. Empirical research on church organizations tends to show that compliance on the basis of normative consensus should be regarded as problematic rather than taken for granted.

It is frequently assumed by the uninitiated (and even by organization theorists who specialize in analysing other types of organizations) that religious organizations are relatively trouble free, simply because they are thought to enjoy a high degree of normative consensus. Thus, Etzioni characterized the Church as a normative organization in which compliance rests on the internalization of directives which are accepted as legitimate by the lower participants. And that, correspondingly, a moral involvement on the part of the lower participants exists and is a positive orientation of high intensity.[88] But the process of internalization of directives which are accepted as legitimate would only be unproblematic if legitimacy was granted unequivocally to power-holders in religious organizations. The research that we have discussed show that this is far from being the case.

The problem of internalization and legitimacy are the same as the problems of communication and authority. Hopkins has also demonstrated that the problem of communication emphasized in the organization theory of Barnard, and the problem of authority discussed by Weber, are likewise but two sides of the same coin.[89] Weber examines the status of the administrator (the office), attributes authority to this unit, and explains the effective exercise of authority mainly in terms of other attributes of the office or in terms of attributes brought to it by officials. Barnard, in contrast, examines the role relation (channel of communication), attributes authority to communications (which thus become more or less authoritative), and explains effectiveness in terms of other attributes of communications or in terms of role relations that transmit communications.

The problems of communication experienced by many religious organizations illustrate the close relation between communication processes and authority. Communication between the central administration and the local congregation is often hindered by the reservations which many local clergy have about the types of rationality and legitimacy upon which the central organization depends. The communications of the central administration are frequently ignored because the clergy (or groups of them) do not find them consistent with their conception of the ultimate goals, and they do not accept the authority of the communicators.[90]

Perhaps the opening text for all studies of religious organization should be this quotation from a report of a speech given by the secretary of the Parochial Clergy Association in the Church of England on 22nd March 1965:

> The Hon. Secretary gave a brief history of the build-up of the central organization of the Church—which was costing around £1,000,000 per year—but did not necessarily add one soul to the Church. It was more than ever essential today for the existence of an organization like the P.C.A. to resist this crushing machine . . . and reassert the freedom of the Clergy to proclaim the Church as a spiritual organism.[91]

It provides a forceful reminder that consensus cannot be assumed to exist in a religious organization any more than it can be assumed for other social systems. Thus the sociology of organizations has a great deal to offer the sociology of religion and—as we have attempted to demonstrate—*vice versa*.

References and notes

1. For a critique of "methodological amateurism" in the sociology of religion, and an outline of an alternative research strategy based on comparative studies of middle-range units, see Ivan Vallier, "Comparative studies of Roman Catholicism: dioceses as strategic units", *Soc. Compass*, **16,** (2) (1969), 147–184.

2. This use of the term "anthropological" is similar to that of Talcott Parsons, who defines the anthropological focus as "the analytical study of phenomena of culture, of the patterned symbolic-meaning systems in and by which social systems and personalities are orientated and guided". Parsons *et al.*, *American Sociology*, New York: Basic Books, 1968, p. 321.

3. Philip Selznick, *Leadership in Administration*. Evanston, Ill.: Row, Peterson, pp. 141–142.

4. Kenneth A. Thompson, *Bureaucracy and Church Reform*, Oxford: The Clarendon Press, 1970.
      In one sense this is simply a transposition into an evolutionary and developmental context of Peter Blau's general observation about the study of formal organizations that, "although the defining characteristic of an organiza-tion is that a collectivity is formally organized, what makes it of scientific interest is that the developing social structure inevitably does not completely coincide with the pre-established forms." [Peter M. Blau, "The study of formal organization", in Talcott Parsons (Ed.), *op. cit.*, 54–65, p. 56.]

5. E. Troeltsch, *The Social Teaching of the Christian Churches*, 2 vols., trs. Olive Wyon, London: Allen and Unwin, 1931, vol. 1, p. 331.

6. Other elaborations of the church–sect typology were also proposed by Howard Becker, who distinguished four types: the *ecclesia*, denomination, sect and cult (H. Becker, *Systematic Sociology*, Gary, Indiana: 1950 ed., pp. 624–42; and *Through Values to Social Interpretation*, Durham, N.C.: 1950, pp. 114–118). Joachim Wach concluded that there were three major forms; ecclesiastical bodies, independent bodies or denominations, and sectarian bodies [J. Wach, *Types of Religious Experience: Christian and Non-Christian*, Chicago: Univer-sity of Chicago Press, 1951, pp. 190–196].

7. Cf. H.R. Niebuhr, *The Social Sources of Denominationalism*, Hamden, Conn.: Shoe String Press, 1954 ed., pp. 19–21: Liston Pope, *Millhands and Preachers*, New Haven: Yale University Press, 1942; Earl D. C. Brewer "Sect and church in Methodism", in *Soc. Forces*, **4** (May 1952), 400–408; O. R. Whitley, "The sect-to-denomination process in an American religious movement: the disciples of Christ", in *Southwestern Soc. Sci. Q.*, **36** (1955), 275–281.

8. David O. Moberg, *The Church as a Social Institution*, Englewood Cliffs, N.J.: Prentice-Hall, 1962, p. 101.

9. Cf. J. Milton Yinger, *Religion in the Struggle for Power*, Durham, N.C.: Duke University Press, 1946, pp. 31–34; Earl D.C. Brewer, "Sect and church in Methodism", *Soc. Forces*, **30** (May 1952), 400–408.

10. Thomas F. O'Dea, "Mormonism and the avoidance of sectarian stragnation:

a study of church, sect, and incipient nationality", *Am. J. Sociol.*, **50** (Nov. 1954), pp. 285–293; and T.F. O'Dea, *The Mormons*, Chicago: University of Chicago Press, 1957.

11. Bryan R. Wilson, *Patterns of Sectarianism*, London: Heinemann, 1967, pp. 10–11.

12. Wilson, *op. cit.*, pp. 22–45.

13. *Ibid.*, p. 45.

14. *Ibid.*, pp. 14–15.

15. See Wilson, *op. cit.*, p. 33; also Theodore W. Sprague, "Some notable features in the authority structure of a sect", *Soc. Forces*, **21** (3) (March 1943), 344–350; H.H. Stroup, *Jehovah's Witnesses*, New York: Columbia University Press, 1945; and E. Royston Pike, *Jehovah's Witnesses*, London: Watts, 1954.

16. Neil J. Smelser summarized some of the different criticisms of the sect-to-denomination sequence as: (a) It is too limited a statement of the possible adaptations of religious groups, even within Christianity; (b) it is too limited to particular countries such as the United States; (c) it does not take account of the distinctive influence of the sect's original values, its initial level of insulation or isolation from the parent society (Smelser, *Theory of Collective Behaviour*, London: Routledge & Kegan Paul, 1962, p. 360). Cf. B. Johnson "A critical appraisal of the church–sect typology", in *Am. Sociol. Rev.*, **22** (1957), 88–92; H.W. Pfautz, "The sociology of secularization: religious groups", in *Am. J. Sociol.*, **61** (2) (Sept. 1955), 121–128; and B.R. Wilson, "An analysis of sect development", *Am. Sociol. Rev.*, **24** (1959), 3–15.

17. Friedrich Furstenberg, "Kirchenform und Gesellschaftstructur", in *Sociologisch Bull.*, **3** (1960), 100–112. Cf. Glenn M. Vernon, *Sociology of Religion*, New York: McGraw-Hill, 1962, p. 176, where the Church of England is described as moving toward a denomination status.

18. T. Parsons, "Christianity and modern industrial society", in E.A. Tiryakian (Ed.), *Sociological Theory, Values and Sociocultural Change*, Glencoe, Ill.: The Free Press, 1963, pp. 35–70; and "The patterns of religious organization in the United States", in *Daedalus*, **87** (3) (Summer 1958), 65–85.

19. J.M. Gustafson, *Treasure in Earthen Vessels*, New York: Harper, 1961; and R. Lee, *The Social Sources of Church Unity*, New York: Abingdon Press, 1960.

20. Cf. P.M. Harrison, *Authority and Power in the Free Church Tradition*, Princeton, N.J.: Princeton University Press, 1959; and K.A. Thompson, *Bureaucracy and Church Reform*, Oxford: The Clarendon Press, 1970.

21. Harrison describes this as an "expediential authority", not fully legal nor based on ecclesiastical tradition, but arising out of the immediate needs of the denominational organization (Harrison, *op. cit.*, p. 14).

22. Cf. Thompson, *op. cit.*, ch. 2, for a discussion of the nineteenth century Oxford Movement in the Church of England and its response to organizational reforms.

23. Cf. Paul Harrison, *op. cit.*, chs. 4–5; and Paul M. Harrison "Guidelines for research on inter-Protestant relations", *Inf. Service*, New York: National

Council of the Churches of Christ in the United States of America, **44**, No. 2 (Jan. 1965), 1–8, p. 2.

24. For a fuller discussion of these and other hypotheses, see Harrison (1965), *op. cit.*

25. This distinction was made by Charles H. Page in his seminal essay "Bureaucracy and the liberal church", in *The Review of Religion*, **16,** Nos. 3–4 (Nov. 1951), 137–150.

26. Talcott Parsons, *The Structure of Social Action*, Glencoe, Ill.: The Free Press, 1949, p. 256.

27. Parsons, *op. cit.*, pp. 257–258.

28. An example of such an interposed empirical goal would be that of the Ecclesiastical Commissioners in the nineteenth century Church of England, who had the express purpose of strengthening the parochial unit as an agent of social control and stability. Cf. Thompson, *op. cit.*, ch. 3.

29. Parsons, *op. cit.*, pp. 257–258.

30. F.W. Dillistone, *The Structure of the Divine Society*, London: Lutterworth Press, 1951, p. 169.

    The interposed empirical goals here are social integration and cooperation and symbolic-appropriateness lies in the congruence between the organic model of organization and the New Testament conception of the Body.

31. Paul S. Minear, *Images of the Church in the New Testament*, London: Lutterworth Press, 1961.

32. H. Richard Niebuhr, *Christ and Culture*, London: Faber and Faber, 1952.

33. See Peter F. Rudge, *Ministry and Management*, London: Tavistock, 1968; and also his "Study of Ecclesiastical Administration, Using the Methods and Insights of Public Administration', Unpublished Ph.D. thesis, University of Leeds, 1966.

34. There are obviously certain objections that can be levelled at a typology that is derived from such divergent sources, especially as Weber's categories were ideal types drawn from a wide range of social institutions, whereas management theory has a practical basis and has centred mainly on profit-making firms. A more fundamental criticism, as we will see (and Rudge admits this) is that the typology might mask quite different or alternative approaches to the study of organizations, such as that which considers power to be the main focus for understanding an organization, in contrast to a concern with personal relationships, or the interrelation of task and environment.

35. Weber, *Theory of Social and Economic Organization*, trs. by T. Parsons and A.M. Henderson, London: Oxford University Press, 1947, p. 341.

36. Weber, *op. cit.*, pp. 358–359.

37. *Ibid.*, p. 339.

38. See F.J. Roethlisberger and W.J. Dickson, *Management and the Worker*, Cambridge, Mass.: Harvard University Press, 1939.

39. For an analysis of the two theories in terms of a dichotomy, see Douglas McGregor, *The Human Side of Enterprise*, New York: McGraw-Hill, 1960, pp. 33–37. Rensis Lickert sees them as part of a continuum that can be further

subdivided, e.g. exploitive/authoritative type–benevolent/authoritative–consultative–participative (R. Lickert, *New Patterns of Management*, New York: McGraw-Hill, 1961, pp. 223–233).

40. Warren G. Bennis, "Leadership theory and administrative behaviour"; "The problem of authority", *Admin. Sci. Q.*, **4** (3) (Dec 1959). 259–301.

41. Cf. T. Burns and G.M. Stalker, *The Management of Innovation*, London: Tavistock, 1961, for a detailed analysis of the two ideal types of organization at opposite ends of the flexibility dimension.

42. Cf. Stafford Beer, *Cybernetics and Management*, London: English Universities Press, 1959.

43. A similar correspondence can be found between Niebuhr's list of the different perceptions of the mission of Christ in relation to culture and the theories of organization. Christ against culture corresponds to charismatic theory; Christ the fulfilment of culture corresponds to human relations theory; the Christ of culture, or above culture (Christ enters in from above and culture then enshrines and is enriched by the supernatural) corresponds to traditional theory; Christ the transformer of culture corresponds to Systemic theory (the Church adapts in order to transform society). In this case, however, there is an image that corresponds to classical theory, and that is Christ and culture coexisting—a duality in effect. Holders of this last position would tend to exclude the criterion of symbolic-appropriateness in evaluating the functioning of some branches of ecclesiastical administration.

44. An established or institutionalized sect is one which has come to terms with its societal setting—it is organized on a wider and continuing basis, and has achieved some respectability and power—but it still maintains a conflict with some of the prevailing attitudes.

45. The attraction of the systemic or organic model, as we have seen in the statement by Dillistone, lies in the fact that it seems to achieve a successful combination of the otherwise divergent sets of criteria—calculable efficiency in attaining empirical goals, and symbolic-appropriateness. Unfortunately, it ignores one of the main sources of conflict in religious organization, which is the fact that religious symbols cannot in practice be broken down very easily into specifiable, empirical conditions without generating controversy. The reason for this has been given by Paul Tillich.

   > Religious symbols are distinguished from others by the fact that they are a representation of that which is unconditionally beyond the conceptual sphere; they point to the ultimate reality implied in the religious act, to that which concerns us ultimately.

   Paul Tillich, "The religious symbol", in F.W. Dillistone (Ed.), *Myth and Symbol*, London: SPCK, 1966, p. 17.

46. Ferdinand Tönnies, *Community and Association: Gemeinschaft und Gesellschaft*, trans. and suppl. by Charles P. Loomis, London: Routledge and Kegan Paul, 1955.

47. E.K. Francis, "Toward a typology of religious orders", *Am. J. Sociol.*, **55** (5) (March 1950), 437–449.

48. Andrew M. Greeley, "After secularity: the Neo-Gemeinschaft society: a post-Christian postscript", *Sociol. Anal.*, **27** (3) (Fall 1966), 119–127, p. 125.

49. Cf. Thompson, *op. cit.*, ch. II, for a discussion of the symbols favoured by the different church parties, and the correspondences between the symbols and the main system problems with which the various parties were concerned.

50. Amitai Etzioni, "Two approaches to organizational analysis: a critique and a suggestion", *Admin. Sci. Q.*, **5** (2) (Sept 1960), 257–278, p. 277.

51. Barry Young and John E. Hughes, "Organization theory and the canonical parish", *Sociol. Anal.*, **26** (2) (Summer 1965), 57–71.

52. Young and Hughes, *op. cit.*, p. 70.

53. Leslie Paul, *The Church as an Institution*, London: Prism Publications, n.d.: p. 10. For an account of his investigations into the conditions of the clergy in the Church of England, see his *The Deployment and Payment of the Clergy*, London: Church Information Office, 1964.

54. Paul, *op. cit.*, p. 10.

55. Paul, *op. cit.*, p. 11.

56. Ross P. Scherer, "The ministry and its sources of income", *Seminary Q.*, **6** (11) (Winter 1965), 1–2, p. 1.

57. Sister Marie Augusta Neal. *Values and Interests in Social Change*, Englewood Cliffs, N.J.: Prentice-Hall, 1965, pp. 15–16, 158–159.

58. Cf. Bryan R. Wilson, "The Paul Report examined", *Theology* **68** (536) (Feb 1965), 89–103; and *Theology* **68** (359) (May 1965), 245–246; Leslie Paul, *Theology*, **68** (538) (April 1965), 202–206.

59. Joseph H. Fichter S.J., *Religion as an Occupation*, New York: University of Notre Dame Press, 1961, pp. 213–214.

60. Fichter, *op. cit.*, p. 224.

61. Robert P. Rankin, "The professionalization of the calling: functional implications", paper read at Am. Sociol. Ass. Annual Meeting, August 30, 1962; the materials for this paper were drawn from research incorporated in his "Religious Ideas and Church Administration: A Sociological Study of Methodism", Unpublished Ph.D. dissertation, University of California at Berkeley, 1958.

62. Talcott Parsons, *Essays in Sociological Theory*, Glencoe, Ill.: The Free Press, 1954, pp. 34–49.

　　Cf. Max Weber's use of the term *Beruf* (calling) to refer to the Protestant sense of a higher obligation as applied to an occupation. The term is discussed in Reinhard Bendix, *Max Weber, An Intellectual Portrait*, New York: Doubleday, 1960, p. 73.

63. John Donovan, "The Catholic Priest", Unpublished Ph.D., Harvard University, 1952.

64. Samuel Blizzard, The Minister's Dilemma, *The Christian Century* (25 April 1956), pp. 508–510.

　　Studies of the work-time distribution of Protestant Ministers in America bring out the increasing emphasis on administration. In the early 1930s the percentage distribution of weekly work duties of 687 ministers was homiletical, 28.7; pastoral, 24.9; ministerial, 20.7; administrative, 11.4; educational, 5.4; civic, 5.1; and mechanical, 4.0 (H. Paul Douglass and Edmund de S. Brunner, *The Protestant Church as a Social Institution*, New York: Institute of Social and Religious Research, 1953, p. 119). By mid-century the average working day of 251 rural ministers in 22 Protestant denominations was 9 hours and 17 minutes. The role of administrator took 37 per cent of his time, followed by pastor 26 per cent, preacher and priest 18 per cent, organizer 11 per cent, and teacher 8 per cent [Samuel W. Blizzard, B.B. Maurer and G.A. Lee, "Rural ministers—work long day", *Science for the Farmer* (Pennsylvania State University), **3** (4) (Spring 1956), 14].

65. Cf. Charles Y. Glock and R. Stark, *Religion and Society in Tension*, Chicago: Rand-McNally, 1965, ch. 7.

66. Cf. James M. Gustafson, "An Analysis of the Problem of the Role of the Minister", *J. Relig.*, **34** (July 1954), 187–191; and David O. Moberg, *The Church as a Social Institution*, Englewood Cliffs, N.J.: Prentice-Hall, 1962, ch. 18.

67. Cf. Samuel W. Blizzard, "Self-Image of the Minister as a Community Leader", *Abstract of Papers and Addresses* (11th Meeting, Society for the Scientific Study of Religion, 21 April 1956), pp. 4–5; and "The parish minister's self-image and variability in community culture", *Pastoral Psych.*, **10** (97) (Oct 1959), 27–26. Also W. Seward Salisbury, *Religion in American Culture*, Homeward, Ill.: Dorsey Press, 1964, pp. 215–219.

It is not only the Protestant minister who experiences these role conflicts. Apparently the Jewish Rabbi experiences similar conflicts, especially as his most favoured self-conception, that of scholar, is the one least demanded by his congregation. Cf. Sidney I. Goldstein, "The role of an American rabbi", *Sociol. and Soc. Res.*, **38** (Sept–Oct 1953), 32–37 and Marshall Sklare, *Conservative Judaism*, Glencoe, Ill.: The Free Press, 1955.

For an account of the extra dilemma faced by the military chaplain, see Waldo Burchard, "Role conflicts of military chaplains", *Am. Sociol. Rev.*, **19** (Oct 1954), 528–535.

68. Cf. Bryan R. Wilson, "The Pentecostalist minister: role conflicts and status contradictions", *Am. J. Sociol.*, **64** (March 1959), 494–504.

69. Harry W. Allison, "Ministers: a 200 hour view", in *Christian Century*, **84**, No. 17, (26 April 1967), p. 534.

70. This is the view put forward by J. Snook, "The Protestant clergyman in America. The problems in analysing his career", *Soc. Compass*, **16** (4) (1969), 485–492. Cf. for a discussion of the dilemmas of institutionalization— the "dilemma of mixed motivation", the "symbolic dilemma", the "dilemma of administrative order", the "dilemma of delimitation", and the "dilemma of power"—Thomas O'Dea, "Five dilemmas of the institutionalization of religion", *J. Scientific Study of Religion*, **1**, No. 1 (1961), 30–39. See also Luke Smith, "The clergy: authority structure, ideology, migration", *Am. Sociol. Rev.*, **15** (June 1953), 31–38; and R.J. Menges and J.E. Dittes, *Psychological Studies of Clergymen*, New York, 1965.

71. James B. Ashbrook, "Ministry leadership in Church organization", *Ministry Studies*, **1** (1) (May 1967), A Ministry Studies Board Monograph.

72. William G.T. Douglas, "Predicting Ministerial Effectiveness", Unpublished Ph.D. thesis, Harvard University, 1957. Cf. also John H. Simpson, "A Study of the Role of the Protestant Parish Minister with special reference to organization theory", Unpublished M.Th. thesis, Princeton University, 1965.

73. Roland Robertson, *The Sociological Interpretation of Religion*, Oxford: Blackwell, 1970, p. 138.

74. On the question of whether clergymen are declining in both status and prestige, see Robert Towler, "The Changing Status of the Ministry?" in Roland Robertson (Ed.), *Sociol. of Relig.*, Harmondsworth: Penguin, 1969.

75. Cf. Harrison, *op. cit.*, esp. ch. XI.

76. Ross P. Scherer, "Ministers of the Lutheran Church—Missouri Synod: origins, training, career-lines, perceptions of work and reference", Unpublished Ph.D. thesis, Chicago University, 1965.

77. Ross P. Scherer, *op. cit.*, and "Career patterns in the ministry: The Lutheran Church—Missouri Synod", Paper presented at the American Sociological Association, Annual Meeting, Washington, D.C., 30 Aug–2 Sept 1962.

78. D.H.J. Morgan, "The social and educational background of Anglican bishops—continuities and changes", *Br. J. Sociol.*, **20**, (3) (Sept 1969), 295–310; see also A.P.M. Coxon, "A sociological study of the social recruitment, selection and professional socialization of Anglican ordinands", Unpublished Ph.D. thesis, University of Leeds, 1965.

79. James O. Gibbs and Phyllis A. Ewer, "The external adaptation of religious organizations: Church response to social issues", *Sociol. Anal.*, **30** (4) (Winter 1969), 223–234 (based on data drawn from a larger study of religious organizations by Gibbs, reported in his "Organizational effectiveness: determinants of the flexibility criterion in religious organizations", Unpublished Ph.D. thesis, University of Washington, Seattle, Washington.)

80. William Starbuck, "Organizational growth and development", in James March (Ed.), *Handbook of Organizations*, Chicago: Rand-McNally, 1965, pp. 451–533.

81. In Gibbs' study there was only slight association between organization age and size, and age was unrelated to church response to social issues, but this lack of association may have been due to lack of much variation in organizational age. Eighty per cent of the churches he studied were organized before 1912. However, it seems likely that age, size and adaptability are highly associated, in view of the contrast between the short life expectancy of small sects and the relative durability of large denominations and churches.

82. Vallier, *op. cit.*

83. *Ibid.*, p. 154.

84. Robert Benne, "A study of the regional organizations of the three major Lutheran bodies", unpublished paper, Ethics and Society Research Project, University of Chicago Divinity School, 1963 (made available by Professor

Gibson Winter). This study was part of a larger project examining the emergence of large religious organizations. Some of the results of the project were published in Gibson Winter, *Religious Identity*, New York: Macmillan, 1968.

85. *Ibid.*, p. 37.

86. *Ibid.*, p. 59.

87. It might be worth mentioning the conclusion reached by a research unit looking into the best method of studying work organizations, who considered the respective merits of a "dimensional" method as opposed to classification by types: "The dimensional method of classification has one major advantage over classification by types (ideal or otherwise). Even with a comparatively crude analysis, there is a very large number of theoretically possible profiles (with six dimensions each a ten-point scale, for example, there are a million theoretically possible profiles). Of course many of these theoretical profiles may never appear in reality, and those that are found may cluster into bunches of similarly structured organizations. These bunches may well be labelled "types" but with the knowledge that these types have not been postulated *a priori* but have been evolved with reference to the empirical date." (D.S. Pugh *et al.*, "A conceptual scheme for the empirical study of work organizations", unpublished, Industrial Administration Research Unit, College of Advanced Technology, now University of Aston, Birmingham, n.d. p. 8.

   The unfortunate fact about Etzioni's typology is that it is presented initially as a dimensional approach, but soon proceeds by selection and elimination to the level of a typology.

88. Etzioni, *op. cit.*, p. 10.

   Etzioni also states that in order to have efficiency in normative organizations such as a church (leaving aside the question of whether efficiency is an acceptable criterion of success in a church), high consensus is required with regard to ultimate values, organizational goals and means. Consensus on participation in the organization is desirable but not necessary. But this observation of Etzioni's is clearly false if, in fact, one of the formal goals is to reach just such a consensus on participation. [Cf. for a critique of Etzioni on this point, Jos. Dhooghe, "Organization problems regarding different types of membership in the church", *Soc. Compass*, **15** (2) (1968), 93–99].

89. Terence K. Hopkins, "Bureaucratic authority: the convergence of Weber and Barnard", in A. Etzioni (Ed.), *Complex Organizations*, New York: Holt Rinehart and Winston, 1962, pp. 82 ff; Max Weber, *The Theory of Social and Economic Organization*, and Chester L. Barnard, *The Functions of the Executive*, Cambridge, Mass.: Harvard University Press, 1938, pp. 163–171.

90. For an account of these problems in the Church of England, see Thompson, *op. cit.*, esp. pp. 228–229.

91. Reported in the Parochial Clergy Association's Journal *Parson and Parish* (July 1965), p. 7.

PETER W. MUSGRAVE

THE UNIVERSITY[1]

Peter W. Musgrave *received his M.A. from Canterbury and his Ph.D. from London University. After six years in the woollen textile industry he served as a secondary school teacher, a lecturer at colleges of education and as lecturer/senior lecturer in sociology at Aberdeen University in Scotland. He is presently professor of the Sociology of Education at Monash University in Melbourne, Australia. He is the author of numerous papers and the following books:* The Sociology of Education *(1965, second edition, 1972);* Technical Change, The Labor Force and Education *(1967);* The School as an Organization *(1968);* Society and Education in England Since 1800 *(1968);* The Economic Structure *(1969);* Sociology, History and Education *(1970). His present teaching and research interests include the sociology of the curriculum and the training of teachers.*

> The university ideal, which derives from the corporation of masters and scholars of the Middle Ages, is of a self-governing community concerned with advancing and disseminating knowledge.

When the Vice-Chancellor of Essex University wrote these words he was engaged in creating a new university, but in this task he was deeply influenced by the long history of this particular educational organization. There are, possibly, only two other formal organizations in contemporary Britain whose history is longer than that of the universities, namely the governmental machinery clustering round the monarchy, and the church, both of which, but particularly the latter, were closely connected with the development of the universities. Because of the strong link with the past any consideration of the British universities today must start by examining the legacy of history. This analysis should help to explain some of the characteristic features of the structure of British universities. Why, for instance, are some subjects popular or even taught at all and others excluded? Why are there so few part-time students? and, above all, why are the goals of those running the universities so different from the goals held in comparable societies?

Once the influence of the past has been established (first section) the forces that are today working to change the inherited ideas of a university will be examined. Attention will be given to two social institutions closely linked to the universities that seem today to have particular salience, namely the economy and the polity. The interaction between the past and present has worked, and still works, to create a number of universities, within which there exists an unstable and slowly changing pattern of social positions. This will be discussed in the third section. Recruits to the university, whether staff or students, and their organizational positions are considered in the fourth section, followed by a consideration of their goals. Staff and students are motivated in a variety of ways so that they differentially fulfil the behavioural expectations associated with their positions. The sixth section concerns the process of interaction between members, which results in a number of cultural climates within the universities. As staff and students enter and pass through the universities, they are affected, to a greater or lesser extent, by their experiences. This results in measurable outcomes which vary according to the experiences undergone and the nature of the clients who earlier entered this process, though the results (as will be seen in the seventh section) are no longer very like those in the minds of the creators or those who have developed this particular educational organization, nor are they often the effects intended by those running the universities today. The evidence and ideas discussed in these sections will be summarized, and future directions considered briefly in the conclusion.

The legacy of the past

Until the late 1820s there were two categories of universities in Britain. Firstly, there were the two ancient English universities, Oxford and Cambridge, whose history can be traced back respectively to the twelfth and thirteenth centuries and, secondly, there were the four ancient Scottish universities, the youngest of which, Edinburgh, was founded in 1582, that is whilst Scotland was still an independent country. The major function of all these ancient universities was vocational in that their students were almost entirely destined for the church, though law, largely canon, and medicine were also studied. Furthermore, the educational system of the time was so primitive that much of the educational work of the grammar (secondary) schools was perforce undertaken by the universities, whose students had enrolled to begin their studies often by the age of twelve or thirteen. Very early in the existence of the English universities, fear for the moral welfare of their students forced those in power to find some means of gaining closer control of their students. They solved the problem by building colleges which rapidly became the basic organizational unit of the two English universities. This did not happen in Scotland, possibly because of the greater poverty of that country.

By the late-sixteenth century the Renaissance and the Reformation had deeply influenced the universities in both countries. In the first case the spirit of the teaching given had become humanist, and, though the curriculum was still based entirely on the classics, the aim was rather to produce the cultivated man who, more particularly in England, could take his part in the governing elite of the country. Control was still in clerical hands, but since the Reformation it was the new Church of England that had power in England, as had the Presbyterian Church in Scotland. These religious changes had perhaps more influence on the doctrines permitted in the curriculum than on organizational structure. The four Scottish universities were situated in the main cities and were easier of access to all social strata; they were, therefore, always close to the grassroots of Scottish society. In addition, because of the method of government in early modern times in Scotland there was not the same close link with the ruling elite as was the case in England.

Certainly Oxford and Cambridge were far less prepared for the industrial revolution of the eighteenth century than were Edinburgh and Glasgow. Though there were still students, some relatively poor, preparing for the church at these English universities, the ethos was created by the rich undergraduates for whom their time at university led to no degree, but was seen as a pleasant preparation for the life of gentlemen and members of the ruling class. Simultaneously in Scotland men like Adam Smith were laying the foundations of patterns of thought, philosophical, scientific and ideological, which were to underpin the economic revolution.

During the Napoleonic wars restrictive measures by the government held in check the greater demands for a say in political decisions that the middle class, now growing in numbers and in wealth, was beginning to make. Similarly, the demands of the new industrial working class and the rural labour force, whose way of life was fundamentally altered by the process of industrialization, were repressed. Largely from middle-class pressure, two new universities were founded. First an entirely non-religious university was founded in London, in 1828, as a result of demands for an institution of higher education which would suit the interest of the mainly nonconformist middle class, followed by one in Durham, in 1833, founded by the Church of England, out of fear that its great wealth would be confiscated in a coming and more egalitarian age. Simultaneously, criticism of the two older English universities was growing. Eventually this reached such a pitch that two Royal Commissions were appointed and, despite the unwilling cooperation of Oxford and Cambridge, sufficient reforms of structure, particularly in relation to the links between Church and the colleges, were made to silence much of the criticism. For the reasons outlined above, the Scottish universities were much closer to the needs of a now more egalitarian society, and more able to meet the demands of the expanding international economy, increasingly based on the application of science to technology.

There had been one major innovation in the idea of what a university should be and, though this had been initiated on the Continent, its effect was felt in Britain. After their defeat by Napoleon at Jena in 1806 those in power in Prussia began a reconstruction of their country. As an integral and major part of this policy Humboldt founded the University of Berlin in 1810. The basic principles of this new model of a university were that there should be a high standard of intellectual work, taught in departments led by professors, with the aim of a general education, but that this experience should be seen as relevant to the needs of the professional part of the labour force, namely to the civil service, the legal and medical professions, or even to such vocational occupations as forestry and agriculture.

This type of university was much more nearly suited to the needs of industrialization in the mid-nineteenth century than were the English or even the Scottish universities. The nature of the German university, however, changed as the salience of the economy increased during the nineteenth century. Humboldt's humanism gave way to intellectualism and to a growing stress on empirical scientific research under the leadership of professors who headed each independent department in a rather authoritarian manner.[2]

This new definition of a university was very remote from the ideas ruling at Oxford or Cambridge and initially had no large impact on those universities. Furthermore, for various reasons it had little influence in Scotland, where admittedly there was less need for change. Additionally, the Scottish universities, having less connection with a political elite, had avoided becoming mere finishing schools, and had a more serious intellectual tone. Indeed, they, like the German universities, had a firm belief in the value of a broad general education at first degree level. There were two other reasons why changes were less necessary in the Scottish than the English universities. In Scotland the universities were geographically and socially close to the changes of the times. One Scot in a thousand was a university student, compared with one in 5800 in England, and something over 20 per cent of Scottish students were of manual origin, which was probably twenty times the English proportion.[3] For such reasons the curricula contained more relevant material. Also, the poverty of the universities and their students forced a structure based on large lectures by professors which in some way paralleled the German System.

However, the influence of the new German idea of a university was felt strongly in the new English civic universities which were founded in the second half of the nineteenth century. Owens College (later Manchester University), established in 1851, was the first of these foundations. By the end of the century, several more universities had been created in provincial industrial centres, for example, Newcastle (1871), Leeds (1874), Bristol (1876), Sheffield (1879), Birmingham (1880), and Liverpool (1882). Many of their staff had experience of Oxford or Cambridge. They, therefore, brought to the new foundations some of the humanist, elitist and collegiate emphases of those universities. Yet the original aim of the new foundations was to be "community service stations"[4] and much of the necessary finance came from local industrialists. Thus, there was a stress on such practical and mundane specialisms as metallurgy and the technology of iron and steel or textiles. In addition, many of the professors in the new scientific departments had experience of the German universities and their large research laboratories.

By the turn of the century, therefore, there were three categories of universities in Britain. The two ancient English universities were still collegiate in character, elitist in recruitment and humanist in curriculum and spirit; though science, practical subjects and research were now coming to be accepted, doctorates were still not awarded here, nor, in fact, were they in any British university until after the 1914–1918 war. Secondly, there was the new civic group in which, though doctorates were not granted, they were found amongst the scientific staff who had been to Germany, where a more practical curriculum was taught; yet because these universities had a double inheritance, the new subjects tended to have low status, whilst the disciplines associated with the arts faculty, which had in many ways inherited the functions of sixteenth century humanism, carried into provincial England and to the new middle class, the cultural tradition of Oxford and Cambridge.[5] Thirdly, there were the four Scottish universities, in many ways unaltered by the political and economic upheavals of the nineteenth century and changing rather because Scotland was becoming somewhat less of a separate entity as she was drawn into the national scheme of government, than because of the direct influence of the economic and political forces affecting the English universities.

The ancient universities were wealthy corporate bodies who had large endowments upon which to rely, but the new universities were not in this. independent position and relied heavily upon local goodwill and donations. The war of 1914–1918 caused great dislocations in the latter, since their income from fees dropped suddenly as the majority of their men students joined the armed forces. The government, which had before been providing a small amount of finance, now stepped in to supply a much larger proportion of their needs, and these subsidies involved a real administrative problem. The British universities had by 1900 built a strong tradition of freedom and self-government, but the British method of government had come to rely heavily on the tenets of Gladstonian finance, whereby monies were disbursed sparingly and only for closely specified purposes. How were the universities to be subsidized without encroaching upon academic freedom?

In 1919 there was established the Universities Grants Committee (UGC), a body descended from a wartime committee established for this same purpose. The Treasury allocated monies directly to particular universities on the recommendations of this body who acted as a buffer between state and university, matching available finance and the submissions from its constituent organizations. Thus, until very recently, the Treasury never examined the details of the manner in which the universities spent state money. Freedom of action within their available budgets remained with the universities. This administrative solution was feasible because those who held political power, whether in the government or in the civil service, were largely recruited from the universities, and shared common values and assumptions. Furthermore, there were a number of precedents in Britain especially during the 1914–1918 war, for the establishment of part-time committtees to advise the government. The UGC consisted of part-time members drawn largely from the universities, though with time, notable industrialists and educationalists were also appointed. The convention was that those from the universities spent a fifth of their time on UGC affairs. They were, therefore, in close touch with academic matters, since they were still teaching, writing and administering in their own universities. The UGC developed close cooperation with a large number of similar or closely related bodies. Such were the Medical and Industrial Research Councils and the Board (after 1945 the Ministry) of Education. Within the limits of the finances made available to it, the UGC was, therefore, able to respond to the needs of the universities and to arrange their subsidies in such a way that the state did not make demands that would encroach upon their freedom.[6]

The growth of the universities during the interwar years was slow. There were 42 000 (1.5 per cent of the eligible age group) full-time students in British universities in 1924–1925 and 50 000 (1.7 per cent of the age group) in 1938–1939 (R.15 and 16). After the war of 1939–1945—once the immediate increase of enrolments delayed by service in the forces was past—the rate of expansion seemed to slow down again so that the percentage of those with university entrance qualifications who actually entered universities fell from 74 in 1955 to 61 in 1961, though the proportion of the age group entering rose from 3.4 to 4.1 (R., 12). This was surprising, since many commentators remarked on the increasing need for highly educated manpower in the labour force because of the changing, and especially the more scientific, nature of the processes involved in the economy. These new demands would perhaps have been more easily met by universities organized in the German nineteenth century tradition of professional specialism rather than in the English eighteenth century tradition of humanist elitism. As a partial answer to such needs, specialization had increased greatly within the universities, so that the number of subjects reported in the UGC statistics had grown from 123 in 1928 to 382 in 1953.[7]

Despite the fact that many in the universities still held to views based on the humanist and elitist tradition, the Robbins Committee, whose report "Higher Education", was issued in 1963, put forward strong recommendations for the expansion of universities, particularly in the areas of science and technology, and in the size and composition of the student population. The Conservative government immediately accepted its recommendations that the numbers in the universities should be expanded from 130 000 in 1962–1963 to about 350 000 in 1980–1981 (R. 160).

There was some growth in the late 50s and early 60s in the numbers of students. Between 1954–1955 and 1963–1964 Oxford and Cambridge expanded by 20 per cent, London by 30 per cent, and the Scottish universities by 52 per cent. The main growth was in the civic group, where the larger universities grew by 69 and the smaller by 111 per cent (R., II (a), 20).

What was largely overlooked, even in the universities themselves, was that given natural population increase, this "expansion" would do no more until the 1970s than keep the proportion of students eligible for university each year constant. Whether or not the absolute, recommended expansion would meet the growing needs of technology is uncertain, but certainly it seems that the egalitarian aim of the expansionists was unlikely to be achieved since the intake, even in the 1950s, was still clearly biased against the working class. In 1964 one study found that "the social class composition of the student body in the universities has remained roughly the same during the past three to five decades".[8]

During this same period, decisions were taken that created two new types of university in Britain; these were, (a) what are often called "the new universities" and (b) what eventually, on the recommendation of the Robbins Committee, have become the technological universities. A further set of organizations giving higher education, namely the colleges training teachers, were given the title of Colleges of Education, and became eligible to teach for the degree of Bachelor Education— also the following recommendations in the Robbins Report.

One new university, Keele, founded in 1951, was planned in the English tradition, with the aim of giving a liberal education through close contact both between staff and students, and amongst the students themselves. This was considered particularly necessary for the increasing proportion of working-class entrants who were (in the event, mistakenly) expected to come to the universities.[9] In the new sense of urgency surrounding the appointment and deliberations of the Robbins Committee, other new universities were founded in a number of smaller, residential towns. For example, the Universities of Sussex, Essex and East Anglia were established at Brighton, Colchester and Norwich respectively, and universities were also started at Canterbury, Lancaster and Warwick in England, at Stirling in Scotland and Coleraine in Northern Ireland.

The members of the UGC had two hopes for these new universities, firstly that they would eventually provide for an expansion of numbers, though the rate of growth of each individual university was slow in comparison with similar new foundations in many comparable countries.[10] Secondly, there was an expectation that new ideas in teaching and a new map of knowledge would be developed. Members of the UGC felt that "university education needed a shake-up, an injection of new concepts and methods to shake it out of its complacent routine of specialized single subject honours courses, insular departments . . . and lack of awareness of the needs of students. . .".[11] However, some factors clearly served to strengthen the "English" tradition of the university (as exemplified in the ancient English universities) and worked against the way in which a new tradition had been developed in the more recent civic universities, in which the German influence had been strongest. The main factors were the relative geographical isolation of the new universities, and their emphasis on both the collegiate ideal and on what Weber called "the pedagogy of cultivation".

Among the universities created since 1945, the path by which a number of technical colleges achieved the status of university was long. In the late-50s several of these organizations that were already undertaking advanced work (including teaching for the external degrees of London University) were granted the title of Colleges of Advanced Technology (CATs), but the power to grant degrees was initially withheld. As a result of a recommendation of the Robbins Committee the CATs became technological universities empowered to give degrees. In addition, as a result of the policy of the Labour Party, then in office, new emphasis was put upon the creation of thirty Polytechnics for students who, in the words of Anthony Crosland, Minister of Education at the time, "cannot on entry show that they are of university calibre", but who by strong motivation and good teaching can "subsequently tackle a full-time degree course". These organizations did not have the power to grant their own degrees, unlike the new universities who were awarded this right of the full university from their establishment, and unlike the civic universities who earned this privilege whilst teaching for the external degrees of London University. Therefore, a concurrent development was the creation in 1964—again consequent upon a recommendation of the Robbins Report—of the Council for National Academic Awards. The CNAA established committees, largely recruited from the universities, to examine applications for degree level courses from the Polytechnics and other nonuniversity organizations with the aim of enforcing the seemingly threatened high academic standards.[12]

By the late 1960s there were forty-four full universities in Britain, together with some Colleges of Education, which had a proportion of students reading for the degree of Bachelor Education from the local university to which the College was affiliated. There was also in development a non-university sector at the apex of which were to be thirty Polytechnics where some, but eventually a substantial proportion of students would be reading for CNAA degrees, which, though not awarded by any university, are in some measure within the control of university staff. The organizations providing higher education of solely university level can be put into five categories that reflect differences due to their historical development; the ancient English universities of Oxford and Cambridge, the ancient Scottish universities of St. Andrews, Glasgow, Aberdeen and Edinburgh, the English civic universities including the Universities of London and of Wales, the new universities including Stirling in Scotland and Coleraine in Northern Ireland, and the technological universities, which include establishments in Scotland and Wales.

The problem of controlling this system of higher education had rapidly grown so complex that several important administrative bodies had formed in addition to the UGC. Two will be mentioned. The first, perhaps the lesser in importance, was the creation in the early 1960s of the Universities Central Council on Admissions (UCCA). The demand for places in the universities had become so great that machinery seemed necessary to ration them out, though initially the ancient English and Scottish universities were not members of UCCA. So strong is the stress on the right of each university to chose its own students, however, that this new organization became no more than a clearing-house, which forwarded student applications to the universities according to choice, automatically referring applications to lower choices if the university of first choice did not accept, a bureaucratic device to save time and effort.

More important was the gradual development of the Committee of the Vice-Chancellors of the English, and the Principals of the Scottish universities who had for some time held "an unofficial monthly meeting". Before 1939 its members were few enough for them all to be on friendly terms and the universities were still of a size that the Vice-Chancellors (as the administrative heads) were reasonably well informed about their internal workings. Gradually, especially during the war of 1939–1945, this group became "the body from which 'university opinion' might be sought"[13]. However, the nature of the group changed as its members became more numerous and as the size of universities grew throughout the 1950s and 1960s. By this time what was now known as the Committee of Vice-Chancellors and Principals was admitted to be representative of the universities by the UGC, the Ministry of Education and the public at large, and a permanent administrative organization, with a complex structure of specialized sub-committees, was developed.

Before trying to summarize the characteristic goals of the British universities and to note any differences between the categories that have been isolated, some attention must be given to two major forces working to change the legacy of the past which appear to have exerted some influence on the contemporary British universities.

The contemporary economic and political ethos

At any time any one social institution is liable to be influenced by changes in inter-locking institutions. The view taken here is that in contemporary Britain, edu-cation and specifically the universities, are at present affected by certain economic and political forces, powerful enough to alter key parts of the structural and ideological legacy of the past.

(i) *The economic climate* As was mentioned earlier, the universities have gradually grown to be more dependent upon the Treasury for recurrent grants to keep them in existence. In 1919–1920 £692 000 was granted through the UGC to the univer-sities and this sum represented 28.8 per cent of their income. By 1956–1957 grants had reached 28 millions, representing over 70 per cent of their total income (or 90 per cent if special research grants were excluded). The state was, at this time, directing about 15 per cent of its total educational expenditure towards the universities, representing about 0.8 per cent of the national income.[14] This sum was disbursed, at the request of the UGC, as already described. As a result of this system, the Public Accounts Committee of Parliament were unable to check the efficiency with which this growing sector of public expenditure was used. By the mid-60s, when this grant was over 60 millions, the issue had become politically important. The impact of this situation can, perhaps, be demonstrated in relation to the supply of housing which was still a major problem in Britain in the early 1960s. At that time, the capital cost of housing an entire family on a local authority housing estate was comparable to the £1705 required to provide a residential place for one student in a university college (R., IV, 113). Though many of those in power, being university graduates, were sympathetic to the threat to academic freedom, it was deemed politically no longer possible to exempt so large a segment of public money from the normal routines of government accountancy. In 1968, therefore, the Public Accounts Committee was given access to the books of the UGC and the universities.

Interestingly, the Robbins Committee had recommended the formation of a special ministry for higher education, but this was unacceptable to the government of the day, although certain administrative changes were made, then, in an un-successful attempt to exercise closer governmental control over the universities.

The government, therefore, now has apparent control over the universities, based on its control of the purse strings and such consequent matters as salary scales and staffing ratios. Thus in 1966 the UGC, when allocating the quinquennial grants to each university, sent out a "Memorandum for General Guidance", and when establishing the new universities, this same committee has positively dis-couraged them from developing medicine, dentistry and certain Slavonic, Oriental and African studies (though, for instance, Lancaster ignored this policy by establishing a Centre for Central European studies, financed "entirely out of appeal funds"[15]). However, on another occasion a number of universities in 1966 opposed a demand from the government that fees for overseas students should be raised. The Committee of Vice-Chancellors supported this stand and some universities did not make the change.

However, there can be little argument that the government exercises increasing control over the universities and that the traditional role of the UGC as a buffer between state and university has altered. In fact, the UGC was never an entirely neutral body and under contemporary social conditions, there is a growing need both for a more unitary policy on higher education and for accountability to society for the activities of the universities (UGC, 176–182). Indeed, the academic freedom which appears to have been violated is a relatively modern British tradition. Up to the mid-nineteenth century the English universities were subject to considerable control from the Church of England. The civic universities, growing up in an increasingly secular age and with the help of large private donations, in some ways became freer than the ancient universities, but by 1900 all British universities felt and probably were as free of external control as universities anywhere in the world. Although, today, there exists the bureaucratic machinery for a close control of higher education, the universities do not seem to have been subjected to many attacks so far (UGC, 185), although the Vice-Chancellor of Liverpool University recently retired as a protest against governmental encroachments upon the freedom of the universities, made largely in the interests of economic efficiency.

(ii) *The political climate*   The reason for this resignation is symptomatic of the different contemporary political climates of Britain and, for example, the USA. In the latter, Presidents of universities have recently resigned because of political militancy among their students. Before considering the way in which changes in the political views of students have influenced the British universities one result of the growing political emphasis upon egalitarianism in education must be considered. The development of the Polytechnics and a non-university sector of higher education has already been outlined. This differentiation is usually referred to as "the binary system". The connection of this system with the demands for equality in education can be seen in a passage from a major policy statement made by Anthony Crosland, the Minister of Education, at Woolwich Polytechnic in 1965:

> The Government accepts this dual system as being fundamentally the right one, with each sector making its own distinctive contribution to the whole. We infinitely prefer it to the alternative concept of a unitary system, hierarchically arranged on the ladder principle, with the universities at the top and the other institutions down below.

There are indications that the policy of expanding the non-university sector of this binary system also meets another of the government's policies, namely the provision of more places for the study of specific, often technological, subjects in higher education, more cheaply than in the traditionally free universities that have proved so difficult to control.

The egalitarian ideology that has become so important a force in national politics since 1945, affected the universities much more directly in the late-1960s through the political views and activities of their students. Many students who now come to the universities see higher education no longer as a privilege for an elite, but as a right for all. These students view the traditional and inherited values of the university in a very critical spirit and are no longer willing to defer un-

questioningly to the authority of their teachers and those administering the universities.

There are many possible sources of these changing political views. Students
are in some ways more politically mature than in former generations, since the
great postwar expansion in secondary education has ensured the emergence of a
larger proportion of questioning young adults during a period in which the former
blacks and whites of the international situation have largely disappeared as the
tension in the cold war has lessened, and in which the American involvement in
Vietnam was increasingly criticized. In addition, the hope that a gradualist
policy based on the concept of the Welfare State would solve many of the national
problems of poverty and inequality also seems to have been largely disappointed.
For many students the traditional values and organization of the universities,
always slow to change, have seemed an obvious and handy target for the application of their new found ideology and idealism.[16]

(iii) *The characteristics of the British universities*   As a result of their history and
the social forces at work today, those who have power or work in the British
universities have a complex set of interrelated goals. The weight given to these
purposes changes through time and at any one moment differs between groups or
single individuals. Prominent amongst these aims is that of *scholarship*, which,
even in the ancient English universities around 1800, was always a real way of life
for some members, both senior and junior, of the universities. Often this love of
learning was an offshoot of, or accompanied the process of training students in
their vocation. For centuries this meant a life in the church, whilst today, the
scholarship may be the servant of a modern vocation such as engineering. However, since the middle of last century, scholarship has been competing with (as
well as complementing) research in all fields of knowledge. At the extreme,
research work has encouraged fact finding and experimentation of the most trivial
sort, at the same time possibly encouraging criticism of established theory merely
for the sake of criticism. This process may have further undermined a deference
to the authority of the past which was historically associated with the universities—
a process of erosion also supported by the contemporary political version of the
ideology of egalitarianism.

A further important goal in all universities has been that of *moral development*.
Particularly in the ancient English universities, the college system was devised
with this purpose in mind, and the civic universities imitated Oxford and Cambridge in building some halls of residence. The new universities were very conscious of this purpose and even in Scotland such halls have become more common
since 1945. But the ending of the age of deference has made this goal more difficult
to accomplish. Staff are now no longer seen by students as *in loco parentis*. Yet
the more favourable staff-student ratio in Britain of one to eight compared with
one to thirteen in the USA or one to thirty-five in Germany (R., 41) at least permits
closer interaction in the general work of teaching and learning. Though this
closeness might well lead to a clearer definition of differences—political or otherwise—in the interests of staff and students, in Britain it would also seem to make

for easier influencing of students, though perhaps the process is less obstrusive in normal teaching than in a college or a hall.

The emphasis placed on the university as a *community* which should influence its students is still evident in the siting of the new universities in small towns. A striking example was in the decision to put the University of Essex at Wivenhoe Park, a few miles from Colchester, rather than in Chelmsford, which would have been too easy of access to London, and, in the words of the Vice-Chancellor would have "made it difficult for the university to build up a strong corporate life"; not only was the student to stay the course and pass his exams, but he was to have "the intellectual and social experience of being a member of an academic community".[17]

To many, the university is seen as a "mechanism for the inheritance of the western style of civilization"[18] and there are, therefore, powerful residues of tradition in the minds of those filling the positions of staff or student. This influences the ways in which the universities are gradually adapting to the demands of the technological society.[19] The ideal of a *humanist and general education* is so strong that once technological institutions have achieved university status they tend to legitimate their position by introducing subjects in the humanities and arts. The technological universities are thus themselves seen, and come to see themselves, as elitist in aim. This probably results partly from the concept of the universities as institutions for the education of the elite and partly from the consequent fierce competition for university places in Britain (places are provided for never more than about half of all those who are qualified). Similarly, the new universities whose purpose was largely non-elitist, in that their creation was in part to cope with an expanded proportion of the age group in higher education, have taken their place in the upper echelons of "the pyramid of prestige"[20] together with the older universities, whose connections with the political and business elite of Britain have not diminished since 1945.[21]

The humanist tradition has also been a powerful support to the emergence of a hierarchy of disciplines within higher education. Until recently, arts had much greater prestige than the sciences; the status of the classics is evident in the common deference given to, and often assumed by, the man with a "first in Greats at Oxford". Similarly, the "pure" sciences still tend to have higher standing than the applied sciences or technology.[22] The social sciences, until recently, stood low in the hierarchy with education perhaps lowest of all, as being applied, social, and comparative newcomers to the academic field. These recent changes and conflicts in goals are warning enough to any analyst of the universities to avoid a view too oriented towards consensus. There are disagreements among both staff and students, as well as between staff and students. Yet despite the presence of much conflict within the British universities, the historical legacy is so powerful that an American academic sociologist who also has considerable experience of teaching in Britain can truthfully observe:

> Whatever the cleavage between the ancient universities and the modern, between the English and the Scottish, the range of variation of the British universities from the highest to the lowest is very narrow in comparison with the American.[23]

Positions within the universities

Acting on their definitions of the goals of their particular university members of the academic staff have in the past created a structure of positions for staff and students. This has gradually changed through time and is still changing under the impact of social forces such as the political and economic influences that have been shown to be strong today. Because the British universities, despite their differences, draw largely on a common heritage, there are many common features in the structures of each of the five groups defined in the last section. We will consider here those relating to university government, staff, students, types of residence and the teaching situation.

The system of government evolved in the universities is extremely complex and representatives of five groups play some part in the process of setting or changing the goals of these organizations and their administration. Teachers have always been prominent in this task. Students in some medieval continental universities had considerable power, but until recently only in Scotland can there be said to be any long tradition in Britain of students taking part in university government. In the Scottish universities the students elect a Rector who during his period of office sits on Court, the supreme seat of power in their universities. The Government, originally in the form of ecclesiastical authority, and more recently, in the form of representatives of local government, have also normally been represented on university governing bodies. With the growth of the feeling that the universities had a responsibility to society at large, such members of the nonacademic community as industrialists or prominent citizens have been included as well. Finally, particularly in the older universities, special assemblies of the university's own graduates have been given certain, limited power in the governmental machinery.

These five elements play their part in higher levels of university government, usually, except in the case of the graduates, on a body called Council in England, or Court in Scotland, which is supposedly responsible for making the ultimate decisions in the university. Certainly financial decisions, on which so much else turns, are at least formally made here. Answerable only to Council is a body consisting entirely of academics, usually known as Senate, which is responsible in the main for articulating academic policy. Next down the hierarchy are the various Faculties, or, in some of the new universities, Schools, within which are specialized Departments, each with its own governing body. Where these lower divisions are accompanied by geographical separation in different buildings, or on separate sites, a feeling of the corporateness of the university sometimes becomes hard to sustain.

Each level of the governing machinery is served by a secretariat. At the upper levels there is a body of specialized administrators; at the lower level departments have one or more secretaries. This structure with its many committees and its rigidly established procedures by which matters are referred up and down, has been a target for criticism from both students and staff so that, especially in the new and the technological universities, attempts have been made to enfranchise all members of the university.

In 1966–1967 there were 23 609 full-time university staff of whom 8.4 per cent were in the ancient English universities, 12.6 in the Scottish universities, 59.0 in the civic group (31.3 of whom were at London), 5.5 in the new universities and 14.5 per cent in the technological universities (UGC, 203–204). These staff members are organized in a hierarchy of a bureaucratic nature in that there is a well-defined career structure. There is a probationary grade of assistant lecturer (13.6 per cent of all staff in 1966–1967 (UGC, 25)) prior to appointment with tenure, usually after three years, as a lecturer (46.3 per cent); in this latter position earnings increase annually for six to seven years, at which point there is a rarely enforced "efficiency bar". Once at the top of the scale, a teacher, at the level of lecturer or higher, serves until the retirement age of sixty-five with dismissal as an extremely remote possibility. In 1967 the UGC laid down that, except in medical faculties, up to 35 per cent of all positions might be senior posts, with the rank of senior lecturer or reader or professor. This ratio was intended to equalize the career opportunities in each university and to decrease competition, but it has also been incorporated into the system of financial control operated by the UGC (UGC, 28–30). The exception made in the case of medicine, together with the higher salary scales operating in that faculty, are intended to counteract the attraction of high earnings for medical practitioners outside the universities.

Despite these changes, there has been a marked diminution in the chances of promotion to the position of professor over the last forty years. Thus in 1927–1928 22 per cent of university teachers were professors; by 1961–1962 the proportion was 12 per cent and this figure had fallen to 9.8 per cent by 1965–1966 (R., III, 13). There is, however, more chance of becoming a professor in some of the smaller or the newer than in the larger or more established subjects (R., III, 32). Thus, in 1961–1962 there were, on average, 4.8 teachers per head of department in medicine, 6.8 in arts and social science, 9.9 in pure science, and 10.9 in applied science (R., III, 18). However, in another way the difference in status between members in the academic hierarchy is lessening. As a result of the pay award of 1969 the lower ranks were given substantially bigger increases than professors, thereby diminishing the income differentials. The status of academic positions may also be compared with similar positions outside the universities. In the interwar years the normal professorial salary was £1000—less than a principal in the civil service, and the starting salary for an assistant lecturer was £250 as against £300 for a civil servant. Today a professor earns about £5600 which is more than an assistant secretary, who is one grade higher than a principal, whilst an Assistant Lecturer starts at a higher salary than a Principal.[24] Thus, since 1945, despite lessening chances of high promotion, there has been a big increase in the number of academic positions, differentials within the university seem to have diminished and the general social status of all university teachers appears to have risen.

The positions available for staff and students, and the machinery to administer these organizations have been created largely with the specific purposes of teaching and research in mind. There are a number of different learning positions available in the universities. Students may undertake either an honours course specializing in one or two fields, or an ordinary degree which is usually wider in scope and hence tends to go to less depth in any one subject. The proportion of students completing honours courses has grown since 1945 so that whereas in 1955–1956 64 per cent of all first degrees from British universities were in honours, by 1965–1966 the percentage had risen to 74. In line with their emphasis on general education the Scottish universities have always had a high proportion of their students, particularly women, reading for the Scottish Ordinary M.A.[25] In 1959, 24.8 per cent of students in Britain did not take the honours degrees. In Oxford and Cambridge 9.4 per cent took ordinary degrees but in the Scottish universities 59.2 per cent did so, including 45 per cent in science and 65 per cent in arts, the majority of the latter being women (R., II a, 140). The number of positions available to postgraduate students has also increased rapidly since 1945, to over 17 per cent in 1961–1962.

The resources of staff available for teaching are very much more favourable for students than in most other countries. In 1966–1967 the ratio of full-time staff to full-time students was 1 to 7.8 (UGC, 24), though, staff–student ratios vary considerably by faculty. In 1961–1962 (excluding the two ancient English universities) there was one member of staff to 8.8 students in arts, 7.0 in science, 8.8 in applied science, 3.0 in agriculture and 6.0 in medicine (R., III, 5).

Teaching resources are used in different ways in different universities and faculties. The average number of hours per week during which students were taught in 1961–1962 was 14.8, of which 8.1 hours were spent in lectures, 0.5 in tutorials, 1.1 in seminars and 4.6 in practicals. Traditionally, much teaching has been in the form of lectures in Scotland, whilst tutorials have been emphasized at Oxford and Cambridge (R., 116, 253). Usually for students lectures are "straightforwardly informative . . . ordered . . . in a way which gives the audience an opportunity to see a subject in perspective", whereas "the purpose of the tutorial . . . is not to convey information, but to teach the pupil how to think, by exposing himself to the stimulation of an older scholar".[26] Recently there has been an increasing volume of criticism of the lecture as a teaching device by students and by some young staff on the grounds that it is an authoritarian and frequently abused method allowing for little participation by the learner, and restricting the possibilities of clarifying misunderstandings or following up individual interests. However, although students want more tutorials and seminars, this form of teaching appears to be viewed by many students as a loosely structured discussion group rather than as an organized situation requiring considerable preparation by all the participants.[27]

Mechanical aids to learning are, as yet, rare in British universities, although the recently established Open University relies principally upon a combination of television and correspondence courses. This new organization has recruited the usual type of staff and aims to teach non-residential students for general degrees of the traditional British pattern.

Only in the new universities has much thought been given to devising new combinations of subjects so that the accepted image of learning is redrawn. The hope is that students put in these new learning situations will come to view the world differently. This group of universities have not, however, pioneered new subjects except in the field of "business technology". (For instance, marketing departments have been established with part-time staff from industry, and money has been donated for such purposes, and also to finance research.) And these developments have aroused fears for academic freedom in the minds of many, on the grounds that control of an academic organization is passing into the hands of vested outside interests.[28]

The pattern of residence of students varies greatly by university group. In 1961–1962 at Oxford and Cambridge 62 per cent were in colleges, 1 per cent lived at home, 1 per cent were in lodgings with board, and 36 per cent in independent lodgings, whilst at the other extreme, corresponding percentages in Scotland were: 15 in colleges, 14 at home, 20 in lodgings with board, and 18 in independent lodgings (R., IIa, 178). Here can be seen quite clearly the legacy of the past in the importance given to residential colleges in the ancient English, in contrast to the ancient Scottish, universities.

The development of the system of grants, which support the majority of students studying for first degrees, has had the effect of increasing the percentage of students living away from home from 72 per cent in 1955–1956 to 82 per cent in 1965–1966, at a time when criticism of authority in the family and elsewhere has grown more strong. The college or hall of residence provides residential positions in a corporate ethos that is also often perceived as formal and hierarchical. For this reason, places in this type of residence are less in demand today amongst students, who have come to put more emphasis on the facilities for meals, social life and extra-curricular activities that are provided by Students' Unions. Many extra-curricular positions associated with societies, whether political or of some other nature, have been centred in Unions and, therefore, the positions of President and on the committees associated with the Union have grown in importance. So complex is the task of the President of the Students' Union in most large universities that he is granted a paid sabbatical year whilst in office. In many ways it would seem that the integrating positions in modern British universities are found less today in the system of residence and more in the Union, which is likewise financed out of university money. The importance of this student organization is reflected in the large membership of the National Union of Students—by the late 1960s the sixth largest union in Britain.[29]

Patterns of recruitment

The majority of positions in the British universities are for students or academic staff and, since the ultimate aim of this chapter is to discuss what these organizations do to those who fill positions within them, attention must next be given to the nature of those recruited.

(i) *Students*   The universities pride themselves that they choose their own students and, even though the establishment of UCCA has to some extent centralized the process of application, the decision to accept or reject is still made by the individual universities according to the order in which the student has given his preferences. Yet the quantity and the quality of applicants is largely outside the control of those running the universities. Regarding quantity the absolute number of places available to students is largely dependent upon the policy of the government. As a result of the decision to implement the expansion recommended by the Robbins Report, the proportion of the population in the relevant age group who were enrolled in the universities rose from around 4.5 per cent during 1958–1962 to 6.3 per cent during 1962–1967,[30] although Britain still has one of the lowest proportions of the age group in universities amongst the economically developed nations.

Although students are chosen by all universities on a meritocratic basis, the demand for places in some subjects is, of course, greater than in others, so that the acceptance rate varies between subject groups; in 1966, 70.9 per cent of the applicants were accepted in pure science, 50.2 in arts, 38.0 in social science and 22.3 per cent in medicine (UGC, 104). As a result, the academic quality of students at entry, as measured by their success in public examinations at secondary school, varied considerably between faculties.[32]

One result of this meritocratic base of selection and of the availability of adequate subsistence grants is that there is a much larger proportion of children of working-class origins in the British universities than in those of any other European non-communist country. Around 1960, 25 per cent of students came from such backgrounds compared with 5 per cent in France and Western Germany, or 20 per cent in Norway.[33] However, the proportions of men and women from such backgrounds varies as do the proportions in different faculties. In 1955 the percentage of men (26 per cent) with fathers in manual occupations was higher than that for women (19 per cent), while 15 per cent of medical students (only 10 per cent for women) had parents in manual occupations, and 30 per cent of students in both pure science (21 per cent for women) and technology (only 8 per cent for women) were of working-class origin (R., IIb, 428). Interestingly, more working-class students appear to be attracted to the pure and applied sciences, which lead to well-known and traditionally secure occupations than to the subjects which lead to less obvious, middle-class careers. This tendency is particularly the case for such "non-school" subjects as anthropology and sociology.[34]

Social classes were also recruited differentially to university groups. Oxford and Cambridge showed the lowest proportion of working-class students (13 per cent and 9 per cent respectively); the civic universities accepted 30 per cent, with some regional variation, and Scotland 24 per cent (R., IIb, 429). These figures appears to meet expectations based on the histories of these groups except in the case of Scotland, which seems to be less democratic in this respect than previously, the proportion equalling the overall average. One can reasonably infer that the proportion of students from manual homes is higher in the technological than in other universities, since the sector from which this new category was largely created, namely full-time further education, had 42 per cent of its students in 1961–1962 from the working class (though even here, the parents of the majority were in skilled occupations (R., IIb, 92).

Perhaps the greatest anomaly in connection with the social class of students recruited to the British universities is that the new universities, created at a time when one of the major goals of expansion was to increase educational equality between classes, have a lower than average proportion of students from manual backgrounds. During the mid-1960s these universities, with the exception of Lancaster, recuited fewer working-class students than the average for all British universities. In Essex and Keele, where the proportion was the lowest, only 18 per cent of students were children of manual fathers, nearly as low a proportion as that at Oxford.[35]

One characteristic of university students, closely associated with social class, is the amount of schooling undergone by their parents. In the early 60s 70 per cent of students had at least one parent who had experienced selective secondary education, but there were some differences between faculties and university groups. Thus, medicine (78) and humanities (77) had the highest proportion of such parents, and applied science (71) and pure science (69) the lowest, whilst the ancient English universities (87) were the group with the highest percentage and the civic universities (67) the lowest (R., IIb, 2).

The nature of the British educational system is such that almost all entrants to university must come from a selective secondary school of one type or another and the British selective secondary schools dedicate themselves largely to the goal of sending as large a proportion of their pupils as possible to the universities. The result would seem to be that there are a large number of what Bidwell has called "*de facto* students", that is those at the universities with no clear idea of their own aims, or there at another's behest. In a study of a sample of students at Cambridge, Leeds and Southampton universities made between 1961 and 1963 Marris found that four-fifths of those at Cambridge and two-thirds of those at the other two universities had never seriously considered any alternative to going to university on leaving school. "They do not so much choose the university, as fail to choose otherwise."[36] The differences found in the Robbins survey support Marris's findings, since students at Oxford and Cambridge had the lowest percentage (43) of definite choices of occupation; the ancient Scottish universities (60) had the highest (R., 11b, 168).

The differences between commitment to an occupation noted above are reflected in the levels of aspiration of different categories of students within one technological university. At Bradford, Musgrove found that linguists and social scientists had lower levels of aspirations than those of scientists and technologists. Another study at this university noted that all groups of students tended to see themselves primarily as potential members of a profession or in their future vocational role rather than primarily as students, though the social scientists seemed less committed in this respect than other students.[37] Most British students, largely owing to the operation of the system of grants, attend universities away from their home areas. By 1961–1962 the proportion living within thirty miles of home had dropped somewhat to less than one-third. This proportion was much the same in all universities except for the 5 per cent at Oxford and Cambridge, with their great national reputation, and 52 per cent in the ancient Scottish universities, which are sited in the large areas of population and have always tended to recuit locally (R., IIa, 186).

The overall proportion of women students has changed little since before 1939, remaining at about 25 per cent. At Oxford and Cambridge the slow growth of women's colleges has accounted for a very low 12 per cent. The larger civic universities, the Scottish group and London all have over a quarter of their students who are women, whilst the smaller civic universities have about 35 per cent (R., IIa, 24–25). All the new universities also have more than the national average of women amongst their students, but this is very largely due to their reduced emphasis on the traditionally masculine faculties[38]. In 1961–1962, 42 per cent of all British students in humanities were women, compared with only 3 per cent of those in the applied sciences (R., IIa, 26).

In summary, all British students are highly qualified on entry, since there are many more applicants than available places, but many are uncertain of their ultimate goal. While students reading the less popular subjects, namely the pure and applied sciences, have somewhat lower qualifications, as measured by their examination records at school, more appear certain of their future in life, than those studying the humanities. Moreover, British students are more often male and middle-class with at least one parent who has had experience of secondary education, and tend to be at a university some distance from their home. A substantial minority, especially at the ancient and the new English universities, still come from independent schools. Students from working-class families and from grammar schools are common in the pure and applied science faculties and in the civic universities. Although the ancient Scottish universities tend to recruit from their own densely populated hinterlands, they are less democratic than their cultural tradition would lead one to predict.

(ii) *Academic staff* Almost all academic staff in British universities are recruited through open advertisement in the national press. Applications are then referred to appointment committees, consisting of senior members of the department and the faculty concerned, together with one or two academics from elsewhere in the university. These committees, while usually recommending to court or to some other senior governmental body, are the real selecting bodies, as it is extremely rare for a recommendation to be refused.

Over the last thirty years, the growth in the number of universities has allowed a widening of sources of recruitment to the very senior positions. The titular head of a university, the Chancellor, still tends to be a member of the royal family, but others, such as eminent retired academics, are now more often invited. The function of such appointees is to serve as a crucial link to those close to the sources of power where decisions affecting growth of universities are made. The social and educational backgrounds of Vice-Chancellors and Principals (the operational heads) are still closely linked to the universities which had high status three decades ago, namely Oxford, Cambridge, Edinburgh and Glasgow, and to the faculty which then had highest prestige, namely arts. However, the creation of the technological universities out of the former CATs has allowed the emergence of a group of Vice-Chancellors with a different career pattern, more closely linked to the applied sciences.[39]

In 1961–1962 Oxford and Cambridge were still the main source of staff, supplying 31 per cent of all university teachers and 42 per cent of professors. This distribution is changing, since a higher proportion of older than of younger teachers took their first degree at Oxford or Cambridge. The proportion of those coming from the civic universities is rising; whereas 18 per cent of those over fifty were graduates of civic universities, for those under thirty the percentage was 29 (R., III, 36–38). University groups, particularly Oxford and Cambridge, tend to be self-recruiting. Thus, in 1961–1962 78 per cent of the teachers in Oxford and Cambridge graduated in those universities, whilst 40 per cent of those in civic universities (48 per cent for London) held first degrees of those universities. Perhaps surprisingly, in view of the supposed connection between the Scottish universities and the preservation of the Scottish national culture, only 51 per cent of their staff had graduated in Scotland (R., III, 182).

One crude index of the quality of staff is the proportion of those with first-class honours in their first degrees. The proportion of those holding first-class honours degrees who were recruited between 1959 and 1961 was 52 per cent, compared with 61 per cent for teachers recruited earlier. Since there is reason to believe that wastage is biased towards those with lower qualifications, the standard of the profession may not in fact be falling (R., III, 21).

Perhaps more important than a possible slight lowering in the academic quality of new entrants to the profession of university teaching is the changed nature of their prior social experience. Until very recently, a small proportion of former students was recruited from a student body who did not question the assumptions upon which the universities rested their government and their teaching. More recently larger numbers of young staff have entered the universities, coming from a generation which, since the 1950s has had a cultural experience markedly different from that of former generations, and which, since the mid-60s, has been increasingly questioning of many established political and intellectual orthodoxies.[40]

There is a marked lack of information about the nature of those recruited to full-time administrative positions in the universities. As inspection of handbooks and calenders indicates that at the higher level all, and at the middle level many, administrators hold degrees. Senior positions in Scotland are frequently held by those holding law degrees, but in England, recruitment seems more diverse. On the financial side chartered accountants are common.

University teachers, then, are, like their students subject to a process of meritocratic selection, through the workings of appointment committees and references. The former predominance of the ancient English universities and of the Humanities among academic appointments seems to be lessening as the other groups of universities and subjects grow more rapidly. The present, general expansion of the universities indicates clearly the interrelationship between those recruited to the positions of both staff and students, since a proportion of the ablest of the latter eventually move into positions as teachers. If the quality of these students alters, whether intellectually or in any other way relevant to their future vocation, then there is at least a strong possibility that the nature of the universities will eventually change.

Role expectations in the university

(i) *Academic staff* The behavioural expectations of the positions in British universities are ill-defined for their incumbents. Contracts of service signed by academic staff on appointment are usually worded in such vague terms as "to teach, examine and undertake such other duties as the head of department may direct, and to advance his subject by research . . ." or for a professor "to organize and administer the department, and to teach and carry out research". Yet the expectations of others for those filling these roles are very complex, including, in addition to the behaviour so far specified, writing, keeping up-to-date with the relevant literature, pastoral care of students and serving on committees. Some indication of the weight given to various sections of this role are indicated by the findings of the survey of university teachers made for the Robbins Committee in 1962. Average hours worked were 40.5 per week, of which 13.3 were in connection with teaching, 11 research, 4.4 private study, 4.4 administration and 2.4 work outside the university. There were, of course, variations by grade-professors spent more time on administration and less on research—and by faculty—scientists gave more time to research (R., III, 56).

However, for all grades of staff, there appears to be considerable difficulty in satisfactorily apportioning time between the various role sectors, since the rewards available differ. Academics have regarded themselves primarily as either scholars, teachers, tutors or researchers, according to the priority that they gave to the historic goals of the universities. The role of scholar—a man of deep and wide learning gained by long and constant private study—was predominant until the nineteenth century, but today the pressures to acquire new knowledge and to *apply* it are so great that true scholars are probably rare. During the mid-nineteenth century the role of the tutor who gave his main energy to the pastoral care and development of the personality of his students was developed in Oxford and Cambridge. This role was less easy to play in the mainly non-residential universities. Yet so powerful was its influence (largely because of the recruitment of graduates from the two ancient English universities) that similar systems for pastoral care of students were created in the civic, and even the Scottish, universities. Under contemporary conditions many students see such arrangements as paternalistic and, therefore, as unacceptable. Even in 1961–1962 there was evidence that throws doubt on the popularity of the system of personal tutors, since only 39 per cent of British students reported consulting with academic staff in the week prior to the survey, other than in periods of formal instruction and apart from casual remarks and greetings. Interestingly, students of the Scottish universities and those of Oxford and Cambridge had the same low figure—35 per cent (R., IIb, 504).

The role of teacher has also been given more prominence since the mid-nineteenth century as university courses have been seen to be relevant for a success-ful career. Teachers use different styles. Some rely on the authority of their office, others on their own personality, others again focus entirely upon the student rather than on their discipline or their own personal characteristics.[41] Yet there is little attention to method. The panel of the Association of University Teachers on teaching techniques found "a deep-rooted suspicion of any attempt to model in-service training in higher education on the lines of that carried out (for intending school teachers) in departments of education"; many academics thought that time spent on such courses might better be given to research.[42] A number of university departments of education now run brief courses on teaching methods, but in 1962 only 17 per cent of a sample of staff claimed that they "had even had any instruction or guidance on the teaching of university students"; moreover, only 43 per cent of assistant lectures, claimed to have "checked the efficiency of their teaching technique".[43] Clearly for many teaching is a "necessary evil". The reason usually given for this attitude is that the main rewards to academics lie outside teaching, since research and publication are prerequisites for promotion and status within their specialities. The low status of the role of teacher has recently received much adverse comment, so that in 1969 when the Prices and Incomes Board recommended a pay rise for university staff, this body advocated amongst other measures a special bonus tied to success in teaching. There was much oppo-sition to this suggestion, mainly on the grounds that such success is difficult to measure, and the recommendation was not adopted.

The role of researcher is largely a twentieth century development, influenced by the nineteenth century German universities. Thus, promotion to the position of professor usually results from outstanding research although, paradoxically, the professor is then expected to administer and lead a department—behaviour calling for very different capabilities than those ensuring successful research. It is clear from previous sections, that the growing size of the universities has forced another role upon some (particularly more senior academics), namely that of administrator. Though, as noted, some full-time administrators are employed, academics have tended to distrust such professionals. Not only is there a fear of academic freedom in handing administration to specialists, but there is perhaps—true to a British tradition—a preference for employing the amateur rather than the expert.

The conflict inherent in playing such complex roles is well summed up in the following words: "A simple and undivided loyalty is a luxury which is not within the reach of the members of any university."[44] This role strain is further complicated by an increasing number of links that exist with the outside world (such as industry, government and mass media) as the universities have moved from relatively closed to more open institutions. In 1961–1962 half the professors who answered the questionnaire for the Robbins Committee spent some time at meetings of committees outside their universities during the two weeks covered by the survey, as did 18 per cent of the academic profession as a whole; such work was more common for those in the social sciences than in any other faculty (R., III, 65).

This strain is further increased in two ways. *First,* growing numbers of new recruits to the profession, either openly or implicitly by their actions, are questioning the role of the academic as it has been played by this generation of teachers. In addition, students no longer expect their teachers to behave as was accepted by the last generation of students. Until the mid-1960s any questioning on the part of students appeared to assume the continuance of the social and the university system as it was—the present rules of the game were accepted. Now, with questioning of the very system, confusion frequently results. Thus, for example, the Board of Discipline of the London School of Economics met in 1951 to deal with the case of a student who had sold books stolen from the library to second-hand bookshops, but, when it next became necessary to convene this Board, fifteen years later, with the occurrence of serious trouble in 1966, its exact procedures were very unclear.[45]

Little is known about the role of the full-time administrator in the university. A growing number of academic and financial administrative officers are employed in universities, as are many "service" officers, such as those running student health services, appointments and careers offices, or catering and sporting facilities. While this complicated administrative system has frequently been criticized by students as excessively rigid and bureaucratic, the university administrator himself is the centre of many conflicting forces. In the *first* place he is supposedly a full-time professional, but he serves part-time, amateur masters, who tend to distrust experts. *Secondly*, students, and even staff, are often uncertain of the exact responsibilities of any one officer, so that misunderstandings can arise through approaching the wrong administrator. This seems to occur frequently over matters relating to grants and examination entries. *Third*, though the administrator should not make policy, clearly considerable power could lie with those who draw up agenda and act as guardians of the rules, whether these are academic or disciplinary. Since there is now a lower proportion of professors to undertake the greater burden of the amateur role of administering the larger universities, and since the pressure to do research on those below the rank of professor has grown, it would seem that the full-time administrator now has access to more power and, by default, may even formulate policy. This could be a *fourth* source of strain for those who play this as yet unmapped role, since the academic staff tend to be very jealous of any loss of freedom in the running of the universities.

(ii) *Students* The uncertainty in staff members about their role expectations, naturally leads to uncertainties for their students, but there are important additional problems for the latter. During the years since 1945, the latent roles played by students have gradually become more important so that students have become less of a separate group cut off from the outside world. Thus, what seems deviant behaviour to members of staff may well be conformity to the norms of a group outside the university of which the student concerned is a member. In the last few years, political roles, particularly of a radical nature, have assumed more salience for many students, and the public image of students has altered so that many may well now include an element of violence in their behavioural expectations.[46]

Enrolment in a university "signifies a desire (or at least an acquiescence to parental desire) to assume a student role, and with it a willingness to conform with student norms". The role of scholar is one important public view of the student and some Australian students themselves saw as most important those *academic* requirements specified by the university, namely punctuality and attendance at classes, and as least important, those not directly connected with the classroom.[47] Indeed, particularly in Scottish universities, students may initially tend to equate the university teacher with a master at school who punishes and rewards. Thus, one former student at Glasgow later commented "At the University I read Classics. The course did not make any radically different demands, except in quantity from those I had experienced at school."[48] In one of the technological universities, at a time when it still had the status of a CAT, students preferred to keep their relation with staff purely academic. To move outside such a role was harmful because it "confused attitudes of deference and authority appropriate to the classroom".[49] Clearly the figures already quoted for average hours of teaching per week (14.8 hours) are relevant here. During this period, the student is displaying what many see to be his typical behaviour, namely studying. The undergraduate is also frequently expected to study in vacation, but the student expects, and on the whole, is now expected to spend at least some of his time in the labour force. In the sixteen weeks of the summer vacation of 1961, 53 per cent of a large sample of students spent an average of one hour or less per day on academic work, and 62 per cent took paid work not related to their academic course, of whom three-quarters worked for more than four weeks.[50]

Some students particularly in the more senior years, adopting a self-concept made available to them by the example of staff, see themselves primarily as researchers. A study of honours chemistry students at London University, for example, found a number who clearly saw their role in such terms.[51] Moreover, the growing stress on the individual and his right to choose his own course has in many departments (particularly if large) encouraged the development of optional courses, often requiring a dissertation or major essay. This is perceived by many students as "research", a word whose meaning seems to have become somewhat widened in recent years. This role concept has possibly been encouraged by the increasing proportion of postgraduate students in the British universities. Six types of such students have been identified. The greatest proportion are "dedicated scholars", "would-be academics", or seek a qualification for some career outside the university. There are, however, in addition, around 15 per cent of "drifters", for whom life has as yet offered no other attraction, and a very small percentage who are either "Peter Pans" (perpetual students) or are covering up for a poor first degree.[52]

Rarely today, do students regard themselves as members of a superior finishing school for the ruling elite, as was the case in the nineteenth century (and even in the twentieth for a minority of students at Oxford and Cambridge). Though a few may play the dilettante or the hearty games player, some academic work leading to success in examinations is essential since in 1962–1963, 98 per cent of students reading for first degrees or diplomas were receiving public awards which are normally withdrawn for persistent academic failure. A growing concern of the local grant-giving councils has also been the way in which students, subsidized out of the revenue from local rates, have become either radicals or behaved in a manner seen by local councillors as deviant. Though no awards appear to have been withdrawn yet for such reasons, the system of student grants certainly acts as an effective sanction, to reinforce the expectations of study and academic achievement amongst most students.

The final student role to be considered here is that of politician. With the growing importance of the Union and the increasing political orientation of student life there has been increasing participation in the government of the university, whether at departmental or even at Court level, as well as in the administration of the Union. A minority group, however, tend to be involved. Thus, at the highly political London School of Economics, where over 3 000 students are enrolled, "the total number of votes cast in even a hotly contested election for the President of the Union has rarely much exceeded one thousand".[53] Such officers as the Union President tend to be older than most students represented and are now, as noted above, usually granted a paid sabbatical year, during which they find themselves a sometimes unwilling part of the system which many students criticize so forcibly. This traditional, restricted political role as responsible administrator/politician has over the last few years been extended, so that there are now a greater number of politically involved "progressive" students. Such groups act as a model that reinforces, in the minds of the public, the image of the student as violent, and also as a group to which many of their less politically minded peers may be drawn on occasions. Despite the comparatively minor scale of student unrest so far in Britain, this added dimension to the political role of the student seems an established social reality.[54]

For the student, as for the member of staff, there is a complex array of behavioural expectations available and choice is difficult. For many students, there is complete discontinuity between school and university. As a working-class student commented, "from being at school one of nature's chosen few, I had become overnight at Cambridge a C-streamer". Furthermore, where freedom is rated highly, little advice is generally given as to how to choose between various alternatives offered. Another working-class student summed up the implicit strain in these words,

> Nobody had told me that the Oxford principle was, and still largely is, to give its students unlimited freedom, including, if they wish, the freedom to make a complete mess of things. Significantly, Oxford does still talk of 'men' going up, regardless of the fact that only a few short weeks before they were boys at school. . . .[55]

The sanctions present in the official system of the university, as well as those resulting from the grant system force the student into playing to a greater or lesser extent some version of the academic role, particularly if he is a postgraduate student. This tendency is reinforced for many a student by his knowledge that his future career and standard of life is very dependent upon how well he does in his studies. But the reward of status amongst his peers can also attract him so that he adopts some sector of the role of the radical political student, thereby taking on the part in which the public has cast him, and ensuring what Rock and Heidensohn have termed "the politicization of deviance".

Interaction in informal cultures

Staff and students with the particular characteristics that have been outlined, interact with each other and with their peers so that a number of loosely structured, often overlapping, culture patterns have come to exist. These cultures, once in being, provide support so that their members may legitimately play somewhat different versions of the role of student or staff member.[56] Very few British studies, however, have been reported, which show either how the norms and values associated with such patterns come into being, or how, once formed, they are passed on from one generation of students to the next, or what is the nature of the sanctions employed in either of these processes.

Work in the United States has attempted to delineate cultures for whole colleges, but a comprehensive study in universities in NSW has shown that staff do not hold norms which are necessarily the same as those held by students. More particularly they "are more prone to see themselves in an active and productive capacity than are students, whereas they are less likely to recognize student involvement and activity within the university".[57] A recent report on senior British academics finds "evidence of the moral conservatism of the academic profession . . . a conservatism that can accommodate a measure of reform and change: some degree of expansion, though not so much that will threaten the existing character and standard of British universities: some growth in the number of Professors to handle increased administrative burdens, but not so many as to change the elite status of the rank".[58] This attitude to the universities is very different from that held by many students or younger members of staff.

There are, also, differences between universities in staff cultures. The two ancient English universities have held more firmly to traditional approaches to knowledge, whereas the new universities have been keener on cross-disciplinary approaches. The Scottish universities, including the new University of Stirling, have retained a belief in the value of a broad general education, as represented by the degree of the Ordinary M.A. Cross-cutting these variations between universities there are differences due to the fact that academic disciplines may be seen as cultures. Thus, all historians, sociologists or physicists have been initiated into the social system of their disciplines, each of which has its own authority figures, language and view of reality. These differences are frequently symbolized by the existence of the two worlds of Arts and Science. Members of the latter culture today tend to have a sure position in the world outside the universities, whilst those from the former are less certain of their position, especially those from Oxford, Cambridge or London.[59]

Students enter universities knowing that they must come into contact with and to some extent depend on staff from these cultures and, therefore, in some sense, they are positively oriented towards the staff and administration who see as their aim the socialization of the students.[60] Staff have two strong utilitarian sanctions in that they largely control both the formal granting of a degree and also that they write references to support applications for postgraduate scholarships or for future jobs, whether in the universities or outside them. Students are, however, strongly attracted towards the cultures of their peers, whose aims to a greater or lesser extent may be other than academic, and who may have available various rewards and punishments, especially sanctions associated with the availability of social intercourse. One American analysis that has received empirical support suggests that four main student cultures exist, namely the collegiate, the vocational, the academic and the nonconformist.[61] British equivalents would be respectively, the small group who still see the universities as finishing schools; the majority of those in the technological universities or faculties, who, as we have noted, contain a high proportion already committed to a career; thirdly, both a large group of post-graduates and the small group of students who think of themselves as researchers; and, lastly, the radical and political group, who, though seen as typical students by the general public, form a minority culture within the university.

On the arrival at the university the freshman has a number of possible pathways before him. He may opt to play roles within the various cultures available in his university, and may identify more or less strongly with staff or student cultures. Though staff are largely responsible for structuring the situation and for the allocation of formal rewards, for many students the rewards of their peers, who often are, or seem, socially less distant than staff, are a very powerful attraction. The sanctions used in the student cultures put greater emphasis on the gratifications that are more immediately available from their fellow students than those made available by the staff, whose system of sanctions largely depends upon the continuing capacity of the student to defer gratification until his university course is over.[62]

Further, the outside world impinges strongly upon students. At the lowest level there is implicit coercion in the potential withdrawal of a grant, but at the normative level there is the strong feeling amongst many students that the university and their career in it has, in a very wide sense, relevance to the world outside. Thus, Marris found that both at the universities he studied (Cambridge, Leeds and Southampton) and at the CAT (now City University), two-fifths of his sample of students thought their studies would be directly useful to their future work. There was little difference between those reading arts or science, because many of the former intended to become teachers. Further support for this view comes from a more recent investigator at Birmingham University who concluded:

> . . . we have at University a population of students, the great majority of whom tend to plan ahead with a clear reference to professional and social goals. The emphasis of this milieu is obviously in a direction of vocational orientation . . . In view of this strong trend amongst students to orientate themselves towards vocational education, it seems that the conception of University education as an "activity for activity's sake" or as "learning for learning's sake" may be difficult to sustain without experimental data to the contrary.[63]

In view of both the evidence of Marris and of the Robbins Report on the proportions coming to universities without any definite choice of career, and also of data (yet to be quoted) relating to recruitment to political roles, this view, though a healthy reminder of how greatly British universities may have changed from their still often stated very general goals, may be somewhat extreme.

The social situation of the majority of students differs in one major respect from that of most individuals who enter a position in which choice between various ways of playing the role is possible. The role of the student is one of the few *total role situations* in modern society. He has very few other social commitments to which he must give consideration when opting to stress one rather than another style of his role. Because, in general, he has no wife or children to support and he is financially comparatively secure, he has little to lose if he uses his freedom to commit himself deeply to a political or a bohemian role.[64] When one considers this comparative lack of commitment to the social structure outside the university, and the possibility of strong support from peer cultures within the very tolerant ethos of the university, the immunity of students to public criticism of seemingly deviant activity (increasingly of a political nature) becomes understandable. Furthermore, students have more opportunity than most members of a society to learn and think about their nation's ideals and values. Any failure by their elders to live up to these values, whether by the government or by the university itself, may seem more worthy of their questioning and, since they have few adult responsibilities and less need to compromise than their elders, some students may act, or appear to act in an extremely radical manner as a result.[65]

The survival of various cultures, often based on apparently very different values, within a modern university is facilitated by size. Comments such as the following, made by students about Manchester University, are typical, "It's too big and impersonal", and "too scattered, there is no centre apart from the Union, which is overcrowded".[66] There seem to be differing possible foci for the smaller cliques that exist within universities. Thus, Marris found that students considered that such groups did not centre on faculties, or even departments, but at Cambridge around sport, at Southampton around societies and sports clubs, and at Leeds around Union officials and their assistants.[67]

Those running the universities have always seen colleges and halls of residence as important agencies, providing a controlled environment within which a culture consonant with their goals may be passed on to students. Since many of those who live in these halls are resident for longer than one academic year, some students always remain to pass the culture on to the newcomers. In an investigation of the influence of accommodation upon students at Reading University, halls were contrasted with lodgings. The conclusion was reached that the already existing social structure of halls facilitated participation in activities of the type meeting the goals of the "humanist don"—activities generally inaccessible to the student in lodgings. The student in hall could more easily meet those in other faculties or departments, and learn of meetings of societies (often held in hall) which some of those around him would attend, thereby making it easier for him to conform to the culture. There was a distinct pattern of interaction within the hall, marked by conversation between students and with staff, the joining of university clubs and societies, and the reading of non-fiction books. Lodging students, however, visited the cinema more often and took part more frequently in team games. The culture of the hall could be seen as "a pattern of common activities" which facilitated a favourable response to university authority rather than of rebellion against it.[68]

Within such a hall at Hull University in the 1950s, for example, there existed a strongly structured informal hierarchy of cliques, based mainly on geographical factors (such as residential blocks or floors) but also upon common interests. A system of sanctions existed whereby the older students, through age or residence in the hall, ensured that newcomers behaved as the culture demanded. Thus, a typescript document, entitled "The Ancient Rights", laid down important norms, and a ritual ceremony of judgement, "The Trial", followed upon infringement. There were, also, initiation rites for newcomers which gave those who had undergone them a stake in preserving the system. Norms concerning work were so strong that "some students disguise(d) the actual amount of study that they did, or disclaim(ed) that they did any work in the vacations when, in fact, they worked quite hard at their studies".[69] Clearly, if, as seems the case, a substantial proportion of British students have a serious commitment to doing at least some academic work to avoid complete failure, then the possibility in some halls of this anti-intellectualism creates yet another conflict to be faced by many students. This is particularly the case since halls are more akin to total institutions and, therefore, sanctions from peers will have considerable power over many students. This result was certainly not in the minds of those who today are responsible for the running of such places of residence.

Against this background, a number of the changes in the British universities (to which reference has already been made) are working to transform the nature of the existing cultures. Firstly, there are more universities and, therefore, the chances of variety are greater; furthermore, many of the new creations fall within the two categories of the new or the technological universities which were purposefully created to have different cultures from those of the older or civic universities. Next, there has been an expansion in the number of departments and subjects, thereby increasing the number of possible foci for separate cultures for both staff and students. Lastly, the nature of staff, and particularly of students, who enter the universities has been influenced by the growth of a strong generational youth culture, one of the central values of which is an emphasis on separateness. One result of this change in the nature of recruitment is that an attitude of "Us/Them" can flourish more easily, as illustrated in the Hull University situation.

In turning, finally, to a consideration of the outcomes for students of attendance at British universities, we should do well to keep in mind the possibility of the displacement of goals, evident from the previous discussion.

Outcomes

What matters most at a university is the meeting of the minds of pupil and teacher, and of scholars with those of other scholars.

Lord Annan, *Times Literary Supplement*,
30th April, 1970.

Though this statement by the Provost of University College, London may be true, it is clearly only part of the whole truth. The effect on the minds of those who pass through universities depends upon the characteristics of the relevant university, upon the nature of the students or staff, and, finally, upon the set of experiences, amongst several possible options, that is chosen.

Here the possible outcomes will be examined from a number of points of view. In the first three subsections some of the general socializing effects for students of their time at the university and more particularly, the changes in their views about society and their future careers will be examined. The next five sections will consider the effects of attending different universities and faculties, of different teaching methods and forms of residence, and of membership of either sex. Finally, and briefly, some ways in which staff are affected by being members of a university will be examined.

(i) *General socialization*   Students who come to university nowadays are generally away from home, separated from the influences of their families, schools and former friends, and mixing with staff and fellow students who hold a diverse set of opinions. Their teachers clearly have the power to change their behaviour and attitudes within a narrow range of academic matters, but outside this area students are open to the influences of their peers. Learning largely takes place through membership of a community within which students interact, and it is the quality of this community which largely governs the quality of the learning. For many students their experiences on arriving at a university differ from their expectations. In Marris' sample a quarter found the university as expected, another 15 per cent had approached the university with an open mind, but the remaining majority were "more often disappointed than pleasantly surprised".[70]

Although the move to a university may be seen as one part of the long and gradual movement from adolescence to adulthood, during which a number of developmental tasks must be achieved, the demands put upon students by their new environment are great. They suddenly find themselves with considerable freedom and confronted with the choice of many possible modes of behaviour, all advertised with great verve during the orientation week normally held by most universities at the start of the academic year. Among other tastes, the student must become emancipated from his or her family of origin, must continue the process recently begun of establishing intimate heterosexual relationships, must usually participate and gain acceptance in a peer group, and must achieve economic independence.[71] The last problem is much eased by the grant system for students, and the second and third problems have usually already been tackled to some extent whilst still at school. But the problem of achieving independence from the family is for many a new one. Very often it is the return to the family at the end of the first term which shows a student most clearly how far he has moved in thought, word and deed away from his family and earlier life style. In many cases it is only after a further two years at university that students are secure enough in their new independent identity that they can again see their parents as human beings who can be accepted as different.[72] The frequency of difficulties over relationships with the family is indicated by the finding that 94.7 per cent of a sample of students at Birmingham University, who were experiencing difficulties in their studies, mentioned family relationships as a problem.[73]

Once the initial adjustment to life at the university and to independence from the family has been made, the student can consolidate his new identity, incorporating new values and attitudes into his personality. Katz and others found that the major part of this process of change for students at the University of New England (New South Wales) seemed to occur during their first year and that it was only during the last six months at university that further change was really noticeable, when there were signs that the student was anticipating his move out of the student role into his future occupational role. During the middle, major period as a student the problem of acceptance into a peer group must for many be solved. Marris noted that at Cambridge, students usually made friendships within their own year and their own school groups; thus ex-grammar or public school boys tended to group together. At the CAT on the other hand, friendships were clearly related to the structure of the course—half of his sample had no close friends outside the course and only a third made close friends outside their own lecture courses compared with 90 per cent of the university students in this study.[74] For those in halls or colleges there is, of course, greater ease in finding friends, and a number of studies in addition to that done at Hull (quoted above) have commented on the way in which physicial proximity determines friendships.[75] In his study of the intake into University College, London, in 1953, Malleson reported that 15.1 per cent of students could be classed as "isolates". These students were found more often in science and engineering, lived less often in halls, and had higher academic achievements.[76]

Although students have usually begun the process of establishing a satisfactory relationship with the other sex prior to coming to university, contemporary social pressures are such that engaged and married students are now common. In the sample investigated for the Robbins Committee, 18 per cent of all British post-graduate students and 3 per cent of all undergraduate students were married; figures for overseas students were some three times higher (R., IIa, 54). Marris found that two-fifths of his sample had a boy or girl friend outside the university who was as important to them as their studies. For half of these students the relationship involved some disparity of education—if not of intellectual interests—though this was less likely in the case of women students. The students who were married or engaged generally achieved higher academic results than others.[77]

A university degree has in the past been seen as more than a mere guarantee of a minimum standard of academic competence. A graduate was felt to be in some sense socially acceptable. He had learnt certain values of tolerance that were rated highly especially amongst the governing elite and by members of the pro-fessions. There are a number of studies done in the United States which show a steady growth in liberalmindedness amongst students during their years at university.[78]

The index most commonly used in Britain for measuring the move to a more liberal view is the indirect one of the proportion changing their political allegiance from the Conservative to the Labour Party. In the early 1960s amongst the upper and middle sections of the middle-classes, 9 per cent of Conservatives, but 26 per cent of Labour supporters were graduates. Surveys at the universities of Nottingham in 1962 and Manchester in 1963 have shown a move from Conservative to Labour amongst students during their courses. At Nottingham a fifth of students made such a switch and three times as many moved from right to left as changed in the other direction. Within the universities, those studying different subjects may react differently since at Manchester, amongst engineers, support for Conservatives was two to one against Labour, whilst there was three to one support for Labour among those in the social sciences. This latter result may, of course, be due to differential recruitment of students with prior commitments. Moreover, the social class of students at Manchester seemed important since those who came from working-class homes supported Labour in the proportion of two to one, whereas those from middle-class homes supported the Conservatives in the proportion of four to three.[79]

(ii) *Social class* By virtue of their academic success, students from a working-class background achieve an occupation of higher status than that of their parents. They are, therefore, on entering university, at least capable of upward social mobility. What effect does this experience have upon them? In a study by Abbott of three northern universities (Durham, Newcastle and Edinburgh) 14 per cent of a sample of 1303 students considered that their social status had altered since entering the university. 6 per cent of upper middle-class students said that they had moved down in class on becoming students but would return to a higher status on leaving university. Some students with working-class fathers clearly felt that they had already moved into the middle-class by going to grammar school, whilst the majority of others thought that their social class would change only on leaving the university. Many were clearly in a "zone of transition". Marris found that a considerable number defined themselves as "students rather than recruits to a career".[80] For such students, going to university allowed the postponement of final identification with a social class.

Many do, however, admit of a change. Zweig reported an Oxford student as saying, "Oxford brought me up a class" and a Manchester student "I am from a working-class background, but I feel I am entering a new class". One such student at Cambridge reported that there were "pressures moulding you to be an acceptable undergraduate; I behave more naturally at home".[81] These pressures appear to be acting towards the social goals of the universities, and are found particularly in the residential colleges and halls. The hope is that by mixing working- and middle-class students together the former will come to accept many of the norms and values of the latter and the latter will more fully understand the former. This process does to some extent take place. One ex-public school boy at Edinburgh commented, "You know I have a friend who is a miner's son, and do you know he is quite intelligent"; another in similar amazement remarked, "I thought people from grammar schools were the scum of the earth until I met one". But there are forces working against the achievement of this goal. Working-class students are concentrated in certain faculties, for example, in science rather than in medicine, particularly in Edinburgh. Further, Scottish working-class students tend to live more often at home than do their English equivalents, and, perhaps consequently, there appears to be differential recruitment to university societies and clubs.[82]

Despite these various pressures, there was little difference between the social classes in wastage rates except in Scotland, where there was a higher rate for children of manual workers than amongst other students (R., IIa, 136). Of those who completed courses, children of working-class parents achieved as high academic results as did those from middle-class homes (R., IIa, 155). Indeed, in one respect middle-class students were at some disadvantage at university, since they comprised the majority of those from boarding schools, who, on the whole, exhibited a considerably higher wastage rate than those from the day secondary schools attended by most working-class students (R., IIa, 134).[83] Once in a university, the student from a working-class family seems capable of taking the academic benefits offered to him, even if the university sometimes fails to fulfil its social goals in his case.

(iii) *Orientation towards a career* Though the present system of grants for students gives reasonable temporary economic independence, ultimately the majority of students must face the problem of finding employment—hopefully a career. Some students choose their faculty or subject with their future in mind. This is most clearly the case in such vocational faculties as medicine and law, in such departments as those training social workers or amongst those reading for the degree of Bachelor of Education in Colleges of Education.

As mentioned earlier, some subjects tend to appeal more to one social class than to another. One study has shown that socialization into the clearly defined role of dedicated scientist provides an apt response for working-class chemistry students, who may be experiencing some crisis of identity in this middle-class milieux.[84] The suggestion is that this may explain at least part of the comparatively high proportion of working-class students in scientific subjects. Further, middle-class students seem more able to take the risk of an uncertain future in their preference for the humanities and social sciences.

The protracted study of non-vocational subjects will, of course, decrease the chance of students learning an occupational self-concept. The author believes both that society may not have a place for all the "cosmopolitans" that are produced by universities with the traditional humanist goals and that courses based on such aims lead to uncertainty of identity amongst students.[85] In this context, Wankowski at Birmingham University found that certainty about future goals was "conducive to success in studies even when study difficulties are experienced", and high achievement was significantly associated with clarity of aim.[86] This finding is further reinforced by the recent work of Musgrove in Bradford—one of the technological universities. Here he found an indication that the students "appear to take their role as students very seriously, but not as a refuge from the world of work".[87]

The sample of students investigated on behalf of the Robbins Committee were asked whether they had a specific occupation in mind on going to the university and students in their final year were asked whether they had changed this choice during their time as students. While 23 per cent had no occupation in mind on entry, this proportion had not changed for those students in their final year. Uncertainty in the final year was more common amongst science students largely because high proportions in these subjects go on to postgraduate courses (R., IIb, 180). Amongst those students in their first year who had made a decision about half the men and two-thirds of the women in humanities and one-fifth of the men and just under half the women in science planned to teach. The majority of the remainder wanted to go into research, development or production outside the university. In a longitudinal study of the making of decisions among those who entered the arts faculty of Aberdeen University in 1953, about a third had made their final decision before entry to the university, a third during the course and a third after graduation. A very few able students who wanted to do research or further academic study deferred their decision until they knew their degree results. Apart from these students, there seemed to be no difference in degree of certainty about career between those who did more or less well academically. Whether their decision was made early or late depended upon both the nature of the person and of the job. "Teaching and law are examples where familiarity and specific forms of training encourage(d) early decision; research and management (were) opposite examples."[88] Certainly, the majority of students would appear to adhere to their choice of the general area in which they wished to work, though they could change their choice of a specific job.

There is some evidence that the teaching profession attracts a number from Arts of those who can think of nothing else to do, particularly in the case of women, who tend not to regard this choice as a commitment to a lifelong career. At least two other forces may be at work to channel graduates into this area of teaching and social work. Marris noted that some of the greater than expected numbers of intending teachers amongst upwardly socially mobile students seemed to be seeking a career with a similar air of classlessness to that experienced at the university. In addition, Parkin commented that "the welfare and creative professions provide acceptable sanctuaries to those who wish to avoid direct involvement in capitalist enterprises by affording outlets for the exercise of their talents which entail no compromise of political ideals."[89]

(iv) *University type* Wastage rates differ quite widely between universities. For the 1957 entrants in the Robbins sample of British universities, the variations in arts, science and biology were respectively from 4 to 34 per cent. The two ancient English universities had the lowest rates with only 4 per cent at Cambridge and 7 per cent at Oxford (R., IIa, 128). The Robbins Report does not give full details about the failure rates at various universities, but the civic universities seem to have rates about two to three times and the Scottish universities about three times higher than those at Oxford and Cambridge (R., IIa, 135), and, despite these the variations between universities, the rates seem to steady through time (R., IIa, 129). From this, one may make a number of inferences. There are in all probability differing norms about what proportion should fail despite the British system of using external examiners with the aim of ensuring equal standards between universities. Secondly, there are differences in the standards of students on entry to the universities which influence wastage rates. Lastly, there may be some effect due to differences in teaching methods. Face to face teaching of the tutorial type is, as has been noted, most common at the two ancient universities and least common in the Scottish universities, though in the latter case the opportunity to re-sit examinations for the M.A. (Ordinary) lowers the wastage rate by allowing second chances.

About one-fifth of entrants to Scottish universities in 1955 were from England or Wales and there is some evidence that those from south of the border do better academically than the Scots.[90] A further factor that offsets the higher Scottish wastage rate is that a higher proportion of the relevant age group in Scotland enters the universities so that the percentage ultimately attaining a first degree is about the same as in England (R., 57).

In contrast, the two ancient English Universities have for centuries now maintained links with the political elite, and do not lay sole emphasis on academic achievement. Success in the Unions, or debating societies, of these universities has often acted as an entrée to national politics.[91] Furthermore, success in one other non-academic area of performance, namely games, has tended to enhance social and occupational chances after leaving these universities.[92] Despite their scientific and technological links with the economy and their very real attempts to broaden the nature of their student body, these universities still perform a distinct class function in maintaining and transmitting an elitist style of life, and tend to select students accordingly, if only because some do not bother to apply.

Most of the new universities have tried to plan their courses so that their students might gain as wide an education as possible. This has been done both because a broad humanist or scientific education is seen as desirable in itself and because thereby specialization may be delayed till the student can choose with confidence in such a way that he will be fully involved and that he can find employment for the resulting skills. The university may well in this way be enabled to match the needs of the economy more efficiently, but delaying the final choice may increase the chance of the student feeling insecure, through lack of a firm occupational identity. Indeed, in some ways even the economic argument may be hard to sustain in view of experience at Keele University. Here all students spend their first year in a foundation course and net migration out of science into arts at the end of this period is almost inevitable as the necessity for prior knowledge in the sciences (gained at school) generally precludes movement in the opposite direction. Thus, those responsible for selection allow for a 40 per cent loss of students from science departments to arts at the end of the foundation year.[93]

On the other hand, the technological universities have a practical orientation and a link with the world of work. This is particularly the case where students are doing "sandwich courses" which demand alternating periods in industry and in the university. Such an atmosphere seems "socially acceptable to a boy from a working-class background who would not consider a full time university course." Yet there are signs, certainly at Bath University, that, as a technological university grows older, it changes its emphases and presents a more middle-class and alien image which attracts a decreasing proportion of those for whom the traditional university is an uncongenial place.[94] Moreover, entry qualifications seem to be somewhat lower, a fact which may well explain the high proportion of withdrawals during the course on grounds of academic failure. Indeed, in the late-1960s all the new technological universities had a wastage rate in excess of 20 per cent, that is, half as high again as the average for all universities; the range was from 22.5 for Heriot-Watt to 28.7 for Strathclyde.[95]

(v) *Faculties* Wastage rates also differ between faculties in much the same way as the academic quality of the students recruited to the faculties was seen earlier to vary. In 1968, wastage rates ranged from 6.3 and 6.5 per cent for arts and social studies through figures of about 10–12 per cent for the pure sciences and 20.1 per cent for engineering.[96] Medicine had the lowest rate of 5.9 per cent. This last rate can probably be related to the methods of teaching in that faculty where the staffing ratio is very favourable and the re-sitting of examinations is frequently allowed (R., IIa, 128). In general, about half of those who fail to complete their courses regardless of faculty do so during their first year (R., IIa, 131).

In the study carried out by Katz and others at the University of New England (NSW) there were no major changes in the values of students measured two and a half years after entry except amongst those in the Arts faculty who became less dogmatic in their attitudes to controversial issues and more cosmopolitan in outlook. These changes seemed to occur largely during the first year.[97] Existing British evidence supports this finding that those who complete a course in arts are most changed in attitude. Thus, for example, amongst the members of the Campaign for Nuclear Disarmament in Parkin's survey, which was made in the early 1960s "of those in higher education 70 per cent were specializing in humanities or social sciences, and especially sociology, while only 17 per cent were in pure and applied sciences". However, as indicated earlier, a process of self-selection seemed to be operating since those in sixth forms who hoped to enter higher education were heavily biased to choosing the two former subjects. But what was true of students was also true of staff, since sociology teachers were "especially well disposed to CND".[98] Thus, at least for sociology students, role models with authority existed. A recent comparison between engineering and sociology students enrolled for degree courses in a polytechnic reveals a somewhat similar situation. A "high degree of conservatism" existed, even among sociologists, though they were less right wing in attitude. Yet a degree of socialization seems to take place since sociologists in their third year, especially the women, were less conservative than those in their first year. Again, a difference existed in their experience prior to entry, since most students of sociology came direct from grammar schools, whilst the engineers more often had attended less prestigious modern or comprehensive schools, or had worked in industry.[99]

A framework for explaining the way in which faculties have differential effects upon their students would seem best built around two foci. Firstly, the nature of those who enter the faculties differs, both in academic quality and in embryonic political ideology. Secondly, those in arts and the social sciences do not on the whole have the same chance to develop an occupational identity as those in pure and especially applied sciences.

(vi) *Teaching methods* The average wastage rate in Britain, which is less than 20 per cent, is much lower than the rate of 40–50 per cent which is the average in, for example, the universities of France or the United States (R., 190). Possible reasons for this are: the high level of students' qualifications at entry, the favourable staff–student ratio in the British universities which allows more intensive teaching, and more rigidly structured courses than in countries like Germany with a strong tradition of *Lernfreiheit*, or the United States where many options are possible in first degree courses. British students, particularly in honours courses, usually opt for a *subject*, the curriculum, length of course and timing of examinations following automatically.

The teaching methods used vary considerably among universities, and departments within universities, but the lecture, tutorial, seminar and, in the sciences, practical classes are common. In large lecture classes, such as are common for the Scottish undergraduate, the lecturer may well fail to communicate to his students either the exact criteria of attainment in his subject, or the humanist love for and commitment to learning that are often advanced as the rationale for these broad courses—47.6 per cent of a group of final-year medical students reported that they had not known what was expected of them in the first year of their course.[100] Thus, mere success in the yearly examinations may become the aim of many students, in a process of goal displacement.

By tradition, much stress is put on tutorials in the two ancient English universities as the principal means whereby "the meeting of minds", emphasized by Lord Annan as a major goal in the quotation at the head of this section, may take place. Seminars are more frequent in other universities, but Marris found signs that the social processes involved in this method of teaching can work against this aim. The successful tutorial or seminar depends largely upon the cut and thrust of the critical talk that follows an essay or paper, but this demands that the students are confident enough to expose themselves. Halsey writes of the "agonies of gauche discomfort" which students undergo when they are forced outside "the established and familiar rules of intercourse in classroom or laboratory". As a result of such discomfort, one student at Oxford, in an interview with Zweig, is reported to have said, "The life of a student makes me feel insecure and immature".[101]

In the same context, examination procedures are relevant, since they may affect the circumstances under which a student works and, hence his motivation. Often in British universities other than Oxford and Cambridge the student attends seminars or tutorials with the staff member who will eventually examine him. Thus he may feel even less confident to expose his views to the criticism of a teacher who in another, crucial role—that of examiner—may well remember to his disadvantage his poor past performances. The suggestion has often been made that at the two ancient English universities, where the tutor (usually allocated by the student's college) is rarely the examiner, who is appointed by the university department concerned, the tutor and student tend to cooperate, in an attempt to beat the "mutual enemy"—the examiner.[102] There are changes, particularly in the new universities, towards various forms of continuous assessment of course work, though opinions differ as to whether students are overworked as a result.[103] However, four out of five of the university teachers who replied to a survey in 1962 thought that examinations were the best practicable way of motivating students to work hard, and three-quarters also felt that they were the best method for measuring the intellectual quality of students; there were, of course, differences between universities, by subject and especially by age, Assistant-Lecturers generally being less certain.[104]

The plight of weak students as they pass through this structured pathway of learning experiences has in recent years been given more attention. The system does cool out some students judged not to possess the capacity to complete the course, while others, who perhaps could have completed a course may also fail. Wankowski found that many weak students could be identified quite easily by the end of their first term at university and at Aberdeen University an early warning system has been established which, at this early stage, identifies about 80 or 90 per cent of those at risk of failure by the end of the first year. The failure rate in the science faculty where the system was initially established fell markedly subsequent to the introduction of this system as well as methods for helping those identified, though whether the higher pass rates could be directly attributed to these changes is uncertain.[105]

Much work has been done in the United States on the formation of occupational identity in medical faculties.[106] In Britain the clinical training given in hospitals provides an equally interesting, but comparatively unexplored, situation. In this country, students work in small groups for several years. One study found no association between studying in small groups and such indices as "difficulty in learning medicine, or in forming relationships, or in success in examinations". Yet the investigators still felt that such a method of learning "is likely to have a marked effect on the educational experience of the students, and perhaps on their development as individuals". They are given some support by the fact that 48.8 per cent of all the students in the sample had needed guidance in their course, and 40.7 per cent got this mainly from other students, specifically stating this on their own initiative.[107]

Academic difficulty or loss of interest, particularly when an unsatisfactory initial choice of course has been made, may lead a student to withdraw from the university on his own initiative. This is more frequently the case amongst first-year students. Psychological disorder is more often the reason for withdrawal amongst second- and third-year students.[108] The Student Health Service can perform an important supportive function in the teaching situation for many students with academic difficulties, though it is not usually until the particularly stressful period of annual examinations that students approach this service. "Effecting a rapprochement" in a situation where there is "hostility between teacher and student" is one of the most useful jobs a student health physician can do". The major period of stress appears to occur at the end of the third year when, at University College London, "about 10 per cent of those about to sit final examinations came to the Student Health Centre for some kind of help.[109] At the start of this section on teaching methods the low staff–student ratio in comparison with other countries was noted. In such a favourable situation, more attention is likely to be given to the student's problems as learner. In this context since the mid-1950s a number of universities, for example, London, Essex and Lancaster, have established Higher Education Research Units, which should produce information relevant to the sociology of learning in the university.

(vii) *Residence*   The assumption that residence in a college will change the values of the student has been a strong influence on the growth of the structure of the English, and more recently, even of the Scottish universities. In 1961–1962, 24 per cent of men and 43 per cent of women students were in colleges, halls or hostels. The highest proportion was 62 per cent for Oxford and Cambridge, the lowest, 15 per cent for the Scottish universities (R., IIa, 177). The socializing effect of colleges is to some extent lessened if the students are near enough to their homes to visit at weekends. Zweig found that 65 per cent of his sample at Manchester University lived in neighbouring countries so that frequent contact with their home was possible.[110]

There is a tendency to contrast the conditions in colleges or halls with the frequently poor living conditions in lodgings, or with the emotional strains suffered by students who live at home. However, in a study of Newcastle University, Eden found that 28 per cent of those in lodgings and 47 per cent of those living at home were "entirely satisfied". Some students became part of the family where they lodged. As one said, "I am lucky with my landlady. I'm completely assimilated to the family. I can even spank the child."[111]

Amongst the 1955 entrants to British universities studied for the Robbins Committee, there seemed "to be no marked relation between students' living accommodation in the final year and degree performance. Students in residence, especially those from manual working-class homes, did slightly worse than others in terms of the proportions obtaining firsts and upper second class degrees" (R., IIa, 198–199). Though a comparison of academic success rates may affect the economic arguments for and against providing expensive halls of residence, the case has traditionally rested on what was supposed to happen in the two ancient English universities where the college system was first established. The comparison, already quoted, that was made at Reading between students in hall and lodgings showed that on the whole the intended effects did occur. Students in hall talked about their work more frequently with their peers, read more non-fiction, attended more university clubs and societies, and studied more. The conclusion was that "the ready made social structure of hall . . . gives a freedom for culture not possessed by lodgings students. Those in lodgings have to go out and make those social contacts themselves."[112] Other work supports these findings, and Abbott also noted that for working-class students at Durham membership of a college tended to intensify the process whereby such students took up middle-class values, even when the student was in lodgings, but ate meals in college, a common arrangement at this university where all students are members of a college.[113]

An important part of the argument for the collegiate system rests on the assumption that the "meeting of minds", stressed by Lord Annan, will be more frequent for those living in colleges. The evidence here is contradictory. Warr and Marris did not find this to be the case for "pupil and teacher". At Cambridge, Leeds and Southampton there was no difference by type of residence in social contact between staff and students. Though the chances are there, the contacts seem to be artificial.[114] But, as Albrow noted, friendships are more easily made between "scholars", and the intellectual rubbing of shoulders with those in other faculties or departments seems to occur readily for those in some form of residence. For example, Thoday found at Birmingham that 90 per cent of those in hall first met the majority of their friends from other faculties in hall, whereas only 46 per cent of those in lodgings first met such friends in their lodgings. Marris noted that students in halls had a greater proportion of their friends reading subjects other than their own.[115] Yet many students today prefer forms of residence which are less formal and hierarchical in structure. In this context it is worthy of note that even in Marris' work, carried out in 1961–1963, students in residence commented that the relationship between teacher and student in a hall often seemed paternalistic. Despite these attitudes, colleges and halls, though costly, do seem to be having, to some extent, the intended effects.

(viii) *Sex*   Before considering staff, one or two differences in the way the sexes react to university will be noted. Wastage rates in all faculties are much the same for women as for men (R., IIa, 133) and there is little difference between the proportions of both sexes gaining first- or second-class degrees as a whole. The proportion of men gaining firsts or upper seconds is considerably higher, largely because a higher proportion of women read arts, where the proportion of students gaining first and upper seconds is below average (R., IIa, 155). In Scotland, two-thirds of those gaining Ordinary M.A.s are women, but this would seem to be due to normative pressures (this degree is seen as the means of entry to a traditional occupational role for women—primary teaching) rather than due to a lower standard of achievement among women students.

A recent study noted a tendency for women students to change significantly "their beliefs about the importance of participating in university cultural societies and clubs" during their time at Bradford University. Women students in both arts and science faculties appeared to move towards the intensity of beliefs commonly found among men students in these areas.[116] Generally, universities seem to reduce, rather than intensify, some of the differences between the sex roles.

(ix) *Staff*   Universities also influence their own staff in a variety of ways. First of all future teachers in universities inevitably undergo the experience of being students, albeit successful ones. Second, teachers already within the university control the mechanisms admitting new members to their ranks. One aspect of this control is the fact that they teach the postgraduate students from whom new staff are largely drawn, thus frequently imposing on the postgraduate student the difficult task of undertaking so-called original research, at the same time not being so divergent that his teacher will condemn his work as deviant rather than label it brilliant. Further, the senior members of any university control the appointment boards, whose members take up verbal and written references, judge work done to date, and if satisfied, admit newcomers as teachers. The sanctions that can be brought to bear on the aspiring member of staff to match contemporary academic orthodoxy may be strong. However, within the boundaries of permitted tolerance, the teacher, once appointed, has great freeedom in what he teaches. Though the British student can not lay claim to the degree of *Lernfreiheit* that his continental peer has, his teachers can boast of their right to *Lehrfreiheit*.

The rapid growth of the British universities is also affecting the structure of the academic profession. As noted earlier, of all university teachers, 31 per cent in 1961–1962 were graduates of Oxford or Cambridge, although this proportion was higher among the older teachers than among more recent recruits. The two ancient English universities have, in each generation, produced a higher proportion of teachers than graduates, but this proportion is now falling (R., III, 36–38). As the civic and new universities grow, the proportion of university teachers drawn from Oxford and Cambridge will in all probability diminish.

Despite this over-representation of the ancient universities, the prospects of promotion to the rank of professor does seem to have been much the same for graduates from any university. Promotion chances in 1961–1962 seemed very much as they were in 1956–1957 and the Robbins Committee concluded that expansion on the scale that they recommended could not, given the present balance between goals, greatly change these chances (R., III, 32). For many academics, promotion raises a conflict of loyalties, since movement to a more senior position in another university may be necessary. The teacher must decide whether his loyalty is to his present university, or to the wider reference group of his professional peers. "An almost unique aspect of universities . . . is their dual prestige system." Status is derived both from position in the local organization and also from standing in the professional academic community of, for instance, physicists or sociologists. Work in the United States has shown that university teachers balance a number of rewards in deciding whether to seek "an academic paradise" elsewhere and that economic benefits are not the only consideration. Teaching and research facilities, local amenities, both on and off campus, are also factors.[117] In Britain the academic pull of Oxford and Cambridge, the many amenities of London, and the propinquity of the mountainous country of Scotland can all act as constraints on decisions about academic careers.

By the age of fifty-five, chances of promotion are slim and what has been called "the process of becoming 'deadwood' " can take place. It has been maintained that such demoralization is especially easy for academics because of the special conditions of their work. The teacher has great freedom, his specific goals are often vague, and exact responsibility for how the student achieves is rarely attributable to one man.[118] Therefore, evaluation, difficult at any time, becomes almost impossible. Thus, teachers who do not know clearly what they want to do or have done may, in later years, become indifferent to their performance. Those few who are promoted to the position of professor have been shown to develop attitudes about professorial power which seem related to their views on national political affairs. However, their views about academic status appear to be rather "related to expansionist or elitist views of the university system".[119]

In general, for staff—whether teachers or administrators, male or female—as for students, the influences of the positions held in various categories of British universities is influenced both by the experiences undergone within these organizations and also by the latent roles that they bring to their work from their lives outside the universities.

Conclusions

The influence of the two English ancient universities upon the other British universities has remained particularly strong. The four ancient Scottish universities have had less impact, their structure being considerably modified as Scotland has been drawn within the (basically) English, governmental system. The traditional English idea of a university, developed in Oxford and Cambridge, was modified somewhat in the nineteenth century under the impact of the new German definition of what a university should be. Yet the group of civic universities which were in the main created at this time, were and still are recognizably British universities, concentrating on the general education of an elite. Furthermore, the new universities, founded in a large measure to change the pervading definition of a university, appear to have failed both to become less elitist in aim and recruitment and to redraw the map of learning to any major extent. There are even signs that the former CATs, having once gained the status of universities, are tending to imitate the well-established model. One hesitates to predict that institutions within the recently established binary system will follow the same pathway, but basically the powerful hold of the idea of what a university should be on the minds of many within these organizations is thwarting the goals of egalitarianism and closer economic links held by many with political power.

Yet, interestingly specific economic factors are causing changes in the structure of the British universities. Expansion is demanded on the grounds that research and trained manpower are both needed by the economy, but, although such growth matched the beliefs and interests of many within the universities, this has only been achieved by greatly increased financial dependence upon the state, which in its turn has demanded a greater say in controlling the universities. The place of the UGC as a buffer between government and universities has already been substantially altered, though so far the comparatively recent, but nevertheless very strong, tradition of academic freedom has prevented any substantial intervention in purely academic affairs, despite substantial fears that this would occur.

This same belief in academic freedom has also protected the universities during the more recent difficulties associated with demands for student power. So wide is the range of tolerated behaviour in staff and students that up to the middle of 1970 despite some public demands no student had suffered as a result of a public body withdrawing his grant for non-academic reasons. Also, only one member of staff of any university had been dismissed as a result of actions in pursuit of his political beliefs.

Clearly the nature of those recruited to the positions of staff or student is a crucial factor in determining what effect the universities have on those within them. In Britain what is known about recruits mainly relates to the academic achievements of both staff and students at entry, and to the social class of origin of students. Little attention has been given to attitudes, except perhaps to those relating to politics. Least of all have any attempts been made to discover the beliefs of newly recruited staff, who would seem to be particularly important in this regard. Because they represent recent and successful students, they may well have much influence on the present generation of students. Also they are new staff, albeit young, and in the present climate of opinion may have some influence on their older and more senior colleagues.

In general, the role expectations of those in British universities have also been neglected as a topic for research. This is especially true of administrative staff, about whom extremely little of any systematic nature is known. Even the Robbins Report more or less ignored their presence. Yet at a time of expansion and unrest, often focused on administrative and legalistic issues, their position is central as a focus of conflict. Even from the meagre evidence gathered here, staff and students alike seem to experience much conflict in their expectations of how to behave. Staff must balance the demands of their responsibilities as teachers and as researchers; students must decide whether to relate to academic staff or to their peers. As a result, interaction between the incumbents of two positions which closely interrelate, will most probably lead to further conflict between them. However, at the moment, extremely little is known about such conflicts or the sanctions used by staff and students in the process of reaching a truce situation with their peers and between each other.

Nor is much known about the informal social systems of students within the universities or of the systems latent to the playing of the role of student. Clearly such systems have powerful sanctions which could affect the degree of involvement that the student has in the formal goals of the university. There are hints in the data presented above that the influence of peers is in some respects such that these official goals are not achieved. Thus, the attraction of political activities, either at a national level or within the university, may distract excessively from academic goals or, again, the influence of peers may prevent "the intellectual shoulder rubbing" desired by those running the university or may even lead to some form of anti-intellectualism within an organization dedicated primarily to the intellectual life.

Other factors clearly influence the success of the universities in achieving the goals set by those in power. Some have been explored particularly in the work done for the Robbins Report. There attention was given to the traditional British topics of social class, academic achievement and halls of residence. However, little research has yet been done in other areas, especially on the values, beliefs and attitudes of staff and students, whether at entry, during, or at the conclusion of their stay at university.[120] One central question about which very little is known relates to the whole purpose of the British universities, namely: What is the effect on students of undertaking and on staff of teaching a course for a degree that is seen as non-vocational—particularly in those subjects usually included under the headings of arts or social sciences? The interpretation put here on what little evidence is available is that the effects may be the opposite of what is intended, since the student may gain neither a firm personal identity nor more than a superficial acquaintance with the academic culture.

Paradoxically, one of the main reasons why we know so little about many of these questions is that there is much opposition *within* the universities to research *on* the university. There would seem to be three main explanations for this. Firstly, personal interests and styles of life are probably perceived as being threatened. Next, many consider that time spent in being investigated could better be spent on one's own research. Lastly, and perhaps most important, the sociology of the university is often a concern of two departments low in the academic pecking order—those of sociology and education. Despite such drawbacks to research, increasing pressure from students, teachers and society itself will require answers to the above questions (among others) and will eventually lead to more radical change in university organization.

References and notes

1. I wish to thank the following of my colleagues at Monash University for comments made on various drafts of this chapter: Professors S.S. Dunn and R. Selby Smith, Dr. N.J. Ryan, S.J., and Associate Professor R.W. McCulloch. Final responsibility naturally is mine.

2. E. Ashby, "The future of the nineteenth century idea of a university", *Minerva*, **6** (1) (Autumn 1967), 5; and see also P.W. Musgrave, *Technical Change, the Labour Force and Education*, Oxford: Pergamon, 1967, esp. part I.

3. See A.F. McPherson, "Selections and survivals: A sociology of the ancient Scottish universities", in R. Brown (Ed.), *Knowledge, Education and Cultural Change*, 1973, London: Tavistock. See also L.J. Saunders, *Scottish Democracy, 1815–1840*. Edinburgh: Oliver and Boyd, 1950; G.E. Davie, *The Democratic Intellect—Scotland and her Universities in the Nineteenth Century*, Edinburgh: Edinburgh University Press, 1961; W.M. Mathew, "The origins and occupations of Glasgow students, 1740–1839", *Past and Present* (33) (July 1966).

4. W.H.G. Armytage, *The Civic Universities: Aspects of a British Tradition*, London: Benn, 1955. See also the same author's *The German Influence on English Education*, London: Routledge and Kegan Paul, 1969.

5. A.H. Halsey, "British universities and intellectual life", *University Q.*, **12** (2) (Feb 1958).

6. For a consideration of academic freedom and the UGC see Lord Robbins, *Of Academic Freedom*, London: Oxford University Press, 1966, esp. pp. 11–15. Lord Robbins was Chairman of the Committee which produced the

so-called Robbins Report, *Higher Education*, London: HMSO, 1963. The Report and the five Appendices of this committee provide the most up-to-date complete description of the British universities and will be cited frequently in this chapter. In order to avoid constant footnotes sources will be indicated in the text in the following manner "R., II(b), 37" will stand for "Higher Education, Appendix II(b), p. 37".

7. A.H. Halsey and M. Trow, "University teaching; the structure of a profession", in D. Martin (Ed.), *Anarchy and Culture*, London: John Murray, 1969, p. 47.

8. A. Little and J. Westergaard, "The trend of class differentials in educational opportunity in England and Wales", *Br. J. Sociol.*, **15** (4) (Dec 1964).

9. R.L. Jobling, "Some sociological aspects of university development in England", *Sociol. Rev.*, **17** (1) (March 1969).

10. Keele University, founded in 1951, had 1410 students by 1966–1967, whereas Monash University, Victoria, founded in 1958 had over 5804 full-time and 1316 part-time stdents by mid-1967, and over 10 000 students in total by 1970.

11. H.J. Perkin, *New Universities in the United Kingdom*, Paris: OECD, 1969, p. 70.

12. For the whole non-university sector see E. Robinson, *The New Universities*, Harmondsworth: Penguin, 1968.

13. *UGC: University Development, 1962–1967*, London: HMSO, 1968, p. 191. Although this report will not be cited as often as the Robbins Report, the number of footnotes will be lessened further by citing it in the text as "UGC" with a page number. See also R. Aitkin, "The Vice-Chancellors' Committee and the U.G.C.", *Universities Q.*, **23** (2) (Spring 1969), esp. p. 169.

14. S. Caine, *British Universities*, London: Bodley Head, 1969, pp. 15 and pp. 186–189.

15. H.J. Perkin, *op. cit.*, p. 135.

16. There is a growing literature on "the student problem" in the British universities. See, for instance, A. Cockburn and R. Blackburn (Eds), *Student Power*, Harmondsworth: Penguin, 1969; D. Martin (Ed.), *op. cit.*; J. Nagel, *Student Power*, London: Merlin, 1969.

17. A.E. Sloman, *op. cit.*, pp. 14 and 50.

18. E. Ashby, *op. cit.*, p. 3.

19. A.H. Halsey, "The changing functions of universities", *Harvard Educ. Rev.*, **30** (3) (Spring 1960).

20. A.H. Halsey, "A pyramid of prestige", *Universities Q.*, **15** (4) (Sept 1961).

21. For political data see W.L. Guttsman, *The British Political Elite*, London: McGibbon and Kee, 1963, esp. pp. 105–106 and for economic data see, for instance, *Management Succession*, London: Acton Society Trust, 1956.

22. P.W. Musgrave, "Some constant factors in the demand for technical education, 1860–1960", *Br. J. Educ. Studies*, **14** (2) (May 1966).

23. E. Shils, "Observations on the American university", *Universities Q.*, **17** (2) (March 1963), 183.

24. S. Caine, *op. cit.*, p. 12.
25. In Scotland pupils have traditionally left school at 17, a year younger than in the rest of the United Kingdom, and an M.A. (honours) degree takes four years, as opposed to three elsewhere so that throughout the U.K. those graduating with honours degrees do so at 21 years of age. However, in Scotland after three years students may take a general degree, the Ordinary M.A., which is equivalent in standard to a general B.A./B.Sc. degree of an English university, but may be gained a year earlier in Scotland than elsewhere in the U.K.
26. *Report of Commission of Inquiry*, vol. 1, Oxford, University of Oxford: 1966, pp. 104 and 107.
27. UGC Report of the Committee on University Teaching Methods, London: HMSO, 1964, pp. 45–50; see also I. Watt, "The seminar", *Universities Q.*, **18** (4) (Sept 1964).
28. For a case study see E.P. Thompson, *Warwick University Limited*, Harmondsworth: Penguin, 1970.
29. E. Rudd, "What students spend", *Universities Q.*, **16** (4) (Sept 1962); for some views on the NUS see D. Widgery, "The Students' Muffler", in A. Cockburn and R. Blackburn (Eds), *Student Power*, Harmondsworth: Penguin, 1969, pp. 119–120.
30. R. Layard, J. King, and C. Moser, *The Impact of Robbins*, Harmondsworth: Penguin, 1969, pp. 24–25.
31. E. Ashby, *op. cit.*, p. 9.
32. Statistical Supplements of UCCA, 1967, quoted by A. Pollard, "O and A Level: Keeping up the standard", in C.B. Cox and A.E. Dyson (Eds), "*Black Paper Two*", London: Critical Quarterly Society, 1969, p. 78. The percentage in Medicine was 39.9, a case contrary to the general trend.
33. "*Conference of Ministers of Education of European Member States on Access to Higher Education, Vienna, 1967*", Paris: UNESCO, 1967, vol. 4, table 6, quoted by H.J. Perkin, *op. cit.*, p. 103.
34. J. Abbott, *Employment of Sociology and Anthropology Graduates, 1966–1967*, London: British Sociological Association, 1970.
35. H.J. Perkin, *op. cit.*, p. 107; M. Cross and R.G. Jobling, "The English new universities—a preliminary enquiry", *Universities Q.*, **23** (2) (Spring 1969).
36. P. Marris, "*The Experience of Higher Education*", London: Routledge and Kegan Paul, 1964, p. 14; C.E. Bidwell, "The school as a formal organization", in J.G. March (Ed.), "*Handbook of Organizations*", Chicago: Rand-McNally, 1965.
37. F. Musgrove, "Social class and levels of aspiration in a technological university", *Sociol. Rev.*, **15** (3) (Nov 1967); D. Child and F. Musgrove, "Career orientation of some university freshmen", *Educ. Res.*, **21** (3) (June 1969).
38. H.J. Perkin, *op. cit.*, p. 112.
39. P. Collison and J. Millen, "University chancellors, vice-chancellors and college principals: a social profile", *Sociol.*, 3 (1) (Jan 1969).

40. R. Chester, "Role conflict and the junior academic" in D. Martin (Ed.), *op. cit.*

41. J. Adelson, "The teacher as a model", in N. Sandford (Ed.), *The American College*, New York: Wiley, 1962.

42. H.J. Perkin, *op. cit.*, p. 179.

43. UGC, "*Report of the Committee on Teaching Method*", London: HMSO, 1964, pp. 103–105.

44. *Report of Commission of Inquiry*, vol. I, Oxford: Oxford University Press, 1966, p. 97.

45. H. Kidd, *The trouble at LSE, 1966–1967*, London: Oxford University Press, 1969, p. 10.

46. P. Rock and F. Heidensohn, "New reflections on violence", in D. Martin (Ed.), *op. cit.*

47. C. Katz, F.M. Katz and W.B. Oliphert, *What Happens to students: A study of students at the University of New England, 1961–1964*, Armidale, N.S.W.: University of New England (Mimeographed), 1965, pp. 109–110; F.M. Katz and M.E. Poole, "Role definition by university students", *Australian J. Educ.*, **13** (1) (March 1969).

48. J. Mitchell, in R. Goldman (Ed.), *Breakthrough*, London: Routledge and Kegan Paul, 1968, p. 138.

49. P. Marris, *op. cit.*, p. 105.

50. UGC Committee on Teaching Methods: *Use of Vacations by Students*, London: HMSO, 1963.

51. S. Box and S. Cotgrove, "Scientific Identity, Occupational Selection and Role Strain", *Br. J. Sociol.*, **17** (1) (March 1966).

52. E. Rudd, "The troubles of graduate students", in D. Martin (Ed.), *op. cit.*

53. S. Caine, *op. cit.*, p. 145.

54. See P. Rock and F. Heidensohn, *op. cit.*

55. D. Marsden and D. Davies, in R. Goldman (Ed.), *op. cit.*

56. E.C. Hughes, H.S. Becker and B. Geer, "Student culture and academic effort", in N. Sandford (Ed.), *op. cit.* The study by H.S. Becker, B. Geer, E.C. Hughes and A.L. Strauss, *Boys in White*, Chicago: University of Chicago Press, 1961, is one of the few accounts of the creation of a student culture, in this case in a medical school.

57. F.M. Katz, D.J. Magin and P.S. Arbib, *Role divergence in the University*, Sydney: Tertiary Education Research Centre, University of N.S.W., 1969, p. 43.

58. M. Trow and A.H. Halsey, "British academics and the professorship", *Sociology*, **3** (3) (Sept 1969), 330–331.

59. A.H. Halsey, "The study of the university teacher", *Universities Q.*, **17**, 2 (March 1963).

60. B.R. Wilson, "The needs of students", in M. Reeves (Ed.), *Eighteen Plus*, London: Faber & Faber, 1965.

61. B.R. Clark, "Student culture in college", being ch. 6 in *Educating the Expert in Society*, San Francisco: 1962. See also, for example, K.G. Hillman,

"Student valuation of academic achievement" *Sociol. Q.*, **10** (3) (Summer 1969).

62. See W.L. Wallace, "Faculty and fraternities: organizational influences on student achievement", *Admin. Sci. Q.*, **11** (4) (March 1967).

63. P. Marris, *op. cit.*, p. 38; J.A. Wankowski, *Students—Why Some Fail*, Birmingham: University of Birmingham Educational Survey, 1969, pp. 17–18.

64. T. Burns, *The Revolt of the Privileged*, London: Social Sciences Research Council Newsletter, Nov 1968.

65. See F. Parkin, *Middle Class Radicalism*, London: Manchester University Press, 1968—chs. 7 and 8 for an analysis of students' part in the Campaign for Nuclear Disarmament along these lines.

66. F. Zweig, *The Student in the Age of Anxiety*, London: Heinemann Educational, 1963, p. 99.

67. P. Marris, *op. cit.*, p. 92.

68. M.C. Albrow, "The influence of accommodation upon sixty-four Reading University students", *Br. J. Sociol.*, **17** (4) (Dec 1966), p. 410.

69. A. Giddens, "Aspects of the social structure of a university hall of residence", *Sociol. Rev.*, **8** (1) (July 1960), 106; See also P.B. Warr, "Attitudes and behaviour in a hall of residence", *Universities Q.*, **19** (11) (Dec 1964), 67, where the culture of a Birmingham hall "was found to be essentially tough-minded".

70. P. Marris, *op. cit.*, p. 32.

71. M. Hutt, "Undergraduates and their problems", in D. Daiches (Ed.), *The Idea of a New University*, London: Deutsch, 1964, p. 41.

72. C. Katz, F.M. Katz and W.B. Olphert, *op. cit.*, pp. 53, 71, 91–93 and pp. 124–125 are relevant to the next paragraph. See also, P. Marris, *op. cit.*, pp. 142–146.

73. J.A. Wankowski, *op. cit.*, p. 13.

74. P. Marris, *op. cit.*, pp. 78 and 103.

75. A. Giddens, *op. cit.*, and see also, for example, D. Thoday, "Halls of residence", *Universities Q.*, **12** (1) (March 1957), and T. Newcombe, "Student peer-group influence", in N. Sandford, *op. cit.*

76. N. Malleson, "Different sorts of students", *Universities Q.*, **15** (1) (Dec 1960).

77. P. Marris, *op. cit.*, pp. 149–152. Malleson, *op. cit.*, pp. 61–62 also found that married or engaged students did better academically.

78. See, for example, H.C. Selvin and W.O. Hagstrom, "Determination of support for civil liberties", *Br. J. Sociol.*, **11** (1) (March 1960).

79. M. Abrams, "Politics and the British middle class", *Socialist Commentary* (Oct 1962); N. Barnes and G. Paton, "Redbrick student", *Socialist Commentary* (Nov 1962); R. Rose, "Students and society", *New Society* (2 Jan 1964).

80. J. Abbott, "The concept of motility", *Sociol. Rev.*, **14** (2) (July 1966); P. Marris, *op. cit.*, pp. 154–156.

81. F. Zweig, *op. cit.*, pp. 41 and 113; P. Marris, *op. cit.*, p. 147.

82. J. Abbott, "Students' social class in three northern universities", *Br. J. Soc.*, **16** (3) (Sept 1965); a rather outré instance of the third structural point is that there is differential social class recruitment to the two forms of football at Oxford and Cambridge, association being biased to the working and rugby to the middle class, see S.J. Eggleston, "Secondary schools and Oxbridge blues", *Br. J. Sociol.*, **16** (3) (Sept 1965).

83. A more recent investigation concerning medical students also found a higher wastage rate among students from boarding compared with day schools, but did not find a lower wastage rate amongst the working than the middle class; see Report of the Royal Commission of Medical Education, Appendix 19, Survey of Medical Students in 1966, London: HMSO, 1968, pp. 354–355.

84. S. Box and S. Cotgrove, "Committment to science: A solution to student marginality", *Sociology* **1** (3) (Sept 1967).

85. F. Musgrove, "Self concepts and occupational identities", *Universities Q.*, **23** (3) (Summer 1969), 342–343.

86. J.A. Wankowski, *op. cit.*, p. 16.

87. See, for example, details of exact choices and interests of first and final year medical students in Rep. of R.C. on Medical Education, p. 356; and R. Williams, "Industry as a career: What students think", *New Society* (26 March 1970).

88. J.D. Nisbet and W. Grant, "Vocational intentions and decisions of Aberdeen arts graduates", *Occup. Psychol.*, **39** (4) (Oct 1965), 219.

89. M. Collins, *Women Graduates and the Teaching Profession*, Manchester; Manchester University Press, 1964; A.F. Skinner, "Scotland, Part 1. Professional Education", *The Yearbook of Education*, London: Evans Bros., 1963; P. Marris, *op. cit.*, p. 157, F. Parkin, *op. cit.*, p. 192.

90. A.F. McPherson, *op. cit.*, p. 20.

91. W. Guttsman, *op. cit.*

92. S.J. Eggleston, *op. cit.*

93. H.J. Perkin, *op. cit.*, pp. 128–129 and 170.

94. C.T. Sandford, M.E. Couper, S. Griffin, "Class influences in higher education", *Br. J. Ed. Studies*, **35,** 2 (June 1965) and M.E. Couper and C. Harris, "C.A.T. to university: The changing student intake", *Educ. Res.* **12** (2) (Feb 1970). See also H. Dickinson, "Students in a C.A.T.: Qualifications and success", *Universities Q.*, **18** (4) (Sept 1964).

95. *Enquiry into Student Progress*, Table 10, UGC, 1968.

96. *Ibid.*, table 29.

97. C. Katz *et al.*, *op. cit.*, pp. 103–105.

98. F. Parkin, *op. cit.*, pp. 172.

99. G. Payne and J. Bird, "The newest universities, 2: What are their students like?", *New Society* (23 Oct 1969).

100. See UGC; Report of the Committee on Teaching Methods, ch. VI, in which surveys carried out by the NUS and its Scottish equivalent both showed a demand for fewer and better lectures, but; the Committee's own survey

did not reveal so critical a spirit amongst students. *Report of R.C. on Medical Education*, p. 340.

101. P. Marris, *op. cit.*, p. 119; A.H. Halsey, "Universities expansion and the collegiate idea", *Universities Q.*, **16** (1) (Dec 1961), 58; F. Zweig, *op. cit.*, p. 6.

102. See, for example, P. Marris, *op. cit.*, pp. 62–63.

103. H.J. Perkin, *op. cit.*, p. 87.

104. UGC: Report of the Committee on University Teaching Methods, p. 87.

105. J.D. Nisbet and J. Walsh, "Predicting student performance", *Universities Q.*, **20** (4) (Sept 1966).

106. See, for example, H.S. Becker, B. Geer, E.C. Hughes and A.L. Strauss, *op. cit.*, and R.K. Merton, G.C. Reader, and P.L. Kendall, "*The Student Physician*", Cambridge, Mass.: Harvard University Press, 1957.

107. *Report of R.C. on Medical Education*, pp. 343 and 351–352.

108. J.A. Wankowski, *op. cit.*, pp. 11–12.

109. N. Malleson, "The influence of emotional factors on achievement in university education", in *Sociol. Rev.*, *Monograph*, No. 7 (Oct 1963).

110. F. Zweig, *op. cit.*, p. 90.

111. A. Eden, "Social life in a provincial university, *Br. J. Sociol.*, **10** (4) (Dec 1959).

112. M.C. Albrow, *op. cit.*

113. J. Abbott, *op. cit.*, p. 213. For support for Albrow's conclusions, see also A. Eden, *op. cit.*, and for Sheffield, P.B. Warr, *op. cit.*

114. P.B. Warr, *op. cit.*, p. 60; P. Marris, *op. cit.*, pp. 80 and 124–125.

115. D. Thoday, *op. cit.*; P. Marris, *op. cit.*, p. 76. See also P.B. Warr, *op. cit.*, p. 60.

116. L. Cohen and A. Batcock, "Female university students and social influence", *Educ. Res.*, **21** (3) (June 1969).

117. L.S. Lewis, "On prestige and loyalty of university faculty", *Admin. Sci. Q.*, **11** (4) (March 1967).

118. J. Katz, "Personality and interpersonal relations in the college classroom", in N. Sandford (Ed.), *op. cit.*

119. M. Trow and A.H. Halsey, *op. cit.*, pp. 329 and 335–338.

120. One book, A.H. Halsey and M. Trow, *The British Academics*, London, 1973, which is due for publication at the time of writing and is based on an empirical investigation made in 1964, should tell us much in this respect about the staff of British universities.

ANTHONY J. ELGER

INDUSTRIAL ORGANIZATIONS—a processual perspective

Anthony J. Elger *has recently joined the Department of Sociology, University of Warwick, having previously taught in the Department of Sociology, University of Aberdeen, Scotland. He received his B.A. in Sociology and Psychology at the University of Hull and, after postgraduate research at the University of Durham, is completing research on the orientations and strategies of engineering workers in a declining industrial area. His current interests include industrial sociology, generative models of social processes and critical perspectives in sociology.*

This chapter discusses the social processes through which participants in industrial organizations sustain and transform the patterns of social relations in which they are implicated and which constitute the organization. This processual viewpoint implies that "organizational structure", as a pattern of social relations and social constraints, should be seen as the ongoing product of social processes enacted by organization members rather than as some form of "given" which furnishes automatic constraints on the lines of actions of those members. Thus any analysis of industrial concerns must consider the ways in which the interpretations and resources which participants bring to, or develop within, their organizational involvements support or subvert particular institutional arrangements. Constraining characteristics of organizational arrangements must then be related to features of actors' perspectives, resources and commitments.

In emphasizing processes of social interaction as a crucial focus of organizational analysis this chapter follows those recent students who have criticized systems theories of organizations and who have provided some guidelines for alternative styles of analysis. As some of these critics have emphasized, this debate involves more than simply theoretical controversy, for the dominance of systems theory coincides with a sophisticated commitment among "organization theorists" to the problems and policies of upper management.[1] In recognition of the value-imbued character of sociological analysis, and in contrast with those features of social life celebrated by the systems theorists, the perspective adopted in this chapter emphasizes the humanly created and sustained character of social institutions, and attends to the conflicts of interest generated by the typical social relations of industrial concerns, together with those social processes which mitigate, conceal, contain, organize or intensify these conflicts.

The theoretical arguments which will be advanced in support of a processual perspective have general relevance and could be considered in relation to any type of organization. However this chapter is concerned specifically with industrial concerns—that is, those organizations that produce goods to be sold on the market, which involve participants as employees who take on organizational obligations in return for economic rewards, and which are regulated in terms of economic priorities. The manner in which these defining features are treated within different theoretical perspectives, and the patterns of social processes for which they serve as parameters, will be given more detailed consideration in the course of the discussion.[2]

The first section of the chapter reviews the debate between systems theorists and their critics. This affords an opportunity to identify the theoretical issues in dispute and the distinctive features of the different approaches. Some of the theoretical themes outlined in this discussion are then considered more concretely in an appraisal of a small number of substantial empirical studies. The later part of the chapter traces some of the implications of a processual perspective, focusing on the formation and implementation of organizational policies, and on the formation and transformation of occupational milieux. The initial abstract theoretical overview thus provides a point of departure for a more substantive consideration of social process in industrial concerns.

Theoretical perspectives

Silverman has persuasively identified a "systems-orthodoxy" underlying a variety of system models and informing much organizational research.[3] However, in the shadow of this orthodoxy, critics have during the last decade provided increasingly more positive arguments for the relevance of alternative perspectives. Thus an overview of theoretical positions can most usefully be organized in terms of an outline of the main features of systems approaches, followed by consideration of some of the proposed alternatives. This brief review is intended to sensitize the reader to some of the theoretical concerns which inform the interpretation of empirical studies which follows, and thus makes no claim to exhaustiveness in its treatment of the various approaches.

(a) *Systems analyses*

As might be expected, given its importance on the general sociological scene over the last thirty years, Parsonian "normative functionalism" provides the most abstract statement of a sociological "systems analysis" of organizations.[4] In this analysis organizations, including industrial concerns, are viewed as social systems—specialized subsystems of the wider society—oriented primarily to particular societal needs and structured in terms of the normative prescriptions for such orientation. This view follows from the assumption that societies are characterized by consensus concerning generalized values, which specify structural solutions to general functional problems. The linkages between structure, function and normative order are considered to be particularly clear in the case of organizations as they are crystallized in an explicit organizational goal and operating procedures.

For Parsons this view implies that the relevant values, signified by the organizational goal, inform all aspects of organizational structure. Values and norms pattern the procurement and disposal of inanimate resources (input and output) so that "boundary interchanges" between the organization and its environment proceed smoothly in so far as they coincide with societal values (e.g. use accepted exchange media). They structure the internal mobilization of resources ("throughput") through the "media" of direction and decision-making, which flow from authority and which facilitate the organization of roles and resources to realize system goals. Finally they govern the involvements of employees through (a) the contract, which embodies socially sanctioned appeals for commitment through the provision of socially accepted rewards; (b) non-contingent loyalties, which arise when "social needs" find a site for fulfilment in the organization; and (c) authority, which sanctions particular types of coercion ("in that penalties for non-cooperation are set") and therapy in the cause of goal attainment.

Industrial, and other economic, organizations are located in this schema in terms of their "function" as production units. Thus the criterion of social function, interpreted by reference to the supposed value consensus, serves to justify a focus on organizational "production tasks" as such, while the interest of organizational leaders in profitability criteria is given secondary attention because such concerns are not "functions on behalf of the society as a system". The boundary interchanges, which subsume the contributions and rewards of organization members, are identified with the conventional economic categories of factors of production and shares of income, these also being assimilated into an equilibriating consensus-bound analysis.

In this analysis Parsons identifies several sources of tension. "Relative to the goals of the organization it is reasonable to postulate an inherent centrifugal tendency of subunits of the organization, a tendency reflecting pulls deriving from the personalities of the participants, from the special adaptive exigencies of their particular job structures, and possible from other sources, such as the pressure of other roles in which they are involved." In this scheme the first factor—personality—is considered to be the fundamental source of disequilibrium in the organization, and is countered by the machinery of pattern maintenance which controls employee involvement in the ways outlined above. The second factor—adaptive exigencies—provides the stimulus for structural elaboration, when organizational structure is modified to match changing resources but realize stable system goals. If pattern maintenance is effective such elaboration, in which "a given structure moves towards becoming more like what it basically is",[5] appears the only type of organizational change possible.

Cybernetic systems analysts of industrial organizations have generally borrowed or taken for granted the functionalist conception of organizations as co-operative systems oriented to the pursuit of a system goal which coincides with the production task.[6] They are most concerned to extend the analysis of input and output processes and their impact on organizational structure—a concern well represented by the concept of "open socio-technical systems". The notion of open system stresses the possibility of organizational response to a changed environment. This response is typically considered to be one of structural elaboration while the organization remains genotypically similar—that is, continues to achieve the organizational goal. In socio-technical systems theory industrial technology is depicted as being the crucial intervening variable between feedback and "adequate" organizational structure, an idea which makes a distinctive contribution to systems analysis.[7]

Thus Trist *et al.* suggest that organizations have economic, technical and social dimensions which exist in a complex interdependence determined in the last instance by the "primary task" of the organization.[8] While technology appears as a resource for managements facing changed environments it also "sets limits and creates demands" which are reflected in organizational structure. Both features—resource and constraint—are given meaning in relation to task priorities, that is through a connection with levels of goal attainment.[9]

(b) *Criticisms*

The central criticism of systems theories can be summarized in the charge that, by framing their analyses in terms of organizational "tasks" or "functions", they reify the organization as an entity with characteristics independent of the social processes through which organizational members construct and construe social reality.[10] The systems theorist assumes that the organizational "function", generally equated with the organizational goal, provides an unambiguous and virtually unchallenged referent for action within the organization, and thus neglects the ways in which actors' purposes and perspectives intervene in the interpretation and contesting of goal-related prescriptions for action. A notable congruence between theorists' and administrators' perspectives is evident in this equation of functions and goals, and in the related conception of the docility of organizational members *vis-à-vis* administrative instructions.[11] The theoretical underpinning for this reified conception of the organization is provided by the postulate of an overarching consensus which informs all organizational processes. This consensus postulate asserts the pervasive influence of common or complementary normative standards as justification for the emphasis, in systems models, on equilibriating processes and the enactment of role-determined behaviour by organizational participants.

The cybernetic models of organizations as systems do not escape the consensus assumption for the sensing and feedback mechanisms so crucial to a cybernetic approach are assumed to be oriented to organizational purposes. The prescriptive elements of this assumption are nicely revealed in Katz and Kahn's response to the factual failure of organizations to satisfy their model. The finding that "various compromises are attempted by organizational leaders to provide some degree of systematic intelligence without an adequate allocation of resources and manpower to their function" does not prompt a re-examination of their model but stimulates complaints about the failure of organizations to use the services of social science consultants for such duties.[12]

The premise that there is consensus around generalized values not only promotes the reification of organizational goals and structure but also constricts the analysis of participants involvements and lines of action. This is clearly demonstrated in the conception of role-conformity utilised by the systems theorists. This conception gives little attention to possible bargaining or conflict over conduct to be included in the role, or over the manner of role performance, since the "maintenance" mechanisms of socialization and control are assumed to produce role-conformity. Similarly, the extent to which different patterns of experience and differential resources subvert stipulated role-performance is minimized. Together these aspects of the analysis limit consideration of actors' perspectives and actions to the simple dichotomy between formal and informal, which contrasts rational, legitimate, goal-oriented behaviour with sentimental, illegitimate, deviant behaviour without exploring the various rationales and alternative patterns of action conceived of and practised by organizational members.

It is sometimes asserted that these crucial faults of the systems perspective are incidental to the claimed advantages of such a perspective. In this regard proponents of systems models, in their polemics with human relations and "one-best way" theorists, have stressed their concern with organization–environment relations and the ways in which various environmental circumstances are translated into "suitable" organizational structures.[13] But even at this high-point of their analyses their contributions are limited by the assumptions discussed above. Thus the consensus postulate leads to the assumption that the "organization" monitors the environment in a uniform manner to select goal-relevant features of the resource and product markets as the major constraints on organizational structure and change. And the analysis of labour power at the "boundary interchange" is conducted in terms of compliance mechanisms informed by generalized values and residual, frictional, informal action, thus bypassing analysis of the worker as a rational actor, constrained by practical as well as moral circumstances and guided by conceptions of individual and collective futures which may cross-cut organizational plans.

Thus the treatment of organization–environment relations affords a further example of the way in which, by the reification of organizational tasks and treatment of organizational participants as compliant conformists (apart from a few disruptive deviants) the systems perspective shows a close correspondence with the interest and ideology of administrators.[14] This correspondence provides more than an ideological justification for elite policies and perspectives because it also furnishes a vocabulary of organizational design—a conception of efficient organizational forms and how they are to be achieved. Thus the emphasis in systems models on the fluid but equilibrating processes of response to environmental exigencies corresponds closely to the *idealized* depiction of working relationships in project-oriented management teams *proposed* as suitable for innovating organizations, and this emphasis affords a justification and guide for policies and techniques designed to mould personnel as suitable units for such fluid response. In addition the socio-technical systems version of the perspective identifies for managers some "prime manipulable movers" (as Gouldner terms them) such as technology and work group organization, which serve as levers available to "charge agents" in their efforts to improve the efficient pursuit of "organizational tasks".[15]

(c) *Proposed alternatives*

In accord with the general criticisms of functionalist and consensus-based explanations of social structures, the critics of systems analyses of industrial concerns and other organizations have attempted to provide a reappraisal of the importance of organizational goals and formal procedures in organizations, and they have treated actors' involvements and interests as having a problematic relationship to such goals and procedures. Thus the postulate of common values has been replaced by an analysis of the manner in which actors actively and variously interpret and, through the deployment of resources, control social settings within organizations. The explanatory framework emphasizing systemic constraints rooted in normative order has been replaced by one which sees both constraints and accomplishments as socially constructed by interactants.[16] This alternative approach to the analysis of industrial organizations emphasizes that the impact of organizational goals on organizational action is mediated by processes of interpretation and negotiation in which the various groups of participants attempt to protect and advance their special interests. Thus the social relations which characterize industrial, and other, going concerns are to be understood as outcomes of the typical social processes which are generated by the intersection of organizational designs and decision rules on one hand and actors' involvements on the other.

This intersection can be approached schematically by considering the foundation and perpetuation of organizations from the point of view of those involved, by asking how the notions of organizational goals, roles and structure come into play in actors' decisions about what counts as an organization and what constitutes organizational involvement.[17] Both commonsense and legal criteria suggest that particular actors may sponsor a projected social apparatus as an organizational instrument for some purpose, and in this context other categories of actors may be implicated in organizational arrangements in terms of rather various exchanges of contributions and returns, which are envisaged and can be accommodated with the organizational design purveyed by the "founders". Thus the establishment of an organization implies bringing various participants within the jurisdiction of such a goal-oriented social apparatus, which involves diverse organizational arrangements constructed in the interplay of the interests and resources conceived by the various participants. These features of the establishment of an organizational form remain characteristic also of ongoing organizations, and in each case other going concerns may provide models of viable organizational designs, arrangements and contractual relationships to which sponsors and other participants appeal in interpreting, evaluating and negotiating their involvement.[18]

In these terms *industrial* organizations are characteristically intended by their sponsors as effective instruments for the generation of profits through the production of marketable products, the particular products and markets being more or less clearly defined at different junctures in the organizations history. Other participants are involved in the organization through specific contractual relationships (which outline economic returns and conditions of employment) as these are surrounded by diverse assumptions and expectations about the course of organizational affairs and their possible implications for particular categories of employees. These contractual relationships thus reflect, and are interpreted in terms of, the contrasting interests and perspectives of those different categories of participants who control distinctive types of organizational resource. The pattern of organizational arrangements which constitutes the social structure of any industrial concern must thus be analysed as an emergent product of processes of negotiation and interpretation enacted by such differentially placed participants within the jurisdiction of organizational decision-rules and administrative programmes.

Further implications of this approach to organizational analysis will now be considered through a discussion of organizational goals and participants involvements. This discussion provides the basis for a more detailed characterization of organizational social structure.

Organizational goals

While organizational goal orientation is a recognized feature of organizations, conceded by all organizational participants, the terms in which the goal is conceived may diverge considerably for different groups of participants, and the nature of attachment to the recognized purpose varies with the sorts of employment relationships through which participants are implicated in organizational arrangements. Thus the sponsors and controllers of organizations such as business enterprises must actively attempt to order organizational arrangements in ways they deem appropriate to their intended goals—both through the presentation of some version of the goal as having jurisdiction over organizational actions, and through techniques of implementation and control of their preferred organizational designs for goal achievement. Other participants recognize in some form the sponsors assumed goals as a point of reference for actions, but may often construe their involvements and assess the appropriateness of organizational arrangements in other terms, such as the exercise of particular skills or the protection and extension of individual or collective rights. Similarly other social units, having dealings with the organization as outside agencies, will take account of the goal-relevant features of organizational arrangements while initiating bargains about such arrangements informed by their own distinctive interests.

Such an alteration in the status to be accorded organizational goals and associated administrative designs stresses that the linkage of organizational arrangements to sponsors' goals is an accomplishment conditioned by the resources and tactics of the organizational elite in relation to bargaining with and controlling lower participants. Thus the formalized organizational arrangements indicated by job descriptions, organization charts and the like will be influenced by the involvements, perspectives and bargaining power of these members *vis-à-vis* the elite rather than being the simple product of organizational designs sponsored from above, while the avowed goals of the organization may themselves be restated as a consequence of bargaining with organizational members. Outside agencies may also influence organizational procedures and routines in ways unintended by organizational designers.

This argument may seem to veer towards a simple "contractual exchange" theory of organizational arrangements in which organizational goals appear as epiphenomena. However this position is avoided if recognition is given to the ways in which those features of the social setting "taken-for-granted" by the various participants define the context of "givens" within which they bargain over what they construe as the socially contrived and problematic features of organizational designs.[19] What is taken as "given" by the different groups of participants may vary, so that what is seen as inevitable by one group may form the topic of conscious deliberation for another—a point which underlines the importance of examining the awareness relationships existing between the various groups and the ways in which these are sustained and transformed through subterfuge and surveillance.[20] With specific reference to organizational goals and procedures such analysis would focus on the complex relations among publicly avowed, overtly espoused and practically pursued goals of organizational controllers and their possible impact on the bargaining perspectives of lower participants.

Thus analysis of the bargaining processes which intervene in the formulation of organizational procedures deemed appropriate to the organizations goal (and which sometimes lead to reformulation of the goal itself) must identify the perspectives of the various participants, as these condition their assessment of relative bargaining strengths and inform aspirations and strategies. This would then provide the basis for an account of the ways in which the perspectives and strategies of the various groups intermesh in the going concern and the feedback effect of such interrelationships on the reformulation of such strategies and perspectives.

The above discussion has concerned the social processes which mediate between goals and administrative practices proposed by organizational sponsors and controllers and the formal terms in which these are institutionalized in organizational rules and procedures. However, the negotiation of such procedures leaves them to be implemented in day-to-day organizational activities, and here again attention must be given to the social processes of interpretation and negotiation through which such implementation occurs and through which the jurisdiction of organizational goals and policies is demonstrated.[21]

One approach which pays attention to these mediating social processes, through which goals and procedures susceptible to a variety of interpretations are related to particular organizational actions and settings, is that which conceives of organizations as "negotiated orders".[22] This conception takes the ambiguities of organizational goals and rules together with the conditional nature of agreements and contracts between members as points of reference in the analysis of ongoing social processes of interpretation and bargaining through which participants "make" organizational actions. Thus it is recognized that the organizational goal furnishes a "generalized mandate" which, since organizational actions must fall under its jurisdiction, is respected and given formal precedence. At the same time the necessity of specification and translation of the meaning of the goal in relation to each organizational encounter provides opportunities for the relevant parties to institute distinctive interpretations, influenced by their particular interests and bargaining resources, under the aegis of the mandate.[23] Strauss *et al.* thus portray the goal as a symbolic referent under which locally bargained lines of action— informed by interests, opportunities and resources of the interactants—count as organizational procedures. It is in this sense that the organization can be said to consist of "the combination of rules and policies, along with agreements, under- standings, pacts, contracts and other working agreements, which currently obtains". These locally negotiated and constantly reworked interpretations of the "sense" of the organizational goal and procedures are circumscribed by the relative power of the various participants to authorize or exclude particular conceptions, and also by the finite repertoire of usages which the various participants take for granted as possibilities.

This discussion of the social processes of interpretation and negotiation, through which organizational goals and designs are incorporated in organizational procedures which are in turn made to subsume members' organizational activities, shows that substantial resources buttress particular versions of organizational purpose and delimit the variety of activities through which such purpose can be said to be realized.[24] This feature of organizational process, especially as it relates to the capacity of the organizational elite to bring organizational arrangements into alignment with its designs and priorities, underlines the reified nature of the systems perspective which at best locates such capability in a normative consensus. Re- cognition of ways in which higher authorities develop mechanisms intended to sustain organizational activities which match their priorities must thus be coupled with an assessment of the knowledge and resources deployed in such strategies, appreciation of the strategies employed by lower participants in response to such managerial initiatives, and the practical limits to recalcitrance which the elite will tolerate before disbanding the organization as no longer capable of providing the returns which they intended of it.[25]

Thus the analysis of organizational goals and procedures, as they are embedded in social processes of organizational practice, continually reaffirms the impact of participant's involvements—their perspectives, resources and expected benefits—on the organizational "negotiated order".

Participants' involvements

The foregoing discussion recognizes that organizational arrangements are accom- plished, sustained and transformed in encounters between participants who, as individuals and groups, bring distinctive perspectives, interests and resources to such encounters. These perspectives and interests which inform the interpretation and management of working relationships, are not simply the outcome of organiza- tional experiences. Rather they are rooted in the multiple work and non-work relationships in which social actors form and reform their conceptions of themselves and their social worlds, and thus they mediate the impact of diverse circumstances on the stance which actors adopt in organizational affairs.[26] Similarly resources, defined as skills and hardware deployed by any set of actors and acknowledged by others, are generated in extra-organizational as well as organizational processes.[27] Since the perspectives and resources which participants hold in organizational encounters are developed by such participants as actors on a wider social scene—in the context of a network of acquaintanceships and affiliations which includes involvements in various organizations[28]—sociological analysis cannot be limited by "organizational boundaries" which are problematic in their status for, and impact on, organization members.

Among critics of systems perspectives there can be discerned two somewhat distinctive approaches to the analysis of actors' perspectives and their impact on organizational arrangements, each having a characteristic theoretical and substantive focus. One approach focuses on the typical "projects of action" which individuals and groups pursue in the organization—implying an interest in relatively enduring collective aspirations and perspectives founded in common work and community experience.[29] The other tradition attends in particular to the vicissitudes of the "subjective careers" of organization members—with detailed analyses of the transformation of definitions of self and situation as individuals orient themselves amid the changing circumstances of an organizational career.[30]

Though they appeal to different theoretical traditions these approaches can effectively be regarded as complementary in their contributions to the analysis of actors' perspectives in relation to organizational process, for in combination they suggest a complex interplay between the perspectives and demands articulated by organized groups, and the specific conceptions of self and situation developed by organization members.

The focus on "projects of action" directs attention to common circumstances providing an enduring background for common expectations and demands, which override the particularities of organizational experience, inform actors' responses to organizational arrangements, and may through time become built into the pattern of such arrangements. Within this framework the impact of individually experienced changes in working arrangements is recognized but receives little consideration alongside the critical junctures through which transformations in collective definitions and strategies occur.[31] Students of "subjective careers", on the other hand, have focused on the patterning of actors' experiences as a series of individual phases and "turning-points", with emphasis on the discrete perspectives and tactics which actors may adopt as they move from one organizational setting to another. They have emphasized the refractory aspects of organizational arrangements and the contingencies of adaptation to these aspects and have been somewhat less concerned with the articulation of common experiences and collective responses.[32]

Thus each approach identifies important aspects of the dynamic relationship between organizational or occupational experience and patterns of organizational arrangements. Together they suggest that particular work experiences—as they are affected by management strategies and the involvements of other participants—

may subvert or sponsor demands based in conceptions of common interest, while the articulation and implementation, or failure, of such demands will alter the nature of these work experiences.

The approach which emerges from these conceptions differs sharply from contractual models of organizational order in emphasizing the ongoing formation and remaking of actors' perspectives and demands in individual and collective responses to organizational experiences, and in thus underlining the problematic nature of those interests which actors may seek to accommodate within organizational arrangements. And just as interests and demands may be transformed so may the resources which enable actors to establish their claims—for the varied conceptions of organizational purposes and relevant accomplishments, within which individual and collective contributions are evaluated as resources, are also open to persistent reinterpretation and renegotiation. There is no theoretical warrant for Blau's suggestion that lower participants will routinely comply with administrative commands in return for the distribution of rewards which have accrued to the administrator because of organizational accomplishments based on earlier compliant actions, nor for any postulate of congruence between "compliance structures" and "organizational goals", for involvements are problematic outcomes of ongoing interpretive and negotiative processes informed by diverse conceptions of purposes, procedures, services, rewards, opportunities and "taken-for-granted" features of organization.[33] Formalised contractual agreements, which embody stated services and rewards, are to be understood as negotiable rulings within such a matrix of assumed organizational purposes and envisaged individual and collective prospects.

The view of organizational involvements discussed above suggests that any analysis of organizational relationships must attend to the ways in which actors protect or develop their positions within the enterprise. This requires consideration of, on the one hand those overt strategies, involving explicit reference to some version of the organizational goal, by which members may defend or advance their interests in organizational bargaining; and on the other those less explicit manoeuvres which are also important in defining the position of members, but which avoid reference to the jurisdiction of organizational mandates.

The patterning of bargaining strategies can be considered in terms of the resources and alliances available to the various organization members. With reference to resources, some participants are able successfully to identify their peculiar skills with one or another critical "organizational problem", and thus lodge their own interests within a rhetoric of organizational priorities—such strategies are typical of the "micropolitical" phase of organizational activity. Other participants succeed only in pressing claims for more limited recognition of their value in organizational work, so that interaction between themselves and organizational controllers characteristically reveals an awareness of both conflicts of interest and interdependences.[34] These distinctive patterns of claims and recognitions are accompanied by varied formations of group action. Thus some actors are implicated in vertical alliances which are sustained by patronage and sponsorship, while others are drawn into horizontal alliances which are commonly underpinned by collective solidarities.[35] It is through the interplay of such claims and alliances that the individual and collective involvements of participants are formed and reformed under the jurisdiction of organizational goals and programmes.

However these overt bargaining strategies do not exhaust the lines of action through which organization members may pursue their interests. Thus actors with appreciable resources may successfully exclude "issues" from the bargaining arena by advancing what they appreciate are mutable arrangements as "givens" which set the limits *within* which manoeuvring may occur.[36] Similarly participants with more meagre resources may renegotiate their involvements with others in particular organizational enclaves covertly, without reference to, or in opposition to, organizational designs and priorities.[37]

Organizational structure

This discussion of organizational goals and actors' involvements has emphasized that the patterns of social relationships which constitute organizational structure are ongoing products of processes of negotiation and interpretation, through which participants with differential resources and discrepant interests construct organizational social realities under the jurisdiction of organizational priorities and programmes. The implications of this approach for conventional treatments of social structure can be concisely traced out by considering the status of "organizational roles" within a processual perspective.

While in the systems perspective organizational roles are conceived of as units of institutional integration defined by common norms, from the viewpoint outlined above such roles may best be considered as elements of organizational designs and procedures recognized by organization members. As such they are (a) subject to bargaining directed at the modification of expected performances and rewards, and (b) dependent for their implementation on the mutual interpretation of their meaning in particular episodes. Thus the enactment of organizational roles by participants involves them in attempts to reconcile or "manage" the diverse demands which arise, not only from the organizational design, but from a wider array of work and non-work social relationships; and also requires of them ongoing interpretations of the sense and relevance of espoused roles.[38] The enactment of such roles may, therefore, involve a narrow delimitation of possible lines of action, when incumbents, as individuals and groups have few resources with which to bargain and when the variety of interpretations tolerated by others is closely circumscribed; but in other circumstances actors may have more room for manoeuvre in the reconstruction of role-performances and in the reconceptualization of role-categories.[39]

The ongoing process of role-enactment therefore differentially accommodates the interests and self-conceptions of participants within an extant pattern of working arrangements. While some participants may embrace a role they themselves have partially made, others are constrained to occupy roles on terms unresponsive to their interests and concerns. In response to experienced role-constraints actors may declare the discrepancy between role and self-conceptions by displaying "role distance" and may seek to develop strategies of independence in cooperation with others.[40] Thus the perspectives and interests generated in a wider range of social relationships inform the management of role-performances and associated organizational arrangements, though in rather different ways according to the autonomy or constraint which inheres in the enacted role.

These characteristics of organizational role construction and performance underline the inadequacy of systems perspectives which identify such roles as consensually defined clusters of rights and obligations, unambiguously linked with "organizational tasks" and untouched by personal concerns and collective interests. They recommend instead a conception of social structure as the present product of social processes of interpretation, negotiation, conflict and accommodation, among diverse sets of participants who possess distinctive conceptions of their interests within the organization, and differential resources which can be deployed in the pursuit of those interests. This conception of organizational structure informs the discussion in the following section, where some empirical studies are considered which allow a more substantive examination of social process in industrial concerns.

Organizational structure and processual analyses: some major empirical studies

The previous discussion of systems theories and processual perspectives as alternative approaches to organizational analysis has necessarily been rather abstract as it has focused on those general issues of conceptualization and theoretical stance which form the major areas of disagreement between systems theorists and their critics. However, in this section an attempt is made to illustrate the processual approach discussed in the previous section, through a fairly detailed discussion of a selection of "classic" empirical studies in industrial sociology. This should provide a more empirically based review of the patterning of organizational arrangements by participants pursuing diverse and conflicting purposes under the jurisdiction of organizational goals and procedures.

Of the studies considered in this section two involve inter-firm comparisons which illuminate patterns of variation and change in organizational structure, while the remainder are more intensive case studies which thoroughly portray the character and dynamics of participants' involvements and strategies in industrial milieux. The wider comparative studies which are examined first provide a context for discussion of the case study findings.

Woodward

Woodward's study—an examination of the management structure of a sample of manufacturing firms in relation to the "business tasks" and effectiveness of the various firms—exemplifies a concern among recent industrial sociologists to develop a comparative structural analysis of industrial organizations. This concern for comparative analysis has been prompted in particular by an interest in typologies of organizations which may subsume and qualify the numerous small-scale studies of work groups and occupations which were the characteristic products of earlier research orientations.[41]

Woodward's research suggested that a typology of systems of production technology ordered considerable variations in features of formal organization, and their relation to business success (see figure 1). Thus "the technical demands of the production system shaped the organization of the firm to a greater extent than previously recognized, limiting and controlling the behaviour of the people employed, while particular administrative expedients were linked with success in one system and failure in another".[42] The ambiguity of several key terms in this summary is resolved in terms of a "task analysis"—the production system is seen as the product of business goals and available techniques for their realization which thus limit, more or less strictly, management actions. Since conscious planning appeared to have only a limited impact on the relationship between technology and organization Woodward stressed the impact of "situational demands" made by technology on people. The implications of this focus are traced out in more detailed studies of each major type of production category and various types of technical change; these must be examined before any overall assessment of the approach.

Figure 1

Unit Production	Mass Production	Process Production
(1) Measures indicate progressive increase in importance of middle management through stages. This reflects trend in interrelation of management functions:		
Closely linked functions	Formally coordinated functions	Largely autonomous functions
(2) Specialization of production supervision and line-staff relationships greatest in mass production. This is related to the character of the technology and its apparent connection with organizational goals:		
Technology defines organizational tasks	Technology formally administered in terms of sectional targets	Technology delineates production and organizational goals

Woodward suggests that in Unit production *development* is the management "function" most critical to the firm's success since it links customers' novel requests to production possibilities, while the firm's objectives and manufacturing policy are set in numerous short-term decisions by the chief executive. These characteristics of the production system imply the inapplicability of rigorous controls and allow considerable supervisory discretion and in turn high involvement in work and commitment to the firm on the part of employees. Management forms a cohesive team, integrated through technical concerns around the development engineering elite, and able to use informal contacts to smooth interaction. While discretion and informality prompt "distorted" production schedules (e.g. by pressure from "sales" for urgent jobs) high commitment and management solidarity limit such developments.

In mass production *production* is the dominant "function", policy-making is divorced from planning and there is considerable specialization of functional divisions and line and staff departments. The specialization and independence of tasks with distinctive criteria of performance produces complex interdepartmental rivalries, in which departmental loyalties are reinforced because interdepartmental contacts are characterized by conflicts. It also means fragmented work tasks and contradictory priorities on the shop-floor, which necessitate "interpreting the mood and balance of power in senior management as the relative importance of subsidiary objectives vary from time to time". In this setting strategies of independence developed by workers are combated by various explicit control structures. These control structures Woodward treats as additional situational demands in the interstices of technical constraints.[43]

In process production, research, marketing and production constitute "three distinct and autonomous stages" with relations between the production department and the autonomous research and marketing groups mediated by various on-site development departments. *Marketing* decisions are critical in high-level policies on products and processes and thus become incorporated into plant construction. In this situation interdepartmental conflicts are slight because of lack of production pressure, similarity of training and circulation of on-site (production and development) managers, and the mediation of marketing pressures by liaison departments and physical plant. Production is depicted as relatively routine yet satisfying, with pressure only during crises, though production and maintenance priorities conflict.

In these analyses, and in the studies of technical change which show manoeuvring and bargaining as intrinsic features of such change, Woodward seeks to explain informal and shop-floor behaviour (as well as the formal structure already mentioned) in terms of the situational demands engendered by management goals and techniques. She offers a dual—and ambiguous—explanation, concerned firstly with technology and control structures as direct constraints which are factual outcomes of past managerial decisions, and more generally with a "task analysis" which implies the acceptance of socially defined goals and constraints as such when participants commit themselves to organizational roles.[44]

However the case studies show that the definition of the situation, together with the constraints and purposes this implies for participants, is an ongoing process informed by theoretical schemes (e.g. impact of management ideology), private aspirations, established rhetorics and sanctions (e.g. the continued importance of the development department in the case studies of change from unit to mass production) and internal logics of political manoeuvre (e.g. micropolitical implications of departmental origins of the chief executive). Only when these features of organizational process are considered can the links between what are after all socially defined and redefined market conditions, indicators of success, requisite technologies and control strategies, and the further organizational features outlined in the case studies, be explained.[45] In these terms the findings may fruitfully be considered alongside other studies which provide an explicit treatment of organizational process.

Burns and Stalker

Another influential study—that of Burns and Stalker among innovating electronics firms—begins from a juxtaposition of environmental (particularly market) constraints and organizational forms similar to that of Woodward, but develops an explanatory model which makes actors' orientations and strategies a central concern.[46] Their discussion pivots around contrasting "mechanistic" and "organic" organizational designs (see figure 2) which differ in the following respects crucial to various of the organizational participants. For managing directors facing an organizational environment characterized by uncertainty, and the need for innovation, organic structure *may* offer the advantages of wide-ranging discussion and creative problem-solving behaviour by managers committed to a broad vision of the firm's dilemmas. For managers the "mechanistic" form of organization may offer opportunities for the clear definition of minimum commitments and specific criteria for performance appraisal.[47]

These possible implications of differing organizational designs and changes from one to another provide only the baselines for an analysis which is centrally concerned to explain the development and persistence of various empirically observed "abnormal" forms which conform to the logic of neither ideal type. Such explanations focus on "the kinds of behaviour which members of an organization treat as appropriate in their dealings with each other" and the various rhetorics and sanctions which define such appropriateness. These will be examined in the abstract before looking at typical "abnormal forms".

Figure 2

Mechanistic	*Organic*
Hierarchy of Authority and Control	Network of Authority and Control
Specialization of "technical" duties	Contribution of skills
Vertical command communication	Horizontal information communication
Distinct role obligations	Generalized task commitment

Burns begins from the fact that "members of a corporation are at one and the same time cooperators in a common enterprise and rivals for the material and intangible rewards of successful competition with each other". Since participants are hired as resources but legitimately entertain career aspirations, these aspirations may most effectively be pursued by extending the value of themselves as resources. Individual and collective attempts to redefine the value of their contributions—and the consequent rewards—may be interpreted, by opponents, as "political" manoeuvres which cloak advantage in the guise of organizational valuables. Such imputations do, however, carry risks of appearing transparently political where counter-claims about alternative organization resource priorities do not. These circumstances generate varied definitions of the situation and contrasting accounts for action which managers may invoke in their construction of organizational arrangements.[48] Most such constructions sincerely appeal to top management views of organizational "needs" (since they control crucial resources including criteria for advancement and comprehensive information about the firm) though some perspectives are sustained in retreat or opposition to such views, while managing directors may themselves become implicated in factional imputation of "political" motives. Thus Burns suggests that through actions within such plural perspectives managers with multiple commitments to and inside organizations deploy resources to promote organizational continuity and change.

Turning to the actual structural developments documented in the case studies Burns and Stalker found that in the Scottish firms no change toward organicism occurred but "instead strenuous efforts were made to maintain the mechanistic system, or to reinforce it more stringently than had previously been the case", while the English firms were typically involved in series of expedient adaptations which showed "signs of spontaneous development of organic procedures" alongside "recurrent endeavour to reconstitute a mechanistic system".[49]

A composite picture of some of the processes involved in such partial or limited change can be assembled from the case studies. The managing director claims, and is generally accredited with, the responsibility for setting organizational tasks. This involves defining the sorts of goals and dilemmas facing the firm together with the requisite codes of conduct for their settlement. Though the firms were all in some sense committed by their directors to innovation as a response to perceived opportunities and threats (decline of old markets, new "commercial" opportunities, competitors' moves) both organizational goals and suitable organizational designs and programmes were variously perceived by different directors. These differences related to the established ways in which they managed the isolation and omnipotence characteristic of directorship, together with the impact of such internal dilemmas as those posed by succession.[50]

Some directors promoted the distinctive "organic" style of interaction which was intended to neutralize status and political differences and establish wide-ranging cooperative responsibility—often by adopting a strategy of involvement with subordinates via committees or assistants through which they sought to define the source of managerial dilemmas in the firms' environment rather than in directoral initiatives. However, such moves held penalties for both directors (loss of control) and their subordinates (greater commitments). Thus most directors adopted alternative policies through which they retained greater control while those who did promote an organic "ethos" faced sponsorship of bureaucratic arrangements and defensive measures taken by cliques in organized retreat from increased commitments. In cases of partial adoption of organic patterns some managers experienced increased insecurity but also found advantages for political action in the increased room for manoeuvre—which, when systematized in expansionist cabals and tactics of information control, stimulated renewed efforts by other participants at bureaucratic regulation.[51]

Among the diverse organizational arrangements generated in such processes of negotiation and interpretation, and informed by the distinctive interests of directors (in increased flexibility but sustained control) and managers (in defined commitments and/or improved promotion prospects), the most important were those which involved obvious and recurrent political conflicts, between whole departmental groups, and which focused on positive changes in the structure of the firms policy priorities within the jurisdiction of the organizational goal. Such conflict is exemplified in the fate of the development departments discussed by Burns and Stalker and summarized below. The directors' initial commitment to lab. work posed problems of disturbing the established status hierarchy and ethos, at the same time directly threatening to curtail the directors' control. A typical response to this was *isolation* of the development department which had claimed special status, as a crucial resource based on special skills, and had sponsored new and threatening organizational forms based on colleagueship.

In some cases this separation was accompanied by a thoroughgoing *limitation of its role* to that of "consultants", technical salesmen and equipment testers; moves which commonly precipitated resignation of the development manager. Though this outcome commonly occurred in the context of a mechanistic administration, Burns mentions a similar result even in an overtly "organic" firm because of the threat offered by the department to the established innovating role of the director. More often the concern of upper management for clear job specifications and duties among subordinates prompted the *establishment of intermediaries* assigned special translation duties to mediate the conflicting standards and priorities of development and production. The existence of such intermediaries, with vested interests in perpetuating problems, nurtured distinctive departmental loyalties (exemplified by development's idealization of the model shop as what production should really be like, and by the stereotyped images of "long-haired boffins" and "production clots"). Intermediaries were themselves captured by these political cleavages (instance the "engineering" department circumvented by the laboratory) though in some circumstances they could successfully advance their own claims to resources (as did a development department by the adoption of informal strategies *vis-à-vis* research and formalism in production contacts).[52] In any case the outcome was coloured by political manoeuvrings to change or retain organizational priorities in the name of organizational goals but with manifest career and status ramifications.

The research and development departments in most of the Scottish firms had little success in altering organizational priorities and failed to transform their organizational structure. However, among the English firms, the sales departments introduced by upper managements to service new types of markets did, in some cases, succeed through comparable "political" conflicts in reorientating organizational priorities about the distribution of rights and resources and in subordinating the development departments within a structure of product divisions. These outcomes are shown to be the product of micropolitical processes through which organizational change is made by organizational participants harbouring diverse interests and developing strategies for their pursuit within the jurisdiction of organizational goals. Though Burns and Stalker take the tradition of systems typologies as their point of departure (and have been widely discussed within that framework) they develop, in relation to a rich array of empirical materials, a processual analysis which treats actors' allegiances, perspectives and strategies as problematic features of organizational action. In this context organizational structure and operative goals are seen as the outcome of negotiation and inter-pretation processes among organizational members with differential resources.

This style of analysis finds support in detailed case studies of particular firms, conducted by Crozier, Dalton and Gouldner.[53] The Crozier and Dalton studies, of firms in rather contrasting settings, afford further insight into the social processes which generate and sustain the varied patterns of organizational arrangements discussed by Woodward and Burns. In addition these studies, together with Gouldner's classic investigation of the dynamics of bureaucracy in a Gypsum plant, provide a more explicit discussion of the part played by "shop-floor" workers in the perpetuation and change of organizational arrangements.

Crozier

In this monograph Crozier provides an analysis of the "mechanisms of social control and processes of social change" patterned out of the involvement strategies of participants in two French state bureaucracies. Since these revealed certain common features the more detailed study of the "Industrial Monopoly" provides a focus for discussion. Crozier suggests that benefits for both superiors and subordinates underpin the pattern of bureaucracy, while mentioning power-plays as an integral part of the bureaucratization process. Thus bureaucratic job specifications, while offering organizational advantages for upper management, also bring the paradoxical benefit of clearly defined minimal levels of involvement for subordinates.[54] In turn workers sponsor job-allocation seniority provisions to limit the discretion of superiors, which, though vigorously resisted as a curtailment of managerial prerogatives, provide scope for avoidance of onerous discretion among supervisors.[55] The outcome of intense bureaucratization of work and per-sonnel routines is a rigid organizational hierarchy of distinct occupational echelons, each free from dependence on others and possessing a clearly defined "subculture" with standard perspectives and strategies. Among the consequences of rule applica-tion both (a) the minimization of commitments leading to output control, and (b) the directors' role of distant arbitrator under suspicion of favouritism, promote further elaboration of rules.[56]

This spiral process of increasing bureaucratic rigidity is limited to the extent that certain groups can protect their claims to discretion and remain unthreatened by equivalent exercises of discretion on the part of other groups. In the extremely sheltered market environment of the industrial monopoly, and once the prerogatives of management are matched to some extent by organized action, few claims to exercise discretion can be effectively sustained. Expertise in managing problems posed by environmental uncertainties—which must be recognized as relevant to the perceived objectives and recognized techniques of the organization and as susceptible to such expert control[57]—is successfully claimed only by the maintenance engineers and workers, and on occasion by the director (when he can promote "large-scale transformations of the plant").

Thus interaction in the line hierarchy involves minimal discretion in the face of "extremely limiting rules" though the tactic of "rule exemption" can, especially for the director in the role of arbitrator, convert the established rights of rule enforcement into a reservoir of uncertainty. Subordinates defend their position by studied rule observance and output control. Thus mutual tolerance coexists with a "war of position". The uncertainty sustained by the disciplined maintenance team intrudes on the shop floor in the form of a tense alliance with production workers (dramatized by maintenance workers' hints about forming a separate craft union and the covert hostility of production workers) and in persistent antagonism vis-à-vis supervisors.[58] In the management group it is reflected in the assertion of informal power and complaints about official status by technical engineers in relation to the director and, especially, the assistant director. Clearly the uncertainties of machine breakdown provide a peculiarly valuable resource in the monopoly because of the bureaucratic routinization of other organizational features, but nevertheless maintenance are constrained (as are the other occupational categories) by the acceptance of the present interdependent enjoyment of advantages accruing to those in the state monopoly, particularly in regard to the curtailment of dependence relationships and fairly secure wages and working conditions.[59] The cultural validation of claims to independence also affects the pattern of relationships between categories of participants.

Thus Crozier portrays a peculiarly rigid organizational structure constructed and sustained by participants' strategies of minimal commitment and intransigent defence of past gains in an apparently placid environment—but within which certain groups gain considerable informal power through the monopoly of expertise in managing the only recognized source of uncertainty.

Dalton

In contrast to Crozier's case the complex and cross-cutting "political" conflicts and alliances analysed by Dalton are informed by diverse claims for particular organizational priorities in an environment probably construed as much more uncertain.[60] Typically different departments view their jurisdictions as crucial sources of manageable uncertainty while any career or similar advantages which might accrue to them from the general adoption of their perspective only reinforce the rhetoric of organizational priorities.[61] In the fluid situations studied by Dalton, where managers were not fatally allied to their present departments, cliques defending or sponsoring particular organizational priorities spanned a range of departments and levels in the hierarchy. Such alliances, and particularly the "vertical symbiotic" cliques, provided "coaching in the finesse of workable illegalities"—in legitimation of actions by appeal to obscure rules, the development of pretexts and justifications, and unofficial sponsorship of informal action through subordinates—intended to "loosen controls on themselves and tighten them on others".[62] While formal criteria and advertised mandates provide the currency for managerial conflicts, pervasive power-plays and information management allow more overt pursuit of advantages on occasion and also produce defensive groupings with a marginal or formalist stance.

Upper management intervention takes the form of curtailment (often through strengthening of opponents) or cooption of initiatives by utilization of their control of vital resources and rights of mediation—within the limits of their awareness of such initiatives. Since lower-level compromises typically take the form of collusive deviation from high-level regulations, and cliques become skilled in information management (e.g. the secret preparation for nominal surprise visits from head office), such limits provide subordinates considerable room to manoeuvre.[63] Among such arrangements Dalton describes tacit agreements between managers, foremen, stewards and workers based on mutual benefits gained from working outside contracts which were considered "too general and inflexible". Production pressures on management and inability of unions to make further broad gains constrained parties to make private bargains. In particular, simulated conformity and the exploitation of contract ambiguity provided advantages for shop-floor participants. Foremen were relieved from processing grievances and gained cooperation in difficult production tasks while stewards won benefits for certain constituents and increased security and chances of re-election for themselves. Thus the variety of uncertainties and resultant opportunities for individual or clique advantage penetrated even to the shop floor to weaken collective solidarities and strengthen individualist orientations, though the limitations to such advantage for most manual workers meant that occupational group strategies retained major importance.

Following the approach suggested by Burns and Stalker, comparison of the organizational processes depicted by Dalton and Crozier provides further documentation of the ways in which organizational arrangements are patterned out of the resources and strategies deployed by differentially involved participants pursuing diverse purposes within the jurisdiction of organizational goals set by upper management. The "negotiated order" analysed in these studies arose not from any automatic systemic response to unambiguous environmental demands, but through processes of interpretation and negotiation among members over the salient characteristics of organizational context and concerning appropriate administrative procedures and occupational relationships. It is in these terms that certain features of market and technology—for example, "uncertainty"—assume a "taken-for-granted" relevance for organizational arrangements and, informed by the diverse perspectives and resources of the various participant categories, come to pattern distinctive modes of organizational involvement—fostering, for example, individual and clique competitiveness or collective stratum solidarities.[64]

Gouldner

Though Dalton and Crozier discuss the patterns of conflict and accommodation characterizing management–worker interaction in the concerns they studied, Gouldner's analysis of the transformation of organizational arrangements in the course of a series of bargaining episodes between management and workers provides a more detailed review of the dynamics of such interaction and underlines key features of the social processes which sustain and change organizational structures.[65]

This study traced the development of new control strategies, in a works hitherto characterized by an "indulgency pattern", as an outcome of top management succession and intensified head-office productivity demands as these interplayed with various strategies of worker response.[66] The new manager faced the task of "productivity improvement", in the context of technical changes, as a stranger ignorant of informal understandings and alliances. Thus he was both sponsor of and dependent on formalization of controls over workers, while some among middle management, partly as a consequence of frustrated ambitions, opposed such new developments. The direct enforcement of rules by the successor coupled with his "strategic replacement" of recalcitrant middle managers, generated resentment, resistance and effort withdrawal on the shop floor. In turn the management instituted further bureaucratic procedures (paper reports and disciplinary warnings) intended to produce intensification of effort but which, through more predictable and universalistic rule application, "served to mitigate tensions *derivative* of close supervision" but also generated further "apathy preservation" (see figure 3).[67]

Figure 3

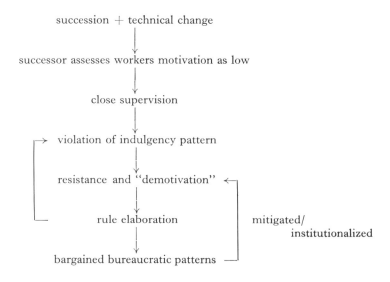

succession + technical change

successor assesses workers motivation as low

close supervision

violation of indulgency pattern

reinforced   resistance and "demotivation"

rule elaboration   mitigated/
                                   institutionalized

bargained bureaucratic patterns

The process of bureaucratization initiated by the successor was met on the part of workers by both resistance and bargaining over the scope of the rules, so that its outcome—the extent to which management objectives were achieved or administrative features valued by workers were preserved—constituted a negotiated order contrived between differentially powerful conflicting interest groups. This is demonstrated by the contrast between the miners, who successfully denied the legitimacy of bureaucratic rules and resisted the management initiatives, and the surface workers, who did not.[68] The miners' strategy was based on the claim, underpinned by the support of a cohesive community, that only group expertise (which implied diffuse spheres of competence and a service role for supervisors) matched the difficult and dangerous work environment.

As the bureaucratic pattern institutionalized under the successor balanced contradictory interests and pressures it was vulnerable to changed circumstances and aspirations. Continuing pressures from top management (e.g. machinery speed up, close supervision in the mine, threatened overtime opportunities) provoked comparisons with past managements and with the financial compensation of other workers (and the money spent on the new machinery) and prompted a pay claim but no formal grievance about stringency. Gouldner suggests that this stemmed from the difficulty of managing claims of ambiguous legitimacy in public confrontations, but in consequence fundamental grievances persisted.[69] These were intensified by a second succession and further round of strategic replacements accompanied by machine pace experimentation.

Gouldner distinguished two perspectives underlying worker responses. Both focused on the disruption of established expectations through bureaucratization and particularly speed-up, but while " 'the traditionalists' wanted a return to the old indulgency pattern the 'market men' were willing to set aside the informal privileges of the indulgency pattern in exchange for new, formally acknowledged, "union powers". The market-oriented union leaders represented claims to management in contractual terms—they wanted favourable bureaucratic rules, worked for a strengthened union to negotiate contractual changes, and emphasized wages. In consequence non-wage grievances which management judged as threatening their "prerogatives", got "lost" in the grievance machinery. Hence, in a crisis precipitated by the intervention of the "roving engineer" (who personified many of the managerial initiatives) the market-oriented clique was discredited and a wildcat strike was led by the traditionalists because of the "run around" on such grievances. Nevertheless the strike settlement incorporated a "market-oriented" solution of further bureaucratization which "segregated supervisors and workers who did not share complementary expectations of each other's role" and increased the control of management and union over the shop-floor without resolving conflicts of interest. Thus management initiated bureaucratic rules were accompanied by union initiated rules, both enforced through the deployment of sanctions by their sponsors.[70.]

Gouldner's study, in focusing directly on social change, demonstrates particularly clearly the way in which patterns of organizational arrangements are sustained and transformed through complex processes of interpretation and negotiation enacted by participants who bring to the working organization distinctive interests, and differential resources through which these can be pursued. The intimate relation between negotiative and interpretive phases of organizational action is underlined in the impact on interest group conflict of not only the capacity to organize and deploy resources, but also (a) the validating rhetorics which actors use to locate their claims within some widely accredited framework (such as occupational equities or organizational efficiency) and (b) those features of the occupational setting which may for the time being be presented and taken as "givens" within which participants assume their room for manoeuvre exists.[71]

In summary, the case studies of Gouldner, Dalton and Crozier, which in different ways focus on participants' attempts to organize and control organizational arrangements, afford an insight into the micropolitical process through which regularities in such arrangements are accomplished, maintained and altered by those participants. As Burns has suggested such insight is a prerequisite for realistic analysis of the interplay between (a) top management attempts to align organizational practice with their designated objectives, and (b) the organizational activities of the various categories of participants, with their distinctive involvements, interests and resources, through which varieties of environmental circumstances are mediated in their repercussions for organizational structure.

This discussion of organizational process also suggests a reappraisal of the dominant approaches to comparative analysis sponsored by systems perspectives. Such analyses have generally been based on typologies of organizational "goals", or, among socio-technical theorists, "task-appropriate technologies"—these goals and technologies being considered unambiguous, stable and above organizational bargaining and conflict.[72] In contrast a recognition of the processual features of the organizational structure of industrial concerns underlines the importance of the diverse perspectives, resources and strategies of participants as these generate extant organizational arrangements and qualify the meaning of organizational priorities and programmes (including technical designs) advanced by upper management.[73] In this sense the detailed case studies of Crozier, Dalton and Gouldner provide a more adequate guide to comparative analysis than those explicitly comparative studies which slight these organizational features.

Topics and issues in the sociology of industry

The first section of this chapter compared the theoretical models advanced by systems theorists with those implied in critiques of the "systems orthodoxy", and suggested that many of the critics could be placed within a broadly "processual" approach. This processual perspective emphasizes that the social structures of industrial concerns are patterned by negotiation and interpretation among participants with diverse interests and resources, so that analyses of variations and changes in such structures must attend to those sustaining and transforming processes. This point was pursued in the second section of the chapter, through an appraisal of key empirical studies which together provide a fairly comprehensive overview of organizational processes which underpin regularities and changes in the structure of a variety of industrial concerns.

In this final section issues raised in the previous sections are discussed by reviewing selected topics drawn from the array of discrete research which constitutes the bulk of the literature of industrial sociology.[74] The following topics are considered in turn: management policies and the environment; administrative designs and management career concerns; and management–worker conflict and accommodation. In each case the discussion draws selectively on the literature to suggest relevant analytical issues within a processual perspective.

Organizational policies

The formation, character and application of organizational policies has received particular attention in the context of the "managerialism debate". This debate concerns the impact of a limited dispersal of stock ownership and the supposed professionalization of management on the relationships among managers, directors, and shareholders in their determination of organizational policies at the most general level of the decision-rules (embracing for example, "profitability" or "growth") which are applied in the adjudication of alternatives lines of organizational action.[75] A central criticism advanced against those who detect the emergence into dominance of self-interested (or possible benevolent) management groups with a critical decline in the influence exercised by owners, concerns the inadequacy of their analyses of (a) the interests and sanctions of the various groups involved in forming and interpreting organizational policies and (b) the process through which such interests and sanctions impinge on decision-making.

A crucial feature of the managerialist position is the claim that managers have interests which are coherently opposed to those of owners, and backed by distinctive resources. However, as Nichols has stressed, the patterns of recruitment and career contingencies experienced by upper management are most likely to generate perspectives which are congruent, rather than in conflict, with those of shareholders. For, while executives are drawn substantially from business and shareholder backgrounds and often retain significant shareholdings (though often a small percentage of the concerns shares) and on these grounds may be oriented to shareholder interests, the internal control mechanisms and standards of success applied by top management similarly reinforce such an identification. In particular managers are selected, rewarded and promoted according to conceptions of "soundness" and "effectiveness" which are usually operationalized in terms of economic performance criteria.[76] Though managers may monopolize various technical competences and sources of information which might serve to limit the range of options open to boards of directors these sources of power remain of limited utility in the context of the legal rights of board members and the absence of any distinctive "managerial interests". Thus conceptions of expertise are generally defined *within* the framework of organizational policies in that specialists come to define their contributions in terms of their relevance for the effective pursuit of organizational objectives, while directors may foster competition between management groups who control comparable competences or information sources, and so retain the capacity to reject particular proposals or practitioners.[77] Only in the limiting case of a monolithic management cadre, which monopolizes some key resources and defines its interests as opposed to those of the directorate is directoral power threatened, and such a combination appears unlikely to develop in the typical environment of business concerns.

This analysis of the perspectives and resources of upper management provides a background for consideration of the resources available to shareholders, directors and managers, and the contingencies of their deployment in policy-making. The formal representation of shareholders' interests on the board takes the form of nominees of substantial shareholder blocs, while the actual or potential intervention of other major shareholders at such junctures as merger attempts, proxy fights, or the search for financing encourages the incorporation of shareholder interests in directoral decision-premises in anticipation of such events. The impact of such potential or irregular incursions by shareholders together with the generally shareholder-oriented perspectives of directors who "represent" funding agencies, senior executives, suppliers and the like undermines the utility of mechanical models of voting majorities of the sort used by theorists of managerialism and underlines the importance of processual analyses of the interests, resources, alliances and contingencies which play on the determination of company policies. The predominance, in business firms, of decision-rules which promote secure profitability can thus be understood as a product of the social processes outlined above.[78]

The critics of managerialism are concerned to trace the working perspectives, interests and sanctions of the various participants in policy-formation, to distinguish rhetorical from enacted claims, and to locate organizational decision-making within a realistic model of organizational processes—one which recognizes in particular the impact of organizational socialization on the orientations of managers, and the importance of such strategic contingencies as mergers and management successions in the patterning of organizational policies. This processual perspective suggests that in general terms the decision-rules operative in modern capitalist enterprises are similar to those pursued by earlier entrepreneurs, though in consequence of the specialization of administrative and investment activities the profitability criterion may be applied with more rigour and sophistication by modern boards of directors.[79]

While the controlling elites of business enterprises may thus espouse similar generalized decision-rules, the bearing of such criteria on organizational designs and working procedures is mediated by elite conceptions of feasible methods of work, and their interpretation of the opportunities and problems posed by the environment. These conceptions and interpretations are products of past experience as it is informed and mediated by prior preconceptions and ideological commitments, for the organization does not simply respond to unambiguous environmental stimuli but, rather, search procedures and reactions to impinging environmental events are themselves developed within the limiting assumptions and selective perception of key personnel. Thus organizational crises such as merger bids, major management–worker conflicts, or bankruptcy may command a reorientation of elite assumptions and perspectives, but the nature of such crises and reorientations must be analysed in terms of actors' perspectives, resources and strategies in interaction with other actors and cannot be reduced simply to "functional system responses".[80]

This processual emphasis suggests that selective search and interpretation procedures adopted by top management will have important effects on organizational planning and administration, especially since they may simultaneously depend on and reinforce preconceptions about relevant information and appropriate policies.[81] This approach also draws attention to the interpretative and strategic features of interorganizational relationships, whether they be with competitors, sources of resources, or regulating agencies, and the manner in which shifts in such relationships may prompt changes in organizational designs and arrangements.[82]

Finally it underlines the impact of those limiting assumptions, concerning for example appropriate technologies and administrative arrangements, which inform the commitments of organizational controllers to particular organizational designs. Such limiting assumptions are evidenced in the impact of organizational ideologies and traditions on organizational plans and procedures, and by the manner in which new departures in organizational design are sponsored by particular elite groups and often await changes in elite personnel.[83]

These features of organizational process—selective investigation and interpretation of the environment, the accommodations which characterize the various interorganizational relationships in which industrial firms are implicated, and the context of socially constructed limiting assumptions within which decisions are made—which mediate the relationship between organizational design, decision-rules, and the environment, evidence the inadequacy of systems approaches and indicate some facets of a more adequate analysis.

Administrative designs and management career concerns

The administrative apparatus which is intended to organize, service and control manufacturing and distribution activities represents a crucial component of the organizational design of industrial concerns. However, the manner in which that apparatus operates does not follow unambiguously from the organizational design and its stipulations concerning the scope and limits of managerial initiative, but represents the interplay of such design features and those managerial career concerns which inform the conduct of managers within, and beyond, these stipulated limits. Thus an analysis of the detailed procedures and patterned social relationships which constitute the actualities of the administrative process must attend to the character of this interplay in the process of managerial "micropolitics".

The previous discussion of the process of organizational socialization among industrial managers suggests that such managers will commonly come to orient themselves to a rhetoric of organizational priorities and concerns within which they lodge their claims to competence and their resultant value as organizational

resources. Where such "careerist" orientations predominate managers will participate in administrative debates over the interpretation of organizational priorities
through shifting alliances of departmental and interdepartmental cliques, which
sponsor distinctive competences identified with one or another interpretation of
priorities. Thus, in the context of elite adjudication of competing claims, those
cliques which succeed in claiming special competences gain an influential position
and favourable conditions for their members in comparison with those groups
which come to be considered as of subsidiary importance.[84]

However comparative study of a variety of industrial concerns reveals variations in the distribution and dominance of such "careerist" orientations among
management personnel, and documents the importance of alternative managerial
perspectives. Such comparisons suggest that managers who find themselves unable
to advance their career through "careerist" manoeuvres may adopt more defensive
postures, either as small groups of colleagues in personal retreat from the dominant
ethos, or, more important, as organized departmental units which seek through
bureaucratic regulations more specific guarantees of their rights and obligations.[85]

The case studies discussed in section two suggest that the diversity of sources
of uncertainty acknowledged by top management and affording opportunities for
management cliques to advance their claims in terms of relevant competences, is a
key factor in the balance of "careerist" and bureaucratic postures. Similarly, the
degree of coincidence between departmental memberships and foci of claimed
competence may influence the amount of department-based rather than cross-
cutting clique activity while the manner in which such claims and activities are
developed is influenced by the prior orientations and expectations of management
personnel (related in particular to their assessment of alternative career prospects
and to typical patterns of personal commitments), as these confront and respond
to organizational selection and promotion policies.[86]

Thus the presentation of departmental and other groups claims, with the
associated mobilization of sponsorship and deployment of organizational rhetorics,
may vary between different firms in relation to the commitments of managers to
flexible and expansionist career orientations and in relation to the scope afforded
to departmental groups for the development of specialized perspectives and claims
around problematic features of organizational design. Where careerist orientations
predominate and ample sources of uncertainty provide scope for specialist contributions the process of presentation and adjudication of competing claims for
priority among management groups, with the associated fateful consequences in
the allocation of resources and the generation and closure of career prospects,
becomes endemic.[87] However, in most industrial firms such processes result only
rarely in major shifts in organizational priorities and routinely assume the character of distinctive departmental postures around the everyday tensions and
conflicts of organizational operations.[88]

These postures and the distinctive interests they represent are pursued and
defended not only in representations to top management but also in practical
strategies of control, developed to cope with both interdepartmental relationships
and the interventions of upper management as these may threaten those interests.

Thus powerful departments will reiterate the value of their own contributions in relation to those of others, develop formal control mechanisms such as intermediaries or counterpart units in response to threats to their dominance, and deploy other more covert tactics to circumvent or dominate other groups. More marginal departments may seek an expanded definition of their spheres of competence, appeal for procedures designed to protect their autonomy, and seek compromises and alliances with other similar groups.[89]

This characterization of the varied patterns of micropolitical action among industrial managements provides the setting for processual analyses of the manner in which organizational designs and procedures are implemented in organizational arrangements. Thus a sociological analysis of the "administrative process" must trace the intersection of management career concerns and top management priorities in the formulation of new policies by particular management groups, and the processes of sponsorship and resistance which influence the adoption, modification or shelving of such proposals. Similarly the ongoing generation of authoritative interpretations of "acceptable" and "deviant" management practice represents the outcome of the operation of top management controls as these are enforced and lapse at particular junctures in the development of organizational arrangements, and as they may be more or less readily subverted or resisted by organized management groups. The complex interplay between officially sponsored actions, covert arrangements which are revealed only to allies but which may be assimilable to recognized procedures, and subterfuges guided by avowedly sectional interests in the patterning of interdepartmental and other management relationships must thus be analysed in terms of the strategies of sponsorship and control pursued by both upper and lower management groups.[90]

The processual character of the intersection of organizational designs and management career concerns suggested in the above discussion is nicely underlined in recent contributions to the debate about professionals, and more specifically scientists, in industrial managements. Such studies have moved away from a simple juxtaposition of scientific norms and organizational demands, and towards a processual analysis of the interpretive and strategic character of career concerns and organizational controls, in explanations of distinctive patterns of the organization of scientific work in industrial enterprises. Thus new attention has been given to the situated character of normative attachments among those trained as scientists. These attachments develop in the context of changing perspectives on prospective career opportunities, rather than involving an abstract espousal of "scientific norms", so that many who become organizational scientists do not cherish expectations which contradict the rationale of industrial research. Once recruited, participants in industrial research and development may become increasingly concerned with science as a source of distinctive competences which furnish the rationale for claims to career prospects and work autonomy. Such developments in the orientations of industrial scientists interplay with top management policies on selection and promotion opportunities, and the operation of surveillance procedures, to generate distinctive work patterns and variable orientations towards the general jurisdiction of organizational goals and priorities. Thus the extent to which industrial scientists develop more covert strategies of independence and codify their representations in claims to professional status in the process of negotiation and interpretation over the value and rewards of scientific competences, depends upon the patterning of orientations and policies involved, so that professionally oriented individuals and organizational units represent but one outcome of these processes.[91]

This work on industrial scientists suggests that professional claims may represent defensive or offensive efforts to institutionalize particular competences (and associated benefits) in terms of parallels drawn with the characteristics of recognized professional competences accredited in the wider society. The fate of such appeals must thus be analysed in terms of the processes through which relevant audiences may come to extend or withhold recognition, the manner in which claimants fabricate appropriate occupational characteristics, and the complex and tenuous relationships between occupational rhetorics and practices (whether professional status is accorded or denied) in the relevant organizational locales. This implies that professional status is not simply "given" in consequence of some correspondence to abstract criteria, but is rather socially constructed and maintained in processes of negotiation and interpretation concerning the grounds and character of such status. These processes and hence the meaning given to professional status may vary among organizational locales and with changes in organizational arrangements, while the actual practices adopted by professional claimants also differ, with varying visibility and negotiability of performances.[92]

Management–Worker Conflict and Accommodation

The manner in which such "organizational objectives" as production plans or payment policies, designed by top management and mediated through the activities of middle managers, are implemented on the shop-floor is an outcome of interaction between managers commanding resources buttressed by legal and customary managerial prerogatives and workers commanding resources which flow from the character of their labour. Thus a processual orientation to the sociological study of work experience and occupational conduct directs attention to the processes of bargaining and interpretation that generate, sustain and transform occupational milieux. This orientation moves away from the conventional focus on technical and administrative constraints *per se* and towards an analysis of the processes of interpretation and negotiation within which such constraints are embedded, so that renewed attention is given to the interests, perspectives and resources of organizational participants as these enter into the social construction of work-settings and condition work experience.

These processual concerns are illustrated in recent studies of aspects of worker involvement and bargaining processes in the motor industry, which qualify in different ways technical determinist views of the assembly-line and its impact on workers in the industry.[93] Thus Goldthorpes' analysis of the work-orientations of geographically mobile and relatively affluent manual workers stresses that within their instrumentalist, "cash-nexus" based, pattern of work involvement, these workers regarded assembly-line work as a "necessary deprivation". Though this study revealed little of the vicissitudes of such orientations in the course of work experience it has prompted a wider reappraisal of the character of workers' perspectives; and this reappraisal suggests that such perspectives, rather than being narrowly patterned by the work-setting itself, develop in relation to wider patterns of personal and collective experience, within and beyond the workplace. Thus the patterns of recruitment and nonwork relationships of workers, the meanings they give to their experience of past and present job changes, and the course of management–worker bargaining and conflict all inform workers' conceptions of their interests, and the strategies by which these interests might be pursued.[94]

Processual analyses of work milieux are not only concerned with the complex determinants of workers' orientations to work-technologies but also direct attention to the manner in which technical features of organizational designs are conceived, interpreted and modified in the course of organizational interaction. Since ongoing administrative decisions, about such matters as manning arrangements and work pace, mediate the impact of any chosen technology on the nature and distribution of work tasks, variations in those decisions will influence the character of work experience. And, to the extent that workers can effectively press their interests, management–worker bargaining itself comes to influence the conception and application of work-technologies and thus the character of the constraints which workers experience in their work. These processes of negotiation and interpretation surrounding any technical design imply that "technical constraints" cannot be regarded as constant in relation to specified production objectives, for different patterns of implementation will generate significant variations in the character of work settings. Thus, drawing once again on the motor industry for examples, significant variations exist in the character of conventional assembly-line working arrangements in that industry, while more radical departures from the assembly-line format have also occurred in particular bargaining contexts.[95]

These studies affirm that the character of administrative and technical work constraints, and the patterns of worker response which they may evoke, must be located within a wider appraisal of the interests and resources of different organizational participants, and the manner in which these are implicated in the construction and interpretation of technical, and other, features of organizational arrangements. Thus analyses of work relationships must consider the manner in which employment relations, career contingencies, occupational institutions and bargaining episodes influence the perspectives and actions of industrial workers, and must place the impact of "technical constraints" in the context of these influences.[96]

This recognition of the socially constructed and problematic character of work settings and occupational conduct underlines the fact that organizational designs and employment contracts stipulate only in general and ambiguous terms the obligations and work conditions of employees. Thus a processual perspective (unlike socio-technical theorists who see organizational roles as being defined in the casual operation of technical and administrative constraints) must be concerned to trace the social processes through which these general stipulations bear on, and are made relevant to, the actions of organizational participants.[97] The character of such mediating social processes will now be considered in relation to empirical investigations of (a) shop-floor administration and (b) patterns of formal bargaining by occupational groups.

(a) *Conflict and accommodation on the shop-floor*   Studies of the day-to-day affairs of shop-floor administration focus on the point of contact between a range of managerial control mechanisms and the perspectives and resources of shop-floor workers. It is at this point of contact that the general stipulations of the employment contract assume the specificity of particular work routines and rewards.[98] Since the processes of routine bargaining and accommodation on the shop-floor have received most specific attention among students of "effort bargaining" their analyses of the practical operation of payment schemes provide the most detailed and illuminating guide to the character of these processes.[99]

Managers view piecework methods of payment as financial gearing devices designed to furnish detailed controls over work-pace and associated rewards— these pay schemes are intended to facilitate the minimization of production costs and the coordination of complex production routines by specifying and enforcing managerial conceptions of appropriate workmanship.[100] The dominant pattern of worker response to such designs involves collective efforts to protect and develop the room for manoeuvre within which their own conceptions of workmanship may be sustained. In particular, workers' interests in controlling the rhythm and method of work conflict with the detailed specifications of pace and technique implied by incentive schemes, while their concern for secure and equitable financial compensation confronts the provision of payments which are susceptible to the vicissitudes of production problems. Among workers who lack strong collective institutions and traditions—perhaps because of heterogeneous patterns of work involvement or envisaged individual mobility opportunities—employers' conceptions of workmanship may become institutionalized along with a variety of individualistic responses to production pressures and inequities (e.g. personal complaints, accusations of favouritism, absenteeism). In the more usual case, where they share some conception of common interests against management, workers develop concerted strategies for weakening or circumventing management controls so that covert manipulation and overt pressure tactics typify the routine application of incentive schemes.[101]

Studies of the character of collective response to incentive schemes reveal typical patterns of conflict and cooperation, generated by the distinctive interests and resources of workers and managers, which underpin the differential stringency and enforcement of such schemes.[102] Thus one line of collective response involves appeals to one or another management level for concessions within the operating scheme. Such claims commonly emphasize the critical nature of particular work-group contributions and stress the inconsistencies which arise in the application of incentive controls amid a variety of production contingencies, and their acceptance by managers implies some compelling mixture of reasons and sanctions which justify alterations in the stringency of piecework controls. In this manner certain interests may be accommodated within the formal procedures of incentive payment, initially through tacit recognition of some special case and eventually, perhaps, through alterations in the conceptions of customary workmanship used by time-study men in their application of the pay scheme. Such claims are most often and successfully pursued with supervisors and other low-level administrators, for whom they may be particularly compelling in the context of immediate production pressures and reliance on a cooperative workforce. These administrators may conceal low-level compromises from upper management to protect their positions, and maintain a semblance of correct procedure by manipulating production plans and records. In this positive manner and through wider practices of encouraging and/or ignoring deviations from stated rules, low-level administrators may be implicated in collusive alliances which seek to protect shop-floor practices which depart from the policies and procedures laid down by upper management.[103]

Such lower-level compromises and innovations take their character from the sorts of interdependence which relate the various participants, and from the scope for subterfuge which they can discover in the interstices, or by the manipulation, of administrative controls. Thus supervisors—who are typically committed to management policies through both reward prospects and career concerns—may, in the face of worker demands or production crises, seek to moderate the impact of various of the management control mechanisms in an attempt to devise "realistic" production arrangements.[104] However, since such moves are designed to ease supervisory tasks within the framework of management priorities, shop-floor administration remains a crucial focus of conflict between management and workers. The character of this conflict over the "effort bargain" is most clearly revealed at those crucial junctures in the administrative process, such as time-studies, when the concerted ingenuity of shop-floor workers confronts administrative actions intended to specify the nature of work-performance. In such bargaining the extent to which workers are able to sustain their control over work practices, and gain room for manoeuvre in coping with production contingencies and earnings fluctuations, depends on the patterns of alliance, solidarity and discipline of the workgroups involved.[105]

This review of research on the practical application of incentive schemes underlines the fact that patterns of organizational arrangements, and in particular specifications of work tasks and rewards, are ongoing accomplishments of manage-ment–worker conflict and accommodation. These studies reveal some of the social processes of interpretation and negotiation through which the perspectives and resources of managers and workers generate distinctive organizational arrangements, and through which changes in perspectives and resources may come to alter those arrangements.[106] And, since the artful practices of worker alliance and organization in management–worker conflict are shown to furnish central themes in workshop lore, this research also suggests the manner in which the activities through which participants sustain and change organizational arrangements themselves feed back into the perspectives and interests of those participants.[107]

(b) *Occupational bargaining strategies*   The autonomy gained by different groups of workers in the course of shop-floor bargaining, and the concessions won in more formalized bargaining episodes, depend on the distinctive bargaining sanctions and occupational claims developed by the various groups. Thus the ongoing processess of shop-floor management–worker interaction must be seen in the context of the emergence and dynamics of occupational bargaining strategies, and the manner in which these strategies impinge on the organization of work routines.[108]

The bargaining strategies adopted by different groups of workers depend most directly on the distinctive resources controlled by such groups. The impact of such differing resources is revealed even in broad comparisons of the contrasting demands and strategies of "skilled" and "unskilled" workers, while detailed studies of particular bargaining episodes trace the ramifications of differential resource control in specific configurations of bargaining positions. These comparisons suggest that "skilled workers", in virtue of their command over scarce and acknow-ledged competences, have been able to sustain claims to work autonomy and have these claims institutionalized in organizational procedures. By contrast "unskilled workers", who do not possess some recognized and enduring expertise, typically seek to specify minimum obligations within the framework of formal administrative controls, while exploiting particular production contingencies which provide them with leverage for limited concessions.[109]

However, these contrasting bargaining practices cannot be explained by reference simply to the "resources" inhering in technical competences or pro-duction contingencies, for these technical properties are themselves embedded in a matrix of social processes. Thus occupational skill claims, though developed around supposed technical competences which may be to some extent institutionalized in organizational arrangements, are buttressed by occupational institutions which facilitate craft controls over the supply and exercise of relevant competences.[110] Similarly, the less institutionalized pressure tactics developed by workers who lack accredited skills depend for their effectiveness on appropriate patterns of worker solidarity which underpin the "disruptiveness" of work group sanctions.[111] Thus "recognized skills" and "critical work tasks" *may* come to be seen as "givens" by particular organizational participants at certain junctures in organizational affairs, and may because of this furnish extremely effective bargaining sanctions, but these "givens" remain suscepitble to reinterpretation and rearrangement should the occupational institutions which sustain them weaken. The relationship between technical circumstances and bargaining strategies is further mediated by the character of workers' involvements and by the nature of managerial initiatives, changes in which may alter the strategies of particular groups by reducing or amplifying their *concern* for bargaining sanctions.[112]

These considerations reveal a complex interplay between occupational institutions and technical "givens" in the generation of bargaining strategies. Thus the institutionalized competences of skilled workers coupled with their homogeneity and solidarity as workgroups, and the relative heterogeneity and resourcelessness of less-skilled groups, may serve to perpetuate or reinforce the pattern of bargaining strategies outlined earlier.[113] However, at certain junctures rather transient bargaining advantages may, through the imposition of occupational controls over labour supply, be transformed into more enduring "skills", while once-skilled groups which fail to sustain coherent occupational claims may suffer "deskilling" in the course of technical changes.[114] And new occupational demands and strategies emerge from new patterns of worker alliance and organization in the context of administrative and technical changes.[115]

These commentaries on *shop-floor administration* and *occupational bargaining strategies* serve to underline the manner in which workers' interests and resources are implicated in, and in turn influenced by, the social construction of work settings and job routines in ongoing processes of management–worker conflict and accommodation. This suggests that an adequate sociology of industry must locate identifiable types of occupational milieux and work experience as the products of these processes of conflict and accommodation rather than treating them as technically or administratively given.

The character of work in "process-production" industries affords a summary example of what this might imply for the analysis of particular work settings. Thus the conception of "responsible work tasks" which has been associated with process-production may be seen as a negotiated definition of the situation which interprets ambiguous and contradictory features of work tasks (e.g. pleasant working conditions, little supervisory or work-pace pressure, extensive shift working, tedious monitoring routines) in a manner which effectively embodies managerial conceptions of workmanship. However this conception is generated and sustained, in the context of a pliant workforce with heterogenous backgrounds and instrumental orientations, by the operation of manning and pay policies designed to foster company loyalties (i.e. "career" opportunities in stratified work teams, high pay and fringe benefits).[116] In changed circumstances managerial policies of rationalization of job categories, and the application of "responsibility" conceptions in the context of financial stringency, may generate general work dissatisfactions and worker bargaining tactics designed to increase their control over their working environment. Thus the various meanings and implications of job "responsibility" can only be properly understood in terms of the ongoing encounter between management policies and resources and the aspirations and bargaining strategies of workers.[117]

Summary

This section has drawn on the theoretical discussion developed and applied in sections one and two, to consider in more detail the social processes which operate in the formulation and interpretation of organizational policies, in the application of those policies by an administrative staff, and in the implementation of production plans and the specification of work obligations on the shop-floor. Together these topics provide an outline of the social processes through which the interests and resources of organizational participants may sustain and transform the patterns of organizational relationships and arrangements which constitute the structure of industrial concerns. Though the discussion has focused on the internal processes of interpretation and negotiation through which participants are implicated in the affairs of business concerns in capitalist societies, and on the typical patterns of conflict and accommodation within the firm, wider implications of a processual perspective have also been suggested. Thus the outline of the processes involved in the specification of profit-oriented commercial policies points to the importance of the wider context of inter-firm alliances, shareholder surveillance, and the vagaries of resource and product markets in the formulation of business policies. Similarly the development of specific perspectives and strategies among workers, and indeed the organization of work itself, must be placed in the context of wider community affiliations, labour market circumstances, and occupational associations. In this respect a processual perspective underlines the interpenetration of organization and society and emphasizes that the relationship between an "organization" and its "environment" are constituted through ongoing processes of interpretation and negotiation which cannot adequately be conceptualized in "systems" terms.[118]

References and notes

I wish to thank Mr. R.K. Brown and Mr. Alan Davies for discussions which helped me in the preparation of this chapter.

1. The relation between theoretical and practical concerns is, of course, complex. Thus many "managerial sociologists" are of an empiricist bent and focus their researches on particular "problem areas", such as technical change and payment systems, but the usual integrating framework remains one or another version of systems thinking. Another complication concerns the somewhat various roles that such academics play in relation to business oligarchies—as ideologists, codifiers of conventional wisdoms, or practical "change agents" or "trouble shooters". The most extended discussions of managerial sociology have focused on the "human relations" school: R. Bendix, *Work and Authority in Industry*, New York: Harper and Row, 1963; L. Baritz, *The Servants of Power*, New York: Wiley, 1965; and C.W. Mills, "The contribution of sociology to the study of industrial relations", *Berkeley J. Sociol.*, **15** (1970), 11–32, discuss the human relations movement, while H.A. Landsberger, *Hawthorne Revisited*, New York: Cornell University Press, 1958; W. Gomberg, "The trouble with democratic management", *Transaction* (July/Aug 1966), 30–35; and A. Carey, "The Hawthorne Studies: a radical criticism", *Am. Sociol. Rev.*, **32** (1967), 403–416, assess particular pieces of research in that tradition. However relevant comments on "systems perspectives" are made by S.R. Krupp, *Pattern in Organizational Analysis*, Philadelphia: Chilton, 1961; R. Mayntz, "The study of organizations", *Current Sociol.*, **13**, 3, 1964; and M. Albrow, "The study of organizations: objectivity or bias?" in J. Gould (Ed.), *Penguin Social Sciences Survey 1968*, Harmondsworth: Penguin, pp. 146–167; while R.K. Brown, "Research and consultancy in industrial enterprises", *Sociology*, **1** (1967), 33–60, provides a specific commentary on "socio-technical" systems analysis.

2. The character and importance of these defining features, which demarcate the subject matter of this chapter, are discussed further in section three. The relevance of these defining features can, of course, only be fully assessed

in the context of historical and comparative analyses of both industrial and non-industrial organizations.

3. D. Silverman, in *The Theory of Organizations*, London: Heinemann, 1970; and "Formal organizations or industrial sociology", *Sociology*, **2** (1968), 221–238, provides an extended discussion of systems theories, on which this section draws. Of course, there are important theoretical differences between variants of the systems approach—in particular, between "normative functionalist" and "cybernetic" models (see W. Buckley, *Sociology and Modern Systems Theory*, Englewood Cliffs, N.J.: Prentice-Hall, 1967) and between various ways of specifying the relation of formal or espoused goals to system functions (see the "rational" and "natural" systems approaches discussed by A. Gouldner, "Organizational analysis" in R.K. Merton (Ed.), *Sociology Today*, New York: Basic Books, 1959, pp. 400–428)—but these differences appear marginal beside the disagreements with their critics, especially in view of the rather eclectic utilization of systems thinking in much teaching and research (see the amalgamation of diverse variants of systems thinking in D. Katz and R. Kahn, *The Social Psychology of Organizations*, New York: Wiley, 1966).

4. The Parsonian model is set out in T. Parsons, "A sociological approach to the theory of organizations" in T. Parsons, *Structure and Process in Modern Societies*, Glencoe, Ill.: The Free Press, 1960; and in T. Parsons and N.J. Smelser, *Economy and Society*, London: Routledge and Kegan Paul, 1956. General appraisals of Parsons are found in M. Black (Ed.), *The Social Theories of Talcott Parsons*, Englewood Cliffs, N.J.: Prentice-Hall, 1961; and A. Gouldner, *The Coming Crisis of Western Sociology*, London: Heinemann, 1971; while H.A. Landsberger, "Parson's theory of organizations", pp. 214–219 in Black, *op. cit.*, provides a specific discussion.

5. Parsons, "A Sociological Approach to the Theory of Organizations"; and Katz and Kahn, *Social Psychology of Organizations*.

6. Thus Katz and Kahn, in *Social Psychology of Organizations*, suggest that the legitimacy of managerial decisions informs all organizational action. This legitimacy is considered to have immediate force for the individual because his behaviour is role-determined: "each person in an organization is linked to some set of other members by virtue of the functional requirements of the system which are heavily implemented through the expectations these member have of him". Nevertheless there are imperfections in compliance so "the authority structure is bolstered by an ancillary system of rewards and punishments". See also Brown, "Research and consultancy", for a discussion of the emphasis on "primary tasks" in the socio-technical systems approach.

7. See Brown, "Research and consultancy". Among those who draw on the socio-technical systems conception are Katz and Kahn, *Social Psychology of Organizations*; E. Schein, *Organizational Psychology*, Englewood Cliffs, N.J.: Prentice-Hall, 1965; R. Blauner, *Alienation and Freedom*, Chicago: Chicago University Press, 1964; and J. Woodward, *Industrial Organization: Theory and Practice*, London: Oxford University Press, 1965; though in

their own analyses Blauner and Woodward emphasize technical determinism, with little consideration of technology as a resource.

8. E.L. Trist *et al.*, *Organizational Choice*, London: Tavistock, 1963, part 1; and F.E. Emery and E.L. Trist, "Socio-technical systems", in C.W. Churchman and M. Verhulst (Eds), *Management Sciences: Models and Techniques*, vol. 2, Oxford: Pergamon, 1960, pp. 83–97.

9. Emery and Trist, "Socio-technical systems", esp. pp. 90–91; and E.J. Miller and A.K. Rice, *Systems of Organization*, London: Tavistock, 1967, part 1.

10. Prominent critics are: Krupp, *Organizational Analysis*; Mayntz, "Study of organizations"; Albrow, "Study of organizations"; and Silverman, *Theory of Organizations*.

11. However, sophisticated systems theorists claim to emancipate their analyses from the terms of reference of organizational controllers by focusing on "latent functions". These claims either fall back on consensus assumptions, or lead directly to thoroughgoing reification—as in Etzioni's use of "commitment of resources" as an indicator of "real goals" (A. Etzioni, *Modern Organizations*, Englewood Cliffs, N.J.: Prentice-Hall, 1964, ch.1.).

12. H. Aldrich, "Organizational Boundaries and Inter-organizational Conflict", *Hum. Relat.*, **24** (1971), 279–293, suggests, as an alternative to the "consensus-oriented monitor" in the cybernetic approach, a treatment in terms of the generation and extinction of variant forms of organization, taking a population of organizations as the unit of analysis. However, little effort has been made to explore these processes, or to study the actions of organizational members through which they would be mediated—for instance the patterns of response of diverse participants to threatened organizational collapse, and consequences of these response patterns. See also E. Penrose, "Biological analogies in the theory of the firm", *Am. Econom. Rev.*, **42** (1952), 804–819.

13. See, for example, P.R. Lawrence and J. Lorsch, *Organization and Environment*, Cambridge, Mass.: Harvard University Press, 1967; and the Tavistock research appraised by Brown, "Research and Consultancy", in particular Emery and Trist, "Socio-technical Systems".

14. It is interesting to speculate on the popularity of systems perspectives, which have absorbed later variants of human relations theory [for example C.M. Arensberg and B. Tootall, "Plant sociology: real discoveries and new problems" in M. Komarovsky (Ed.), *Common Frontiers of the Social Sciences*, Glencoe, Ill.: The Free Press, 1957, pp. 310–337] and have been adopted by "technical sociologists" in Eastern Europe [see A. Matejko, "Some sociological problems of socialist factories", *Soc. Res.*, **36** (1969), 448–480] in terms of just this correspondence.

15. These points are discussed by Mayntz, "Study of organizations", and A. Gouldner, "Theoretical requirements of the applied social sciences", *Am. Sociol. Rev.*, **22** (1957), 92–102; while R. Boguslaw in *The New Utopians*, Englewood Cliffs, N.J.: Prentice-Hall, 1965, begins an appraisal of the design-oriented features of systems-thinking. For an example of a "personnel-

changing programme" designed and legitimated within a systems framework see R.R. Blake *et al.*, *The Managerial Grid*, Houston: Gulf Publishing Co., 1967, and the topical account by S. Aris, "The Games Managers Play", *The Sunday Times* (24 Jan 1971), p. 47.

16. Some recent, but diverse, theoretical sponsors of such a shift in perspectives are: J. Rex, *Key Problems of Sociological Theory*, London: Routledge and Kegan Paul, 1961; H. Blumer, *Symbolic Interactionism: Perspective and Method*, Englewood Cliffs, N.J.: Prentice-Hall, 1969; P. Berger and T. Luckmann, *The Social Construction of Reality*, London: Allen Lane, 1967; F. Barth, *Models of Social Organization*, Royal Anthropological Institute of Great Britain, Occasional Paper 23, 1966; and A. Dawe, "The two sociologies", *Br. J. Sociol.*, **21** (1970), 207–218.

17. This and related questions, which consider the *actors' usage* of concepts of "goal", "role" and "organizational structure", are discussed by E. Bittner, "The concept of organization", *Soc. Res.*, **12** (1965), 239–255, and by Albrow, "Study of organization", and Silverman, *Theory of Organizations*, pp. 13–14 and 147–155. They reflect a methodological corollary to the shift in theoretical perspectives mentioned above—a rejection of the conventional assumption that observers definitions of social reality are related in non-problematic ways to those of participants on the social scene [see A. MacIntyre, "The idea of a social science", *Proc. Aristotelian Soc. Suppl.*, **41** (1967), and T.P. Wilson, "Conceptions of interaction and forms of sociological explanation", *Am. Sociol. Rev.*, **35** (1970), 697–710].

18. Albrow ("Study of organizations") gives particular emphasis to these features, and to the fact that sponsors may bring to their proposals extant organizational structures which they seek to remake in accord with their objectives, in stressing that organizational establishment shades into the ongoing process through which organizations are sustained and transformed.

19. Among recent sociological approaches to institutionalization some accounts focus on mutual interpretation (e.g. Blumer, *Symbolic Interactionism*) or negotiation (e.g. Barth, *Models of Organization*) while providing only summary treatments of (a) the differential power of participants in determining outcomes, and (b) the sources of the constraining character of social institutions. Others dramatise sources of these constraining characteristics, and mention the differential power of actors in influencing the pattern of constraint (e.g. Berger and Luckmann, *Construction of Reality*), but omit to analyse the processes of negotiation and manoeuvre in which actors engage in the interstices of the reified social world [cf. T. Burns, "Micropolitics: Mechanisms of institutional change", *Admin. Sci. Q.*, **6** (1961), 257–281; I. Light, "The social construction of uncertainty", *Berkeley J. Sociol.*, **14** (1969)]. Each, thus, provides only a partial guide to discussion of the institutionalization of organizational procedures and arrangements.

20. This point is made by B. Glaser and A. Strauss. "Awareness contexts and social interaction", *Am. Sociol. Rev.*, **29** (1967), 669–679, but has so far received only rudimentary treatment in the literature on industrial organiza-

tions (see H.L. Wilensky, *Organizational Intelligence*, New York: Basic Books, 1967; and B.A. Turner, *Exploring the Industrial Subculture*, London: Macmillan, 1971, ch. 11).

21. Albrow, "Study of organizations", states the point succinctly: "it is the agents' perception and interpretation of a situation which decides whether or not the application of the rule is justified. Compliance with a rule therefore is not removed from the area of disputable judgement. Formal organization is not facilitated or distorted by individual judgement and discretion; these are necessary preconditions for its generation". See also Bittner, "Concept of Organization".

22. A. Strauss *et al.*, "The hospital and its negotiated order", in E. Friedson (Ed.), *The Hospital in Modern Society*, Glencoe, Ill.: The Free Press, 1963, pp. 147–169. This discussion is based on study of psychiatric hospitals where the ambiguities and bargains may be more manifest than in business concerns. However the "negotiated order" conception is presented as a fruitful approach to analyses of any type of organization, since all organizational goals and rules are ambiguous, though the nature of the ambiguity and the manner of its resolution might be expected to vary between types of organization.

23. This may be conceptualized, at the level of organizational encounters, in terms of (a) alternative versions of "working consensus"—each with an associated cluster of social identities—which may sustain the jurisdiction of organizational goals through alternative sets of transformation rules, and (b) the resources deployed by interactants to cast the consensus in terms favourable to their particular purposes [see E. Goffman, "Fun in games" in *Encounters*, Indianapolis: Bobbs-Merrill, 1961; and E. Weinstein and P. Deuschberger, "Tasks, bargains and identities in social interaction", *Soc. Forces*, **42** (1964), 451–456], P. Strong, "Organizational Goals and Organizational Structure", unpublished manuscript, 1971, pp. 1–16, provides a detailed consideration of such encounter-based analyses of the actors conception and use of organizational goals and structure.

24. Since the specification and implementation of organizational procedures varies between different interactants, for different locales, and through time, "deviance" from such procedure is problematic in the ways treated by interactionist theorists of deviance (see E. Lemert, *Human Deviance, Social Problems and Social Control*, Englewood Cliffs, N.J.: Prentice-Hall, 1967). As that approach suggests, the discovery of deviance is a creative act informed by the intent to control the behaviour of subordinates, making it unlikely that mere "lip service to organizational goals" (Silverman, *Theory of Organization*, p. 14) will provide adequate warrant for acts suspected by the elite. It is in this context that subterfuge remains a crucial feature of organizational process.

25. This provides the context for Stinchcombe's statement [A. Stinchcombe, "Sociology of organization and the theory of the firm", *Pacific Sociol. Rev.*, **3** (1960), 75–82] that "when mechanisms fail to mobilize energies, the

higher bodies tend to change the mechanisms in order to make them effective. There is an institutional guarantee that whatever the motives of the underlying population, the top authorities will try to warp the motives into service of the organizational decision rules".

26. This point has been emphasized by T. Lupton and S. Cunnison, "Workshop behaviour", in M. Gluckman and E. Devons (Eds), *Closed Systems and Open*, Edinburgh: Oliver and Boyd, 1964, pp. 115–128; and by A. Touraine, "Towards actionalist sociology", *Social Sciences Information*, **8,** part 5, 147–166. See also the discussion of "orientations to work" in R.K. Brown, "Sources of objectives in work and employment", in J. Child (Ed.), *Man and Organization: The Search for Explanation and Social Relevance*, London: Allen and Unwin, 1973.

27. Burns, "Micropolitics", provides a sophisticated discussion of the nature of resources as *capabilities* mastered by some actors which are *requisites* for some joint action, and emphasizes that it is mastery that makes "givens" into "resources".

28. The manner in which actors form and reformulate their perspectives in a complex of familiar and institutional relationships receives suggestive treatment in E. Bott, *Family and Social Network*, London: Tavistock, 1957; and in D. Lockwood, "Sources of variations in working-class images of society", *Sociol. Rev.*, **14** (1966), 249–267.

29. This approach has been developed by European critics of systems perspectives in particular Touraine, "Actionalist sociology"; Silverman, *Theory of Organizations*; J. Goldthorpe *et al.*, *The Affluent Worker: Industrial Attitudes and Behaviour*, Cambridge: Cambridge University Press, 1968; and H. Popitz *et al.*, "The Workers Image of Society", in T. Burns (Ed.), *Industrial Man*, Harmondsworth: Penguin, 1969, pp. 281–324. See also the discussion in Brown, "Sources of Objectives in Work".

30. This approach can be identified with the symbolic-interactionist critique of systems perspectives and with the Chicago school of occupational sociology, exemplified by E.C. Hughes, *Men and Their Work*, Glencoe, Ill.: The Free Press, 1958; H.S. Becker and A. Strauss, "Careers, personality and adult socialization", *Am. J. Sociol.*, **62** (1956), 253–263; B. Glaser (Ed.), *Organizational Careers: A Sourcebook for Theory*, Chicago: Aldine, 1968; and H.S. Becker *et al.* (Eds), *Institutions and the Person*, Chicago: Aldine, 1968. The analysis of "careers" represents a point of considerable cross-fertilization with interactionist analyses of deviance.

31. Touraine, "Actionalist Sociology", typifies the focus on "generic projects of action". He considers "social relationships are established between actors, insofar as the actors represent the subject when it is refracted and broken up by passing through organizational systems" and proposes "to construct models of social action based on the patterns of involvement of the historic subject". In his use of the "action framework" Goldthorpe [*Affluent Worker: Industrial*; and see also J. Goldthorpe, "Attitudes and behaviour of car assembly workers", *Br. J. Sociol.*, **17** (1966), 227–244] oversimplifies its

contribution by identifying actors' perspectives as *stable* orientations based on *outside-work* features of actors' social settings, and thus fosters a truncated examination of the dynamics of changes in perspectives in relation to work-place experience [see J.H. Westergaard, "The rediscovery of the cash nexus", in R. Milliband and J. Saville (Eds), *The Socialist Register, 1970*, London: Merlin Press; and Brown, "Sources of Objectives in Work"].

32. The symbolic interactionists accord recognition to the formulation of common perspectives among cohorts of organizational members, but their major contribution is to highlight the limited awareness and shifting focal concerns of actors at different points in their organizational careers [see H.S. Becker, "Personal change in adult life", *Sociometry*, **27** (1964), 40–53]. In this light it is important to avoid the reification of "actors' projects"—they may best be regarded as actors' conceptions, available for use by actors in the com-prehension of their own and others experience and actions.

33. These criticisms are addressed to the theoretical perspectives proposed by P. Blau in *Exchange and Power in Social Life*, New York: Wiley, 1964, ch. 5–8 and A. Etzioni in *A Comparative Analysis of Complex Organizations*, Glencoe, Ill.: The Free Press, 1961. Blau's exchange analysis locates the capability of organizers to control subordinates in the obligation of sub-ordinates to comply with organizers demands once indepted, that indepted-ness being based on an initially unequal command over relevant resources. However, subordinates may consider the initial inequity, and the manner of its continuation, to be unfair or exploitative—in which case compliance would be problematic and commitment to organizational goals uncertain [for a more general appraisal of exchange analysis see M. Mulkay, *Function-alism, Exchange and Theoretical Strategy*, London: Routledge and Kegan Paul, 1971; see also A. Heath, "Blau's economics and sociology", *Sociology*, **2** (1968), 273–292]. For comments on the tautologous character of Etzioni's formulation see T. Burns, "The Comparative Study of Organizations", in V. Vroom (Ed.), *Methods of Organizational Research*, Pittsburgh, Pa.: Pittsburgh University Press, 1967, pp. 118–170; and V. Allen, "Etzioni's synthesis in organization theory: A case of defective construction", *Mens en Maatschappij*, **1** (1972), 17–34.

34. Burns, in "Micropolitics", provides a more detailed discussion of the role of "priorities rhetorics" in organizational affairs [see also T. Burns, "On the Plurality of Social Systems" in T. Burns (Ed.), *Industrial Man*, Harmonds-worth: Penguin, 1969, pp. 232–249] while M. Crozier, in *The Bureaucratic Phenomenon*; London: Tavistock, 1964, ch. 7, discusses the importance of conceptions of interdependence. Of course, Dahrendorf's theory of industrial conflict (R. Dahrendorf: *Class and Class Conflict in Industrial Society*, London: Routledge and Kegan Paul, 1959, part 2) is founded on an apprecia-tion of the coincidence of interest conflict and interdependence between subordinates and superiors. However, as Weigart shows [P. Weingart, "Beyond Parsons? A critique of Dahrendorf's conflict theory", *Soc. Forces*, **48** (1969), 151–165], Dahrendorf's conceptual scheme reifies this coincidence

as a uniform and "normatively given" coexistence, and thus (a) fails adequately to consider the various forms it may take in organizations with particular types of controllers or participants (e.g. entrepreneurs and wage workers), and (b) also defines as meaningless actors' perspectives and projects which resolve or transcend this coexistence (see e.g. comments on "structurally justified expectations", *Class and Class Conflict*, p. 267).

35. See M. Dalton, *Men Who Manage*, New York: Wiley, 1959; Silverman, *Theory of Organization*, ch. 8; and for a general discussion of patronage, F.G. Bailey, *Strategems and Spoils*, Oxford: Blackwell, 1969.

36. Thus P. Bacharach and M. Baratz, "The two faces of power", *Am. Polit. Sci. Rev.*, **56** (1962), 947–952, suggest that "mobilization of bias" is characterized by participation of some members in strategies designed to sustain those values, institutional procedures, and facilities which help them to keep certain issues out of the domain of general political action. Of course some facilities may be refied by all participants and constrain everyone's options, though the manner in which such reification is sustained remains a crucial analytical issue.

37. Patterns of covert compromises, and strategies of subterfuge and information control among subordinates, are discussed by D. Mechanic, "Sources of power of lower participants", *Admin. Sc. Q.*, **7** (1962), 349–364; Dalton, *Men Who Manage*; and expecially D. Roy, "Efficiency and 'The Fix'", *Am. J. Sociol.*, **60** (1954–1955), 255–266.

38. Thus the generic processes of role management and interpretation delineated by W. Goode, in "A theory of role strain", *Am. Sociol. Rev.*, **25** (1960), 483–496; and R.H. Turner, in "Role-taking; process vs. conformity", in A.M. Rose (Ed.) *Human Behaviour and Social Processes*, London: Routledge and Kegan Paul, 1962, pp. 22–40, are revealed in the enactment of organizational as other roles. For discussion of these issues with particular reference to organizations, see D.J. Levinson "Role, personality and social structure in organizational settings", *J. Abnorm. soc. Psychol.*, **58** (1959), 170–180; and W. Rushing, *The Psychiatric Professions*, Chapel Hill, N.C.: University of North Carolina Press, 1964, ch. 1 and 2, especially Rushing's discussion of strategies of role formation and protection.

39. This point is conceded by Turner, "Role-taking", in his discussion of the institutionalization of bureaucratic roles, and is recognized by Goode, "Role strain", in his treatment of third-party intervention and "conventional solutions" as constraints on the pattern of strain-management, though both writers tend towards a pluralistic model in which each actors' claims and interpretations are rather easily accommodated.

40. See E. Goffman's discussion ("Role distance" in his *Encounters*, Indianapolis: Bobbs-Merrill, 1961) of role enactment in roles damaging to actors' self-conceptions. Using the metaphor of the actor as an administrator of a holding-company, who manages disparate role-performances according to some theme, Goffman combines an emphasis on the inevitability of being involved in certain sorts of roles (reflecting differential power) with consideration of the

ways in which self-conceptions provide themes which influence the nature of role-performance.

41. J. Woodward, *Management and Technology*, London: HMSO, 1958; and *Industrial Organization: Theory and Practice*, London: Oxford University Press, 1965. See also J. Woodward (Ed.), *Industrial Organization: Behaviour and Control*, London: Oxford University Press, 1970. The managerial orientation of much industrial sociology is reflected in the treatment of typologies of organization as sources of suggestions for management strategies which transcend the "one-best-way" recommendations of earlier theorists. In this regard, too, Woodward is an influential representative.

42. Woodward, *Theory and Practice*.

43. In more recent research these "control structures" have been the focus of study [Woodward (Ed.), *Behaviour and Control*]. The investigation of these administrative devices has prompted an increased theoretical emphasis on conscious managerial planning as both cause of, and response to, organizational constraints, while the empirical work further documents the processes of interpretation and negotiation which mediate the impact of supposed constraints. The importance of managerial strategies is also shown in W. Zwerman, *New Perspectives in Organization Theory*, Westport, Conn.: Greenwood, 1970, ch. 7. In this "replication" of Woodward's study he documents rather tenuous relationships between technology and structure, in a benign economic climate, and emphasizes the impact on this relationship of strategies for controlling and rewarding subordinates.

44. These concerns prompt the attempt to define technology in a non-social "culture-free" way (see Woodward (Ed.), *Behaviour and Control*, ch. 3). The various attempts to produce such definitions have failed to free notions of "variety" and "uncertainty" from the social context in which actors construct and construe technology [cf. C. Perrow, "A framework for comparative analysis of organizations", *Am. Sociol. Rev.*, **32** (1967), 194–208]. In the more recent research on "control systems" Woodward associates her approach more directly with that of "socio-technical systems" and recognizes the assumptions of normative compliance made by that approach [see Woodward (Ed.), *Behaviour and Control*, chs. 1 and 2]. A similar recognition of the consensus assumptions underlying technical determinism is glimpsed fleetingly in M. Meissner, *Technology and the Worker*, San Francisco: Chandler, 1969, esp. pp. 13–16.

45. A convincing argument for the importance of micropolitical processes, in mediating between technology or market and structure, is found in C. Perrow, "Departmental power and perspectives in industrial firms", in M. Zald (Ed.), *Power in Organizations*, Nashville: Vanderbilt University Press, 1970, pp. 59–85. A similar criticism can be advanced against technology typologies which focus on workers' responses to technical constraints—they often fail to consider the impact of administrative policies, managerial ideologies, worker demands and resources, and the like. These points are taken up in a later section of this chapter.

46. T. Burns and G.M. Stalker, *The Management of Innovation* (2nd ed.), London: Tavistock, 1966, esp. the preface and chs. 7–12; T. Burns, "Reference of conduct in small groups; cliques and cabals in occupational milieux", *Hum. Relat.*, **8** (1955), 467–486; "Micropolitics"; and "Plurality of social systems".

47. This is a theme reiterated by A. Gouldner, *Patterns of Industrial Bureaucracy*, London: Routledge and Kegan Paul, 1955; and by Crozier, *Bureaucratic Phenomenon*—see the discussion below.

48. See M. Scott and S. Lyman, "Accounts", *Am. Sociol. Rev.*, **33** (1968), 46–62. Bittner ("Concept of organization") analyses some of the ways in which the notion of "formal organization' is used by participants in the definition of organizational situations and actions, and one of the usages he discusses is the "gambit of compliance"—where performances are related as responses to rules while discovering in the rules the warrant for "necessary" actions.

49. Burns and Stalker, *Management of Innovation*.

50. Prospects of succession invite distinctive interpretations of current superior–subordinate relations—superiors attempt to assert *their* priorities, managers respond to the assessment of conduct by dissembling performances, and cabals mobilize resources to constrain directors' choices. The resultant interaction exemplifies processes of elite monitoring and subordinate information control which play a central part in organizational politics (cf. Gouldner, *Industrial Bureaucracy*, and discussion below).

51. Burns and Stalker, *Management of Innovation*, chs. 7, 10, 11 and 12. This point, and the suggestion that certain managers and departments promote "organic" patterns in a predominantly bureaucratic organization because of potential gains in control over resources and people, parallel the findings of Crozier (*Bureaucratic Phenomenon*).

52. Burns and Stalker, *Management of Innovation*, chs. 8 and 9; and Burns, "Micropolitics".

53. Crozier, *Bureaucratic Phenomenon*; Dalton, *Men Who Manage*; and Gouldner, *Industrial Bureaucracy* and *Wildcat Strike*, London: Routledge and Kegan Paul, 1955. Two general comments should be made on the use made of these studies in the text:
    (a) The differences between the organizations discussed by Crozier, Dalton and Burns are "overdetermined" in the sense that different cultural contexts, market settings, and historical developments all could be seen to contribute to the distinctive characteristics revealed in the analyses. Any particular emphasis must thus await further comparative study—but comparison which recognizes the processes of negotiation, interpretation, conflict and accommodation through which organizational structures are formed.
    (b) The general overview slights the particular interests and limiting assumptions of the different studies. Thus, in Crozier's study much of the discussion is couched in terms of a critical appraisal of the role of power in bureaucracy, while Dalton is most explicitly concerned to undermine the dichotomous concepts of formal and informal organization. R. Krohn, "Conflict and

function: Some basic issues in bureaucratic theory", *Br. J. Sociol.*, **22** (1971), pp. 115–232, has provided an important critical discussion of the theoretical rationales and analytic insights provided by these authors, and suggests that neither properly analyses the organizational designs or patterns of involvement which sustain the processes depicted, and that each gives inadequate attention to those features of organizational process emphasized by the other.

54. This feature of bureaucratic rules is also central to Gouldner's study of *Industrial Bureaucracy*. Crozier posits a general desire, rooted in French culture and character, to avoid relationships of dependence and seek clearly defined involvements; but the other studies discussed in this section suggest that such a desire is an outcome of the bargaining power and strategies of control open to the different participants.

55. See Crozier, *Bureaucratic Phenomenon*, p. 177, footnote: "much of the rationalization process that decisively curtailed the power of the managers and of the supervisors was achieved when workers were able, after a ten-year struggle, to impose the adoption of a carefully written seniority code". Of course supervisory discretion only becomes "onerous" when it leads to successful charges of favouritism, and to retaliatory action.

56. Cf. Gouldner, *Industrial Bureaucracy*.

57. These features spell out some of the socially defined bases for the recognition of expertise as a resource (see Crozier, *Bureaucratic Phenomenon*, p. 158, footnote).

58. The socially contrived nature of such uncertainty is of particular relevance to the type of analysis being outlined. This feature is indicated by the achievement of banishing written maintenance manuals from the works (Crozier, *Bureaucratic Phenomenon*, p. 153), by cooperation between maintenance craftsmen and technical engineers who "support the maintenance men in instituting disregard for any formal written instructions" (p. 156), and in definition of production workers and supervisors as incompetent—a definition backed by strike sanctions (p. 127). See also Perrow, "Departmental power and perspectives".

59. Crozier does not explore the ways in which conceptions of interdependence constrain actors' power-plays, while he admits that other considerations affect such actions among maintenance workers.

60. Dalton, *Men Who Manage*, p. 55, suggests that "a changing market and technology, with plant expansion and turnover of personnel, promotes and requires cliques". See also Crozier's speculations (*Bureaucratic Phenomenon*, ch. 6) on the implications of increased uncertainty.

61. This is also discussed by Stinchcombe, "Sociology of Organizations."

62. These strategies provide evidence for Dalton's theme of the interpenetration of formal and informal action in "a shifting set of contained and ongoing counterphases of action".

63. The resources available to superiors and subordinates, including the ease of information control, furnish parameters for the "room for manoeuvre" of each group.

64. Cf. Krohn, "Conflict and function".
65. See also the discussion by Silverman, *Theory of Organizations*, ch. 7; and Gouldner's comments on the contexts and characteristics of organizational succession [A. Gouldner, "Comment on Guest's 'managerial succession' ", *Am. J. Sociol.*, **68** (1962), 54–56].
66. The "indulgency pattern" involved lenient rule application, management responsiveness to workers requests and a work discipline focused on technical performance; and was related to the integration of workers into the ethos and cross-cutting social relationships of a rural community. It should be noted that the contrast conceptions of "indulgency" and "stringency" patterns slighted the complexities of actual plant administration, though they strongly resembled the developing "myth of the golden past" definition of the situation among workers and middle management. On the problems which stem from an oversimple amalgamation of actors perspectives and structural changes in a similar analysis, see S. Thermstrom, " 'Yankee City' revisited: The perils of Historical naivete", *Am. Sociol. Rev.*, **30** (1965), 234–242.
67. See the diagrammatic summaries in J. March and H.A. Simon, *Organizations*, New York: Wiley, 1958, pp. 37–47; and in Gouldner, *Industrial Bureaucracy*, and *Wildcat Strike*, p. 84.
68. Like Crozier's production workers, in contrast to the maintenance engineers, they did not successfully resist the rules but exploited the apathy preserving features of these rules in output control.
69. This raises the issue of the contexts within which particular rhetorics are credited. Gouldner, in *Industrial Bureaucracy*, also analysed the utilization of rival vocabularies of motive in the interpretation of organizational behaviour by different groups of participants. Thus deviance from rules sponsored by workers or management in conflict was seen as deliberate action in pursuit of sectional interests, while deviance from mutually sponsored rules was seen as an outcome of ignorance or well-intentioned carelessness (hence remedied by "education") and deviance from third-party rules was viewed as expression of "normal human needs" (cf. Scott and Lyman "Accounts").
70. Gouldner, *Wildcat Strike*, chs. 2–8; Gouldner's typology of bureaucratic rules thus distinguishes (a) rules sponsored by both parties (representative bureaucracy), (b) rules sponsored by workers *or* management and backed by sanctions (punishment-centred bureaucracy) and (c) rules sponsored by outside interests (labelled from the perspective of insiders as "mock bureaucracy", though this appears to generalize a special case—of minimal enforcement—to externally imposed rules in general).
71. See Gouldner's remark that "When a person says he is 'unable' to do something, what he seems to be doing is to take certain of the circumstances (e.g. technology) in which he is involved and treat them as givens or unchangeables", *Wildcat Strike*, p. 144—but what may be taken as given may vary between participants and through time, and itself needs analysis in terms of social processes of knowledge-construction (cf. Berger and Luckmann, *Construction of Reality*).

72. See, for example, S. Udy, "The comparative analysis of organizations", in J.G. March (Ed.) *Handbook of Organizations* Chicago: Rand-McNally 1965, pp. 678–709. Perhaps the most austere and sophisticated reification of organizational structures in comparative analyses is found in the work of D.S. Pugh *et al.* [see "A conceptual scheme for organizational analysis", *Admin. Sci. Q.* **8** (1963) 289–315; "Dimensions of organizational structure", *Admin. Sci. Q.* **13** (1968) 65–105; and "The comparative study of organizations" in D. Pym (Ed.) *Industrial Society*, Harmondsworth: Penguin, 1968, pp. 374–396]. These authors (a) identify "organizational structure" with top management designs and related paper-work concerning work-tasks rules and regulations, despite the possibility that these organizational features may be contentious or selectively perceived by informants, and may not be actively implemented; and (b) fail to sustain their analysis of the one feature of their initial imagery (i.e. flexibility) which might have illuminated the manner in which the "structure" represents the outcome of participants' actions, while using the conventional category of "informal organization" to segregate aspects of organizational process from organizational "structure".

73. See J. Child, "Organizational structure, environment and performance; The role of strategic choice", *Sociology*, **5** (1971), 1–22, for a similar argument; also Burns, "Comparative study of organizations", Silverman, *Theory of Organizations*, and Bittner, "Concept of organization".

74. The managerial frame of reference of much of the empirical research, and hence its compartmentalized "problem-oriented" character, has already been noted in the introduction. It is this frame of reference which accounts in large part for the distinct literature on e.g. payment schemes, technical change, plant bargaining and, more recently, industrial scientists and middle management.

75. See in particular the thorough review by T. Nichols, *Ownership, Control and Ideology*, London: Allen and Unwin, 1969 who makes many of the points mentioned in this discussion. Stinchcombe, "Sociology of organizations", reasserts the importance of examining organizational decision-rules rather than simply individual priorities, and underlines the crucial issue of the capacity of top-management to effectively implement such rules in organizational affairs.

76. Nichols, *Ownership, Control and Ideology*, chs. 10 and 11.

77. Burns, "Plurality of social systems", and Stinchcombe, "Sociology of organizations", emphasize the impact of the framework of organizational policies on the definition of special competences, while Wilensky, in *Organizational Intelligence*, discusses the divide and rule strategy. For a trenchant general commentary on these issues, developed as a critique of "managerialism", see H. Gerth and C.W. Mills, "A Marx for the managers", in R.K. Merton *et al.* (Eds), *Reader in Bureaucracy*, Glencoe, Ill.: The Free Press, 1952, pp. 165–178.

78. M. Zald, "Power and functions of boards of directors", *Am. J. Sociol.*, **75** (1969), 97–111; C. Beed, "The separation of ownership and control", *J.*

Econ. Stud., **1** (1966), 29–46; Nichols, *Ownership Control and Ideology*; and for observations on the dominance of profitability criteria, J.S. Earley, "Marginal policies of 'excellently managed' companies", *Am. Econ. Rev.*, **46** (1956), 44–70; and W.L. Baldwin, "Motives of managers, environmental restraints and the theory of managerial enterprise", *Q. J. Econ.*, **78** (1964), 238–256. A recent and substantial empirical study by R.J. Larner, *Management Control and the Large Corporation*, New York: Dunellen, 1970, which compared the profitability performance of ostensibly "management-controlled" firms and "owner-controlled" firms, found a consistently profit-oriented performance pattern for both types of firm.

79. See Nichols, *Ownership, Control and Ideology*; on the increasing rigour of profitability criteria see Earley, "Marginal policies", and J.P. Nettl, "A note on entrepreneurial behaviour", *Rev. Econ. Stud.*, **24** (1957), 87–94; and on the sophistication of these criteria see Baldwin's discussion in "Motives of managers", of the part played by "market shares" and "organizational growth" considerations in longer-term orientations to "secure profitability".

80. See the general strictures of Blumer (*Symbolic Interactionism*) concerning stimulus-response models of social action and social structure.

81. Wilensky, *Organizational Intelligence*, especially his discussion of preconceptions about appropriate information and sources. A preliminary account of selective search procedures utilized by top managers is provided by F.J. Aguilar, *Scanning the Business Environment*, New York: Macmillan, 1967.

82. See J.D. Thompson and W.J. McEwen, "Organizational goals and environment: Goal setting as an interaction process", *Am. Sociol. Rev.*, **23** (1958), 23–31; in particular their discussion of presentations, "sounding out", and the alternative strategies of competition, bargaining, cooptation and coalition, each involving a distinctive pattern of costs and gains for the administrative elite. However, their analysis must be supplemented by empirical studies of inter-firm and enterprise-state agency interaction, to provide an adequate account of the character of employer alliances and cartels, and the impact of legal constraints on "corporate conduct"; among relevant studies are R. Engler, *The Politics of Oil*, New York: Macmillan, 1961, S. Macauly, *Law and the Balance of Power: The Automobile Manufacturers and their Dealers*, New York: Russell Sage Foundation, 1966; R.A. Smith, *Corporations in Crisis*, New York: Doubleday, 1963, esp. sections on "The great electrical conspiracy"; and W. Carson, "White collar crime and the enforcement of factory legislation", *Br. J. Crim.*, **10** (1970), 383–398.

83. The case studies reviewed in section two illustrate the relevance of these features. Organizational ideologies, sponsorship, and changes in top personnel are also discussed by A.D. Chandler (*Strategy and Structure: Chapters in the History of Industrial Enterprise*, Cambridge, Mass.: MIT Press, 1962), with reference to the policy of "decentralization", and by M.Z. Brooke and H.L. Remmers (*The Strategy of Multinational Enterprise: Organization and Finance*, London: Longmans, 1970) in regard to "moves abroad" and related changes in organizational design. These later authors also document the

casual and piece-meal nature of changes which may then become ratified in an explicit alteration of policy or design.

84. Stimulated by the obvious incompleteness of formal job descriptions in relation to these features of management action, studies of "management behaviour" (summarized in R. Dubin, "Business behaviour behaviourally viewed", in G.B. Strother (Ed.), *Social Science Approaches to Business Behaviour*, London: Tavistock, 1962, pp. 11–55; and in R. Stewart, *Managers and their Jobs*, London: Macmillan, 1967) have thrown doubt on various cherished preconceptions about managerial conduct. However, such studies generally lack that concern for organizational process which could animate their typologies of job-profiles, by documenting the meanings assigned to activities by the various actors and by revealing the patterned assumptions and constraints within which the activity proceeds. Nevertheless the best of these studies do underline the complex relations between beliefs, accounts and actions, and thus reveal the importance of studying those interpretive processes through which actors draw their actions under the rubric of organizational rules, roles and priorities [cf. T. Burns, "What managers do", *New Society* (17 Dec 1964), 8–9].

85. See the discussion of case studies in section two, and also Burns, "Cliques and cabals". Burns uses the term "cabal" for expansionist alliances formed around the sponsorship of particular priorities and personnel, reserving the term "clique" for defensive and protective colleague groups who develop a shared account of obstacles and disadvantages blocking their success.

86. Notable among such policies are those designed to sustain "careerist" orientations and weaken group solidarities—by surrounding threatening career contingencies (e.g. demotions and lateral moves) with ambiguities concerning their implications for individual futures [see F. Goldner, "Demotion in industrial management", *Am. Sociol. Rev.*, **30** (1965), 714–724]; by providing "career-oriented" projects alongside routine job obligations (see L. Klein, "Prescription in management control", in Woodward (Ed.), *Behaviour and Control*, pp. 85–107, for an example); or by disaligning the loyalties of organizational colleagues through frequent and disparate moves (see Wilensky, *Organizational Intelligence*). Goldner's functionalist discussion treats the dilemmas and policies open to top managements though he also recognizes the perspectives and interpretive efforts of middle managers, while Wilensky outlines the strategies of top management together with the tactics of information control and "conventionalism" resorted to by junior managers. P. Campanis provides a case study of a thoroughly "careerist" management milieu, and the normatively ambiguous brokerage practices of managers in that milieux ("Normlessness in management", in J. Douglas (Ed.), *Deviance and Respectability*, New York: Basic Books, 1970, pp. 291–325), which can be read as the product of some of the top management strategies mentioned above.

87. R.R. Ritti and F. Goldner, "Professional pluralism in an industrial organization", *Management Science*, **16** (1969), B233–B246. See also Burns "Cliques

and cabals" and "Micropolitics", and Strauss *et al.*, "Hospital and its negotiated order".

88. See H.A. Landsberger, "The horizontal dimension in bureaucracy", *Admin. Sci. Q.*, **6** (1961), 299–332; who does, however, counterpose "realistic dilemmas" posed by the organizational environment to micropolitical representations and rhetoric. In contrast to this dichotomy what is required is consideration of the ways in which micropolitical processes play into the definition of "realistic dilemmas" and influence the character of their management. See also W. Dill, "Environment as an influence on managerial autonomy", *Admin. Sci. Q.*, **2** (1958), 395–420.

89. Numerous examples of these strategies are discussed in Burns and Stalker (*Management of Innovation*) and in Dalton (*Men Who Manage*), while Ritti and Goldner ("Professional pluralism") discuss the actions of newly emergent specialities and those groups which they threaten with routinization. A good account of the tactics and strategy pursued by a marginal specialism is found in G. Strauss, "Tactics of lateral relationship: The purchasing agent", *Admin. Sci. Q.*, **7** (1962), 161–186; and "Workflow frictions, interfunctional rivalry, and professionalism", *Hum. Organiz.*, **23** (1964), 127–149. See also F. Goldner, "The division of labour: process and power"; and R.A. Peterson, "Some consequences of Differentiation", in Zald (Ed.), *Power in Organizations*, pp. 97–149.

90. Among relevant studies A. Flanders, *The Fawley Productivity Agreements*, London: Faber and Faber, 1964, traces the sponsorship of new policies of management control over "manpower utilization". Flanders describes how a management group based in the "employee relations department", and aided by an industrial consultant, turned top management manpower comparisons "to good account" in careerist terms, and came to dominate managerial policy and control most senior management posts (for domination of "maintenance" see p. 73, "technical department", p. 84, and "process", p. 87). Gouldner (*Industrial Bureaucracy*, and *Wildcat Strike*, esp. ch. 7) provides an analysis of policy changes accompanying top management succession, and also portrays contrasting departmental perspectives on policy. Brooke and Remmers (*Multinational Enterprise*) analyse the operation of policies of "decentralization" in multinational firms to show that such policies involve complex control procedures demarcating the limits of managerial autonomy, and discuss the ebb and flow of elite control efforts in this context.

91. Recent discussions of the situated character of scientific orientations and strategies are found in S. Cotgrove and S. Box, *Science, Industry and Society*, London: Allen and Unwin, 1970; and in S.B. Barnes, "Making out in industrial research", *Sci. Stud.*, **1** (1971), 157–175; while selections from earlier research are included in Glaser (Ed.), *Organizational Careers*. Earlier studies of industrial scientists (e.g. W. Kornhauser, *Scientists in Industry*, Berkeley: California University Press, 1962) discuss processes of organizational socialization and accommodation but take as a starting point abstract functionalist characterizations of scientific, professional and organizational

normative orientations, which have a problematical relationship to participants' actual orientations and activities, and may best be regarded as
rhetorics drawn on by organizational interactants. This is very clearly
revealed in recent critiques of the Mertonian characterization of scientific
norms, which match certain features of scientific rhetoric but are uncertainly
related to the practical orientations of accredited scientists [see M. Mulkay,
"Aspects of cultural growth in the natural sciences", *Soc. Res.*, **36** (1969),
22–52; and S.B. Barnes and R.G.A. Dolby, "The scientific ethos: A deviant
viewpoint", *Archiv. Europ. Sociol.*, **11** (1970), 3–25].

92. The symbolic character of professional claims, and the processes of negotiation
and interpretation which mediate such claims, are emphasized by H.S.
Becker, "The nature of a profession", in his *Sociological Work Method and
Substance*, London: Allen Lane, 1971, pp. 87–103; while A. Strauss and L.
Rainwater, in *The Professional Scientist*, Chicago: Aldine, 1962, ch. 12,
sketch some implications of this emphasis for the study of industrial scientists.
Studies addressed to these features of professional claims have given particular attention to the complex relationships between the ideological claims,
institutionalized competences and working practices of professionals, and
their varied and ongoing construction in diverse organizational locales [see
E. Friedson, *Profession of Medicine*, New York: Dodd, Mead, 1970, chs.
1, 4 and 9; The crucial importance of the relative power positions of the
'professionalising' occupation and their clients is underlined by T.J. Johnson,
in *Professions and Power*, London, Macmillan, 1972, especially chapters 3
and 5, in particular in the case of corporate patronage of occupational groups
who provide specialist services but lack any independent power base; while
the implications of varied patterns of industrial patronage of scientific and
technical occupations for job satisfaction and career strategies are discussed
by N.D. Ellis, "The Occupation of Science", in S.B. Barnes (ed) *Sociology
of Science*, London: Penguin, 1972. Finally Ritti and Goldner, "Professional
pluralism"; G. Strauss, "Tactics of lateral relationship", and "Workflow
frictions"; and F. Goldner and R.R. Ritti, "Professionalism as career immobility", *Am. J. Sociol.*, **72** (1967), 489–502, discuss the defensive role of
professionalization in predominantly "careerist" management milieux.

93. Blauner, *Alienation and Freedom*; Woodward, *Theory and Practice*; and Trist
et al., *Organizational Choice* [see also E.L. Trist and K. Bamforth, "Some
social psychological consequences of the longwall method of coal-getting",
Hum. Relat., **4** (1951), 3–38], each provide comparative analyses of work
conditions and experience in various "socio-technical" settings, while C.R.
Walker and R.H. Guest, *The Man on the Assembly Line*, Cambridge, Mass.:
Harvard University Press, 1952, offer a specific account of the impact of
technical constraints in the motor industry. Blauner presents the most
impressive synthesis of aspects of "socio-technical" analyses of occupational
milieux, but his work must be subject to the following reservations: (a) in
discussion of the character of work in different industries he acknowledges
various of the criticisms of technical determinism mentioned in the text—

most obviously in the case of the impact of community settings on the attitudes and behaviour of textile workers—*but* these qualifications remain extraneous to his theoretical model and thus fail to be accommodated within his overall summary of a u-curve of "alienation", and (b) the inadequacy of assimilating "alienation" to psychological dissatisfaction, and of assessing dissatisfaction on the basis of somewhat dubious questionnaire material; the equation of "alienation" and "dissatisfaction" effectively excludes crucial issues concerning the possible "false consciousness" of satisfied workers, who remain alienated in the classic sense (cf. J. Israel, *Alienation: From Marx to Modern Sociology*, Boston: Allyn and Bacon, 1971, esp. ch. 7; and J.E.T. Eldridge, *Sociology and Industrial Life*, London: Michael Joseph, 1971, pp. 183–195).

94. Goldthorpe, "Car assembly workers"; and Goldthorpe *et al.*, *Affluent Worker: Industrial*. Among critics R. Blackburn, "The unequal society", in R. Blackburn and A. Cockburn (Eds), *The Incompatibles*, Harmondsworth: Penguin, 1967, pp. 15–55; and Westergaard, "Rediscovery of the cash nexus", emphasize the dynamic relationships between the collective demands of workers and their ambivalently "instrumental" orientations to work, while W.W. Daniel, "Industrial behaviour and orientations to work—a critique", *J. Management Stud.*, **6** (1969), 366–375, has stressed that the meaning of instrumental involvement for the worker may change at different junctures in individual and collective organizational careers (see also the ensuing debate between Daniel and Goldthorpe in the *J. Management Stud.*, and for an overview, Brown, "Sources of objectives in work"). Earlier studies by E. Chinoy, *Automobile Workers and the American Dream*, New York: Doubleday, 1955, and "Manning the machines", in P. Berger (Ed.), *The Human Shape of Work*, New York: Macmillan, 1964, pp. 51–81; and by R.H. Guest, "Work careers and aspirations of automobile workers", *Am. Sociol. Rev.*, **19** (1954), 155–163, also document changes in the mundane interpretation of "success" in the course of work careers on the assembly-line.

95. H.A. Turner *et al.*, *Labour Relations in the Motor Industry*, London: Allen and Unwin, 1967, discuss variations in the character of assembly-line work tasks, while S. Melman, *Decision Making and Productivity*, Oxford: Blackwell, 1958, describes the design and implementation of a "deviant" type of work organization—"gang work"—in the car industry. Chinoy, *American Dream* and Guest, "Work careers and aspirations", also comment on the impact of union policies concerning differentials, in narrowing the span of the wage structure. The impact of managerial preconceptions on the administration of work organization is well illustrated by A. Willener, in "Payment systems in the French steel and iron mining industry: an exploration in managerial resistance to change", in G. Zollschan and W. Hirsch (Eds), *Explorations in Social Change*, London: Routledge and Kegan Paul, 1964, pp. 593–618.

96. Among British studies of occupational milieux which provide suggestive analyses of some of these influences are: R.K. Brown and P. Brannen,

"Social relations and social perspectives among shipbuilding workers", *Sociology*, **4** (1970), 71–84 and 197–211; S. Cunnison, *Wages and Work Allocation*, London: Tavistock, 1966; N. Dennis *et al.*, *Coal is Our Life*, London: Eyre and Spottiswoode, 1957; P. Duncan, "Conflict and cooperation among trawlermen", *Br. J. Indust. Relat.*, **1** (1963), 331–347; A.J.M. Sykes, "Unity and restrictive practices in the British printing industry", *Sociol. Rev.*, **8** (1960), 239–254; "The cohesion of trade union workshop organization", *Sociology*, **1** (1967), 141–163; and "Navvies: their work attitudes (and) social relations", *Sociology*, **3** (1969), 21–35 and 157–172; J. Tunstall, *The Fishermen*, London: McGibbon and Kee, 1962; and J. Woodward *et al.*, *The Dockworker*, Liverpool: Liverpool University Press, 1954. S. Nosow and W.H. Form (Eds), *Man, Work and Society*, New York: Basic Books, 1962, introduce comparable American occupational ethnographies.

97. Trist *et al.*, *Organizational Choice*, section 6, provides an instructive example of the character of "systems theory" assumptions. In this section workgroup actions which fail to correspond to claimed systemic requirements are defined as irrational, and the course of bargaining is discussed in terms of the reassertion of "realistic" system priorities over against "fantasies" of sectional interest. Compare the contrasting analysis provided by Dennis *et al.*, *Coal is Our Life*, esp. ch. 2.

98. W. Baldamus, *Efficiency and Effort*, London: Tavistock, 1961, provides a formal analysis of the "completion" of the labour contract in the day-to-day affairs of shop-floor administration, as an outcome of the costing and programming concerns of management and of workers interests in improved and secure returns for expended effort. Baldamus stresses that neither "market forces" nor "psychological givens" adequately explain the pattern of institutionalized "effort bargaining", and he underlines the importance of occupational socialization and selection processes in stabilizing effort conceptions, but (despite his sensitive treatment of the equivocal and ambiguous character of experienced effort) he gives little attention to the problematic features of effort norm enactment. Other suggestive analyses of the dynamics of the labour contract are provided by Gouldner, *Wildcat Strike*, ch. 9; Blackburn, "Unequal society", pp. 34–44; and Dennis *et al.*, *Coal is Our Life*, ch. 2.

99. The Hawthorne Studies and the work of Matthewson (see S.B. Matthewson *et al.*, with an introductory commentary by D.F. Roy, *Restriction of Output Among Unorganized Workers*, Carbondale, Ill.: Southern Illinois University Press, 1969) represent the beginnings of this line of investigation, while a central theme of critics of Hawthorne [e.g. A Carey., "The Hawthorne studies: a radical criticism", *Am. Sociol. Rev.*, **32** (1967), 403–416] and among recent students of effort bargaining (e.g. T. Lupton, *On the Shop Floor*, Oxford: Pergamon, 1963), concerns the rational and sophisticated character of workers' interests and strategies. A general bibliography of the "wage payment" literature is provided in R. Mariott, updated by S. Shimmin, *Incentive Payment Systems*, London: Staples Press, 1968.

100. H. Behrend, "Financial incentives as the expression of a system of beliefs", *Br. J. Sociol.*, **10** (1959), 137–147, provides a detailed discussion of managerial orientations to incentive schemes; while W. Brown, *Piecework Abandoned*, London: Heinemann, 1962, in the course of a managerial polemic against payment-by-results, underlines the central concern with managerial control and "prerogatives" which has prompted both the adoption and the replacement of such schemes.

101. Cunnison, *Wages and Work Allocation*, discusses the setting and character of responses to piecework which are informed by a "militant individualism". Other studies of individualistic responses to payment schemes include W. Goode and I. Fowler, "Incentive factors in a low-morale plant", *Am. Sociol. Rev.*, **14** (1949), 618–624; D. Gowler, "Socio-cultural influences on a wage payment system" in D. Robinson (Ed.), *Local Labour Markets and Wages Structures*, London: Gower Press, 1970, pp. 100–125; and Lupton, *On the Shop Floor*. Among the best accounts of collective responses to pay schemes and other management controls are L. Klein, *Multiproducts Ltd*, London: HMSO, 1964; S. Lerner *et al.*, *Workshop Wage Determination*, Oxford: Pergamon, 1969, appendix 2—"A case study of procedures used to raise P. by R. earnings"; J. Rosser and C. Barker, "A working class defeat: ENV", *Int. Socialism*, **31**, 1967–1968, 21–32; D.F. Roy, "Work satisfaction and social reward in quota achievement", *Am. Sociol. Rev.*, **18** (1953), 507–514, and "Efficiency and 'the fix' ", *Am. J. Sociol.*, **60** (1955), 255–266; and the study by Lupton. See also W.F. Whyte, *Money and Motivation*, New York: Harper and Row, 1955.

102. R.A. Peterson and M.J. Rath, "Structural determinants of piecework rates", *Indust. Relat.*, **4** (1964), 92–103, provides an outline of patterns of differential stringency and enforcement.

103. See in particular Roy, "Efficiency and 'the fix' "; and Klein, *Multiproducts Ltd*, and the discussion of "awareness contexts" in Glaser and Strauss, "Awareness contexts and social interaction". These same processes of low-level alliance and collusion in the subversion of management controls, and shifts in the character of subterfuge, confrontation and accommodation to match changing elite control strategies, are also documented in other literature on shop-floor administration: for examples see J. Bensman and I. Gerver, "Crime and punishment in the factory", *Am. Sociol. Rev.*, **28** (1963), 588–598; D.S. Pugh, "Role-activation conflict: study of industrial inspection", *Am. Sociol. Rev.*, **31** (1966), 835–842; and B.A. Turner, "Control systems: development and interaction", and T.K. Reeves, "Control of manufacture in a garment factory", in Woodward (Ed.), *Behaviour and Control*, pp. 59–84, 108–129. See also Goldner, "Division of Labour: Process and Power".

104. Klein, *Multiproducts Ltd*. Thus distinctive patterns of supervisory action are generated by the interplay of varied supervisory career commitments and administrative designs—compare the supervisors in the organizations discussed by Crozier, Dalton and Gouldner. See also C. Fletcher, "The man

in the middle: A reformulation of the thesis", *Sociol. Rev.*, **19** (1969), 341–354.

105. See the references listed in footnote 101.

106. See in particular the theoretical discussion by Burns, "Micropolitics".

107. See Roy, "Work satisfaction and social reward". Of course, other themes also serve to invest work routines with meaning and thus inform the character of work experience—see the discussions by D.F. Roy, "Banana time: job satisfaction and informal interaction", *Hum. Organiz.*, **18** (1960), 156–168; L. Street, "Game forms in the factory group", *Berkeley Publications in Society and Institutions*, **4** (1958), 44–55; and D. Marsden, "In the mill", in B. Jackson (Ed.), *Working Class Community*, London: Routledge and Kagen Paul, 1968, pp. 69–97.

108. Discussion of *occupational* bargaining strategies is not intended to prejudge the character of the effective bases of bargaining in the workplace, as these may variously involve workgroups, departmental or occupational collectivities or other patterns of alliance, but indicates the wider frames of reference within which such strategies are developed, recognized and justified.

     Analyses of bargaining strategies in the workplace must be situated within a more general consideration of the sociology of occupational associations, and especially trade unions—among students of the sociology of trade unions the following authors illuminate the relationships between bargaining strategies, forms of collective organization, and occupational milieux: H.A. Turner, *Trade Union Growth, Structure and Policy*, London: Allen and Unwin, 1962, esp. books III and IV, weaves into a comparison of "open" and "closed" union organizations a sophisticated discussion of occupational institutions, member–official relations, interunion relationships and union policy and growth; E. Hobsbawm, *Labouring Men*, London: Weidenfeld and Nicolson, 1964, esp. chs. 9–11, 16 and 17, provides a historically situated analysis of the development and character of craft and general unionism and associated shop-floor bargaining strategies; and R. Hyman, *The Workers Union*, Oxford: Clarendon Press, 1971, pp. 173–226, provides a review of themes and issues which is focused on the dynamics of organizing processes, membership demands, union control and policy formation.

109. See especially the work of Crozier, *Bureaucratic Phenomenon*; and Gouldner, *Industrial Bureaucracy* and *Wildcat Strike*, discussed in section 2. W.H. Scott *et al.*, *Technical Change and Industrial Relations*, Liverpool: Liverpool University Press, 1956, chs. 3 and 4; and Flanders, *Fawley Productivity Agreements*, chs. 3 and 4, also depict configurations of bargaining strategies among "shop-floor" workers which approximate to these patterns.

     In particular Flander's study, which traces the impact of a managerial strategy—"productivity bargaining"—designed to weaken workers controls over shop-floor conduct and strengthen managerial controls over manpower utilization, documents the more or less effective resistance of craft groups depending on their control over job-entry and recognized skills, and the broad acceptance by non-craft workers of the agreements, and their interpretation on the shop-floor, as negotiated by the crafts. For a more detailed discussion of this study see the important critical commentary by T. Topham, "New types of bargaining", in Blackburn and Cockburn (Eds), *The Incompatibles*, Harmondsworth: Penguin, pp. 133–159.

110. Compare the discussions by Hobsbawm, *Labouring Men*, ch. 17; N.W. Chamberlain, "Determinants of collective bargaining structures", in A. Weber (Ed.), *The Structure of Collective Bargaining*, New York: The Free Press, 1961, pp. 3–19; and H.M. Levinson, "Wage Determination under collective bargaining", in A. Flanders (Ed.), *Collective Bargaining*, Harmondsworth: Penguin, 1969, pp. 86–118.

111. Despite their programmatic claims for "technical determinism" students of fractional bargaining have provided useful analyses of such strategies. Thus J.W. Kuhn, in *Bargaining in Grievance Settlement*, New York: Columbia University Press, 1961, invokes technical determinants, but his discussion of workgroup strategies—as they evolve around "immediate parochial interests of workers and supervisors on the shop-floor", are informed by union and management politics, and are legitimated by appeals to custom and practice or by reference to the "run-around" over grievances—belies such a crude explanation. L. Sayles, in *Behaviour of Industrial Workgroups*, New York: Wiley, 1958, also focuses on technical determinants in his discussion of the impact of differential solidarity and "importance" on workgroup bargaining strategies—and relates "conservative", "strategic", "erratic" and "apathetic" bargaining *reputations* to such determinants—but he recognizes that (a) solidarity is influenced by manning arrangements and promotion pathways as well as by technical settings, and (b) that "the 'criticalness' of skill depends on intrinsic job characteristics as well as *fellow worker support*". J.E.T. Eldridge, *Industrial Disputes*, London: Routledge and Kegan Paul, 1968, ch. 1, provides a critical evaluation of these studies, while Lerner *et al.*, "Case study of procedures used to raise P. by R. earnings", provides a telling counter-example to the narrow occupational sectionalism usually imputed to workers by fractional bargaining theorists.

112. This again qualifies the "fractional bargaining" analysis which stresses the role of technical obstacles to interaction in retarding solidarity. The dynamics of organisation and demands among workers confronting such obstacles receives definitive treatment in H. Beynon, *Working for Ford*, London: Penguin, 1973.

113. W.H. Scott *et al.*, *Coal and Conflict*, Liverpool: Liverpool University Press, 1963, esp. chaps. 3 and 4, provide an empirical study of such processes in their analysis of the distinctive attitudes and bargaining strategies of various occupational groups in coal-mining. Thus high-status face-workers labour in conditions which provide numerous negotiable issues, and their homogeneity and solidarity as workgroups and "critical" place in production underpin aggressive bargaining strategies, to preserve their status and control over work routines; low-status occupations, with non-crucial worktasks and heterogeneous and changing memberships, adopt individualistic responses to

work pressures, which effectively perpetuate their subordinate positions. While these different bargaining stances reinforce established occupational positions Scott *et al.*, also note the manner in which new tactics and aspirations can impinge to alter those positions. See Silverman's discussion in *Theory of Organizations*, ch. 9.

114. Crozier, *Bureaucratic Phenomenon*, documents a specific case of the construction of valued competences in his discussion of the maintenance engineers (see section 2). More generally Turner, *Trade Union Growth*, has commented on the social processes whereby "a 'skill' may be quite artificially created, by workers gradual imposition of labour supply controls on a formerly 'unskilled' occupation" (p. 114 and his example of Strippers and Grinders on p. 164). An example of the bargaining processes surrounding and informing the "deskilling" of an occupational task is discussed, within a socio-technical framework, by P.J. Fensham and D. Hooper, *The Dynamics of a Changing Technology*, London: Tavistock, 1964, especially chs. 6 and 8: they compare *weavers*, who, faced with increased pace, routine monitoring work and isolation on automated looms (seen as "degradation of the weavers role"), but having limited coherence as an interest group, compromised with managerial demands for "responsible" workmanship in return for financial "compensations", while controlling output levels; and *overlookers*, who, as a more cohesive group, succeeded in maintaining their skilled status when confronted with similar management initiatives.

These examples of the social construction and reconstruction of skills suggest that the meanings given to "skill", "responsibility", "competence" and so on, cannot be treated as given and uniform but rather as negotiable and variable across different organizational locales.

115. The emergence of new demands and strategies is traced in some detail, in relation to workers in the motor industry, by Turner *et al.* in *Labour Relations in the Motor Industry*. They describe the interplay between developing occupational institutions on the shop-floor and the application of technical and administrative managerial controls, and the importance of the evolution of shop-steward organizations into elaborate semi-autonomous factory and combine committees bargaining over wage-structure changes and anomalies, in the generation of new shop-floor aspirations and strategies involving the challenging of entrenched "managerial prerogatives" (see esp. pp. 154–159 and 192–223). However these authors (a) give little systematic attention to the sources of bargaining strength and patterns of comparisons underpinning these institutional developments, and (b) tend to *dismiss* talk about "the tensions of the track" as "part of the preparatory ritual of workplace bargaining" without considering its meaning for actors in such bargaining, and in the formation of occupational and class identities.

Sensitivity to the emergence of new bargaining strategies and demands in management–worker conflict has led students of occupational bargaining to analyse the social bases of cross-cutting and changing, patterns of alliance, solidarity and schism among occupational groups [see, especially, R.K.

Brown *et al.*, "The contours of solidarity: Social stratification and industrial relations in shipbuilding", *Br. J. Indust. Relat.*, **10** (1972), 12–41; Brown and Brannen, "Shipbuilding workers"; and Duncan, "Conflict and co-operation among trawlermen"], and to pay increasing attention to the meanings given particular bargaining strategies and sanctions by participants [see, for example, W. Brown, "A consideration of 'Custom and Practice' ", *Br. J. Indust. Relat.*, **10** (1972), 42–61; Eldridge, *Industrial Disputes*, London: Routledge and Kegan Paul; T. Lane and K. Roberts, *Strike at Pilkingtons*, London: Collins-Fontana, 1971; and L. Taylor and P. Walton, "Sabotage: motives and meanings", in S. Cohen (Ed.), *Images of Deviance*, Harmondsworth: Penguin, 1971, 219–245]. A useful discussion of the rationality of workers' strategies is found in R. Hyman, *Strikes*, London: Fontana, 1972.

116. Blauner, *Alienation and Freedom*, esp. pp. 159–165, recognizes some of the ambiguities surrounding the "occupational identity" of process production workers, but does not consider the context of power and perspectives within which those ambiguities are resolved. Other studies of "technical change to automated production", in their preoccupations with the technical setting, also fail to consider the power contexts of such changes—for example, F.C. Mann and L.R. Hoffman, *Automation and the Worker*, New York: Holt, 1960, whose study suggests that "responsibility" conceptions find only qualified acceptance among workers, fail to explore the implications of managerial siting, recruitment and selection policies which ensured that the automated plant—the "after" in their "before–after" comparison—became "non-union". On the character of workers definitions of, and responses to, process technology see also M.A. Smith, "Process technology and powerlessness", *Br. J. Sociol.*, **19** (1968), 76–88.

117. See Flanders *Fawley Productivity Agreements*; and Goldthorpe *et al.*, *Affluent Worker: Industrial*. The most adequate and comprehensive overview of the sociological literature on technical change, from within a broadly processual perspective, is A. Touraine *et al.*, *Workers' Attitudes to Technical Change*, Paris: OECD, 1965. See also R.K. Brown, "Technology, technical change and automation", in S.R. Parker *et al.*, *The Sociology of Industry*, London: Allen and Unwin, 1967, pp. 113–125.

118. Implications of this point of view, and in particular, the treatment of the firm as a power centre which confronts and may control its 'environment', are sharply outlined by A. Sales in "The Firm and the Control of its Environment", *International Studies of Management and Organization*, vol. 2 no. 3, Fall 1972, pp. 230–256.

RICHARD HYMAN and BOB FRYER

TRADE UNIONS—sociology and political economy

Richard Hyman *is at present Lecturer in Industrial Relations at the University of Warwick and an Associate Fellow in the Social Science Research Council's Industrial Relations Research Unit. He completed his B.A. in Politics, Philosophy and Economics at Balliol College Oxford, and his Doctor of Philosophy at Nuffield College. His present research interests include ideological influences in industrial relations, and the historical development of union bureaucracy. Among his most recent publications are* The Workers' Union (*1971*); Marxism and the Sociology of Trade Unionism (*1971*); Disputes Procedure in Action (*1972*); Strikes (*1972*) *as well as several articles in the field of industrial sociology.*

Robert Fryer *is a graduate of Oxford and Cambridge and is at present a Lecturer in Sociology at the University of Warwick. His current research activities are focused on an organizational analysis of the National Union of Public Employees and the construction of the job of the Trade Union Officer, as well as on ideology and the State in industrial relations. He has published in the fields of organizational analysis, redundancy, sociology of law and values in industrial relations. His most recent work includes* Redundancy and Paternalist Capitalism (*with R. Martin*) *and* Rolls Royce and the White Collar Workers (*with D. Wedderburn*).

A trade union, wrote the Webbs in their classic *History of Trade Unionism*, "is a continuous association of wage-earners for the purpose of improving the conditions of their working lives".[1] Since they provided this much quoted definition, union organization has extended beyond wage-earners narrowly defined to a wide range of salaried occupations. The Webbs' specification of union functions is also open to challenge; as will be seen, this has been and remains the focus of considerable controversy. Nevertheless, their identification in terms of "continuous association" has never been seriously questioned, and places the trade union firmly within the analytical field of the student of organizations.

This brief introduction is intended merely to provide an outline of the coverage, structure and government of British trade unionism; greater detail is readily accessible in the existing literature on industrial relations.[2] Since our principal concern is with problems of organizational sociology, rather than the detail of industrial relations, many of the points touched on here will not be developed further. Instead, the remainder of the chapter will focus mainly on three related areas: the theoretical presuppositions underlying analysis of trade unionism and industrial relations; the processes through which union goals are defined;

and the dynamics of power and control in trade unions' internal and external relations.

Government statistics show that at the end of 1970 there were an estimated 481 unions in the United Kingdom, with a combined membership of 11 million.[3] In size and importance their range is enormous: over 75 per cent of total membership is shared by 23 unions with over 100 000 members; at the other extreme, 256 unions (over half the total number) contain together less than 1 per cent of total membership. The distribution is shown in table 1.[4]

Table 1   Unions and membership in Britain at 31 December 1970

Number of members		Number of unions	Total member-ship	Percentage of	
				Total number of all unions	Total member-ship of all unions
Under 100		90	4 000	18.7	0.0
100 and under	500	116	29 000	24.1	0.3
500 and under	1 000	50	35 000	10.4	0.3
1 000 and under	2 500	59	99 000	12.3	0.9
2 500 and under	5 000	50	172 000	10.4	1.6
5 000 and under	10 000	30	199 000	6.2	1.8
10 000 and under	15 000	13	155 000	2.7	1.4
15 000 and under	25 000	21	403 000	4.4	3.7
25 000 and under	50 000	13	452 000	2.7	4.1
50 000 and under	100 000	16	1 111 000	3.3	10.1
100 000 and under	250 000	14	2 188 000	2.9	19.9
250 000 and more		9	6 155 000	1.9	55.9
Totals		481	11 000 000	100.0	100.0

Source: *Department of Employment Gazette*, November 1971.

Almost all the major organizations (though only a minority of the smaller bodies) are affiliated to the Trades Union Congress (TUC), which in 1970 contained 142 unions with a total membership of 10 million.[5] As table 2 shows, the number of unions in Britain has been declining for many years, even when total membership has been increasing—mainly as a result of amalgamations. TUC affiliations have reflected the same trends.

Aggregate union membership in 1970 represented some 47 per cent of a total labour force of 23.4 million. As is shown by table 2, this is the highest level of

Table 2 Unions, union membership and density in the United Kingdom: selected years 1892–1970

Year	Number of trade unions	Total union membership ('000)	Labour force ('000)	Membership density (%)
1892	1 233	1 576	14 126	11.2
1901	1 322	2 025	16 101	12.6
1911	1 290	3 139	17 762	17.7
1913	1 269	4 135	17 920	23.1
1917	1 241	5 499	18 234	30.2
1920	1 384	8 348	18 469	45.2
1923	1 192	5 429	17 965	30.2
1933	1 081	4 392	19 422	22.6
1938	1 024	6 053	19 829	30.5
1945	781	7 875	20 400	45.2
1948	749	9 362	20 732	45.2
1950	732	9 289	21 055	44.1
1952	723	9 588	21 252	45.1
1954	711	9 566	21 658	44.2
1956	685	9 778	22 180	44.1
1958	675	9 639	22 290	43.2
1960	664	9 835	22 817	43.1
1962	626	9 887	23 432	42.2
1964	598	10 079	23 706	42.5
1966	574	10 111	24 065	42.0
1968	534	10 036	23 667	42.4
1970	481	11 000	23 446	46.9

Source: Bain and Price, *Br. J. Indust. Relat.* (Nov 1972); and Department of Employment, *British Labour Statistics*, HMSO, 1971.

organization—or "density"—ever attained in Britain.[6] The proportion is high by comparison with most Western nations, though international experience reveals great variation: in Sweden roughly 75 per cent of the labour force is unionized, in the United States only 25 per cent. In part the comparatively wide coverage of British unionism reflects its deep historical roots. Organization among skilled artisans existed as early as the eighteenth century, surviving and increasing despite severe legal repression.[7] From the 1850s can be traced the consolidation of the craft societies into impressive national associations, and the emergence of stable organization among workers in such large-scale industries as coal-mining, cotton and iron and steel. The turn of the century saw a further wave of unionization, covering in particular the bulk of manufacturing industry. The extension of organization to white-collar workers, particularly in the public sector, is largely the achievement of the present century.

To a large extent, British trade unionism had achieved its current pattern of organization by 1920, when total membership reached 8.3 million, or 45 per cent of the labour force. Mass unemployment between the wars caused severe losses, yet density never fell as low as 20 per cent. Since the Second World War these losses have been more than recovered, though recent progress has been relatively slow. One reason for this is the changing structure of the labour force: a decline in employment in industries and occupations which have been traditionally strongly organized (such as coal-mining, cotton textiles, docks and railways); and growth in service industries and white-collar occupations which have always been more weakly unionized.

The statistics cited so far represent the *overall* density of union organization; this does not indicate the considerable variations that exist between different sections of the working class. Taking male manual workers only, 60 per cent are trade union members. In some industries, such as mining, the proportion is virtually 100 per cent. On the other hand, unionization is below average among women, in many white-collar occupations, and in a number of industries characterized by numerous small employers. Where organization is strong an important support is often provided by the "closed shop"—an obligation on all workers in a factory or department to hold a union card and pay their subscriptions regularly. Such a system covers about half the trade unionists in the country, usually being enforced "unofficially" by workers at shop-floor level; managements comply rather than provoking a possible strike by employing non-unionists.

Table 3   The largest British trade unions: 1971 membership ('000)

Transport and General Workers' Union	1 723
Amalgamated Union of Engineering Workers	1 386
General and Municipal Workers' Union	842
National and Local Government Officers' Association	464
Electrical Electronic Telecommunication and Plumbing Union	420
National Union of Public Employees	397
Union of Shop, Distributive and Allied Workers	319
National Union of Teachers	277
National Union of Mineworkers	276
Union of Construction, Allied Trades and Technicians	260
Association of Scientific, Technical and Managerial Staffs	250

Source: Trades Union Congress *Report*, 1972.

The structure of British unionism bears the imprint of its history: a protracted and wholly unplanned process of development. No single principle of organization underlies the movement—as is clear from a glance at a list of the largest unions (see table 3). A simplified account of union structure would point, first, to the craft unions: associations of skilled artisans, such as printers or engineering mechanics. Second, one can cite industrial unions, as in coal, steel or the railways. Thirdly, there are the general unions, organizing regardless of skill or industry. But such a simple model requires considerable qualification.[8] There are no pure industrial unions in Britain, in the sense of organizations which recruit within only one industry and have exclusive jurisdiction over every grade of labour. The nearest approximation is the Mineworkers; but its monopoly does not extend to clerical or supervisory grades. There are also very few pure craft unions; most bodies once composed exclusively of apprenticed craftsmen have long since opened their ranks to other grades of labour. An obvious example is the Engineers, which for half a century has admitted all grades of male labour, and for thirty years women also; through recent amalgamations it has also extended its coverage to foundry workers, constructional engineers, and technicians. As for the general unions, their main function has been to fill the numerous gaps left by the earlier structure of trade unionism; though their coverage does overlap considerably with that of other bodies, in the main they have avoided recruiting where another organization was already well established.

The growth of white-collar unionism has further complicated the picture. Though some salaried employees are members of predominantly manual unions, the larger number are separately organized. White-collar associations are the most rapidly growing section of the movement; since the recent affiliation of the Local Government Officers and the Teachers, most of the larger white-collar unions are now attached to the TUC.

The complexity of British union structure is most clearly seen in engineering, where some 20 unions share roughly 2 million members (just over half the industry's labour force). These may be divided into four broad categories. First, the Engineers—a multi-occupational union within engineering, where it has the bulk of its membership (the remainder consisting mainly of maintenance workers in other industries). Second, the two large general unions: the Transport and General, which since its amalgamation with the National Union of Vehicle Builders has some 300 000 of its membership in engineering; and the General and Municipal. Thirdly, the white-collar unions: notably the Scientific, Technical and Managerial Staffs and the Association of Professional, Executive, Clerical and Computer Staffs; in addition there are white-collar sections in the Transport and General and the Engineers. Most members of the latter derive from the former Draughtsmen's and Allied Technicians' Association. Finally, there are a number of sectional organizations with members in specific trades or crafts: for example the Metal Mechanics, the Sheet Metal Workers, and—the largest in this category— the Electricians, which has a majority of its members outside engineering.[9]

On occasion, this structure can create a complex situation at company level; thus at one time, twenty-two unions were recognized for manual workers at Ford's Dagenham factory. But in most engineering factories, at most four or five manual unions would have members, most workers belonging to only one or two of these. A recent study in the motor industry showed that almost 90 per cent of manual workers belonged to one of the three leading unions; this number has since been reduced by amalgamation to two.[10]

In the popular press, the structure of numerous competing unions is seen as a cause of recurrent conflict. But in practice, inter-union conflict is rare; at shop-floor level it is usually thought more important that a worker should belong to *some* union than that he should be a member of one specific organization. There are however two significant consequences of multi-unionism. First, fear of competition may oblige union officials to pay more attention to their members' wishes than would otherwise be the case. And second, the scope for autonomous shop-floor activity is increased. For where, as normally happens, the shop stewards of different unions in the same factory act jointly, control from above by the full-time officials of the various unions is very difficult. This point is of some relevance for the question of control by union leadership, which will receive detailed attention below.

If the structure of British trade unionism is complex, so is its system of internal government, for no two unions have identical institutional arrangements. Some generalizations are however possible. Normally, the basic unit of organization is the branch. In unions of an industrial or general character, this normally comprises all members in a single place of work; but in those with a craft background, branches are more often geographically based—each covering the town or part of town in which its members live, irrespective of where they work. In most unions the branch is responsible for a considerable amount of routine administration, normally carried out by elected lay officers. Regular meetings are held, and can take decisions relating to union affairs or other issues of concern to the members; but attendance is often poor (as many as 10 per cent is unusual), and few union branches genuinely function as instruments of intra-union democracy. Voting for representatives at higher levels of union government often takes place in the branches; here again, membership participation is usually very low, and considerable scope may exist for manipulation of ballots.

At national level, union policy is normally determined by a delegate conference —usually elected by the branches, and meeting every one or two years. Again, there is considerable variation in the amount of real power and initiative which the conference can exercise. In most unions there is too little time, and there are too many delegates (in many cases, several hundred), for effective control from below; conference can then be largely manipulated by the "platform" or leading officials. This is not universally true, however; in the Engineers, for example, the conference is smaller and meets for a longer period than in most unions, and it functions as a very important body.

All unions have in addition at national level an elected executive committee or council, responsible for the central administration of the union, and usually deciding policy in the period between conferences. The composition of such committees is another factor which varies between unions: in the Engineers, the seven members become full-time officials of the union during their period of office; in the Transport and General, the 40-man committee is composed entirely of lay members. (This is at first sight a highly democratic system; but the committee can meet only rarely, and considerable policy-making power is therefore held by the national full-time officials.)

All main unions have a sizeable staff of full-time officers. The most important of these is usually the General Secretary (in a few unions, such as the Engineers, the President is more important); he is normally elected by the membership as a whole, or at least by those who bother to vote. Lower grades of officials are also elected by the members in some unions, but in others they are appointed to their positions by the executive. Unions with a craft background are often particularly committed to the electoral system: it is common for all officers to be elected, and to have to stand for re-election every few years (though it is rare for sitting officials to be defeated). In the Transport and General, by contrast, the General Secretary is the only elected official, and once chosen does not have to face re-election.[11]

The extremes of union size and the bewildering variety of structure and organizational form are eloquent testimony to the *complexity* of British unionism. Yet another complicating factor is the range of historical experience of the movement. As Turner has argued,[12]

> the character of organizations, like that of people, is very much a product of their ancestry and the circumstances of their early growth. . . . British trade unions, more than those of most countries perhaps, are historical deposits and repositories of history and anyone with close experience of trade unionism will be aware of the extent to which every union possesses a personality of its own.

This does not render generalization impossible, any more than does the uniqueness of each human personality. But it does make valid generalization far more difficult than the outsider is liable to imagine. Since our intention in what follows is primarily to develop a general analysis, the unstated qualification will often be that we are seeking to highlight certain tendencies manifest in trade union activity rather than offering a precise description applicable to every organization.

By the same token, our analysis of the sociology of British trade unionism—which we regard as in many respects of far wider relevance—would inevitably require modification before application in other national settings. For example, union administration in the United States is far more "professionalized" than in Britain: the ratio of full-time officials to members is much higher, and they tend to receive "managerial" salaries. British unions rely heavily on the administrative work of "lay" officers (who may receive a small financial commission), while the salaries of first-line full-time officials are rarely substantially above the earnings of the members they represent. Differences of this kind—which may be related to contrasting cultural traditions and social and political institutions—are inevitably reflected in the internal and external functioning of trade unions in each country.[13]

Trade Unions and organization theory

We began by indicating that trade unions match the conventional definition of organizations. The student might therefore expect valuable theoretical insights into the dynamics of trade unionism from the burgeoning literature on "organization theory". He would be disappointed. For what is remarkable about the bulk of writing in this *genre*, despite the broad definitions usually offered for the concept of organization, is its narrow preoccupation with the problems of a specific social grouping within a specific type of organization. In brief, the predominant orientation of most "organization theorists" is towards problems of administration and control within economic enterprises; or by extension, such organizations as hospitals or government departments which appear to generate analogous managerial concerns. What is normally taken for granted is that "organizational goals" are more or less unproblematically defined, usually by those in supreme hierarchical positions; that organizational "members" are employed full-time for the purpose of goal-attainment; and that the principal areas of analytical interest are the "functions" and "dysfunctions" of particular patterns of organizational structure, and the problems associated with the "recalcitrance of the tools of action".[14] Most writers, in other words, are concerned principally with the managerial tasks of achieving the smooth, continuous and efficient cooperation of all employees in pursuit of the official objectives of the organization; ensuring the obedience of subordinates to those in positions of authority; and motivating maximum performance.

This perspective is not readily applicable to trade unions. Perhaps wisely, they are therefore ignored altogether by most exponents of organization theory. Others refer to the trade union only as a problem for managements. Thus March and Simon have one reference to it, as "an extraorganizational group".[15] Thompson discusses unionism briefly in a chapter entitled "the variable human".[16] One of the few writers to attempt to *analyse* trade unions within the framework of organization theory is Etzioni;[17] and his main achievement is to demonstrate, unintentionally, the limitations of this approach.

For many aspects of union organization and activity require analysis in terms quite distinct from those appropriate to the management of economic enterprises. The most obvious is their formal democratic character. The rationale of a union is that it pursues the interests of its members and is in the last resort controlled by them. While the full-time officials (and any lay executive officers) who form its leadership may possess specific authority over the rank and file, this is itself constitutionally derived from the members themselves, who can assert their will through such processes as conferences and elections. Union leaders may even, in their humbler moments, describe themselves as mere servants of the membership. Thus trade union structure is not the comparatively simple hierarchy of most organizations: it involves a *two-way* process of control. Of course the actual practice of a union may diverge from the democratic ideal—the nature and limits of this divergence form an important part of our subsequent discussion—but no union can escape the profound influence of its democratic rationale.

For this reason it is wholly inadequate to analyse trade unionism, as does Etzioni, solely in terms of the "compliance of lower participants".[18] For this is to focus attention exclusively on the problem of control from above: to adopt the perspective of a union leader seeking to manipulate his membership. Not surprisingly, Etzioni's abstracted discussion of "lower participants" fails even to hint at the most obvious factor differentiating the member's relationship to his union from that between patient and hospital or worker and company.

One significant attempt to take account of the democratic character of trade

unionism is Blau and Scott's typology based on the concept of "prime beneficiary".[19] They class trade unions as "mutual-benefit associations" on the grounds
that their primary purpose is to serve the interests of their members, rather than
those of their leaders or the employers with whom they deal (or, one might add,
some hypothetical "public interest").[20] Yet the principal focus of Blau and Scott,
like Etzioni and the generality of organization theorists, is on hierarchical organizations; their discussion of "mutual-benefit associations" is brief and, in our view,
scarcely integrated into their broader analytical framework. This might perhaps
be taken as an indication of the impossibility of constructing a distinctive discipline
of organization theory which is both comprehensive and at the same time
integrated.

A second important characteristic of trade unions is the ambiguity which
surrounds their goals. The assumption that "organizational goals" can be specified
simply, questionable in any organizational setting, is particularly unrealistic in the
case of trade unions. The question "what are trade unions for?" is regularly posed
because the answer is genuinely uncertain. In part this reflects our previous point:
insofar as unions are democratic, their goals are shaped by their members in a
manner which may change over time and vary from union to union. To return to
the Webbs' definition of union purposes, quoted at the beginning of this chapter:
in their first edition of 1894 they referred narrowly to the aim of "improving the
conditions of their [members'] employment". The broader definition offered a
quarter of a century later reflected the heightened aspirations of trade unionists
themselves, as well as a shift in the Webbs' own attitudes. The variety of trade
union objectives is well illustrated in Hoxie's famous classification of "functional
types", the most important being "business", "uplift" and "ideological" unionism.[21]
The first sought merely to influence the terms of the employment relationship; the
second aimed also to foster members' social welfare and status; the third strove to
transform society.[22] Each conception of union function has its fervent proponents;
and the debate on this issue (though mediated by powerful structural influences)
helps shape the actual character of specific unions. The problematics of trade union
goals will be considered in more detail later.

The final peculiarity of trade unions is that they may be termed *secondary*
organizations: their existence and activity presuppose the existence of economic
institutions employing wage-labour. This in turn entails a form of social and
economic organization which is historically specific, even though its existence is
often regarded as timeless and inevitable. Its characteristic is a radical division
between those subject to the insecurity, subordination and exploitation inherent
in the employment relationship, and those for whom labour is merely a cost of
production and a resource to be manipulated.

It follows from the secondary nature of unionism that a union's temporal and
geographical location is derived almost wholly from the organizations which
employ its members: only a fraction of union organization and activity is represented by full-time officials based on a union office (and even *their* activities are
largely oriented towards employers). The trade union lacks the physical facticity
of the factory or hospital or prison. What then does it mean to say that "the union"

adopts a particular policy or engages in a particular action? Organizations, it is often emphasized, do not act. The danger of reification cannot be evaded simply by explaining such references as implying that union members adopt policies or engage in actions *in their role of trade unionists*; for this role is itself imprecise. A shop steward is a union representative, but at the same time an employee of his company; yet his activities cannot be neatly allocated to each role in turn. The ordinary worker acts unambiguously in his role as union member only when (and if) he attends union meetings, usually at a time and place detached from his employment. But if, when at work, he and his mates stage a spontaneous strike in protest against unsafe working conditions, are they performing a trade union role? On the answer to such questions have hung the judgments of so weighty a political institution as the National Industrial Relations Court. Yet whether a man's relations with his employer and his fellow workers are to be regarded as "union activities" must depend largely on his own consciousness of these relations, and this is rarely articulated in a precise manner; hence the answer to such questions is to an important degree subjective and even arbitrary. This necessarily creates problems for sociological analysis.

It may be helpful to summarize our arguments so far—and anticipate some of those that are to follow—by specifying concisely some of the similarities and differences between trade unions and other forms of social organization. Certain similarities are almost defining characteristics of organization: unions are social units which have been purposefully created; they exhibit continuity despite changes in membership and officials; and they possess a formally defined structure of decision-making and administration. Two other features of trade unions are empirically to be found in virtually every type of organization (though their implications are normally very different). First, those in positions of leadership face problems of internal and external administration and control which parallel those confronting other types of leaders, managers or officials. (Hence *they* at least may find some value and relevance in "organization theory".) Second, the members of a union may experience it in certain situations as an oppressive entity which threatens or constrains them. As Gramsci put it:

> The workers feel that the complex of "their" organization, the trade union, has become such an enormous apparatus that it now obeys laws internal to its structure and its complicated functions, but foreign to the masses. . . . These *de facto* conditions irritate the workers, but as individuals they are powerless to change them.[23]

We have already stressed many of the differences between trade unions and such organizations as factories which are commonly the paradigm for organizational analysis. They have only a limited number of full-time employees. Their "management" exhibits little professionalization and specialization (hence such problems as "staff" and "line" relationships are virtually non-existent). The processes of "goal-attainment", or indeed unambiguously "trade union" activities of any sort, occupy the majority of their members only intermittently. The problems of identifying "organizational goals", as we shall see, are particularly acute. Some of these characteristics trade unions share with other organizations:

hospitals and prisons, religious and educational institutions, political parties. But the combination of these factors makes unions virtually unique. Moreover: while the rank and file and lower-level officials of trade unions—like "lower participants" in organizations of every kind—adopt a variety of strategies to achieve a measure of autonomy and control, such strategies acquire a special status from the democratic rationale of unionism. For while the counter-authoritarian processes devised by prison inmates or mental patients, for example, are essentially *deviant*, membership control in trade unions has the vital advantage of *legitimacy*. (Conversely, where trade unionists feel they lack control over "their" organization, the situation holds a special poignancy and gives rise to special problems, both practical and theoretical.)

One final peculiarity of trade unions requires special emphasis. Because of their secondary nature—the fact that they represent workers' response to the deprivations inherent in their role as employees within a capitalist economy—opposition and conflict cannot be divorced from their existence and activity. They constitute a constant challenge to the "rights of capital": first, to hire labour in the cheapest market; second, to deploy, manage and control labour irrespective of workers' own wishes and aspirations. Individually, few workers have the power to assert their interests against those of the employer. Collectively, they can exert greater influence.

Trade unions—workers' collective organizations—are thus first and foremost a source and medium of power: and processes of power are central to their internal and external relations. This fact must recur throughout our analysis. The notions of power, control and dependence which are essential for any proper understanding of trade unionism are of course the subject of intense theoretical controversy. While this is not the place to pursue at length the conceptual debate over the nature and meaning of power, we must state explicitly how we propose to employ the concept. First, we would emphasize that any definition which focuses on a distinction between "power" and "authority" seems to us of secondary importance. Second, we are unimpressed by attempts to interpret power relations as relationships of exchange: for the latter presuppose the *prior* existence of rules, rates and currency of exchange, and the determination of this prior framework is itself typically the outcome of power relations. In our view the critical focus of any analysis of power must be *the differential distribution of control over and access to resources and sanctions, both material and ideological.* This methodological presupposition, which distinguishes us from most writers on the sociology of organizations, should be evident in much of our argument.

A power relationship between individuals or groups with competing or opposing goals and interests necessarily generates conflict, overt or latent. Conflict in industry—the outcome of the pursuit by employers and workers of incompatible demands and objectives—can assume a wide variety of forms.

> Its means of expression are as unlimited as the ingenuity of man. The strike is the most common and most visible expression. But conflict with the employer may also take the form of peaceful bargaining and grievance handling, of boycotts, of political action, of restriction of output, of sabotage, of absenteeism, or of personnel turnover.

Several of these forms, such as sabotage, restriction of output, absenteeism, and turn-over, may take place on an individual as well as on an organized basis and constitute alternatives to collective action. Even the strike is of many varieties. It may involve all the workers or only key men. It may take the form of refusal to work overtime or to perform a certain process. It may even involve such rigid adherence to the rules that output is stifled.[24]

Only those forms of conflict which assume an organized form are normally associated with trade unionism, at least when it has achieved any strength and viability. Moreover, different unions may prefer different methods—pure industrial action to political involvement, peaceful bargaining to militancy: such differences underlie in part the typologies produced by such writers as Hoxie.[25] As is shown in a later section, there exist pressures which often induce trade union officials to moderate and contain the conflictual aspects of their activity. Nevertheless, the conflict inherent in industrial relations can never be wholly suppressed.

Because of the centrality of power and conflict to their functions and activities, there is only limited value—far less, probably, than in the case of any other kind of organization—in studying trade unions simply as "formal organizations" wrenched from their social context. To understand trade unions it is essential to analyse the environing institutions of power with which they interact: an adequate analysis of trade unions and trade unionism must also be, in large measure, an analysis of the political economy within which they operate. For the same reason, theories of trade unions as organizations are intimately related to broader theories of industry and society: thus we shall need to examine the dominant theoretical perspectives on both in some detail. First, however, we will summarize very briefly some of the determinants of the power which unions can exercise and that which is deployed against them.

The starting point for any realistic analysis must be the massive power imbalance between capital and labour. This derives from the very fact that the productive system is, in the main, the private property of a tiny minority of the population, and that profit is its basic dynamic. Confronting this concentrated economic power, the great majority who depend on their own labour for a living are at an inevitable disadvantage.[26] Marshall's classic argument remains valid: "labour is often sold under special disadvantages, arising from the closely connected group of facts that labour power is 'perishable', that the sellers of it are commonly poor and have no reserve fund, and that they cannot easily withhold it from the market".[27] Put simply, the employer can normally survive without labour for longer than the worker can survive without employment. How overwhelming this purely economic predominance may be depends in part on the state of the labour and product markets. A single employer (or tightly knit group of employers) in an isolated community may be able to exercise almost feudal power. In periods of heavy unemployment, workers' ability to influence their terms and conditions of employment even by collective action may be minimal. By contrast, in a context of relatively full employment and a variety of alternative job opportunities, the imbalance may be considerably reduced. Whatever the economic climate, more-over, workers with scarce technical skills or professional qualifications will be in a stronger position than those lacking such assets. The state of the market for the employer's products or services may affect the balance of power by raising or reducing the cost to him of a withdrawal of labour or other forms of conflict. Yet despite all these qualifications, the economic imbalance remains real and pervasive. In the last resort, the employer can threaten to shut up shop and take his capital elsewhere; but while the individual employee may move home and family to a different labour market, a labour force collectively has no such option.

Moreover, this economic predominance is doubly reinforced. First, capital normally has privileged access to the coercive sanctions of the state. In the everyday relationship between employer and worker, the law underwrites a contract which authorizes the former to give orders and obliges the latter to obey. In less routine circumstances, where the collective power of labour seriously threatens employer interests, governments typically intervene to restore the normal imbalance. This is a point to which we return in more detail. Second, unequal economic and political power gives capital a crucial influence over processes of *ideological* formation: legitimating its own predominance and inhibiting effective challenge on the part of labour.

The countervailing power of union organization, at its most successful, can only partially redress this imbalance. The main determinants of union power are of two types: objective and subjective. Of the former, the most significant are the strength or density of organization among the potential membership, and the strategic importance of the workers covered. The importance of intensive organization is obvious: where a significant proportion of the relevant employee group are outside the union and unlikely to follow its policies and instructions, or where there exists an alternative labour force of non-unionists, the ability to exert effective pressure on the employer is considerably reduced.[28] Strategic importance increases the impact of any forms of overt conflict in which union members engage. Thus a group of assembly-line workers may be able to disrupt an integrated production process; or newspaper printers may be able to cause immediate and substantial damage to the employer because of the perishable nature of their product. Such groups as dockers or electricity supply workers, whose work is vital to the entire economy, may have the power to oblige the government to intervene in any dispute to achieve terms acceptable to them.

While such objective factors as intensive organization and strategic importance are among the preconditions of powerful unionism, power also depends on the manner in which workers perceive their situation and interests, and the solidarity and determination with which they pursue their objectives. Workers who perceive no major conflict of interests with their employers are unlikely to organize effectively. Those who define their interests primarily in narrow sectional terms may succeed in winning improvements in relation to other groups; but the consequence may be division and disunity at a broader collective level, and hence a weakening of workers' power as against that of their employers.[29] In practice, there are powerful ideological pressures inducing workers to conceive their interests, on the one hand in limited and parochial terms, on the other as merely part of some all-embracing "national interest"; consciousness on the part of wage-

and salary-earners that they have substantial common interests *as employees* is systematically inhibited. The solidarity[30] and resolve with which workers engage in open industrial conflict—particularly if they possess significant strategic strength—is also commonly exposed to powerful ideological onslaught. A notable example was provided during the electricity workers' dispute of 1971: the disruptive potential demonstrated by even limited industrial action provoked so hostile an ideological reaction by politicians and the media that the Electrical Union ended the dispute with what at the time appeared minimal gains.[31]

Unionism and industrial relations: the dominant perspectives

Although the various versions of "organization theory" have seldom been seriously applied to the study of trade unions, other theoretical frames of reference commonly underlie their analysis. A feature of most of these perspectives is their semi-articulated and only partially developed nature. Partly in consequence, there might appear to exist a considerable variety of approaches; but this variety is largely superficial. For it is possible to discern an orthodoxy of view which consists, more or less clearly, of an amalgam of pragmatism, systems theory and the unitary and pluralistic frames of reference. Combinations of these perspectives are applied not only to the internal dynamics of trade unions but also to their external relations, particularly with employers. This latter aspect of the dominant analytical approaches . is often of particular significance.

It is true that everyday discussion of industrial relations and trade unionism is commonly predicated on a *denial* of any explicit theoretical orientation. Many commentators insist that their concern is only with immediate practical problems: they eschew as "academic" and irrelevant any analysis not directly related to the formulation of policy decisions. Politicians, managers and trade union officials, being men of action, may be particularly ready to dismiss theory as mere idle speculation.

Yet sociologists are well aware that, rather than excluding theoretical presuppositions, pragmatism merely drives these underground; and they are all the more potent for being unrecognized and thus uncriticized. Thus the specification of the main problems of trade unionism and industrial relations may seem at first sight a simple matter. Common sense informs the pragmatist that these centre around the issue of wage drift, the goal of more efficient labour utilization, the need to curb unofficial strikes, or the aim of exercising greater control over shop stewards; and that it is primarily a technical question to provide "fair" and "effective" solutions. But as one sociologist has observed, a problem "consists not only of a fixed and given condition but the perception and definition by certain people that this condition poses a threat which is against their interests and that something should be done about it".[32] And although industrial relationships constitute an area of *conflicting* interests and perspectives, of power competition and ideological controversy, pragmatism adopts a remarkably restricted and one-sided conception of industrial relations problems. Given the aim of influencing "practical policy", it follows naturally that the pragmatist should turn to those in positions of control (in management, government, or trade union leadership) for his definitions both of the problems and of the channels available for their resolution. The *workers'* problems, where these differ (as they often do), necessarily fall outside the pragmatist's terms of reference.[33]

We wish to argue that the one-sided perspectives of pragmatism continue to dominate the analysis of trade unionism and industrial relations. However, pragmatism alone lacks academic respectability; and recent years have witnessed a search for a more articulated theoretical frame of reference which would underwrite the status of industrial relations as an academic discipline. In common with many other areas of social science enquiry, industrial relations analysis has drawn increasingly upon systems theory and, to a lesser extent, the related perspectives of functionalism. Yet one consequence has been to incorporate, with much linguistic obfuscation, many of the assumptions which underlie the common sense approach to industrial relations. This may indeed be one reason why the concept of an industrial relations system, elaborated by Dunlop in the 1950s, should have become so widely adopted.

The argument that systems theory has close affinities with pragmatism may seem at first sight surprising. While pragmatism is problem-centred, systems theory is proclaimed for its analytical value and is often criticized for its abstraction. According to Parsons' familiar definition, "the most general and fundamental property of a system is the interdependence of parts and variables. . . . Interdependence is *order* in the relationship among the components which enter into a system. This order must have a tendency to self-maintenance, which is very generally expressed in the concept of equilibrium."[34] These notions of interdependence and equilibrium are often supported by analogy; for example, social systems may be likened to physical organisms in that they are born, grow, mature, wither and die.[35] From here it is an easy transition to pronouncements about the "health" and "pathology" of the system—judged principally by the effectiveness of the system and its constituent subsystems in satisfying system "needs" and "goals". These in turn are adduced by reference to common values or inferred "from the statements of top executives if they appear to be frank and consistent with other information". The concept of system goal or need is thus employed "as if there were no question concerning its legitimacy".[36] Any activities or processes with "observed consequences which lessen the adaptation or adjustment of the system" are labelled "dysfunctional" and are accordingly to be neutralized or eliminated. In industrial relations, Dunlop's endorsement of the notion of equilibrium inherent in systems theory is explicit when he writes that "the idea of an industrial-relations system implies a unity, an interdependence, and an internal balance which is likely to be restored if the system is displaced".[37]

From this perspective power, rather than being basic to the origin, definition and proposed remedy of system problems, is portrayed as the institutionalized outcome of a common value system which legitimizes both the system goals and the social relations established for their attainment. In short, power is "the generalized capacity of a social system to get things done in the interests of collective goals".[38] In the industrial context, Parsons adds, the power of management is legitimized "by the expectation that management will be competent and that there will be an identity of interest between management and other employees in giving management the power it needs to do the job effectively . . .".[39] Parsons' assumptions are again incorporated into industrial relations systems theory by Dunlop. Value-consensus is inherent in his concept of "ideology", which he defines as "a set of ideas and beliefs commonly held by the actors that helps to bind or integrate the system together as an entity".[40] By simply ignoring the possibility of *conflicting* interests, values or perspectives, industrial relations systems theory is thus able to incorporate the mystifying notions of "public" or "national" interest so commonly utilized by pragmatists.

Viewed from a systems perspective, trade unions can be seen as a key sub-system both within the more immediate Industrial System and the wider Social System. The aims and activities of trade unionists may be assessed for their contribution to the goals of industrial organization and their congruence with the political order of the day. Similarly, at a different level of analysis, the trade union itself may be conceived as a system with the officers, lay officials, shop stewards and membership as subunits of the organization. Within this framework, for example, the unofficial strike (often regarded as the central problem of the British industrial relations system) might be said to threaten the equilibrium of the Trade Union System, Industrial System, Economic System and Political System in that it challenges the legitimate authority of trade union leadership, obstructs the pursuit of managerial rationality, feeds the fire of inflation and threatens the whole fabric of democratic political life. Action taken to eliminate this dysfunctional aspect of trade unionism would serve the public interest at a number of levels by facilitating the achievement of collective goals and system integration.

Thus systems analysis offers an ideologically acceptable alternative to those who embrace the perspectives of the pragmatist but eschew his unsophisticated language and concepts. The selfsame problems of efficiency, practicality, constructive adaption to change and the "orderly" reform of industrial relations can be tackled in either framework. The principal concerns of Parsons' sociology parallel closely the chief worries of those in authority in industry.

Yet this entails that pragmatism and systems theory share common flaws. Neither approach probes behind its definition of problems and solutions to analyse whose interests are at stake and thus who will gain and who will lose from particular proposals and strategies. Thus the way in which men at all levels in a given structure, industrial relations system or trade union define their own situation and articulate their own needs is ignored either in preference for common sense and "what everybody knows" or for the predefined functional imperatives of the system and the views of those assumed to exercise legitimate control. This omission is, as we shall see, particularly serious where the goals of trade unions are in question.

It follows naturally that neither frame of reference examines systematically the underlying motives and origins of social action; their basic concern is merely with its symptoms and consequences for a structure which is normally taken for granted. To return to the example of unofficial strikes in defiance of management and union bureaucracies: these are considered primarily in respect of their impact on the "orderly" functioning of the system or society and the achievement of societal (systemic) goals. The level of analysis normally focuses on such matters as the malfunctioning of payment systems, the fragmentation of collective bargaining, and the inadequacy of communications.[41] Thus the normal assumption is that the "problem" of the unofficial strike can be resolved through reforms to institutions and processes within the industrial relations system itself. From the perspective of the overall social structure, in other words, it is assumed that only marginal adjustments are required.

Yet to regard unofficial strikes as the consequence of minor institutional malfunctioning, rather than a reflection of grievances and aspirations on the part of workers which extend beyond the confines of industrial relations narrowly defined, is to adopt a patently restricted conception of rationality. Within the perspectives of pragmatism and systems theory it is impossible seriously to consider whether unofficial strike action—and indeed the whole panoply of payment systems, collective bargaining institutions, and machinery of communication —might not be epiphenomena of a more fundamental and inherently divisive, irrational and contradictory pattern of social relations. Neither pragmatism nor systems theory can tolerate the idea of a basic and irreconcilable cleavage in society. For the pragmatist could no longer accept as unproblematic such concepts as "effective", "practical" and "orderly", but would have to ask "effective and practical *for whom* and orderly from *whose* point of view?" Systems theory, for its part, could no longer include those presuppositions of integration and adaptation that are basic to the concept of system itself. As for power, common sense either accepts its distribution as one of the "facts" of life to be taken for granted and left unanalysed or, more rarely, by focusing upon power relations within industry alone, fails to consider the impact of power in the wider social structure upon the actions of men in industry. The systems theorist either regards such wider social power as an exogeneous but in itself uninteresting variable that impinges upon industry (as in industrial relations systems theory) or, as in Parsons' approach, conceives of power as the product of value consensus. For neither does the critical analysis of power in its many and often non-obvious forms constitute a key problem.

One of the main advantages of both pragmatism and systems theory, their applicability to almost any aspect of social life, also constitutes a serious disadvantage. The flexibility of the two approaches means that there is no definitive application of either to the specific subject of trade unionism. But two approaches which do adopt a more specifically industrial focus are often combined with elements of pragmatism and systems theory: the unitary and pluralistic frames of reference.[42]

In common with systems theory, both these conceptions of industrial relations and the internal dynamics of trade unions make liberal use of analogy. Favourite units of comparison from the unitary view are the family and well-functioning team with their emphasis on common purpose, undivided loyalty, hierarchy and undisputed and responsible leadership. Conflict is deplored as unnecessary and avoidable, given that the interests of all are harmonious. For the same reason, independent worker representation—which challenges managerial authority and questions the principle that the needs of lower participants will be best served (and indeed defined) by their superiors—is rejected as an unjustified intrusion.

Thus the very presence of trade unions in the workplace or—at a different level—of unofficial movements within trade unions is portrayed not as the natural outcome of legitimate sectional interests but as the wilful disruption of what should be a unified and undivided structure. Horizontal links with workers in other establishments are particularly resented, as is shown in the violent reactions engendered by sympathetic strikes and the use of the so-called secondary boycott and the suspicion and hostility provoked by the unofficial creation by members of different unions of shop-floor liaison committees and multi-plant combine committees.

If it is conceded that there is any case at all for trade unions, then this is only insofar as they contribute to cohesion and control in industry.' Of necessity, any organization of workers which performed this function would parallel the unitary and hierarchical structure of the industrial corporation itself, the rank and file foregoing any control of the determination and implementation of policy. Thus unions may be tolerable if they seek to further the aims of industry (that is, the aims of those who own and control) by exercising "responsible" leadership in pursuit of "moderate" and "constructive" policies. Otherwise their influence must be minimized or eliminated altogether.

It is easy to see how the central assumptions of the unitary frame of reference may be combined with systems theory and pragmatism. Whether the focus is the relationship between workers and employers or the internal dynamics of trade unionism, the language of practicality and functional integration marries easily with ideological assertions of common purpose and undisputed authority. But rich though its emotional yield may be to managers faced by persistent industrial conflict or union leaders challenged by internal dissension, the unitary frame of reference, by its very remoteness from reality, is an inadequate source of *practical* guidance. For the effective management of conflict—whether within trade unions or in their external relations with employers—requires some appreciation of the underlying realities of power and interests. Fortunately, a frame of reference lies to hand which, while still ideologically acceptable, can more readily cope with the challenge of shop-floor power and the existence of cleavages in industrial relations and trade union organization. This, the pluralistic frame of reference, has dominated recent industrial relations theory and has informed sophisticated managerial practice.

Pluralism's basic premise is that the aims and definitions of sectional groups legitimately diverge. The pattern of relations between capital and labour or between different groups and levels within trade unions is thus conceived not as a pre-established but as a negotiated order. The norms which govern the behaviour of participants are shaped and modified, defined and redefined, through processes of competition and compromise. The pluralist insists that trade unions, or sectional groups within unions, far from *introducing* conflict into industrial relations actually provide it with an organized form and hence limit its disruptive effects. He normally adds that the substantive and procedural norms which result from the process of negotiation and compromise can properly be imposed by those in positions of authority—since those whose conformity is enforced have had a hand in constructing the norms and have access to the appropriate channels for their amendment.

The analogy for the enterprise or union which is readily employed by the industrial pluralist is the "miniature democratic state" in which the social structure is shot through with many conflicting, overlapping and interlocking interest groups. All, or almost all, opinion has some collectivized means of expression within a structure of countervailing and balancing power; alliances are shifting and contingent so that no permanent or fundamental cleavages exist; the overall structure is thus represented as "a coalition of interests . . . over which the government tries to maintain some kind of dynamic equilibrium".[43] The government, as a special kind of interest group, has a vital role in pluralist analysis, ensuring that the cross-cutting tensions and competing claims are so resolved that all, or nearly all, interest groups can pursue their aims with at least some success. At the same time it ensures that the common interest of all groups in maintaining the system is safeguarded.

Industrial relations for the pluralist thus represent a process of antagonistic cooperation. Managements and workers, full-time officials and rank and file, legitimately pursue the highest level of satisfaction for their respective aspirations that is compatible with the maintenance of their mutual relationship. In its institutionalized form the reconciliation of their divergent interests through collective bargaining represents a positive, functional and constructive exercise in social conflict.[44] Far from indicating malintegration, such institutionalized conflict demonstrates to each group its involvement in the creation of the norms which govern its behaviour, is associated with heightened morale, and indicates the healthy functioning of the system. The wider the range of issues over which interest groups bargain, always bearing in mind their common commitment to mutual survival, the more likely the achievement of broad-based and universally legitimized solutions. The more that inter-group relations assume a collaborative character—involving a process of "integrative bargaining" or "positive-sum game"—the less likely that any legitimate interest group will feel seriously aggrieved at the partial frustration of its ideal objectives.[45]

The ways in which pluralism differs from the authoritarian assertions of the unitary frame of reference are obvious. Yet in their treatment of industrial relations in general and the internal dynamics of trade unions in particular there are surprising affinities between the two perspectives; while both can readily be accommodated to many of the assumptions of common sense and systems theory. For the fundamental guiding assumption of pluralism is the existence of a *legitimate* government managing from above the relations of various interest groups (themselves legitimate) with itself and with each other. The propriety of the overall political structure is therefore taken for granted. When the pluralist considers management-as-government, he thus assumes that workers must accept the impossibility and indeed the undesirability of transforming or abolishing the rule and political economy of the present owners and controllers of industry. If each side is committed to the ideal of mutual survival, how could trade unionists possibly entertain such aspirations?[46] In fact, as we show in the following section, such goals have motivated trade unionists in the past and continue to do so.

When the pluralist applies this perspective to the union-bureaucracy-as-government, he implicitly denies the relevance of the two-way structure of control of union policy and activity to which we have already referred. Union democracy—control from below by the rank and file—would otherwise form the starting point of analysis, whereas it is typically disregarded as a serious issue. Hence pluralists are normally extremely equivocal in specifying what types of participation in pursuit of what types of demand may legitimately be undertaken by rank-and-file unionists.

Given pluralism's own working assumptions, then, the notion of a "miniature democratic state" is a rhetorical flourish rather than a serious analytical device.[47] Yet if negotiated order is not in fact viewed as the outcome of democratic machinery, it must be predicated on the absence of any *radical* conflict of interests and aspirations among the participants in industry and in trade unions. Thus the awkward postulate of democracy can be discarded by the industrial pluralist only by incorporating—even if in diluted form—one of the central presuppositions of systems theory: a working consensus on goals and values. The pluralist frame of reference, while recognizing the existence of conflicts of interest, is able to assert their reconcilability in part through a *selective* endorsement of the legitimacy of interest groups and their objectives. Those groups and aspirations which challenge the continuation of a collaborative relationship between representatives of rich and poor, exploiting and exploited, are simply denied legitimacy. Those who wish, for example, to develop trade unionism into a vehicle for attacking the status of labour as a commodity and overturning capitalist relations of production can be found no place in the pluralist scheme of industrial relations: in no way can such forms of conflict be regarded as "constructive" or "functional".

Hence the pluralist takes for granted that conflict and negotiation cannot reasonably affect the basic structure of the social order but occur only at the margins. Yet a commitment to the basic institutions of a capitalist political economy has as a corollary the acceptance of a peculiar double standard: for these institutions respond to threats to group interests quite differently according to whether it is "lower participants" or those in positions of control who are affected. An extreme example has been noted by Laski:

> The right to call on the service of the armed forces . . . is normally and naturally regarded as a proper prerogative of the ownership of some physical property that is seen to be in danger . . . [But] we should be overwhelmed if a great trade union, in an industrial dispute, asked for, much less received, the aid of the police or the militia or the federal troops to safeguard it in a claim to the right to work which it argued was as real as the physical right to visible and corporeal property, like a factory.[48]

Some rights, in other words, are more potently legitimate than others: historically the definition of problems requiring state intervention has stemmed consistently from only one of the contending parties in industry, those who own and control the means of production. Thus in the last resort massive inequality in the distribution of power and hence of effective rights falls outside the main focus of pluralist analysis. Its conception of what constitutes an industrial relations problem cannot therefore differ greatly from that of common sense, systems theory, or even the unitary perspective.

Of course industrial relations rarely reach the point of last resort; thus the radical differential in the powers of different groups is not usually so overt, and the reality of power relations is customarily open to considerable mystification. Pluralism itself contributes significantly to this mystification: directly by its assertion that inter-group competition involves a balance of countervailing forces; indirectly by its emphasis on the value of the marginal adjustments and concessions achieved by collective bargaining. In the words of one enthusiastic advocate, collective bargaining

> provides some very substantial support for our system of democratic (*sic*) capitalism. It does this in three ways: first, it provides a drainage channel for the specific dissatisfactions and frustrations which workers experience on the job; second, it helps to "humanize" the operation of an essentially impersonal price system by making it more generally palatable to workers as a group; and, third, it absorbs the energies and interests of the leaders of labor who might be inclined to work for the overthrow of capitalism if this avenue of activity were lacking.[49]

Pluralist ideology, and the institutional processes which that ideology glorifies, thus helps limit workers' aspirations in respect of their jobs and their unions to a level deemed legitimate by those who control economic resources. Such ideological influence (which itself reflects the unequal distribution of social power), insofar as it successfully ensures the modesty of workers' aspirations, frees employers from the need to rely openly on their superior power in their day-to-day relations with their employees. It is the major achievement of industrial pluralists that they have recognized the pivotal role of trade unions in this process. For unions to perform this role, though, the *goals* which they pursue must be of a specific kind: in the language of virtually every orthodox commentator on industrial relations they must be within the bounds of what is orderly, practical, fair and effective—in other words, unlikely to challenge the functional integration of the capitalist social order. We must now consider explicitly how far trade union goals in practice meet these anodyne requirements.

The goals of trade unionism

It has become something of a sociological commonplace, as reference to almost any standard text on "organization theory" will confirm, to argue that organizations are distinguishable from other aspects of social life by their specific creation in respect of and orientation towards particular goals.[50] It is further claimed that the goals of an organization provide a vital key to its character and that "at the least they provide a quick conceptual entry to the organization".[51] Hence the study of union goals should be no exception: providing both a valuable indication of the uniqueness of trade unionism and a convenient starting point for analysis. Thus Olson, whose principal concern is with labour unionism, writes that "the most logical place to begin systematic study of organizations is with their purpose".[52] However, the analysis of the goals of organizations, and especially those of trade unions, is a conceptual and empirical quicksand. This does not mean that the goals of trade unionism are not worth bothering with nor that their analysis should be abandoned in favour of some more effortless task; on the contrary. However, it does mean taking to heart Laski's point that "it is not fanciful . . . to argue that, of all organizations in a community like the United States or Great Britain, the character and purpose of the trade union are the most elusive".[53]

The most immediately obvious problem inherent in the concept of organizational goals, particularly acute in the case of non-imperatively coordinated associations such as trade unions,[54] is the danger of reification. By this is meant the ascription of essentially *human* characteristics to abstractions or to social structures in such a way as to obscure the fundamental part played by genuinely human agencies and values in social action.[55] In short, neither trade unions nor any other kind of organization can be said to have goals outside of those set and pursued in their name by members and other interested parties. And yet the error of reification in the analysis of trade unions is readily understandable, for the very idea of trade unionism entails a minimum notion of the submission of the individual will to that of the collectivity and the overriding of purely personal interests by those of the group as a whole. Thus, it is all too easy to move from a minimally defining characteristic of trade unions to the assumption that such organizations have goals of their own. A further reason why this problem applies particularly to the analysis of behaviour in trade unions is that there are no clear lines of demarcation between actions which can legitimately be termed "trade union" and those which merely deserve the label "worker", "shop-floor", "work-group" or "unofficial".

A further problem is that *all* social action, organizational or otherwise, is purposive. It is true that, in contrast to most social behaviour, the purposes pursued in organizations are frequently given explicit formulation either in their Charter, Rules or Constitution or, as in the case of more ephemeral structures especially, in their rallying cries, slogans or declarations of intent. Moreover, these selfsame aims often constitute internal battle grounds for sectional groups within organizations, trade unions with their conflicting ideological groupings no less than most. But even the goals which emerge in the shape of rules or slogans as a result of these intra-organizational debates and struggles remain mere formal statements, essentially empty and lifeless, until made effective by the constructions put upon them by organization members and significant others. They are open to constant (re)interpretation in which the relative perspectives and power of the different interpreters or participants figure prominently. This is even truer of trade union goals than of those of other kinds of organization. This is due first to the unique pattern of authority relations in trade unions, second to their typical mode of operation in contemporary Britain, and third to the problematics of knowing exactly what actions warrant the epithet "trade union". All these factors illustrate the inextricable and dialectical relationship between trade union goals and other aspects of organizational structure.

The diffuse and multi-layered system of control entails that decisions relating to union goals are taken at a number of different levels. As Fox has observed:

> To refer merely to the individual's membership of a trade union is greatly to simplify a complex pattern of affiliations. He relates himself to a number of collectivities structured into a hierarchy culminating in the national level of the union, which may indeed be related to the even higher collectivity of some central organization such as Britain's Trades Union Congress, or America's AFL-CIO.[56]

The appropriate level of decision-making is in part determined by union policy, but is also shaped by the operating environment of the union, including the internal and external distribution of power. Other features of this environment are the pattern and nature of membership, the organization of work and its accompanying system of controls and the behaviour of management. This complex structure of authority in turn has implications for and is itself affected by the predominant location of trade union activity at shop-floor or workplace level. Not only the interpretation but the very formulation of union goals here takes place outside the formal system established by rule and particularly without the active involvement of the full-time paid official who has increasingly had to give way to shop-floor leadership. The importance of workplace trade unionism is also largely responsible for the lack of any clear distinction between incontrovertibly "union" and other worker-based but "non-union" goals and activities (a distinction which only the National Industrial Relations Court, prompted by expedience and armed with legalistic and moralistic argument, has so far ventured to draw with any confidence).[57]

The conceptions of goals and values to be pursued through the medium of trade unions are, then, likely to be manifold and are just as likely to embody conflicts as to express uniformity and consensus. Such differing conceptions of its purpose lend the union its essentially dynamic character as "groups with differing goals seek to use [the] organization of power, resources and symbols in the service of their own interests".[58] Not surprisingly, the sources of these conflicting definitions of goals are no less bafflingly legion than the goals themselves. As a minimum, these sources include experiences and influences from both work and non-work, from conceptions of self and personal biographies and projects, from the community and from the union itself, from fellow workers, unionists and kith and kin and from the mass media and "public opinion". Of course, each of these influences has its own dynamic and none is entirely autonomous, for not only is each linked to and affected by the other, but all are located within a particular historical conjuncture.

These points have relevance to the specific analysis of white-collar unionism, which as we saw in the introduction is a particularly rapidly growing sector of the British trade union movement. Many writers have argued that the *character* of white-collar unionism (by which is meant, primarily, the nature of the goals pursued and the means adopted) differs systematically from that of manual unionism, as a consequence of systematic differences in the social status and work situation of manual and non-manual employees. It is a common assumption that the social origins of professional and other non-manual occupational groups generate social and political orientations unfavourable to trade unionism: for example, a belief in individual rather than collective achievement, and a particularly firm commitment to the norms and institutions of capitalist society. Blackburn has suggested that, because of a reluctance on the part of non-manual employees to identify with the conflictual, "working-class" image which they associate with trade unionism, extensive recruitment is possible only by organizations which play down the parallels between their goals and activities and those of manual unions.[59] Lockwood has also emphasized the distinctiveness of non-manual attitudes towards trade unionism and hence of the character of white-collar unionism itself. Such differences he attributes less to the social origins of non-manual employees than to their privileged position, by comparison with manual workers, in terms of income, job security, working conditions, and status and autonomy within work. Insofar as such objective differences are declining in importance, he suggests, the distinctiveness of attitudes to unionism will also diminish.[60]

While the literature on white-collar union character contains important insights into the dialectic between the objective situation of an occupation and the character of the unionism it supports, we would reject as inadequate any simple dichotomy between manual and non-manual organizations in respect of (for example) the militancy of their goals and methods. Thus the draughtsmen have for many years been more prominent for their militancy than most manual occupations; the Scientific, Technical and Managerial Staffs, one of the fastest growing unions in Britain, has assiduously cultivated a militant image; while in recent years such previously staid bodies as the Teachers and Local Government Officers have been involved in prominent confrontations with government pay policies. This is not to argue that there is *no* basis for the common assumption that white-collar organization is distinctive. But the distinctiveness which does exist is in large measure a reflection of situational factors which are neither peculiar to nor universal among non-manual workers.[61] For example, organization among such employees is for the most part comparatively recent; this is in part attributable to the rapid growth of the white-collar labour force, and the degree of "proletarianization" that has affected many formerly high-status non-manual occupations. Partly because such unionism *is* comparatively novel, employers have often fiercely opposed the unionization of their non-manual staffs, sometimes creating dependent "staff associations" to forestall the growth of independent organization. Moreover, many white-collar occupations lack the strategic ability to disrupt production which has formed the basis for militant and powerful organization (both nationally and at shop-floor level) among various sections of manual workers. Finally, the scope for individual control and advancement which still exists for some categories of non-manual employees reduces the range of issues in respect of which they are dependent on collective representation. Such objective factors may induce a "realistically" restricted set of trade union aspirations among any group of workers, white-collar *or* manual. And while worker perceptions of what is realistic can and do alter, such practically rooted occupational ideologies may be sufficiently firm and persistent to exert a profound influence on the goals pursued by workers' collective organizations.

In addition to the potential multiplicity of goals that are manifested *within* trade unions, members of other social groups who consider their fortunes to be affected by trade unionism and the actions of trade unionists—such as employers, managers and politicians—also make it their business to concern themselves with the definition of union goals. Extreme examples of successful intervention by such groups are employer-dominated "company unions" and the spurious trade unionism created by totalitarian political regimes. But less dramatic forms of intervention are far more widespread. Thus employers of the unitary persuasion will strive to convince their workmen (perhaps forcibly) that trade unions are unnecessary and that their sectional goals run counter to the natural common interest of employer and employed. The more pluralistically minded may seek to harness the efforts of the union to the goal of greater productivity by way of the constructive conflict of the "non-zero sum" game, arguing that trade and competition are the country's lifeblood and that a bigger cake at lower unit costs necessarily means larger slices all round. Similarly, especially at times of economic crisis or political upheaval, government ministers may have a special interest in exhorting trade unions to seek "reasonable" earnings for their members or to exercise "responsible" leadership in the face of those dissident militants who threaten law and order. They may even go so far as to declare that certain aims and policies of the unions jeopardise the "national interest" and must be curbed by one means or another. Such intervention may take the form of positing a distinction between legitimate "trade union" action and illegitimate (or even illegal) "political" aims or methods. We examine the role of the government in more detail in a later section; but it should be clear already that discussion of union goals normally transcends disinterested academic debate and can constitute a crucial political argument (perhaps backed by powerful sactions) about the *proper* purposes of union organization.

Evidently, then, debates about trade union functions are typically mediated by the various ideological frames of reference outlined earlier. One of these perspectives, the pragmatic or "common sense" approach, might well question the very idea of close scrutiny of union goals; for the plain man would argue that emphasis should be placed not so much on intention as on activity and achievement. Yet as we have seen, to identify a specific social activity as "trade union action" *presupposes* a definition of trade unionism; by refusing to confront this problem explicitly the pragmatist relies on implicit, taken-for-granted definitions and paradoxically ignores the very practical question of the structure of interests and deployment of power involved in the prevailing definition and implementation of trade union goals. In short, such pragmatism involves a mystification of important facts of social life.

A related danger is that, sometimes deliberately but more often unconsciously, union goals are *inferred* from what is assumed to be trade union action. Thus, irrespective of the avowed aims of organization, the rationale of trade unionism is deduced from its achievements. We do not doubt the importance of studying the activities of trade unionists, and some degree of inference may be necessary where aims and policies have not been clearly formulated. However, part of the study of trade union activity must include an analysis of the relation between aims and activities, between prior orientation and actual behaviour. As Hoxie put it:

> What one must do is to study constitutions, working rules, rules for discipline and, above all, agreements with employers . . . in order to discover demands and methods and then with the help of declarations in constitutions and literature to try to build up principles and aims—putting the whole thing finally into shape.[62]

In this respect, the typical concerns of the pragmatic approach to trade union organization are unduly restrictive even in its own terms. As ethnomethodologists have pointed out, it is likely that an essential part of the very practical organizational behaviour of such immediate interest to the pragmatist will be some account by trade unionists of the relationship between the purpose of unionism and their immediate activity; and students of unions ought, quite properly to interest themselves in such verbalization.

In common with pragmatism, ethnomethodology offers not so much a theory of organizations as a programme for enquiry into problems. Where ethnomethodologists claim to diverge from pragmatism (and indeed from all varieties of what they label "positivism", including conventional sociology and Marxism), is in their orientation to the nature of common sense and the taken-for-granted world. Where pragmatism uncritically employs common sense for the proposed resolution of "practical" problems, ethnomethology depicts everyday common sense usage as its chief problematic. What interests the ethnomethologist is not the grounding of such common sense in social values which we have emphasized, but the way in which reference to "what everybody knows" forms an essential part of all social interaction, especially communication. Thus, attention is focused upon the lingual techniques commonly utilized by competent organizational members to inform, direct, justify, explain or sanction the actions of themselves and other members of social situations.[63] In the field of organizational analysis the "primary concern is to investigate the variety of practices and mundane considerations involved in the determinations of the operational meaning and situational relevance of policies and procedures for ongoing, everyday organizational activities".[64] Typically, members' organizational activities entail "accounting" for behaviour in respect of organizational rules and aims; hence the ethnomethological problematic dictates that the relationship of the formal plan of the organization to actual conduct should be investigated with specific reference to *how* members of the organization reconcile the two on a day-to-day basis. Again, the relevance of this for the study of trade union goals needs no elaboration.

However, the legitimate attention thus accorded to verbal activity is, by itself, inadequate as an explanation of organizational behaviour. The main shortcomings of ethnomethology in this respect are twofold. Firstly, as some ethnomethodologists acknowledge, in taking as their own problematic the competent use of rules in socially sanctionable situations they leave unanswered pivotal questions and take for granted certain fundamental presuppositions. No explanation is offered as to *why* members of organizations are constrained to act in accord with pre-established rules and goals (except by way of the unhelpful tautology that such behaviour is part of the taken-for-granted world of organizational life). Thus the ethnomethodological perspective *presupposes* the existence of a structure of power in which superordinates are able both to establish rules and to judge and sanction actions of subordinate organizational members in the light of those rules. Such a presupposition can be avoided only by the combination of psychological reductionism and the assumption of common values, whereby we may suppose that all social actors are driven by some "need" to conform with "socially agreed" rules. Secondly, lingual activity, like all other social action, cannot be torn from its structural context. Thus, analysis should seek not only to throw light upon the accounting and reporting procedures emphasized by ethnomethodologists, but also upon the structural context of constraints and opportunities through which both goals and action are mediated. Furthermore, analysis of this context should also attempt to illuminate the manner in which the very accounts of action in respect of goals are themselves shaped by the environing configuration of power and the socially available vocabularies of motive utilized by trade unionists and others to lend legitimacy to their activities. The language and, more importantly, concepts available to trade unionists in setting and reviewing the goals of their organizations have themselves to be understood within a social context.

We have already argued that men are constrained by the material world and by the objective availability of opportunities and by the power of other men; but they are constrained also by their access to socially legitimate accounts for their actions.

> Along with the conduct patterns appropriate for various occasions, we learn the appropriate motives, and these are the motives we will use in dealing with others and with ourselves. The motives we use to justify or to criticize an act thus link our conduct with that of significant others, and line up our conduct with the standardized expectations, often backed up by sanctions, that we call norms.[65]

It is by reference to such motives that men mobilize not only their own actions but also the potential response of others to those actions. However, conceptions of the world and motives for action in the world are equally the products of social processes and are related to the distribution of social power:

> Specifically, the success of particular conceptual machineries is related to the power possessed by those who operate them. . . . He who has the bigger stick has the better chance of imposing his definition of reality.[66]

The forms this power may take are manifold, but include control over the processes and institutions of socialization, education and politicization and access to the influential apparatus of the communications industry, including the mass media, publication and advertising. The language and concepts employed by trade unionists in the social construction of their world are closely intertwined with evaluations, legitimations and belief-systems that owe their shape to the distribution of social power and its historical development. Consequently, it is dangerous and inadequate to impute over-much autonomy to the communicative inventiveness of social actors.

> The construction of realities may be more influenced by power relations, socialization processes, and class structures than by the creative interpretation of the actors engated in interaction. In fact communicative behaviour rests on work and power relations as well as on language. . . . The social world is not only structured by language but also by the modes and forces of material production and by the systems of domination.[67]

The confidence with which goals are embraced and actions pursued can be easily corroded by the hostility of influential others. Even those who can take refuge in a coherent oppositional world-view may still suffer: not so much at the hands of the definitions of disapproving others as such as by the access of those others to power to enforce their condemnation. Thus power and definitions are locked in an unfolding dialectic. It is precisely to this relationship between the social production of language and the social relations of production that Marx and Engels were referring when they pointed to the association between the ruling ideas and the ruling class of a given epoch.

> The class which has the means of material production at its disposal, has control at the same time over the means of mental production, so that thereby, generally speaking, the ideas of those who lack the means of mental production are subject to it.[68]

The relevance of this social process for the establishment of trade union goals needs little elaboration. If the pursuit of certain goals might threaten social dislocation and even, perhaps, radical political and economic change, employers and governments (and indeed those functionaries of trade unions who benefit from current arrangements) all have an interest in influencing the selection of goals by convincing trade unionists of the universal benefit to be derived from the pursuit of "reasonable" and "constructive" aims. As Allen has argued, most trade unionists act on the basis of assumptions that at best accommodate the aims of unions to the needs of the beneficiaries of the established order and at worst deny the validity of their very existence.

> This socializing process, which is the process of learning on the basis of given analyses about situations, is the main obstacle to militant action. . . . Hence the guilt complex about strike action and the myth of achievement which glorifies the method not the result and causes niggardly advances to be acclaimed as tremendous victories.[69]

Under such conditions, it is incumbent upon those trade unionists and outside sympathizers who perceive the limitations that can be imposed upon union goals to engage in the task of the "resocialization" of trade unionists—a task which represents a formidable struggle for the consciousness of workers and one which, of course, has long exercised the theories and strategies of socialist thinkers.

The consciousness of workers thus cannot escape the influence of the dominant vocabularies shaped by those in power both within trade unions and in the wider society. One consequence of this is that, in attempting to make sense of the immediate experiences of their workaday world, rank-and-file trade unionists may be faced by a series of contradictions, involving a stark contrast between their everyday experience and the rhetoric conventionally applied to industrial life. One outcome of this contradiction may be to stimulate workgroup inventiveness. With the aid of shop-floor leadership, experiences are sifted and resolved into unofficial tactics to be revealed through shop-floor demands and action; while workers develop new vocabularies, concepts, norms and values which may even percolate upwards through the union to gain eventual recognition well beyond their point of origin.

A good example of such a process is the recent shop-floor reaction to redundancies. Ever since the Beveridge reforms and the widespread adoption of Keynesian economics, successive British governments have been in principle committed to a policy of "full employment".[70] Furthermore, again since the Second World War, British public policy has been unswervingly directed towards the goal of greater productivity and increased flexibility and adaptability of labour, exemplified best by the exhortation to widespread adoption of "productivity agreements". This policy was pursued with particular devotion by the Labour governments of 1964–1970 which declared the need for a "shake-out" of labour and introduced legislation—the Redundancy Payments Act, 1965—to hasten this process and to aid managements in their search for greater efficiency.[71] For their part, the officials and executive leadership of trade unions have been unclear as to the precise role they should play in respect of changes in the organization of work, especially where redundancy ensues. While official policy has been confused, trade unionists at the main point of impact of these developments—the workplace—have been caught in the series of contradictions to which we have referred. Not unnaturally, these workers have assumed that their trade union organizations are there to protect their interests; equally, they are fully aware of the governmental policy of "full employment" and the claims that legislation, in the shape of the Redundancy Payments Act, has now recognized a worker's "property" in his job.[72] Very often these selfsame workers have cooperated with management in the introduction of change, perhaps through a formal agreement, and have seen an increase in their productivity. And yet, in recent years, upwards of a million workers annually have been faced by the prospect of redundancy, the majority of them without any statutory financial compensation. The full-time officials of their representative organizations, upon whom even the most seasoned shop stewards and convenors rely at times of such crisis, have thrown up their hands in despair and accepted that redundancy is unavoidable both in the long and short term.[73] Faced with such an attitude by union officialdom and confronted by the prospect of an increasingly bleak labour market, shop-floor unionists in industries ranging from ship-building to printing and electrical components have initiated what is arguably the most significant development in recent industrial relations, namely the "work-in" and factory occupation to fight redundancy.[74] In doing this they have utilized both those elements of the dominant vocabulary of motives which vindicated their actions—full employment, increased productivity and economic viability—and the demands which have been forged by the experiences and values of working-class life, particularly the cry of the "right to work".

The example of redundancy illustrates both the achievements and limitations of shop-floor consciousness in the pursuit of union goals.[75] In particular, the widespread absence of a call for greater shop-floor control once the immediate problem of redundancy has been resolved appears to lend weight to the arguments propounded by Goldthorpe and his colleagues in respect of the contemporary development of trade union consciousness.[76] Research into workers' own definitions of their work situation at three plants in Luton led the authors to conclude that the proto-typical consciousness of British workers—manual and non-manual alike—is veering towards what they call "instrumental collectivism". In so far as workers come to look upon their jobs purely as a means to an end beyond the workplace and to define their relationship with both their work and their employer in pecuniary terms, so increasingly "the unionism of these workers is to be understood in terms of the characteristic attitudes which they bring to their employment: that is, as unionism of a markedly instrumental type".[77]

Just as work does not constitute a "central life interest" for these workers, so neither does their attachment to trade unionism indicate a belief in unionism in itself. Their instrumental unionism appears to echo the "business unionism" celebrated by Perlman forty years earlier and contrasts, according to Goldthorpe and his colleagues, with the collective solidarism of those, particularly "traditional" workers, for whom trade unionism carries an emotional appeal, moral force and the potential for extending the social and political horizons of the working class. According to the thesis advanced by these authors, such traditional unionism, in which workers adhere to a power model of society and which carries the connotations of advancing the frontiers of workshop control, is in decline. Collective power is giving way to individual economics as the main rationale and dynamic of trade union organization.

Leaving aside the serious questions that can be levelled at the adequacy and interpretation of data in the Luton research,[78] the conclusions of Goldthorpe and his fellow researchers in respect of trade unionism are a telling example of the dangers of refusing to go beyond the workers' own definition of the situation to get at the reality which their words seek to describe. Such unwillingness inclines the researcher to an almost infinite relativism and a kind of ethereal idealism. No matter how the worker may define his world, it remains true that he is obliged to sell his labour and engage in relationships of subordination in return for economic reward. This very fact of the treatment of labour in exchange terms, as a commodity, in capitalist employment relations means that to a large extent the goals that workers are able to pursue through trade unions are constrained by the dominant pattern of industrial life and its accompanying concepts. As the main manifestation of the forces that bind labour to capital is the cash nexus, it is hardly surprising that the most immediate expression of the conflict of interest between the two is the struggle over the distribution of the economic product of their relationship. The predominance of consumption values in the non-work world—to which the affluent workers are reportedly so positively disposed—clearly reinforces this same tendency.

Yet before accepting the simple diagnosis of economic instrumentalism it is necessary to consider the non-economic *effects* of an economic orientation to work amongst trade unionists. In the capitalist business enterprise, financial decisions and changes in the deployment of money affect managerial autonomy in at least three ways. In the first place, successful demands by shop-floor workers for an increased rate of pay may cause management to reduce manning levels or speed up production. In other words economic demands, through their impact on managerial decision-making, may have immediate non-economic consequences on the shop-floor. Secondly, as one government after another has constantly emphasized, changes in the wages bill, especially in labour-intensive industries, can impose severe restrictions on management's freedom of action in defining and implementing policy in respect of dividend distribution, investment, the purchase of materials, advertising and all the other capital-centred activities which require a readily available cash-flow. It is possible then to trace the impact of *market* relations, or the terms on which labour is hired, upon *managerial* relations, or what management seeks to do with its labour having hired it.

Thirdly, and most importantly, the expression of union–management relations in financial terms does not modify the fact that those relationships are essentially, both in form and method, relationships of power. The portrayal of economic man and instrumental unionism offered by Goldthorpe *et al.* must be set in a framework of collective bargaining in which the crucial process is the establishment of rules that, of necessity, constrain management's freedom to act.

As Flanders has persuasively argued, the term "collective bargaining" is in many ways a misnomer for what should more appropriately be termed "joint regulation": it is essentially a rule-making process entailing a political as much as an economic relationship in which they very processes whereby collective agreements are struck are the embodiment of conflict and power. Hence whether or not workers define their union activities in terms of a power relationship, the practical consequences of these activities necessarily transcend any purely economic or instrumental intentions.

While it is thus wrong to suppose that viable trade unionism can in principle be limited to goals of a purely instrumental or "business" nature, the pluralist emphasis on "joint regulation" is itself inadequate. Flanders has shown that joint agreement between management and union is but one of a number of methods of rule-making: rules may also be established unilaterally by one side or the other, be imposed by an outside agency, emerge from tripartite negotiation, or may simply reflect the persistence of traditional and customary arrangements. Yet elsewhere he appears to dismiss these alternatives, arguing that

> As in other countries, trade unions in Great Britain came into being, established themselves on firm foundations and extended their power and social influence mainly on account of their achievements in collective bargaining. . . . All the other activities which the trade unions have undertaken and all the other purposes they have acquired must be regarded as a by-product and auxiliary to this their major activity and purpose, since success in it has been the condition for their survival and the basis of their growth.[79]

There is no necessary reason, however, why unions should pursue their members' interests solely through the channels of collective bargaining. Trade union action might properly be oriented towards the establishment of rules with the greatest possible independence and freedom from constraint: unilateral control rather than joint regulation. "Invasion, not admission, should be the trade unionist's watchword", is a sentiment with deep roots in the British labour movement.[80] It may involve two distinct assumptions: that independent action is the most acceptable means by which workers collectively can defend and improve their conditions *within* capitalism; and that trade union action should aim ultimately at *transcending* capitalism altogether.

The trade unionist objection to collective bargaining as a *method* is clearly expressed in the following criticism:

> It surprises me when I hear "collective bargaining" spoken of . . . as the "first principle" of trade unionism. You may search the "objects" of the older unions for this precious "first principle", but you will not find it. The object of trade unionism used to be to uphold the price of labour *against* the encroachments of the employers, not in agreement with them.[81]

The objection to collective bargaining as an *end in itself* has been stated by the recently retired General Secretary of the Mineworkers:

> Although the primary purpose of trade unions is to maintain and improve the working lives of their members, most unions include, in the objectives outlined in their constitutions, the political aim of "abolishing capitalism". This . . . is not just a pious or nebulous aspiration. . . . Not only is the prize considerable economic power, but considerable political power as well. A fundamental change in capitalism involves measures to abolish private ownership of the means of production, distribution and exchange and the political power associated with it. . . . Capitalism is still capitalism and, although there have been changes, its basic character of exploitation and class struggle remains.[82]

These two objections have been powerfully linked in this classic assertion of trade union action as a means to workers' control:

> There must be no alliance or compromise with the employer. We shall be obliged, indeed, to negotiate with him through his representatives in the daily routine of the workshop, but not to espouse his interests, or to advance them in any way when it lies in our power to do otherwise. Our policy is that of invaders of our native province of industry, now in the hands of an arrogant and tyrannical usurper, and what we win in our advance we control *exclusively and independently*.[83]

It is of course true that such ambitious objectives have often been eroded in the actual practice of trade unionism. To understand why this is so it is necessary to consider in detail the relationship between goals, activities and constraints to which we have previously referred. Historically of crucial importance has been the growth of a mutual dependence between union and management representatives, creating a commitment to the maintenance of the bargaining relationship so salient as to mediate all other union objectives. The effect is to suppress the aspect of trade unionism as a protest and challenge to capitalist relations of production: in the extreme situation union involvement in joint regulation may transform it into "part of the control system of management".[84] The institutional pressures which can thus sublimate the original purposes of unionism are discussed in detail in the following section. The principal objection to advocates of pluralism must be, not that they fail to recognize these pressures—for many writers have indeed considered them[85]—but that they assume that it is both inevitable and desirable that trade unionism should succumb to them. Trade unionism is thus *defined* in terms of goals which take for granted its incorporation into the political economy of capitalism.

Institutional pressures and union policy

The wide range of potential union goals, and the absence of any general consensus on their proper objectives, create particular scope for the process of goal displacement. It is a commonplace of organizational analysis that the original purposes of organizations often tend, over time, to become supplemented and extended; procedures devised for the efficient attainment of these goals become sanctified as ends in themselves; and those in charge of the organization become committed to "institutional" goals which are considered necessary for its security and stability but may conflict with its overt purposes. That such tendencies are particularly evident in trade unions has been emphasized by Ross:

> As an institution expands in strength and status, it outgrows its formal purpose. It experiences its own needs, develops its own ambitions, and faces it own problems. These become differentiated from the needs, ambitions, and problems of its rank and file. The trade union is no exception. It is the beginning of wisdom in the study of industrial relations to understand that the union, as an organization, is not identical with its members, as individuals.[86]

It is worth repeating that the notion that institutions have needs, ambitions and problems—like the idea that organizations act—is a reification which carries with it a serious danger of obfuscation of the actual social processes involved. The concept of "institutional needs" is a metaphor which makes sense only to the extent that it is based on an implicit reference to the wants and interests of real people. In one sense, the "needs" of trade unions might be understood in terms of those of the members themselves. In so far as a union exists to serve the interests of its members, they have at least an instrumental interest in its organizational strength and survival. Yet there are three important reasons why such institutional needs may conflict with the actual wishes of trade unionists and hence the manifest purposes of the union. First, workers as individuals may be able to benefit personally from policies or actions which, if pursued by members generally, would result in a reduction in collective union strength and hence be to the ultimate disadvantage of all.[87] Second, the benefits of strong organization may accrue only in the long term, and may be obtained only at the expense of members' short-term wishes. A simple example might be a proposal to increase membership subscriptions. Where such conflict exists, the priority to be assigned to long-term institutional as against immediate membership interests is itself an important policy issue. And third, policies oriented towards organizational needs may become ends pursued for their own sake rather than through any calculation of long-term membership interests. This is especially likely where organizational interests become intrinsically linked with the fate of a union's leaders; for them, the demands of union strength and security will acquire major salience, and may come to provide a simple rationalization for any policy against the wishes or immediate interests of the rank and file.

There are four main types of institutional goal which can readily displace the overt objectives of a union: security and stability; financial solvency and strength; unity and cohesion; and administrative efficiency.

The problematics of institutional security and survival, important in any organization, are particularly salient within trade unionism: for unions by their very nature represent a challenge to the structure of power within the political economy of capitalism. Their purely economic objectives conflict with the capitalist's desire to minimize costs of production; their involvement in a struggle for control challenges his managerial autonomy; while any connection between trade unionism and socialist politics is a potential threat to his very existence. The more ambitious and extensive a union's objectives, the more likely it is to attract the hostility of those in positions of economic and social dominance. Hence the formative period of trade unionism in many countries has been marked by violent employer opposition, and often governmental repression—which has in turn rendered union organization itself precarious. Conversely, if a union can curb those of its objectives which seriously challenge the *status quo* it may be able to win the acquiescence and even goodwill of employers and the state, in a manner which considerably enhances its security. In practice, unions which have become firmly established have typically been drawn inexorably towards policies which are relatively acceptable to these significant others. Thus it is rare indeed for trade union commitment to major social change to be an operational one, in the sense of influencing day-to-day industrial policies or serious long-term strategies: the socialist attachments of British unions are in general confined to the rhetoric of rulebook preambles and conference speeches.[88] Similar pressures normally affect industrial policies in such manner that interference with managerial control does not go "too far",[89] while economic demands are characterized by "moderation".[90] Where unions are willing to confine their objectives within these comparatively innocuous limits, far-sighted managements have little reason to resist, and much reason to welcome, union involvement in job regulation. For by articulating the many discontents generated by the workers' role within capitalist employment a union makes their behaviour more predictable and manageable. Resentment is not permitted to accumulate explosively, but is formulated in a manner which facilitates at least temporary solution; and union involvement in any settlement increases the likelihood that its members will feel committed to the agreed terms.[91]

An accommodative relationship between union and employer—in which the former acts, in Wright Mills' famous phrase, as a "manager of discontent"[92]— thus has obvious pay-offs for the employer. He may thus be keen to reciprocate in a manner which assists union security. The closed shop is one such response. "The union shop, or other forms of compulsion, are highly important to the strength and stability of labor unions. It is the union as an organization, not the worker directly, that needs the 'job control'."[93] It follows that a trade-off between union moderation and employer goodwill may appear particularly attractive to union officials, even where the advantages for the ordinary member are far less obvious. The future of the bargaining relationship forms an important consideration whenever demands are formulated or strategies devised. In some circumstances such long-term concerns may impose so severe a constraint on union action that, like a miser who refuses to enjoy his wealth, the potential achievements of union strength are never realized.[94]

The importance of financial solvency as an organizational objective is clearly shown in the history of British unionism. In the earliest associations financial administration and control largely devolved upon the individual branches. Yet these tended to exhaust their funds in over-liberal benefits or injudicious strike action; it was impossible to accumulate sufficient funds to support an effective long-term industrial strategy, and at times the existence of the organization itself was threatened by bankruptcy. Hence there was an inexorable trend towards the centralization of financial control, which extended—since strike pay could constitute a major drain on union funds—to centralization of power to authorize strike action and central coordination of industrial policy.[95] Yet the pursuit of financial solvency and strength easily became an end in itself: a policy originally justified as a prerequisite of effective militancy could be used as an argument *against* militancy. It was a common complaint against the late nineteenth century British craft unions that their leaders were preoccupied with accumulating massive bank balances; they were reluctant, their critics alleged, to support strike action or even pursue demands which involved a risk of confrontation, for fear of reducing the financial reserves. In contemporary industrial relations there is little evidence that such considerations induce a "peace-at-any-price" attitude among union leaders; nevertheless, they can exert a noticeable influence on industrial policy.

"Unity is strength" is a common trade union maxim, and internal unity and cohesion is thus a natural organizational goal. Conversely, division and dissension within a union may well be regarded as undesirable and even dangerous. Yet a concern to maintain unity may conflict with the democratic control which overtly characterizes trade unions: for criticism of leadership actions and decisions, or attempts by sectional groups to obtain greater attention to their special interests, may be suppressed as disruptive and subversive.[96] Unity is most likely to be assigned priority over democracy where a union's membership is heterogeneous: for there may be no strong feeling of common identity, while bargaining strategy may require a judicious balancing of divergent sectional interests. In such a context, "excessive" internal democracy may be viewed by its leaders as a threat to the integrity of the whole union. On the other hand, the open articulation of opposing viewpoints is far more likely to be tolerated in societies with a homogeneous membership: these often constitute what Turner has described as "exclusive democracies".[97]

The goal of efficiency has been at least part of the rationale of most of the changes in the internal organization and functioning of trade unions since the early nineteenth century: centralization, the rise of the full-time organizer, the gradual professionalization of many of the leadership functions.[98] Again, as is discussed in the following section, there is an apparent conflict with the democratic character of trade unionism. Union leadership, it need hardly be said, would be in many ways a simpler task if the wishes of the members themselves could be ignored—or at least, if the scope for their articulation could be as narrowly circumscribed as possible. And it is significant that many of the most vocal critics of trade union "inefficiency" (often themselves associated with employer interests) are in reality attacking trade union democracy.[99]

The theory that institutional pressures divert trade unions from their overt objectives and confer on their policies "a profoundly conservative character" was first explicitly stated by Michels in his *Political Parties*.[100] The original goals, he argued, "are, whenever requisite, attenuated and deformed in accordance with the external needs of the organization. Organization becomes the vital essence. . . . More and more invincible becomes its aversion to all aggressive action. . . . Thus, from a means, organization becomes an end."[101] For Michels, such goal displacement was inevitable: an intrinsic element in an "iron law of oligarchy". Yet while Michels' sociological insight was of immense theoretical importance, we would deny the operation of any "iron law". The pressures which formed the stimulus for the emergence and growth of union organization—which are rooted in the experience of workers within capitalist wage-labour—inevitably set limits to the process of goal displacement.[102] The relative strength of conservative and oligarchic tendencies on the one hand, and countervailing pressures on the other, itself varies between unions and may be seen as in large measure situationally determined. But before pursuing this argument further it is necessary to turn explicitly to the question of union democracy on which we have already commented briefly.

Union policy and union democracy

Implicit in any analysis of goal displacement, as we have seen, is the appreciation that trade unions develop "official" policies which can diverge from members' conceptions of their own interests. The danger is that the membership may become merely the object, rather than the prime beneficiary, of job regulation. Thus our previous discussion leads naturally to a consideration of problems of internal union government.

One theme pervades the voluminous literature on this topic: the conflict between the goals of efficient and effective organization on the one hand, and membership control of union policy and its implementation on the other: a conflict which becomes manifest as soon as a bureaucratic hierarchy of full-time officials is established.[103] A related finding often emphasized is the fact of rank-and-file apathy: in most situations only a small minority participate in the official processes of union government.

Michels' famous (or notorious) conclusion was of course that democratic control[104] is in practice impossible. While the primary concern of his *Political Parties*—as the title indicates—was with the political organizations of the working class, he insisted that "in the trade-union movement, the authoritative character of the leaders and their tendency to rule democratic organizations on oligarchic lines, are even more pronounced than in the political organizations".[105] Unions, he argued, could not operate on the basis of "direct democracy"; for the conduct of negotiations and disputes required an organization, led by officials with specialized experience and knowledge. The privileges of office naturally led union leaders to cling to their positions; even if subject to re-election, the experience and political skills which they developed constituted an overwhelming advantage over any rivals. Social isolation from the rank and file led to ideological differentiation, undermining any socialist commitment the officials might originally have had: "their own social revolution has already been effected".[106]

Thus far, Michels' argument is in line with the earlier analysis of the Webbs (with which he was himself familiar). Historically, they noted, "with every increase in the society's membership, with every extension or elaboration of its financial system or trade policy, the position of the salaried official became . . . more and more secure". By the turn of the century, when they were writing, chief officers of trade unions had come to enjoy a "permanence of tenure exceeding even that of the English civil servant". They added that "the paramount necessity of efficient administration has co-operated with this permanence in producing a progressive differentiation of an official governing class, more and more marked off by character, training and duties from the bulk of the members".[107] In these circumstances, the Webbs insisted, any attempt to maintain the traditional procedures of "direct democracy" would lead "straight either to inefficiency and disintegration, or to the uncontrolled dominance of a personal dictator or an expert bureaucracy".[108]

For the Webbs, though, specific institutional arrangements could safeguard trade unions against this sad fate. (Their Fabian political philosophy made them fervent if disingenuous advocates of quasi-parliamentary representative institutions as the key to union democracy.) Michels, by contrast, brushed aside such qualifications to his "iron law". "Uncontrolled dominance", he insisted, was inevitable; and the leaders' power permitted them to impose their conservative policies, even where these were "disapproved of by the majority of the workers they are supposed to represent".[109] Such "abuse of power" in general provoked little resistance. Lacking adequate information or experience on which to base any serious criticism of leadership policies, most members accepted that their officials had a "customary right" to their positions and were willing to allow them to take the difficult decisions. Thus oligarchic control was reinforced by mass apathy.[110]

Any study of contemporary trade unionism which examined only the official mechanisms of internal government would appear to offer considerable support for Michels' diagnosis of an "iron law of oligarchy".[111] Where unions require the regular re-election of officials, "the defeat of the incumbent is a relatively rare event";[112] and there has been a discernible trend in recent years for several unions to limit or remove even the formality of election. Hence the emergence of a leadership caste is repeatedly emphasized:

> In sum, whether we consider the objective pattern of organizations, recruitment and reward or the subjective orientations and career expectations of the staff experts or the characteristics of those who are selected for high influence, the picture is one of slowly growing yet embryonic bureaucracy.[113]

By contrast, the formal processes of union democracy seem frail indeed. Most union conferences, as we saw in the introduction, are dominated by the leadership "platform" and thus fail to function as a genuine means of rank-and-file determination of policy. The branch, the one formal link between the ordinary member and his union, is more often concerned with routine administration than with decision-making on issues which might encourage membership involvement. Thus it is not surprising that membership apathy is regularly documented:[114] in most unions only some 5–10 per cent of members are in any sense active participants in the official processes of union democracy, regularly attending branch meetings and voting in union elections.

Undoubtedly the general factors discussed by Michels provide part of the explanation for this state of affairs. But in addition it is possible to mention a number of more specific influences on the degree to which internal union government deviates from the democratic ideal.[115] Perhaps the most important of these is membership composition. As was seen in the previous section, the degree of membership homogeneity is likely to affect internal democracy. Where a union represents a variety of occupational groups with divergent and in some respects even conflicting interests, open articulation of these sectional interests may threaten organizational unity; where membership is more homogeneous this is far less a danger. Moreover, members of a diverse union may lack any real basis for judgment on those aspects of policy which do not affect their immediate interests. (Some unions—notably the Transport and General—attempt to overcome this difficulty by means of separate "trade groups" which determine the industrial policy for the various sections of membership.)

Membership participation and control are also affected by such factors as skill, status, educational qualifications, and strength of occupational identity. Higher-skilled groups, or those that form cohesive occupational communities, are often associated with a high degree of union democracy. Conversely, lower-skilled occupations, women, and occupations marked by casual employment or high labour turnover, are often organized by unions which fit Turner's category of "popular bossdom"—strong leadership control and little rank-and-file participation.[116] Where a union contains both types of membership, the former normally dominates its internal government. Hence in the Engineers, a disproportionate number of activists and officials come from the skilled section. Or in most unions in which women form a large majority of the membership—the Public Employees, the Teachers, the Shopworkers, the Tailors and Garment Workers, the Civil and Public Services Association—most leading positions are occupied by men.

Union democracy is also affected by the size and distribution of membership. The scope for direct participation and control by the rank and file in central decision-making is clearly greatest where membership is small and geographically concentrated. The larger and more dispersed the membership, normally, the larger is its bureaucratic apparatus and the more fragmented its rank and file. Either the individual branch is very large, and itself prone to oligarchic control; or the branch is only one of many striving to influence higher union policy—and coordination of initiative from the various branches is then difficult (and may even be prohibited by union rules); or there exist several intermediate levels between branch and national executive, so that the central leadership is particularly remote from the rank and file.

Union government is affected not only by the nature of the membership but also by the prevailing conception of union *purpose*. The more restricted a union's objectives, the less likely it is to manifest extensive democratic control. This relationship was noted by Hoxie in his original characterization of business unionism: "in harmony with its business character it tends to emphasize discipline within the organization, and is prone to develop strong leadership and to become somewhat autocratic in government".[117] If the function of a union is merely to provide its members with a limited economic service, it is less unreasonable to judge its operation by the standards of an ordinary commercial enterprise, and the case for democracy is accordingly weakened. Where union goals are so narrow and thus so unproblematic, technical expertise is the most important requirement on the part of the union official: and it follows from this perspective that "trade union wage policy is inevitably a leadership function".[118] This is to advocate the radical division between leadership and membership which was condemned by the authors of *The Miners' Next Step*: "this power of initiative, this sense of responsibility, the self-respect which comes from expressed manhood, is taken from the men, and consolidated in the leader. The sum of *their* initiative, *their* responsibility, *their* self-respect becomes his".[119]

Not surprisingly, then, a narrow conception of union function provides little incentive for membership participation.

> Participation in any organization appears to be related to the number and saliency of the functions which it performs for its members and the extent to which they require personal involvement. In most cases, trade unions perform only one major function for their members—collective bargaining, which can be handled by a more or less efficient union administration without requiring any membership participation, except during major conflicts. In such unions, we would not expect continuous participation by more than the handful of members who are involved in administration.[120]

Hence an attempt by union leaders to confine activities to the pursuit of limited economic improvements may, by encouraging membership apathy, reinforce their own predominance. This would seem to represent the vicious circle diagnosed by Michels: oligarchy, mass apathy and narrow and conservative policy each stemming from and at the same time perpetuating the other.

Yet we would deny, as against Michels, that there is any inevitability in such a vicious circle. Indeed, recent developments in industrial relations demonstrate the absurdity of such an assumption: for neither oligarchy, nor apathy, nor conservatism can be regarded in any simple fashion as characteristic of trade unionism. Structural pressures inhibiting democracy are not irresistible; they can be counterbalanced, for example, by a union constitution which facilitates rank-and-file control, a tradition of democracy, or the existence of rival factions each ready to mobilize opposition to autocratic action on the part of the other. The Engineers is one example of a union in which all three of these factors are important. Union leaders themselves may hold a genuine commitment to demo-

cracy and extensive union functions, and hence encourage rank-and-file participation. There has certainly been a tendency in this direction in Britain in recent
years, particularly in the two largest unions. And perhaps most important of all,
membership apathy in respect of the formal machinery of union government may
coexist with rank-and-file involvement in other forms of organization and activity.
The importance of shop-floor organization in a wide area of British industry is
a case in point: and its significance for the whole operation of trade unionism is
immense. It is to this that we now turn.

Shop stewards and domestic bargaining

"Britain has two systems of industrial relations", wrote the Royal Commission
on Trade Unions and Employers' Associations in its *Report* (the Donovan Report).
"The one is the formal system embodied in the official institutions. The other is
the informal system created by the actual behaviour of trade unions and employers'
associations, of managers, shop stewards and workers."[121]

The official structure of collective bargaining, established in most industries
for at least half a century, normally involves regular negotiations at national level
between officials of the union or unions concerned and the relevant federation or
association of employers. The resulting national agreements specify rates of pay,
hours of work, and other conditions of employment for the industry. In theory,
this process determines all important aspects of the employment relationship that
are negotiable: all that is left for discussion at local or workplace level are questions
of the implementation of national agreements, and minor problems of domestic
concern.

The reality is very different: in most industries with strong organization
the national agreements set a bare minimum standard for wages and conditions;
the worker relies primarily on domestic bargaining to win acceptable terms. The
clearest evidence of the impact of shop-floor bargaining is the gap between officially
negotiated wage rates and workers' actual earnings. The Donovan Report contrasted basic rates in engineering in October 1967—£9.37 for a labourer and
£11.08 for a fitter—with actual average earnings of £21.39 for men in engineering
and electrical goods and £24.42 in vehicle manufacturing.[122] This striking
difference derives from three main sources. Systems of payment by result, or
piecework, apply to roughly a third of all wage-earners,[123] and provide considerable
scope for domestic bargaining; strong shop-floor organization may be essential
if workers are to achieve acceptable earnings. Overtime, for which payment is
made at an enhanced rate, is extensively worked—an average of roughly 6 hours
a week for male manual employees.[124] Its amount and allocation are often controlled by shop-floor bargaining. Finally, the nationally agreed rates may be
increased by straightforward supplements negotiated at workplace level.

Domestic bargaining has less obvious but nevertheless important consequences
in respect of control over the process of production. Formally and legally, employers
possess almost unlimited authority over their labour force. Trade union attempts
to achieve constraints on these "managerial prerogatives" through official negotia-

tions have rarely achieved significant success. As a protection against arbitrary managerial control, and a means of winning an element of autonomy within their working lives, trade unionists are obliged to act collectively at the point of production. Where shop-floor organization is strong, workers can indeed impose important limitations on managerial autonomy: affecting such issues as who shall be employed or dismissed, how machinery shall be manned, what shall be the rate of production, whether men shall be moved from one job to another.

The prevalence of informal shop-floor bargaining, and the strength of organization at the place of work, are reflected in the British strike pattern. For most of the postwar period at least 95 per cent of all strikes have been "unofficial", in the sense that they occur without the formal approval of the union executive (though this is sometimes accorded retrospectively). An unofficial strike is not necessarily one of which the union leadership disapproves (though this is indeed true in some cases); often the workers merely see no need to seek official support before stopping work. Most stoppages are small and short, and occur relatively spontaneously; and even in a major dispute, official support is of limited value since strike pay in most unions is so small (often about £5 a week). In addition, such actions as overtime bans and going-slow may be even more common than actual strikes, and are probably even more overwhelmingly unofficial.[125]

The pattern of unofficial action is directly related to the pattern of industrial relations in Britain. Since the most important issues concerning workers' employment are settled at the place of work, it is natural that sanctions should be applied at this level when the results of negotiation are unsatisfactory. Since the official representatives of the national union are rarely involved in negotiations at workplace level, it is hardly surprising that workers should commonly see no reason to seek official approval before stopping work. This is obviously of central importance when we evaluate the significance of "apathy" or "oligarchy" in the official union machinery; for given the structure of British industrial relations, this official machinery is of very little direct significance to the ordinary member.

"The Shop Steward is for most rank-and-file members their first and only contact with the Union. To them the Shop Steward rather than the Branch is the Union."[126] The rise of the shop steward to his key position in British unionism has been a slow one. Since the nineteenth century, some unions have had representatives at the workplace to carry out such functions as checking that all workers are paid-up members, collecting subscriptions, and reporting to the branch or district on conditions within the factory. Such stewards came gradually to act as representatives of their fellow-workers when urgent issues arose within the workship, and this function became particularly important during the 1914–18 war. The danger of victimization by employers limited their negotiating role during the interwar depression; but in the past three decades there has been a great expansion in their number and influence. Today there are probably over 250 000 shop stewards in Britain, about a third of these in engineering.

By definition the steward is a shop-floor employee, typically chosen directly by his fellow-workers because he enjoys their trust. His authority as a negotiator does not derive from the union of which he is a member; until very recently, few union-rule books even mentioned the steward's bargaining functions. Nor, in the main, does it derive from formal procedure agreements: most of these define the steward's role in a manner far more restrictive than occurs in practice. His powers stem primarily from the fact that he shares the aspirations of his members, is personally involved in their experiences and grievances at the point of production, and is expected to represent their interests closely in negotiation with management. Should he fail to do so adequately, it is relatively easy for the rank and file to reassert control, through shop-floor meetings or less formal pressures. In the last resort, workers can replace a steward whose competence or integrity they doubt by one in whom they have greater confidence.

There are thus very important differences between the workers' relationship with his shop steward and with his full-time union official; yet at the same time these differences should not lead us to ignore certain similarities. In some situations, particularly in the largest factories, the shop steward organization can itself display considerable bureaucratization. Management will often permit one or more chief stewards (or convenors) to act full-time as union representatives, even though they may be nominally employed in a specific shop-floor job. Important negotiations may be largely monoplized by a committee of leading stewards and convenors, who may make little effort to maintain effective contacts with the rank and file or even with the remaining stewards. Highly bureaucratic shop steward organization may be made possible by and in turn encourage membership apathy. Thus there is rarely much competition for the steward's position: most are elected unopposed, or else "emerge" without the formality of an election.

In addition, shop stewards are subject to the same institutional pressures in microcosm as affect union officers. Despite popular stereotypes, the Donovan Report insisted that "it is often wide of the mark to describe shop stewards as 'troublemakers'. . . . Quite commonly they are supporters of order exercising a restraining influence on their members in conditions which promote disorder".[127] For the steward, as for the full-time official, the bargaining relationship with management is necessarily a salient consideration during negotiations. In addition, a number of specific facilities may be dependent on management goodwill: permission to carry out shop steward duties without loss of pay; provision of office and telephone facilities; opportunities to recruit members, collect subscriptions and hold meetings; above all, perhaps, the mere readiness to allow access to discuss any issue or grievance arising. Not surprisingly, then, most stewards are reluctant to act in a manner which might alienate management goodwill; the natural predisposition is to seek a mutually satisfactory outcome to issues which arise—to view them, like management, as "problems" to be resolved rather than as disputed ground in a continuing relationship of conflict.[128]

Necessary as these qualifications are, however, it remains true that the shop steward is, potentially at least, far more closely attuned to the wishes of his members and subject to their control than is normally the case with the full-time official. Yet the steward is himself involved in a relationship with the official, and this relationship may exercise a considerable influence on the activities of each. We turn to consider this in detail.

Shop stewards and full-time Officials

A consequence of the narrow focus of the dominant definition of industrial relations problems, involving an emphasis on the need to "reconstruct" workplace relations around a formalized shop steward role, has been a comparative neglect of the full-time union official.[129] The Donovan Report devotes a mere three pages to him; while earlier studies of trade unionism, as we have seen, reserved their attention for the minority of chief officers and national officials of the movement. Yet first-line officers, representing the first level of paid, full-time officialdom beyond the workplace, occupy a key position in the interface between the rank and file and the union bureaucracy. Of course, both their formal powers and responsibilities and less institutionalized activities vary from union to union and location to location. Overall, however, these full-time officials continue to play an important part both in the internal life of the trade union and in its relationships with employers. They frequently have the responsibility of convening district and other supra-workplace committees and executing their decisions; they may figure centrally in union arrangements for the supervision of ballots and elections, signature of agreements or processing of grievances through a procedure operated jointly with employers; very often they are responsible for the initial establishment of union organization and negotiating arrangements within the workplace. In some circumstances employers may prefer to deal with outside full-time officers. In any case their relative ease to movement, breadth and facility of contact and acquaintance with administrative techniques normally permit them to exert considerable influence in internal union affairs.

How powerful this influence may be depends in part on the official's own goals and self-conception. Some see themselves purely as the servants of the members and stewards with whom they have contact, others as the guardians of official union policy and still others as "professionals" answerable largely to their own professional morality and the judgment of their peers. Whatever the circumstances of their work and the exact nature of their own self-image, these officials will be engaged in relationships of power; "upwards" with national officers and union executive, "sideways" with fellow officers and "downwards" with shop stewards and, through them, with rank-and-file members.

The specific relationship between full-time official and the shop stewards within his area of responsibility must logically fall within one of four patterns. Their activities may be largely autonomous, so that each is independent of the other; the stewards may be dependent on and subordinate to the officer; the official may be controlled from below by the stewards and the members they represent; or the relationship may be characterized by mutual dependence and control.

The main influences on the relative power of shop stewards and full-time official are represented by the structure and traditions of the union itself; the composition and work situation of the membership; and the policies and actions of the employer and the structure of collective bargaining—all interrelated factors which we have considered in detail previously. Thus in a union such as the Engineers, where the full-time official works closely with a district committee composed largely of shop stewards, and is subject to periodic re-election in which he requires their good offices to ensure the support of the activist membership, his dependence on them may be considerable. By contrast, in a union with a less democratic structure or tradition the official may be able to act in a far more authoritarian manner. Where the membership is willing and able to participate actively in union affairs, at least at the level of the workplace, the shop steward who enjoys their trust is in a powerful position in his relationship with the outside official. The steward in such a situation can rely on the members to follow *his* advice when deciding whether to pursue a demand, accept an agreement, or declare a strike; while the official may have to depend on the stewards for his flow of work from the plant, and seek and rely on their information and guidance. By contrast, in industries, occupations or unions where the membership is more passive, the officer need have little fear that a disgruntled steward can mobilize effective sanctions against him. Finally, the structure of collective bargaining (in part reflecting the preferences of management) helps determine how far the steward can acquire influence and prestige in the eyes of his members through frequent and successful involvement in plant-level negotiation; or how far the full-time official has the key role in negotiations (or has at least to right to accord or withold formal approval of domestic agreements), and can use this power in such a way as to discredit an "awkward" steward. Here there is an obvious contrast between trade unionism among manual workers in private manufacturing, particularly engineering, and the far more formalized bargaining structure in the public sector, particularly for white-collar occupations. In addition, certain bargaining issues call for the detailed parochial knowledge of the steward, while others require the more technical expertise of the full-time official.

The respective political skills of full-time officials and shop stewards and their members will also affect their relationship. For example, an official may be adept in the exercise of "controlled militancy". Thus where members are clearly angry and aggrieved, he may encourage them to take limited industrial action, in the hope that this may "relieve their feelings" and prevent more disruptive militancy which might make his own position more difficult. (The one-day token strike is an increasingly popular example.) Or he may be skilled in the strategy of "intra-organizational bargaining", using subtle methods to persuade members that while he supports their aims in principle they are in practice unrealistic.[130] A rank and file which is relatively inexperienced may be at a considerable disadvantage in its relations with an official adept in such tactics.

In practice, the relationship between stewards and full-time official rarely falls within the pattern of pure one-way control or total autonomy: normally there is some degree of mutual dependence. Moreover, this relationship may be in the process of change from one pattern to another; while typically, different aspects of their activities may be characterized by different varieties of dependence. One consequence of this complexity is that the same relationship may be open to many conflicting interpretations. Some commentators see power residing, uncontrolled, on the shop-floor; others argue that the oligarchic tendencies diagnosed by Michels operate at the level of the first-line officer; yet others insist that the relationship between official and shop steward exists in name only, each operating in a world of his own.[131] It should be unnecessary to spell out how devotees of each of the ideologies we have analysed construct their reactions to these varying diagnoses and their typical proposals for "reform".

It is important to conclude this discussion by emphasizing that the power, influence and activities of steward or official are only partly determined by their mutual relationship. Officials who dominate their members and shop stewards may have little power in the face of the employer; stewards who largely control the preferences of full-time officials may owe this power to the consent of their constituents or the acquiescence of management, either of which, as we have seen, may be withdrawn. As Tannenbaum and Kahn have argued, the distribution of control *within* a union must be distinguished from the total control exercised in *external* relationships.[132] As we have emphasized earlier, the influence of employers on a union's strength and activities is, potentially at least, particularly great; and how this influence is exercised is likely to reflect the *manner* in which members and officials seek to use the control at their disposal. Thus most employers have considerable scope for choice, not only whether to deal primarily with stewards or full-time officials and hence how to structure their relative influence, but also whether to foster the prestige of the union as such in the eyes of their employees. And as has already been remarked, the power which employers can exert may extend even to the definition of the goals of trade unionism and the proper relationship between leaders and members. In exerting this influence, employers have in recent years made increasing resort to a further agency the role of which we must now consider.

Government policy and trade unionism

The main focus of our discussion so far has been on the three-way relationship between workers, employers and union officials. This has been analysed without detailed attention to the broader context of the relationship and the impact of outside agencies. In particular, little has been said of the role of the state in industrial relations. One reason is that, traditionally, government action has had only a limited role in British industrial relations—certainly by comparison with most other countries.

> There is, perhaps, no major country in the world in which the law has played a less significant role in the shaping of these relations than in Great Britain and in which today the law and the legal profession have less to do with labour relations. . . . British industrial relations have, in the main, developed by way of industrial autonomy. This notion of autonomy is fundamental and . . . it means that employers and employees have formulated their own codes of conduct and devised their own machinery for enforcing them.[133]

It would be wrong to suggest that there has ever been complete legal abstention, for a considerable volume of law has applied to British industrial relations throughout the present century; but its principal function has been to support at the margins a system of collective bargaining based primarily on the autonomy of the parties directly involved.

The support of trade unions for this tradition of "voluntarism" is understandable. Historically, as was seen earlier, their experience of judicial intervention in their affairs was such as to provoke the natural response that the law should merely leave them alone. (Trade unionists have indeed been prepared to demand legislation to deal with specific problems not easily resoluble through collective bargaining —factory safety, for example; but they have normally been reluctant to advocate any extensive legislation, even in a form favourable to union aims, for fear that this might open the way for more hostile legislative initiatives.) Voluntarism was accepted by employers and governments for rather different reasons. Employers— or at least those who had learned that it was possible to come to terms with trade unions—felt that they had could handle their relations with them without requiring the outside support of the state. Insofar as they espoused the general philosophy of *laissez faire*, this too suggested that collective bargaining arrangements should operate with the minimum of governmental interference. Governments for their part had no cause to adopt an interventionist line so long as the results of voluntary collective bargaining posed no threat to their own policies. Yet the precondition of government and employer acquiescence in voluntarism is easily stated: unions should lack the power to endanger the stability of the political economy of British capitalism; or, if they possessed this power, should refrain from exercising it. This was indeed the case in the years when voluntarism was largely unquestioned. Before 1914 union organization covered only a relatively small proportion of the labour force, while between the wars mass unemployment attenuated the economic power of labour; during the period of both world wars, and up until the last decade, though union organization was stronger, its national leadership was on the whole characterized by considerable restraint in bargaining.

In recent years this precondition has ceased to obtain, and in consequence the whole strategy of voluntarism has been under growing attack.[134] The decade of the 1960s saw the onset of "explosions" in industrial militancy, and in consequence, in the rate of increase in wages. The average annual increase in money incomes rose from 4.8 per cent in the period 1956–1960 to 5.6 per cent during 1960–1964, 6.4 per cent in 1964–1968, and 10.2 per cent in 1968–1970.[135] While the precise dynamics of this trend are disputed, part of the explanation is clearly that the process of shop-floor organization and bargaining, described previously, has broken through the self-imposed limits of postwar union officialdom. Paradoxically, this process has coincided with—and has probably been accentuated by—government attempts to restrain wage increases. An "incomes policy" was central to the policy of the Labour government elected in 1964, and was pursued with varying degrees of firmness throughout its period of office.[136] Yet its effect was uneven. Strongly organized groups could continue to push up earnings through bargaining on the factory floor; pieceworkers in particular were largely immune from the effects of governmental policy. The main victims were thus workers (most notably in the public sector) who were dependent on official, industry-wide negotiations for their wage improvements. Two additional factors complicated the situation. Government policy permitted above-average pay settlements as part of a "productivity deal" in which workers accepted major changes in working arrangements or payment systems.[137] This led to occasional highly publicized instances of apparently spectacular wage advances.[138] At the same time, the policy challenged traditional assumptions about "fair" wage relationships by precluding the principle of "comparability" whereby pay in industries largely dependent on official national bargaining was maintained in line with earnings in other industries.

The overall effect of these developments was that workers with strong shop-floor organization became more ambitious in their demands, and in their readiness to support these with militant action; while traditionally passive trade unionists (particularly in white-collar occupations and the public sector), from 1969, became involved in strike action in protest at the decline in their relative earnings. Eminently respectable unions, which had not called an official strike in half a century or more—the Miners, the Teachers, the Postal Workers—became involved in confrontations with the government, their leaders often fearing that they would otherwise lose control of their membership to rank-and-file militants. The consequence was apparent in the strike statistics: the number of recorded stoppages rose to an all-time record of 3 906 in 1970 (compared with a postwar average of around 2 000); while the number of striker-days rose progressively to 24 million in 1972 (compared with a post war average of between 2 and 3 million).

This process has coincided with an increase in the economic constraints on British employers and governments. Profitability appears to have been decreasing at the same time as international competition has intensified.[139] The development of large-scale transnational corporations, the integration of diverse productive activities, the decreasing life-span of capital equipment which is itself escalating in cost and complexity: all these trends create a need for long-term company planning. This in turn creates urgent pressures for new levels of predictability in labour costs and intensity in labour utilization.[140] Yet recent trends in industrial relations jeopardize both objectives. Not surprisingly, then, managements which have long abandoned the old ideology of *laissez faire* have turned to the state for assistance.

Governments have proved responsive because for them too, recent industrial relations have had unacceptable implications. It should be unnecessary here to argue in detail against the naive view that the state is a neutral agency mediating impartially in the conflict between capital and labour:[141] the trend in recent decades has been towards increasing interdependence between governments and industrialists. The success of government economic strategy is intimately linked to the welfare of the owners of capital. Virtual stagnation has meant that increased real wages cannot be financed painlessly out of economic growth; ideally, from the government viewpoint, the share of profits should increase in order to finance faster investment. The pressures of international economic management set stringent limits to the level of tolerable price inflation. Hence the desired objective is a firm restraint on money wage increases and a more intensive exploitation of labour; and actions by workers and their unions which threaten managerial goals are a challenge to government policy also.

Governments can respond to this challenge in either of two ways. The first is founded on an appreciation of trade union "institutional needs". Just as sophisticated employers have preferred a collaborative relationship with union officials to one of open conflict, so governments—particularly in time of war or economic stringency—have sought to cultivate the goodwill of union leaders. Consultation, representation on a wide range of official committees, "honours" for individual leaders, have been willingly offered in exchange for union "moderation" and "responsibility"[142]—in other words, a refusal to exercise the full potential of union strength, to offer any serious challenge to managerial control, or to contest the existing (grossly unequal) distribution of wealth and income.[143]

For the Donovan Commission, as for most academic authorities on industrial relations, the approach to industrial relations most likely to prove effective was the intensification of the attempt to "incorporate" trade unionism. The Donovan diagnosis of the central "problem" of British industrial relations centred on the "anarchy and disorder"—in other words, the undermining of managerial control—at shop-floor level. The recommended solution was the elaboration within the workplace of those pressures which had traditionally proved effective at the level of national union leadership. Essentially, the aim was to exploit the ambivalence in the shop steward's position: his desire for a stable relationship with management, his natural tendency to treat disputes as "problems" to be solved, his exposure to precisely the same moderating pressures as operate upon the full-time official. The mechanisms suggested were the formalization of the steward's role within the factory, substituting "joint regulation" for areas of control exercised auto-nomously by workers (the strategy of productivity bargaining and procedural reform); a greater involvement of full-time officials (in conjunction with higher management) in supervising industrial relations at the point of production; and the closer integration of shop stewards within the official structures of trade unionism. Such a re-integration of "formal" and "informal" systems of industrial relations would permit union–government collaboration at national level to exert a genuine impact on the shop floor, and would in particular permit a viable "incomes policy" to underwrite the existing distribution between wages and profits.

The alternative approach, advocated extensively within the media[144] and by the more militant employers, is more overtly coercive. This, the strategy adopted by the Conservative government elected in 1970, involves attacks on trade unionism at three distinct but related points. The Industrial Relations Act of 1971 attempts to weaken union *organization* through its prohibition of the closed shop and interference with internal union rules and relationships. The same legislation seeks to emasculate union *action* by hedging industrial militancy of every kind with an array of restrictions and prohibitions. Union *objectives* are trammelled by compulsory controls on wages. (In addition, proposals are apparently being considered to undermine the trade union defence of workers against arbitrary managerial control by the outlawing of so-called "restrictive practices".)

In recent years, government policy has tended to rely on an admixture of *both* approaches. The 1964–70 Labour government was primarily concerned—understandably, in view of the traditional links between the unions and the Labour Party—to achieve union *cooperation* in restraining wage increases and reducing strikes. A whole panoply of agencies—the Department of Employment and

Productivity, the National Board for Prices and Incomes, the Commission on Industrial Relations—were constructed to this end (while the National Economic Development Council, set up in 1962, had a similar function). Most union leaders, doubly concerned to win government goodwill, were inclined to cooperate. But the success of the government strategy was vitiated by the inability of union leaders to deliver the compliance of their members. As already seen: the period was marked by heightened rank-and-file aspirations, and the manifest limitations of leadership control. By the end of the decade few union leaders were *openly* adopting a restraining role, and several appeared publicly to encourage militancy.

Yet a strategy of coercion contains no guarantee of success. The action of the Labour Government, in 1966–7, in giving compulsory force to its incomes policy was effective in the short run, but may have contributed to eventual union disillusionment with the whole policy. Its subsequent attempt to include sanctions against strikers in its industrial relations legislation was a fiasco. Union hostility to the "penal clauses" prevented the implementation of the proposals as a whole (based largely on the Donovan recommendations); and while official union opposition was purely verbal, the mood of confrontation helped encourage extensive unofficial strike action against the government's Bill. (This was itself a significant development, given the traditional taboo of British unionism against the use of "industrial" action for "political" purposes.) The more draconian legislation of the Conservatives carried confrontation a stage further; and some union leaders (even though only a minority) endorsed protest strike action. One lesson of these episodes would seem to be that if governments force the trade union leadership into overt opposition, this may not in itself involve serious perils; but an indirect consequence is to add a veneer of legitimacy to more vigorous resistance led by shop-floor militants, and to undermine still further the ability of officialdom to exercise its traditional restraining influence. This helps explain why the new government, after two years, decided on a more conciliatory approach—which was in large measure reciprocated.

If the above analysis is correct, the relationship between governments, union leaders and the rank and file is necessarily ambivalent. Where governments regard industrial relations as a major problem, the choice of collaborative or coercive policies involves a genuine dilemma, and oscillation between the two is predictable. Union leaderships are necessarily torn between conflicting pressures: the goal of cordial relations with the institutions of political power (particularly important at the level of the TUC, perhaps the primary function of which is to consult and negotiate with governments), and the sometimes urgent expectations of their own members. In this dialectic, then, it is the nature of rank-and-file attitudes and expectations which appears to represent the crucial determinant.

The dynamics of contemporary trade unionism

British trade unions, we have argued, under the pressure of their members' unwontedly ambitious material aspirations and militant temper (though in view of the dehumanization and exploitation involved in the worker's position in capitalist society their aspirations and actions still reveal amazing restraint), have come to produce dangerous instability for the political economy within which they operate. Yet this consequence is wholly unintended: in almost every case trade unionists' particular conflicts with specific segments of the political economy are unrelated to any *general* questioning of its basic character. This would appear to underline Lenin's classic argument that it is natural for trade union action to involve the unquestioned acceptance of the framework of capitalism, and to be directed merely to the pursuit of improvements within this framework. "The history of all countries shows that the working class, exclusively by its own effort, is able to develop only trade-union consciousness, i.e. the conviction that it is necessary to combine in unions, fight the employers, and strive to compel the government to pass necessary labour legislation, etc."[145] By contrast, an explicit challenge to "the whole of the modern political and social system" presupposes a sophisticated theoretical understanding which could not develop spontaneously out of trade union activity alone.[146]

Such an argument is based on the belief that *ideology* is of critical importance in the persistence of capitalist social and economic relations. "The ideas of the ruling class", wrote Marx and Engels, "are in every epoch the ruling ideas, i.e. the class which is the ruling *material* force of society, is at the same time its ruling *intellectual* force."[147] The importance of this factor has been emphasized by Parkin:

> Members of the underclass are continually exposed to the influence of dominant values by way of the educational system, newspapers, radio and television, and the like. By virtue of the powerful institutional backing they receive these values are not readily negated by those lacking other sources of knowledge and information. However, since such values are the moral representation of the interests and opportunities of more privileged groups, their "appropriateness" as far as the less privileged are concerned is problematic. The tendency among the under-privileged is not to reject these values, and thus create an entirely different normative system, but to negotiate or modify them in the light of their own existential conditions.[148]

This helps explain the *inconsistencies* in working-class attitudes revealed by a wide range of sociological studies.[149] Typically, workers do not question the dominant ideology when formulated in abstract and general terms; yet in respect of their concrete and specific experience they fail to endorse its implications. Hence they may adopt cynical attitudes towards those in positions of authority, and engage in actions (going on strike, for example) deprecated by those whole-heartedly committed to the prevailing ideological perspective.

This then involves current trade unionism in a profound contradiction: workers have adopted aims and methods intolerable to the custodians of the social and moral order, even though no explicit or coordinated challenge to this order is intended. Clearly this intensifies the problematics of trade union goals, to which we have already devoted considerable attention: objectives are implicit in workers collective actions which are not explicitly articulated and may well be explicitly disavowed. Accepting the conventional maxim that strike action for "political" ends is illegitimate, trade unionists are often at pains to deny the manifest political significance of the struggles in which they are engaged.

There can be little doubt that such ideological confusion imposes a serious handicap on effective trade union action. Moreover, it creates an inherently unstable situation out of which two diametrically opposite routes may lead. The strategy of governments and employers, if necessary intensified, may prove (at least temporarily) successful. Despite the considerable strength of shop-floor union organization in many industries, its fundamental weakness is its fragmentation. It is by no means uncommon for each sectional group within a workplace to pursue its own interests and fight its own battles with little regard for those of other sections, and even at cross purposes with them. Where companies could afford piecemeal concessions on the shop-floor, were vulnerable to small stoppages which could disrupt an integrated production process, and had no coordinated industrial relations policy to cope with such problems, sectional action by workers proved highly effective. But sectionalism may constitute a fatal weakness where managements and government intervene in industrial relations with a relatively coordinated strategy. Thus the current situation contains the possibility that organized workers, meeting an increasingly concerted offensive in a fragmented manner, might sustain a series of sectional defeats which could transform self-confidence into demoralization. This may be all the more likely where a physical attack on shop-floor union organization is combined with an *ideological* offensive aimed at persuading workers to accept the particular implications of the generalized capitalist value system. Such notions as "fairness", "efficiency", etc., interpreted in a manner hostile to workers' interests, may be used to restrain the specific goals pursued by trade unionists; so may particular interpretations of what constitute "realistic" and "unrealistic" aspirations.[150] In particularizing the dominant ideology in this manner, union officialdom may well play a key role.

Yet such a process is by no means inevitable. One reason for the general working-class acquiescence in the dominant interpretations of society is that the economic and political structure of modern capitalism is relatively opaque.[151] But if governments and employers are impelled to adopt an abnormally coercive policy towards trade unionism, the transparency of class and power relations is likely to increase. This could initiate a "vicious circle" analogous to that analysed by Fox in situations in which managements are unable to obtain sufficient worker cooperation and obedience even though there is no explicit questioning of their "right to manage". "Finding its authority failing, management falls back on the coercive sanctions of power, only to find that this further undermines its own legitimacy, which in turn prompts the intensified use of power".[152] Such a cumulative devaluation of legitimacy in respect of not only managerial authority but the whole structure of political control, is one possible outcome of the current crisis in British industrial relations. Were the dominant ideology even in its most generalized form to lose its hold, industrial militancy might be expected to assume the aspect of an explicit challenge to the structure of control in industry and society. In the process, workers through their objectives and activities would be redefining trade unionism itself.[153] Such a development would however meet the opposition not only of those in positions of social and economic dominance, but also of those in the trade union hierarchy committed to their existing status and functions.

Which direction is followed in the future development of trade unionism and working-class consciousness depends on the conjuncture of a complex array of factors. If it is academically unsatisfactory to regard the outcome as indeterminate, this is nevertheless the only realistic conclusion. "History is at its least automatic when it is the consciousness of the proletariat that is at issue".[154]

References and notes

1. S. and B. Webb, *The History of Trade Unionism*, London: Longmans Green, 1920 ed., p. 1 (first edition 1894). In this work, together with their *Industrial Democracy*, London: Longmans Green, 1897, the Webbs provide the classic analytical study of British unionism.
2. Among the most important recent studies of British unionism are the following: G.D.H. Cole, *An Introduction to Trade Unionism*, London: George Allen and Unwin, 1953 ed.; J.D.M. Bell, "Trade unions", in A. Flanders and H.A. Clegg (Eds), *The System of Industrial Relations in Great Britain*, Oxford: Blackwell, 1954; H.A. Turner, *Trade Union Growth, Structure and Policy*, London: George Allen and Unwin, 1962 (primarily a history of the cotton unions but containing important insights into the sociology of British trade unionism in general); A. Flanders, *Trade Unions*, London: Hutchinson, 1968 ed., H.A. Clegg, *The System of Industrial Relations in Great Britain*, Oxford: Blackwell, 1972 ed.
3. *Department of Employment Gazette*, **79** (Nov 1971), p. 1022.
4. Comparative data from other countries are being compiled under the direction of G.S. Bain and R.J. Price and will shortly be published, probably as *Profits of Union Growth: a Comparative Statistical Study of Eight Counties.*
5. Trades Union Congress, *Report*, 1971. In 1972 a number of unions were suspended from the TUC for registering under the Industrial Relations Act.
6. G.S. Bain and R.J. Price, "Union growth and employment trends in the United Kingdom, 1964–1970", *Br. J. Indust. Relat.*, **10** (Nov 1972), p. 376.
7. The law has constituted a persistent obstacle to trade unionism in Britain. The Combination Acts of 1799 and 1800, which were themselves a supplement to older and in some ways more repressive laws, remained in force until 1824. Serious obstacles to union activity remained inherent in common as well as statute law, becoming particularly evident in the 1860s. New statutes in 1871 and 1875 were intended to legalize union organization and activity; but at the end of the century a series of judicial decisions cast doubt on the legality of most forms of collective action by workers. The Trade Disputes Act of 1906 appeared to underwrite union freedom; but this has again been threatened, first by a further succession of hostile judicial decisions in the 1960s, then by the anti-union provisions of the Industrial Relations Act of 1971.
8. Turner (*Trade Union Growth, Structure and Policy*) has suggested a distinction between "closed" and "open" unionism as an analytical device more appropriate than the conventional craft/industrial/general trichotomy.

9. See Clegg, *System of Industrial Relations*, ch. 2 for a detailed discussion of the coverage of each of the main British unions.

10. H.A. Turner, G. Clack and G. Roberts, *Labour Relations in the Motor Industry*, London: George Allen and Unwin, 1967, p. 195.

11. For a more detailed discussion see Clegg, *System of Industrial Relations*, ch. 3.

12. *Trade Union Growth, Structure and Policy*, p. 14.

13. Such national variations are discussed by S.M. Lipset, "Trade unions and social structure", *Indust. Relat.*, **1** (1961–1962). Because of these variations, much American literature on trade union sociology is of limited relevance to Britain; in general we ignore those writers whose analysis reflects the specifically United States context. A useful survey which focuses principally on American writing is A.S. Tannenbaum, "Unions", in J.G. March (Ed.), *Handbook of Organizations*, Chicago: Rand-McNally, 1965.

14. P. Selznick, "Foundations of the theory of organization", *Am. Sociol. Rev.*, **13** (Feb 1948), p. 32. Selznick's famous phrase indicates that employees are human beings, not impersonal occupants of "organizational roles".

15. J.G. March and H.A. Simon, *Organizations*, New York: Wiley, 1958, p. 72.

16. J.D. Thompson, *Organizations in Action*, New York: McGraw-Hill, 1967.

17. A. Etzioni, *A Comparative Analysis of Complex Organizations*, Glencoe: The Free Press, 1961.

18. *Comparative Analysis*.

19. P.M. Blau and W.R. Scott, *Formal Organizations: a Comparative Approach*, London: Routledge and Kegan Paul, 1963 ed.

20. "The first and overriding responsibility of all trade unions is to the welfare of their own members. That is their primary commitment; not to a firm, not to an industry, not to the nation. . . . Once trade unions appear to be acting as servants of employers or servants of the government, they are bound to be written off by their own members" (A. Flanders, *Management and Unions*, London: Faber and Faber, 1970, pp. 40–41). Nevertheless, the argument that there exists a "national interest" transcending sectional and class conflicts—yet which surprisingly also appears to be in line with the interests of the rich and powerful and hostile to those of ordinary workers—*does* exert a significant influence on trade union action. This point is considered in more detail later in our discussion.

21. R.F. Hoxie, *Trade Unionism in the United States*, New York: Appleton, 1917. For a famous analysis and defence of "business unionism" see S. Perlman, *A Theory of the Labor Movement*, New York: Macmillan, 1928.

22. Where a trade union is "ideologically" oriented in Hoxie's sense—and almost all British unions express some commitment to social change which would benefit not merely their own members—Blau and Scott's label "mutual-benefit association" is clearly inadequate. Hoxie's own terminology is unsatisfactory, since "business unionism" embodies as real an ideology as "ideological unionism", even if this is not consciously recognized.

23. A. Gramsci, "Soviets in Italy" (1919–1920), *New Left Rev.*, **51** (Oct 1968), p. 35.

24. C. Kerr, *Labor and Management in Industrial Society*, New York: Doubleday, 1964, p. 171.
25. For another classic analysis of trade union methods see the Webbs' *Industrial Democracy*; also the critique by Flanders in *Management and Unions*.
26. Only 4 per cent of the adult population in Britain own shares, and 1 per cent own 81 per cent of all privately owned shares. For data and an important analysis of the inequality of economic power and its implications, see R. Blackburn, "The unequal society" in R. Blackburn and A. Cockburn (Eds), *The Incompatibles: Trade Union Militancy and the Consensus*, Harmondsworth: Penguin, 1967. While any analysis of the power of private capital must take account of the existence of a "public sector" of employment, major qualification is unnecessary: for to a large extent it functions to service the private sector and it is subject to policy norms which parallel those of private capitalism. And while the power of capital is mediated by the existence of a professional, often "propertyless" managerial hierarchy, its basic nature remains unaltered (see in this connection the powerful critique of "managerialist" and "post-capitalist" ideologies by T. Nichols, *Ownership, Control and Ideology*, London: Allen and Unwin, 1969.
27. A. Marshall, *Principles of Economics*, 8th ed., London: Macmillan, 1920, p. 567.
28. It is worth noting that size in itself is probably a less important source of union power than membership density: intensive organization may well be more powerful than extensive. Thus a small but tightly-knit union of strategically located workers may be more powerful, for some purposes at least, than a larger body with less intensive coverage. Many trade union amalgamations seem to make little significant contribution to the power of their members *vis-à-vis* their employers; but they may well enhance the personal positions of union leaders (particularly within the inner councils of such bodies as the Trades Union Congress).
29. As D. Lockwood has noted (*The Blackcoated Worker*, London: George Allen and Unwin, 1958, p. 137), trade unionism may well represent a consciousness of sectional rather than class interests. For an illuminating discussion of the interrelationship of sectional and broader collective consciousness and action see R.K. Brown, P. Brannen, J.M. Cousins and M.L. Samphier, "The contours of solidarity: social stratification and industrial relations in shipbuilding", *Br. J. Indust. Relat.*, **10** (March 1971). The question of levels of rationality involved in various perceptions of interests and the related strategies is discussed by R. Hyman, *Strikes*, London: Fontana, 1972, pp. 132–139.
30. Solidarity action by workers not directly involved in an industrial dispute has recently been viewed as a particularly serious threat by employer interests; and most actions of this kind are (at least in theory) outlawed by the Industrial Relations Act.
31. Trade unions also attempt to exert ideological influence: arguing, for example, that "good employers" must observe certain minimum conditions and practices. Such arguments have certainly achieved some effect—particularly

in government employment, where unions have traditionally felt inhibited from engaging in overt conflict. But on balance, the ideological influence of unions on their opponents is limited, and by comparison with that exerted in the reverse direction it may well be declining.

32. S. Cohen (Ed.), *Images of Deviance*, Harmondsworth: Penguin, 1971. For a critical use of this insight with respect to the strike and redundancy "problems" see R. Hyman, *Strikes* and R.H. Fryer, "Redundancy, values and public policy", *Indust. Relat. J.*, **4** (Summer 1973).

33. Particularly clear examples of the "pure" pragmatist perspective are provided by the reports of Courts of Inquiry and the various government agencies involved in investigating industrial relations matters. Our argument that pragmatism is closely associated with the adoption of a managerial definition of industrial relations problems does not entail that such reports assume an uncritical attitude towards particular managerial actions and practices: on the contrary. It is the *institution* of management, and the *objectives* of the capitalist enterprise, which are taken for granted; and when managements are criticized it is normally for failing to pursue these objectives effectively.

34. T. Parsons, *Toward a General Theory of Action*, Cambridge, Mass.: Harvard University Press, 1951, p. 107.

35. Of course, systems theorists have also employed mechanical and, more recently, cybernetic analogies. As Gouldner has ironically noted: "there is a hint of a Rousseaueanism here: social systems are born as living organisms, but everywhere they are becoming machines" (A.W. Gouldner, *The Coming Crisis of Western Sociology*, New York: Basic Books, 1970, p. 210). For other critiques of the systems approach to sociology see M. Black (Ed.), *The Social Theories of Talcott Parsons*, Englewood Cliffs, N.J.: Prentice-Hall, 1961; and W. Buckley, *Sociology and Modern Systems Theory*, Englewood Cliffs, N.J.: Prentice-Hall, 1967.

36. C. Perrow, *Organizational Analysis*, London: Tavistock, 1970, p. 134. Perrow's argument that "our present state of conceptual development, linguistic practices and ontology offers us no alternative" is open to socio-logical challenge, as the section on goals below indicates.

37. J.T. Dunlop, *Industrial Relations Systems*, New York: Holt, 1958, p. 27. It is true that some writers who employ the concept of an industrial relations system deny any presupposition of functional interdependence or common purpose. Yet if these assumptions are removed, the notion of system is drained of meaning: systems theory becomes *merely* a new label for prag-matism.

38. Parsons, *Structure and Process in Modern Societies*, New York: The Free Press, 1960, p. 181.

39. Parsons, "Suggestions for a sociological approach to the theory of organiza-tions", *Admin. Sci. Q.*, **1** (1956), pp. 234–235.

40. Dunlop, *Industrial Relations Systems*, p. 16.

41. These arguments are rehearsed in almost any standard work on industrial relations. See for example H.A. Clegg, *op. cit.* and, most importantly, the

Report of the Royal Commission on Trade Unions and Employers' Associations, Cmnd. 3623, London: HMSO, 1968—generally known as the Donovan Report after the name of its chairman.

42. For a concise statement of both frames of reference, see A. Fox, *Industrial Sociology and Industrial Relations*, London: HMSO, 1966. In this work, which was one of the Donovan Commission's research papers, Fox strongly advocates the pluralistic frame of reference. In a later paper ("Industrial relations: a social critique of pluralist ideology", in J. Child (Ed.), *Man and Organization*, London: George Allen and Unwin, 1973), he presents an important and far more critical analysis of pluralism (in terms which we follow in part in our own discussion). Yet while he demonstrates that pluralism is ideologically loaded and conceptually inadequate, he concludes (p. 231) that "unquestionably the pluralistic perspective has vital uses as a working instrument when we involve ourselves in public policy". Fox makes it obvious that such "public policy" will necessarily share the objectionable features of the theory on which it is based. Moreover, Fox makes explicit (pp. 219–220) the political significance of such imvolvement: "those working within a pluralist framework implicitly accept the master institutions, principles and assumptions of the *status quo* as non-problematical. In doing so they add their professional status, personal prestige, and influencial involvement in public policy making to the forces and influences which lead subordinate groups to continue seeing the *status quo* as legitimate, inevitable, unchangeable, 'only to be expected', subject only to changes at the margin".

43. Fox, *Industrial Sociology and Industrial Relations*, p. 2.

44. The "positive functions" of social conflict have been elaborated by Coser, drawing upon the work of Simmel; see L.A. Coser, *The Functions of Social Conflict*, London: Routledge and Kegan Paul, 1956. For studies which focus upon the constructive value of institutionalized conflict in industry see R. Dubin, "Constructive aspects of conflict" in A. Kornhauser, R. Dubin and A.M. Ross (Eds), *Industrial Conflict*, New York: McGraw-Hill, 1954; W.H. Scott, E. Mumford, I.C. McGivering and J.M. Kirkby, *Coal and Conflict*, Liverpool: University of Liverpool, 1963; and N.S. Ross, *Constructive Conflict*, Edinburgh: Oliver and Boyd, 1969.

45. There are obvious parallels between the pluralist perspective in industrial relations and such developments as "open systems theory" and the "behavioural theory of the firm". All were elaborated as attempts to transcend the over-simplistic character of prevailing orthodoxy in their respective areas of analysis. We would argue that none of these attempts in practice escape the inadequacies of the approaches they were designed to supersede.

46. As Dahrendorf has argued (R. Dahrendorf, *Class and Class Conflict in Industrial Society*, London: Routledge and Kegan Paul, 1959), "constructive conflict" requires that each party recognizes the legitimacy of the other, and hence is committed both to mutual survival and to the maintenance and stability of the framework of rules through which disagreements are mediated. Necessarily these rules will themselves be the product of earlier conflicts

and will have been profoundly influenced by the distribution of power and availability of sanctions to the parties to the conflict. The implications of these assumptions are rarely revealed as explicitly as in the following statement by a leading pluralist (O. Kahn-Freund, *Labour and the Law*, London: Stevens and Sons, 1972, pp. 52–53):

> Management can legitimately expect that labour will be available at a price which permits a reasonable margin for investment, and labour can equally legitimately expect that the level of real wages will not only be maintained but steadily increased. Management can claim a legitimate interest in obtaining for each job the most qualified worker available; labour can claim a legitimate interest in obtaining a job for each worker who is unemployed. Management can and must always expect that the arrangements of society (through law or otherwise) ensure that labour is as mobile as possible in the geographical as well as in the occupational sense; labour must always insist that workers enjoy a reasonable measure of job security so as to be able to plan their own and their families' lives. . . . Management's interest in planning production and in being protected against its interruption is the exact equivalent to the worker's interest in planning his and his family's life and in being protected against an interruption in his mode of existence, either through a fall of his real income or through the loss of his job. All this is palpably obvious, except for a person blinded by class hatred either way.

This conception of "legitimate expectations' clearly takes for granted a political economy in which the power of capital outweighs that of labour. Briefly translated, the argument is that the dependence of the owners of capital on profit (though remarkably, profit is not explicitly mentioned) is "the exact equivalent" of workers' dependence on wages. Managements have a natural right to exploit workers, workers have a highly qualified right not to be *excessively* exploited; and anyone who questions this simple equation must expect the full weight of the pluralist's impassioned and moralistic invective.

47. See, for example, Dubin's abandonment of the full implications of democracy on the grounds of the inappropriateness of "majority rule" in industry ("Constructive aspects of conflict", p. 38): "should such a process be adopted, it seems clear that the workers, constituting the largest single group within the enterprise, would ordinarily outvote all other groups".

48. H.J. Laski, *Trade Unions in the New Society*, London: George Allen and Unwin, 1950, pp. 66–67.

49. F.H. Harbison, "Collective bargaining and American capitalism", in Kornhauser *et al.*, *Industrial Conflict*, p. 276.

50. For a useful discussion of the analysis of organizational goals see M. Albrow, "The study of organizations: objectivity or bias?" in J. Gould (Ed.), *Penguin Survey of the Social Sciences*, Harmondsworth: Penguin, 1968.

51. Perrow, *Organizational Analysis*, p. 171.

52. M. Olson, *The Logic of Collective Action*, Cambridge, Mass.: Harvard University Press, 1965, p. 5.

53. *Trade Unions in the New Society*, p. 4.

54. For an application of Weber's notion of "imperatively coordinated association" to industrial relations, see Dahrendorf, *Class and Class Conflict*.

55. For a discussion of reification see P. L. Berger and T. Luckman, *The Social Construction of Reality*, Harmondsworth: Penguin, 1971. D. Silverman has pointed out the dangers of reification in organizational analysis, *The Theory of Organizations*, London: Heinemann, 1970.

56. Fox, *A Sociology of Work in Industry*, London: Collier-Macmillan, 1971, p. 110.

57. See for example the judgment on the case of *Heaton's Transport Limited v. TGWU*, reported in *Industrial Court Reports*, part 3, Nov. 1972.

58. Fox, *A Sociology of Work in Industry*, p. 114.

59. R.M. Blackburn, *Union Character and Social Class*, London: Batsford, 1967. The proposition that union density varies inversely with "unionateness" is further elaborated in a later paper: R.M. Blackburn and K. Prandy, "White-collar unionization: a conceptual framework", *Br. J. Sociol.*, **16** (June 1965). Here they specify seven criteria of "unionateness", including the willingness of an organization to engage in strike action, the use of the name "union" in its title, and affiliation to the Trades Union Congress and the Labour Party. Blackburn's arguments on union character are criticized in detail in the work by Bain *et al.*, cited below.

60. Lockwood, *The Blackcoated Worker*. Lockwood suggests (pp. 195–198) that white-collar workers typically unionize for "instrumental" reasons (to further their sectional economic interests) whereas manual workers have traditionally organized for "ideological" reasons (out of feelings of solidarity and class consciousness). A later paper (J.H. Goldthorpe and D. Lockwood, "Affluence and the British class structure", *Sociol. Rev.*, **11** (July 1963), suggests that a process of "normative convergence" is occurring. The "radical individualism" of the traditional white-collar worker and the "solidaristic collectivism" of the traditional manual worker, they argue, are both giving way to an "instrumental collectivism" in which workers accept the need for collective organization, but for limited economic rather than ideological reasons. This argument, as it applies to manual workers, is further developed in the Luton studies, which we consider below. We would argue that the dichotomy between "instrumental" and "ideological" motives for unionization is a false one. The defence and advancement of workers' material interests is a *universal* motive for unionization; it is a separate question how broadly or narrowly workers define their common interests, and hence how far they are prepared to act in concert with other trade unionists; and a further question again whether they consider participation in a working-class political party as a necessary and effective way of furthering their interests. As many critics of Goldthorpe and Lockwood have argued, it is a myth to assume that the "traditional" manual trade unionist was class-conscious and politically radical; equally, as we argue below, the notion of the exclusively and narrowly "instrumental" worker is unsatisfactory. For *any* group of workers, the relationship between a consciousness of narrow, sectional economic interests and of broader, class and political ones is typically volatile and imprecise.

61. For a cogent critique of the simple notion that there exists a distinctive white-collar union character see G.S. Bain, *The Growth of White-Collar*

Unionism, Oxford: Clarendon, 1970; and G.S. Bain, D. Coates and V. Ellis, *Social Stratification and Trade Unionism: a Critique*, London: Heinemann, 1973.

62. Hoxie, *Trade Unionism in the United States*, p. 279.

63. See, for example, the seminal paper by E. Bittner, "The concept of organization", *Soc. Res.*, **32** (1965).

64. D.H. Zimmerman, "The practicalities of rule use", in J.D. Douglas (Ed.), *Understanding Everyday Life*, London: Routledge and Kegan Paul, 1971, p. 222.

65. H. Gerth and C. Wright Mills, *Character and Social Structure*, London: Routledge and Kegan Paul, 1954, pp. 116–118.

66. Berger and Luckman, *Social Construction of Reality*, pp. 126–127.

67. H.P. Dreitzel (Ed.), *Recent Sociology 2*, London: Macmillan, 1970, pp. xvi–xvii.

68. K. Marx and F. Engels, *The German Ideology*, London: Lawrence and Wishart, 1970, p. 64. (Originally written 1846, first published 1932.)

69. V.L. Allen, *Militant Trade Unionism*, London: Merlin, 1966, p. 157.

70. See W.H. Beveridge, *Full Employment in a Free Society*, London: George Allen and Unwin, 1944.

71. For an elaboration of this argument see Fryer, "Redundancy, values and public policy".

72. For a critique of this claim see R.H. Fryer, "The myths of the redundancy payments act", *Indust. Law J.*, **2** (Spring 1973).

73. In a recent study by S.R. Parker *et al.*, *The effects of the Redundancy Payments Act*, London: HMSO, 1971, it is reported that 47 per cent of trade union officers said that redundancies among their members were "entirely unavoidable" in the short term. Similarly, 49 per cent thought they were "entirely unavoidable" in the long term. In stark contrast, the numbers of officers thinking that redundancies were entirely avoidable were 6 per cent and 5 per cent respectively.

74. So far there are few analyses of this phenomenon. For somewhat unsatisfactory accounts of the Upper Clyde "work-in" see W. Thompson and F. Hart, *The UCS Work-In*, London: Lawrence and Wishart, 1972; and A. Buchan, *The Right to Work*, London: Calder and Boyars, 1972.

75. For a more general discussion of the potential of such action and also the structural constraints see P. Anderson, "The limits and possibilities of Trade Union action", in Blackburn and Cockburn (Eds), *The Incompatibles*, Harmondsworth: Penguin, 1967.

76. See J.H. Goldthorpe, D. Lockwood, F. Bechhofer and J. Platt, *The Affluent Worker*, vols. I and III, Cambridge: Cambridge University Press, 1968–1969.

77. Vol. I, p. 107.

78. For a comprehensive critique see J. Westergaard, "The rediscovery of the cash nexus" in R. Miliband and J. Saville (Eds), *Socialist Register 1970*, London: Merlin.

79. *Trade Unions*, p. 75.

80. C.L. Goodrich, *The Frontier of Control*, London: Bell, 1920, p. 253.
81. F. Knee, "The Revolt of Labour", 1910, reprinted in K. Coates and A. Topham, *Industrial Democracy in Great Britain*, London: MacGibbon and Kee, 1968, p. 24. This collection of readings, republished 1970 as *Workers' Control*, is an important source of documentation on historical and contemporary debate over the purpose of trade unionism.
82. W. Paynter, *British Trade Unions and Problem of Change*, London: George Allen and Unwin, 1970, pp. 15–16. For trade unions in newly industrializing countries, political action is often far more salient an activity than collective bargaining; but it would be sheer linguistic imperialism to argue that such bodies are not therefore "real" trade unions.
83. W. Gallacher and J. Paton, *Towards Industrial Democracy*, 1917, reprinted in Coates and Topham, p. 109.
84. D. Bell, "The capitalism of the proletariat" in *The End of Ideology*, New York: The Free Press, 1962 ed, pp. 214–215.
85. Thus pluralist writers have often argued that joint regulation provides a means to *increased managerial control:* "the paradox, whose truth managements have found it so difficult to accept, is that they can only regain control by sharing it" (Flanders, *Management and Unions*, p. 172). Pluralists have made it clear why employers should welcome joint regulation; by the same token they offer no convincing evidence why it should be the primary goal of trade unionists. Their main argument would probably be that some unions (particularly in white-collar occupations) lack the power to exercise effective autonomous control; yet if workers are so powerless, it is questionable what concrete gains they will achieve through collective bargaining.
86. A.M. Ross, *Trade Union Wage Policy*, Berkeley: University of California Press, 1948, p. 23.
87. For a discussion of this point see M. Olson, *The Logic of Collective Action*. He suggests (p. 87) that many members' attitude to their union is "analogous to the characteristic attitude of citizens toward their government. Voters are often willing to vote for higher taxes to finance additional government services, but as individuals they strive to contribute as little as the tax laws allow (and on occasion even less)".
88. It is interesting that while most American unions have explicitly disavowed socialist objectives and embraced the ideology of business unionism, this has not occurred in Britain. But their broader overt aims do not appear to make a significant difference to the actual policies of British unions.
89. This is discussed by Hyman, *Strikes*, pp. 95–97.
90. This point is strongly emphasized by Allen, *Militant Trade Unionism*, pp. 29–30.
91. As we have seen, the stabilization of capitalism resulting from this process of "antagonistic cooperation" has fascinated writers in the functionalist-pluralist tradition.
92. C. Wright Mills, *The New Men of Power*, New York: Harcourt Brace, 1948, pp. 8–9.

93. Olson, *Logic of Collective Action*, p. 87.
94. The process of goal displacement in a specific British union is examined by R. Hyman, *The Workers' Union*, Oxford: Clarendon Press, 1971, pp. 195–205.
95. The classic discussion of this trend is in S. and B. Webb, *Industrial Democracy*.
96. See for example J.R. Coleman, "The compulsive pressures of democracy in unionism", *Am. J. Sociol.*, **61** (May 1956), reprinted in W. Galenson and S.M. Lipset (Eds), *Labor and Trade Unionism*, New York: Wiley, 1960.
97. Turner, *Trade Union Growth, Structure and Policy*, pp. 289, 304–305.
98. Again, the classic analysis is provided by the Webbs.
99. A clear example is M. Shanks, *The Stagnant Society*, Harmondsworth: Penguin, 1961.
100. R.W.E. Michels, *Political Parties*, 1915 (original German edition 1911). Reprinted, New York: Dover, 1959.
101. Pp. 369–373.
102. This argument is developed in detail in R. Hyman, *Marxism and the Sociology of Trade Unionism*, London: Pluto Press, 1971.
103. Our discussion in this section focuses principally on problems associated with the development of professional trade union *leadership*. The relationship between rank and file and lower-level full-time officials is considered in a later section.
104. The proper definition of the concept of democracy is as contentious an issue in industrial relations as in political theory. In particular it is persistently debated whether active participative control by the rank and file is a pre-requisite of union democracy, or whether passive membership consent, supplemented by the occurrence of periodic elections, is a sufficient condition. For a consideration of this issue see Hyman, *The Workers' Union*, pp. 206 ff.
105. P. 143.
106. P. 305.
107. *Industrial Democracy*, p. 16.
108. P. 36.
109. *Political Parties*, p. 143.
110. Elsewhere Michels characterizes the attitude of rank-and-file members to their leaders not as apathy but as virtual hero-worship: they felt they owed them a "sacred duty" of loyalty. A strong sense of personal loyalty towards officials is certainly a notable feature of the British trade union movement, and one no doubt deliberately cultivated by many leaders. But conversely, the bureaucratic aspects of modern union leadership may tend towards the "routinization of charisma" analysed by Weber.
111. Only one empirical study has claimed to provide an important counter-example to Michels: S.M. Lipset, M.A. Trow and J.S. Coleman, *Union Democracy*, Glencoe, Ill.: The Free Press, 1956. This examination of the International Typographical Union in the USA emphasizes the two-party system which has allowed alternating control of union government for over half a century, and also the high degree of rank-and-file participation. But

the authors add that there are many features of this union which make it virtually unique.

112. Clegg, *The System of Industrial Relations in Great Britain*, p. 82.

113. H.L. Wilensky, "The trade union as a bureaucracy" in A. Etzioni (Ed.), *Complex Organizations: a Sociological Reader*, New York: Holt, Rinehart and Winston, 1961, p. 223.

114. Findings are summarized by Clegg, *The System of Industrial Relations* and Hyman, *The Workers' Union*; see also Government Social Survey, *Workshop Industrial Relations*, London: HMSO, 1968.

115. Among general discussions of these influences see, for America, W. Spinrad, "Correlates of trade union participation", *Am. Sociol. Rev.*, **25** (1960); S.M. Lipset, "The political process in trade unions: a theoretical statement" in Galenson and Lipset, *Labor and Trade Unionism*; and A.S. Tannenbaum, "Unions". More recent British discussions are Turner, *Trade Union Growth, Structure and Policy*; J. Hughes, *Membership Participation and Trade Union Government*, Royal Commission Research Paper 5 (Part 2), London: HMSO, 1968; and R. Martin, "Union Democracy: an Explanatory Framework", *Sociology*, **2** (1968).

116. *Trade Union Growth, Structure and Policy*, pp. 290–291.

117. *Trade Unionism in the United States*, p. 47.

118. Ross, *Trade Union Wage Policy*, p. 39.

119. Unofficial Reform Committee (of the South Wales Miners' Federation), *The Miners' Next Step*, 1912, Tonypandy: Davies, pp. 13–14.

120. Lipset, in Galenson and Lipset, p. 226.

121. P. 12.

122. P. 15.

123. National Board for Prices and Incomes, *Report 65: Payment by Results Systems*, Cmnd. 3627, London: HMSO, 1968, p. 7. The proportion of workers paid by results may have declined more recently, with the introduction by a number of employers of forms of measured day work.

124. E.G. Whybrew, *Overtime Working in Britain*, Royal Commission Research Paper 9, London: HMSO, 1968.

125. For a more detailed discussion see Hyman, *Strikes*. In recent years there has been a revival of large-scale official strikes largely attributable to the developments discussed in a later section.

126. J. Goldstein, *The Government of British Trade Unions*, London: Allen and Unwin, 1952, p. 241.

127. Pp. 28–29. The findings of the survey conducted for the Commission are revealing: 46 per cent of managers thought their stewards were less militant than ordinary members, only 16 per cent that they were more militant; while 70 per cent preferred negotiating with shop stewards to full-time union officials; only 3 per cent thought stewards "unreasonable" (Government Social Survey, *Workplace Industrial Relations*, pp. 85–86).

128. A number of recent publications discuss shop steward activities and organization, and consider factors underlying variations in stewards' influence. See

for example W.E.J. McCarthy, *The Role of Shop Stewards in British Industrial Relations*, and McCarthy and S.R. Parker, *Shop Stewards and Workshop Relations*, Royal Commission Research Papers 1 and 10, London: HMSO, 1966 and 1968; Clegg, *The System of Industrial Relations in Great Britain*; J.F.B. Goodman and T.G. Whittingham, *Shop Stewards in British Industry*, London: McGraw Hill, 1969; W.A. Brown, *Piecework Bargaining*, London: Heinemann, 1973.

129. The one notable exception is H.A. Clegg, A.J. Killick and R. Adams, *Trade Union Officers*, Oxford: Blackwell, 1961. Current research at the SSRC Industrial Relations Research Unit at the University of Warwick is giving detailed attention to the role of the full-time official.

130. For a discussion of "intra-organizational bargaining" see R.E. Walton and R.B. McKersie, *A Behavioral Theory of Labor Negotiations*, New York: McGraw-Hill, 1965; and R. Hyman, *Disputes Procedure in Action*, London: Heinemann, 1972, ch. 5.

131. For examples of these respective positions see B.C. Roberts (Ed.), *Industrial Relations: Contemporary Problems and Perspectives*, London: Methuen 1962; T. Cliff and C. Barker, *Incomes Policy, Legislation and Shop Stewards*, London: Shop Stewards' Defence Committee, 1966; and the Donovan Report.

132. A.S. Tannenbaum and R.L. Kahn, "Organizational control structure", *Hum. Relat.*, **10** (1957).

133. O. Kahn-Freund, "Legal framework", in H.A. Clegg and A. Flanders (Eds), *The System of Industrial Relations in Great Britain*, Oxford: Blackwell, 1954, p. 44. For other discussions of the tradition of "voluntarism" see K.W. Wedderburn, *The Worker and the Law*, Harmondsworth: Penguin, 1965 (revised ed., 1971) and Flanders, *Management and Unions*.

134. An analysis which draws very similar conclusions, though from a totally different perspective, is provided by A. Fox and A. Flanders, "The reform of collective bargaining: from Donovan to Durkheim", *Br. J. Indust. Relat.*, **7** (1969).

135. D. Jackson, H.A. Turner and F. Wilkinson, *Do Trade Unions Cause Inflation?*, Cambridge: Cambridge University Press, 1972, p. 67.

136. Two analyses of the Labour incomes policy are H.A. Clegg, *How to Run an Incomes Policy and Why We Made Such a Mess of the Last One*, London, Heinemann, 1971; and A. Fels, *The British Prices and Incomes Board*, Cambridge: Cambridge University Press, 1972.

137. An influential early study is A. Flanders, *The Fawley Productivity Agreements*, London: Faber and Faber, 1964. For a critical appraisal see T. Cliff, *The Employers' Offensive*, London: Pluto Press, 1970.

138. A notable example was the agreement in 1969 at the Chrysler works in Coventry, giving production workers a weekly wage of £35 on the intro- duction of measured day work in place of piecework; this figure then became a target for car workers throughout Britain.

139. For a detailed analysis see A. Glyn and B. Sutcliffe, *British Capitalism, Workers and the Profits Squeeze*, Harmondsworth: Penguin, 1972.

140. For one analysis of this trend see M. Kidron, *Western Capitalism Since the War*, Harmondsworth: Penguin, 1970.

141. For a valuable critique of the role of the state, including its involvement in industrial relations, see R. Miliband, *The State in Capitalist Society*, London: Weidenfeld and Nicholson, 1969. See also Blackburn, "The unequal society".

142. For a union to be generally regarded as "responsible" it must suppress attention to the interests of its members out of concern for what is conventionally termed the "national interest". See the critique of "the meaning of responsibility" by Allen, *Militant Trade Unionism*.

143. For a detailed examination of the effect of such pressure on union leaders see V.L. Allen, *Trade Unions and the Government*, London: Longmans, 1960, and *Militant Trade Unionism*.

144. For a discussion of the role of the media in industrial relations, and in particular their manipulation of "public opinion", see Hyman, *Strikes*.

145. V.I. Lenin, "What is to be done?", 1902, in *Collected Works*, vol. V, Moscow: Foreign Languages Publishing House, 1961, p 375.

146. In "What is to be done?" Lenin presented this argument in an extreme form which he qualified elsewhere; for details see Hyman, *Marxism and the Sociology of Trade Unionism*. A recent elaboration of Lenin's argument and its relevance to contemporary trade unionism is P. Anderson, "Limits and possibilities of trade union action".

147. *The German Ideology*, p. 64.

148. F. Parkin, *Class Inequality and Political Order*, London: MacGibbon and Kee, 1971, p. 92.

149. For a survey of relevant studies see M. Mann, "The social cohesion of liberal democracy", *Am. Sociol. Rev.*, **35** (1970).

150. Thus the provisions of the second stage of the Conservative government's wage freeze (Jan 1973) were widely proclaimed as "fair", even though they *increased* inequality: a worker earning £20 was entitled to a rise of only £1.80, whereas one earning £100 was allowed an extra £5. For a more detailed discussion of such ideological influences see R. Hyman, *Inequality and Industrial Relations*, forthcoming.

151. The concepts of opacity and transparency in respect of social structure are discussed by Parkin, *Class Inequality and Political Order*, pp. 160–163.

152. Fox, *A Sociology of Work in Industry*, p. 38.

153. "Although I'm a working man/ I can ruin the government's plan/ I'm not too hard/ But the sight of my card/ Makes me some kind of superman" runs in part a popular song climbing the British hit parade in early 1973 (J. Ford and R. Hudson, *Part of the Union*). If such sentiments, with their intimations of hegemonic consciousness, were to become widespread, the implications for trade union goals and methods could be considerable.

154. G. Lukacs, *History and Class Consciousness*, London: Merlin Press, 1971, p. 208. (Original German edition 1923.)

ANNE R. EDWARDS

THE PRISON

Anne R. Edwards *received her training in sociology at Bedford College, University of London. Following work at the Rutherford College of Technology, Newcastle-upon-Tyne and at Durham University, she moved to Australia where she is now Senior Lecturer in the Department of Anthropology and Sociology at Monash University. Her research and teaching interests include sociology of deviance, mental illness and sociological theory. She has recently completed research on adaptations and socialization in prison.*

> A prison is a physical structure in a geographical location where a number of people, living under highly specialized conditions, utilize the resources and adjust to the alternatives presented to them by a unique kind of social environment.[1]

Penal systems in general, and prisons in particular, have been and are required to perform some or all of a variety of functions on behalf of society: punishment, protection of society, deterrence (general and individual), reformation, rehabilitation, retribution and restitution. Cressey adds a further, usually "unstated" goal: protection of prisoners from outside society and from others (staff and prisoners) inside the prison.[2] Galtung identifies twelve social functions, distinguishing between two broad categories: the first concerned with the "prevention of crime" by various means ("physical", "biological" and "normative constraints") and the second covering the symbolic, social, economic and psychological needs of the society or of specific sections of the population. He observed: "It is remarkable how efficient the prison may be in fulfilling all functions except the internalization of norms in the violator";[3] but particular types of penal institutions can also be seen to concentrate on different combinations of the various functions, such as punishment versus correction or the needs and interests of prisoners versus those of the wider society. The prison, which has existed in something like its present form since the latter half of the nineteenth century in Britain and the United States,[4] has from the 1930s onwards attracted the attention of an increasing number of social scientists; of those writing in English most are Americans but there are also a few from Britain and Scandinavia.

1. The prison as an organization in society

Usually the framework for these prison studies has been one taken from organization theory with comparisons made particularly with the mental hospital;[5] but some writers include penal institutions in a broadly defined category of organiza-tions, variously termed "total institutions",[6] "people-changing",[7] "people-handling",[8] "integrative",[9] or "service"[10] organizations. The common features are the purposes or functions such organizations fulfil and the material with which they work: their primary purpose being to produce people in a predetermined mould and specifically, in the case of penal and also psychiatric institutions, to ensure, for society, the control of and, if possible, a reduction in antisocial (especially law-breaking) behaviour. In other words, prisons can only be defined initially in relation to the tasks they are required to perform for the wider society to which they belong. The methods used may be variable (for instance, solitary confinement, work training, military discipline or psychotherapy) and at different times and places the relative ordering of the various socially approved subsidiary goals may alter, the most frequently discussed recent change being from custody and contain-ment of inmates towards some attempt at treatment and rehabilitation.[11]

This movement has been usefully analysed in general theoretical terms as involving a shift from one basic type of organization to another; for example, this is seen by Blau and Scott as being from a "commonweal" to a "service" type of organization,[12] by Etzioni as from a "coercive" to a "normative" basis of compliance[13] and by Wilson in terms of a contrast between"bureaucratic" and "participative" styles of management.[14] Although these writers are operating with different theoretical typologies of organizations, differentiated according to various structural features, all emphasize the fact that a treatment orientation implies a more open, flexible, "democratic" system of decision-making (for staff if not for inmates), a concern for the welfare of the "clients" of the organization as being at least as important as the interests of the wider society and a corresponding change in commitment to or involvement in their organization on the part of inmates and rank-and-file staff. Specific studies have been undertaken to explicate the inter-relationships between goals, regimes, strategies, staff roles and inmate responses in penal institutions categorized as being either mainly custodial or mainly treatment or a mixture of the two.[15]

An additional type is the "work-" or "production-" centred prison,[16] which is characterized as an attempt to move away from an exclusive preoccupation with security and order (achieved by physical and coercive means) towards a system where prisoners are induced to work sufficiently hard to guarantee the economic self-sufficiency of the institution.[17] Mouledous describes two systems of "coordina-tion" existing side by side on the same prison farm, one based on threat and the other on exchange, each with its own distinct aims (order or production) and each giving rise to quite different typical inmates (the "gunman" or the "guard-trusty").

To return to the two major types of penal institution, the custodial and the treatment-oriented, some doubts have been raised as to whether any actual cases of the pure treatment type do or can exist. All that have been found empirically to date are some institutions that place relatively greater emphasis on treatment as compared to their other goals or functions. Janowitz claims that, even in juvenile institutions, treatment regimes remain "experimental" and include a variety of programmes.[18] Emery, referring to the British penal system, makes the following assertion:

> Given the requirement of medium or maximum *security*, the prison regime cannot be expected to be a reformative agent. . . . It is, however, a moot point whether therapeutic techniques are as yet effective, even in an *open* prison.[19]

Perrow, who shares the view that a "therapeutic community" would be extremely difficult, if not impossible, to create in a penal institution, offers an alternative interpretation of the widely noted apparent movement away from strictly custodial regimes. He introduces the concept of a "humane care" organization to cover the case of the institution "in which custodial practices have been largely discarded, but therapeutic ones barely developed, despite considerable effort."[20] In other words, he is describing an intermediate type of institution where "punitive, repressive methods of handling inmates" are absent, but no positive attempts have been made to replace them with a constructive, systematic treatment programme. Rose makes a similar kind of distinction between "active" and "passive treatment" and argues that passive treatment "shades off" into "passive deterrence", where "while there is always work provided there is no organized and deliberate attempt at individual treatment" (and which in turn is differentiated from "active deterrence").[21] Passive treatment, on the other hand, is "where there are constructive facilities for work, education, leisure, welfare and so on, but no real attempt at individualized treatment planning based upon continuous consultation". Street, Vintner and Perrow delineate some of the characteristics of this type of institution when catering for juveniles: its emphasis lies on re-education and development, and the basic technique used is training, which should be distinguished from the fundamental resocialization processes needed in a treatment programme.[22] The crucial factor is clearly the involuntary nature of confinement for all prisoners and some mental patients; this fact makes it problematic whether the kind of moral and social commitment to the institution, the staff and the programme, required before fundamental resocialization can occur, can be expected to exist or can even be induced in more than a small minority of inmates. It is in relation to this question of "reformation" or not that the role of an inmate social system or inmate group becomes critical.

2. Organization within the Prison

The most consistent finding to emerge from the prison literature is the existence of some sort of social system among the inmates. Organizational analysis generally has drawn attention to the fact that organizations contain at least two major systems: one, the formal, official administrative system and the other, an informal society comprising the "lower participants" of the organization—in the case of prisons and mental hospitals, the inmates. The members or employees of such organizations (both staff and administration) and the inmates can initially be seen as constituting two caste-like groups; there is an absolute barrier within any one institution to mobility between the two groups, minimal and impersonal communication across the dividing line and authority totally in the hands of one group. On further examination, however, this appears to be an oversimplification. On the one hand, staff and administration may not in fact constitute a single and united body on many issues: frequently, divisions have been noted between the top administrators and the ordinary staff,[23] and, especially where some rehabilitation programmes have been instituted, between the professional staff and the custodial or "line" officers.[24] On the other hand, inmate society too consists of a number of large and small groups, often with different attitudes and values and it may have to try to represent the interests of any of a wide variety of types of prisoners, differentiated according to degree of criminalization and previous institutional experience, among other characteristics. Further, as the classic study by Sykes has demonstrated, the apparently total dominance of the staff is defective as their "authority" suffers from "corruption", to a large extent as a result of the activities of inmates but also because, for various reasons, custodians fail to exercise some of their powers.[25]

Comparisons, such as those in Berk and Grusky (who studied adult prisons) and in Street *et al.* (juveniles), between institutions differing in the weight they give to treatment (relative to order and custody), reveal that the general orientation of the "inmate organization" or the "inmate group" varies from cooperation to hostility in relation to the institution and its staff. As Berk states:

> Two different types of informal organization developed: the inmate subsystem performed contrasting functions in treatment and custodial institutions.[26]

These were "supportive" and "oppositional" respectively. He also found that informal leadership patterns reflected the goal and structural differences between organizations. The kinds of adaptations and roles found among inmates also tended to vary by institution in a similar fashion,[27] as does the nature of their prison socialization.

Up to now, the main impression given here of the sociology of the prison is one of harmony and consistency: the ordered and progressive accumulation of empirical data and a single, widely used and all-embracing interpretive schema. In fact, however, as in most substantive areas of study in sociology, the material so far published contains a considerable number of confusions, contradictions and discrepant findings on many of the important and well-researched issues, such as the solidarity of inmate society, types of inmate adaptation and the nature and effects of prison socialization.

Before starting on a systematic analysis of the published studies of penal institutions, therefore, some discussion on the possible logical explanations for such differences and disagreements seems justified. The two main alternatives are academic or empirical explanations. The academic line of approach includes both theoretical and conceptual issues and methodological considerations; the two major empirical sources of possible variation are differences in the kinds of penal institution and in types of prisoners. In other words, where two or more studies have come up with different and incompatible results, the variations can be attributed either to the theoretical orientation guiding the research or the particular methods adopted or to "real" empirical differences in the nature of the phenomena under investigation or to a combination of all three.

3. Academic sources of diversity: concepts, theoretical perspectives and methods

Diversity can be illustrated by writers' choices of particular concepts, the varied meanings and uses of their concepts,[28] their underlying theoretical perspectives and their "domain assumptions"[29] (the related question of methodological differences is to be discussed later).

A. *Concepts*

The following list includes the most commonly used basic concepts to be found in the prison literature (dealing with both the whole organization and inmate society) and is arranged in three sections:
(i) the prison as a totality or a "microcosm of the larger society"[30]—organization, system, community (qualified by terms such as "prison" or "correctional"), culture;
(ii) the collective, structural and cultural arrangements of inmates (all qualified by epithets such as "inmate", "prisoner", "informal", "unofficial" or "sub rosa")—society, social system, community, social structure, organization, group, social role, culture, subculture, contra-culture, counter-culture, code, ideology, belief system;
(iii) socialization processes affecting inmates—socialization, resocialization, prisonization, rehabilitation, institutionalization, internalization, criminalization.

Conceptual preferences are significantly revealed by an emphasis being placed primarily on either the structural or the cultural aspects of inmate society, though some authors do make attempts to integrate the two.[31] Structural phenomena are groups, relationships, status hierarchies, social positions, leadership, power, action and interaction and "cultural" covers norms, values, beliefs, attitudes, perceptions and roles (defined as role-expectations). This analytical distinction is also reflected in the methods and types of data used in different studies: participant observation or questionnaire, and actions or attitudes. In another context, Lerman put this distinction to illuminating and profitable use in connection with the question of delinquent subcultures producing law-breaking behaviour among young, urban males.[32]

Referring to the various concepts implying a socialization process of some kind for prisoners, McCorkle and Korn make this basic logical point:

As the concept "socialization" implies group membership, so the derivative concept, "resocialization", implies changes in group membership.[33]

A further differentiation is needed, based on the content of the socialization or resocialization, between criminalistic attitudes and habits and prison-specific norms and patterns of behaviour. The two processes may be termed "criminalization" and "prisonization".[34] To what extent prisonization involves institutionalization is another issue, one which seems to require a multi-stage or multi-level concept of prisonization[35] for its resolution. Whether prisonization and criminalization constitute a socialization or a resocialization experience for any particular inmate depends on his previously acquired habits, expectations and beliefs (and thus on his past reference and membership groups and subcultural involvements). For instance, the "accidental" offender, with no previous record or criminal associates, may find himself during a long prison sentence learning both criminalistic and prison-specific attitudes and practices in a "double" resocialization experience, while, at the opposite extreme, a recidivist, who has served many previous sentences, simply responds to a familiar situation without the need to undergo any resocialization at all. From a treatment-oriented perspective, prison socialization takes on quite a different meaning and must be separated conceptually from rehabilitation. Galtung defines them as follows:

> Penologically and socially the most important fact is whether a released convict commits a new crime or not. If he does not, *rehabilitation* may be said to have taken place, but this is not the same as resocialization. *Resocialization* means that he abstains from criminal acts when these acts are in his action-space, but are excluded because of the constraints from anticipated personal sanctions. Thus, resocialization implies rehabilitation, *but the converse need not be true.* According to our scheme, there are three other ways in which the criminal acts may be excluded, but more significantly: *Rehabilitation may result from the disappearance of the illegal acts from the action-space.*[36]

It must be remembered, therefore, that, like Grygier's concept of "social progression",[37] socialization is basically neutral and empty of content, which must be supplied by empirical investigation in any given case.

B. *Theoretical Perspectives*

Conceptual clarification is of limited value without an analysis of the theoretical perspectives that accompany the concepts and give them their meaning. Fundamentally, two main theoretical approaches are available to the sociologist: those of structural-functionalism and of interactionism. Which of these two stances is adopted determines a range of general orientations and theoretical concerns, for example, in the case of organizations, the questions of goal determination, of change and stability, of the bases of social order, of organizational viability, the role of the individual and the relationship of the organization to the external environment.

The major characteristics of these "two sociologies" (which may be regarded as complementary or conflicting alternatives)[38] have been described by, among others, Dawe, who argues that they each incorporate also a distinct and different social philosophy.[39] Man and society are perceived in quite a different manner by the various followers of the two approaches and, even where the same concepts are used or the same phenomena are examined, this is done in different ways and to different ends.

Specifically, striking differences can be discerned between the two theoretical stances in their attitudes to two fundamental sociological questions: micro versus macro levels of analysis and total or partial determinism of human conduct. Structural-functionalism tends to favour the macro or holistic perspective and to see individuals as puppets manipulated by external and constraining social forces; in the organizational context, actors *are* their roles. It has, therefore, been variously criticized for being "rationalistic" and "apolitical",[40] static, consensual,[41] dehumanizing, closed and exclusive, "positivistic" or "absolutist"[42] and prone to reification and mystification.[43] The "action" frame of reference, by contrast, starts from the basic concept of an actor in a social situation interpreting its meaning for him and acting on that meaning. Such actors are believed to exercise some limited degree of autonomy and to be capable of evaluating and creating their social reality as well as responding to external pressures. Although located initially at a micro level, such a theoretical framework need not be restricted in its application to the sphere of interpersonal relationships only, but can be extended to deal with more general, structural and macro categories of phenomena. However, there is continuity between concepts at the various levels of analysis; in particular the concepts of structure and culture can be derived from concepts of social action, interaction, meaning and typification.[44]

Recently, the implications of this state of affairs for the sociology of organizations have been spelled out by Silverman, who claims that up to now organization analysis has utilized almost exclusively a systems (and frequently a specifically structural-functionalist) frame of reference. He develops an alternative (based on "action" theory and drawing heavily on the ideas of Weber, Schütz and Berger and Luckmann) and contrasts the two perspectives:

> (The former) emphasized explanations of behaviour in terms of the interaction of systems attempting to satisfy their needs, and often made use of an organic analogy to explain the nature of the relationship between system-parts. (The latter) argued that attention should be first paid to the orientations of the participants who might be differentially attached to any aspect of social life and who themselves create, sustain and change the rules of the social game.[45]

These two views of the relationship between man and his social situation can be expressed as a contrast between "fate" and "way of life". These alternative conceptions are well illustrated, in the case of the hospitalized mental patient, by making a comparison between the interpretations of Goffman and of Braginsky, Braginsky and Ring. Goffman sees patients as puppets at the mercy of their relatives rendered impotent by virtue of the dehumanizing and disenfranchizing effects of being diagnosed mentally ill and having such a label medically or legally affixed, and subjected to the systematic "mortification of self" practices characteristic of "total institutions".[46] By contrast, Braginsky *et al.* choose to stress the "purposeful, coherent and effective" courses of action pursued even by mental patients, who engaged successfully in "impression-management" in order to "establish personally satisfying and quite rational styles of life within the hospital".[47] With specific reference to their theoretical model for understanding patients' behaviour, they identify the concepts of "context" and "meaning" as the basic elements.

In the case of the prison, a different but comparable situation is discernible.

The predominant emphasis, particularly in the 1950s, was placed on an informal inmate society with a strongly anti-staff and anti-institution normative system and organized markets in scarce goods and services under inmate control. In this context, the assumption was made that inmate social organization was a semi-automatic reaction against the deprived and degrading conditions of prisoners and that reducing the degree of deprivation experienced in prisons would have little or no effect on the basically oppositional character of inmate society.[48] A contrary picture, however, is emerging from two sources: on the one hand, studies comparing treatment and custodial prisons by Berk, Grusky and Street found inmates modifying their attitudes and behaviour in accordance with the goals and regimes of particular institutions and, on the other hand, Garabedian, Giallombardo, Morris and Morris, Polsky, Sykes and others have drawn attention to the variety of different roles and adaptations portrayed by the occupants of a single prison, suggesting that prisoners differentially perceive and respond to the same set of "objective" conditions.[49]

Associated with these fundamental issues faced by the two dominant perspectives are two further differences between them: (i) the questions of stability and change and (ii) the different perceptions of the relationship between the organization and its external environment.[50]

(i) *Stability and change* This question deals with what has also been called the problem of "static" versus "dynamic" analysis; static analysis is largely concerned with describing and analysing all or most of the aspects or parts of a system and their interrelationships, but at a single point of time, and may use survey techniques only and/or more social anthropological methods. Such "snap-shots" of separate institutions may be examined singly or compared with others (taken at different times or in different places).[51] The dynamic type of approach, which emphasizes "process" as much as or more than "structure", can operate at two possible levels: prisoners may be studied during the various phases of their prison sentence and after release (cross-sectionally or longitudinally)[52] or the prison as an organization (including all its participants—administration, staff and inmates) may be observed over a prolonged period of time, during which specific innovations or changes may be introduced either deliberately or incidentally to the research.[53] Mathiesen claims that to date writers have paid too much attention to the "stable aspects of the social structure of prisons" at the cost of studies of change.[54] He described two "aspects of organizational change": firstly, "the recurring processes which take place over time within a custodial social structure" (the striking exception to the general neglect of this topic being Sykes); and, secondly, "the question of change in structure" especially from a custodial to a treatment orientation (this latter providing the central focus for Mathiesen's own analysis of a Norwegian prison).

(ii) *External environment* This question too can be dealt with on different levels. As regards the inmates, it can be seen in the controversy over whether their responses to prison life are explicable primarily in intra-organizational terms (the "deprivations" hypothesis) or only by considering the sorts of people they are, that is the kinds of experiences, habits, attitudes, values and needs each individual prisoner has acquired outside and brought with him into prison (the "importation" hypothesis).[55] The staff[56] and the administrators also have lives apart from their occupations and their orientations to and conduct in the everyday work situation cannot be understood in isolation.[57] Finally, the prison, as a "living" social institution, is perceived and treated in certain ways by the different members of the society in which it is located and this fact has consequences for its general internal workings as well as for the various categories of individuals whose lives are bound up with it.

Before ending this discussion of alternative theoretical frameworks for the sociological analysis of organizations and particularly prisons, two brief points need to be made concerning the concepts of socialization and social role.

Social role

The concept of social role is the subject of much debate and some disagreement. At least three different aspects of the concept have each provided the basis of a definition and have led to its varying uses and meanings in current sociology; to use Levinson's words:

> a. Role may be defined as the structurally given demands (norms, expectations, taboos, responsibilities, and the like) associated with a given social position. Role is, in this sense, something outside the given individual, a set of pressures and facilitations that channel, guide, impede, support his functioning in the organization.
> b. Role may be defined as the member's *orientation* or *conception* of the part he is to play in the organization. It is, so to say, his inner definition of what someone in his social position is supposed to think and do about it . . .
> c. Role is commonly defined as the actions of the individual members—actions seen in terms of their relevance for the social structure (that is, seen in relation to the prevailing norms). In this sense, role refers to the ways in which members of a position act (with or without conscious intention) *in accord with or in violation of a given set of organizational norms*. Here, as in (b), role is defined as a characteristic of the actor rather than of his normative environment.[58]

There are fundamental differences between functionalists and interactionists (especially symbolic interactionists) in their conceptions and uses of the term. For functionalists, following Linton, roles and their interrelationships are "primary components of social institutions, social systems, and social structures"; within the alternative theoretical perspective (and stemming from Mead), role is seen as "the mediating link" between the individual and society.[59] Put another way, in the former case of "a unitary, all embracing, conception of role", the assumption is being made "that there is a 1 : 1 relationship, or at least a high degree of congruence, between the three role aspects noted above".[60] In the latter, however, no such unity is assumed or expected and the three separate dimensions are investigated empirically. Levinson goes on to argue for a more systematic analysis of the influence of personality on individuals in organizations, and presumably in sociology generally, to redress the balance:

Just as social structure presents massive forces which influence the individual from without toward certain forms of adaptation, so does personality present massive forces from within which lead him to select, create, and synthesize certain forms of adaptation rather than others.[61]

Socialization

An earlier discussion of the concepts of socialization and resocialization prepared the ground for a more theoretical analysis of their various meanings and uses. Socialization, in structuralist and consensus theories, is perceived as a process emanating from society of moulding the individual so that both his overt behaviour and his internal feelings, beliefs, values and expectations are consistent with the requirements of the social system in which he lives and with its core value system. Socialization or "internalization", in theories emphasizing "the social construction of reality" and the reciprocal, symbolic and fluid nature of social interaction, is regarded as only one of three interdependent and equally important processes: the others being externalization and objectivation.[62] Having thus located the role of socialization in their general theoretical framework, Berger and Luckmann differentiate the various constituent processes. "Primary" socialization refers to the basic and universal process starting at birth and by means of which the individual "becomes a member of society". "Secondary socialization is any subsequent process that inducts an already socialized individual into new sectors of the objective world of his society", and involves the "internalization of institutional or institution-based 'subworlds' ".[63] Whereas secondary socialization entails diversifying within or building on to a pre-existing "symbolic universe", resocialization demands a total or partial "transformation" in which the individual "switches worlds".[64] Prisonization and criminalization may, therefore, approximate a resocialization process for some, but secondary socialization for others (who have had elements of institutional living or criminality respectively in their primary socialization experiences).

The preference of the present writer is for the interactionist theoretical perspective; very briefly this perspective stresses the following aspects of the prison as an organization:
(i) The prison cannot be satisfactorily understood without attention being paid to its external environment; since no prison exists in a social vacuum, societal pressures and constraints (both prescriptive and proscriptive) exercise considerable influence over the internal functioning of the prison at the levels of staff and inmate.
(ii) Like any social institution, the prison is undergoing a continuous process of adaptation and change—partly in response to specific and changing demands made on it by the wider society, partly because of its shifting population composition, but also because it is a "living social organism".[65]
(iii) Internally a prison should be analysed as a collection of individuals, dyads, cliques, and groups (of varying degrees of permanence) arranged from time to time in coalitions and factions of various types; each of these units may or may

not rest on and share with any others a common "symbolic world" or "sub-universe".[66] Thus, instead of dividing each prison *a priori* into a formal and an informal system,[67] the investigator seeks to identify the significant persons and groups as they emerge and change empirically in a particular institution (not always maintaining a rigid separation of staff and inmate)[68] and then studies them all. Here the issues raised by Becker and Gouldner over taking "sides" are highly relevant.[69] Up to now, there has been a tendency to concentrate on either the "underdog" or the "middledog". However desirable and theoretically necessary a comprehensive picture of the prison from all sides may be, it must be conceded that the peculiar nature of the "total institution" (particularly the caste-like features and the resulting conflict) makes this objective hard to attain in practice.

(iv) Looking at the individual in an organization, he is seen as capable of creating his social reality (within limits) as well as responding to that presented to him by others (particularly those among the staff and the inmates with power over him). Why and how an inmate accepts or rejects a particular role or style of adaptation,[70] and how he chooses or finds reference and membership groups are crucial questions. So too are the issues of role conflict and ambiguity experienced by staff (especially custodial staff in a treatment-oriented prison), but seen from their points of view.

(v) The types and levels of inmate socialization/resocialization need to be regarded as inseparable from the past and present experiences, attachments and orientations of each individual and not as simple, universal, linear and externally enforced processes of "reformation", "corruption" or "institutionalization". Thus, socialization is integrally related to the "definition of the situation" of each prisoner, which in turn is importantly linked to his inside and outside membership and reference groups.

C. *Methodological differences*

The two theoretical perspectives outlined above lead to somewhat different types of methodology: put simply, one based on analysing the system and the relationships between the system parts and the other, actors in social situations. Two major methodological implications of the interactionist perspective can be identified. Firstly, the subjective definition of the situation is a crucial variable in the understanding of social action (and eventually of an "emergent social structure"), which requires a conscious movement in the direction of phenomenology, as has been discussed by, for example, Douglas.[71] Secondly, data specifically based on observed behaviour and interaction are an essential addition to the more common use of self-reports of conduct, relationships and attitudes, such material usually gathered by questionnaire and interview methods; and thus sociologists need to utilize more of the techniques traditionally associated with social anthropology and which were used in the pioneering study by Clemmer.

The empirical investigation of the existence of inmate subcultures, in particular, requires a complex and varied research strategy and cannot simply be inferred from the finding that a number of individuals share the same attitudes and values.[72] Similarly, assertions about the degrees of solidarity or organization among inmates demand a wide range of different types of empirical evidence and should not, as in the case of Glaser for instance,[73] be based solely on answers by individual prisoners to questions, a source of information which is inevitably restricted to each individual's personal perception and experience of the social world in which he lives (and which cannot be used to detect a case of "pluralistic ignorance" when it occurs).[74]

The majority of prison research to date has opted for one or the other of two main methodological techniques available: either participant observation over one or more years and the utilization of a wide variety of sources of material (for example, Giallombardo, Mathiesen, McCleery, Morris and Morris and Polsky) or the collection of "hard" questionnaire data (whether by interview or self-administered) from, often relatively large, samples of prisoners and/or staff in a number of different institutions (examples of such studies where the focus was on prisoners are Cline and Glaser, while Brown *et al.* and Kassebaum *et al.* surveyed institutional and general correctional staff respectively).[75]

Individual case studies and the comparative approach, however, need to be combined. Limitations of time and other resources may force compromises either at the cost of the wealth and depth of material obtained from each institution or in the range and types of comparisons made. At the least, material derived from the study of one institution should be rendered more meaningful by being contrasted with any available material from others' studies of other institutions.

A diachronic approach is of central importance in studies of inmate adaptations and socialization or as an alternative form of comparative analysis. In the former case, panel and longitudinal data is essential (covering the whole period of prisoners' sentences as well as a follow-up after release) and cross-sectional surveys of prisoners are only a poor substitute. In the latter, Street *et al.*, for instance, reached a deeper understanding of their institutions by conducting at least two separate investigations at different points of time, whilst McCleery and Sykes in America and Emery in England achieved equivalent results by maintaining a continuous interest over a long period.

The adequate interpretation of the analyses given in different studies requires knowledge of how the investigator was perceived by the various individuals and groups in the institution. As was pointed out above, simultaneous identification with both staff and inmates or even with all staff or all inmates is a near-impossibility; and thus, at any one time, the researcher will find himself defined as being "on one side" or another, "with" one group or "for" one individual rather than others,[76] which will directly affect the quality and the meaning of any data gathered. A "full" picture of the whole institution is not to be gained by feigning objectivity and neutrality (which is never believed by more than a few of the subjects of the research anyway), but rather by differential and selective involvement at various times with different categories of persons and preferably with the joint participation of several investigators in each institution, and by the self-conscious and critical evaluation of all empirical data.

4. Empirical differences

These can be regarded as falling into two general categories, which are not mutually exclusive: differences between types of prisons at an institutional level and variations in the kinds of prisoners, as individuals, within and between prisons.[77]

A. *Prisons*

All penal institutions play out their particular roles within a given penal system, which in turn is located in a broad spatial and temporal, socio-cultural setting. In view of this, cross-cultural comparisons (either between countries or between states in a federal structure or between localities) as always must be treated with caution. The countries from which comparative material is drawn for present purposes are the United States, Britain and Scandinavia (only publications which are available in the English language were considered). A distinction must also be made between institutions according to the positions they occupy in the total penal system of each country: in England, between (in the case of males) local prisons (general and special), training prisons and central prisons and in America principally between federal and state institutions.[78]

However, an assumption of homogeneity of institutions within each society or even within each sector of a prison system would be totally incorrect. Earlier at least three "ideal types" of prisons (custodial, treatment and "humane care" or mixed) were delineated, to all of which some empirical approximations can be found. Such institutions are more usefully conceived of as points on a continuum ranging between a purely punitive, custodial regime at one extreme and a "therapeutic community" at the other.[79]

Other relevant variables are: physical layout and architecture, determinate or indeterminate sentences, and size (numbers of inmates and of staff) especially in relation to the practicability of various types of programme;[80] the opportunities offered by different sorts of regime or organization (specifically the proportions of time spent in solitary confinement and in communal activities) for association and communication among inmates and informally between staff and inmates; and the various grades of security or custody and the degree of insulation and segregation of prisoners from the outside world (the distinction between open and closed institutions and variations in the permitted numbers of letters, visits, home leaves and accepted reasons for going outside the prison).[81]

Various characteristics of the inmate population, however, may act as "limiting" factors in relation to the viability of some of the types of regimes outlined, thus affecting both the chances of their being introduced and the nature of their operation: for example, the homogeneity or heterogeneity of a prison population in regard to age, length of sentence, criminality and previous institutional history.

B. *Prisoners*

Individuals vary in their biological and psychological make-up and in their social and cultural background (which includes involvement in crime and experience of institutional life). Separate penal institutions are provided for juveniles and adults (though the cut-off points are not standardized or firm and some young offenders may find themselves in adult prisons) and for the two sexes.[82] Age, sex and race[83] reflect important social and cultural differences in the experiences and life-styles of individuals. The concepts of "latent" culture, role and social identity can be applied to the analysis of these differences. Glaser discusses the relationship between age and stages in the "criminal career cycle".[84] Giallombardo and Ward and Kassebaum argue that the striking variations between male and female prisoners mirror the different social roles played by the two sexes generally in society. Similarly, Irwin and Cressey utilize these concepts to help account for three distinct types of inmate subculture (thief, convict and legitimate).[85] In this last example even if degree and type of criminality and previous prison experience cannot be simply reduced to two subcultural variables, they are clearly factors of some importance in understanding how the composition of the inmate population affects the prison at the formal and the informal levels. Associated with these factors is the question of the varying lengths of sentences being served by prisoners; whether an institution is for short-term, longer-term or a mixture of offenders has a direct influence on the nature of inmate society, the types of leaders and the predominant orientation of the inmate code.[86]

The well-authenticated existence of a variety of inmate roles and social patterns of adaptation in every kind of penal institution (whether for males or females, juveniles or adults and whether treatment-oriented or custodial)[87] and also in mental hospitals[88] suggests that the particular roles or clusters of roles prevalent in each institution (for instance the relative proportions of "alienative" and "cohesive" types of roles)[89] may be key factors in determining the structural features and the cultural climate of the inmate social system and the nature of prison socialization.

Underlying all these socio-cultural differences between individual prisoners are personality factors. They exercise an important influence over the choice or allocation of roles to individual inmates and the styles of behaviour exhibited by particular role-players and, therefore, indirectly over inmate society. Empirically, however, it may prove difficult to differentiate between such variables as personality, socio-cultural background and type of institution.

The state of confusion and disagreement in the sociological literature on the prison and particularly concerning the inmate social system can be illustrated by the following eight questions:

(a) Is the inmate social system characterized by solidarity or anomie?

(b) Is the inmate code in practice an unattainable ideal or a realistic guide to inmate conduct?

(c) Under what conditions, if any, can inmate groups and social systems be expected or persuaded to support and participate in treatment programmes?[90]

(d) Are the typical inmate roles and adaptation to prison life (such as homosexuality) "healthy" or "sick"? Do they help or hinder rehabilitation and re-socialization and thus, following release, a future free of crime?[91]

(e) Questions relating to the content and pervasiveness of prison and prisoner cultures and to the nature and variability of the processes of prison socialization.

(f) Does repeated and/or prolonged incarceration cause progressive and irreversible prisonization or does each sentence of whatever length only result in a relatively superficial and temporary, non-linear, adaptive learning process specific to the particular intra-prison problems and the stage of the sentence reached?

(g) How far does prison socialization involve in fact a "disculturation" or "untraining" process rather than a reformative one? What is the relationship between prisonization and recidivism?[92]

(h) Are inmates' collective and individual responses to prison life determined by such background factors as outside attitudes, values and roles, past knowledge and experience, criminal and institutional history and personality or by intra-institutional variables such as type of regime and the need to counteract the shared "pains" of imprisonment?[93]

The next sections of this paper will deal with these issues under the following two headings:

(i) The Inmate Society, Leadership and Social Roles [questions (a) to (d) and (h)].

(ii) Prison Socialization Processes [questions (e) to (g)].

It is intended to follow the recommendation of several writers, who stress the need to place greater emphasis than hitherto on differences between penal institutions. The main focus of discussion is, therefore, on comparisons within and between institutions, highlighting, in particular, age, sex and cross-cultural variations. Most of the published material refers to the American context; there are, however, several systematic sociological analyses of Scandinavian institutions (Bondeson, Cline, Mathiesen and Stürup), but only two of English prisons (Emery and Morris and Morris), both adult, male prisons and both carried out in the late 1950s.[94]

5. The inmate society, leadership and social roles

All people-changing or total institutions share certain basic organizational features, designed to ensure the total—if temporary—detachment (psychologically as well as physically) of inmates from their previous social worlds and self-identities and to provide a total social environment within which resocialization into the required mould is facilitated under the direction of more or less trained staff. To these ends, "self-mortification" and "degradation ceremonies" greet all inmates on admission to the institution[95] and their daily existence is characterized by the impersonal regimentation of people and activities, constant surveillance, denial of individuality and autonomy and (theoretically) total authority and power in the hands of the staff. From the viewpoint of the individual inmate, life in such an institution is experienced as a continuous process of regulation, deprivation and attacks on personal identity. He may accept or deny that this is necessary, depending largely on whether he entered voluntarily, sharing the official objectives and methods of the institution and wanting to "be changed" (for instance some mental patients and entrants to closed religious orders take this view), or was forcibly incarcerated and resists attempts to change him for whatever reason (inmates of penal institutions and concentration camps and other mental patients are in this category).

Goffman explicitly placed his analysis of the effects of such institutional procedures on the inmate's self in a symbolic-interaction framework. The processes of mortification he described are associated with loss of roles (available in outside society), desegregation of audiences and roles, losses of property, name, identity, and control over personal appearance and physical postures, violation of privacy, interpersonal contamination and the importance of disidentifying roles which inmates are forced to play.

Writers dealing specifically with the prison have detailed the mortifications and pains of imprisonment. Sykes was the first to examine systematically the experience of imprisonment in a male, maximum security prison from the inmate's standpoint and he pointed to five major, socio-psychological "deprivations or frustrations" which constitute as serious a threat to the individual prisoner as did brutal physical treatment in the past: these are the deprivations of liberty, of goods and services, of heterosexual relationships, of automony and of security. Such deprivations have effects at two levels: firstly, the painfulness of having desired and customary social and psychological satisfactions denied and, secondly, the implications of such frustrations for the fundamental sense of personal identity and self-respect as a human being, which individuals constantly reinforce in a "free" community, by acting as more or less autonomous agents and daily expressing their individuality through their chosen relationships and activities. A similar approach is to be found in Cassel and Van Vorst who describes the situation of the female prisoner.[96] They talk of "psychological needs" but the sources of stress and deprivation they identify are largely social. They categorize needs under three types of adjustment problems—self, family and general social; the full list is as follows: (a) self-adjustment—affectional starvation, tension and anxiety, exaggerated symbiotic needs, psycho-sexual needs, sexual needs, depression and despondency and spiritual and religious needs; (b) family adjustment—deterioration of member interrelationships, unity of family, family status and security decline, fidelity of spouse, and inter-family rivalry; (c) social adjustment—inequality of justice, reconciling personal and cultural philosophy, effective peer affiliation, social stigma on self, social stigma on family, community education and acceptance of rehabilitated persons, and satisfactory relations with parole officer. They add two other categories of needs which are not only found among prisoners nor are found among all prisoners: supportive therapy (for example for drug addicts) and self-development (vocational guidance and education). In fact, except for a reference to family-based satisfactions being more important to women than to men, their account could apply equally well to male prisoners.

Underlying these specific pains and deprivations for the prisoner is a further negative and personally threatening aspect. Imprisonment itself is a mark of social condemnation and life in prison serves to remind the inmate constantly of his rejection by the wider society, in particular the fact of his social rejection is kept alive by the attitudes to and treatment of him by staff members acting as the physical embodiments of general social norms. As Sykes and Messinger express it:

> The isolation of the prisoner from the free community means that he has been rejected
> by society. His rejection is underscored in some prisons by his shaven head; in almost

all, by his uniform and the degradation of no longer having a name but a number. The prisoner is confronted daily by the fact that he has been stripped of his membership in society at large, and now stands condemned as an outcast, an outlaw, a deviant so dangerous that he must be kept behind closely guarded walls and watched both day and night. He has lost the privilege of being *trusted* and his every act is viewed with suspicion by the guards, the surrogates of the conforming social order. Constantly aware of lawful society's disapproval, his picture of himself (is) challenged by frequent reminders of his moral unworthiness.[97]

At this point one of the major criticisms of the total institution concept becomes relevant, namely that institutions are rarely total in reality. Prisons and mental hospitals are linked to the wider society in at least two different ways; firstly, the whole institution is accountable in a general sense to an outside authority and must be sensitive to some extent to external pressures; secondly, personnel (both staff and inmates) enter such institutions at the earliest as adolescents and in greater numbers as adults, bringing with them attitudes, expectations and habits which they have acquired outside; staff continue to reside and maintain a non-work life outside the institution and, though temporarily segregated in a physically closed environment, prisoners and patients mostly return in due course to the wider society (meantime retaining some psychological links through letters and visits). It is this latter fact that is of concern here. A number of writers have stressed the differential impact of imprisonment on prisoners, depending on individuals' personalities, social and cultural backgrounds and previous experiences of penal institutions. Morris and Morris consistently regard each prisoner's perceptions of the "objective facts of his custodial situation" as so variable that generalizations about pains are made impossible.[98] Giallombardo, in considering sex differences in the nature of prison experiences, observes that, though "the evidence clearly suggests that prison life is depriving and frustrating" for female inmates (with respect to liberty, autonomy, goods—especially clothing—and services, heterosexual relationships, and security), it is not experienced in exactly the same way by men and women.[99] Rather the meanings given to imprisonment and the relative degrees of frustration of different needs felt by male and female prisoners are related to their general, culturally defined, sex roles. Ward and Kassebaum write:

> Men come to prison as husbands and fathers but more importantly as breadwinners— the principal determiners of the social status of the family. Their self-definitions give greater emphasis to their occupational roles. . . . Women prisoners suffer more from separation from families and disruption of familial roles. Women bring to prison with them identities and self-conceptions which are based principally on familial roles as wives, mothers, and daughters, and their related roles (fiancées and girl friends).[100]

A similar general argument about the origins of inmate subcultures can be found in Irwin and Cressey. They point out that prior criminal involvement and previous prison experience provide inmates with a pre-existing set of norms and expectations. Without denying the obvious functional and problem-solving nature of inmate social systems, they maintain that three main types of subcultures exist in a prison which derive from sources outside any particular prison: "thief" or "criminal", "convict" and "legitimate". Critics such as Roebuck,[101] have focused on the details of how difficult it is to separate the attitudes and membership of the thief and convict subcultures, how the thief category oversimplifies and conceals "real" differences between the various types of career, professional and committed criminals, and how diverse and disunited are prisoners with a legitimate orientation and how rarely they are to be found in American prisons anyway. However such criticisms should not be allowed to totally invalidate the fundamental thesis that inmates enter prisons with their own preconceptions and expectations or world-views and that some may share similar world-views based on similar prior experiences and socialization processes and that this affects in turn the collective and individual responses of inmates to the pains of imprisonment.

Cline, in collaboration with Wheeler, attempted an empirical test of the two basic hypotheses that have been suggested to account for the anti-staff orientation of most inmate social systems and subcultures: the "deprivation" and the "direct importation" explanations. They gathered data from fifteen widely different types of Scandinavian institutions—juvenile, preventive detention and special institutions, and normal prisons. They used three measures of importation and six variables relating to deprivation and found their importation hypothesis supported, and a negative correlation between degree of social deprivation and anti-staff climate. Until comparable studies are undertaken in a number of American and British penal institutions, it is impossible to know whether the Scandinavian situation is peculiar to those countries or is common to other modern industrial societies. [This whole discussion refers to question (h) which was outlined in the previous section.]

Whether, however, it is functioning solely to mitigate the pains and shared deprivations of prison life or whether some similar experiences and characteristics of prisoners (as individuals and as criminals in the outside world) are also important, some sort of inmate society seems to be universal in penal institutions. Such a society operates on two interrelated levels:

(i) psychologically, through the values and attitudes of a common culture, it furnishes mechanisms whereby the individual prisoner can come to terms with his situation, control aggression and maintain, in an environment of condemnation and rejection, some self-respect and sense of identity;[102]

(ii) socially, in offering opportunities for roles, relationships and activities, it serves both to bind the inmates together as a body, however loosely and temporarily, and also to reduce some of their material as well as emotional deprivations by the provision of markets in scarce goods and services.[103]

Beyond this general statement, however, there are differences and disagreements. The form taken by inmate social systems, the actual values embodied in inmate codes and the degrees of solidarity or cohesion all vary between prisons and over time within a single institution. Striking differences have been reported between male and female prisons, juvenile and adult institutions, between custodial and treatment-oriented institutions and between countries.

(i) Sex

Male prisoners construct a collective system (of greater or lesser solidarity) focused around a wide range of different needs and interests, such as power, sex, material goods and protection from staff intervention. Roles are defined in relation to such concerns and the social mechanisms utilized by inmates to achieve their ends reflect those available to men in the outside world, principally economic transactions, contractual relationships, and the use of threatened or actual physical violence. As Sykes pointed out, in prison these tactics are largely exploitative involving "force, fraud, and chicanery".[104] The characteristic male inmate roles are "merchant", "politician", and "tough", all different routes to a position of dominance of the inmate world. The inmate code usually tacitly recognizes that most inmates are primarily self-seeking and individualistic (though this can take either an assertive form, for instance, the "Robber Baron",[105] or a detached and uninvolved one such as the "real man"[106] role, and aims only to check inmate conduct which betrays the whole inmate social system to staff members (especially "ratting"). Some prisons seem to have a somewhat more collectivity-oriented inmate society in which the "right guy", or "Robin Hood" typifies the ideal roles for the inmate, or the inmate leader.[107]

Female prisons, on the other hand, seem to produce a collective inmate response structured along the lines of marriage and the family. The affectional and mutually supportive dyad relationship constitutes the basic unit in the institutions studied by Giallombardo, Halleck and Hersko,[108] Ward and Kassebaum and others; and, though a physical, sexual element is often involved, it has been found that unlike male prisoners, sex usually occurs between women who have already formed an emotional relationship. In some juvenile institutions for girls,[109] in the Alderson federal reformatory investigated by Giallombardo, and in another reformatory studied by Hefferman,[110] wide social networks of "families" were also discovered. Psychological support, material gifts, advice and status all appeared to be channelled via the "marital" or homosexual dyad and, where it exists, the family. The only exception is the "homey" role where a high degree of mutual aid and reciprocity obtains without any homosexuality.[111] Often, Giallombardo found, other roles, such as "pinners" (lookouts) and inmates with access to scarce goods, would also operate within the family context wherever possible. Kosofsky and Ellis and Ward and Kassebaum argue that the "family" only appears in juvenile institutions or where inmates have been deprived of a secure, complete family life outside and is therefore serving as a substitute under these circumstances. But the thesis that outside roles carry over into intra-prison life suggests that "families" are created by females in institutions, because these are the social units most familiar to women and the usual sources of need–satisfaction, and because, as Giallombardo points out,[112] the dyad is too unstable a base upon which to build the whole inmate social system. The relatively isolated and self-controlled "ideal" male role has no counterpart in women's prisons.[113]

Tittle discusses the whole question of male/female differences in inmate organization and points to various possible reasons, such as different types of male and female prisoners, different prison conditions for the two sexes, and different staff–inmate relationships between male and female institutions. His study was undertaken in a single institution (a federal hospital taking imprisoned narcotic addicts) which accepted both sexes. His main findings were: homosexual activity between women was more affective and occurred more often within stable relationships, while among men it was more casual and concerned with simple physical gratification;[114] women subscribed less to a "system-wide normative code"; and men showed a greater degree of group cohesion. After having controlled for certain institutional and background factors (such as age, criminality and prior incarcerations), Tittle still found a significant association between sex and the nature of inmate organization.

(ii) *Age*

Age, which has already been mentioned in regard to female prisoners, is another important inmate characteristic which directly influences the nature of the inmate social system. Adolescents, simply by virtue of their age, may be more responsive to the particular orientations and goals of their institution and staff members; thus treatment institutions may be more successful with juvenile inmates than with adults.[115] However the writers who have provided some evidence to support this argument are also, as a result of studying different institutions, confronted with variable intra-organizational factors (such as goals, regimes, staff characteristics and attitudes).[116] Some data are nevertheless available to suggest that similar criteria form the basis for the allocation of prestige and power in juvenile and adult male institutions: knowledge, criminal experience and sophistication, strength and aggressiveness.[117] One role that seems to be lacking in juvenile institutions is that of merchant or trader, which may well be explicable in terms of the relative inexperience in or total lack of opportunity to play such roles which are characteristic of the adult male in the economic and occupational spheres of "free" society. The examination of age differences should not, however, be confined to a juvenile/adult dichotomy. The concept of maturation as a process has been utilized by various theorists (such as Matza)[118] in order to help explain an apparently widespread tendency to "grow out of" crime. Glaser sees age as a significant index of shifts in reference group allegiances or the sorts of people individuals of different ages (other factors being equal) might be "interested in developing social relationships with".[119]

(iii) *Custodial versus treatment-orientations*

As has already been observed, inmate organization and inmate orientations to staff are correlated with the predominant official goals and strategies of particular types of institution. Whether inmate society is largely supportive of or oppositional to the staff and the programme in any institution is partly determined by the extent to which the institution favours a custodial, humane or treatment orientation. Also the degree of solidarity of the inmate social system is partly the result of the structure and climate of the official administrative system. This, however, does not mean that formal organizational variables are the sole or even the main determinants of inmates' values and their individual and collective arrangements. Berk, Grusky and Street *et al.*, have separately investigated these relationships: Grusky in an experimental prison camp, Berk in three adult male institutions (occupying differing positions on a continuum between a strong custodial and a strong treatment orientation) and Street *et al.* in a similar range of juvenile institutions. All three studies confirmed the general thesis: in particular, where an institution is pursuing treatment goals, inmate groups and leaders adopt a noticeably more cooperative attitude to the staff and the programme.

Emery and Stürup give some corroborative evidence for this thesis from a British prison and a small special institution in Denmark respectively. Following the introduction of changes in the amount of time inmates could spend with each other, mainly in leisure activities, Emery noted a significant reduction in the level of tension between staff and inmates (especially the younger ones), an increase in the general stability of inmate–staff relationships, and this occurred without the greater freedom of association permitted to prisoners leading to abuse by inmates of either the regulations or each other. Stürup described an attempt at "treating the untreatable" and recorded no instances of hostile inmates banding together to thwart the purposes of the institution.

Earlier writers in particular have questioned whether greater permissiveness by staff and a reduction in harsh and punitive measures would in fact result in greater cooperation between inmates and staff. McCorkle and Korn claimed rather that a more likely consequence would be for inmates to continue to oppose the regime, since their opposition stemmed from a psychological need to protest and to externalize their hostility on to the system in order to protect themselves from the effects of being socially rejected. Glaser argues that:

> Where staff permissiveness includes nonsurveillance, it may simply create a power vacuum which the more prisonized components of the inmate population will fill. Inmate surveillance replaces staff surveillance, and inmate life may become less permissive in terms of the freedom available to choose between alternative modes of behaviour.[120]

Cloward attacks the thesis from another viewpoint. He claims that positive "incentives to rehabilitation and social reintegration" fail as forms of social control exercised by the staff, because "the goals to which prisoners are enjoined to aspire are largely unavailable to them . . . The society in which he (the prisoner) seeks to become reintegrated continues to reject him . . . and thus perpetuates his inferior status".[121] Thus the inmate elite group adopts a highly "conservative" ideological stance and opposes any changes which might threaten the *status quo* and its position. Grosser comes to a similar conclusion:

> (Inmate) organization produces, in response to their psychological needs, precisely the conditions that make identification with noncriminal values highly improbable. It is the isolate and the precariously adjusted prisoner, holding at best a marginal position between the inmate group and the administration, who is most likely to be open to rehabilitative influence. Since this influence is often not forthcoming, or the prisoners are intimidated by the power of the inmate organization, their stability is more often jeopardized than reinforced. As long as the inmate social organization presents the only reference group powerful and accessible enough to offer the recruit some sense of security, a change in his values can hardly be expected.[122]

This whole issue remains to be finally resolved. It is, however, worth noting that those arguing on the grounds of the "intractability" of prisoners are not, by and large, basing their case on systematic empirical evidence but on theoretical assumptions.

Mathiesen and Street attempt to take the whole question a stage further by postulating some underlying factors which "condition" inmates' collective responses to imprisonment. Street identifies two such factors which differentiate between types of institutional environment: (a) variations in the balance of gratifications and deprivations (the relative scarcity of valued licit and illicit objects and opportunities) and (b) variations in staff patterns of control and authority (for example rigidity, punitiveness and social distance). He uses these factors to distinguish between custodial and treatment institutions and to act as the independent variables in his subsequent analysis of the varying orientations of the inmate groups in different juvenile institutions. Mathiesen argues along similar lines.[123] He hypothesizes two factors in the inmate's subjective perceptions of his situation which also intervene between the goals and structure of the formal organization and the inmates' responses to imprisonment. The first factor is his perceived strength or weakness in terms of "maximum bargaining potential" and the second is the degree of "background honour of a salient membership group" (i.e. the inmate population). He uses these two variables to help account for an inmate response of "censoriousness" (which he observed in his Norwegian, "mildly treatment-oriented" institution) rather than the more commonly found counter-culture and social cohesion among inmates. He suggests that the treatment-oriented nature of the institution (where individualization of treatment comes to be defined as "illegitimate patriarchalism" by prisoners[124]) and general cultural factors specific to Norway were largely responsible for what he found.

(iv) *International comparisons*

Some, relatively minor, national differences have emerged in comparisons between the American literature and the only comparable British study, that of Pentonville prison by Morris and Morris. They draw mainly on Sykes' research and comment throughout their book on points of similarity and difference between the two prisons. For instance, they criticize Sykes' interpretation of the failure by staff to assert their absolute authority over the prisoners and offer an alternative hypothesis which better fits the British situation, in terms of understaffing and a certain degree of "cynicism or apathy" among staff members.[125]

Cross-cultural differences have already been cited as a possible source of variations in types of inmate social system and inmate orientations to the staff and the institution in general. It is certainly of some significance that the first and to date only study, which has yielded quite divergent and even apparently conflicting findings on inmate attitudes and adaptations, is that by Mathiesen. His main discovery was that, instead of the expected anti-staff counter-culture and cohesive inmate society, the inmates in his institution shared the general norms and values of the authorities, but used these standards to criticize the staff "for lack of adherence to their own established principles"; this he termed "censoriousness". He further isolated three types of censors: "formalists", "indignants" and "exploders" (differentiated according to the degrees of strategy and conviction involved in each).

In general, as has already been observed, international variations must be due either to differences in types of institutions (size, goals, regimes, staff and so on) or to differences in the types of prisoners in such institutions, or both. What is obviously needed at this point are systematic, sociological replication studies undertaken with similar theoretical orientations and methodologies to investigate cross-culturally these hypothesized relationships.

Returning to the more specific and limited question of the nature of the inmate social system in the American context, one is still faced with considerable variation and disagreement. Five separate, but overlapping, dimensions can be distinguished on which differences between institutions have been found; four relate to the internal structure of the inmate society and one to its relationship to the formal aspects of the prison system and to the staff. These are: consensus–dissensus, organization–anomie, cohesion or solidarity–alienation, and collectivism–individualism; the fifth is cooperation–conflict or opposition. [These dimensions are concerned with questions (a) to (c) which were described in the previous section of this paper.] As Cressey and Krassowski state:

> Two principal kinds of relationship appear among prisoners. First, the majority of inmates live in social conditions which have been termed anomie, unorganization, individualism, and "pluralistic ignorance". . . Second, there are strong tendencies toward organization and interdependence among inmates. . . Leaders of various types including "right guys" or "real men", and "politicians" or "merchants", and "gorillas" or "toughs" emerge. These elites, who ordinarily are the least improbable offenders, attempt to enforce a code which puts emphasis upon being an astute criminal, upon maintaining social distance from the guards and other employees, and upon inmate solidarity.[126]

They note that both types of relationship result from the goals set for the organization and that both are found in institutions where inmates suffer serious deprivations.

For all the reasons already stated, differences in this regard between institutions and within one institution over time are to be expected. Thus, whether an inmate code (of a pro- or anti-staff orientation) is widely obeyed depends largely on the position a particular inmate society occupies on each of the other four continua or dimensions. These in turn are determined by organizational factors on one hand and background and personality characteristics of prisoners on the other. Sykes suggests that at any single point of time the "society of captives lies balanced in an uneasy compromise" between "perfect solidarity" and being simply "a warring aggregate", with a balance too between alienative and cohesive roles and styles of leadership (Morris and Morris analyse Pentonville in a similar manner), but that over time the balance point is constantly moving.

Inmate society comprises a number of aspects only some of which are readily and directly ascertainable. Data on social interaction patterns, social roles and types of adaptation, social groupings, styles of leadership and status evaluations can be obtained by participant observation and by questioning inmates. The more fundamental questions relating to the distribution of power, stratification hierarchies, internalization of roles and values, social cohesion and indeed whether an inmate "system" exists at all can only be inferred by using various indicators as indirect measures. One can quarrel with Clemmer's conclusion that "the prison world is not a like-minded, highly integrated collectivity, but is, on the other hand a diffuse aggregation wherein impersonal relations abound, and consensus of a high degree is absent due to the individuation of most of the personalities involved" on these very grounds.[127] To support his case he cites data on fragmentation, the existence of social cleavages, socio-cultural differences and the physical separation of prisoners, but this seems to be a highly selective use of the available evidence, since he also provides data which seem to point in the opposite direction.[128]

Mathiesen attempts to handle this whole issue in a more theoretical fashion and presents a table (see table 1) giving the conditions necessary for solidarity among inmates (consensus and dissensus are measured against staff norms).

Table 1 Consensus and dissensus: a typology[129]

		Consensus absent	*Consensus present*
	Institutionalized	1. Pure peer solidarity	2. Peer solidarity and censoriousness
Dissensus	Present but uninstitutionalized	3. Disruption "without alternative"	4. Disruption and censoriousness ("individual censoriousness")
	absent	5. Disruption and indifference	6. Hierarchical solidarity

The controversy in the American literature relates to types 1 and 3, while those who seek examples of inmate groups which are supportive of treatment programmes and staff are concerned with type 6. Mathiesen's own study provided an instance of type 4. Such a model, further refined and developed, seems to provide the most illuminating general framework within which these questions can be examined and, hopefully, eventually resolved.

Inmate Roles and Individual Adaptations [question (d)]

Reference has already been made to the existence in most prisons (both male and female) and a few mental hospitals of a range of inmate social roles. Sykes has given the fullest list of roles in a male prison, which can be differentiated according to sphere of activity (exercise of power and influence, economic transactions, homosexuality and so on) in which the inmate operates, the methods used, whether he is working for or against the main body of prisoners and whether his activities are generally approved, tolerated or condemned by the inmate code and most inmates. The positive and negative evaluations of different roles clearly will vary from prison to prison and therefore roles must be defined in relation to a specific inmate normative system. Sykes was describing an inmate society whose dominant orientation was criminalistic and anti-staff. The roles he delineated were: (i) approved and/or accepted roles—"real man", "right guy", "politician", "fish", "wolf", "tough", "gorilla", "merchant or peddler", and "square John" (some of these are despised but regarded as indispensable or unavoidable); (ii) disapproved and sanctioned roles (those that are deviant according to the general inmate norms and threaten inmate society)—"rat", "centre man", "ball-buster", "punk", "fag", "hipster", "ding" and "outlaw".

Giallombardo and Ward and Kassebaum describe the choice of roles available to the female prisoner, all pointing out that most are associated with homosexuality; Giallombardo gives argot terms for the "male" and "female" partners, for "true" homosexuals, those heterosexuals who adopt homosexuality as a temporary response to imprisonment and for the uninitiated, and for prostitutes, among others (eleven roles in all are listed). Female prisons also have their equivalents of rats and centre men ("snitchers and inmate cops"), square Johns and weaklings ("squares"), ball-busters ("jive bitches"), peddlers ("boosters"), but not of gorillas and toughs.[130] Interestingly Ward and Kassebaum report a high proportion of "true" homosexuals among the small number of inmates playing politician and merchant roles.[131]

Alternative typologies of individual responses and adaptations to the prison situation have been offered by Schrag, Morris and Morris, Wilson and the present

		Membership group Sphere of social relations		
		Staff	Prisoners	None
		---	---	---
Reference group	Staff	1	2	3
Primary source	Prisoners	4	5	6
of values	Outside World	7	8	9

Numbers	General Types	
1	(a) Staff Man	(b) Reforming Character
2	Opportunist	
3	(a) Lone Informer	(b) Prison Patient
4	Inmate Representative	
5	Career Criminal	
6	Inadequate Recidivist	
7	Penitent	
8	Situational Adaptive	
9	Non-Participant	

writer. Schrag suggests four basic social types, based on orientation to general social (or societal) norms: prosocial, antisocial, pseudosocial and asocial.[132] These correspond very closely to the square John, right guy, politician and outlaw roles respectively, which are used by various researchers, some of whom have added a fifth category which is largely residual and includes the "shunned" or the "dings".[133] The present writer has developed a nine-category, theoretical typology, incorporating most of the previous classifications which is based on a differentiation between the membership and reference groups inmates affiliate with both inside and outside the prison. This typology, which relates to males in custodial and treatment-oriented prisons, is summarized here:[134]

Profiles of the nine types

1(a) *Staff Man*—the "centre man" or the "redband" (the Pentonville equivalent) in a custodial prison. He is protected by the staff because he is useful to them but is at the same time regarded with some contempt. He is totally rejected by inmate society.

1(b) *Reforming Character*—in a treatment-oriented prison, this type, through his involvement with the staff, is the most committed to some concept of rehabilitation and reform both in general and for himself. He is the justification for the existence of a treatment policy and thus important to the staff. He may be rejected by the more criminalistic members of the inmate population, but not necessarily by the majority.

2. *Opportunist*—any values or norms temporarily adopted by him come from the staff (treatment or custodial) whose power position he respects. He mixes with inmates so as to avoid trouble.

3(a) *Lone Informer*—in a traditional custodial prison, he also shows some normative bias towards the staff. He probably has personality problems (possibly associated with his criminal record, for example a sexual offender) which have led to his taking such an unpopular and isolating role. Once committed to helping the official administration, he finds himself increasingly needing the support and approval of the staff having forfeited that of the inmates.

3(b) *Prison Patient*—he may have very similar characteristics to the Lone Informer but shows a different set of responses when in a treatment-oriented prison. His record may here be the reason for his presence in such a prison and psychiatric treatment may be required. Because of his receptiveness to the attitudes and standards of the staff, he too may be promising material. His role in the eyes of the inmates will therefore change from being considered deviant to being at the least tolerated and possibly approved (depending on the nature of his offences and the general attitude of the inmates towards treatment).

4. *Inmate Representative*—the "politician". He is chosen from among the most trustworthy of inmates to act as the official spokesman of the inmate society in any dealings with the staff, and therefore must be seen as having a shared preference for relations with both staff and inmates. He comes nearest of all the types to being treated on equal terms by the staff.

5. *Career Criminal*—for him, crime is a profession and prison an occupational risk. He is part of an outside criminal network and may use his time in prison to recruit for it. He is a well-integrated person, his values and relations being consistent. In some prison situations his involvement in the outside criminal world may lead him to opt out of active participation in inmate groups.

6. *Inadequate Recidivist*—he is usually an habitual petty thief who lacks any external social ties or real alternatives to a life of largely unsuccessful crime. He is tolerated by the leaders of inmate society, but regarded as inferior by their standards and unreliable.

7. *Penitent*—"conventional morality-directed". He sees imprisonment as an atonement for his crime. He will take on staff standards of judgment and will seek to avoid any chance of inmate contamination. This is often possible with a short sentence.

8. *Situational adaptive*—"other-directed". He is a nominal conformer who tries, wherever he finds himself, not to be too involved or to be conspicuously different. His main identification is with outside groups.

9. *Non-participant*—"inner-directed". He has a strong and self-sufficient personality and withdraws from prison life as far as possible, relying on his inner resources and outside ties. This again is feasible for a short period. Like type 5, he is a relatively well-integrated person.

Morris and Morris adopt a somewhat different, though related, typology, derived from Merton's adaptations to anomie (ritualism, retreatism, rebellion, and innovation) and they add a further category, into which most prisoners fall, that they term "manipulation" (working within the system to achieve one's own ends). Cutting across this typology is another distinction they make between two basic forms of prisonized response—participation and withdrawal. Their conception of inmate adaptations has features in common with Goffman's classification of the ways in which mental patients face their situation. He distinguishes collective and individual responses: the former incorporate the means whereby inmates obtain desired but forbidden commodities, "buddies", sexual relationships and the ubiquitous "rat"; the latter include five main adaptations: situational withdrawal intransigence, colonization, conversion, a combination of these or "playing it cool" (the commonest course of action), and a separate category for those already "immunized" or institutionalized by prior experiences.

Ward and Kassebaum briefly discuss other female adaptations to imprisonment (apart from homosexuality) in terms of the framework employed by Goffman and Morris and Morris; they talk of psychological withdrawal, rebellion, colonization and various combinations of the different adaptations.

Wilson seems to be operating in the same general area as Schrag and Merton in between structural or organizational conditions and individual personality. He talks of the individual's *adaptations to his role* and delineates three such adaptations: cooperative, opportunistic and alienated. These are derived from "the relationships between the individual's own personal goals, together with the means employed to pursue them, and the organizational structure".[135]

Unfortunately, there is little or no discussion in the prison literature generally of a number of fundamental questions about inmate roles and adaptations: how and when roles are allocated or chosen; whether inmates in fact usually select their roles or are labelled or categorized by other inmates and/or staff members; how far the behaviour and the accompanying attitudes are internalized either in prison or previously; or whether most inmates simply conform outwardly in order to avoid being noticed as different and penalized for it; and whether and how roles can be changed.

One rare exception is Wellford, who explicitly stated that one of the problems "becomes one of determining the criteria to be used to establish which role an inmate is playing".[136] However, in answering his own question he simply reiterates that, as Garrity, Giallombardo, Schrag and others have already observed, inmate responses reflect background, situational and personality variables. No more specific hypotheses are offered about which particular prison conditions and personal factors are responsible for each of the various role-adaptations being adopted. A combination of theorization and careful, empirical investigations is obviously necessary before it is possible to identify some of the patterns and processes involved.

The question of inmate cohesion cannot be separated from that of inmate roles and adaptations. The predominant orientation of most roles in a given institution (whether alienative and individualistic or cohesive and collectivistic) is one of the major determinants of the degree of solidarity of the inmate social system. An additional factor is the prevalence among the inmate population of deviance from the inmate code (whether tolerated or heavily sanctioned) and the extent of non-involvement (even where this is not regarded as deviance) in inmate society and its prescribed activities.

The more general issue of whether adaptations to prison life are likely to aid or hinder the rehabilitation process can only be answered by reference to what the adaptations are, how deeply internalized they are, what they are responses to, what sort of rehabilitation one has in mind and what kind of outside world each inmate is returning to. A prisoner, who comes from a criminal environment and whose life is centred around a criminal occupation, may or may not find his adjustments to prison life help him in his chosen career: if he has adopted familiar or compatible patterns of behaviour, subscribed to the collective inmate code and made friends or contacts among those of a similar persuasion, his prison experiences can simply be regarded as a temporary episode of no great lasting significance. If he has been seriously affected by imprisonment, either by becoming withdrawn and asocial or by being converted to the official, staff view of crime, he will not find it easy or even possible to fit into his previous style of life. Conversely, a first or occasional offender may not only not be deterred by his term of imprisonment, he may become criminalized, prisonized or both and thus be changed in the opposite direction from reformation. For many prisoners, however, the adjustments they make to the pains of imprisonment may not have any lasting effects and in fact may assist inmates in avoiding some of the damaging social and psychological effects of stigmatization and incarceration. In this event, they would have to be judged positive or even "healthy" responses to an "abnormal" situation. For instance, Giallombardo's account of homosexuality within a certain social climate and as part of a wider "family" nexus, backed by a strong, conditional acceptance of such behaviour only within certain types of relationships and under exceptional circumstances (such as in prison), suggests that such an adaptation cannot be regarded as detrimental, corrupting or "unhealthy". Nevertheless, this particular issue is largely a normative one, and cannot be answered on the basis of "objective" empirical evidence of what goes on in prisons alone.

6. Prison socialization processes [questions (e) to (g)]

Though it may be desirable or convenient to distinguish analytically between the nature of individual adaptations and roles in prison, the inmate code and the whole inmate social system, on one hand, and inmate socialization processes on the other, in reality the two sets of phenomena are closely interrelated. Such a distinction gives the illusion that the "static" aspects of the inmate's situation can be separated from the "dynamic". But, in fact, from an interactionist perspective, roles particularly—but also the whole inmate culture and social structure—are constantly undergoing change and modification. The classic differentiation of "structure" from "process" cannot thus be maintained.

In practical terms, this means that the preceding discussion about membership and reference groups, frequency and intensity of interaction, prior criminal and general subcultural affiliations, previous prison and other institutional experience, current prison roles, and the dominant orientation of the inmate code and inmate society are all directly relevant as the major determinants of the character of the prison socialization process experienced by each inmate. Some researchers (for example Garabedian, Morris and Morris, Schrag and Wheeler) have explicitly made this connection and more or less systematically utilized these variables in their analyses of socialization processes.

In a previous section on concepts and theoretical perspectives, distinctions were made between socialization and resocialization, and between prisonization and criminalization. Whether prison-specific assimilation or *prisonization* constitutes a secondary socialization or a resocialization process (and whether or not inmate culture is congruent with previous socialization), and whether this exposure reforms or reinforces a pre-existing world-view depends both on the individual's previous socialization and on the content of the prison's inmate normative system or systems (which itself is partly related to the official organizational goals and structure). Simultaneously, a *criminalization* process may be occurring, which may also either feed into the pre-existing symbolic world of the individual prisoner or require a further type of resocialization.

> The unqualified claims that prisons are breedings grounds for crime and that imprisonment adversely affects all prisoners do not appear to be warranted. Continued prison experience minimizes the chances that some prisoners will refrain from crime upon release, but it increases the chances of successful adjustment in society for others. The data on parole adjustment do not support the general contention that extended exposure to the prison community decreases the chances of successful adjustment on parole. On the contrary, for many classes of offenders increasing length of the period of incarceration either does not affect the chances of successful parole at all or tends to increase the chances of successful parole. In general, it was observed that property offenders corresponded most closely to the expectations developed from the concept of prisonization, that individuals who were most stable appear to be negatively affected by prolonged incarceration, and that individuals who were relatively unstable appear to be positively affected by prolonged incarceration.[137]

The fundamental issue, therefore, is what part is played by the experience of imprisonment and the socialization process, which is an unavoidable concomitant of that experience, in an individual's whole life and "career": a career as a confirmed deviant or as a generally law-abiding citizen (with single or occasional law-breaking episodes) or involving an alternation of criminal and non-criminal phases.[138] The significance of court convictions and sentences of imprisonment for the careers of different types of individuals lies in the attendant effects of being publicly labelled and socially condemned,[139] of suffering the disruption of family and other social ties, of enforced segregation and exposure to prison life in all its aspects, and of facing the consequences, when released, of such stigmatization and prolonged absence from "free" society. The problems, which the ex-prisoner encounters, include deterioration in family and personal relationships, difficulties in obtaining employment and an income,[140] general personal and social disorientation, and feelings of resentment against the members of a society which continues to distrust and penalize him for his past crime. Indeed, in this respect, the confirmed career criminal is the only type of ex-prisoner who can avoid most of these deleterious effects.[141] Paradoxically, he is the least likely to seek full re-acceptance into conventional society; those who do wish to try a legitimate style of life find that the consequences of having served a prison term are serious obstacles to the accomplishment of their objective.

It is now necessary to look more closely at some of the published studies of prison socialization. Clemmer first introduced the concept of prisonization, which he defined as follows:

> The taking on, in greater or lesser degree, of the folkways, mores, customs and general culture of the penitentiary. (A) slow, gradual, more or less unconscious process during which a person learns enough of the culture of a social unit into which he is placed to make him characteristic of it.[142]

He differentiated between criminality and prisonization and held that prisonization is universally experienced by prisoners and is of an anti-reformative nature, but that the degree is variable. He identified several stages and suggested a number of determining factors, such as personality, outside primary relationships, degree of involvement in inmate groups, and acceptance or rejection of the inmate code. Clemmer considered that prisonization constituted a linear process: as time passed, the inmate became increasingly deeply prisonized.

It is this assumption that Wheeler investigated. As he points out:

> His position that prisonization is the most important determinant of parole adjustment is based on the assumption that processes observed during the early and middle phases of incarceration continue until the inmate is paroled.[143]

Wheeler's research utilizes another measure of the time variable, namely, length of time *remaining* to be served, and he divides his sample into three categories accordingly: "(a) those who have served less than six months . . . and are thus in an *early phase* of their commitment; (b) those who have less than six months remaining to serve—the *late phase* inmates; and (c) those who have served more than six months and have more than six months left to serve—the *middle phase* inmates." Wheeler also has three categories based on the more usual measure—length of time served—less than six months, six months to two years and over two years.

These two indices of the passage of time yield quite divergent results. The longer the time prisoners have served, the smaller the percentage who express conformity to staff norms: among first-timers, over the first year of their sentence there is a steady reduction in the proportion of high conformers to staff norms. Wheeler also confirmed that primary group contacts were significantly related to this process: those highly involved in groups experienced a more rapid reduction in the percentage of high conformers than did the relatively uninvolved. He argues that these two variables are interdependent and result in a "polarization" of two types of inmate: the "non-involved conformist" and the "involved non-conformist" who become "progressively isolated" or "progressively prisonized" respectively.

The second measure (based on time remaining to be served) suggests a more complex set of processes: (i) "a steady increase in the percentage of low conformity responses" over the three phases and (ii) "a U-shaped distribution of high conformity responses". Wheeler claims that the former is prisonization, but that the latter is a process of "differential attachment to the values of the broader society." Mid-sentence, there is maximum sensitivity to inmate culture and anti-staff norms, while the early and late phases reflect a stronger attachment to outside, conventional values. He points out that different types of inmate may be differentially involved in these various processes and that panel studies are necessary to investigate this possibility (though he does demonstrate the applicability of his findings to both first-termers and recidivists). Elsewhere Wheeler examines the extent to which each inmate perceived inmates generally to be strongly anti-staff (though this data provided a picture of inmates as significantly more anti-staff than each inmate personally admitted to in his own case) which is clearly relevant to the socialization issue.[144]

Most other studies confirm or elaborate on Clemmer's and Wheeler's findings. Garabedian, following Wheeler closely, corroborated the existence of a U-shaped or curvilinear prisonization process. Glaser also found that (though there are variations between institutions) more inmates generally favoured friendships and social contacts with their fellows mid-sentence than early on or near release; he too prefers a reference group explanation for this pattern. Glaser and Stratton reported U-shaped trends in relation to interests among inmates in vocational and educational pursuits and in religious participation.

Garabedian (in his 1963 article) then analysed the three phases of the socialization process separately for five basic types of prisoner (square John, right guy, outlaw, politician and ding). He found that socialization followed a curvilinear trend only for the first two role types; in the case of the outlaw it was a linear trend, politicians seemed to maintain a stable conforming orientation to staff and dings experienced what Wheeler termed "delayed rehabilitation". Garabedian also obtained evidence of a differential retention of various roles: though the proportions of square Johns, right guys and politicians remained fairly constant over the three phases of confinement, there was a proportionate increase in the number of dings and decrease in the number of outlaws in the later phase. The five types exhibited different patterns of association with inmates and with staff, especially during the middle phase. Schrag too provides evidence that prisonization varies according to the prisoner's social type, with the normative orientations of both the pro-social and the antisocial types showing the familiar U-shaped trend.

Other writers (such as Garrity and Morris and Morris) have developed the idea of different *levels* and *degrees* of prison socialization, originally mooted by Clemmer, which further complicates the picture. However, in order to estimate the relationships between prison socialization and post-release adjustment, for different types of prisoners, such refinements are clearly essential.

There are, however, some discrepant findings on prisonization. Ward and Kassebaum in their women's prison, found no evidence of either a general linear or a curvilinear trend; age at first arrest was the major determinant of degree of support for the inmate code.[145] Tittle examined "inmate code subscription" and primary group affiliation among the male and female inmates at a federal hospital for narcotic addicts, differentiating between those with a "weak" and a "strong criminal orientation" and between early, middle and late phases of confinement. His findings confirmed again an overall curvilinear pattern for both sexes, with, at all three phases, a smaller proportion of women than men expressing strong support for the inmate code. This sex difference, moreover, cannot be attributed to a higher percentage of isolate women, since higher proportions of women than men belonged to primary groups at the middle and late phases. The distinction between those with weak or strong criminal orientations brings out further interesting results. Among men with a strong criminal orientation, the percentage in primary groups remains constant, while in the weak group there is an increase in the middle phase (coinciding with the increase in support for the inmate code); among women, there are substantially higher proportions of the strong criminal group keenly supporting the inmate code than of the weak category, and than of men.

No suitable data for comparative purposes were gathered by Morris and Morris and so far these prisonization theses have not been tested in British penal institutions. Mathiesen found in Norway that both number of confinements and time spent in a single institution affected inmate attitudes to staff. The number of incarcerations and time in prison resulted in a steady decline in respect for custodial staff; inmate perceptions of the importance of treatment staff follow a "zigzag movement" in which time in the particular institution led to attitudes becoming more appreciative, but the greater the number of previous confinements the lower the respect inmates had for staff.

Street *et al.* discovered different socialization processes in the various juvenile institutions they were investigating. A slight U-shaped curve appeared in the treatment institutions, but in the custodial ones negative attitudes to staff and to the institution increased steadily over time. Of the two humane institutions, one conformed to the treatment pattern and the other to the custodial. They found that these institutional variations existed independently of differences in the background attributes of their inmate populations, such as age, past delinquency and previous institutional experience.

Wellford also conducted a study to measure the relationships between the three variables, of length of time served, phase of sentence and social type, and the variable prisonization (defined in this case as degree of adoption of the inmate code). The first was not significantly associated with prisonization, but the other two were, and independently of each other. Wellford then questions Wheeler's interpretation, in terms of the pains of imprisonment, of why inmates adopt an inmate code and advocates instead an explanation based on both "situational factors" and "actor characteristics" (for example, in the form of Schrag's concept of social types).

One piece of research has yielded totally contrary results to the general patterns outlined so far. Atchley and McCabe conducted a replication study of Clemmer's and Wheeler's investigations in a federal male treatment institution. *No* relationship emerged between time served and prisonization, there was an increase over time in group involvement for *both* high and low conformers but *no* increase over the three phases of institutional confinement in the percentage of non-conformity and *no* U-shaped curve. The only pattern they found that was similar to Wheeler's observations was the "overall pattern of prisonization", that is the percentages in the prison population of high, medium and low conformers to staff norms. As has already been discussed in considerable detail, various possible explanations can be offered for such contradictory results and Atchley and McCabe devote a major part of their article to this whole question; one theoretical point they make is that "the relationships among interaction, conformity, phase of institutional career and time spent in the institution are much more complex than either Clemmer or Wheeler anticipated." One avenue that has already been explored by other writers (such as Garabedian, Schrag and Wellford) is the question of social and psychological differentiation between types of prisoners within and between institutions; the other main alternative is the analysis of institutional differences in goals, structures, policies, size and other such variables.

Although a substantial number of empirical studies of prisonization (usually measured by nonconformity to staff norms) has been undertaken, this writer has discovered only one which focuses specifically on criminalization. Certainly, in some prisons, the content of the two socialization processes may be very similar, but this is still an empirical question which must be investigated by the researcher in any given case. Bondeson set out to examine the criminalization process in a girls' training school in Sweden. Her index of criminalization was knowledge of criminal argot and she found that extent of argot knowledge was significantly associated with time spent in the institution and total time in different training schools (controlling for amount of previous deviancy, age and intelligence) and with status in the institution. In view of the fact that these are the same variables that have been shown to be related to the degree of prisonization, some studies are urgently needed which would investigate these two processes over time in the same inmate population, and explore some of the interrelationships between them.

7. The staff

In discussing prisons from the inmates' standpoint, it has been implied at times that not only are the staff a homogeneous, monolithic group of individuals, but their attitudes, values, interests and behaviour exactly coincide with those of the administrators and, in some reified sense, with the "institution" as a whole. Earlier in this paper, it was remarked that in practice no such consensus exists among the various grades and occupational categories of correctional staff let alone between the staff and the administration.

In penal and psychiatric institutions, the most significant divisions seem to occur between custodial officers and professional or specialist staff, and between those formally in charge of running the organization (who are also the individuals held responsible for the organization to outside authorities) and all other employees. In adult prisons, further occupational distinctions can be made between various categories of staff: supervisory, specialist (trained professionals), ancillary (e.g. instructors and medical orderlies) and custodial. In juvenile institutions in America, there are three main categories of personnel—cottage-parents, teachers and social workers. In England, Approved schools are staffed mainly by teachers and instructors of various kinds (as befits their predominantly education-based programme); some have psychiatric and psychological staff available and probation officers work closely with the schools. Borstals appear to concentrate mainly on the maintenance of order and discipline, with some provision for trade instruction, and generally resemble prisons; any counselling that is required tends to be carried out by the discipline officers.[146] Most of the following discussion, therefore, will deal with America, except where relevant material is available on British or Scandinavian institutions, and will concentrate on the considerable body of evidence concerning the problems.

> It is coming increasingly to be recognized that the amount and quality of productive output in any organization, be it a business firm, a government agency or a mental hospital, are highly influenced by the relationships among the various staff groupings. In the case of the mental hospital, "productive output" refers to therapeutic change in patients. We are learning that the hospital's effectiveness depends not merely on its

technology—its specific treatment techniques—but as well on the qualities of its administration, the ordering of occupational statuses, and the division of work functions.[147]

This statement, summarizing the major theme of a book on the "Patient and the Mental Hospital", is equally applicable to the prison.

Gilbert and Levinson's analysis of "custodialism" and "humanism" as ideologies provides a useful starting point. They see these two "ideal types" as occupying polar positions on a continuum. Their description of the two types is as follows:

> The model of the custodial orientations is the traditional prison and the "chronic" mental hospital which provide a highly controlled setting concerned mainly with the detention and safekeeping of its inmates. Patients are conceived of in stereotyped terms as categorically different from "normal" people, as totally irrational, insensitive to others, unpredictable and dangerous . . . In consequence, the staff cannot expect to understand the patients, to engage in meaningful relationships with them, nor in most cases do them much good . . . The custodial conception of the hospital is auto-cratic . . . The humanistic orientations, on the other hand, conceive of the hospital as a therapeutic community rather than a custodial institution . . . They view patients in more psychological and less moralistic terms . . . They attempt in varying degrees to democratize the hospital, to maximize the therapeutic functions of nonmedical person-nel, to increase patient self-determination . . . and to open up communication wherever possible.[148]

They also hypothesize a relationship between the custodial and an "authoritarian" personality type, and between the humanistic and an "equalitarian" personality. Further, there is some substantial evidence that custodial orientations are closely associated with a "voluntaristic" view of the causation of human behaviour, within which criminal deviation is seen as "wilful", "intentional or deliberate"; whereas a treatment orientation is accompanied by a "deterministic" view so that individuals are perceived as "sick rather than bad", and their deviations "due to ignorance or inability to conform".[149] Correspondingly, different forms of handling prisoners are recommended by the two schools of thought: "punishment and/or close surveillance" and "treatment", "therapy" or "education" respectively. (Cressey has pointed out that most therapy programmes including so-called group therapy rely on "clinical" rather than "group relations" principles, and are directed towards changing *individuals* but not their groups.) Brown *et al.* put it this way:

> The officer's primary concern is with the community; the community must be protected from the people it has ordered to be separated from itself. The treatment person's primary concern is with the inmate; the individual ordered to be separated from the community must be prepared for his eventual return to that community.[150]

Weber shows that the two types of staff hold different values regarding their own and the other's work:

> The professionals often stressed humanitarianism and service. They thought of themselves as primarily providing a service to the delinquents. . . The professionals thought of themselves as cooperative . . . The professionals saw the non-professionals as holding two sets of values. One view regarded the non-professionals as being a hard-working, simple group of people . . . The other view regarded the non-profes-

sionals as strict disciplinarians who demanded hard work and obedience from the delinquents . . . The non-professionals emphasized kindness, firmness, the ability to get along with people, and hard work as necessary qualities for work with delinquents. They viewed the immediate, the concrete, the practical, and action . . . as important . . . (They) regarded the professionals as generally pseudointellectual and theoretical . . . They also saw the professionals as placing power and status over democratic practices.[151]

Mathiesen notes an important difference between *administrative* and professional staff in a treatment-oriented institution:

Other things being equal, treatment experts are, owing to their less pronounced stress on the client's experience of the situation, less willing than lay administrators to accept the censorious claims of inmates . . . Treatment experts are, owing to their less pronounced concern with the possibility of disobedience, less willing than lay administrators to take into account the censorious claims of inmates.[152]

In addition to the fundamental distinction between custodial and humanistic orientations or ideologies, subdivisions may occur within each broad type, according to perceptions of criminality and its causation, and preferred methods of treatment and control: custodial staff may be solely concerned with order, discipline and security or may seek also to assist in rehabilitation programmes; while treatment staff differ in respect of their preferences for individual group or milieu types of therapy. "Humane care" institutions largely depend not on a high percentage of treatment personnel but on a greater degree of permissiveness and tolerance on the part of custodial staff. In fact there has been increasing pressure for correctional institutions to move in this direction from various sections of the public in most modern western societies. As Grosser has observed: "If repressive and more humane methods can serve equally well to safeguard the community and isolate prisoners, then according to the values of our society the more humane system is preferable."[153] Often though, such a move has brought the opposite reaction that conditions in prisons, as places of punishment, should be austere, harsh and unpleasant. Nevertheless, the "humane" type of institution continues to exist and is certainly more common than the genuine treatment-oriented institution.[154] Morris has suggested that the chronic staff shortages in most British prisons and some American ones may be one major factor responsible for the relative absence of constructive programmes in prisons aimed at the reformation of offenders.

Conflict (which is generally non-violent and often covert) for staff in correctional institutions (as in mental hospitals) can take three forms: (i) conflict between custodial personnel and therapeutic or "humanistic" personnel within the same institution;[155] (ii) conflict between different types of specialist staff (for example teachers and social workers in juvenile institutions or between psychiatric and general medical staff); (iii) role conflicts for particular grades or occupational categories of staff who are subjected to external or organizational demands to perform contradictory tasks, to operate in different and new ways, to take on different attitudes to inmates or to continue to work under a changed regime.[156] In relation to the third form of conflict, frequent mention is made in the literature of custodial staff being required (in traditional prisons) to act also as counsellors, therapists or just good listeners to the inmates or, in treatment institutions, primarily to contribute to the rehabilitation of prisoners by therapy or by introducing a more permissive regime, but nevertheless still to ensure the containment of those same prisoners.[157] The converse situation can also occur where treatment staff find the creation of a truly therapeutic community is incompatible with societally imposed demands that the prison make sure its inmates remain safely inside.

Piliavin suggests three main reasons for such conflicts developing: firstly, lack of education and training; secondly, lack of emotional attributes for the jobs which particular staff members are required to perform; and, thirdly, conflicts between their various "goal and task priorities" which result from having "different responsibilities and problems". He also notes that staff members themselves tend to stress the first two types of reasons in accounting for any problems and conflicts they become aware of.

It is not proposed to deal with these issues in any further detail except to mention briefly some of the suggested methods of coping with the problems. Piliavin argues that different strategies need to be adopted as between traditional and modern correctional institutions. In the former, he observes, greater contact between the various categories of workers may increase conflict; by improving channels of communication and the exchange of views and giving the groups greater knowledge about each other, differences of status and orientation may become more obvious and of greater concern. He recommends (as does Spencer, among others) a different organizational form or structural model, with, in particular, a greater degree of overlapping between the tasks of the various categories of worker, rather than greater separation of functions. Contrary to the usual argument, he claims that some incompatibility of tasks can be tolerated and is ultimately more satisfactory than a total division of labour and a narrow specialization. Zald goes further and argues that not all conflict is automatically "bad" anyway. The ideal milieu treatment institution, he envisages, would inevitably contain some conflict, but hopefully of a different kind. He evaluates conflict according to the institutional context in which it occurs and the issues over which it arises.

> Although the milieu institution or the problem-solving organization may have a high level of conflict, it may be that the conflict is of a kind that works in the service of institutionalized goals rather than as a brake and impediment to organizational effectiveness.[158]

The final topic to be covered in this section concerns staff perceptions of and attitudes to the inmate population. In British prisons these are coloured by the fact that prison officers (whose tasks are largely custodial and disciplinary) share a common cultural and social class background with many of the prisoners. Morris and Morris comment:

> Because the prisoner tends to be the expression of his own worst self rather than a wholly distinct social species—to be the layabout rather than the industrious artisan— the relationships between officers and prisoners are often closer and more intense than those between officers and the senior professional and administrative staff.[159]

Emery argues that this produces considerable problems for both groups: prisoners are condemned by staff for their "immoral" acts and respond to this by making a counter-accusation against the staff that they have surrendered "their autonomy for economic security". Both sides are drawing on a common stock of cultural values in making these moral claims.

The orientations of custodial and treatment staff towards prisoners, and criminals in general, have already been described. And, from the inmate side, considerable hostility has been shown to exist towards the correctional staff in many institutions, though significant differences have been found between institutions (both juvenile and adult) with different goals and formal structures; the more treatment-oriented organizations with, correspondingly, a more "democratic" form of decision-making enjoyed greater inmate support and cooperation than did those with traditional custodial goals. In the great majority, however, the picture given by early writers, such as Weinberg, of two opposing, mutually distrustful groups, each with a negative stereotype of the other and whose interaction with each other is largely determined by the stereotype, is confirmed. Two interesting pieces of research into staff perceptions of the inmate and of inmates' views of the staff are worth reporting briefly. Hazelrigg sampled young male offenders in an institution and, on the basis of self-ratings, estimated their scores on three scales of inmate loyalty, criminality and criminal identification. He then compared the profiles of eight high scorers and six low scorers with staff evaluations of the same individuals, and found that, though staff and inmates agreed on the evaluations of high scorers, staff consistently considered low scorers to be more criminalistic than those inmates' own self-ratings would merit.[160]

Wheeler obtained from inmates and staff (custodial and treatment) in a state reformatory for males their own privately held views of staff and inmate conduct and their perceptions of the attitudes and conduct of the three groups.[161] Inmates, in their personal opinions, were not consistently anti-staff, but in their views of other inmates' attitudes they thought inmates in general were definitely hostile to the staff. Custodial staff agreed with the inmates, but treatment staff believed inmates had a more favourable orientation towards staff. Treatment and custodial staff themselves showed little consensus in their personal views of staff conduct, but agreed that treatment staff were more permissive. Inmates, however, saw all staff as equally custodial in their attitudes. Wheeler offered two possible explanations for the biases in perceptions, particularly the over-perception of conflict between staff and inmates: firstly, a "selective perception" model and, secondly, a "selective visibility" model. He favours the latter, arguing (with some supportive evidence) that staff and inmates exaggerate the degree of inmate hostility to staff, because they generalize from the most visible inmates, who occupy positions of power and status, mix more, and more often violate institutional roles. Hazelrigg, without rejecting this thesis, argues also for the "selective perceptions" explanation with both staff and inmates operating with a stereotypical concept of the inmate. In his study he found no relationship between the incidence of institutional infractions and a high or low score. Clearly this whole question needs further careful investigation and in a variety of institutional contexts.

8. Conclusion

In this concluding section it is proposed to do two things: firstly, to reiterate two general theoretical and methodological comments about the sociology of the prison, which have already been made earlier in this chapter; and, secondly, to summarize the major problem areas on which further research is needed and which have been noted or implied in the course of discussion.

First, to repeat a warning given earlier. Although various aspects of the prison (staff, inmate social system, social roles, socialization, goals and formal organizational structure) have been treated separately, one at a time, a prison is in reality a unity, a complex social system whose parts (i.e. sets of actors) are closely interwoven. Further, the question of the mutual interdependence of the penal institution and its wider socio-cultural, political and economic environment must not be neglected.

Secondly, a restatement of the interactionist perspective. Much of what has been criticized in the literature stems from a basic problem faced by all social research, but which is particularly acute in "closed" organizations and in conflict situations: how to obtain a valid, reliable and comprehensive picture of social reality. Admittedly, there is now some information on life in prison from the standpoint of the inmate (and also from that of staff members) and certainly more than is available in the case of the mental hospital. But surprisingly, even systematic participant observation studies (such as the one by Giallombardo) still rarely give any detailed account of the inmates' conceptions of the prison, except in very general terms or with reference only to the question of the degrees of "deprivation" experienced. Further, the views expressed tend to come from the most prominent, articulate, vociferous or "helpful" prisoners. Detailed data, however, on inmate orientations to and evaluations of the prison are obviously highly relevant, especially to the recidivism question. The need to obtain data on actual behaviour, relationships, groups and so on, which demands the use of more social-anthropological methods, should not result in researchers overlooking the value of repeated, in-depth interviewing of representative samples of all types of inmates (and staff), even if they do largely abandon large-scale survey and questionnaire methods. There is some tentative but suggestive evidence that, as might be expected, inmates of penal and psychiatric institutions may not uniformly and universally regard confinement as a totally unpleasant experience. This is apart from obvious cases such as, in prisons, organizers of profitable rackets, holders of power, socially inadequate recidivists who have been institutionalized, and some homosexuals. Two studies of mental patients have revealed that some inmates consider that the mental hospital compares favourably with their lives outside and, in their "quest for asylum", may choose to reside in such institutions.[162] Comparable data on prisoners are far more shaky and sketchy and, until more systematic research is undertaken, little reliance can be placed on them.[163] All such findings are also open to the criticism that (as Linn expresses it) "such verbalizations are merely indicators of psychological defences employed by the patients" or prisoners and this can only be resolved by collecting other sorts of corroborative evidence.

The following are the topics on which further research is needed; in general they indicate the importance of comparative and longitudinal studies:

1. The factors both in the individual's background and personality and in the prison situation that determine which role or roles, if any, each inmate comes to play, and which adaptation(s) to the experience of imprisonment he employs.

2. The processes by which the inmate finds himself playing a particular role or adopting a particular adaptive pattern; when, how and if inmates change their roles and modes of adaptation.

3. How and why some inmates are not cast in specific roles (as have been identified in the literature) at all.

4. How each inmate perceives his role, other roles, and the various alternative forms of adjustment to prison, and what factors determine his perceptions and evaluations and the degree to which he internalizes his roles and styles of adjustment.

5. How and why deviance from inmate codes, norms and expectations occurs and the factors determining the differential reactions of staff and inmates to such deviant acts and individuals.

6. The interrelationships between the institutional context (organizational goals, structures, staff orientations, etc.), the personalities, past experiences, habits and social attitudes of the inmates and the forms of inmate society which emerge, persist and change (the society's orientations to staff and institution, its solidarity— whether based on collectivism or individualism—and other such features).

7. The interrelationships over time between all the background and personality characteristics of the inmate, his definition of his prison situation, his roles (and adaptations) and his membership and reference groups, on the one hand, and the nature and degree of socialization/resocialization he undergoes, on the other hand; such relationships in turn being dependent on the particular type of organization (formal and inmate) in which they occur.

8. How all these factors combined determine whether prison in each case constitutes a deterrent, reformative or criminalizing experience or is only an unimportant episode.

9. Independent but simultaneous, panel (where possible) studies in the same institutions of prisonization and criminalization processes.

10. The investigation of subsequent post-prison careers, in terms of types of individual, previous life-styles and subcultural involvements, prison relationships, roles, adaptations and socialization experiences, and circumstances encountered after release (what each man *was* like, what happened to him in prison, and what he goes back to).

11. The factors determining staff–inmate relationships and attitudes to each other (e.g. selective perceptions versus selective visibility).

12. Institutional and other variables associated with the effects of increased staff permissiveness and the introduction of more treatment-oriented programmes.

13. The conditions (societal, organizational and personal/human) under which a really "therapeutic community" might be created.

People say, well, they say prisoners should be punished, don't they, locked up for years as a punishment for what they've done? Perhaps they're right. They don't seem to want to know why people commit crimes, and maybe stop them doing it again.[164]

References and notes

1. Lloyd W. McCorkle and Richard Korn, "Resocialization within walls", *Annals*, **293** (1954), 88.
2. Johann Galtung, "The social functions of a prison", *Soc. Problems*, **6** (1) (1958), 128–129.
3. Donald R. Cressey, "Achievement of an unstated organizational goal: An observation on prisons", *Pacific Sociol. Rev.*, **1** (2) (1958), 43–49.
4. For a detailed historical account of prisons in Britain and the United States, see Sir Lionel Fox, *The English Prison and Borstal Systems*, London: Routledge and Kegan Paul, 1952; D.L. Howard, *The English Prison*, London: Stevens and Sons, 1962; and Harry E. Barnes and Negley K. Teeters, *New Horizons in Criminology*, 3rd ed., Englewood Cliffs, N.J.: Prentice-Hall, 1959, chs. 21–26; Richard R. Korn and Lloyd W. McCorkle, *Criminology and Penology*, New York: Holt, Rinehart and Winston, 1959, part 2.
5. The following writers compare prisons and mental hospitals: Donald R. Cressey, "Contradictory theories in correctional group therapy programmes", *Federal Probation*, **18** (2) (1954), 20–26; Norman K. Denzin, "Collective behaviour in total institutions: the case of the mental hospital and the prison", *Soc. Problems*, **15** (3) (1968), 353–365; Galtung, 1958, *op. cit.*, pp. 130–132; Elmer H. Johnson, "Bureaucracy in the rehabilitation institution: Lower level staff as a treatment resource", *Soc. Forces*, **38** (4) (1960), 355–359; Frances G. Scott, "Action theory and research in social organization", *Am. J. Sociol.*, **64** (4) (1959), 386–395; J.C. Spencer, "Problems in transition: From prison to therapeutic community", *Sociol. Rev.*, *Monograph*, No. 9, Paul Halmos (Ed.), Keele: University of Keele, 1965, pp. 13–30. For the sociological analysis of the mental hospital, see, for instance, Ivan Belknap, *Human Problems of a State Mental Hospital*, New York: McGraw-Hill 1956; Erving Goffman, *Asylums*, Harmondsworth: Penguin 1968; Milton Greenblatt, Danield J. Levinson and Richard H. Williams (Eds), *The Patient and the Mental Hospital*, Glencoe, Ill.: The Free Press 1957; Alfred H. Stanton and Morris S. Schwartz, *The Mental Hospital*, New York: Basic Books, 1954.
6. Goffman, 1968, *op. cit.*, pp. 11–12; Goffman describes the job of total institution staff as "people-work" (p. 73).
7. David Street, Robert D. Vintner and Charles Perrow, *Organization for Treatment*, New York: The Free Press, 1966, pp. 1–7 and 15 (note 1). They distinguish between "processing"—which involves *adapting* people—and "changing"—or *altering* them—and therefore between socialization and resocialization.
8. Joseph C. Mouledous, "Organizational goals and structural changes: A study of the organization of a prison social system", *Soc. Forces*, **41** (3) (1963), 284.

9. Talcott Parsons, "Suggestions for a sociological approach to the theory of organizations—11", *Admin. Sci. Q.*, **1** (2) (1956), 229. This concept is developed in relation to the prison by Scott, 1959. *op. cit.*

10. Peter M. Blau and W. Richard Scott, *Formal Organizations*, London: Routledge and Kegan Paul, 1963, pp. 51–57; George H. Grosser, "External setting and internal relations of the prison" (1960), reprinted in Lawrence E. Hazelrigg (Ed.), *Prison Within Society*, New York: Doubleday Anchor, 1968, p. 9.

11. For example, Donald R. Cressey, "The nature and effectiveness of correctional techniques", *Law and Contemporary Problems*, **23** (4) (1958), 754–758; Talcott Parsons, "The mental hospital as a type of organization", in Greenblatt *et al.* (Eds), 1957, *op. cit.*, ch. 7; and Street *et al.*, 1966, *op. cit.*, pp. 18–22.

12. Blau and Scott (1963, *op. cit.*, pp. 52–57 and 79–80) differentiate the two types of organization according to whom they serve: the general population of society or a particular set of clients. Traditional custodial prisons fit their "commonweal" type (where the people being processed are regarded as enemies of society) and more treatment-oriented institutions fall into the "service" category, along with mental hospitals and schools. This view contrasts with that of writers, such as Goffman, who stress the *similarities* between all the various kinds of total institution, and also question whether in practice the mental hospital's first duty is seen as being to its patients or to a wider public. The somewhat arbitrary and selective nature of the particular organizational feature chosen by various writers to serve as the basis of their typologies is also illustrated by the fact that Parsons (unlike Blau and Scott) puts prisons and hospitals together and in a different category from schools (the latter he terms "pattern-maintenance organizations", 1956, *op. cit.*).

13. Amitai Etzioni, *A Comparative Analysis of Complex Organizations*, Glencoe, Ill.: The Free Press, 1961, pp. 27–31 and 50.

14. Thomas P. Wilson, "Patterns of management and adaptations to organizational roles: A study of prison inmates", *Am. J. Sociol.*, **74** (2) (1968), 149.

15. Bernard B. Berk, "Organizational goals and inmate organization", *Am. J. Sociol.*, **71** (5) (1966), 522–534; Cressey, *Pacific Sociol. Rev.*, **1** (2) (1958), 43–49; Oscar Grusky, "Organizational goals and the behavior of informal leaders", *Am. J. Sociol.*, **65** (1) (1959), 59–67; Gene G. Kassebaum *et al.*, "Job related differences in staff attitudes toward treatment in a women's prison", *Pacific Sociol. Rev.*, **5** (2) (1962), 83–88 and "Some correlates of staff ideology in the prisons", *J. Res. in Crime and Delinquency*, **1** (2) (1964), 96–109; Richard H. McCleery, "The governmental process and informal social control", in Donald R. Cressey (Ed.), *The Prison*, New York: Holt, Rinehart and Winston, 1961, ch. 4; Thomas Mathiesen, "The sociology of prisons: problems for future research", *Br. J. Sociol.*, **17** (4) (1966), 364–373; Street *et al.*, 1966, *op. cit.*; George H. Weber, "The organization of camps for delinquent boys", *Am. J. Orthopsychiat.*, **32** (5) (1962), 824–836; Mayer N. Zald, "Power balance and staff conflict in correctional institutions", *Admin. Sci. Q.*, **7** (1) (1962), 22–49.

16. Weber, 1962, *op. cit.* p. 826; and Mouledous, 1963, *op. cit.*, p. 284.
17. Giallombardo points out that a joint concern for custody, internal control and economic self-sufficiency effectively eliminated treatment as a determinant of the programme devised for the women in the prison she studied; see Rose Giallombardo, *Society of Women*, New York: Wiley, 1966, pp. 57–58.
18. Morris Janowitz, in Street *et al.*, 1966, *op. cit.*, pp. x–xi.
19. F.E. Emery, *Freedom and Justice Within Walls*, London: Tavistock, 1970, pp. 96–97 (writer's emphases).
20. Charles Perrow, "Reality adjustment: a young institution settles for humane care", *Soc. Problems*, **14** (1) (1966), 69.
21. Gordon Rose, "Administrative consequences of penal objectives", in Halmos (Ed.), 1965, *op. cit.*, p. 212.
22. Street *et al.*, 1966, *op. cit.*, p. 21. In the case of an adult male prison, however, staff permissiveness and non surveillance may merely increase the degree of inmate control, see Daniel Glaser, *The Effectiveness of a Prison and Parole System*, Indianapolis: Bobbs-Merrill, 1964, pp. 169–170 and 212.
23. See, for example, Emery, 1970, *op. cit.*, pp. 15–20; and Richard McCleery, "Correctional administration and political change", in Hazelrigg (Ed.), 1968, *op. cit.*, ch. 6.
24. Johann Galtung, "Prison: the organization of dilemma", in Cressey (Ed.), 1961, *op. cit.*, pp. 127–133; McCorkle and Korn, 1954, *op. cit.*, pp. 93–95; Spencer, 1965, *op. cit.*, pp. 25–28; Edwin J. Thomas, "Role problems of offenders and correctional workers", *Crime and Delinquency*, **12** (4) (1966), 360–364; George H. Weber, "Conflicts between professional and non-professional personnel in institutional delinquency treatment", *J. Criminal Law, Criminology and Police Sci.*, **48** (1) (1957), 26–43.
25. Gresham G. Sykes, *Society of Captives*, Princeton, N.J.: Princeton University Press, 1958, ch. 3, and "The corruption of authority and rehabilitation", *Soc. Forces*, **34** (3) (1956), 257–262.
26. Berk, 1966, *op. cit.*, p. 531.
27. One example is the variable attitude to inmates supplying information to staff members, which can be termed "informing" or "confessing". See Giallombardo, 1966, *op. cit.*, pp. 106–112; Elmer H. Johnson, "Sociology of confinement: Assimilation and the prison rat", *J. Criminal Law, Criminology and Police Sci.*, **51** (5) (1961), 528–533; McCleery in Cressey (Ed.), *op. cit.*, pp. 280–290; Thomas Mathiesen, *The Defences of the Weak*, London: Tavistock, 1965, pp. 125–136; Richard M. Stephenson and Frank R. Scarpitti, "Argot in a therapeutic correctional milieu", *Soc. Problems*, **15** (3) (1968), 348–395; David A. Ward and Gene K. Kassebaum, *Women's Prison*, London: Weidenfeld and Nicolson, 1966, pp. 32–34; and Harry A. Wilmer, "The role of the 'rat' in the prison", *Federal Probation*, **29** (1) (1965), 44–49.
28. This point has been made by Schrag, who goes on to examine in some detail the concepts, crime, culture, society and social self; see Clarence Schrag, "Some foundations for a theory of corrections", in Cressey (Ed.), 1961, *op. cit.*, pp. 309–331.

29. See Alvin W. Gouldner, *The Coming Crisis of Western Sociology*, London: Heinemann, 1971, pp. 29–37, for a discussion of "background assumptions", divided into "world hypotheses" and "domain assumptions".

30. Cressey (1961, *op. cit.*, p. 3), uses this phrase to introduce his collection of writings on the prison.

31. For example, Donald Clemmer, *The Prison Community*, New York: Holt, Rinehart and Winston, 1958; Mathiesen, 1965, *op. cit.*; Terence and Pauline Morris, *Pentonville*, London: Routledge and Kegan Paul, 1963; Schrag, 1961, in Cressey (Ed.), *op. cit.*; and Stanton Wheeler, "Role conflict in correctional communities", 1961, in Cressey (Ed.), *op. cit.*, pp. 229–259.

32. Paul Lerman, "Gangs, networks and subcultural delinquency", *Am. J. Sociol.*, **73** (1) (1967), 63–72. Lerman queries the widespread tendency for delinquency researchers to equate gangs and subcultures. He argues rather that "interactional" and "subcultural dimensions" need to be distinguished and finds empirically that deviant values, symbols and behaviour patterns can be transmitted by a variety of "structural units" (pairs, triads and groups).

33. McCorkle and Korn, 1954, *op. cit.*, p. 88; Street *et al.*, 1966, *op. cit.*, pp. 6–7 also distinguish between socialization and resocialization.

34. Various authors use these terms; for example, Clemmer, 1958, *op. cit.*, pp. 298–304; Glaser, 1964, *op. cit.*, p. 476, and Charles W. Thomas, "Towards a more inclusive model of the inmate contraculture", *Criminology*, **8** (3) (1970), 261.

35. Clemmer, 1958, *op. cit.*, pp. 298–315 and "Observations on imprisonment as a source of criminality", *J. Criminal Law, Criminology and Police Sci.*, **31** (3) (1950), 311–319; Anne R. Edwards, "Inmate adaptations and socialization in the prison", *Sociology*, **4** (2) (1970), 218; Donald L. Garrity, "The prison as a rehabilitative agency", in Cressey (Ed.), 1961, *op. cit.*, pp. 373–375; Morris and Morris, 1963, *op. cit.*, pp. 169–171 and 174–178.

36. Galtung, 1958, *op. cit.*, p. 129 (original emphases).

37. This concept is explored in Tadeusz Grygier, "The concept of 'social progression' ", in Grygier *et al.* (Eds), *Criminology in Transition*, London: Tavistock, 1965, pp. 153–193.

38. The question whether they are complementary or conflicting is discussed in Percy S. Cohen, *Modern Social Theory*, London: Heinemann, 1968, pp. 14–15; and David Silverman, *The Theory of Organizations*, London: Heinemann, 1970, pp. 142–143.

39. Alan Dawe, "The two sociologies", *Br. J. Sociol.*, **21** (2) (1970), 207–218; a similar line of argument is to be found in Thomas P. Wilson, "Conceptions of interaction and forms of sociological explanation", *Am. Sociol. Rev.*, **35** (4) (1970), 697–710.

40. See the interchange between Sheldon S. Wolin and Philip Selznick in Amitai Etzioni (Ed.), *A Sociological Reader on Complex Organizations*, 2nd ed., New York: Holt, Rinehart and Winston, 1969, pp. 133–154.

41. Jack D. Douglas ("Deviance and order in a pluralistic society", in John C. McKinney and Edward A. Tiryakian (Eds), *Theoretical Sociology*, New

York: Appleton-Century-Crofts, 1970, pp. 368–401) criticizes the consensual views of structural functionalism from a pluralistic perspective.

42. For example, Jack D. Douglas, *American Social Order*, New York: The Free Press, 1971, ch. 2; and Douglas (Ed.), *Understanding Everyday Life*, London: Routledge and Kegan Paul, 1971, ch. 1 (esp. pp. 9–14); Silverman 1970, *op. cit.*, pp. 140–141.

43. See Silverman, 1970, *op. cit.*, pp. 50, 67 and 219; see also Peter L. Berger and Thomas Luckmann, *The Social Construction of Reality*, London: Allen Lane, 1967, pp. 106–109, and 208–209.

44. See particularly Berger and Luckmann, 1967, *op. cit.*, pp. 47, 72, 79 and 149–182; Cohen, 1968, *op. cit.*, p. 70; Silverman, 1970, *op. cit.*, pp. 126–127, 147 and 194.

45. Silverman, 1970, *op. cit.*, pp. 215–216. For his detailed exposition of an "action" theory of organizations, see chs. 6–9.

46. Goffman, 1968, *op. cit.* It is *not* here being argued that Goffman is a structural functionalist. Mouzelis has recently criticized Goffman for his "one-sided picture" of total institutions (betraying the principles of symbolic interactionism); see Nicos P. Mouzelis, "On total institutions", *Sociology*, **5** (1) (1971), 113–120.

47. Benjamin Braginsky, Dorothea D. Braginsky and Kenneth Ring, *Methods of Madness*, New York: Holt, Rinehart and Winston, 1969, p. 34.

48. This is argued particularly by McCorkle and Korn, 1954, *op. cit.*; Sykes, 1958, *op. cit.*; and S. Kirson Weinberg, "Aspects of the prison's social structure", *Am. J. Sociol.*, **47** (5) (1942), 771–726.

49. This point should not be confused with a different issue, namely, whether individual and collective inmate responses are determined by the "pains" of imprisonment or by the attitudes and practices "imported" by inmates from outside. These conflicting views are represented by Charles R. Tittle and Drollene P. Tittle ["Social organization of prisoners: an empirical test", *Soc. Forces*, **43** (2) (1964) 216–221] and Hugh F. Cline ["The determinants of normative patterns in correctional institutions", *Scandinavian Studies in Criminology*, vol. 2, London: Tavistock, 1968, pp. 173–184], who both provide supporting empirical evidence for their respective views, and are part of the separate issue of how organizational behaviour is related to the external environment, see below.

50. See Silverman, 1970, *op. cit.*, pp. 16–18 and 32–38 for an account of the various, possible relationships.

51. Many, if not most, prison studies up to now have been of this type; see, for instance, Clemmer, 1958, *op. cit.*; Morris and Morris, 1963, *op. cit.*; Clarence Schrag, "A preliminary criminal typology", *Pacific Sociol. Rev.*, **4** (1) (1961), 11–16 and Ward and Kassebaum, 1966, *op. cit.*

52. Examples are Robert C. Atchley and M. Patrick McCabe, "Socialization in correctional communities", *Am. Sociol. Rev.*, **33** (5) (1968), 774–785; Peter G. Garabedian, "Western Penitentiary: A Study in Social Organization", unpublished Ph.D. dissertation, University of Washington, 1959 (and

various published articles); Glaser, 1964, *op. cit.*; Charles R. Tittle, 1969, "Inmate organization: Sex differentiation and the influence of criminal subcultures", *Am. Sociol. Rev.*, **34** (4) (1969), 492–505; and Stanton Wheeler, "Socialization in correctional communities", *Am. Sociol. Rev.*, **26** (5) (1961), 697–712.

53. Examples here are Emery, 1970, *op. cit.*; McCleery, 1961, in Cressey (Ed.), *op. cit.*, ch. 4; Street *et al.*, 1966, *op. cit.*; and George H. Weber, "Emotional and defensive reactions of cottage parents", in Cressey (Ed.), 1961, *op. cit.*, ch. 5. In other cases there was participant observation over a considerable period but without any specific change in the situation; see, for instance, Giallombardo, 1966, *op. cit.*; Goffman, 1968, *op. cit.*; Mathiesen, 1965, *op. cit.*, and Morris and Morris, 1963, *op. cit.*; these studies are probably more appropriately considered as coming under the "dynamic" heading, but with the proviso that the dividing line between static and dynamic in this sense is an arbitrary one involving questions of degree not kind, and theoretical orientation not type of data.

54. Mathiesen, 1966, *op. cit.*, p. 361.

55. See note 49 above. Outside society may affect behaviour in various different ways apart from the simple production of "types of people". Giallombardo, 1966, *op. cit.*, pp. 184–189, details the relationships between the sex roles general in society and inmate behaviour in male and female prisons. Other writers, such as Clemmer, 1958, *op. cit.*, pp. 301–302; Glaser, 1964, *op. cit.*, pp. 369–370; Mathiesen, 1965, *op. cit.*, pp. 72–76; and Morris and Morris, 1963, *op. cit.*, ch. 13, stress the importance of outside reference groups.

56. Professional staff particularly are attached to outside groups (their professional organizations) which seek to exercise guidance and control over their members' conduct in their jobs. Discussion of these influences can be found in Elmer H. Johnson, "The professional in correction: Status and prospects", *Soc. Forces*, **40** (2) (1961), 168–176; Kassebaum *et al.*, 1962, *op. cit.* pp. 86–87; Harvey Powelson and Reinhard Bendix, "Psychiatry in prison", *Psychiatry*, **14** (1) (1951), 73–96; Spencer, 1965, *op. cit.*, pp. 26–27; E.J. Thomas, 1966, *op. cit.*, pp. 362–364; and Weber, 1957, *op. cit.* However, most studies of prison staff emphasize the importance of the work situation and actual job tasks in determining attitudes and behaviour at work rather than external or pre-existing factors—one notable exception being Powelson and Bendix, who describe how a particular personality type (namely authoritarian) is well equipped to make the necessary adjustments for psychiatrists practising in a prison in order to handle the contradictions between theory and practice (see pp. 82–83). These issues, of course, relate to the general question of professionals employed in organizations.

57. In their study of another type of organization (the factory), John H. Goldthorpe *et al.* [*The Affluent Worker*, vol. 1, Cambridge: Cambridge University Press, 1968, pp. 8 and 183–186] take the same view. See also (re Goldthorpe *et al.*) Geoffrey K. Ingham, "Organizational size, orientation to work and industrial behaviour", *Sociology*, **1** (3) (1967), 247.

58. Daniel J. Levinson, "Role, personality and social structure in the organizational setting", *J. abnormal soc. Psychol.*, **58** (1959), 172 (original emphases).
59. William A. Rushing, "The role-concept: Assumptions and their methodological implications", *Sociol. and Soc. Res.*, **49** (1) (1964), 47; see also Wilson, 1970, *op. cit.*, pp. 700–701.
60. Levinson, 1959, *op. cit.*, p. 173.
61. *Ibid.*, p. 177. Levinson's conception of personality and interactionists' "subjective" concept of the social actor overlap to a considerable extent. Mathiesen (1966, *op. cit.*, pp. 362 and 374–376) urges greater attention to personality in order to counter the "rather one-sided emphasis on the effects of social roles". He is writing of roles in the functionalist sense of being organizationally or socially defined and imposed on individuals.
62. Berger and Luckmann, 1967, *op. cit.*, pp. 77–79; Burkart Holzner, *Reality Construction in Society*, Cambridge, Mass.: Schenkman, 1968, presents a similar viewpoint.
63. *Ibid.*, pp. 150 and 158.
64. *Ibid.*, p. 176; see also pp. 175–182.
65. Sykes' classic study (1958, *op. cit.*) is a good example of such an orientation.
66. Berger and Luckmann, 1967, *op. cit.*, pp. 102–106 and 110–122.
67. Silverman claims that "this dichotomy is now largely discredited among contemporary organization theorists" (1970, *op. cit.*, p. 7, note 1), but the solution proposed here is totally different from the systems theory approach Silverman describes as having taken over (ch. 2, esp. p. 27).
68. Ida Harper ["The role of the 'Fringer' in a state prison for women", *Soc. Forces*, **31** (1) (1952), 53–60] found, in a women's prison, that the major structural feature was the mutual opposition of two factions, each of which included both staff members and inmates.
69. Howard S. Becker, "Whose side are we on?", *Soc. Problems*, **14** (3) (1967), 239–247; and Alvin W. Gouldner, "The sociologist as partisan: Sociology and the welfare state", *Am. Sociol.*, **3** (2) (1968), 103–116.
70. One of the very few writers who consider questions of this kind is Wilson, 1968, *op. cit.* Wilson talks of "the individual's *adaptation* to his organizational role" (p. 148 original emphasis), defined as "the relation between the individual's own personal goals, together with the means he employs to pursue them, and the organizational structure". Wilson is explicitly using Levinson's framework.
71. Douglas (Ed.), 1971, *op. cit.*, ch. 1; Douglas develops his argument with reference to deviance, see Douglas, 1971, *op. cit.*; and Douglas (Ed.), *Deviance and Respectability*, New York: Basic Books, 1970. A more phenomenologically-oriented sociology could make judicious use of a far wider range of sources, including autobiographical and semi-fictional accounts by individuals of their prison experience (recent examples are Angela Davis *et al.*, *If They Come in the Morning*, London: Orbach and Chambers, 1971; and (in England) Bill Fletcher, *A Menace to Society*, London: Elek, 1972; and Tony Parker, *The Frying-Pan*, London: Hutchinson, 1970).

72. Lerman, 1967, *op. cit.*, discusses this problem in relation to delinquency; Ulla Bondeson ["Argot knowledge as an indicator of criminal socialization", *Scandinavian Studies in Criminology*, **2** (1968), *op. cit.*, pp. 73–107] handles the same topic in a very similar manner in her study of a criminal subculture in a Swedish training school for girls.

73. Glaser himself conceded that "systematic observations of behaviour" would have been preferable sorts of data to opinions and recollections of past experience, supplemented from the official records (1964, *op. cit.*, p. 519).

74. Such a situation can be the result of the selective visibility and power of certain ideas or individuals as is discussed by Wheeler, 1961, in Cressey (Ed.), *op. cit.*, where he attempts to account for his empirical finding that staff–inmate conflict is "overperceived" (when individuals' own views are compared with their perception of others' views). Richard A. Cloward [in Helen L. Witmer and Ruth Kotinsky (Eds), *New Perspectives for Research on Juvenile Delinquency*, U.S. Children's Bureau Publication, 1956, pp. 80–91] first used the concept of "pluralistic ignorance" in this context.

75. Cline (with Wheeler), 1968, *op. cit.*, looked at fifteen different correctional institutions in Scandinavia, and Glaser, 1964, *op. cit.*, five federal male prisons in America; Barry S. Brown *et al.*, "Staff conceptions of inmate characteristics", *Criminology*, **9** (2 and 3) (1971), 316–329; and Kassebaum *et al.*, 1964, *op. cit.*

76. In the Pentonville study, this is explicitly stated by Morris and Morris, 1963, *op. cit.*, pp. 9–11 and 324–328; they achieved considerably better relationships with the prisoners than with the staff, some of whom were openly hostile and obstructive. However, there is no generally agreed strategy for overcoming this problem. Morris and Morris recommend a different, though not necessarily incompatible solution from that of the writer; they advise the researcher to enter prison with an independent, high status role and to maintain his independence (though no suggestions are made as to how this could be done). This problem is also raised by Sykes, 1958, *op. cit.*, p. 136, who also favours neutrality and warns against too great a reliance on participant observation methods. See also Rose Giallombardo ["Interviewing in the prison community", *J. Criminal Law, Criminology and Police Sci.*, **57** (3) (1966), 318–324] where the need for the researcher to "establish a role which is independent of the existing roles in the prison" is reiterated.

77. Atchley and McCabe, 1968, *op. cit.*, pp. 778–783, outline six ways in which differences of these two kinds could account for the discrepancies between their findings on inmate socialization patterns and those of Clemmer and Wheeler: institutional differences are suggested in the forms of staff organization in federal and state reformatories, and inmate differences (again to some extent associated with the federal/state dichotomy) in relation to age, offence patterns, childhood pre- or post-World War II, orientations to imprisonment, types of reference groups, and relationships between interaction and conformity.

78. See Richard F. Sparks, *Local Prisons: The Crisis in the English Penal System*, London: Heinemann, 1971, ch. 2; John P. Conrad, *Crime and Its Correction*,

London: Tavistock, 1965, ch. III (who covers the United States, Britain, Netherlands, Scandinavia, France and Russia): and Korn and McCorkle, 1959, *op. cit.*, pp. 459–464.

79. Spencer, 1965, *op. cit.*, discusses this concept in the context of the prison and argues that a new model is needed. Cressey, 1954, *op. cit.*, and Street *et al.*, 1966, *op. cit.*, point to important institutional differences in staff attitudes, methods used, staff–inmate relationships and inmate responses according to whether the treatment-oriented institution utilizes "clinical" or "sociological" principles (i.e. favours individual or milieu therapy).

80. Size on its own and in conjunction with other variables (such as, respectively, goals, national and sex differences) is mentioned by Berk, 1966, *op. cit.*, p. 523 (note 5), Galtung, in Cressey (Ed.), *op. cit.*, 1961, p. 107 (note 1 on Norwegian prisons), and Giallombardo, 1966, *op. cit.*, pp. 76–77, states that the two federal prisons for women have approximately two hundred and six hundred and fifty inmates only (the inmate totals for the five male prisons studied by Glaser, 1964, *op. cit.*, p. 530 were 500, 700, 1300, 1300 and 2500).

81. The categories of custody used in American federal prisons are given in Glaser, *ibid.*, pp. 160–161 and the similar British classification is described in Sparks, 1971, *op. cit.*, pp. 18–19.

82. The exceptions are mental hospitals and special treatment institutions, such as the narcotic addicts' hospital, in which Tittle did his study (1969, *op. cit.*,) and which took male and female prisoners for treatment.

83. The percentage of Negroes among Federal and State felony prisoners received into institutions in 1946 is 33 per cent (from Korn and McCorkle, 1959, *op. cit.*, p. 237). The percentage obviously varies widely by state and institution. Sociologically, the most interesting recent observation is of a politicization while in prison of Negro offenders convicted originally of "ordinary" crimes; see Eldridge Cleaver, *Soul on Ice*, London: Jonathan Cape, 1969 and *Soledad Brother: The Prison Letters of George Jackson*, Harmondsworth: Penguin, 1971.

84. Glaser, 1964, *op. cit.*, pp. 469–484.

85. See John Irwin and Donald R. Cressey, "Thieves, convicts and the inmate culture", *Soc. Problems*, **10** (2) (1962), 142–155.

86. Various writers mention the dominant role in inmate society played by longer-term, highly antisocial and recidivist prisoners; see, Cloward, in Witmer and Kotinsky (Eds), 1956, *op. cit.*; Glaser, 1964, *op. cit.*, pp. 115–116; Morris and Morris, 1963, *op. cit.*, pp. 225–226 and 242–249; Clarence Schrag, "Leadership among prison inmates", *Am. Sociol. Rev.*, **19** (1) (1954), 37–42; and Wheeler, 1961, in Cressey (Ed.), *op. cit.*, p. 255.

87. See Morris G. Caldwell, "Group dynamics in the prison community", *J. Criminal Law, Criminology and Police Sci.*, **46** (5) (1956), 648–657; Peter G. Garabedian, "Legitimate and illegitimate alternatives in the prison community", *Sociol. Inquiry*, **32** (2) (1962), 172–184; "Social roles and processes of socialization in the prison community", *Soc. Problems*, **11** (2) (1963), 139–152; and "Social roles in a correctional community", *J. Criminal*

Law, Criminology and Police Sci., **55** (3) (1964), 338–347; Giallombardo, 1966, *op. cit.*, ch. 8; Glaser, 1964, *op. cit.*, pp. 575–583; Morris and Morris, 1963, *op. cit.*, chs. 7 and 11; Howard W. Polsky, *Cottage Six*, New York: Wiley, 1965, pp. 74–84; Schrag, 1954 and 1961, *op. cit.*; Sykes, 1958, *op. cit.*, ch. 5; and Ward and Kassebaum, 1966, *op. cit.*, ch. 3.

88. See Goffman, 1968, *op. cit.*, pp. 57–68 and 187–266; Harvey L. Smith and Jean Thrasher, "Roles, cliques and sanctions: Dimensions of patient society", *Int. J. Soc. Psychiat.*, **9** (3) (1963), 184–191.

89. These terms are used by Sykes, 1958, *op. cit.*, pp. 106–108 and Morris and Morris, 1963, *op. cit.*, pp. 242–248; a similar basis for differentiating roles ("self" versus "collectivity orientation") is to be found in Garabedian, 1964, *op. cit.*, p. 340, and Sykes himself uses the terms "individualistic" and "collectivistic" (pp. 82–83).

90. Grosser, in Hazelrigg (Ed.), 1968, *op. cit.*; McCorkle and Korn, 1954, *op. cit.*; and Weinberg, 1942, *op. cit.*, argue never. Other studies, such as those by Berk, Garabedian, Grusky and Street *et al.*, provide instances where such inmate cooperation has occurred [Peter G. Garabedian. "The natural history of an inmate community in a maximum security prison", *J. Criminal Law, Criminology and Police Sci.*, **61** (1) (1970), 78–85].

91. See, for instance, with reference to homosexuality in male and female prisons, the contrasting views of Benjamin Karpman, ["Sex life in prisons", *J. Criminal Law, Criminology and Police Sci.*, **38** (5) (1958), 475–485]; Gresham Sykes and Sheldon L. Messinger, 1960, ["The inmate social code", reprinted in Norman Jonston *et al.* (Eds), *The Sociology of Punishment and Correction*, 2nd ed., New York: Wiley, 1970, pp. 405–406]; Giallombardo, 1966, *op. cit.*, pp. 148–151; and Ward and Kassebaum, 1966, *op. cit.*, pp. 219–227.

92. See Clemmer, 1958, *op. cit.*, ch. 12, and 1950, *op. cit.*, pp. 311–319; Patrick J. Driscoll, "Factors related to the institutional adjustment of prison inmates", *J. abnorm. soc. Psychol.*, **47** (3) (1952), 593–596; Garrity, 1961, in Cressey (Ed.), *op. cit.*, pp. 372–378; Daniel Glaser and John R. Stratton, "Measuring inmate change in prison", in Cressey (Ed.), *op. cit.*, 1961, ch. 10; Goffman, 1968, *op. cit.*, p. 23; Morris and Morris, 1963, *op. cit.*, pp. 169–171 and 175–183; and T.P. Morris, "The sociology of the prison", in Grygier *et al.* (Eds), 1965, *op. cit.*, p. 77; Schrag, 1961, in Cressey (Ed.), *op. cit.*, pp. 347–359; and Marvin E. Wolfgang, "Quantitative analysis of adjustment to the prison community", *J. Criminal Law, Criminology and Police Sci.*, **51** (6) (1961), 610–611.

93. Many writers directly address themselves to this question: Bondeson, Cline, Giallombardo, Mathieson, Jerome Rabow and Albert Elias ["Organizational boundaries, inmates roles, and rehabilitation", *J. Research in Crime and Delinquency*, **6** (1) (1969), 8–16], David Street ["The inmate group in custodial and treatment settings", *Am. Sociol. Rev.*, **30** (1) (1965), 40–55], Sykes, and Tittle and Tittle.

94. Georg K. Stürup, *Treating the "Untreatable"*, Baltimore: Johns Hopkins Press, 1968. There have been a number of empirical studies of various

institutions (e.g. approved schools, detention centres, borstals and prisons) carried out in Britain. But they are restricted to accounts of the history and current regime of each type of institution and a description of the inmates, in terms of their personality characteristics, social backgrounds and criminal and penal histories with, sometimes, a statistical analysis of the "successes" and "failures" measured by reconvictions.

95. Goffman, 1968, *op. cit.*, pp. 24–51 and Harold Garfinkel, "Conditions of successful degradation ceremonies", *Am. J. Sociol.*, **61** (5) (1956), 420–423.

96. Russell N. Cassel and Robert B. Van Vorst, "Psychological needs of women in a correctional institution", *Am. J. Corrections*, **23** (1961), 22–24.

97. Sykes and Messinger, 1960, in Johnston *et al.* (Eds), 1970, *op. cit.*, p. 405 (original emphasis).

98. Morris and Morris, 1963, *op. cit.*, pp. 161–169.

99. Giallombardo, 1966, *op. cit.*, p. 93.

100. Ward and Kassebaum, 1966, *op. cit.*, p. 70; see also pp. 69–74 and Giallombardo, 1966, *op. cit.*, pp. 14–17. This is, of course, an oversimplification and tends to ignore the facts that men are also affected emotionally by separation from their families and that some women are dependent, for various reasons, on paid employment, and thus suffer from the stigma attached to a prison sentence when seeking and keeping a job.

101. Julian Roebuck, "A critique of 'thieves, convicts and the inmate culture' ", *Soc. Problems*, **11** (2) (1963), 193–200.

102. See Grosser, 1960, in Hazelrigg (Ed.), 1968, *op. cit.*, pp. 12–15; McCorkle and Korn, 1954, *op. cit.*, Weinberg, 1942, *op. cit.*; and, on mental hospitals, William Caudill *et al.*, "Social structure and interaction processes on a psychiatric ward", *Am. J. Orthopsychiat.*, **22** (1952), 314–334; Goffman, 1968, *op. cit.*, pp. 55–65; and Smith and Thrasher, 1963, *op. cit.*

103. See Giallombardo, 1966, *op. cit.*, chs. 8–10; Morris and Morris, 1963, *op. cit.*, chs. 7 and 11; Sykes and Messinger, 1960, in Johnston *et al.* (Eds), 1970, *op. cit.*

104. Gresham M. Sykes, "Men, merchants and toughs: a study of reactions to imprisonment", *Soc. Problems*, **4** (2) (1956), 131.

105. Morris and Morris, 1963, *op. cit.*, pp. 244–247.

106. Sykes, 1958, *op. cit.*, pp. 101–102.

107. The "right guy" role is described in Garabedian, 1963 and 1964, *op. cit.*, and the "Robin Hood" in Morris and Morris, 1963, *op. cit.*, pp. 243–244.

108. Seymour, L. Halleck and Mervin Hersko, "Homosexual behaviour in a correctional institution for adolescent girls", *Am. J. Orthopsychiat.*, **32** (5) (1962), 912–917.

109. For example, Sidney Kosofsky and Albert Ellis, "Illegal communication among institutionalized female delinquents", *J. Soc. Psychol.*, **48** (1958), 155–160; and Lowell S. Selling, "The pseudo family", *Am. J. Sociol.*, **37** (2) (1939), 247–253.

110. A report of the research of Sister M. Hefferman is in Ward and Kassebaum, 1966, *op. cit.*, pp. vi and 139–140.

111. Giallombardo, 1966, *op. cit.*, pp. 118–119.

112. *Ibid.*, pp. 155–157. Ward and Kassebaum (1966, *op. cit.*, p. 78) argue that "the women's prison may be viewed as a non-cohesive aggregate of homosexual dyads and friendship cliques".

113. Giallombardo, 1966, *op. cit.*, p. 130.

114. Tittle also found less reported homosexuality than in segregated institutions and a similar incidence for both sexes (approximately 25 per cent) and infers that this is largely the result of having males and females together in the same institution, providing thus more "normal" opportunities for "sexual role fulfilment".

115. See Stephenson and Scarpitti, 1968, *op. cit.* Fisher, on the contrary, found anti-staff orientations persisted even in a treatment institution. See Sethard Fisher, "Informal organization in a correctional setting", *Soc. Problems*, **13** (2) (1965), 214–222.

116. Their studies are American; unfortunately no comparable published material from juvenile institutions in Britain is available. Generally British researchers have concentrated on a descriptive, mainly statistical, account of the backgrounds and characteristics of offenders in different types of institutions and sometimes their reconviction rates. Recent examples are Charlotte Banks, "Boys in detention centres", in C. Banks and P.L. Broadhurst (Eds), Stephanos: *Studies in Psychology*, London: University of London Press, 1965, pp. 173–203; and Helen J. Richardson, *Adolescent Girls in Approved Schools*, London: Routledge and Kegan Paul, 1969.

117. See, for instance, on juvenile institutions, Gordon H. Barker and W. Thomas Adams, "The social structure of a correctional institution", *J. Criminal Law, Criminology and Police Sci.*, **49** (5) (1959), 417–422; Sethard Fisher, "Social organization in a correctional residence", *Pacific Sociol. Rev.*, **4** (2) (1961), 87–93; and Polsky, 1965, *op. cit.*, pp. 55–59 and 75–80.

118. David Matza, *Delinquency and Drift*, New York: Wiley, 1964, pp. 22–26.

119. Glaser, 1964, *op. cit.*, p. 477.

120. *Ibid.*, p. 169.

121. Cloward, 1960, in Hazelrigg (Ed.), 1968, *op. cit.*, pp. 86–89.

122. Grosser, 1960, in Hazelrigg (Ed.), 1968, *op. cit.*, pp. 20–21.

123. Thomas Mathiesen, 1965, *op. cit.*, chs. 1–2 and "A functional equivalent to inmate cohesion", *Hum. Organization*, **27** (2) (1968), 117–124.

124. Mathiesen, 1965, *op. cit.*, pp. 100–101.

125. Morris and Morris, 1963, *op. cit.*, pp: 270–272.

126. Donald R. Cressey and Witold Krassowsky, "Inmate organization and anomie in American prisons and Soviet labour camps", *Soc. Problems*, **5** (3) (1958), 217–218.

127. See Clemmer, 1958, *op. cit.*, p. 150.

128. For example, the very fact of stratification which suggests some value consensus over prestige-conferring qualities such as criminal success and passive resistance to staff; the existence of a prison culture containing well-understood and tolerated, if not prescribed, social roles and a wide range

of social controls; and a single identifiable process of socialization or "cultural assimilation" unique to the prison and the inmates which affects individuals from every stratum and group.

129. Mathiesen, 1965, *op. cit.*, p. 27.

130. Ward and Kassebaum, 1966, *op. cit.*, pp. 54–55.

131. *Ibid.*, p. 118.

132. Schrag, 1961, *op. cit.*, and in Cressey (Ed.), 1961, *op. cit.*, pp. 346–357.

133. See Garabedian, 1963, *op. cit.*; Garrity, 1961, in Cressey (Ed.), *op. cit.*, pp. 375–378; and Norman S. Hayner, "Characteristics of five offender types", *Am. Sociol. Rev.*, **26** (1) (1961), 96–102.

134. See Edwards, 1970, *op. cit.*, pp. 218–221.

135. Wilson, 1968, *op. cit.*, p. 148.

136. Charles Wellford, "Factors associated with adoption of the inmate code: A study of normative socialization", *J. Criminal Law, Criminology and Police Sci.*, **58** (2) (1967), 197–203.

137. Garrity, 1961, in Cressey (Ed.), *op. cit.*, pp. 378–379. Actual statistics on recidivism are relevant at this point. Glaser (1964, *op. cit.*, p. 24) suggests that in America about 33 per cent of ex-prisoners return to prison within two to five years. Figures, based on follow-up studies of Borstal boys and certain categories of prisoners released from English institutions in 1954, show that approximately 60 per cent had recidivated by 1960 (see Morris, 1965, *op. cit.*, pp. 78–79). The proportions of prison populations with previous prison confinements are, of course, much higher—Glaser (p. 15) gives a figure of around 50 per cent for America and Sparks (1971, *op. cit.*, p. 105) quotes around 70 per cent for England.

138. See Glaser, 1964, *op. cit.*, pp. 465–467. For a typology of delinquents and criminals based on the concept of "career", see Don C. Gibbons, *Society, Crime and Criminal Careers*, Englewood Cliffs, N.J.: Prentice-Hall, 1968.

139. For an interesting theoretical discussion of the effects of labelling and treatment on criminals, see Grygier, 1965, *op. cit.*, on the concept of "social progression". The "labelling" or "interactionist" approach applied to the sociology of deviance is rapidly becoming a popular and productive field of study. See, for instance, Howard S. Becker, *Outsiders*, Glencoe, Ill.: The Free Press, 1963; Simon Dinitz, Russell R. Dynes and Alfred C. Clarke (Eds), *Deviance: Studies in the Process of Stigmatization and Societal Reaction*, New York: Oxford University Press, 1969; Edwin M. Lemert, *Human Deviance, Social Problems and Social Control*, Englewood Cliffs, N.J.: Prentice-Hall, 1967; David Matza, *Becoming Deviant*, Englewood Cliffs, N.J.: Prentice-Hall, 1969; Earl Rubington and Martin Weinberg (Eds), *Deviance: An Interactionist Perspective*, New York: Macmillan, 1968; Edwin Schur, *Labelling Deviant Behaviour*, New York: Harper and Row, 1971; and, for the only two contributions from Britain to date, see Stanley Cohen (Ed.), *Images of Deviance*, Harmondsworth: Penguin, 1971; and Laurie Taylor, *Deviance and Society*, London: Michael Joseph, 1971.

140. Glaser (1964, *op. cit.*, p. 475) claims that: "At least 90 per cent of American prison releases seek legitimate careers for a month or more after they leave prison." For a study of employers' attitudes towards "using" unskilled workers who have either been charged and convicted of assault or been tried and acquitted (compared with a no-criminal record control group), see Richard D. Schwartz and Jerome H. Skolnick, "Two studies of legal stigma", *Soc. Problems*, **10** (2) (1962), 133–142.

141. Morris and Morris (1963, *op. cit.*, pp. 175–176) comment: "Garrity . . . suggests, incidentally, that prison is largely an irrelevant interlude in an entrenched criminal career".

142. Clemmer, 1958, *op. cit.*, pp. 298–299; see also the whole of ch. 12.

143. Wheeler, 1961, *op. cit.*, p. 698.

144. Wheeler, 1961, in Cressey (Ed.), *op. cit.*

145. Ward and Kassebaum, "Homosexuality: A mode of adaptation in a prison for women", *Soc. Problems*, **12** (2) (1964), 159–177.

146. See Roger Hood, *Borstal Re-Assessed*, London: Heinemann, 1965, chs. 3 and 5.

147. Greenblatt *et al.* (Eds), 1957, *op. cit.*, p. 9.

148. Doris C. Gilbert and Daniel J. Levinson, " 'Custodialism' and 'humanism' in a mental hospital structure and in staff ideology", in Greenblatt *et al.* (Eds), *op. cit.*, 1957, p. 22; see also pp. 20–35.

149. See Cressey, 1958, *Pacific Sociol. Rev.*, *op. cit.*, pp. 44–46 and "Contradictory directives in complex organizations: The case of the prison", *Admin. Sci. Q.*, **4** (1) (1959), pp. 1–19; Jay Hall *et al.*, "The challenge of correctional change: The interface of conformity and commitment", *J. Criminal Law, Criminology and Police Sci.*, **57** (4) (1966), 493–503, and Kassebaum *et al.*, 1962, *op. cit.*, p. 84.

150. Brown *et al.*, 1971, *op. cit.*, p. 316.

151. Weber, 1967, *op. cit.*, pp. 27–30.

152. Mathiesen, 1965, *op. cit.*, pp. 199–201.

153. Grosser, 1960, in Hazelrigg (Ed.), 1968, *op. cit.*, p. 19.

154. The "Norwich system", which was first introduced into English prisons in the 1950s, can probably be classified as a "humane" type of regime (see Emery, 1970, *op. cit.*, pp. 38–41). "H. Wing" in Pentonville is an example, but seems to have been largely unsuccessful, see Morris and Morris, 1963, *op. cit.*, pp. 272–279 and note 22 above.

155. For example, Brown *et al.*, 1971, *op. cit.*; Kassebaum *et al.*, 1962, *op. cit.*; Weber, 1957, *op. cit.*; Zald, 1962, *Admin. Sci. Q.*, *op. cit.*, and "Organizational control structures in five correctional communities", *Am. J. Sociol.*, **68** (3) (1962), 33–345.

156. For example, Charles Perrow, "Reality shock: A new organization confronts the custody-treatment dilemma", *Soc. Problems*, **10** (4) (1963), 374–382 and 1966, *op. cit.*; Irving Piliavin, "The reduction of custodian–professional conflict in correctional institutions", *Crime and Delinquency*, **12** (2)(1966), 125–134; Street *et al.*, 1966, *op. cit.*, ch. 10; and E.J. Thomas, 1966, *op. cit.*

157. For instance, Cressey, 1959, *op. cit.*, pp. 1–5; Emery, 1970, *op. cit.*, pp. 11–20; Oscar Grusky, "Role conflict in organization: A study of prison camp officials", *Admin. Sci. Q.*, **3** (2) (1959), 452–472; Johnson, 1960, *op. cit.*; Morris and Morris, 1963, *op. cit.*, pp. 80–87; Lloyd E. Ohlin, "The reduction of role conflict in institutional staff", *Children*, **5** (1958), 65–69; and Weber, in Cressey (Ed.), 1961, *op. cit.*

158. Zald, 1962, *Admin. Sci. Q.*, *op. cit.*, pp. 45–48.

159. Morris and Morris, 1963, *op. cit.*; see also Emery, 1970, *op. cit.*, pp. 33–37.

160. Lawrence E. Hazelrigg, "An examination of the accuracy and relevance of staff perceptions of the inmate in the correctional institution", *J. Criminal Law, Criminology and Police Sci.*, **58** (2) (1967), 204–210.

161. Wheeler, 1961, in Cressey (Ed.), *op. cit.*

162. Braginsky *et al.*, 1969, *op. cit.*, esp. ch. 5; and Lawrence S. Linn, "The mental hospital from the patient perspective", *Psychiatry*, **31** (3) (1968), 213–223.

163. For example, Raymond J. Corsini and Kenwood Bartleme, "Penology and the attitudes of prisoners", *Br. J. Delinq.*, **4** (1) (1953), 5–58; Walter C. Reckless, "The Impact of correctional programmes on inmates", *Br. J. Delinq.*, **6** (2) (1955), 138–147; and, on the subjective attitudes of prisoners to parole, see Richard Dembo, "Recidivism: The 'criminal's' reaction to 'treatment' ", *Criminology*, **8** (4) (1971), 345–356; and Donald Rasmussen, "Prisoner opinions about parole", *Am. Sociol. Rev.*, **5** (4) (1940), 584–595.

164. A prisoner, quoted in Parker, 1970, *op. cit.*, p. 4.

DAVID SILVERMAN

ACCOUNTS OF ORGANIZATIONS—organizational "structures" and the accounting process

David Silverman *received his Ph.D. in sociology from the University of London and is currently Senior Lecturer in Sociology at the University of London Goldsmiths' College. His main interests lie in ethnomethodology and in theorizing conceived as a practical activity. He has taught at the London School of Economics and at the University of California, Los Angeles. His books include* The Theory of Organizations (1970) *and the joint publication of* New Directions in Sociological Theory (1972). *He is currently researching on practical decision-making in a large British public sector organization and the research will be published as* Organizational Work *(1974). He is also writing to introduce students to the social sciences,* Re-Membering Castenada: A prologue to the Social Sciences *(forthcoming).*

> Here it is difficult as it were to keep our heads up—to see that we must stick to the subjects of our everyday thinking, and not go astray and imagine that we have to describe extreme subtleties, which in turn we are after all quite unable to describe with the means at our disposal. We feel as if we had to repair a torn spider's web with our fingers.
> (Ludwig Wittgenstein, 1968; para. 106)

The task of this chapter is the exposition of a developing position within sociology which seeks to base the analysis of social structures on a study of what can be called "the accounting process". Because the literature may be somewhat unfamiliar, this chapter will begin by examining some of the features of a traditional sociological study of organizations, in particular the distinction that it posits between social structures and social relations.[1] An analysis of the basis of this distinction leads into a discussion of the commonsense interpretive procedures (the "natural attitude" as outlined by Alfred Schutz) upon which it relies.[2] The main body of the chapter then follows in the form of a review of five studies of organizational activities (by Garfinkel, Bittner, Zimmerman, Sudnow and Cicourel) which embody the theoretical presuppositions that emerge out of a focus upon the natural attitude. The final section, with reference to the author's own research, takes up the relationship of the study of accounting to the concepts of "organization" and "bureaucracy".

Introductory remarks

Something like a consensus characterizes the current state of organizational analysis. While different writers take up a variety of issues (from "micro" to "macro" in perspective) and use a range of research instruments (both qualitative and quantitative), they seem in little doubt of the essentially complementary nature of their work—even if few are prepared to undertake the perilous task of synthesis. The main features of this consensus are a recognition of the need for a division of labour among researchers and an agreement about what constitutes the concerns of the study of organizations as a whole. As a consequence, writers tend to specialize in what are seen as different but entirely legitimate sub-areas of organization analysis. There is every reason to accept Blau's characterization of the three main sub-areas as the character of organizational roles, social relations in organizations and "formal" organizational structures. As he writes:

> Three foci can be distinguished in the study of organizational life; they may be called "role analysis", "group analysis", and "organizational analysis". In the first case, the focus is on the behaviour of individuals in their specific roles as members of organizations, as illustrated by studies of career patterns, work satisfaction and productivity, attitudes of soldiers towards combat, and administrative decision making. The second focus is on the structure of social relations in work groups—for example, the significance of group cohesion for performance, the differentiation of informal status in groups, the exchange of advice for prestige among colleagues, and generally patterns of informal organization. Third, *organizational analysis proper* focuses upon the system of interrelated attributes that characterize the organization itself rather than its component parts, such as its size, the division of labour in it, its bureaucratization, and the degree of centralization of control.[3]

While distinguishing his three foci, Blau acknowledges that they deal with closely related factors and constitute as a whole "the study of organizational life".

The second feature of the consensus which is suggested, arises directly out of the first. This agreement about the subject matter of the study of organizations rests on a commitment, shared by the spectrum of sociological perspectives, from the structural-functionalists to the symbolic interactionists, to a task of describing and explaining organizational structures and relationships. Goffman, for instance, evidences a concern with description while Blau appears to be concerned with explanation.[4]

A feature of the concerns exemplified by both Goffman and Blau is the non-problematic status accorded to the structures and relations which are purportedly being described and explained. The social world, they seem to infer, is somehow "out there" and the role of the sociologist is to catch or to "tap" its component parts which, as it were, await explication. As in most enquiry (whether lay or scientific), the very availability of the phenomenon and of knowledge of its features is not itself an issue. Goffman and Blau might as well, for all practical purposes, be offering descriptions and explanations of the component parts and internal relations of a raincloud.

Yet the analyses of the natural and social scientist have a very different basis. As Schutz notes:

> . . . there is an essential difference in the structure of the thought objects or mental constructs formed by the social sciences and those formed by the natural sciences.

It is up to the natural scientist and to him alone to define, in accordance with the procedural rules of his science, his observational field, and to determine the facts, data and events within it which are relevant for his problem or scientific purpose at hand. Neither are those facts and events preselected, nor is the observational field preinterpreted. The world of nature, as explored by the natural scientist does not "mean" anything to molecules, atoms and electrons. But the observational field of the social scientist—social reality—has a specific meaning and relevance structure for the human beings living, acting and thinking within it. By a series of commonsense constructs they have preselected and preinterpreted this world which they experience as the reality of their daily lives. It is these thought objects of theirs which determine their behaviour by motivating it. The thought objects constructed by the social scientist have to be founded upon the thought objects constructed by the commonsense thinking of men, living their daily life within their social world.[5]

It is clear that Schutz intended the last sentence not as an injunction to social scientists—who, if not so instructed, might do otherwise—but as a statement of a necessary feature of sociological analysis. Inevitably, then, Blau and Goffman, as lay participants in society as well as sociologists, offer descriptions and explanations "founded upon the thought objects constructed by the common sense thinking of men living their daily life within their social world". Yet their "inside" knowledge (and that of their audience), unavailable to the natural scientist (and his audience), is traded upon as a tacit resource to constitute a knowable phenomenon. Their accounts seem convincing, then, peripherally because we assume that they have followed the canons of the scientific method (rigour, precision, etc.) but, more significantly, because both writer and reader already possess background knowledge of the phenomena of the social world glossed as "what everybody knows", "what can be taken for granted", and so on. Paradoxically, in the manner of a self-fulfilling prophecy, their accounts of organizational structures, which, like everyday accounts, purport to describe phenomena which exist separately from anyone attending to them, create the features of a "real", "available" world.

The "sensible", "methodic" character of such accounts does not derive, then, from the intrinsic features of the phenomena in question for neither writer sets out out to analyse the "preselection" and "preinterpretation" that constitute the phenomena. Rather the ordered nature of such accounts arises from the interpretive activities that writers and readers necessarily bring to bear in their tasks of, respectively, creating and understanding texts. That these accounts carry conviction is, then, itself a practical accomplishment whose basis could form the topic for sociological enquiry.

In order to avoid misunderstanding, this is not intended as an irony, still less as a "criticism" of such writers. Whether either Goffman or Blau is "right" or "wrong" is not in issue. For the fact is that, like students of organizations and sociologists in general, they are able to bring off "sensible" accounts. Thus the features of organizational analysis that are discussed in this part of the paper are not at all presented in a "critical" spirit. Neither are remedies suggested for purported "shortcomings". Rather such analysis, like lay analysis, is viewed as an amazing practical accomplishment relying, in unexplicated ways, upon folk knowledge of the processes of preselection and preinterpretation.

Organizational structures and social relations

As has already been noted, the division of labour that is accepted in studies of organizations is reflected in Blau's distinction between "role", "group" and "organizational" analysis. The last area of study, it seems, focuses on the structural features of organizations and the processes that produce them. Unlike the other areas, this, in Blau's terms, constitutes organizational analysis "proper". By reference to a later empirical study which follows on from the research imperatives which Blau had implied earlier, the character of the assumptions, which are employed to bring off the distinction between organizational structures and social relations, will be examined.

In their preface to *The Structure of Organizations*, Blau and Schoenherr note the limitation of single-case studies which, while providing useful material on social relations, fail to analyse with comparative data the interdependence between organizational characteristics. This distinction between knowledge of social structures and of social relations, necessitates, in their view, a strategic choice by the researcher:

> Hence, a choice must be made between examining sociopsychological processes within an organization, taking its basic structure as given, and investigating the interdependence among elements in the structure of organizations, while ignoring the details of daily relations and of human relations.[6]

Blau and Schoenherr opt for the latter alternative not so much as a painful necessity produced by the need for comparative materials, but as a statement of faith based upon an assumption about the dominant position of the concept of "social structure" in sociological analysis. While they recognize that only persons, unlike organizations, can think and act, their argument is that organizational structures serve as constraints on human activities and can be analysed in their own right.

Blau and Schoenherr grant that this omits certain matters (variously and somewhat curiously referred to in different parts of the book as "socio-psychological processes", "human relations", "psychological forces", "the motives of individuals" and "psychological factors", but say that such strategic choices must be made if "social structure" is to receive its due attention. Their study thus sticks exclusively to the identification of structural features in organizations and attempts to explain their interrelations. For example, what is the relationship between "size" and "differentiation", between "formalization of rules" and "bureaucratic rigidity" and "complexity" and "subsystem autonomy" and between "environmental context" and "organizational form"?

Before examining the study further, the approach to be adopted towards it shall be discussed. In many ways, *The Structure of Organizations* provides a sound basis for discussion because its authors are refreshingly self-conscious about the existence of alternatives to what they seek to do and about their basis of choice between different research priorities. Since they set up the question as a choice between "social structures" and "social relations", it ought, however, to be stated at the outset that the view that, by focusing on "social structures", Blau and Schoenherr have, in some sense, made the "wrong" choice has *no part* in this argument. Neither does the contention that "social relations" are too closely interwoven with "social structures" to permit their analytic separation. Rather than "criticize" the distinction, the purpose of this section is to analyse the *grounds* which are available for seeing its "good sense", for "good sense" it undoubtedly has within the paradigm of knowledge of a particular variety of sociology. It is this paradigm which creates the possibility of such versions of the world.

To understand what makes Blau and Schoenherr's position both possible and sensible, a further sentence from the preface deserves examination.

> The assumption implicit in this approach is that formal organizations as well as other social structures, exhibit regularities that can be analyzed in their own right, independent of any knowledge about the individual behaviour of their members.

The sensible character of this proposition resides within a paradigm which provides for the existence of social phenomena with intrinsic features or properties (they "exhibit regularities"), which exist independently of the activities of the participants or of the observer (they "can be analyzed in their own right"). Such a paradigm is a feature of what may be termed "positivistic" sociology and is also a central feature of lay or common sense knowledge of the world (discussed in the following section of this paper).

According to this view of knowledge, as expressed in scientific activity, the regularities are there, as it were, for anybody's view, and the role of the observer is simply that of the "messenger" who reports to other the intrinsic properties of the factual world. This denial of the interpretive activities of the observer is achieved by a nominalist view of the nature of scientific concepts. The observer simply says at the outset something like "by x I am going to mean y", and his study is then assessed in terms of the statistical significance of the relationships between variables —as the researcher has defined them. Since an infinity of definitions or conceptualizations can presumably be produced for any phenomenon, the observer's grounds for the choice of a particular definition or the application of a certain concept to a given piece of data are never themselves the object of enquiry. Or rather, on the basis of our routine knowledge of the everyday world, we are convinced by "sensible" definitions and "reasonable" application of concepts—in much the same manner as the use of terms "makes sense" in the unfolding of natural conversation.

In such accounts, then, the common sense knowledge employed by the observer (and the participants) for defining features, seeing relationships and recognizing regularities is specifically uninteresting. They are things to be glossed as "what may be taken for granted", and the like, so that the "real" business of the exercise (recording instances of relationships and regularities) may proceed. As Cicourel argues, the problem turns on the objectification of data—the ways in which the researcher lays claim to have adequately preserved (for purposes of inference) the materials labelled "data".[7] The "short-circuiting" of the issue of objectification which he describes ensures that the problematic nature of the process, whereby messages are relayed and received from the social world, never arises.

To talk of "regularities that can be analyzed in their own right" presumes a process whereby these regularities routinely display themselves. Yet Blau and Schoenherr's study of the organizational structures of state employment agencies make it clear that the facts hardly jump onto the page. First, the researchers' initial conceptualization of the "basic" features of organizations (differentiation, size, formalization, etc.) ensures that not all materials constitute data. Second, as they make clear, some data must be rejected as "too imprecise" for the purposes of the study. Before the stage of relating "variables" to one another is reached, then, the researchers engage in a process of negotiating what they will take as knowledge, of sifting and evaluating materials to produce depictions of organizational structures which seem "adequate" for their analytic purposes and which fit the theoretical apparatus with which they enter the field.

Since research cannot be conducted on organizational structures "themselves" but on data taken as representations of such structures, the process by which researchers' obtain data which, from their point of view, adequately report social structures can itself be seen as reflection of a socially organized search for knowledge. As they explain in a section called "Data", Blau and Schoenherr's depiction of organizational structures emerged out of a search process which began by obtaining organizational charts, continued with two stages of "explanation" and "clarification" by "key informants" employed by the organizations, and ended with slotting of these materials into operational measures constructed by the researchers. As will be apparent from the discussion below, knowledge of structure was, at each stage, grounded in the interpretive activities of the observer:

(1) *Organizational Charts* The researchers took the basic structure of organizations to be represented by organizational charts. As they write:

> Many of the operational variables needed, though by no means all, could be constructed on the basis of a very detailed and accurate organizational chart.

The negotiation of this material as an adequate representation of organizational structures necessarily glosses lay knowledge of the features that make a chart sensible as a depiction of social order to both laymen and observers—for instance, the concept of "hierarchy" as routinely used in attending to the sensible character of an organizational chart (which we presumably take for granted will show something resembling a pyramid, rather than, say, a square or an inverted pyramid). It would further imply that the chart itself produced, in some predictable manner, a particular structuring of activities in an organization and that researchers need not concern themselves with the manner in which the chart is attended to, if at all, by participants in carrying out their activities. However, even given these assumptions, the researchers did not always feel that their 3000 charts "spoke for themselves" or related sufficiently clearly to their own prior concerns.

(2) *Explication by Key Informants* Even in the early stages of the research, it was felt that additional information was needed in order to make "proper sense" of the charts. So key informants were interviewed in order to elucidate the "meaning" of the charts. It should be noted that such "further" information was a product of the

research activity itself: there is no means of knowing from the report whether such explanations were required by the staff themselves in carrying out their routine activities or how these activities depended upon incomplete knowledge or unstated assumptions.

(3) *Further Clarification* When analysis began, it was speedily recognized that, even with the informants' explanations, there was a need for further clarification. Once again, the interpretive relevances of the researchers are here asserted as the basis for deciding what shall constitute a "fact". The charts are "not sufficiently precise" or "comparable" from the point of view of the researcher ("for our purpose"). Consequently, they must be "revised". The conceptions of precision and comparability employed by the participants to decode organizational charts and the procedures whereby they decide that their knowledge is "sufficient" assume no importance as compared to the researchers' own schemes.

(4) *Operational Measures* The process of "description" reaches its final stage when these refined "facts" are coded in terms of the operational measures determined by the researchers. These coding activities are necessarily based on taken-for-granted knowledge of social structures employed to interpret the "underlying pattern" that any "fact" purportedly reveals. As in the example below, operational definitions tacitly reflect knowledge of the world which "facts" report:

> The major dimensions of the shape of the pyramid *decided on* were the number of hierarchical levels as an indication of vertical differentiation, the number of major subdivisions as the main indication of horizontal differentiation, and the number of sections per division as another indication of horizontal differentiation.

Here what feature counts as an indication of a variable is "decided on" on the basis of knowledge of the routine features of social structures.

In addition, when the researcher comes to apply his categories to data, he is always faced with a series of decisions about the relevance of a category to a given case. As a consequence, he must engage in ad hocing practices which rely for their sensible character upon tacit knowledge of the everyday world. For instance:

> In measuring hierarchical levels, deputy managers or assistant supervisors were not counted . . . Several job titles indicative merely of differences in grade or skill, like statistical clerk I and statistical clerk II, are counted only as one in the measure.

To summarize the argument: however deeply one digs, organizational charts (and other socially produced phenomena) have no intrinsic meaning. Their meaning arises in socially organized attempts (both lay and sociological) to recognize and count them. The "structures" that Blau and Schoenherr report do indeed come to stand "in their own right—but as features of the interpretive activities that create them as observable–reportable phenomena. It should be added that this assertion has nothing to do with charge of "bias", which the authors recognize as a possibility and seek to control. Indeed, within their paradigm of knowledge, once bias has been dealt with, there can be no doubt about the correspondence between their accounts and the intrinsic properties of the world:

> We are convinced that the final charts accurately describe the formal structures.

Notice the sensible nature of this claim, given the extensive search procedures adopted by the researchers, if structures are presumed to exist independently of anybody's (participant or observer) attending to them. For, within such a perspective, the crucial thing is to record accurately the "message" from the real world and the "messenger's" paradigm of knowledge is neither here nor there—providing he controls for "bias".

The everyday world and the accounting process

Part of what has been done in the previous section is to waive the issue of what the facts "really are" in order to raise the question of the manner in which researchers (like Blau and Schoenherr) routinely go about the business of providing for the existence of "facts" in the context of a "factual" world. As has been shown, despite their commitment to the "regularities" which structures "exhibit", the data which they utilize are a product of the *ad hoc* interpretive procedures that they employ to create their "variables". This focus on the interpretive activities of the observer parallels the programmatic statement by Zimmerman and Pollner:

> Thus one would not examine the factual properties of status hierarchies, for example, but rather the *fact* of the factual properties of status hierarchies: one would ask how members provide for the fact that status hierarchies are factual features of the member's world. Similarly, instead of treating statistical rates as representations of trends, processes, and factual states of the society, one would ask how members manage to assemble those statistics, and how they use, read, and rely on those statistics as indications of the states of affairs they are taken to depict.[8]

As Zimmerman and Pollner imply, "practical investigations" and the provision of factual features of the world are equally characteristic of lay and sociological enquiry. Yet organizational research is implicitly committed to "do better" than common sense by describing more "precisely" the character of organizational structures so that their internal relationships can be more fully understood. By his objectivity and statistical rigour, the social scientist can, it is claimed, attain knowledge that is more reliable than everyday knowledge. As a competitor with common sense, then, the social scientist is able to bring off easy victories by the "superiority" of his techniques for describing and explaining what is happening (has happened). Yet sociology shares with common sense an agreement as to the fundamental and ordered character of a factual domain independent of the employment of some method of enquiry. While common sense and sociology offer competing accounts of the world, they are, then, both committed to the existence and availability of a world possessing intrinsic features with ordered properties. Since the "masking" of the manner in which the world is made available in the course of giving an account of it is equally a feature of lay and sociological accounts, in this section of the paper we will sketch out the knowledge of the everyday world upon which they both rely.

The everyday world

The analysis of the central features of the everyday world was the main task of Alfred Schutz. Schutz set out to understand the basis on which men in their everyday lives attend to and create regular and knowable features in their social world. According to Schutz, men attain knowledge of the world by means of what he called the "natural attitude". This contains the following presuppositions:

(1) *Predefinition* Man is born into an already organized, predefined and pre-interpreted social cosmos. This world existed long before one's birth and is already experienced and interpreted by our predecessors as an organized world. These interpretations provide the "objective" features of the world with which we must reckon if we are to attain our ends—they define the actor's sense of social structure.

(2) *Availability* In the natural attitude, there is no doubting the objective, "real" features of the world as we experience them, neither do we doubt its concrete availability for understanding and action—for even if we do not understand, we know that there are experts who possess the necessary knowledge. Moreover, we take-for-granted that the character of the world as we have experienced it is more or less permanent and unchanging, that what appeared to us to be beyond question yesterday will still be beyond question tomorrow. This is not to imply that we never have doubts but rather that such doubts are made sensible in the context of global certainties.

(3) *Intersubjectivity* The world is experienced from the outset not as the private world of a single individual but as an intersubjective world common to us all. We assume a basic reciprocity of perspectives such that, disregarding our own private meanings, we interpret events in a manner which is identical for all practical purposes and assume that we all would have broadly the same experience if we were to change places. In this way, we routinely make sense of the other's talk and action and bring off our own "acceptable" activities.

(4) *Typicality* We make sense of the world by seeking for knowledge of the "typical features" of any social scene. Since we can only personally experience a small fraction of the social world, we rely on typifications, handed down by our predecessors and passed on by our associates, in order to define our environment and to learn how to form our own typical constructs. Everyday language possesses what Schutz calls a "treasure house" of ready-made, preconstituted types and inbuilt relevances which constitute the actor's stock of knowledge. Even unique objects and events became unique within a horizon of typical familiarity and prior knowledge.

(5) *Practical Interests* In the natural attitude, the features of our intersubjective world are addressed with a pragmatic motive. We do not seek "full' knowledge of

the world but merely sufficient knowledge to "get by" and to further our practical interests: as Schutz comments—

> Our practical interest alone, as it arises in a certain situation of our life, and as it will be modified by the change in the situation which is just on the point of occurring, is the only relevant principle in the building up of the perspective structure in which our social world appears to use in daily life.[9]

Practical rationality

Under the auspices of the natural attitude, the world is experienced as a massively real structure, already predefined and recalcitrant when acted upon. Knowledge of this world is gained by applying rules of thumb which have proved successful in the past in order to serve our practical interests. Yet the organization of these rules is not routinely of interest to us.[10] As a consequence, the rationality of our knowledge is routinely sustained insofar as that knowledge can be successfully employed to further our practical interests of the time. The issue for the practical "theorist" is never whether the knowledge does justice to the intricate features of social reality but rather (and more simply) "does it work?".

Schutz employs an analogy of a cookery book to characterize both this knowledge of the everyday world and our search procedures to obtain it:

> This kind of knowledge and its organization I should like to call "cookery-book knowledge". The cookery-book has recipes, lists of ingredients, formulas for mixing them, and directions for finishing off. This is all we need to make an apple pie, and also all we need to deal with the routine matters of daily life. If we enjoy the apple pie so prepared, we do not ask whether the manner of preparing it as indicated by the recipe is the most appropriate from the hygienic or alimentary point of view, or whether it is the shortest, the most economical, or the most efficient. We just eat an enjoy it.[11]

Yet the researcher is equally as dependent on this "cookery-book" knowledge in his attempts to depict the features of the world. Whether he has to make sense of questionnaire answers, officially generated statistics or organizational charts, he will (albeit after what he takes to be a more extensive and detached search for knowledge) apply everyday recipes for success to interpret what, for all practical purposes, the materials really mean. Like his subjects, his ways of attending to the world (interpretive procedures) will, in the manner of a self-fulfilling prophecy, conjure up its objective features. At the same time, the subjects' logic-in-use, the manner in which they proceed on incomplete knowledge by closing the unfolding features of social life in the context of a passing social scene, are excluded from the observer's analysis as, retrospectively, he seeks to read his own sense into materials. Paradoxically, then, sociology typically serves to obscure the actor's logic-in-use as employed in a socially organized setting, while trading upon lay paradigms of knowledge as a tacit resource to constitute "problems" and to do "analyses".

Accounting

Up to this point, a certain circularity may seem apparent in the argument. For, like the participant, one way in which the observer may come to grips with social reality—the use of reports framed in natural language—has inescapable links with the natural attitude. As Schutz comments:

> The typifying medium par excellence by which socially derived knowledge is trans-
> mitted is the vocabulary and syntax of everyday language.[12]

Yet the alternative—descriptions of the world couched in scientific concepts—necessarily possess unknown, negotiated links with the social structures it purportedly describes (this was the argument developed in relation to Blau and Schoenherr's book). As a consequence, accounts, whether in natural or scientific language, report not on external realities but on the interpretive activities that make them possible—most notably those activities associated with the natural attitude. Wittgenstein expressed this most clearly:

> One thinks that one is tracing the outline of the thing's nature over and over again, and
> one is merely tracing round the frame through which we look at it.
>
> A picture held us captive. And we could not get outside it, for it lay in our language and
> language seemed to repeat it inexorably.[13]

The ethnomethodological paradigm implies that the way to address this circle is to treat the "picture" and the "frame" as data and the process by which they are displayed and recognized as the "thing's nature" as the phenomenon for investigation. More specifically, this implies as a policy that the observer "bracket" (put on one side, adopt a position of "official neutrality" towards) the assumptions of "intersubjectivity" and "availability" that were discussed earlier as features of the natural attitude.

First, while sociologists typically assume a reciprocity of perspectives (intersubjectivity) between themselves and their subjects and, thereby, infer a particular rationality (or rule-governed character) in the latter's accounts, actions and records, this is not a necessary basis for analysis:

> No necessity dictates that a definition of rational action be decided in order to conceive
> a field of observable events of conduct. This result has the important and paradoxical
> consequence of permitting us to study the properties of rational action more closely
> than ever before.[14]

Instead of treating the properties of rationality as a basis for interpreting activities, it is possible to examine how such activities *provide for* a sense of their rationality. For instance, how the records of bureaucratic agencies demonstrate that their activities (and their outcomes) are in-accord-with-a-rule. In this way, the rule-governed character of such activities may be seen as a practical accomplishment, employed *ex post facto*.[15]

Second, while, according to the natural attitude, one suspends doubt about the availability of the features of the social world.[16] Thus the sociologist seeks to make problematic the very availability of the world (for reflection or action) which is relied upon in everyday life. Instead his problem becomes how features of reality are attended to, displayed and recognized in lay and professional accounts of the world.

Organizational structures and the accounting process

There is a large and increasing amount of research material on organizations deriving from the ethnomethodological paradigm. As discussed in the last section, such work is *characterized by*:

(1) An attempt to examine the ways in which activities and their outcomes are displayed as in-accord-with-a-rule such that their sensible character may be recognized, and
(2) An examination of the practices and policies through which the features of the real world are provided for in the activities and accounts (both lay and professional) that routinely arise in socially organized settings.

As a consequence, this work specifically *avoids*:

(1) The explanation of talk and actions in terms of purportedly underlying rationalities and sets of rules (roles, norms and cultures) which arise outside such activities and determine their character, and
(2) The treatment of social phenomena (facts, rates and structures) as if they exist independently from anyone's accounting activities and are (in some unknown way) "available" for analysis.

In this section of the paper, we shall review the relevant literature under these auspices. Each work will be considered separately for, while there is much to be gained by comparison, it will be probably easier to follow if there are separate presentations which retain the logic of each argument. In the subsequent section, however, we shall return to their common features in an attempt to clarify the relevance of the concepts of "organization" and "bureaucracy" for sociological analysis.

1. *Garfinkel: jurors' decision-making*

The task of a jury, as Garfinkel describes it, is to decide "harm", "blame" and "remedy".[17] In total, these decisions constitute its 'verdict', i.e. its decision as to the legally enforceable situation.

Jurors' activities may be conceived, says Garfinkel, as a "method of social inquiry" in order to come to decisions about "what really happened" and, therefore, about which of the alternative depictions of past motives and events that are presented to them most nearly accords with the "facts". Common sense models of the world are employed in order to make sense of testimony in terms of common sense knowledge of social structure ("what any competent member of society knows that anyone knows") and of practical procedures for assembling materials and deciding between them (e.g. by reducing to a minimum the number of variables defining the "problem"). These practices and knowledge constitute an available "corpus of knowledge", by providing for "what actually happened", i.e. the "facts" of the "case" rather than possibilities, hypotheses or fanciful imaginings, etc. By the "sorting of claims" on the grounds of common sense knowledge of social structures and of "correct" grounds for inference, jurors call upon and make available (for their practical purposes of decision-making) the features of a real world with stable properties.

However, common sense rules of inference are not the only rules available to the "good juror". According to Garfinkel, jurors also talked about features of decision-making that, from handbooks, from court personnel and from TV films, they learned as the "official juror line". Decision-making that followed this line should, ideally, put to one side everyday conceptions of "fairness" and personal preferences and feelings of sympathy. The good juror will not make snap decisions until the important matters of the trial (including the final speeches of counsel and the directions of the judge) have concluded, neither will he adopt irrevocable commitments that he may be later called upon to defend "out of pride" rather than in terms of the "facts" of the "case". Instead, between what is legal and what is fair, he will do what is legal. For the good juror the "law" and the "evidence" alone form the basis of decisions and the judge's instructions are not innovated upon.

In the event, Garfinkel argues, the adoption of the "official juror line" did not lead to the suspension of everyday practices for deciding upon facts. Jurors did not, overnight, as it were, suspend their intricate knowledge of their massively real world as a basis for sorting fact from fancy. The major impact of the "official line", then, was not upon the grounds for inferring what was a "fact" but upon what "facts" the juror would consider relevant for his present activities. For, unlike the attitude of everyday life, where the search for knowledge is only of importance for immediate practical ends, the juror is interested in facts "for their own sake". As an essentially disinterested observer, he feels obliged to treat the situation as an object of "theoretic interest".

While doing this, the juror nonetheless retains all his common sense grounds for deciding upon the facts—as Garfinkel puts it "becoming a juror does not mean becoming judicious". This creates for the juror many situations in which the conditions of correct choice are ambiguously defined; on many occasions, for instance, it became difficult to sustain the official line of personal disinterestedness. However, in accounts to an interviewer, jurors always identified their procedures with those depicted in the official line.

The role of the official line in terms of the interpretive activities of jurors now becomes clearer. Instead of defining the nature of the outcome of decision-making, conceptions of the "good juror" were used to defend the sense of outcomes, where any outcome that coincided with common sense grounds of inference could have been possible. As Garfinkel argues: "The outcome comes before the decision (as to its grounds)". Only in retrospect, then, did jurors establish the "good sense" of their decisions. Invariably, this good sense was displayed as a product of the application of the official line.

This has important consequences for conceptions of the rule-governed character of social life. For:

> If the above description is accurate, decision making in daily life would thereby have, as a critical feature, the *decision maker's task of justifying a course of action*. The rules of

decision making in daily life, i.e. rules of decision making for more or less socially routinized and respected situations, may be much more preoccupied with the problem of assigning outcomes their legitimate history than with the question of deciding before the actual occasion of choice the conditions under which one, among a set of alternative possible courses of action, will be elected.

Thus the rule-governed character of everyday actions is a practical accomplishment based on the display of activities and outcomes as in-accord-with-a-rule. Accounts and records, by their rewriting of history, provide for the "good sense" of the activities which they report. They do not describe the basis of any decision but display the rationality of the decision-making process.[18]

2. *Bittner: the police on skid row*

Bittner spent one year with the police departments of two large cities, including eleven weeks of observation on Skid Row. His study focuses on the policeman's sense of social structure (the way the police define "typical" features of Skid Row) and the practical skills he employs to handle what he conceives as "problems".[19] Many of these skills can be seen as ad hocing activities adopted to cope with the "troubles" that arise in the unfolding of a social scene. Indeed, the central task that the policeman on Skid Row sets himself—"peace keeping"—is itself almost undefined in official norms.

Bittner notes that the judiciary, while formally in control of police activities, has no authority or means to control or review those activities that do not result in prosecution. Following Banton, he distinguishes police activities related to arrests and prosecutions in the courts (these are under judicial control), from actions that are unrelated to arrest or prosecution and which are carried out under police discretion. In the former case, it is normal to refer to "law officers" concerned with the activity of law enforcement; in the latter, to "peace officers" concerned with peace keeping.

The degree of discretion available to the policeman in justifying any peace keeping activity is emphasized by the following features of official practices: (1) Police manuals refer to "peace keeping" only in passing, while stressing that it is a matter for the individual officer's "common sense"; (2) Police departments generally keep no record of procedures that do not involve making arrests; and (3) No legal directive defines appropriate actions, except in the most general terms. There is, therefore, no officially defined conception of what activities give rise to it, nor what it means to do a good job of "keeping the peace". As Bittner remarks:

"Peace keeping appears to be a solution to an unknown problem arrived at by unknown means".

Peace keeping activities are occasioned, according to Bittner, by "structural determinants". On the face of it, this seems to be according ontological status to social forces. However, it at once becomes clear that Bittner is using the concept of "structural determinants" in a highly specific sense:

. . . in order to place the particular into the overall domain to which it belongs . . . the structural determinants of keeping the peace in general (will) be discussed. By structural determinants are meant the typical situations that policemen perceive as *demand conditions* for action without arrest.

Thus Bittner is *not* calling upon the "social structure" as a tacit resource. Rather, in his interpretation, "structural determinants" arise in the employment by policemen of their *sense* of social structure in order to perceive typical situations which count as "demand conditions" for "peace keeping" rather than "law enforcement".

These demand conditions are seen to arise in the following circumstances: (1) When dealing with licensed services and premises, policemen face few legal directives and are mainly concerned with the moral aspects of these activities, rather than in questions relating to the technical adequacy of their service; (2) When dealing with traffic regulation, the police recognize that it is more important to build good relations with the public than to be "legalistic" in traffic control; (3) In cases of "minor offences" (in the context in which they occur), police may refrain from making an arrest but simply give a warning to the person concerned "not to repeat the offence"; (4) In matters with no criminal and often no legal aspects, such as quarrels or disorders in the home, the police may be called in by public demand. This may seem trivial but:

> . . . no matter how trivial the occasion, the device of "calling the cops" transforms any problem. It implies that a situation is, or is getting, out of hand. Police responses to public demands are always oriented to this implication, and the risk of proliferation of troubles makes every call a potentially serious matter.

In addition, peace keeping arises when: (5) Crowds and demonstrations arise and must be "controlled", yet there are very ill-defined conceptions of "necessary" coercion on such occasions; (6) The police deal with the activities of persons thought to be in need of protection (the young, the mentally ill); and (7) The police have relations with persons occupying a pariah status (inhabitants of ethnic ghettoes, sexual deviants, persons with police records). This last group have to be kept "in order" even when no arrest is likely and the demand condition it creates for the police is particularly relevant to the case of Skid Row.

The police on Skid Row perceive their central task as "containment", achieved by intensive patrolling by policemen assigned on a fairly permanent basis and with a good deal of discretion. Bittner quotes a sergeant in the area who comments: "A good man has things worked out in his own ways on his beat and he doesn't need anybody to tell him what to do". Policemen "work things out" by developing and utilizing a stock of knowledge about Skid Row life. Skid Row is perceived by them as the natural environment of people who cannot or will not lead "normal lives" for any length of time. These dual assumptions of "incompetence" or "disinclination", the police believe, are also held by the inhabitants about their own identity and shape the way in which they expect others routinely to treat them. The police believe that people on Skid Row are only concerned with the present and, accordingly, police activities should be geared primarily to present circumstances. Because relationships or locales have been relatively untroubled in the past, policemen do not assume that this will apply to the present. Relations of "trust" between policeman and citizen, just as such relations between one citizen and another, are only temporary. As a consequence, one must be permanently wary and be able to locate the "predatory" elements in all relationships.

Like the participants, for the policeman on Skid Row, the present itself is an insufficient basis for making predictions about the future. For instance, locating a person in one locale on a given day provides no grounds for a future location. Thus considerations of momentary expediency are seen as having unqualified primacy as maxims of conduct. In this state of "radically reduced visibility", the policeman (like the inhabitants) adopts ad hocing as a general rule.

In the context of the policeman's experience of social structures, he develops the "practical skills" that constitute his "craft". Policemen's sense of social structure is reflected, then, in their conceptions of what counts as doing a good job and what practical skills provide for its accomplishment. But this is not to imply a "mentalistic" account of personal conceptions and motivations. Typifications of "practical skills" are rooted in ways of attending to reality in the intersubjective world of socially organized settings. They stand, then, independently of any one person's views or attitudes. Indeed, such typified ways of attending to the world constitute social facts that persons experience as constraining. For instance, policemen who were perceived to act "differently" would meet sanctions not only from Skid Row but also from fellow officers.

The main features of these skills, as Bittner describes them, are gaining a rich knowledge, knowing when to invoke the law, and ad hocing. (1) Skilled policemen seek to gain a richly particularized knowledge of persons and locales by building personal relations with people working on Skid Row through regular visits and small talk. They adopt "an aggressively personal approach" which involves the conversational skills of not seeming to defer to people or to expect deference. In return, they expect people, as a matter of course, to answer questions of a personal nature without even querying the cause. Since "privacy" is nonexistent in Skid Row such an expectation is not unwarranted. (2) Policemen apply the law only in order to solve a pressing practical problem of peace keeping that cannot be resolved, in the short run, by any other course. When, in such a situation, someone obviously "needs" to be arrested, the practical question then arises of what charge should be made. As we saw in the case of jurors, formal grounds for decisions come *after the event*—the arrest refers not to these grounds but to the practical exigencies of peace keeping. Further, even when all the legal grounds for an arrest are "present", people may not be arrested if peace keeping can be better served by another course of action. In this context, as Bittner puts it, there is an "attenuation of the relevance of culpability" as legal concepts lose their importance during the course of peace keeping". (3) Skilled policemen base their judgments on the possibly unique features of a situation—for instance, relevant questions may be "how far is a drunk from his room?" or "is there a crowd around to observe an attempt to threaten a policeman's authority?". Equally, they feel that they must appear to act without hesitation and seek rapidly to "sum up" situations and come to decisions. Yet they do not feel that they are creating an injustice by rapid actions for practical purposes. For, in their view, being arrested and sent to jail is neither economically nor socially damaging to people on Skid Row. It makes sense to policemen, then, to be more interested in reducing the aggregate total of "troubles" in the area than in dealing "in strict fairness" with individual cases.

As Bittner explains, police activities on Skid Row reflect their routine ways of coming to terms with the world (their stock of knowledge) and the practical skills and socially organized practices which both sustain and are features of that stock of knowledge. The fact that peace keeping, unlike the "official juror line", is poorly defined by officialdom, has little bearing on day-to-day activities. Like jurors, policemen will define the "factual" character of events and act in terms of common sense knowledge of social structures and everyday interpretive procedures. Rather, such ill-definition allows a greater degree of discretion (i.e. less threat of sanctions) in calling up a wide range of materials in displaying that a particular action was in-accord-with-a-rule. While Bittner is not specific on this point, one imagines that, for the police on Skid Row, practically *any* account that does not violate everyday means of drawing inferences will justify most actions—at least from the point of view of officialdom.

3. Zimmerman: "sensible" intake work

Life Garfinkel and Bittner, Zimmerman focuses on the everyday rationality of members of organizations, more especially the way in which they provide for the features of a social structure and display a rule-governed character in their activities. Zimmerman takes as his concern the record-keeping practices at Lakeside, a district office of a state Bureau of Public Assistance.[20]

Before welfare aid can be given, intake workers have to establish a "need", make a decision about the "eligibility" of the applicant in terms of that need and be able to justify that decision in terms of the official requirement of the welfare programme in question. The applicant appears before a receptionist and is directed to fill in the "relevant" form. Before the intake caseworker sees the applicant, the receptionist must "clear" the case by seeing to it that a complete and competent application is executed, by assembling forms into a dossier, and by assigning a caseworker to attend to the case. Only then does the documentation and investigation of the applicant's case begin. In these activities, the caseworker adopts procedures and gives accounts which both provide for and rely upon a sense of social structure. The issue for Zimmerman, then, is not the reliability of these procedures, nor the factual character of such accounts but rather the way in which both provide for their "reliability" and "factual character".

The intake caseworker's task is to assemble and assess information relevant to the applicant's eligibility for assistance. One of the features of this activity, Zimmerman notes, is a treatment of the applicant's "story" as a set of claims which do not stand as "facts" until they are verified. On the other hand, the "story" is allowed to stand as a "fact", where it is seen to have a bearing on a person's ineligibility for assistance—it is presumed that applicants would not invent particulars which might cast doubt on their eligibility. In order to verify applicant's claims, caseworkers marshal evidence drawn from official records (birth certificates, medical records, details of encounters with other agencies, etc.). However, while verbal statements are checked by reference to pieces of paper, clearly not any piece of paper will do. For instance, Zimmerman refers to an anecdote told by an intake caseworker about an applicant who said she could not find the citizenship papers giving her age but that she had at one time copied her date of birth and given it to the caseworker. The other caseworkers, he notes, found this story highly amusing—while paper verification is important, it seems, only official papers will serve that purpose.

On the basis of such search activity, caseworkers build up a dossier (a "case record") which narrates the "case" in terms of relevant transactions with the applicant, makes judgments about their significance in terms of questions of eligibility, and, thereby, prepares the ground for official action. The case record thus involves a transformation of history in terms of the relevances of bureaucratic procedures. It does this, first, by allowing the applicant's history to be seen in terms of eligibility factors—thereby making her affairs, for bureaucratic purposes, into a case, and herself into a client; second, by displaying the caseworker's course of investigation as an activity in accord with legitimate organizational procedures, i.e. as demonstrably in-accord-with-a-rule. The caseworker's activities serve, then, both to assemble a world and to display its rule-governed character:

> The process of assembling a case record proceeds over a series of steps, each one informing the preceding. For reception and casework personnel alike, these steps are features of ordinary work practice which they make happen as observable events over a variety of occasions of concerted work, mutual instruction, discussion, and dispute. The way they are made to happen as observable events is a feature of the work of reconstruction.

As Zimmerman points out the meaning of the past is found in the present—for caseworkers and jurors alike, each step informs the preceding one.

The investigative stance of the intake caseworker is a thorough-going scepticism. Such scepticism serves to display the rationality of her actions. Even if her assumption that clients' claims (in themselves) have no basis turns out to be misguided in a particular instance, this is of no consequence, since claims have to be "proved" in any event:

> From the point of view of experienced personnel, the "stance" consists of a thorough-going skepticism directed to the applicant's claim to be eligible for assistance. As a mode of conducting an investigation, it is encountered in the setting by the observer (and by new personnel) as characterizations of "good work", and as advice extended by supervisors and "old hands" to novices, i.e. to those whose competence as caseworkers is problematic. In relation to the intake worker's task of making the investigation of eligibility an accountably rational enterprise, "being skeptical" is a way of displaying a hard-headed commitment to establishing the "facts of the matter" (as against the applicant's mere *claims*) as well as being a method for locating the courses of documentation which will determine the relevant facts.

While new caseworkers often want to believe the claims of certain clients, their supervisor's insistence that the intake function should be treated as an investigative process, together with personal experience with situations which run counter to applicants' claims and the workers' initial assessment, means that workers soon learn a more "acceptable" stance. In their actions the investigative stance is expressed in the practices of, first, evoking the features of a setting which are investigatable matters (can be settled by a document), and, second, in using typifications of actors and settings in order to pick holes in applicants' accounts (for instance, by asking: "Is that what you would reasonably expect a person needing help to do?"). Moreover, in their accounts and records, the investigative stance is an even more obvious feature. Zimmerman reports that in keeping records and talking to colleagues, caseworkers displayed the central feature of their task as the documentation of claims, thereby providing for a potential discrepancy between the applicant's "subjective" and "interested" claims and "factual" and "objective" records.

Speed as well as "verification" is also central to the intake caseworker's activities. Not only do workers want to keep their case-loads at a manageable level, they also seek to avoid having any case "unresolved" after thirty days—at which point it becomes "delinquent" and official remedies become applicable. As a consequence, they pressure applicants to produce documentation to support their claims and, having obtained such papers, treat official records as self-evidently "plain facts". The problematic status assigned to applicants' claims does not imply routinely expressed open disbelief; indeed, where the applicant is "cooperative" (i.e. respects the bureaucratic relevances of the encounter and produces documentary evidence to support her claims), the transaction can proceed quite "smoothly". Rather caseworkers do not even conceive of the possibility that official records might regularly be wrong or systematically falsified and attend to an applicant's talk on this basis. In their encounters with applicants, then, workers rely on this aspect of their sense of social structure to produce (for them) non-problematic situations. As Zimmerman argues, members' accounting is a feature of the setting it describes by providing for the "sense" of what it accounts.[21]

The status of official documents as "plain facts" is accomplished, first, by seeing certain activities in society as *constituted* by record-keeping; in the cases of getting married or signing a property contract, for instance, the activity is necessarily linked to the record-keeping enterprise. Second, caseworkers ascribe typical motives to both the parties referred to in documents (who may be taken to intend what they do) and to bureaucratic record-keepers (who are taken to be detached, objective, and so on). For instance, an applicant's claim for unemployment benefit was jeopardized because his claim to have diligently sought work could not be "verified". Yet the lack of any record, Zimmerman suggests, might have reflected a lack of interest by organizations offering employment in recording casual and unsuccessful requests for work. However, from within the "plain facts" perspective, there is no basis for doubting the routine reliability of official documents and the ordered properties of the world that they depict and rely upon:

The taken-for-granted use of documents, as analyzed by accounts given in the setting, is dependent on an ordered world—the ordered world of organizations, and the ordered world of the society-at-large. When simply taken-for-granted, the features of these ordered domains are matters of mere recognition for which no accounts are called for or given. Indeed, such routine recognition, and the action and inference proceeding from it, is the mark of the competent worker.

Both these activities and their outcomes are to the participants (and to the observer to make something of agency records) non-problematic outcomes of a largely non-problematic world. Indeed, the end result, as Zimmerman remarks, provides a built-in assumption of its "obvious" character.

Yet this is not to imply that the "documented" case should be contrasted ironically with the "actual state of affairs". For an infinity of "convincing" accounts can be constructed out of any past social scene. Cicourel conveys this by his concept of "indefinite triangulation":

> I use the expression "indefinite triangulation" to suggest that every procedure that seems to "lock in" evidence (thus to claim a level of adequacy) can itself be subjected to the same sort of analysis that will in turn produce yet another indefinite arrangement of new particulars or a rearrangement of previously established particulars in "authoritative", "final", "formal" accounts.[22]

The issue, instead, is to reveal the range of closing procedures employed by participants and observer alike to infer "what happens" and to produce "sensible" accounts which provide for their "rational" particulars.

4. Sudnow: normal crimes

Like Zimmerman, Sudnow is concerned to explore the compilation and display of "documented" cases. He prefaces his study of the routine practices of public defenders (P.D.'s) in United States' courts by noting two approaches towards the utility, for research purposes, of official classificatory schemes.[23] The "revisionist" school (he mentions Cressey and Sutherland) argue that the categories of the criminal law are too clumsy for analytic purposes since they group together different "causes" of crime and people of different backgrounds and styles of activity. As a consequence, they suggest it is necessary to remedy official definitions of categories of crime by introducing specifications which are more sociologically meaningful (e.g. *white collar* crime, *systematic* check forger). The alternative perspective, to which Sudnow subscribes, focuses upon the actual operations of the legal system, including the way in which official categories are called upon by the parties themselves in their routine activities.

Sudnow himself uses the rates of statistics of legal outcomes to analyse the rate producing agencies (the social organization of the criminal law system) and the assembling process (the routine practices of persons concerned with operating that system, notably the Public Defender and the District Attorney). It is well known that the majority of criminal cases never "go to trial" because the defendant pleads guilty. The guilty plea appears as a non-problematic outcome of a system where the police only press charges where they are convinced that a person has committed a crime. However, one event that often seems to intervene between the arrest of a defendant and his appearance in court is the "reduction" of the offence with which he is charged. As Sudnow notes, the law does provide for the recognition of "lesser offences" (offences for which the required period of imprisonment is less) where an offence involves a "necessarily-included-lesser-offence", i.e. where a person by committing one offence (say "robbery"), necessarily commits a lesser offence (say "petty theft"). Once a case is brought to court, two procedural matters affects the issue of "necessary inclusion". First, a person cannot be charged or convicted of two crimes that are necessarily included in the same offence. Second, a judge cannot instruct a jury to decide its verdict on an alternative offence which is not necessarily included in the charged offence. But these considerations have no bearing on what happens to a charge *before* the defendant is brought to trial. In the pre-trial period, then, alterations in the charged offence may be made by the D.A. without reference to the concept of "necessarily-included-lesser-offences":

> The issue of necessary inclusion has no required bearing on (a) what offence(s) will be charged initially by the prosecutor, (b) what the relation is between the charge intially made and "what happened", or (c) what modifications may be made after the initial charge and the relation between initially charged offences and those charged in modified complaints. It is this latter operation, the modification of the complaint, that is central to the guilty plea dispostion.

It still remains, however, to establish why changes should be made at the pre-trial stage and how this is accomplished, since for some offences there is often no statutorily designated crime included in it (for example, drunkenness).

Complaint alterations, Sudnow suggests, are the outcome of a bargaining process between the defendant and the P.D. and D.A. By obtaining a guilty plea, both the P.D. and the D.A. lessen the amount of court work in which they have to engage and obtain general approval for speeding cases through what are generally overcrowded courts. By pleading guilty to a lesser offence, a defendant who does not have much confidence in his acquittal should his case "go to trial" obtains the certainty of less time in prison.

The basis of the instant reduction of the charge is the employment of a concept of typically-situationally-included lesser offences. Such offences, the lawyers believe, typically occur as a feature of the way in which people charged with crimes of a certain nature typically behave. For instance, drunk people typically engage in "disturbing the peace". The grounds of complaint alterations in the pre-trial period do not, then, lie in legal statutes. The penal code does not provide a referent for defining the classes of offences for this process of instant reduction of charge. Rather the lawyers concerned, use their everyday sense of social structure and their "stock" of knowledge of offences-of-this-nature to membership any one case into the class of events into which it typically belongs. In this transformation of the charge, the parties reconstruct the history of the case by asserting features that it will typically have had, irrespective of whether there are grounds for asserting that it happened "that way" in this particular case. That is to say, they refer not to the statutorily defined class of offence but to a typification of *normal crimes*.

As a result of his experience in a community, the P.D. gains knowledge of the regular features of crimes and criminals: the typical manner in which offences are committed, the locales in which they routinely occur, the type of victim normally involved, and the social characteristics of the persons who regularly commit them.

For instance, he learns of the typical career patterns of certain types of criminal. Some will regularly repeat the same crime, others are "once-only" offenders or may vary the types of crimes they commit.

From this background knowledge, the P.D. builds up a picture of typical occurrences, of normal crimes, and by invoking this concept, the public defender can then ask: "Is this a burglary (rape, drug offence) like any other?" Moreover, his superiors will judge his competence in terms of his ability to "draw-out" the typical features of an offence and an offender in order to settle the matter as soon as possible with a "proper" conviction. Clearly, there are parallels here with the kind of knowledge that, according to Bittner and Zimmerman, is at a premium in police work and casework.

The mechanics of the guilty plea procedure are located in certain socially organized practices and the assumptions which these provide for and sustain. During their interactions the attorneys build up a set of unstated recipes to be used for reducing an original charge to a lesser offence where the former is an instance of a "normal crime". For instance, Sudnow notes the "typical "burglary is reduced to petty theft. However, this reduction occurs under the auspices of a generalized conception of what is "reasonable". First, the offence must have the normal features of its type. If it has deviant features, for example an unusually gruesome murder, then the recipe will not be applied. Second, certain kinds of reductions, which would involve changing the "category" of the offence, are not countenanced. Crimes involving assault will not be reduced to or from "money" offences, for instance, while victimless crimes will not be reduced to or from either—provided that they have "normal" features. Third, the reduction of the charge must be great enough to make it likely that the defendant will plead guilty, while at the same time ensuring that he "gets his due".

As already implied, both attorneys are convinced of the guilt of the defendants they deal with. They refer to the criminal records that most of them have and are convinced that the police simply do not "make mistakes". Furthermore, to presume innocence when interviewing an experienced defendant would simply be to give him an opportunity to try an "innocent pitch". As well as presuming guilt, the P.D. relies on certain features of the original charge, as brought by the D.A., for filling him in on the typical or deviant character of a particular case. Where the D.A. judges that it is not a "normal crime", and hence the normal reduction would not provide a sufficient penalty, he will charge various situationally-included, lesser offences as well as the main charge. This indicates to the P.D. that the proper procedure, if there is to be any bargaining at all, is merely to drop the minor charges, while letting the more serious charge stand. Normally, however, the D.A. does not charge all the offences that he might so that when a reduction is proposed it will appear particularly lenient to the defender since it will seem to involve a change in the charge. The "setup" terminates when the alteration of charges is made in open court, on the request of the P.D. and with the prearranged approval of the D.A. In the context of a guilty plea, the details of the case are only briefly referred to, and here only with reference to determination of sentence. As a consequence, the negotiated nature of the charge is not discussed, nor is whether the charge is included in the previous charge—as one P.D. commented to Sudnow: "Nobody thinks twice about [it]".

The crucial aspect of Sudnow's discussion, from the point of view of the accounting process, is the manner in which charges (like jury decisions, arrests, "documented cases" and accounts in general) report not a given series of past events but on the practices which make such charges (accounts) viewable-as-a-report-on-past-events.

5. *Cicourel: juvenile justice*

"Juvenile delinquency" is a topic which has generated both sociological enquiry and officially produced statistics. Often the two have become linked as sociologists, while referring to the features of inaccuracy and bias in such statistics, employ official data in order to construct models and theories of the character and causes of juvenile delinquency. Paralleling Zimmerman, Cicourel, however, seeks to show how the assembling of statistics and files is itself an important feature of socially organized relations. The issue is not the purported "bias" or otherwise of such materials but the assembling process itself, as indicated by Cicourel:

> An understanding of how official statistics are assembled informs the researcher as to how "delinquents" are produced by the socially organized and socially sanctioned activities of members of the community and representatives of law-enforcement agencies. A knowledge of the "praxiology" of the various actors involved in the rate-producing process would presumably supply the researcher with a program for adequately describing how persons in the community come to be defined and processed as "delinquent".[24]

The "praxiology" or sets of accepted practices and customs of officials concerned with "delinquency" involves accounting for delinquent activities in terms of structural "causes". Indeed, the notion of delinquency maintained by parts of officialdom reveals a spill-over of a certain kind of sociological jargon.

As an instance of this spill-over, Cicourel's examination of the files of probation officers shows a preference by the latter for accounting for delinquency in terms of general " 'family problems', for example broken homes, marital strains or weak parental personalities—"factors" typically cited by researchers as contributing to juvenile delinquency.' Thus the way in which both official and sociologist come to terms with delinquency, by positing its existence as a routine "fact" and trading upon a taken-for-granted social structure to supply truncated concepts to account for "it", reveals a profoundly mundane orientation to the social world.

In this context, Cicourel takes his task to be that of examining official procedures for constituting and dealing with the phenomenon of delinquency by calling upon the properties of an "available" social structure to display the "good sense" or "rationality" of activities and their end products. By locating the identification of "delinquency" within the natural attitude, it becomes possible to focus analysis on the language-categories routinely employed by participants for depicting "delinquency" as a feature of a person, a scene or a report. Language-categories thus provide the means both for "closing" the indefinite properties of any social

event and for counting instances of the same "type". However, the closing procedures of the researcher are equally as important as those of the participants for
understanding the managed nature of the relationship between his interpretation
and the materials which it instances. Thus, as well as seeking to reveal the "unstated" and the "seen but unnoticed" background expectancies which give the
"sense" to lay accounts, the observer's task is to analyse the lay knowledge under
whose auspices he constructs his own account:

> I assume the critical task of the researcher is to show the reader how the research
> materials are always understood by reference to unstated and seen (but unnoticed)
> background expectancies both members *and* observers always employ to recognize
> and to understand their activities.

The materials Cicourel discusses are police and probation reports and conversations between the parties, gathered during four years participant-observation
in two police and probation departments and in a juvenile court. In order to
illustrate his analysis, we will take just one case from the rich and extensive
materials that are presented.

Linda, 13, first came to the attention of the police when she reported that she
had been kidnapped by four boys. She said she had been coaxed away from a
dance by them and admitted that she had told them that she would get drunk and
perhaps have sexual intercourse with one of them. After stealing some alcohol, the
boys took her to a club where they all got drunk and she had sexual intercourse with
the youngest boy. She then passed out and was left for two days at the club, food
being brought to her intermittently. After this incident, the police did not form an
immediate impression that Linda was a "bad" girl:

> The males sought to depict the girl as a "slut" who wanted to have sexual intercourse
> with them. Subsequent events supported this view, but I want to underscore the
> following: the police viewed the girl as an "attractive" victim with no prior record and
> family appearances to support a positive perspective.

A few weeks later, however, on the parents' information that Linda had run away
from home the day before and might be at a certain address, the police went to a
house where they found evidence of a drunken party. Linda was seen coming out of
a bedroom, evidently very drunk, and admitted that she had had sexual intercourse with ten boys. As a consequence of this second incident, Linda was charged
as "in danger of leading a lewd and immoral life".

The first of a series of official negotiations of her condition began with an
interview between Linda and a probation officer. Part of that interview went as
follows:

Probation Officer: You're not pregnant?
          Linda: No.
Probation Officer: Have you used anything to prevent a pregnancy?
          Linda: Once he (one of her boyfriends) used one of those things.
Probation Officer: Did you ever feel scared about getting pregnant?
          Linda: No, I was always trying to get even with my parents.
Probation Officer: You sort of wanted to (get) even with them?

> Linda: Yes. I always wanted to get even with other people. My mother gets mad at me. I love my father. I know that's what wrong with me. I talk about this with my parents. I don't know why.

Cicourel notes how the probation officer began the interview with independent knowledge and theories of "what happened" formed from reading Linda's file. Rather than ask Linda for her detailed reconstructions of the "events", she seeks to document "what is known" about her by establishing materials about her personal life (the questions about pregnancy). As becomes clear in the probation officer's later reports, she is also seeking materials upon which to base a "clinical" interpretation of Linda's activities. Notice how she takes up Linda's remark about wanting to "get even" with her parents, while Linda's final remark provides the grounds for a psychoanalytic account of her behaviour—although this is slightly undercut by the impression of prior planning of such a line ("I talk about this with my parents").

In addition to developing information on which to base her subsequent interpretation of Linda, the probation officer also coaches the girl by providing her with a guide to the "proper" answer of her questions. For instance, in the following sequence, after some discussion about Linda's previous promiscuity, the probation officer leaves Linda in no doubt about how to concoct the appropriate answer to official questions:

> Probation Officer: Will you wait until you get married?
> Linda: Yes. I don't want my husband to know.
> Probation Officer: Will you change then?
> Linda: Oh yes. I'm trying to change all the time and I'm trying as hard as I can.
> Probation Officer: Well, if you are really trying hard that's what we want . . .

After her interview with Linda, the probation officer visited the parents. Their remarks, occasioned by the question "Does she feel sorry about what she did?", are presented below:

> 'Father: What's happened to Linda is caused by an emotional factor. After these tests we should know what is wrong. She may need psychiatric help. Why this hearing if there is something wrong with her? We are more interested in her than the court.
> Mother: She does this, but she doesn't know why'.

In these comments, Cicourel suggests, the family seek to encourage a "psychiatric" interpretation of Linda's "condition". The probation officer, on the other hand, uses the interview as a means of assessing the "home situation". At this stage she is more interested in Linda's parents than in Linda herself. As a result of the interview (together with other materials gathered by another probation officer), she forms an impression, mentioned to the other probation officer, of the father as potentially "sicker" than Linda. It seems that the father had remarked that he had practised hypnotism on Linda and encouraged her to drink at home. Moreover, Linda had said that her father asked her to describe "in detail" her affairs with boys.

In writing her report for the court, the probation officer recommends that Linda be institutionalized for three to six months for extensive treatment on the grounds that the parents could not afford to pay for individual psychotherapy administered while Linda was living at home. Yet she provides no statement from the parents about their willingness to pay, apparently because of her conviction that the girl ought not to stay at home.

As a consequence of the hearing, the probation officer's recommendations are largely observed and Linda is sent to the state mental hospital for one month.

The conversations and documents to which Cicourel refers reveal how impressions of events are formed in routine inter-personal situations and how these become depicted, for bureaucratic purposes, as authoritative accounts of "what happened". Hence history is continually created as member's produce records which provide for the latter's sensible and "correct" character: In the course of this practical decision-making about "what happened", members make available through their accounts the social structure which provides the grounds for reading their "sense" of their talk and reports. As a consequence, the situations and activities to which their accounts refer are displayed as demonstrably in-accord-with-a-rule. The competences involved, as Cicourel recognizes, rely on considerably more that dictionary knowledge of the meaning of language-categories:

> The various expressions used by the police, probation and school officials for depicting juveniles do not depend for their meaning on some dictionary or literal interpretation of lexical items, but require an open texture of what "anyone knows" and assumes "others know" . . . The significance of the notion of "natural social order" is not to be found in the presumption of predetermined or divine forces, but in how members (layman scientists) decide order, make decisions assert "facts", label and depict moral character, "good families", "defiance of authority", "a bad attitude", assume a policy or rule applies, and so on.

"Organization" and "Bureaucracy"

The studies which have been reviewed in the previous section of this chapter are centrally concerned with the practices whereby social structures are provided for and activities revealed to be in-accord-with-a-rule. In short the topic of such studies is the accounting process. In a book which is concerned with organizations, it is entirely legitimate for the reader to expect a statement about the relationship of the study of accounting to the study of organizations. The position adopted here, then, is that the concepts of "organization" and "bureaucracy" are firmly grounded in the "natural attitude". Within that attitude (whose main features were discussed earlier), such concepts refer to lay schemes of interpretation whereby the "sensible" and "rational" nature of activities is provided for and recognized, i.e. whereby activities are constituted as observable reportable phenomena. The concept of "organization" thus provides the possibility of one kind of account, which, like other accounts, makes available the features of a non-problematic social world.

It will be recognized at once that this kind of argument is entirely unlike the manner in which the logic of the sociology of organizations has developed. In this section an attempt will be made to show that the latter relies on a particular reading of the Weberian concept of bureaucracy; a reading which it is by no means clear that Weber himself would have supported.

Almost uniformly in the literature on "organizations", Weber's ideal-type of bureaucracy is, albeit implicitly, taken to refer to the instrinsic features of some visible object. It is as if Weber were offering to the world a painting of some object, say a table, and the question that should be correctly addressed to his portrayal should be: "has he got it right?", i.e. has he captured the intrinsic features which make a thing a "bureaucracy?". On this basis, subsequent writers point to studies which note the existence of "informal" patterns to which Weber's conceptualization does not refer and of internal inefficiencies and "dysfunctions" in bureaucracy. As a consequence, the concepts of bureaucracy and organization have been re-formulated and distinctions between "formal" and "informal" patterns of activities have been instituted. The picture of "bureaucracy" has, then, been altered with the aim of establishing a better correspondence between it and the "object" to which it purportedly refers.

Yet Weber's whole conception of the social sciences was based on a differentiation between the character of physical and social relations. As is well known, he was concerned in his empirical work to emphasize the uniquely meaningful character of social life and to produce interpretations of social action in terms of their subjective meaning. Weber makes an attempt, then, to base his ideal-types on interlinked patterns of meaning which define the character of social phenomena; as he says, ideal-types must be judged in terms of their "adequacy on the level of meaning". Furthermore, as many writers on bureaucracy apparently ignore, Weber's own analysis arose in the context of a study of the bases on which authority is claimed to be (and recognized as) "legitimate". For Weber, then, the sense of labelling activities "bureaucratic" arises within a rational-legal system of authority which provides a means of justifying (legitimating) a course of action by an appeal to the sanctity of enacted rules. In the sequence below, for instance, he implies that social life proceeds on the basis of interpretive procedures which specify what may be taken to be the case rather than upon what, in some ontological sense, is "really so":

> "Obedience" will be taken to mean that the action of the person obeying follows in essentials such a course that the content of the command may be taken to have become the basis of action for its own sake. Furthermore, the fact that it is so taken is referable only to the formal obligation, without regard to the actor's own attitude to the value or lack of value of the content of the command as such.[25]

The issue here, clearly, is that social objects become recognized by imputing motives to parties and inferring regularities in their activities. In this sense alone do social phenomena have "intrinsic" features or possess ontological status. However, Weber's sociology does not provide for an analysis of the common sense practices through which both participants and observers come to impute social meanings (this is a point which will be returned to shortly).

If the sociologist's knowledge of organizations is contrasted with that of the lay participants in organizations, a difference and a similarity can be viewed. First, the layman manages without "precise" or "complete" definitions of "bureaucracy" and "organization". Second, like the sociologist, the laymen is committed to the existence of "bureaucracy" as a "natural fact", as an object "out there" in the world—like the atmosphere or, indeed, a table. Sociologists, then, cannot make claims to possess sole knowledge of organizations and bureaucracies. Yet this is damaging to their pretensions in ways which do not threaten the natural scientist. While the latter can justifiably dismiss lay conceptions of natural regularities (e.g. movements of the stars, meteorological events), social regularities are preconstituted by lay conceptions. For, through the categories of natural language, laymen have predefined social structures, including bureaucracies. On the basis of their interpretive procedures, "bureaucracy" thus comes to stand as a depiction of the intrinsic features of an object. To apply the concept is, then, to give evidence of membership of a language-community in which the definition of "certain" activities in this way "make sense". Its use does *not* refer to the intrinsic features of some available object—structures or relations are not, in themselves, "really" bureaucratic (or otherwise)—for both the recognition of social relations (as the product of underlying structures) and their display (as bureaucratic) depend upon interpretive practices which provide ways of attending to the world. The conventional sociological treatment of "organizations" and "bureaucracy" thus trades upon such practices in its task of producing "sensible" and "rational" descriptions. It is worth repeating a passage in which Wittgenstein captures this precisely:

> One thinks that one is tracing the outline of the thing's nature over and over again, and one is merely tracing round the frame through which we look at it.

It is possible, however, to treat "bureaucracy" not as, in itself, an object, but as a language-category which provides for the object-like qualities of an activity. Rather than seeking clearer specifications of what bureaucracy "really means" or attempting to formulate "operational definitions", the object of investigation becomes the manner in which a concept of bureaucracy is called upon, usually as a tacit resource, to display and to acknowledge the "sense" of actions. For, as suggested earlier, laymen do not worry themselves over much about scientific definitions of bureaucracy; nor, indeed, do they probably use the term frequently in the course of natural conversation. Rather, in carrying out their routine business, competent members bring off comprehensible talk and action by relying on taken-for-granted knowledge of social structures (including organizational structures). The reader has only to think of the truncated conversations that regularly pass between himself and "office-holders" (post office clerks, sales assistants, bus drivers) to realize the manner in which the encoding and decoding of such talk relies on a sense of social structures which includes knowledge of bureaucratic "routines". Such knowledge is typically *tacit*: as Garfinkel has shown, to ask the other party to spell out the assumptions on which their talk proceeds is simply to invite disruption.

In a paper called "The Concept of Organization", Bittner develops an alternative posture parallel to that implied here. The central feature of organizational analysis, as he sees it, is a reliance on common sense knowledge of the world. For instance, post-Weberian sociologists have distinguished between "formal organization" (programmatic constructions that prospectively define conduct) and "informal structures" which seem to grow spontaneously in ways not provided for in the programme. Yet laymen too account for their activities in terms of rules and so the sociologist's analysis tacitly mirrors common sense. As Bittner comments:

> In general, there is nothing wrong with borrowing a commonsense concept for the purposes of sociological inquiry. Up to a certain point it is, indeed, unavoidable. The warrant for this procedure is the sociologist's interest in exploring the common-sense perspective. The point at which the use of commonsense concepts becomes a transgression is where such concepts *are expected to do the the analytical work of theoretical concepts.* When the actor is treated as a permanent auxiliary to the enterprise of sociological inquiry at the same time that he is the object of its inquiry, there arise ambiguities that defy clarification.[26]

By tacitly relying on actors' theories of the world, the student of organizations confuses, then, the use of the social world as a *topic* of enquiry with its employment as an unacknowledged *resource* in developing explanations and theories.

Despite his commitment to a sociology of meaning, Max Weber, according to Bittner, relied on everyday knowledge of "bureaucracy" to produce his ideal-type. Rather than analyse the common-sense presuppositions of his theory, he offers a truncated account of bureaucracy which glosses how competent actors make sense of "rules", "offices", and "hierarchies" in the context of actual social scenes. This attempt to develop "refined" operational definitions of bureaucracy, as well as analyses of interactions which trade upon what-everyone-knows about organizational structures, necessarily involves what Bittner calls a "theoretical shortcut". The alternative is to consider the methods by which competent members employ everyday knowledge of bureaucracy to provide for the "sensible" and "rational" nature of their encounters and the outcomes which these produce:

> . . . the formal organizational designs are schemes of interpretation that competent and entitled users can invoke in yet unknown ways whenever it suits their purposes. The varieties of ways in which the scheme can be invoked for information, direction, justification, and so on, without incurring the risk of sanction, constitute the scheme's methodical use.

In itself, then, bureaucracy has neither an intrinsic meaning nor is it the determinant of actions—it does not have this kind of ontological status. Rather the concept of bureaucracy exists in and through the socially sanctioned occasions of its use. Thus sociologists who point to differences in the rule-governed nature of "formal" and "informal" practices, mirror everyday accounting activities which also routinely seek to depict the "sense" of "what is happening". The issue for analysis is rather the interpretive procedures and socially organised activities which *provide for* the sense of "some-thing" having happened—for instance, by laying claim to the rule-governed character of events.

To conclude this section of the chapter, reference will be made to some materials gathered in the course of research on a large public sector organization.[27] One routine activity in which senior members of the organization engage is the selection of recruits for junior administrative positions from a much greater number of applicants. A three man Selection Board interviews each candidate. On the occasion at which the following transcript was obtained, however, one of the members of the Board, a newcomer to the selection process, was being "filled in" by the Chairman about the order of questioning and, more specifically, was learning that newcomers must expect to come last:

> Chairman: Bob, look, I'm going to ask you to go second. Not for any reasons of seniority . . .
> Bob: Mm
> Chairman: or anything like that but because he and I do so many of these things together that to a certain extent we complement each other.
> Bob: Mm.
> Chairman: And therefore I want someone to be, in soccer terms, the sweeper-upper. Will you be the sweeper-upper? Do you mind?
> Bob: Where do you want me? Second-phase possession?
> Chairman: Will you do second-phase possession?
> Bob: I'll be inside wing-forward.
> Chairman: Ha, ha, ha. Right ho.

One of the ways of inferring the sense of this exchange is by employing lay knowledge of how persons "bring off" their talk by using it to locate their position in hierarchies. It could be argued, then, that there are grounds for identifying one talker as the senior person and the other as the junior even if that information had not otherwise been provided. First, one person introduces the new topic at the beginning of the exchange (his "Bob, look" followed a pause in conversation) and also closes the topic ("Right ho"). Second, the same person gives an instruction to the other ("I'm going to ask you to go second"), which the latter seems to accept without questioning the authority of the speaker to give instructions. Bob is already asking "Where do you want me" before the Chairman has asked "Do you mind?". At the same time, the Chairman's instructions do not come over as "pulling rank" both because this possibility is specifically excluded ("Not for reasons of seniority or anything like that") and because, rather than issue a "command", the Chairman provides rational grounds for his instruction ("but because he and I do so many of these things together . . ."). The football analogy also allows his instruction to be seen in a light-hearted manner. Even so, the final politeness ("Do you mind?") hardly allows, given the fact that a senior is issuing an instruction, for the junior to refuse. As already noted, Bob complies even before he is asked whether he "minds" and, by continuing with the football analogy, allows the exchange to end as a joke.

By examining what makes this exchange sensible, rather than treating it as a self-evidently sensible conversation reporting on a recognizable set of events, the author has sought to show how the production and comprehension of talk always proceeds by employing a sense of social structure. Each utterance provides for a context in which it would be sensible, while the listener (or reader) makes sense of the talk by assigning it a knowable context. In this exchange, such a context is provided by the notion of "hierarchy". Thus the two parties talk to each other as a "senior" and a "junior" by displaying through their utterances the features of hierarchies. It should be stressed that hierarchies are relevant socially *only* to the extent that members attend to their existence as a relevant means for bringing off interactions. This is not, however, to engage in a solipsistic denial of the factual character of hierarchies. Rather the author is pointing out that only in and through members' activities do hierarchies acquire their facticity.

If bureaucrats accomplish their activities by attending to hierarchies, they also rely on the "objectivity" of official records. As Zimmerman shows, bureaucratic routines are carried out on the basis of the "plain fact" character of what records depict.[28] Officials are assumed to have no material interest in the "cases" which they handle and their decisions are purportedly a faithful reflection of the "facts" rather than of their personal biases. Thus Weber's spirit of "formalistic impersonality" exists as a members' interpretive rule—but not as a "description" of a self-constituted phenomenon—available for displaying and inferring the sense of activities accepted as bureaucratic (a rule which, incidentally, is also available for understanding "scientific" activities).

As in all talk, then, bureaucrats concern themselves with displaying what will be currently understood as rational grounds for past actions and as sensible descriptions of past social scenes. Furthermore, this sensible character of the past is found in what "finally" is seen to transpire—so that, for all practical purposes, the meaning of the past is found in the present. However, in the case of bureaucratic activities, official outcomes rather than the personal recollections of the parties, provide the crucial "clue" for understanding the sense of past events. Once such outcomes are negotiated and recorded, past interactions are re-read to find grounds for seeing the official outcome as sensible, appropriate, necessary, and so on.

In the following example, an administrator, who was asked to listen (with two colleagues) to tapes of selection interviews in which he was not a participant, adjusts his account as we inform him of official decisions and as the comments of colleagues suggest that he might have made the "wrong" inference about these decisions:

1. (His first comment after hearing an initial interview between James, the organization's interviewer, and a candidate for an administrative job) I certainly wouldn't recommed calling that guy for group selection, neither would you or James I imagine.
2. (After hearing the other auditors' more favourable comments) I would have thought you would have put it down as a hold . . . I would like to have seen the guy and seen his reactions.
3. (After hearing a tape of James' comments and being informed of his "accept" decision) I reckon I must have got an anti feeling to this guy.
4. (After hearing the same candidate's second interview at the offices of the organization) I got a slightly better impression of the guy.
5. (After hearing the Board's comments). I had missed his sense of humour.
6. (After hearing a tape of the candidate's account—to a research—of "what happened"). He showed awareness of complexity.
7. (On being asked by a researcher to summarize his reactions to the candidate) My impression of him got steadily better . . . I was very surprised about his ability to sum up what was wanted of him. It was quite out of keeping with my impression of him . . . This is all frightfully confusing . . .

As early as Time 2, the administrator, on hearing the other auditors' comments, is providing for grounds upon which his reject decision might be inaccurate—because of inadequate information ("I would like to have seen the guy and seen his reactions"). By the end, he favours acceptance without hesitation and finds grounds to justify his interpretation ("I was very surprised about his ability to sum up what was wanted of him"). Thus knowledge of the official outcome provided him with a view of the "real" features of the interviews, i.e. even though there are other features available to any competent person in the talk, they are irrelevant if they do not help substantiate official decisions.

Concluding remarks

It was stated earlier—and probably bears repeating—that the analysis offered here should in no way be seen as a rebuke to sociologists nor as a corrective of which account can be taken in subsequent work. It has been no part if the argument to maintain that any aspect of the sociology of organizations is "wrong", "one-sided", or "unrealistic". Indeed, within the frame of the natural attitude, there is every reason to view its accomplishments as "right", "complete", and eminently "realistic". For while the issue remains "what is happening (has happened)?", there is equally no basis for doubting lay or professional accounts of social phenomena—although this is not to say that participants or practitioners may not doubt some accounts from within their paradigm of knowledge.

As has been argued, the "sensible" nature of such accounts derives not from the phenomena to which they refer but from the way in which the account makes available the features of some phenomenon and display its rational properties. It has been the central contention of this chapter that the latter—the accounting process—is itself a worthwhile topic for sociological investigation. Because this analysis of accounting will necessarily have to refer to the forgotten common sense grounds of our activities (lay and professional), it is entirely appropriate to end, as the chapter began, with Wittgenstein's comment:

> We feel as if we had to repair a torn spider's web with our fingers.

References and notes

1. See P. Blau and R. Schoenherr, *The Structure of Organizations*, New York: Basic Books, 1971.
2. This concept of "natural attitude" is expounded in the two chapters by A. Schutz appearing in D. Emmet and A. MacIntyre (Eds), *Sociological Theory and Philosophical Analysis*, London: Macmillan, 1970. The chapters are entitled "Concept and theory formation in the social sciences", and "The problem of rationality in the social world".
3. P. Blau, "Theories of organizations", *International Encyclopaedia of Social Sciences*, New York: Collier-Macmillan, 1968, p. 303 (the emphasis in the text is superimposed by the author).
4. See E. Goffman, *Asylums*, Harmondsworth: Penguin, 1968, p. 22; and Blau, 1968, *op. cit.*
5. Schutz, 1970, *op. cit.*, pp. 11–12.
6. This and following quotations in this section are from Blau and Schoenherr, 1971, *op. cit.*

7. A. Cicourel, *The Social Organization of Juvenile Justice*, New York: Wiley, 1968, pp. 4–5.
8. D. Zimmerman and M. Pollner, "On the everyday world as a phenomenon", in J. Douglas (Ed.), *Understanding Everyday Life*, London: Routledge and Kegan Paul, 1971.
9. Schutz, 1970, *op. cit.*, p. 97.
10. See Zimmerman and Pollner, 1971, *op. cit.*, and Schutz, 1970, *op. cit.*, p. 98.
11. Schutz, 1970, *op. cit.*, pp. 98–99.
12. Schutz, 1970, *op. cit.*, p. 96.
13. L. Wittgenstein, *Philosophical Investigations*, Oxford: Blackwell, 1968, paras. 114–115.
14. H. Garfinkel, *Studies in Ethnomethodology*, Englewood Cliffs, N.J.: Prentice-Hall, 1967, p. 281.
15. See Cicourel, 1968, *op. cit.* and D. Zimmerman, "Record-keeping and the intake process in a public welfare organization", in S. Wheeler (Ed.), *On Record*, New York: Russell Sage Foundation. Both these texts are discussed in the next section.
16. As expressed by Garfinkel, 1967, *op. cit.*, "in the activities of scientific theorizing quite a different rule of interpretive procedure is used. It provides that interpretation be conducted while holding a position of 'official neutrality' toward the belief that the objects of the world are as they appear", pp. 272–273.
17. This discussion of Garfinkel's work refers principally to Garfinkel, 1967, *op. cit.*, pp. 104–114.
18. See D. Silverman and J. Jones, "Getting in: the managed accomplishment of 'Correct, Selection Outcomes", in J. Child (Ed.), *Man and Organization: The Search for Explanation and Social Relevance"*, London: Allen and Unwin, 1973, for an account of "selection" decisions in these terms.
19. The following quotations are from E. Bittner, "The police on Skid Row: a study of peace-keeping", *Am. Sociol. Rev.*, **32** (1967), 699–715, on which article this discussion is based.
20. The ensuing discussion and quotations are from Zimmerman, 1970, *op. cit.*
21. This refers to Garfinkel's notion of the essential reflexivity of accounts (Garfinkel, 1967, *op. cit.*).
22. Cicourel, 1968, *op. cit.*
23. The discussion and following quotation are from D. Sudnow, "Normal crimes", in E. Rubington and M. Weinberg (Eds), *Deviance: The Interactionist Perspective*, New York: Macmillan, 1968.
24. This and the ensuing quotations are from Cicourel, 1968, *op. cit.*, pp. 27, 15, 294, 296, 299, 301, 335, respectively.
25. M. Weber, *The Theory of Social and Economic Organization*, New York: The Free Press, 1964, p. 327 (the author's emphasis).
26. This and the following quotation are from E. Bittner, "The concept of organization", *Soc. Research*, **31** (1965), 240–255. (The author's emphasis).
27. This study is more fully discussed in Silverman and Jones, *op. cit.*
28. Zimmerman, 1970, *op. cit.*

Suggestions for further reading

The main texts from which this chapter has emerged are Cicourel, *Method and Measurement in Sociology*, New York: The Free Press, 1964, and (1968) and Garfinkel (1967). Since, however, some of these materials are sometimes found to be difficult reading, P. Filmer *et al.*, *New Directions in Sociological Theory*, London: Collier-Macmillan, 1972, is a useful text at an introductory level, while H. Wagner (Ed.), *Alfred Schutz on Phenomenology and Social Relations*, Chicago: Chicago University Press, 1971, provides a helpful introduction to the work of Alfred Schutz. Collections of readings, which include papers by Cicourel, Zimmerman and Pollner are available in Douglas (1971) and H. Dreitzel (Ed.), 1970, *Recent Sociology No 2*, New York: Macmillan, 1970. Relevant studies of organizations, in addition to the five presented here, include Cicourel and Kitsuse, *The Educational Decision Makers*, Indianapolis: Bobbs-Merrill, 1963; Silverman and Jones (forthcoming); and Sudnow, *Passing-On: The Social Organization of Death and Dying*, Englewood Cliffs, N.J.: Prentice-Hall, 1968. For a fuller account of the research from which the materials are given in the later sections of this chapter are drawn, see D. Silverman and J. Jones, *Organizational Word: The Language of Grading/The Grading of Language* (1974).

ARLENE KAPLAN DANIELS

PROFESSIONALISM IN FORMAL ORGANIZATIONS

Arlene Kaplan Daniels *received her doctorate in sociology from the Univer-*
sity of California at Berkeley and is currently Chief for the Center of the
Study of Women in Society at the Scientific Analysis Corporation, San
Francisco, California. Previously she was an Associate Professor in the
Department of Sociology at San Francisco State College. Dr Daniels is
mainly concerned with issues in the field of occupations and professions,
focusing in particular on problems of military psychiatrists. She has recently
completed work on a comparative study of psychiatrists, social workers and
certified public accountants, as well as a study of ethics in psychiatry. She
has also published reports of studies concerning dentists and folksingers.
Her most recent book is entitled Academics on the Line *(with R. Kahn-*
Hut, 1970).

The following essay is designed to raise some critical questions about the study of professionals in organizations. Generally professionals are viewed as a very special set of workers; and introduction of these workers into large organizations is expected to produce a special set of advantages—and problems. The advantages are related to the special skills and the high motivation to perform correctly and to maintain ethical standards expected of professionals. The problems are related to the importance professionals attach to their special prerogatives and their resistance to external (lay) authorities. And both the high motivation to maintain standards and the resistance to authority are indoctrinated in professional aspirants from the beginning of their training.

Most individuals anticipating professional work are attracted to the status and prerogatives of members of the most clearly prestigeful profession in the United States today, medicine. The image of professional prerogative is based upon that possessed by the physician. This image not only influences the professionals in other fields, with their own goals or purposes in mind, it also influences sociological inquiry about professions. For the picture of what a profession is or can be is modeled upon the example provided by the more powerful professions like medicine.

In the first section, the concept of professionalism is examined critically to see how it might help—or hinder—the study of professionals in organizations. For the essence of professionalism is generally understood to imply autonomy (freedom from external, non-professional control) for practitioners. And this understanding is brought to the study of professionals in organizations. Such studies generally take the perspective that professional autonomy is, to some extent, an intrinsic requirement of proper or effective practice. Though the usefulness of this assumption is rarely questioned in the literature on professions, it is questioned in this first section of the chapter.

In the second section it will be shown how, given the usual understandings distinguishing professionals from other types of workers, professionals do have a special place in organizational structures. The types of organizations will be considered, within which professionals may be found, in order to see how they affect the professional's own perspective on his activities and career opportunities. As professionals expect a certain amount of autonomy in their work—and fight to achieve it (or complain about not having it) when their expectations are not met, organizations containing professionals will be examined with this problem of autonomy in mind.

But the emphasis on the necessity for professional autonomy obscures the importance of a major organizational concern—that of accountability. The discussion will therefore turn from the usual perspective taken on professionals in organizations—which focuses upon the professional's own assessment of his place—and attempt a larger analysis. This analysis considers a wide variety of judgments: the interaction of judgments by the professional, the client, and the agency within which professional service is offered. And so the third section is devoted to an analysis of the structural components of an accountability system—that is, the process by which the work of the professional may be judged. The difficulties in formulating standards for judgment acceptable to all concerned parties and the difficulties involved in enforcing whatever standards have been decided upon are discussed in detail. In the final section some of the unfortunate consequences of professionalism for the client–consumer are presented and questions for future research are suggested.

I. What is professionalism? A critical discussion of the concept

The idea of professionalism has always contained within it an invidious distinction. Persons who are professional are more capable, reliable and well-trained than persons who are amateurs. Or, alternatively, persons who are professional are dedicated and motivated by higher ideals of service than mere craftsmen or businessmen. From this perspective, some conflicts between professionals and other workers are almost "natural" and expected. For professionals, with their high standards of practice and their high ideals, will inevitably come to some disagreement with others practicing their trades and following more mundane interests in the workaday world. In this section the strengths and weaknesses of this perspective shall be reviewed, showing how this concept of professionals and professionalism has developed and how that development has influenced the studies of professionals in organizations that are available today.

How are professionals distinguished from other workers and how useful is the concept of professionalism? The classic works by the pioneers (notably Carr-Saunders and Wilson) in the discussion of professions attempted historical reviews of the development of the groups generally referred to as professionals in a search for their common elements.[1]

Since this early work, the characteristics discovered in these historical and comparative reviews have taken on an added importance. That is to say, those characteristics which have been found to be *associated* with occupations known as professions come to be thought of as *intrinsic* to the distinction between professions and other occupations. From this perspective has emerged what Roth has termed the "attribute approach".[2] One surveys professions for common elements and then determines the degree of professionalism in any occupation by the presence or absence of a certain number of these common elements. An important example of this approach is provided by Greenwood[3] who argues that necessary criteria for delineation as a profession are: a systematic body of theory requiring lengthy training; a professional authority leaving the client no choice but to accept professional judgment; professional control over admission to the field; a regulative code of ethics which actually compels proper behavior from members; and a professional culture distinct from other worlds of work. Other lists of professional attributes are commonly found,[4] but no comparisons of these overlapping lists of characteristics will be attempted here, for all of them have the same weakness. They fail to distinguish empirically verifiable facts from statements of ideology.

Thus far, most of the literature on the professions has not been sufficiently critical of the attribute approach. In the search for common elements, the statements produced by professional spokesmen of established professions have been accepted without any serious attempt to discover if such statements *can* be empirically verified. The ideology presents lengthy training as part of a necessary process in the development of expertise and ideals of service. Professional groups may consciously foster certain characteristics (such as a period of lengthy training) in order to strengthen a claim to professionalism and/or to restrict competition and regulate the flow of new entrants into the field. Social workers and school teachers, for example, often complain that they learn little or nothing in their formal training, but it is an ordeal required of them in order to acquire the certification which enables them to practice. They feel that they begin learning only when they go into the field to begin practice and not before. Whatever the validity of these perceptions it is clear that a lengthy training can enhance the power of the profession. And the fact that there *is* a long period of training is used to argue that such a period is necessary. But the fact remains that long training may become an artifact for advancing status and not a condition of real requirement for professional expertise.

Following suggestions by Hughes,[5] the attribute approach may not be the best perspective for a sociologist. The focus is too much upon the definition of professionalism as the professions themselves define the term and as professionals set the standards for determining which groups may or may not fall within the category of profession. As Hughes says,[6]

> Basing one's study upon a conventional term such as profession may lead one to group together and observe only those occupations which, since they cherish and publish a common stereotype of themselves, engage in a common concealment.

Thus, by accepting too readily the attribute approach, researchers fail to examine the relationship between behavior and ideology in professions. They see what professional spokesmen want them to see—such as the growth of professional schools and the extension of training. But insufficient consideration is given to the practical uses of such training or to the power struggles involved in forcing new professional recruits to take it.

Another issue, which may be neglected, when professionals are viewed only as they wish to be viewed, is the efforts which occupational groups make to improve their image. The process of "collecting" professional attributes may be part of the strategy involved in what Hughes[7] has called "career straightening". The humble origins of a profession may be glossed over and a new image of a more honorific career can be produced through this process.

> The first people to practice a new line of work come into it from other occupations . . . At some point these irregulars, having become aware of themselves as a new group with a social identity, set about settling the terms of entry of their successors, the second generation. Almost invariably they seek to straighten the career line. They set up devices to require their successors to choose the occupation earlier, to make them follow a set course of study and training, to enter into the work as a sole and continued way of making a living, and to do the work under institutional arrangements defined and enforced by the members of the occupation.

While these phenomena of creating attributes and straightening careers can be found in many occupations, they are particularly apparent in those aspiring to professional status. And the history of even the best-established professions can be viewed from this perspective. It is always argued, of course, that these efforts also ensure that better service will be provided to clients. But the evidence for this assertion is not decisive. Again, as with other aspects of the attribute approach, assertions are made that this process is associated with professionalism without much supporting data.

Of course there are exceptions to the tendency to accept ideology as reality.[8] Among these exceptions, Freidson's work is particularly useful, for it shows in some detail just why it is that autonomy need not be connected to the ideals of disinterested service entailed in the definition of professionalism. In his discussion of "The Formal Characteristics of a Profession" Freidson[9] points to the ways in which professions gain autonomy and preserve it. He argues that formal criteria to designate what is a profession have little to do with service, though they do not preclude it. Instead the process by which appropriate criteria are shown to exist in any particular profession is a political one designed to show the public that this occupational group deserves the power and privilege (and autonomy) associated with professional status. Once the public—and its representatives—become convinced, the profession wins such benefits as the right of certification and licensing recruits. Extending the length of training to justify assertions of professionalism may thus be seen as part of that political process and not inevitably related to high standards of performance or to a service ethic.

We do not know the extent to which this political orientation is equal to or more important than the service ethic. Again we suffer from the limitations imposed upon us by accepting without question assumptions present in professional ideology. For as Freidson astutely points out, we really have no well-corroborated data on the extent of the service orientation among professionals nor whether this service orientation exists to any greater or lesser extent in other occupations as well. The difficulties of disentangling the ideology of service from the political advantages of the professional label become clearer when we examine the concept of professional autonomy in some detail.

One of the ironies posed by any study of professionals in organizations is that, by their very definition, professions are supposed to be "free". The ideal, typical professional exists in an independent relationship with his client who desires to receive the benefits of professional service. And this service is expected to differ from any simply commercial service in that the purveyor has a special type of knowledge and is a special type of person. The notion that persons in a profession follow a calling, or *"Beruf"* as it is described by Weber[10] suggests that they are uniquely and personally dedicated to offering service, even at the cost of some self-sacrifice. The heroes in medicine and epidemiology who gave their lives for science are glorified in the writings of Hans Zinsser and Paul De Kruif;[11] the dedicated men and women in medicine and nursing, the engineers who risked death and destruction to complete great public works, the religious teachers and comforters who endured much to follow their vocation are the types of persons who are generally associated with the notion of calling. But the idea of profession also has implications of an elite position—for persons who are "free" to pursue their calling are also free to disregard the opinions of others, free to select their own line of work and their own clientele. Thus professionals should be free from the judgments of others—particularly non-professionals. And one of the things which characterizes all who are established professionals or who aspire to that position is the desire for this freedom.

If one examines the ideology of professional groups one finds that the basis of the argument is that freedom from evaluation by non-professionals is necessary not in self-interest, but in order best to serve the public. The professional *needs* the room to make independent evaluation because the nature of the service he performs requires that he take into account many facts, potentialities and nuances not readily understandable to a layman. Particularly in moments of danger or crisis— as when a surgeon performs a difficult operation and some unexpected difficulty arises—the professional needs to be unquestioned in the performance of his duties. One knows the professional's worth by his successes. If a client is dissatisfied with the results of the professional judgment, he takes his problem elsewhere. This view of the room necessary for the professional to work rests upon certain assumptions about the nature of the relation between professional and client, symbolized by the fee-for-service relationship found in the profession of medicine, particularly as that profession developed in the United States.[12] This model of the independent professional is pervasive even in professions which never resembled the medical model—the military, teaching, librarianship, social work—and all professionals will argue from it. Of course, professional groups vary in the success with which they make their argument. Physicians are more successful than nurses in imposing their professional perspectives on laymen and other professionals in hospitals. And professors are generally more successful than librarians in imposing their perspectives on laymen and other professionals in universities.

But whatever the political success of the argument, the model of how a professional ought to retain control over his work remains much the same. The literature produced by professions as well as that on professions by sociologists suggests that professions present three main arguments to justify their claim for professional autonomy. These arguments involve: (1) the assumed power of ethical codes, (2) the assumed beneficial consequences of control over recruitment and certification, (3) the professional review boards and the assumption that they control the behaviour of individual practitioners. It is argued that occupational groups which have developed sufficiently to possess all these characteristics require no further control by the public nor by employing organizations. Let us consider each aspect of this three part argument in turn.[13]

1. The power of ethical codes

The idea of professional callings[14] suggests that individuals enter professions to serve humanity, their country, or God. The necessary inhibitions against too great a concern for self-interest will be self-imposed when the notion of service is uppermost. But one must be trained to turn idealistic notions into appropriate practice. In training, aspiring professionals internalize appropriate attitudes and values toward clients along with learning techniques. Thus appropriate behavior becomes "natural" so that elaborate systems for social control will not be required later. In any case, ethics are based not only on idealism but also on practicality. A reputation for honesty and competence enhances the worth of a practitioner to his clients and the rewards available in a professional career. When students emerge from training to enter practice, they will discover that altruism is good business.[15]

These assumptions are embodied in the ethical code developed by all professions. Codes contain some general statements about the service offered to humanity or to some special public. They contain exhortations to the practitioner to maintain standards of conduct appropriate to a professional. And they suggest the relevant publics to which these standards apply: the client, the public at large, fellow professionals, professionals in related or neighboring fields.

But codes show more variety than similarity. They vary in the specificity or detail in instructions to guide practitioners. Some codes, as in the more established professions, have developed over time; others have been developed by professional commissions with relative speed. Why is there so much variety?

Where new professions emerge—or old occupations are upwardly mobile—ethical codes are useful in the construction of ideology to support the move to greater power. They seem to be constructed as much to serve as evidence of professional intentions and ideals as they are to provide behavioral guidelines to practitioners concerned with providing ethical service. Greenwood,[16] in his analysis of the elements of a profession, may have unwittingly contributed to the proliferation of ethical codes. Since he states that the possession of an ethical code is an important requirement of every profession, any upwardly mobile occupation need only construct one, point to it, and proclaim itself a profession according to Greenwood's criterion. For the newer professions, formation of professional codes may be viewed as part of a defensive strategy. The occupation "proves" that it is a profession by presenting its credentials (i.e. the code of ethics).[17]

A way to gauge the intent of ethical codes is through content analysis of their focus. As Taeusch notes, for example, the code of medical ethics announces that the key responsibility of a physician is disinterested service to patients. Yet the largest number of sections in the code for physicians are devoted to regulation of fees and the proper regulation of relations with colleagues, i.e. the regulation of competition between practitioners.[18] One may also question the rationale for the emphasis placed upon describing or differentiating the proper practitioner from others which appears in many codes. Some of the exhortations in the principles of medical ethics which urge physicians to denounce quacks and to fight charlatans may be viewed as a preoccupation with preventing undesired competitors from encroaching upon the professional territory. (The history of medical association battles with chiropractors and osteopaths illustrates this preoccupation.) These adjurations also warn off accredited professionals in bordering jurisdictions.[19] Alternatively, codes may indicate that professionals should never encroach upon the territory of more powerful groups. (In the code of ethics adopted by psychology, clinical practitioners are warned against trying to treat cases which should be referred to a medical specialist.) Finally, ethical codes may caution members to stand firm against a more powerful profession, if necessary. In the Principles of Conduct for Hospital Administrators, for example, the seventh principle reads:

> In his relationship with the medical staff of the hospital he will support that which is constructive, sound and in the interests of good hospital professional practice. *He will resist and oppose that which is, in his judgment, harmful, destructive, or unwise.*
> (italics added)

In social work, considerable emphasis is given to appropriate relations with employers; engineering devotes much space in its code to the responsibility of the practitioner to the public at large for the preservation of public safety.

Differing emphasis on various audiences in these codes suggest that the problems faced by each profession are different. But it may also be that professions have different concerns in bolstering their public image which are reflected in their ethical codes. If so, codes do not simply fulfill the functions suggested by the professional ideology. Rather, they may be part of the ideology, designed for public relations and justification for the status and prestige which professions assume *vis-à-vis* more lowly occupations. Roth[20] sums up this position in a rather sharp letter at the onset of a movement to produce an ethical code for sociologists.

> I want to register my protest against the latest effort to push through a code of ethics for sociologists. It seems to me that sociologists' own studies of occupational spheres, including the use of codes of ethics by various professional and business groups, should have convinced them that this is a fruitless undertaking. But apparently this is not the case. When we examine the codes of ethics of medicine, real estate, psychology, and a variety of other spheres of activities, we find that such codes are primarily designed to do the following:

(1) Reduce the conflict among members of a professional or business fraternity (or at least the public manifestations of such conflict);
(2) Maintain a monopoly of lucrative professional tasks;
(3) Ward off criticism from outside the fraternity.

Insofar as codes of ethics make a claim to protecting the public against improper professional or business practices, the codes are a fraud. The way in which they are actually used tends to protect the fraternity against the public rather than the other way around.   `

2. Control over recruitment and certification

It is argued that appropriate service can only be assured if the values and methods are learned properly from other members of the profession. All professionals strive to control recruitment and certification of their membership. It is assumed that teachers in professional schools are the most capable of any to survey the crop of trainees and to weed out those who seem inappropriately motivated as well as technically inadequate.[21] Where students do not respond well to this instruction, they are expected to leave. Generally, such systems depend upon attrition through self-selection. It is believed that those who leave were the "wrong kind" for that field in the first place.

In the most advanced, accepted, and powerful professions, this concern with proper education culminates in complete control of the flow of practitioners into practice. Professional associations set the standards for entrants, control admission, education, and examination requirements and the state certification process by which practitioners are officially licensed to practice. The profession has the power to state just what a practitioner is, how he is identified, and where he may be found in society. No other prospective practitioners have the right to encroach on this territory.

But how reasonable is this argument that professional training assures competent practitioners? If we examine some of the studies of medical education—the system of professional education with the tightest control over the aspirants to a career in the field—we find many serious questions raised. First, the system of education into which the prospective doctors are thrown does not tend to enforce idealism. Instead, many studies[22] indicate that students become more cynical as they progress through their professional education. Neither the professional models, the message they impart, nor the conditions of training enforce an idealistic commitment to the service of humanity. In addition, some studies indicate that many students, from the very first, enter medicine with the primary goal of making money and acquiring prestige rather than that of offering service.[23] It can just as easily be argued that the tendency toward increasing cynicism as one progresses through professional training in medicine encourages the most idealistic, rather than the least qualified, to abandon medicine. Self-selection processes, then, may have been working to the disadvantage rather than to the advantage of the patients waiting for the doctor at the end of this training.

Second, the tight control which medicine holds over professional education has not been a guarantee of uniformly high standards of clinical practice. Once the first two difficult years of medical school have been passed, very few students are ever dropped from the program. And so poor students develop bad habits and remain ignorant when permitted to continue unchecked. Finally, it is widely recognized that medical schools, as well as internship and residency programs, do not approach a standardized level of competence and vary widely in the quality of teaching and experience which they provide. Thus, whatever the advantages of such control in training and licensing professionals, the right to control training creates a monopoly for a given credential or type of education which, in the absence of uniform professional control, encourages abuses and laxness within the system.

3. Professional review boards

The core of professional autonomy is that professional representatives have sole power to police the membership once they are practicing in the field. Professions which possess this autonomy receive it from the state. That is, society delegates legal power to a profession to give, suspend, and revoke the license to practice. Generally, this power is entrusted to state boards of examiners who are responsible for certifying entrants and sanctioning practitioners for any improper performance called to their attention.

Each board is composed mainly of practitioners in the field who are appointed by an elected official—usually the governor of the state. The board reviews cases of poor or unethical practice arising among those who are licensed.[24] In medicine, for instance, the state board may deprive a practitioner of his licence or suspend it for a stated interval. Other professions do not have such a centralized authority over members. In law and accounting, for example, the state board is supplemented by professional organizations with power to supervise and sanction colleagues.[25] And other professions are vulnerable to external regulatory agencies which may or may not contain professional peers in the review structure. In addition to legislative review[26] the Internal Revenue Service and the Security Exchange Commission, for example, may review practices and initiate proceedings against unethical practitioners of law or certified public accounting in the courts as well as by asking professional associates to review the behaviour of questionable members.

These forms of supplemental review and sanction suggest that professional review systems are often recognized as insufficient to provide necessary regulation. Some of the weaknesses in a strictly professional review system are quite clear. First, the profession makes the assumption that all its members are practicing properly. Therefore, no regular or routine pattern of supervision and review is established. In other words, there is no system similar to the regularly recurring driver's license examination required for motorists, who are expected to vary or lapse in their driving ability over time. Thus, incompetent or unethical performance may remain undected by the autonomous professional surveillance system unless a client brings it forward. It is curious to find such complete dependence on the client when the ideology of professionalism has stressed that no client can ever properly judge professional practice. Clearly, it is not sufficient for a profession to depend upon its clients, for they are often cowed or awed by professional prestige, authority and knowledge. Accordingly, they may not use what judgment they do have to complain as often or as determinedly as they might otherwise. Furthermore, unless they are persistent in pressing complaints through formal channels, clients may be ignored. The authority of colleagues, and the belief in their ability, also influences professional review; in consequence the importance of a client's complaint may not be sufficiently recognized.

One of the problems is that professional autonomy does not permit any check on the quality of service. Really powerful professions cannot even provide systematic data on incidents of poor service so that practitioners might be warned or advised about pitfalls before they unwittingly fall into them. Since no data are available, professionals simply assume that the system for the transmittal of proper professional service is working when they are personally satisfied with the level of service they produce. Systems of periodic review—and systems which provide external supervision—may not guarantee high professional standards in performance; but they may guarantee a minimal standard of services for protection of the client—something for which the emphasis on professional autonomy does not allow.

Apparently, the assumption that members of a profession should cooperate within an association (much like a guild in structure) has some unfortunate consequences for the effectiveness of colleague control. Loyalty to one's colleagues may outweigh responsibility to clients. Professionals vary in how explicitly they set standards of behaviour toward clients, but every profession states quite explicitly that professionals should not criticize one another before non-professionals. While codes state that criticism of a colleague to an outsider is a gross breach of professional etiquette, they do not offer another clear alternative when discovering incompetence in a colleague. The codes suggest that violations of professional conduct should be reported; but they are rather vague. They never explain exactly what responsibilities a professional does have in those cases where he detects or suspects a breach in the proper professional conduct of a colleague. As a result, only the grossest misbehavior, or the most severe pressures from external sources, move professionals to discipline their own members.[27] In law, for example, Carlin suggests that only highly unfavourable publicity assures action against erring attorneys.[28]

The point of the preceding discussion is to suggest that there is really no reason to accept the contention that professional autonomy is a necessary component of professional service. For, whatever the rhetoric of professionalism, all the evidence seems to indicate that professional autonomy does not encourage the development of practical or workable systems of control. In medicine, for example, the ideal, typical model of solo practice in a fee-for-service structure activity precludes the possibility of professional review.[29] As a consequence, this profession, with the greatest autonomy of any, has a most fragmented system of professional control, while professions such as law and certified public accounting, which are not so independent and which must render account to extraprofessional reviews also possess more well-developed professional review systems.

Such observations raise the serious question of whether or not autonomy is indeed vital for the performance of high-level professional service. There are some indications that supervision from outside the profession can at some times really improve the quality of service. Comparisons in transmittal of health care services, where physicians are supervised and where they are not, provide some suggestive evidence. Some successes in utilization indicate that controlled surveillance and supervision by peers and *also* by other health care practitioners and by consumers can result in a better quality of medicine, more economically practiced. Paradoxically, higher standards of performance may some day be found in professions which *are* closely regulated than in those which are not.[30] The history of professions and professionalism does not really seem to support the contention that professional autonomy contributes to high standards of professional service. Instead, the more powerful the profession, the more serious appear the charges of laxness in concern for public service and zealousness in promoting the individual interests of the practitioners.[31]

Nevertheless, a persistent belief in the crucial importance of professional autonomy to the delivery of good service influences or colors our studies of professionals in organizations. If professionals have to be autonomous in order to practice at their best, how could it be otherwise? In consequence, an implicit assumption in such studies is that bureaucracy (with its emphasis on hierarchy and supervision) and professionalism are antithetical. In the following section we shall consider some of these bureaucratic settings in which professionals operate to see what arguments have developed by professional spokesmen, and spokesmen for bureaucracies, in presenting the rationale for how professionals should be treated and what may be expected from them when they practice in organizations.

II. The effect of organizational structure on professional working conditions

When discussions of professionals in organizations are considered, it is clear that such issues as the right to autonomy and independent judgment within the organizational structure are important to the professionals involved. Professionals strive to avoid clearly demarcated levels of supervision whenever practicable, arguing that this evasion is necessary to the production of good service. While total independence is clearly not possible, the notion of professional autonomy and its connection to ideal standards of service can be retained to some extent if only colleagues judge one another. The question of whether or not professional standards are best recognized and maintained by eliminating external authority and substituting peer review will be considered through an examination of two "model" types of organizations—first those composed primarily of (and administered by) the professionals involved, as in law firms, followed by large-scale organizations which hire professionals for their own rather than professional purposes. Examples of the latter type are found in the military and other branches of the federal government, as well as in large commercial enterprises.

1. Professional organizations

Conflicts within organizations between professional and other goals should be minimized (if we follow the line of argument for professional autonomy) when the head of the organization who formulates goals and sets priorities is himself a professional. Professionals should be able to share and work toward common goals. After all, they share a common training, a common socialization process. With this view in mind, the first hospital administrators were doctors, and university presidents were generally former professors and distinguished scholars. Of course these organizations contained many more interested parties than just doctors and professors. The clientele (students and patients) required certain safeguards. And formal representatives of their interests—or the interests of the public at large—were generally served by boards of directors who were laymen. These diverse concerns have necessitated organizational policies which are not always in accord with strictly professional aims and interests.[32] For example, physicians at one hospital may wish to elaborate their expertise through the purchase of expensive radiological equipment already available to the public at a neighbouring hospital. And the administration or board of directors may have to curtail such professional aspirations in the interests of public economy. And, as a matter of fact, such organizations as hospitals or universities are less and less frequently administered by members of the dominant professional group in the organization. The famous phrase: "war is too serious a matter to be left in the hands of the generals" has often been paraphrased to include such statements as: "hospitals are too necessary to be left in the hands of the doctors"; "universities are too important to be left in the control of the professors".

Other such organizations composed principally of professionals carrying out professional aims and goals which have been examined are law firms,[33] CPA firms,[34] architectural[35] and engineering firms[36] and medical group practices.[37] Ideally, such organizations follow lines of "collegial" or guild organization rather than hierarchical patterns of administration requiring supervision and subordination. Though practically speaking, the work of professional specialists may be so specialized that colleagues really cannot supervise their juniors. Morris Daniels[38] reports that sometimes in large CPA firms senior accountants, managers, and partners may each be so specialized from long experience with a set of technical problems in their field that, strictly speaking, a hierarchical system of supervision is impractical. But whether or not a knowledgeable form of supervision is possible, all (or most) members of the organization are colleagues. Therefore communications which are advisory rather than directive set the tone and style of organization. Goss[39] presents such a model in her description of how medical doctors deal with one another even when one has the authority of attending physician and the other is a resident, intern, or other doctor in a somewhat subordinate position. Even when an authority hierarchy does exist, the higher ranking physician will adopt a conciliatory tone. If the lower ranking doctor does not choose to follow advice, he is not pressed to do so.[40]

While such practices may be common in medicine, they are less so in other professional associations. Law, certified public accounting, architecture and engineering firms, for example, generally distinguish clearly between junior and senior men, between employees and partners. The interests of these two strata are not always complementary and subordinates may find that their notions of appropriate professional goals and techniques are not always parallel to those of their senior colleagues. Not all juniors escape dismissal or are invited into partnership; not all partners remain with the firm. Some of the charges and counter-charges in these conflicts imply that one side or the other is less than professional in its activity or motivation. For instance, the "old timers" may complain that young men or women nowadays won't work as hard and as self-sacrificingly to perfect their skills and to get ahead in the field as they did. (In academic departments sometimes the charges are reversed: the young are working hard and the old are "sitting pretty".) The young in some professional firms may see themselves as exploited and neglected by senior colleagues who are no better than any other set of rapacious employers might be.[41]

In some cases these differences may lead juniors to rebel and even to question the value of professionalism. In consequence they may unite to gain strength in unionization and thereby combat what they see as unreasonable exploitation.[42] Occasionally the juniors may see the true spirit or purpose of their profession evaporating under the traditionalism or short-sightedness of their superiors. They may unite to force a return to professional standards. Such a trend may now be present, for example, among the junior clergy in the Catholic Church. Despite the structure of hierarchical authority in the Church, it is a collectivity of professionals. And these professionals all presumably share the same larger concerns. But today the pressures to make the Church responsive to modern day problems comes in large part from the juniors.[43]

In sum, one might expect that the establishment of an organization of colleagues bypasses many of the problems or potential areas of conflict to be found in what are more commonly seen as bureaucracies. But in fact, professional self-images are not generally amenable to closely coordinated work. For one thing the ideological emphasis on autonomy which pervades professional training and practice does not generally encourage the notion that cooperative work is necessary or desirable. Nor does this ideology encourage professionals to be amenable to the kind of routinized or specialized division of labor which many professional firms may require. As Scott[44] points out, one of the potential areas of conflict between professional and bureaucratic forms of organization is that professional tasks are regarded as complex and requiring considerable independent judgment in their completion while many bureaucratic tasks are rationalized into separate parts which, like production line work, can be learned through technical training and then performed with a minimum array of skills and capacity for judgment. Thus professionals have an ideology to use when they resist organization within a rational bureaucratic system of work. When they do specialize they may be able to hide behind technical proficiency, which by mystifying a potential supervisor, still permits the individual technician to order his work as he pleases.

In professional firms the price for such specialization may be a secure position but a ceiling on promotion or advancement. The literature on associations of professions in large firms already cited contains many examples of persons in "dead end" positions: auditors who refused to take on the more perplexing and uncharted problems of management service may not be able to rise within CPA firms; lawyers who specialize in particular kinds of background legal research may not be seen as partnership material in the large corporation firms where skill in managing relations with clients and public presentations may be necessary for advancement.

And so it may be argued that professionals working within their own organizations face some problems which beset members of many large business organizations. (1) Employers may wish to secure effort from employees which provides insufficient payment or gratification for the workers. CPAs or lawyers do not all wish to work desperately hard in order to prove their value to the firm. And some see the testing period for potential partners as a time of unfair exploitation. In this regard they are no different from aspirants in business organizations who wonder if loyalty to the firm is really worthwhile. (2) Skills required to start up the success ladder need to be discarded as one climbs. At the same time, new skills may need to be developed quickly. Hard-working young auditors who are efficient and conscientious at detail work may be valued for their effort. However if they do not learn how to manage contacts with clients, they may have no future with their CPA firm. Conscientious attention to many small details may not be required in a senior partner. In facing these problems it may be small consolation that at least fellow professionals rather than laymen have set the terms for the performance of aspirants. What happens when even this consolation is removed? Large-scale organizations like the various levels of public government and the service agencies they control, as well as private industry, hire all sorts of professionals to offer service or provide consultation. And nonprofessionals make many of the important decisions affecting these professionals. These issues are discussed in the next section.

2. Professionals in organizations

The concept of professionals in organizations does not, in general refer to the professional firms discussed in the previous section. Instead it is the professional in some subordinate or advisory position to lay administrators or owners that comes to mind, and much of the literature concerned with role conflicts for professionals in organizations focuses upon the predicament of these persons.

The issues for professionals *in* organizations center around the definition of tasks. Who has the right to say what a professional (with his understanding about the value of autonomy) should or shouldn't do as he practices in his field? Professional and larger organizational goals cannot always be assumed to be complementary. Which set of goals takes precedence in moments of conflict? The typical pattern of organization found in professional associations as presented in Part I generally will not adapt well to problems of other organizations. For example, colleagues are typically willing to give their peers the benefit of the doubt, offering leniency and minor penalties to wrongdoers whenever possible. But large organizations, responsible to the public interest or concerned with maximizing profits, are not always able to accept such a collegial perspective; it may be too expensive. The accommodations which are made between professional and other organizational perspectives vary widely. The more powerful professions, like medicine, have been successful in imposing limits upon the encroachments of any nonprofessional authority.[44a] For example, physicians of whatever specialty and, in some cases, engineers, have been placed in relatively invulnerable or unquestioned positions by virtue of the social value placed upon their particular professional expertise and judgment. This social value is translated, in institutional terms, into leaving them alone or into offering them leeway in practice and judgment that ordinary employees in organizations would not receive.

The less powerful professions leave their practitioners more vulnerable to the demand of employers and lay administrators. Such persons as social workers, lawyers, city planners and public health workers in governmental agencies (and also in the military) provide examples of this type of professional employee. Librarians in universities, nurses in hospitals, teachers in school districts, engineers, chemists, and other scientists in industry are also the types of professionals that come to mind when examining professionals *in* organizations.

In considering the role of professionals in organizations, where role conflicts are expected to arise and where dilemmas are often discussed, the main focus in the literature involves the *differences* between bureaucratic and professional goals *as they affect the professional*.[45] A professional has a particular self-image, a notion of how his duties should be arranged, an ideal of something like craftsmanship which he wishes his work to match. But bureaucracies have larger purposes. Elegant or careful service may have to be subordinated to strictures imposed by limited time or money; the values of the profession and those expressed in organizational goals may be at odds. And so the following kinds of problems arise and are discussed in the literature. Social workers protest the imposition of too heavy a caseload by bureaucratic authorities trying to save money, and such orders as the one requiring them to make "midnight raids" on welfare mothers to assure that no man is in the house.[46] Lawyers resist control by powerful clients.[47] City planners[48] and public health workers[49] face somewhat different but equally vexing problems in asserting *their* conception of the professional role within the bureaucratic system. In these cases the bureaucracy tends to set a somewhat different standard for his behaviour from what the professional considers appropriate. As already noted, when the professional comes from a field with a relatively long and prestigious history, the problem is somewhat mitigated.[50] There are, for example, general understandings —developed in the private practice arena—of what doctors and lawyers do. They cannot be expected to reveal what clients have told them in confidence and employing agencies may find that such professionals become recalcitrant when expected to breach confidences. The *amour propre* of such practitioners is bolstered by these understandings. They can point with pride to historical accomplishments of their colleagues, resist suggestions that they do anything they may term unprofessional or unethical, and, in the last resort, turn to private practice when bureaucratic agencies deal too harshly with them. Thus, while in the field of public health, the problems of physicians who do not have control over their working conditions may be professionally vexing and damaging to status,[51] they are not nearly so vexing for the physician as they are for the nurses, health educators, and others who have no history of independence and, in some cases, *do* have a history of subordination. Nurses, for example, have always been subordinate, first to doctors and then to hospital administration.[52] Generally, professions created by fiat are created subordinate, as servants of a governmental agency. This is certainly the case for social workers.[53] In consequence, the practitioners have no history of independence and find it difficult to assert professional goals or values in the face of bureaucratic opposition. There is, after all, no other place readily available in which they may practice. Teachers are in much the same subordinate position as employees of local school districts where they are under the supervision of principal[54] and superintendents appointed by the board of education. And even the more academically distinguished professor is in a similar position—serving, until he has tenure, at the pleasure of administrators and trustees irrespective of what his colleagues in departments or academic senates may say. His true position in the power struggle is shown by his inability—tenured or not—to enforce demands for higher wages or better working conditions.[55] In this respect he is like the primary and secondary school teacher in that he cannot control the size of classes nor procure the necessary materials for teaching when governing boards unilaterally insist upon budget cuts. And in this respect he is also like his colleague the librarian who also has little power to influence working conditions. For when the librarian cannot protect his budget he cannot maintain the purchase of journals and editions of books which are often irreplaceable if not acquired when they are current. In this situation the librarian cannot protect the quality of his collection which some see as the core of his professional responsibility.[56]

All of these problems suggest that the value a professional places on his service may not be recognized by employing organizations. Because the professional cannot request funds, organize work, set priorities, he cannot control his working conditions, the product created, nor the service offered. Such problems are also faced by scientists in industry who serve as advisors (in staff rather than line positions) or who work as technicians. Kornhauser[57] has pointed to the conflicts these scientists face, as have others.[58] Perhaps the best statement of one solution to the problem as it arises in industry can be found in Melville Dalton's classic work *Men Who Manage*.[59] Professionals are forced, through their own initiative, to reconcile very difficult problems or conflicts inherent within the very nature of the organization. If they make the wrong decision they can then stand as scapegoats for the internal strains or inconsistencies in the organization which are never resolved. The conflicts continue and the individual does the best he can to cope with them, knowing that he will be punished if he does not. In mental hospitals, for example, superintendents know they may be fired if a scandal erupts within their jurisdiction. If some patient dies under mysterious circumstances the public outcry will be propitiated by their forced resignation. The internal difficulties created by trying to combine custodial and rehabilitative aims in one organization need never be resolved; the figurehead will change and the inconsistencies continue to be juggled as best they can by the next administrator. Thus, the first resolution for professionals who face conflicts in bureaucratic organizations between professional and organizational values may be to take the brunt of responsibility for resolution upon themselves. In any case, as long as bureaucracies face no serious crises these conflicts may not surface.

In happy (boom) economic times many problems between professionals and bureaucratic authority are only latent, while in hard times, when priorities must be set, the issues are joined. Then professionals add their complaints to those of others who are denied "proper" working conditions or simply fired. At such times, other forces than professional associations of colleagues determine the ordering of priorities—and the laying off of staff.

But these conflicts or difficulties which may arise are always there—and they are highlighted in the military. Here an arm of the government decrees how professionals shall be used, where and when, and the general part they shall play within the overriding "mission".[60] The power of this bureaucracy is great. And this power suggests a second alternative professionals may use in organizations to resolve bureaucratic and professional differences: that is, see their work as some scientists do—as the work of technicians.

The professional does what he is told to do by his primary client, the organization. The organization makes judgments about how the professional is to use his skills. And therefore it is perfectly appropriate for the professional to treat the second client—whatever persons the organization refers to him—in accord with organizational directives. Any potential role conflicts are thus resolved or ignored. For instance, Burchard found that military chaplains viewed themselves as agents of the military and so simply saw no problem in counseling soldiers to fight—in spite of their allegience to the principles against killing embodied in the ten commandments. And these findings were supported at a later period by Zahn.[60a] The work of Clausen and Daniels on military psychiatrists also indicates that the professional minimizes ethical dilemmas and role conflicts when viewing himself as an agent of a larger organization with standards and programs he has little power to influence.[61]

One consequence of the "technician" resolution of the professional dilemma in organizational roles is that the professional practitioner can take this resolution a step further and so become a partisan supporter of organizational (as opposed to professional) goals. In essence, then, an effective resolution of the dilemma is for the professional to become entirely "coopted."[62] The notion of cooption is discussed in the sociological literature; but the real meaning of the term can best be seen by examining an example in the popular literature. Consider the following excerpt from an interview with an Army chaplain in Hawaii by a reporter for *The New Yorker*.[63]

What do you learn in your chaplaincy course, Reverend?
Oh, mostly to read maps and not make fools of ourselves in the military.
Anything else?
Well, we're taught to handle all those kids parroting the antiEstablishment line. We get to learn how to turn them around. We learn to say to them, "It's not killing that is good, it's defending your country that is good".

Do you like the military chaplaincy, Reverend?

It sure is rewarding. It's not that I love the Army, but I think soldiers are just great. I've just finished a six month tour with the Green Berets. You should see how they beam at you when they get out of the helicopter, those boys so hungry for the Gospel! . . . Any special problems you encounter, Reverend?

Well, last year we'd average one guy a week who refused to take the plane back to Saigon. He was usually a guy who'd seen a buddy killed. We'd take him to the psychiatric ward at the military hospital, and in three days he'd be just fine, ready to get back on that plane to Vietnam.

Such resolutions to the problems of role conflicts also raise some interesting questions of the way one kind of primary allegiance slips over into another. The professional can struggle over conflicting values, taking the brunt of his decisions personally and accepting punishment from the most powerful agency—organizational leaders—when he fails. In this way he can maintain allegience to professional values if he chooses to do so. If he sidesteps responsibility by remaining neutral: i.e. seeing himself as a technician carrying out orders, he can avoid direct confrontation between two value systems. However this alternative may pull the professional into the organizational value system so that when conflicts arise he will side with the organization rather than professional values. The more powerful the organization, of course, the more pressure the professional faces to make this third resolution his own. Thus the question of how valuable autonomy may be to any particular professional is resolved when the conflict between professional and bureaucratic values is joined. The professional may claim autonomy (and allegiance to professional values) at his peril. Or he may sidestep the issue when he sees himself "free" to follow organizational goals.

III Supervision of professionals in organizations

In the previous section the focus has been upon how organizations impede or enhance *professional* perspectives of appropriate working conditions. In this section attention is focused on the consideration of a larger question: what are the general problems involved in establishing any adequate system of supervision of professional activity, regardless of where professionals practice? Obviously, the major question is: what are the criteria for judgment and how are standards enforced?

There are five factors in practice which appear to influence any system for setting standards and judging how well practitioners meet them. These five factors are: (1) opportunity for observability of the practitioner while he is performing his service; (2) clarity of goals for the service; (3) clarity of techniques involved in the service; (4) clarity of the relationship of techniques to goals; and finally (5) the power of the client—either the direct client or the employing bureaucracy—to express and enforce his view of appropriate service.

1. Observability

A necessary (though not sufficient) part of any accountability system is the extent to which professional behaviour can be observed. Some professional activities can be observed while they are being performed—as when a teacher lectures to an audience. While other activities are not so easy to see, their products are visible enough—as when a scientist makes a great medical discovery embodied in a "miracle" drug, or an academic writes articles which may be read, or at least counted. Still other activities, such as the administration of an agency, must be taken pretty much on faith. The absence of negative evidence (no riots or public scandals) may be all the evidence which exists.

The issue of observability raises the question of to what audience the professional is observable: to a direct client? or to the "public" as client? to colleagues and related professionals? or to some combination of all of these?

2. Clarity of goals

Some difficulties arise because of the difficulty in delineating appropriate goals or outcomes for the professional activity. Problems in clarity of goals are minimal if public expectations of the profession are relatively specifiable. However, they rarely are. For example, doctors are supposed to heal the sick or at least to minimize suffering. In our society these goals are greatly valued; but doctors often find it difficult to order priorities when such matters as the age, ability to pay, and social worth of the patient are at issue.[64] Should the aged be kept alive at any cost or should they be permitted to die? Should more efforts be made to save the socially valuable over those who are social burdens? When scarce resources are in question —as the facilities for open heart surgery or hemodialysis—these questions are open to public and professional debate. It may also be clear that architects are expected to design buildings which will be functional. However, questions of aesthetics and appropriate land use may confuse the issue, i.e. what kind of building should be built and where?

Thus, goals may not be clear, or they may not be clearly related to a broader set of expectations. Engineers are expected to design plans for buildings or bridges or other public works so that stress and other factors will be taken into account. It is expected that the edifice will remain standing under various atmospheric pressures and changes, and that it will withstand the use for which it was designed. But engineering goals do not specify the value of using land for highways or some other purpose.

All of these differences in opinion about appropriate, overriding goals indicate the conflicting values abroad in the society. In pluralistic societies where conflicting values are common, professionals will always have the problem of defending or validating any particular set of goals to which they adhere.[65]

3. Clarity of techniques

Professions vary in just how specific the techniques they use may be and how easily anyone outside the profession can evaluate them. And they also vary in the clarity with which the application of specific techniques may be related to the goals of the profession.

When techniques are very esoteric or specialized, there may be no way for persons outside the profession to evaluate them—and they rarely try. Stock-holders rarely attempt to read complex budgetary reports, much less judge the technical proficiency of the CPA who prepared them. Current efforts in the CPA profession to make reports more "readable" and useful to a potential audience of investors suggest that professionals fear becoming obsolete when they are *too* arcane or mystifying. They run the risk of placing themselves outside the world of desired services if these specialized tasks are no longer required. For example, the CPA profession might lose the auditing field if computer technology eventually allows the audit to be mechanized. But if the professionals have prepared for the possibility by developing new goals (advising businesses rather than supervising them), and new techniques through which they are attained (new forms of budgetary analysis), they may attract a new clientele with their skill as budget analysts and economic commentators on the state of business finance.

Similarly, the future of a profession may be jeopardized by a practice which is perceived as too ordinary and unspecialized by the public. Professionals may see as special and technically difficult a service which does not appear so to the layman. The professional skills required for therapeutic interviewing may be considered difficult to acquire. Yet to the public, psychiatrists or social welfare caseworkers may seem only to be talking to people about their troubles. The distinction may not be sufficiently clear between these professional activities and what any bar-tender can do to warrant much time, faith or money spent on such services. This view may be reflected in somewhat cavalier treatment of the professional within organiza-tions. For example: librarians only order and stamp books; their views carry little weight when the university budget has to be cut, and their advice carries no implications of expertise to which an administrator must attend. Accordingly it is sometimes difficult to persuade organizational spokesmen about the value of what they are receiving. They may have to be "educated" to understand it.[67]

4. Relation of clarity of techniques to goals

The ability to evaluate professionals when they are observed at their work, or assumed to be working (if they are not observable), is related to the clarity of the relationship between goals and techniques. Where goals and techniques are clear and the outcome of the service is not problematic, evaluators (clients or others) will be most able to judge whether or not the techniques are suitable and the practitioner competent. For example, when a patient appears with a cut finger, the goal of the physician is clearly to stop bleeding, prevent infection, promote healing, and minimize scarring. General expectations are that these goals can be met by a competent physician using standard techniques of cleaning and stitching or clamping. Incompetence may be easily detached and recognized if the wound becomes infected or gangrenous, or leaves unnecessary scars.

On the other hand, if goals and techniques are unclear, the outcome of the service is also problematic, and it will be more difficult to judge competence. The goals and techniques of the psychotherapist, for example, are so vague that it is extremely difficult for anyone to evaluate his competence.

Where goals are clear, but techniques are difficult to specify (as in some aspects of teaching languages or mathematics) or when goals are difficult to specify but techniques are clear (as in technical specialties like electron microscopy, computer programing), it will also be difficult to evaluate the service. Where there is either a clear goal or a clear technique, outsiders will have some basis for evaluation, but the vague complement will make evaluation problematic. In architecture, for example, the techniques of design are clear, but the goals of design may be extremely vague. The client's or the professional's desire for an aesthetic, prestigious, or functional edifice is difficult to specify and the professional's fulfillment of the goal is open to debate. Thus it is sometimes difficult to determine whether or not the architect had rendered "competent" services.[68] Thus far the issues involved in achieving an accountability system, have been discussed. Observability and clarity provide some of the basic conditions, but they are not enough. The relationship of the professional and the client is an important additional consideration. If the client has no power to insist upon his rights, no amount of clarity and observability will ensure the existence of an accountability system.

5. *Power of the Client*

The power of the professional in even such powerful professions as medicine or law is always moderated when the professional faces a direct client in a fee-for-service relationship; for the client may withold his custom (or even the fee) once the professional service has been performed. Professionals such as engineers, architects, and entire corporate law firms who serve a few clients (or only one large corporate client) are particularly vulnerable to such client control. Their clients may not only be excessively demanding and irritating, but they may also desire services considered of dubious professional worth, services which the professional thinks may actually harm them, and which raise ethical and legal questions. The prevalence of such problems is indicated by the scandals which arise from time to time, resulting in court action, fines, and even imprisonment of professionals who have colluded or conspired with unscrupulous and determined clients.[69]

The relative power of professional and client is most particularly changed when a professional is employed or regulated by a bureaucracy within which he performs some professional service as its agent. In these situations, the power of the client is magnified so that the professional's responsibility (and his accountability for his actions) are not limited to the direct client for whom he may be performing the service; it is probably the indirect client employer, overseer or contractor of services) who wins the primary allegiance of the professional.

The professional–client relationship within a bureaucracy

Today, third parties increasingly enter into professional–client relationships— whatever the nature of the service offered. The free, solo practitioner is becoming rarer,[70] and many services can now only be offered in technically equipped and properly staffed bureaucracies, such as hospitals, law courts, libraries, universities, computer centers and research laboratories, where the professional must come to practice. Still others such as certified public accountants and tax lawyers are regulated or controlled by governmental agencies. Extraprofessiona lauthority may be responsible for allocation of resources, predictions of required expenditures of time and money, the protection of the public welfare and other matters directly connected with the manner in which professional services are transmitted. When professionals are directly employed, the bureaucratic organizations come to assume responsibility for certain aspects of practice carried on within their domain, and, because of their responsibility, they find it necessary to assess performance. So extraprofessional authorities (sometimes in conjunction with professional representatives) try to develop accountability in order to meet this responsibility. When extraprofessional authorities make this effort, they face many of·the same problems that any client faces in attempting to assess the worth of the professional service he receives. In order to see the differences in types of accountability structures, available to direct clients and bureaucratic agents, the five components of structural accountability suggested from the perspective of "management" (or any outsider concerned with the level of service available) may be useful, particularly in explaining how critical variables in these settings affect the structure of an accountability system. Such variables include the following; the power of an extraprofessional authority structure (e.g. the military bureaucracy has great power over professionals who are members but the public university does not); the alliances which each may draw upon (e.g. the physician may call upon his powerful professional association to protect him in a way that a college professor may not); as professionals move into bureaucracies, accountability structures develop which may or may not use criteria for evaluation and methods for sanctioning deviation which are endorsed by the professional associations. Thus an important factor to consider is the extent to which bureaucratic goals and methods are congruent with those of the profession.

1. Observability

Observability is always important in bureaucratic structures, for some system of categorizing and assessing a functionary's individual activity is generally required. Records of events, time clocks, signed reports are all efforts to codify the array of activities in which members have been engaged. Where the activities of the professional are performed in private or involve so much judgment and independent decision that the practitioner cannot be judged on the spot, some record of his behavior is often substituted. Thus, for example, medical records as well as medical behavior figure crucially in the accreditation of hospitals, In this case, medical records are accepted as the functional equivalent of the behaviour which is assumed to have occurred for these facts now to be detailed in the record; e.g. the hospital record shows the doctor to have performed his task appropriately when the record discloses what was wrong with the patient at time of admission, what the doctor planned as therapy, and how the patient progressed under this treatment. Records may serve the same purpose for accountants or lawyers who draw up documents and then "attest" to the credibility of their content. Their signatures indicate that the professionals have examined all pertinent data (as testimony or sworn depositions, inventory or invoices) before giving their certification. Managers of bureaucracies dependent upon professional services are particularly anxious that all records be in order: assuming that records are adequate, professionals, for all practical purposes, may be assumed to be as observable as other functionaries in the performance of their duties.

But such criteria for observability are often resisted by professionals. Resistance is usually based on the claim that their work involves amorphous areas of judgment and decision-making which regulations cannot take into account when criteria are formulated for observability. What has to be recorded may be seen as unrelated to professional service. Thus, for example, college professors sometimes balk at attendance records which they feel are, like time clocks, unsuitable and irrelevant for their status and function.[71] Professionals may feel discomfort and conflict when they must submit to regulations and requirements which they see as unrelated to attaining their professional goals, but which are designed to assure compliance with other institutional goals. Psychiatrists in state or military hospitals, for example, sometimes complain that keeping records and signing forms are activities which severely curtail the actual amount of time available to help patients.

Even in bureaucracies controlled by colleagues, practitioners may find that the bureaucratic controlling system imposes rules and regulations which delimit the activities of the individual; as Weber[72] points out, this is inherent in any organizational practice. However, these formal requirements may be more gracefully received within professionally dominated bureaucracies (such as corporate law or accounting firms) since distinctions between the goals of the organization and those of the individual practitioner should be lessened; at the same time there will be greater consensus over techniques and systems of review. Young lawyers and accountants expect to progress through the hierarchy of professional firms; someday as junior or senior partners, they will supervise others as they are now supervised.[73]

Yet problems of observability exist whether within professionally or nonprofessionally controlled organizational hierarchies. Such problems are one indicator of the extent and type of resistance professionals raise to supervision or coordination of activity.

2. Clarity of goals

Many problems of making records adequate for observability stem from the difficulty of assessing what one has seen. For example, administrative staff in organizations may observe professionals on their way to or from the special location within the organization where the professional activity is performed. Similarly, colleagues and other members of the role set (assistants, subjects, clients, and related professionals) may casually or carefully observe the professional at his work. Operating room attendants have many opportunities to observe the work of surgeons and anesthesiologists, for instance, and will usually make assessments. While this assessment may be informal, or while the nonprofessional observers may not be sufficiently adept to be informed observers, these others are certainly knowledgeable enough to note gross inadequacies or problems in professional performance.

When resisting social controls from outsiders, professions with relatively clear goals can have an advantage, particularly if they can argue that endangering their autonomy will endanger that goal which even bureaucratic officials desire. Physicians refuse to sign orders or perform duties in situations where they feel lives would be endangered or illness would be needlessly prolonged. Architects and engineers can point out the folly of disregarding their advice on design and construction when pressured to cut costs, speed up deadlines, or please powerful interest groups in some other way. Furthermore, they may refuse to certify plans which they believe to be substandard. An appeal to ultimate common goals may be useful to professionals who feel they cannot accommodate requests to meet short-term, immediate goals set by current pressures.

In all such cases, professional associations tend to support embattled colleagues against outside interference. The rights of professionals to hold opposing views or to seek a variety of goals is often defended as a legitimate area of variation. And arguments in favor of the professional's right to argue for (and attempt to enforce) his particular decision in a given situation are bolstered by the ideology that professional decisions are discretionary acts, and intimate knowledge of the particular situation is required to judge professional decisions. Such discretion extends to the right to interpret how the goals of the profession are to be understood to relate to any particular situation.

Of course, in some instances where the mandate is not clear and where the professional group does not possess consensus—where the profession itself is seriously divided—practitioners may not be supported when facing resistance from bureaucratic authority and other agents in the society. These problems are particularly acute today within educational institutions where the goals of the professional and the expectations of the client are not clear. Is the purpose of education to influence thought, convey knowledge, prepare students for an occupational career, or to socialize individuals into conventional roles? Whatever the goals, the methods utilized to attain them are correspondingly unclear. In higher education it is often argued that the value of the learning experience may not be realized by a student until many years later. Thus the goal of teaching is not attained now, but in the future. Unfortunately, the student may hate the experience now and also hate the dedicated teacher. It is only later that the student will appreciate what he has learned. In a similar vein, it is argued that the popular teacher may not be particularly effective in conveying his subject matter, despite the fact that his students find him entertaining or enjoyable. The indicators of effectiveness and the signs that a teacher has accomplished (or is accomplishing) the aim of teaching are thus unclear.

Sometimes it is the specification of goals which is not clear and sometimes even the statement of the most general, ultimate aim does not create agreement. Understandably, when standards of performance are not easily related to a specific goal it is tempting for the organization to formulate some other goal which *is* specifiable.

Under these circumstances, as in the case of teaching, it is tempting to substitute standards for evaluating teacher performance which *at least* meet bureaucratic standards. In this view adequate performance may be judged by neatness, conformity to rules, and punctuality; for these criteria are readily accessible to examination and review. When such criteria are imposed by bureaucratic authority, professionals without a strong association, such as teachers, cannot easily resist.

3. Clarity of Techniques

The conflicts described above are compounded when professions do not possess a clear array of techniques. Neither layman (potential direct client) nor extraprofessional authority can readily assess the scope and worth of the professional activity under these circumstances. This confusion may be reflected in the views of extraprofessional analysts or experts at time and motion studies who cannot see what special worthwhile activity is occurring through the use of professional techniques. Such problems in definition and assignment of social value are especially likely when resources are scarce: professionals in bureaucracies may be stripped of their perquisites and their numbers curtailed when appropriations are cut or budgetary allocations are rearranged. Professionals in bureaucracies can fight for and maintain their place in the organization only if they can show the relationship between their techniques and the overriding organizational goals. Chemists, for example, must show that their quality control studies increase the detection of substandard products and thereby improve the reputation and profit of the company to insure continued use of their services during economic recessions when professional staffs are cut.

4. The Power to Define the Relation of Clarity of Techniques to Goals

Problems in relationships between techniques and goals only come clearly into focus when the professional service is bureaucratically regulated. For the relationship between professionals and their clients then requires some specification in terms of organizational policy as well as in terms of their mutual expectations about appropriate goals and techniques.

   When one attempts to describe some of the possible relationships that can be found between bureaucratic requirements and professional standards in the empirical world, one also becomes involved in a discussion of the relative power of professionals and the bureaucracies containing them. Which agency has the power to insist upon a system of priorities? Which has the power to insist upon a definition of goals and techniques? Of course, when goals and techniques of the bureaucracy and the profession are both clear and complementary, there seems to be relatively little difficulty. Such conditions are most likely to be present when the professional and the bureaucratic organization are one and the same. In this case professionals can rationalize their work, making it more efficient while minimizing the possibilities of external control—and disputes about methods of control—by internal controls and accountability systems established within their own bureaucracies.

Thus, members of the priesthood[74] may acquiesce to bureaucratic control over their professional affairs because of their sense of responsibility to and membership in their heirarchy. They understand that such interference is "suitable" within their profession. Similarly, professional firms composed of certified public accountants perform a wide variety of business audits; law firms with large staffs of colleagues solve complex problems in corporate or tax law. This work is supervised and standardized through a system of internal review, which practitioners may expect and even welcome as collegial interaction.

Bureaucratic control over professionals can also be low and generally undisputed as long as goals and techniques are vague and relatively unspecified by either professionals or bureaucratic authorities. Thus the areas of potential conflict or disagreement never become formulated. For example, even within organizations, professional practice may be modeled on the lines of the free professional offering a fee for service. Psychiatry in clinics can often resemble private practice in that the professional and client draw up a contract to their mutual satisfaction. There are technical and financial limitations in the parallel (intensive, long-term therapy usually cannot be offered in this setting); nonetheless the bureaucratic intervention in the professional–client relationship is considered to be slight. Except in times of social revolution and widespread academic unrest, this same situation applies in college teaching. The hierarchy within the bureaucracy follows a "hands off" policy leaving professors and students to work out whatever accommodations they wish. It is only when the bureaucracy makes explicit demands that professors and administrators discover their basic differences.[75]

Thus, when there is conflict about appropriate goals and techniques used by the professional, bureaucratic and professional power are in contest and the relative power of the professional group *vis-à-vis* the organization decides the extent to which bureaucratic control can be enforced. Professionals with relatively little power (such as elementary school teachers) will find techniques and procedures structured for them by the bureaucratic hierarchy attempting to rationalize their organization and make it efficient. The ensuing conflicts illustrate how control of the direction of professional activity may be contested. Really serious conflicts often arise in such jurisdictional disputes. And teachers sometimes reject the "traditional" professional image sufficiently to unionize and strike when they feel that bureaucratic goals set by administrators and members of lay boards of education keep them from meeting what they define as professional goals for teaching.[76] But the administrative staff and board members may charge, or countercharge, that they are in fact attempting to force teachers to take professional responsibility for their students, a responsibility which is now threatened by unionization and striking. In such cases, the power to define appropriate professional goals, behavior, and techniques for reaching goals remains undecided. Similar problems arise today in higher education where professors protest infringements upon their academic freedom and expertise from regents or trustees. At the same time these authorities question the bases for independent authority and "tenure" among professors.[77]

Relatively strong professionals (like specialists in medicine) will be more successful in forcing their definitions of appropriate professional functions upon the bureaucracy. The power of the medical profession in certifying and licensing its practitioners, in effect, provides a very strong union for the membership. In consequence bureaucratic authorities, when they have to act as "management" to such "workers," negotiate very cautiously.

In some cases (as in computer programming or munitions development) jockeying between professionals and bureaucratic authorities often depends upon changes in larger policies beyond the immediate relationship. Changes in such policies for the establishment of priority systems may alternately give the advantage to one group or the other. In periods of national expansion and development, in time of defense spending, or in wartime, professionals in these fields are much in demand. But as of today in 1974 for example economic recession and governmental cutbacks put professionals in areas like aerospace dynamics, computers, or arms development in a poor position to assert their authority and practice their techniques.

5. The Power of External Authority (The Indirect Client)

In the previous section, an attempt has been made to show how the relative power of contesting authorities in the bureaucratic and professional spheres inevitably affects definitions as well as relationships between goals and techniques. Thus the power of some indirect client (or interested party) to enforce some standard of professional service has already been discussed. For any standards made possible by aspects of observability or clarity in professional service have no real meaning without the power to sanction those who depart from these standards. And any power which bureaucratic authorities may possess can only be understood in relation to the supporting, opposing, or neutralizing power of the profession.

Regulatory systems initiated by external authority constantly run afoul of the collegial network or guild structure of professions. If the external authorities are powerful (as is frequently the case in educational institutions) the professionals may be overruled or their protests and arguments ignored. Sometimes, professionals are seriously punished by bureaucratic authorities for what they term "unprofessional" conduct. These occurrences are common in such jurisdictions as social work and teaching despite protestations from professional leaders that the conduct under attack is acceptable and may even be praiseworthy. These eventualities are, however, much rarer when the professional association is powerful and the guild type of structure is more pronounced. Medicine or dentistry, for example, are quick to defend members against sanctions by outsiders. The argument, of course, is that any punitive actions for "unprofessional" or "incompetent" behaviour may only come after peer review. In such instances, professional colleagues are the best judges of what may be observed in a colleague's behaviour, according to professional ideology. The necessity to protect a colleague or to give him every benefit of the doubt may limit the capacities of professional colleagues to make judgments in this area. As noted earlier in Part I, professionals rely heavily upon the idea of individual professional judgment. They are reluctant to suggest that any questionable practice is sufficiently debatable to warrant collegial intervention—even such minor steps as asking a colleague to clarify his motives or to explain his methods may seem too severe. The reluctance of colleagues to question one another—combined with the touchiness of colleagues when they are questioned—limits the utility of observability by colleagues in any accountability structure. These difficulties of collegial policing are exacerbated by the general difficulties which have already been noted (particularly when the relations of goals to techniques are vague), for colleagues may reason that all variation is appropriate and equally acceptable. Such a view promotes professional solidarity but does little to prevent or appease criticism from outsiders.

The significance of the efforts to regulate professional performance clearly depends upon the power mustered by those who make them. The regulations of the Security Exchange Commission or the Internal Revenue Service, have the effect of orders which are sufficiently important to have a considerable effect on the ways in which corporate and tax law are practiced. But where the power of the professional is as great or greater than that of the assessor—as is the case for doctors in hospitals—then the extraprofessional authority does not "order." It must appeal to the practitioners in terms of their own standards. Requests that practitioners accept and then meet performance standards and insistence upon sanctioning violators are only operative in those circumstances if professional groups (such as hospital medical staffs) are willing to act as mediators between bureaucratic hierarchy and practitioners.

Paradoxically the more powerful the profession, the less authority it really does exercise internally over the behaviour of individual practitioners. In a profession as powerful as medicine, practitioners may overrule even the most powerful authority structure by claiming the prerogatives of self-control but then giving little attention to the responsibilities required for internal regulation. For example, medicine in the United States has been expected to supervise and control utilization in such federal programs as Medicare and Medicaid. Yet the crisis in the economics of health care distribution in this country is partially attributed to overuse of the system by physicians, who were supposed to have been controlled by a system of peer review. The medical profession appears to have given lip service to the idea of supervision, but little real supervision has materialized, even though this control mechanism was specifically written into the original legislation as the best means of guarding against excessive use.

Summary and conclusion

These widely varied patterns of adaptation between professional and other organizational systems suggest that virtually all professional systems of review may have to be reorganized: some to be given more power—and some to be given less—when facing outside authorities. In medicine, to continue with that example, even physicians sometimes argue that the problems of control and review of medical performance are only successfully resolved when nonmedical professionals join in the review procedure.[78] It is argued that only "outsiders" can fully represent client interests when they conflict with professional and colleague interests. In contrast, teachers at all levels of the educational hierarchy are requesting a greater

voice in the definition of educational goals, the organization of efforts to attain them, and greater control over educational performance. In this case it is argued that only professionals can protect educational standards against certain elements in the public.

The crucial issue in any accountability system for evaluation of professional service may, however, revolve around what Haug and Sussman[79] have called "The Revolt of the Client". As increasing numbers of persons appear to be dissatisfied with the type of professional services they receive, questions about the established or normative order arise more frequently. The assumption that professional– adhere to ethical standards of behaviour and, therefore, do not require outside supervision is questioned by both direct and indirect clients. Regulatory agencies as representatives of the public are increasingly monitoring aspects of professional– client transactions (in hospital care and health insurance, in banking and investments, in science and teaching).

These trends suggest that new types of accountability systems may be required in the future where professional judgments and client demands (both from direct and indirect clients) will have to be balanced together in a joint review system. Welfare systems, for example, will need to be monitored by welfare clients as well as by legislators and agency administrations. Perhaps no accountability system can ever be really effective without a check and balance system permitting all those affected by the professional service to have a voice in its evaluation and manner of transmittal. Unfortunately, it is just such questions, and the research which they might suggest, which are too often neglected in studies of professions.

At the start of this discussion, a question about the usefulness of professionalism as a sociological concept was raised. Perhaps the limitations of this concept in sociological research can now be better understood. The main consequence of the concept seems to be to put persons who are professionals outside the reach of any accountability system, thus providing the rationale for a "hands off" policy towards the activities of professionals. When issues in the maintenance of standards and the distribution of service are examined, it appears that the crucial issues are autonomy and the power any particular professional group can wield in acquiring or preserving it. If quality of service were *really* a significant issue to professionals, they might be sponsoring research on such matters as the incidence of incompetence or unethical behaviour among their colleagues, and the existence of a service ethic as discerned in actual behaviour among professionals. Instead, the only indications of this ethic are found through attitudinal surveys which, offer opportunity for the expression of pieties. It may or may not be significant that *professionals* do not appear to be sponsoring such studies, but certainly *sociologists of the professions* should be attempting these and related studies. The few now available, which have already been cited (for example those of Becker, Freidson, and Roth) should stand as examples to point the way for further research.

Such research is needed not only for theoretical but also for practical, social programatic reasons. Where individuals do not always have a choice whether or not to accept their services, professionals should be required to justify their claims that benefit will result from the service. Many current problems surrounding the use of mental health and other health care or social service professionals with unwilling

clients (in ghettos, prisons, and state hospitals for example) are involved in this issue. But even more generally, the public is entitled to a more comprehensive understanding of what services professionals can and do really offer them. It seems clear that more research into the actual practices of professionals is needed, rather than unquestioned acceptance of professional ideology, in order to provide information about these issues. This research is particularly important today when increasing numbers of professionals are engaged in some type of public service within an organizational framework. And sociological research can and should contribute empirically verified knowledge to consumers in this area.

References and notes

My first acknowledgement is to Morris J. Daniels of the Department of Sociology at San Diego State College. Many of the ideas expressed in this chapter were first developed with this colleague when we were co-investigators (1967–1970) on an NIH Grant HD 02776–02 to study problems of social change and social control in three professions: psychiatrists, social workers, and certified public accountants. My later thinking on problems of professionalism was most strongly influenced by Eliot Freidson and Julius Roth; therefore I wish to acknowledge my debt to these men as well. Finally, I am indebted once again to Rachel Kahn-Hut for her invaluable editorial and substantive criticisms in this as in all other writing projects of recent years.

1. A.M. Carr-Saunders and P.A. Wilson, *The Professions*, New York: Oxford Clarendon Press, 1933. See also Roy Lewis and Angus Maude, *Professional People*, London: Phoenix House, 1952.
2. Julius A. Roth, Sheryl K. Ruzek, and Arlene K. Daniels, "Current state of the sociology of occupations", *The Sociol. Q.* (Summer 1973), 309–333.
3. Ernest Greenwood, "Attributes of a profession", *Soc. Work*, 2 (July 1957), 45–55.
4. See for example Edward Gross, *Work and Society*, New York: Thomas Y. Crowell-Collier, 1958; Robert Perrucci and Joel E. Gerstl, *Profession without Community: Engineers in American Society*, New York; Random House, 1969; Bernard R. Blishen, *Doctors and Doctrines. The Ideology of Medical Care in Canada*, Toronto: University of Toronto Press, 1969; and Nicholas Alex, *Black in Blue. A Study of the Negro Policeman*, New York: Appleton-Century-Crofts, 1969.
5. See Everett C. Hughes, *Men and Their Work*, Glencoe, Ill.: The Free Press, 1958; and also Hughes, *The Sociological Eye*, Chicago: Aldine-Atherton, 1971.
6. Hughes, *The Sociological Eye*, op. cit., p. 301.
7. *Ibid.*, p. 465.
8. See particularly Howard Becker, "The nature of a profession", *Education for the Professions*, Chicago: National Society for the Study of Education, 1962, pp. 24–46. And see Eliot Freidson, *The Profession of Medicine. A Study of the Sociology of Applied Knowledge*, New York: Dodd, Mead, 1970.

9. *Ibid.*, pp. 71–84.

10. Max Weber, "Politics as a vocation" (pp. 77–128) and "Science as a vocation" (pp. 129–156), in H.H. Gerth and C.W. Mills (Eds), *From Max Weber: Essays in Sociology*, New York: Oxford University Press, 1946.

11. See for example, Hans Zinsser, *Rats, Lice and History*, Boston: Little Brown for the Atlantic Monthly Press, 1935: or Paul De Kruif, *Microbe Hunters*, New York: Harcourt, Brace & Co., 1926.

12. Freidson, *op. cit.*

13. For a more detailed consideration of this particular argument see Arlene K. Daniels, "How free should professions be?", in Eliot Freidson (Ed.), *The Professions and their Prospects*, Beverly Hills, Calif.: Sage Publications, 1974.

14. Weber, *op. cit.*

15. Talcott Parsons, *The Social System*, Glencoe, Ill.: The Free Press, 1951, pp. 428–473; Harold Wilensky, "The professionalization of everyone?", *Am. J. Sociol.*, **70** (Sept 1964), 137–158.

16. Greenwood, *op. cit.*

17. Wilbert E. Moore, *The Professions; Roles and Rules*, New York: Russell Sage Foundation, 1970, pp. 118–119.

18. C.F. Taeusch, *Professional and Business Ethics*, New York; Henry Holt, 1926.

19. See "The Relation between Psychiatrists and Psychologists"—section 6.9—of the 1969 revision of the AMA Principles of Medical Ethics.

20. Julius Roth, "Letter to the Editor", *Am. Sociol.*, **4** (May 1969), 159.

21. Everett Hughes, "Stress and strain in professional education", *Harv. Educ. Rev.*, **29** (Fall 1959), 319–329.

22. See for example, Robert K. Merton, George G. Reader, and Patricia L. Kendall, *The Student Physician*, Cambridge, Mass.: Harvard University Press, 1957; Leonard Eron, "Effect of medical education on medical students' attitudes", *J. Med. Educ.*, **30** (Oct 1955), 559–566; Howard Becker, Blanche Geer, Everett Hughes, and Anselm Strauss, *Boys in White*, Chicago: University of Chicago Press, 1961.

23. See Samuel Bloom, "The process of becoming a physician", *Ann. Am. Acad. Polit. Soc. Sci.*, **346** (March 1963), 77–87; and Seymour E. Harris, *The Economics of American Medicine*, New York: MacMillan, 1964.

24. See Corinne Gibb, *Hidden Hierarchies*, New York: Harper and Row, 1966, for an excellent comparative review of professional licensing practices.

25. See Martin Mayer, *The Lawyers*, New York: Harper and Row, 1966; and D.J. Casler, *The Evolution of CPA Ethics*, Occasional Paper No. 12, East Lansing: Michigan State University, 1964.

26. See Lawrence M. Friedman, "Freedom of contract and occupational licensing 1890–1910: A legal and social study", *Calif. Law Rev.*, **53** (May 1965), 487–534, and Ronald L. Akers, "The professional association and the legal regulations of practice", *Law. Soc. Rev.*, **11** (May 1968), 463–482.

27. For a discussion of how difficult doctors find it to attempt to curb one another see Eliot Freidson and Buford Rhea, "Processes of control in a company of equals", *Soc. Problems*, **11** (Fall 1963), 119–131.

28. Jerome E. Carlin, *Lawyers on their Own*, New Jersey: Rutgers University Press, 1962.
29. E. Freidson (1970), *op. cit.*
30. Experiments and trial programs illustrating these possibilities; for medicine are reported in the *Carnegie Q.*, Carnegie Corporation of New York, **18** (Summer 1970).
31. Richard H. Hall, "Professionalization and bureaucratization," *Am. Sociol. Rev.*, **33** (Feb 1968), 92–104.
32. For a discussion of the power of lay boards in charitable organizations see Mayer N. Zald, "The power and functions of boards of directors; A theoretical synthesis", *Am. J. Sociol.*, **75** (July 1969), 97–111. For some interesting observations on the relative power in hospitals of boards of directors, hospital administrators, and doctors, see Charles Perrow, "The analysis of goals in complex organizations", *Am. Sociol. Rev.*, **26** (Dec 1961), 854–866. For a discussion of the powers of college trustees see James Benét, "The regents as a window on the ruling class", *Change*, **4** (Feb 1972), 22.
33. Carlin, *op. cit.*, and *Lawyer's Ethics*, New York: Russell Sage Foundation, 1966; Arthur L. Wood, *Criminal Lawyer*, New Haven, Conn.: College and University Press, 1967; Erwin O. Smigel, *The Wall Street Lawyer*, Bloomington: Indiana University Press, 1969.
34. Paul D. Montagna, "The public accounting profession; organization, ideology and social power," *Am. Behav. Sci.*, **14** (March–April 1971), 475–491; and "Professionalization and bureaucratization in large professions", *Am. J. Sociol.*, **74** (Sept 1968), 138–145. See also Morris J. Daniels' Monograph on the CPA Profession, San Diego State College (forthcoming).
35. See Barrington Kaye, *The Development of the Architectural Profession in Great Britain*, London: Allen and Unwin, 1960; Alan Lipman, "The architectural belief system and social behaviour", *Br. J. Sociol.*, **20** (June 1969), 190–204. See also the unsigned article "The architects want a voice in redesigning America", *Fortune* (Nov 1971).
36. Robert Perruci and Joel E. Gerstl (Eds), *The Engineers of the Social System*, New York: Wiley, 1969; L.B. Barnes, *Organizational Systems and Engineering Groups*, Boston, Mass.: Harvard Business School, 1960.
37. Eliot Freidson, *Patients' Views of Medical Practice*, New York: Russell Sage Foundation, 1961; and Freidson, *Doctoring Together*, Chicago: Aldine (forthcoming).
38. Morris J. Daniels, *op. cit.*
39. See Mary E.W. Goss, "Influence and authority among physicians in an outpatient clinic", *Am. Sociol. Rev.*, **26** (Feb 1961), 39–50; and "Patterns of bureaucracy among hospital staff physicians", in Eliot Freidson (Ed.), *The Hospital in Modern Society*, Glencoe Ill.: The Free Press, 1963, pp. 170–194; see also Eliot Freidson and Buford Rhea, *op. cit.*
40. Bucher and Stelling argue that the ideas of bureaucratic organization are not entirely relevant to professionals in organizations, for professionals can build their own organizations within the larger system. In the professional frame-

work negotiation and shifting alliances are more important concepts than hierarchical models of authority and subordination. Rue Bucher and Joan Stelling, "Characteristics of professional organizations", *J. Health Soc. Behav.*, **10**, (March 1969), 3–15.

41. Interesting examples of these arguments in law firms may be found in Mayer and Smigel, *op. cit.*

42. See Kenneth Prandy, *Professional Employees—A Study of Scientists and Engineers*, London: Faber and Faber, 1965. His findings indicate that those with less responsibility and authority tend to have a trade union orientation while the engineers with more responsibility and authority keep the "professional" stance and join professional associations rather than trade unions. See also E.J. Dvorak, "Will engineers unionize?" *Indust. Relat.*, **2** (May 1963), 45–66. Efforts at unionizing architectural employees have recently begun in the San Francisco Bay area with some success (two offices are already unionized, while the union has petitioned the NLRB for elections in several others). An interesting contrast of tendencies appears to be emerging between those who follow the traditional labor emphasis on "bread and butter issues", and those union members who strive towards a redefinition of the profession. These latter are concerned with formulating clearer career lines and creating greater participation in the decision-making process of the architectural firm. Some of these issued are discussed—directly and indirectly—in such documents as the *Report of the Task Force on Employer–Employee Relations*, San Francisco, 1970; reported by the American Institute of Architects and the Organization of Architectural Employees: *Profile of Bay Area Architectural Employees*, San Francisco, 1970–1971.

43. See Terance P. Ference, Fred H. Goldner, and Richard R. Ritti, "Priests and Church; The professionalization of an organization", *Am. Behav. Sci.*, **14** (March–April 1971), 507–524.

44. W. Richard Scott, "Professionals in bureaucracies—areas of conflict", in Howard Vollmer and Donald Mills (Eds), *Professionalization*, Englewood Cliffs, N.J.: Prentice-Hall, 1966, pp. 265–274.

44a. See Eliot Freidson, *Professional Dominance*, New York: Atherton Press, 1970.

45. See, for this approach, the work of Scott, *ibid.*, and the collection of essays in Amitai Etzioni (Ed.), *The Semi-Professions and their Organization: Teachers, Nurses, Social Workers*, New York: The Free Press, 1969.

46. For a discussion of some of the conflicts involved in trying to fulfill professional and bureaucratic goals in social work see Archie Hanlan, "Counteracting problems of bureaucracy in public welfare", *Soc. Work*, **12** (July 1967), 88–94; Ralph W. Morgan, "Role performance by social workers in a bureaucracy", *Soc. Work Practice* (1962), 11–126; Sidney Z. Moss and Miriam S. Moss, "When a Caseworker leaves an agency; The impact on worker and client", *Soc. Casework*, **48** (July 1967), 433–437; and Nina Toren, "Semi-professionalism and social work: A theoretical perspective", in Etzioni, *op. cit.*, pp. 141–195.

47. Glenn Greenwood and Robert Frederickson, *Specialization in the Medical and Legal Professions*, Mundelein, Ill.: Callaghan, 1964, discuss the house-counsel briefly; but James F. Davis *et al.* (Eds), in *Society and the Law*, Glencoe, Ill.: The Free Press, 1962 provides a more detailed discussion of the attorney's direct relationship to the organization and notes how formerly he was referred to as a "kept" lawyer by his Wall Street colleagues.

48. See Martin Rein, "Social planning; The search for legitimacy", *J. Am. Inst. Plan.* (July 1969), 233–244; Francis Fox Piven, "Whom does the advocate planner serve?", *Soc. Policy*, (May–June 1970), 32–37; Paul Davidoff and Thomas Reiner, "A choice theory of planning", *JAIP* (May 1962), 103–115.

49. See, for example, the following: John J. Hanlon, *Principles of Public Health Administration*, St. Louis: Mosby, 1965; Mary F. Arnold, "Perceptions of professional role activities in the local health department", *Public Health Reports*, **77** (1962), 80–88; E.M. Cohart and W.R. Willard, "Experience of public health workers", *Public Health Reports*, **70** (1955), 1116–1124.

50. For a discussion of some variations on this problem in other societies see Mark G. Field "The doctor-patient relationship in the perspective of fee for service and third-party medicine", *J. Health Hum. Behav.*, **2** (Winter 1961), 252–262; Joseph Ben-David, "The professional role of the physician in bureaucratized medicine: A study of role conflict", *Hum. Relat.*, **2**, 3 (1958), 255–274.

51. See Kurt W. Back *et. al.*, "Public health as a career of medicine; secondary choice within a profession", *Am. Sociol Rev.*, **23** (Oct 1958), 533–541.

52. Freidson, in his discussion of Florence Nightingale, points out that she refused to allow nurses to serve at their own initiative but only under doctor's orders. From its inception then, "Nursing was thus defined as a subordinate part of the technical division of labor surrounding medicine". Freidson, 1970, *op. cit.*, p. 61. See also Donna F. Ver Steeg, "The fictional nurse . . . Is she for real?" *Nurs. Outlook*, **16**, 8 (Aug 1968), 20–23 for an interesting and amusing account of how the subordination of nurses appears in romantic novels produced for the mass media.

53. See Sheryl K. Ruzek, "Making social work accountable", in Eliot Freidson (Ed.), *The Professions and Their Prospects*, Beverly Hills, Calif: Sage Publications, 1974; David J. Kallen, Dorothy Miller, and Arlene K. Daniels, "Sociology, social work and social problems", *Am. Sociol.*, **3** (Aug 1968), 235–239; Harold Wilensky and Charles Lebeaux, *Social Welfare and Industrial Society*, New York: Russell Sage Foundation, 1958.

54. See Harmon Ziegler, *The Political World of the High School Teacher*, Eugene, Oregon: Center for the Advanced Study of Educational Administration, University of Oregon, 1966; Harmon Ziegler, *The Political Life of American Teachers*, Englewood Cliffs, N.J.: Prentice-Hall, 1967; see also Stephen Cole, *The Unionization of Teachers: A Case Study of the UFT*, New York: Praeger, 1969; Ronald G. Corwin, *Militant Professionalism—A Study of Organizational Conflict in High Schools*, New York: Appleton-Century-Crofts, 1970.

55. See Arlene K. Daniels, and Rachel Kahn-Hut, *Academics on the Line*, San Francisco: Jossey-Bass, 1970 and Robert Smith, Richard Axen, and Devere Pentony, *By Any Means Necessary*, San Francisco: Jossey-Bass, 1970.

56. See William J. Goode, "The librarian: From occupation to profession?", *The Library Q.*, **31** (Oct 1961), 306–318, reprinted in *Professionalization*, Vollmer and Mills (Eds), *op. cit.*, pp. 34–43, See also Guy F. Lyle *et al.*, *The Administration of the College Library*, New York: Wilson, 1961.

57. William Kornhauser, *Scientists in Industry: Conflict and Accommodation*, Berkeley: University of California Press, 1962.

58. Barney G. Glazer, *Organizational Scientists. Their Professional Careers*, Indianapolis: Bobbs-Merrill, 1964, and see also Mark Abrahamson, "Informal groups in the research laboratory", in *The Professional in the Organization*, Chicago: Rand-McNally, 1967, pp. 63–70. For a most amusing, satiric view of scientists in organizations see Robert Sommer, *Expertland*, Garden City, New York: Doubleday, 1963.

59. Melville Dalton, *Men Who Manage*, New York: Wiley, 1959.

60. For a discussion of how one profession fits into the military mission see Arlene K. Daniels, "A sub-specialty within a professional specialty: Military psychiatry", in Eliot Freidson and Judith Lorber (Eds), *Medical Men and Their Work*, Chicago: Aldine-Atherton, 1972.

60a. Waldo W. Burchard, "Role conflicts of military chaplains", *Am. Sociol. Rev.*, **19** (Oct 1954), 528–535; Gordon Z. Zahn, *The military chaplaincy: A study of role tension in the air force*", Toronto: University of Toronto Press, 1969.

61. Roy E. Clausen and Arlene K. Daniels, "Role conflicts and their ideological resolution in military psychiatric practice, *Am. J. Psychiat.*, **123** (Sept 1966), 280–287. See also Arlene K. Daniels, "Normal mental illness and understandable excuses: The philosophy of combat psychiatry", *Am. Behav. Sci.*, **14** (Nov–Dec 1970), 167–184.

62. Philip Selznick, *The Organizational Weapon*, New York: McGraw-Hill, 1952. See also Selznick's *Leadership in Administration*, Evanston, Ill.: Row, Peterson, 1957, for a discussion of how "professionalism", in organizations is expected to solve administrative problems.

63. Francine Du Plessix Gray, "The sugar-coated fortress", *The New Yorker*, **48** (March 4, 1972), 46.

64. See Julius A. Roth and Elizabeth M. Eddy, *Rehabilitation for the Unwanted*, New York: Atherton Press, 1967; Renee Fox, "A sociological perspective on organ transplantation and hemodialysis", *Ann. N.Y. Acad. Sci.*, **196** (Jan 1970), 406–428.

65. In societies with strong, centralized powers, professionals should have fewer difficulties in validating the legitimacy of their goals. The Soviet physician, for example, should find little overt resistance to the view that treating the sick should occur within a value system which gives prominence to the productive individual who rapidly returns to work after an illness. See Mark Field, *Doctor and Patient in Soviet Russia*, Cambridge Mass.: Harvard University Press, 1957.

66. See, for example, Charles Kadushin, *Why People Go to Psychiatrists*, New York: Atherton Press, 1969.

67. In California, arguments about these matters have raged for some time. Governor Ronald Reagan made headlines when he suggested that the University Rare Book Collection could be auctioned off in order to help meet the expenses of the library. More recently, there have been accusations and denials of extravagance over just what books the library ought to buy. The Reagan administration charged it was a waste of money to purchase seven copies of 19th Century British Parliamentary Papers for $350 000. (*S.F. Chronicle*, Tuesday, Feb 29, 1972). The following day the acting librarian defended the purchase on the grounds that such volumes are widely used by students in many specialties and that microfilms are much too difficult to use—and too costly in themselves—to be a successful alternative. Eldred Smith, the acting librarian, summed up his professional judgment of the necessity for such purchases by saying: "If a campus is going to attempt to provide substantial graduate instruction, it must have readily available library sources". (*S.F. Chronicle*, Wednesday, March 1, 1972).

68. See J.A.N. Ellis, "The sociologist as interpreter on an interdisciplinary team, The use of social research in architectural planning". Paper presented at the American Sociological Association Convention, Washington D.C., 1970. See also T.E. Lasswell and C.M. Deasy, "The measurement of values, goals and strains in architectural programming". Paper presented at the American Sociological Association Convention, Washington D.C., 1970.

69. See Carlin, 1966, *op. cit.*

70. See, C. Wright Mills, *White Collar*, New York: Oxford University Press, 1953; Hall, 1968, *op. cit.*

71. See John W. Kinch, "The Failure of Gentlemen's Agreements", in Daniels and Kahn-Hut, *op. cit.*, 130–139.

72. Weber in Gerth and Shils, "Bureaucracy", *op. cit.*, 196–230.

73. See Smigel and Mayer, *op. cit.*

74. Except in times of social revolution, see Ference *et al.*, *op. cit.*

75. See Sherri Cavan, "Aristocratic workers," in Daniels and Kahn-Hut, *op. cit.*, pp. 170–181.

76. See Marie Haug and Marvin Sussman, "Professionalization and unionism", in Eliot Freidson (Ed.), *The Professions and Their Prospects*, Beverly Hills, Calif.: Sage Publications (forthcoming).
    See also Cole, Corwin, and Zeigler, *op. cit.*

77. Daniels and Kahn-Hut, *op. cit.*

78. See John Knowles, Statement Reported in the Convention Bulletin, American Hospital Association (Sept 16), 1970.

79. See Marie Haug, and Marvin Sussman, "Professional autonomy and the revolt of the client", *Soc. Problems*, **17** (Fall 1969), 153–160.

JOHN B. McKINLAY

CLIENTS AND ORGANIZATIONS

John B. McKinlay *is an Associate Professor of Sociology at Boston Univer-*
sity. He received his B.A. from the Victoria University of Wellington in
New Zealand, and his Ph.D. from Aberdeen University in Scotland. He is
interested in the sociology of medicine and social welfare, the formation of
subcultures among members of total institutions and the philosophy of social
science. Before moving to Boston, he was Visiting Professor at the University
of California, Los Angeles. His current teaching and research includes
professions and clients, social stratification and poverty.

This chapter aims to sensitize the reader to a body of literature which, in the author's view, is illustrative of a newly emerging orientation to formal organizations. No attempt will be made either to comprehensively review all the literature pertaining to this new orientation, or to trace out its various antecedents. Rather, the author will be quite selective and concentrate on a body of literature which highlights particular problems and developments.

No one can doubt that twentieth century Western societies have witnessed a phenomenal growth and expansion of formal organizations—be it education, entertainment, employment, health care—nearly every area of social life is being affected.[1] Clearly, formal organizations have been with us for a relatively long time but some observers suggest that the characteristic form of organizations has changed somewhat—from charismatic and traditional organizations to large-scale bureaucracies and professional organizations—and pervade our lives in new and previously unforeseen ways. As Boulding (among others) has warned, the "organizational revolution" is upon us.[2]

Paralleling this trend has been the body of social theory—developed mainly within a political context—concerning the emergence of "mass" society.[3] Very briefly, this theory holds that the destruction of old community life has separated the individual from binding social ties and that his or her isolation results in a sense of powerlessness which can be both personally devastating as well as destructive of democratic processes.[4] It is further proposed that organizations mediating between the individual and the wider society serve as a bulwark against the development of such alienation.[5] One of the major protagonists of this view, Kornhauser, claims that:

> Meaningful and effective participation in the larger society requires a structure of groups intermediate between the family and the nation: without such groups the

individual cannot readily perceive himself as having the capacity to determine his life and to affect the lives of others.[6]

In a recent empirical study of this organization mediation thesis, it was found that membership in a work-based organization is associated with a feeling of relatively strong control over events, and that the greater perceived powerlessness of the unorganized worker is not simply a function of socio-economic status.[7] Although the results from this study appear fairly clear, they illustrate along with other findings, the difficulty of not specifying the direction of causality. One would like to know, for example, whether participation in or association with organizations actually reduces feelings of alienation or whether in fact the nonalienated are more likely to become involved with organizations. If the former interpretation is correct, and there is supportive evidence for it, then it becomes clear that the estrangement of certain groups from organizational life can be regarded as a serious disadvantage, and the current trend towards increasing bureaucretization can only result in further alienation from the mainstream of social life.

It should be emphasized that there is still considerable debate over the tenability of the mass society thesis and the plausibility of some of its assumptions and implications. Some theorists subscribe to the view that, far from becoming mediating forces allowing individual expression and control, formal organizations are simply agencies for further alienation.[8] Mills espouses this view and even attributes it to voluntary activity when he writes:

> Voluntary associations . . . have lost their grip on the individual. As more people are drawn into the political arena, these associations become mass in scale; and as the power of the individual becomes more dependent upon such mass associations they are less accessible to the individual's influence.[9]

Certainly, since the early writings of Marx appeared, one of the major themes of sociology and social philosophy has been the attempt to locate the antecedents of alienation.[10] There now appears to be widespread agreement that industrialization and its concomitant bureaucratization, are primary contributors to alienation in various spheres of social life and their influence extends far beyond the workplace. However, with few exceptions, there has been a tendency in the literature to postulate a direct relationship between bureaucratization and alienation without specifying the bureaucratic *characteristics* related to different forms or *dimensions* of alienation.[11] Bonjean and Grimes have recently tackled this question by examining the relationships between five bureaucratic characteristics and six forms of alienation among separate samples of hourly paid workers, salaried managers and independent businessmen.[12] The authors conclude that their data do not support the broad generalization that a direct relationship exists between bureaucratization and alienation. They do, however, propose the following modifications: (a) that bureaucracy may be directly related to alienation among blue-collar workers, but not among salaried managers or independent businessmen; (b) that the authority dimensions of bureaucracy are more closely related to measures of alienation that other bureaucratic characteristics, among hourly paid workers; and (c) the form of alienation among hourly paid workers is self-estrangement. In general, therefore, it does seem that bureaucratization and alienation may be in some way related to each other, but the precise form and direction of the relationship, as well as the social situations in which the relationship appears more manifest, are just beginning to be described and systematically researched.

Indeed, many unanswered—and often unformulated—questions present themselves when attention is directed towards formal organizations, particularly in relation to clients. For instance, one may ask in what ways (if at all) do client, patient, or inmate characteristics affect the structure of organizations? Do lower status employees and inmates (clients) exert any influence on organizational functioning? To what extent can professionals in organizations be regarded as "free" to operate solely in the client's interests? What purposes may "creaming" serve for both officials in organizations and the success of organizational practice? Does the nature of client–official interaction vary in different organizational contexts? How do various caretaker organizations retain control over "difficult cases", with what results for inmates or clients subsequent self concept and behavior? It is to these and related questions that this chapter addresses itself.

Client characteristic and structural outcomes

Many of the ideas in this section of the present chapter have been strongly influenced by the work of Lefton and Rosengren. My debt to them will become obvious, and is here gratefully acknowledged.

While researching and teaching in the area loosely termed "formal organizations" in both Great Britain and the United States, the author has found it useful to distinguish between five separate perspectives on organizations. They are listed here and briefly discussed in order that they may form a backdrop for discriminating between the central concerns of each of the preceding chapters, as well as clearly separating the foci of the present chapter from those concerned with other areas. Although not exhaustive, the following categorization has been developed in order to indicate both the range and scope of different approaches, and a number of new directions in current sociological research. Clearly, many studies and writings do not fall easily into only one, or even several, of the categories which follow. Additionally, each perspective listed involves a somewhat different set of theoretical concerns and methodological strategies.

Very briefly then, the five general perspectives are as follows:

(a) *From the outside looking in*—here the central focus is on the way in which the social, demographic and cultural characteristics of the surrounding community influence both the structure and functioning of various organizations.[13]

(b) *From the top looking down*—here one often conceives of organizations as hierarchical, "flow chart" type structures and attention is directed at the problems of top administration and management in maintaining the system by setting and realizing goals.[14]

(c) *From the inside looking around*—here attention is directed at aspects of the social behavior of staff within the organization.[15] Studies concerning, for example, organization and marginal man, bureaucratic personality, employee role behavior, worker satisfaction, etc. could be categorized under this heading.

(d) *From the bottom looking up*—here the central concern is with the behavior of "external" clients with regard to some formal organization.[16] Much of the literature on the utilization behavior of certain social categories, for example, would be included in this general category.

(e) *Insides Out*—of primary importance for this perspective is the behavior of "internal" clients in what have come to be termed "total institutions."[17] The literature concerning degradation and self-mortification in mental hospitals and prisons would fall into this category.

These five general approaches may be regrouped into two main orientations. The first three give emphasis to certian *characteristics of organizations themselves*, while the latter two approaches emphasize the perspective of external or internal *clients in relation to organizations*. Generally speaking, the literature on organizations has been biased towards the first orientation, particularly the "top looking down" and "inside looking around" perspectives. Despite this continued bias however, there are many signs of an emerging interest in the client and inmate orientation. Reflecting, to some extent, this bias in available work, most of the contributors to his volume have quite naturally opted for aspects of the first three approaches. The principal concerns of the present chapter are with the latter two perspectives on organizations ("bottom looking up" and "insides out"). This interest is, of course, not entirely new. Such well known theorists as Parsons, Blau and Scott, Perrow, Etzioni, Eisenstadt, Glaser, and Strauss (among others) have all underlined the influence of client characteristics on the structure of organizations.[18]

There are, of course, many alternative ways in which different perspectives on formal organizations can be analytically distinguished. Lefton and Rosengren, for example, have isolated what they regard as four distinct traditions in the study of formal organizations.[19] *Firstly*, there are those studies and writings, perhaps best represented by the bureaucratic models developed from Weber's ideal-type conception.[20] The prime concern of this approach has been with the operating functionaries of organizations, rather than with the clients they serve. *Secondly*, there is the "community structure" tradition, which emphasizes the impact of the demographic and ecological characteristics of the surrounding community upon the structure and functioning of organizations.[21] *Thirdly*, there is what Lefton and Rosengren call the "social system approach" which focuses primarily upon the structural linkages by which the functional prerequisites of organizations— seen as subsystems—are integrated with and accommodated to the institutional system of the larger social order.[22] This particular approach appears to preclude any direct concern with the role of clients in organizations, precisely because of the abstract level of analysis at which such concerns are generally expressed. *Finally*, there is the tradition represented by the work of symbolic interactionists. This approach conceives of formal organizational structures and processes as having only secondary importance, providing merely a contextual backdrop against which processes of self-identity, situational definitions, role emergence, and symbolic verification are, for various interactants, brought into bold relief.[23]

Lefton and Rosengren argue that none of these four distinct traditions attempt to describe the linkages between clients on the one hand, and formal organizational structures on the other. With some empirical justification, they proceed from the premise that organizations vary in their concern with the careers of their clients along two major dimensions. One primary concern is with the length of contact between the client and the organization which may range from a highly truncated span of time (as in the casualty department or emergency room of a general hospital) to a nearly indeterminate span of time (as in a long-term prison). This concern for the client's biographical time is termed the *longitudinal* dimension. There is a second range of interests concerning the client's biographical space. Here the organization may have an interest in but a limited aspect of the client's social life or milieu. This concern for the client's biographical space is termed the *lateral* dimension. The short-term remand home or approved school is one example of this lateral interest. Other organizations have a broader scope of interest in clients, as in the care offered by, say, a psychiatric outpatient clinic. In such a situation the longitudinal dimension usually concerns social time, and the lateral dimension, social space.[24]

Lefton and Rosengren emphasize that lateral and longitudinal interest in the biographical careers of clients may vary independently of each other. They distinguish between four logically different patterns, each of which is thought to affect the internal structural and interpersonal processes of organizations, as well as extra-organizational relationships. The notion of *plus-laterality*(+) expresses the extent to which a client-serving organization takes the "whole" person into account in its efforts to effect given social, psychological or physical changes. Its converse, *minus-laterality*(−) describes a purposively restricted focus on specific or segmented features of clients. A comparable distinction can also be made between plus and minus longitudinally. The four biographical variants with illustrations from the area of medical care are depicted in table 1.

Table 1

Empirical examples	Lateral (social space)	Longitudinal (social time)
Acute general hospital	—	—
T.B. hospital, Rehabilitation hospital, etc.	—	+
Short-term therapeutic psychiatric hospital	+	—
Long-term therapeutic hospital	+	+

After a valuable discussion of these four biographical variants, along with supportive examples, Lefton and Rosengren consider the consequences of such variation in terms of, among other areas, client compliance, staff consensus and inter-organizational collaboration. It remains for researchers to follow up some of the theoretical and empirical ramifications of this noteworthy contribution, and to test its applicability to other organizations such as schools, prisons and welfare agencies. The purpose of describing in some detail the work of Lefton and Rosengren at this point has been twofold. *First*, it reinforces the earlier discussion of the importance of redressing the present imbalance in current analyses by considering the ways in which clients influence and shape organizational structure. *Second*, to acquaint the reader with a body of work which, in the author's view, holds considerable promise for future studies and supports the emerging client orientation.

Professionals in organizations

Increasingly, skepticism is being voiced concerning the professed activity of certain formal organizations. There is a body of evidence accumulating which suggests that organizations seldom accomplish what their formal charter and the claims of administrators or representatives suggest.[25] Although, of course, formal organizations have both manifest and latent functions, with many it is difficult to determine what precise latent functions its members subscribe to. Such organizations, with a variety of resources, manpower, access to mass media, etc., are able to persuade the public that their manifest functions are, in fact, the real and only functions of the organization. So we see in the United States for example, that EXXON oil is primarily interested in dissolving oil slicks and purifying water, Ford Motors is "concerned" to reduce exhaust emission and minimize air pollution and Chevrolet is anxious to ensure that every American has a "better way in which to see the U.S.A."[26] If one was to take such claims seriously, it would seem that the generation of hollow consumer needs and the desire for profit are the very last interests of the giant corporations. However, the closer one looks, the more one finds that, despite claims to the contrary, hospitals are really not patient-oriented, prisons seldom rehabilitate inmates, universities and schools are prey to market rather than educational demands, industrial concerns are really only interested in maximizing profits, and that even voluntary organizations serve to dissolve employee conscience pangs as much as they improve the lot of those they are supposedly assisting.

These rather superficial and somewhat ephemeral organizational "concerns" for certain groups and issues illustrate the way in which organizations use ideologies with the explicit intention of energizing certain groups toward acting in the organization's interests, and perhaps those of groups who are in a position to benefit from such action. With this phenomenon in mind, Krause investigated the ways in which the concept "citizen participation" is being used by certain bureaucracies (urban renewal and community action programs) in the United States in an ideological manner.[27] He suggests that certain target groups (usually the poor) may be placed in an invidious position when bureaucracies offer them the "citizen participation" ideology. They may lose if they participate, and they sometimes lose if they do not participate. Krause concludes that participation in the manifest activities espoused by the bureaucracy are *either* directly detrimental to the welfare of those asked to participate (urban renewal) *or* the bureaucracy becomes involved on behalf of a powerless or unliked target group (Office of Economic Opportunity) which activity is unacceptable to the wider population. Rather than dying away in Western societies, as Bell has suggested, Krause claims that ideologies are becoming primary tools used by large and powerful bureaucracies.[28] If his conclusions are correct, and present trends continue, then the use of ideologies by large-scale formal organizations constitute a threat to the individual's capacity to exercise some control over development in his society.

Faced with manifestly deceptive or exaggerated claims by organizations, clients may decide to reject the publically presented ideology. In such a situation, according to Fisher, the organization or helping group may move in four different ways: it may try to alter its ideology and the nature of the helping claim; it may try to alter its structure in order to effect its claims; it may seek to change the response of its clients; or it may attempt to change the make-up of its clientele.[29] It is suggested that changes in any one or more of these directions are ultimately far-reaching, for they all involve some change in the organization or helping group itself.

Fisher divides the ways in which organizations may alter their ideologies or claims into six main categories: (1) *scale*—how much the organization claims it will do for its clients; (2) *scope*—how wide a group or how many sorts of clients the organization promises to service; (3) *time schedule*—when or over what periods of time the organization claims it has serviced or will service its clients; (4) *location*—the place at which service is claimed to be best given; (5) *technique*—what technological or organizational measures the organization claims will result in the most effective means of service; and (6) *the end*—for which the organization claims it is undertaking its service work.

Given the apparent disparity between the claims and performance of certain organizations there appears to be a general public tendency to turn to and place reliance on the role of professionals as a counterbalance to this emphasis.[30] This public conception of professionals and the general credibility given to the altruistic claims of professionals underlies a central theoretical question which is presently claiming the attention of many sociologists. Simply put it is: How autonomous are professionals in formal organizations? Various aspects of this question are, of course, addressed by Daniels in an earlier chapter.

The traditional model of the professional has always been one of the free agent contracting to perform a service for a client.[31] It is thought that the client can choose his own professional and the first loyalty of the professional is always to his/her client. This conception has recently been challenged, however, on the grounds that it gives little attention to the numbers of professionals who have always been employed in organizations and the changes which such employment brings about in the professional relationship over time.[32] Unfortunately, the notion of the "free professional" ignores the ways in which conflicting values exert pressures upon the professional particularly where third parties intervene in a relationship with a client. Professionals with a basic mandate to provide a personal service to some individual may find this mandate directly or indirectly challenged by organizational priorities which require either the practitioner or his client to give primacy to other considerations. Recent sociological studies of professionals in organizations seriously question how "free" professionals really are.

Where the rewards are high enough, professionals may adapt their professional ideas of competence, rewards and status to the value system of the organization they serve.[33] Kornhauser shows, for example, that scientists in industry are pressured to subordinate their basic research interests to applied commercial problems of concern to their employers.[34] Goldner and Ritti show how readily professionals abandon their own work for administrative duties so as to rise within the status hierarchy of their employing organization.[35] Merton has suggested that intellectuals who enter the government service face similar predicaments.[36] In the area of psychiatry, Szasz has argued that once the professional moves into a bureaucratic setting he becomes unrecognizable.[37] The focus of the psychiatrist's concern can no longer be on helping the patient since his professional rights and duties have been redefined by his organizational context. Indeed, Burchard observed that conflicts in basic differences between the professional and organizational values are sometimes so readily resolved in favor of the organization that often no conflict is seen.[38] When military chaplains were asked how they resolved the discrepancy between Biblical commandments against killing and their loyalty to the military organization, most reported that they did not see any conflict. Barber and his colleagues show that the social structure of competition and reward in science for priority of discovery and recognition and prestige that go with it leads to the devaluation of therapy and to more permissive behavior in the use of human subjects for experimentation.[39]

Returning to the concept of professionals as mediators between the client and some formal organization, many researchers have noted and described the breakdown in communication between clients on the one hand, and professionals on the other. Culpability for this breakdown is generally attributed to the characteristics of clients, the argument usually being as follows:

> (1) The gap between client culture (values, beliefs, definitions of situations and patterns of response) on the one hand, and the orientations of professionals and the basic rationale of organizations on the other is enormous, and is reinforced in bureaucratic encounters.[40]
> (2) Because clients often have a limited role repertoire, with few opportunities to rehearse or adopt new roles in different settings, they misunderstand the formalism of the official, are unable to adopt the role of the listener and are limited in their ability to display role distance.[41]
> (3) With a truncated education, certain clients often have no facility with form filling, experience difficulty in verbalizing feelings and thoughts, and have limited access to information sources regarding both their eligibility for services and where to receive what they believe they are entitled.[42]

It is now clear, from studies of lower-class life styles in particular, as well as from certain aspects of formal organizations, that not all subgroups of a society have an equal facility with and the requisite expertise for performing effectively in certain types of formal organizations.[43] As a consequence, clients from various social categories have been labeled "ignorant", "lazy", "irresponsible"—often in quotation marks, perhaps to denote their nonpejorative sophistication—like "multi-problem", "unstable family", "culturally deprived", and "culture of poverty". Nearly all of these labels imply that something is lacking in clients who experience difficulty with professionals and agencies.[44]

Perhaps it is understandable that professionals and the administrators of formal organizations tend to ascribe culpability to potential consumers for the failure of misconceived programs. Unfortunately, blaming clients does not take one very far—indeed some claim it does more harm than good. A group of researchers working mainly in the area of the sociology of deviance suggest that the process of labeling an offender and making him conscious of himself as a deviant may reinforce the very behaviour which is regarded as "inappropriate".[45] Merton, although concerned with a different type of problem, has described such a process as a "self-fulfilling prophecy" and Lemert has coined the phrase "secondary deviance" to draw attention to the possibility that a person may act in an even more extreme fashion as a consequence of the definition and labeling of his behavior by mandated labelers.[46] Such subsequent behavior, according to the "labeling" theorists, may be substantially similar to the original, primary deviance, but has as its source the individual's revised self-conception of him in the community.[47]

While there is then a body of evidence supporting the view that certain clients experience "communication problems" with professionals and agencies, this can only be regarded as a partial explanation of the communication breakdown. Such a view overlooks or deemphasizes certain professional and organizational factors which foster, and perhaps even encourage, the difficulties.

Increasingly, attention is being directed at the ways in which aspects of the behavior of officials and of professionals may influence client–professional encounters. This perspective contrasts sharply with traditional research (which ascribes culpability to patients for the breakdown of interaction) and focuses on the treatment stereotypes—professional's or "official's" hold of clients and conditions, and the ways in which these may influence the treatment process. Balint, for example, has described the activity of doctors with regard to patients, as "apostolic", to draw attention to the way in which they seek to proselytize their patients into having the diseases that the doctor thinks appropriate in their case:

> Apostolic mission or function means in the first place that every doctor has a vague, but almost unshakably firm, idea of how a patient ought to behave when ill. Although this idea is anything but explicit and concrete, it is immensely powerful, and influences, as we have found, practically every detail of the doctor's work with his patients. It was almost as if every doctor had revealed knowledge of what was right and what was wrong for patients to expect and to endure, and further, as if he had a sacred duty to convert to his faith all the ignorant and unbelieving among his patients.[48]

The use of such stereotypes has been further explored in some detail by Sudnow who studied the processing of cases by a public defender in the court of a large city in the United States.[49] He suggests that for the public defender, the effective diagnostic unit is the *typical* kind of crime for the city at a given point in time. Sudnow showed how the public defender thinks in terms of stereotypic crimes, and how his questioning of a defendant is not so much an attempt to find the unique facts of the case, but to discover the extent to which the defendant fits the court's stereotyped category of criminal. It is suggested that the categories employed by the public defender help to maintain the smooth-running of the court, without gross violation of either the courts' concepts of punishment, or the defendant's own rights.

After discussing earlier work in this area Scheff has suggested that diagnostic stereotypes operate in many kinds of treatment, control and welfare agencies, with differential consequencies.[50] He argues that in, say, a surgical ward, diagnostic stereotypes may be used as preliminary hypotheses which are subsequently retained or rejected after further clinical examination. In the kind of situation already described by Sudnow, he suggests that diagnostic stereotypes appear to be not only first hypotheses, but also the final result of the investigation, with a marked tendency for the medical profession to accept these stereotypes with a minimal attempt to determine their goodness of fit with the case at hand.

Scheff has presented the following set of propositions in an attempt to relate the type of situation, the type of organization, and the functional importance of the diagnostic stereotypes:

(1) The more numerous the stereotypes that are actually used in the agency, the more precise they will be; and the more precise, the more valid they will be.

(2) The more the status of the client is inferior to and different from that of the staff, whether because of economic position, ethnicity, race, education, etc., the more inaccurate and final the normal cases will be.

(3) The less dependent the agent is on the client's good will, the less precise and valid the stereotypes will be.

(4) The more substantial or scientific the body of knowledge (in the agency or profession handling the clients), the more valid and accurate the conceptual packages.

(5) The successfulness of staff members' socialization into an agency can be determined by the extent to which he employs the prevailing conceptual packages.

(6) In terms of the agency's criteria, proficiency, effectivness and eligibility for promotion are determined by the consistency with which staff members employ the prevailing conceptual packages.[51]

Emphasis has already been given to the importance of studying what actually goes on between clients and professionals and/or agencies. It is now clear that organizational factors, and aspects of professional behavior, may be just as important as, if not more important than, the characterological features of clients, in understanding the nature of client relationships with officials and organizations. There is no doubt that much of the work to date has been undertaken from an organizational or "official" perspective. To employ sociological jargon, past research has been primarily concerned with *professionals' typifications of clients* and the social, structural and psychological factors which foster their emergence, reinforce and perpetuate their existence.[52] The importance of understanding the nature of officials' definitions of clients, of locating their sources, and of considering their subsequent effect on service provision should not, of course, be underemphasized. However, it is equally important that the counter or oppositional *typifications of professionals and agencies by clients* be examined. These two aspects are equally important because, in a sense, they appear to have their source one in another, and seemingly reinforce one another.

An area therefore, which in the author's view deserves the increasing attention of researchers, relates to the study of clients themselves, and organizational impedimenta from the clients' perspective. While there is a considerable amount of knowledge relating to the organizational structural basis of professionals' definitions of clients, we have hardly any information at all about the types or sources of clients' definitions of professionals and agencies. It would be valuable, for example, to know whether, and to what extent, certain client definitions or typifications of agencies are specific to certain types of organization, or specific to a certain area of activity regardless or organizational type. Useful also in this respect would be information regarding whether and under what circumstances certain definitions are transferred from agency to agency and the subsequent effect on the interpersonal strategies adopted to obtain services. Research on clients and organizations in the seventies will probably become increasingly preoccupied with various organizational effects on behavior. One would hope that the current imbalance, will not be perpetuated and that clients themselves, in relation to the organizations they utilize, will be studied.

Who controls organizations?

Reflecting the ideologies of the very entities they were studying, sociologists for a long time have conceived of or fostered an image of formal organizations as a fairly rigid hierarchical system whose daily operations are controlled from the top. Such a perspective views top administrators and officials as formulating policy and practice and initiating a downward flow of information with people in the lower echelons ensuring compliance with administrative directives. This somewhat rigid and simplistic formulation has largely resulted from "ivory tower" theorizing and has little empirical support. Unfortunately, it is also a conception which, for a variety of reasons, is congenial to and widely accepted by administrators and planners. In relation to the author's five basic perspectives on formal organizations, this could be termed the "top looking down approach".

However, it appears, from considerable field research, that in reality formal organizations are influenced (perhaps even controlled) from the bottom, as well as, or instead of, from the top. Certainly, it seems that both inmates or clients and lower employees within formal organizations wield considerable power and influence not associated with their formally defined position. Such participants may be said to have informal personal power, but little formal authority. Generally speaking, this personal power does not result from the unique characteristics or personalities of its wielders (although these may be relevant) but rather from particular aspects of their position within the organization, and additional features of the organization itself.

Several studies may be cited which illustrate this complementary (not necessarily conflicting) "bottom looking up" perspective. Scheff, for example, has described the failure of a state mental hospital to implement change through the opposition of hospital attendants.[53] From this study, it seems that the power of the attendants resulted mainly from dependence on them by the hospital's physicians—a dependence fostered by such factors as the physician's short tenure and his disinterest in administrative tasks, etc. An implicit agreement appeared to develop between the physicians and the attendants, whereby the latter would take on some of the responsibilities and obligations of the ward physician in return for increased power in decision-making processes concerning the patients.

From a similar study of prison guards, Sykes found that although guards could report inmates for disobedience, frequent reporting appeared to give prison officials the impression that the guard was unable to command obedience from the inmates.[54] The guards therefore, had some stake in ensuring the good behavior of prisoners without the use of formal sanctions against them. According to Sykes, this resulted in an informal agreement whereby the guards allowed minor violations of certain rules in return for cooperative behavior from the inmates—an example of control wielded by "internal" clients. A similar situation has been experienced by the author in respect to both secondary schooling—where students challenged a reluctant teacher to inform "the boss" (headmaster) of their misbehavior—and approved schools (where trainees challenged housemasters to inform "Big Dad" (principal) of some misdemeanor). In both cases, the use of a nickname, in addition to the issuance of a challenge further distanced the challenger (client) from the formal expectations of the organization. Several other researchers have investigated the ways in which patients in hospitals obtain information which is pertinent to their case and the ways in which they use this information to bargain or negotiate with medical staff over the precise scheduling of important events within the hospital.[55]

Mechanic also supports this interpretation and regards the power which clients or members may assume within formal organizations, as a consequence of access to and control of a person's, information, and instrumentalities.[56] The aspects of organizational structure which Mechanic sees as conducive to the assumption of power by such participants are: the time spent in the organization, the centrality of the participant's position, duality of power structures, and the replaceability of people.

Contrary to what one might expect, the balance of power between, say, internal inmates, low status employees and higher status administrators does not appear dependent on the type of formal organization involved. The logical concept that the more closed an institution is, the more limited the power of the lower participants in it, does not appear to hold. At first sight of course one would think that internal inmates would have very limited power (if any at all) in say, a prison or concentration camp. Even in these situations however it has been found that inmates are able to exercise some maneuverability—admittedly usually by subtle and surreptitious means—and influence organizational outcomes.[57] In more open situations, where internal inmates or external clients are not continually present (e.g. a university or public welfare agency) there may be, of course, more freedom for the exercise of informally assumed power. The ways in which students obtain extensions for course papers, or have professors accept late papers, may provide good illustrations of such manipulation by clients. Even terminally ill or dead patients or patients under anesthesia have been found to exert some influence on the organizational structure of a hospital and the routine activities of its staff.[58]

It is of course not suggested that the actual state of affairs existing in any formal organization is solely the product of the interactional bargains struck between clients and the organizational employees only. The negotiated state— which is probably in constant flux—may also be influenced by other interests within the organization, according to their relative strength and the issues involved. Smith's study of the two lines of authority in a hospital (the dual authority structure) may be viewed as one attempt to describe the negotiations between two groups with formal authority.[59] It may be useful however to extend this work by conceiving of multiple authority or power structures (which would include both inmates or clients and employees) each of which exerts some influence on structure and outcome depending on (among other things) the nature of the issue involved.

The precise techniques by which various power groups *within* organizations assume and retain power will also probably vary between open and closed institutions (for example, a voluntary organization compared with the military)—as well as between comparable organizations which serve different functions (for example, a prison compared with a hospital for the criminally insane). Unfortunately, little information is available on such techniques, from research to date.

One noteworthy exception, from another area of inquiry, is Parson's typology of "Ways of Getting Results" in which he distinguishes between "situational" and "intentional" attempts to influence, on the one hand, and between "positive" and "negative" attempts on the other.[60] If the attempt is "situational" X seeks to induce Y to perform in a certain way by either offering (positive) or threatening (negative) to change his situation (e.g. pay him or to block his promotion). In "intentional" attempts, X may influence Y by suggesting the ways in which Y would reward *himself* by complying (positive). Conversely, X may point out that if Y does *not* comply, he will punish himself in some way by violating a commitment he has already made (negative). These four types are labeled as follows: "Inducements" (situational-positive), "Deterrents" (situational-negative), "Persuasion" (intentional-positive), "Activation of commitments" (intentional-negative). Parson's typology may profitably serve as a starting point to investigate in empirical detail various negotiating strategies employed by different groups, in a variety of organizational contexts and in relation to a number of different issues. There has been a recent attempt by Danet and her colleagues to isolate and describe the attempts by *external participants* (clients) to influence bureaucratic decisions in their favor.[61] More specifically they focused on the kinds of reasons or "persuasive appeals" which clients offered to substantiate their requests to officials in formal organizations, and they list five sets of organizational circumstances, in which "persuasive appeals" may occur. (1) In many situations, it is legitimate and even necessary to present a "reason" designed to activate an organizational obligation, as when a client, requesting a loan from a bank, is asked to state why he needs the money. (2) Whenever the roles do not guarantee the automatic transfer of resources, and officials have discretionary power, we may expect persuasive appeals to appear. (3) Clients may attempt to influence an official's decision after a refusal, or when they know they have no legal right to what they want. If a request (accompanied by an appropriate strategy) fails on the first try, the client is likely to increase his efforts to influence officials and to switch to an illegitimate appeal such as a bribe or a request for a favor. (4) People who lack experience with formal organizations may offer reasons, even when these are unnecessary or inappropriate, simply because they are unfamiliar with the role of client and continue to behave as they would in informal interaction. (5) Clients, familiar with their role and the organization, may break the rules of the game intentionally in order to get what they want.

Danet also isolated the following types of appeals. *First*, there are appeals to *reciprocity*, in both positive and negative forms (inducements and threats, respectively). This type of appeal takes the form: "if you grant the request, I will reward you" or, "if you don't, I will deprive you". *Second*, there are appeals based on pure *persuasion* as in "you will reward yourself". *Third*, are appeals to *altruism*, the form of which is "if you grant the request, you will reward me". These three persuasive strategies all appeal to someone's profit, as well as depending on some aspects of the personal exchange relationship of the two parties involved, and compliance with them is, in principle, voluntary. The two remaining types of appeals listed are both normative in character, and compliance with them is supposedly obligatory. Danet distinguishes between appeals to the norm of reciprocity and appeals to impersonal norms. While appeals to the norm of reciprocity say "I will reward you" (future tense), appeals to the *norm of reciprocity* say "You owe it to me now because I have rewarded you in the past". Although this latter type of appeal also involves an exchange relationship between the parties, compliance is presumably experienced as obligatory. In the case of appeals to *impersonal norms*, which is the fifth basic type of persuasive appeal, compliance is also obligatory but *independent* of past interaction or personal acquaintance between the two parties. ("You owe it to me because some abstract principle you have internalized obliges you to do so".)

In one study, Katz and Danet investigated the relationship between background characteristics of clients and variations in the use of these different types of appeals, as well as the relationship between different appeals and different organizations.[62] Four hypothetical situations, in which a client seeks services from an official, were presented to a heterogeneous sample of Israeli army reservists. These men were all asked to state what should be said in each case, in order to get the official to grant the request. In particular, the authors were interested in the *variability* of persuasive appeals, and whether some clients discriminated more than others in what they said to different organizations, as well as to whether certain organizations were distinguishably similar or different judging from the variability in types of appeals addressed to them. The arguments or persuasive appeals suggested by the reservists were found to vary depending on both personal background and the type of organization involved. In general, it seemed from the evidence presented that the nature of the organization did influence the types of persuasive appeals of clients in trying to get what they wanted. It is perhaps noteworthy that the content of these appeals appeared to be influenced more by the normative basis on which the organization rested (the prime beneficiary whom it was serving) than on the client's ability to offer his resources in exchange for the services offered by the organization.

In a subsequent report Danet, employing a very promising methodological technique, examined the patterns of variation in the language of persuasive appeals to the Israeli custom authorities.[63] Persuasive appeals were chosen as the focus of the study on the grounds that they would reflect clients' orientations to bureaucracy. It was found that, in the case of customs, there were no appeals to reciprocity or attempts at pure persuasion. They neither offered inducements, nor did they threaten customs officials. Moreover, of the three basic types of appeal which were common, appeals to impersonal norms (e.g. "the customs owes me rights") were least frequent. It was found that only 15 percent of all appeals were to normative obligations, compared with 32 percent to the norm of reciprocity and a high 41 percent to altruism. The proportion of appeals to altruism is perhaps an indication of the weakness of external clients in this particular organizational situation. Since appeals to impersonal norms were low it was suggested that in this situation, clients lack both bargaining power, which would be best expressed with appeals to reciprocity, and normative power, as expressed by appeals to impersonal norms. Given the data, Danet suggests that even in a powerful commonweal organization, the properly socialized client feels equal to the official before the law in some ultimate sense, while those less socialized define themselves as more subservient and do not hesitate to appeal in a style that the socialized would regard as degrading and perhaps obsequious.

There have been some recent attempts to study the strategies designed to gain or maintain personal power, using laboratory experimentation. Perhaps more than any other, Jones has developed a promising approach to what he terms "strategic behaviours".[64] He points out that all interpersonal relationships involve some mutual dependence and that each party to a social interchange has potential influence over certain rewards available to and costs incurred by some other. If the dependences of one on the other are not only mutual but approximately equal, then there is a balance of power in which each can either enforce a minimal set of rewards through his capacity to act, or fail to enact the responses sought by the other. When the power, in a two-person relationship is asymmetrical, Jones suggests that a repertoire of strategic alternatives is open to the dependent person which guarantee him a certain minimum of rewards but do so at the expense of confirming or strengthening the power asymmetry which defines his dependence. An example suggested is compliance—the use of overt obedience to avoid punishment and secure available rewards. Other strategies however may be effective in modifying the asymmetry itself so that the dependent person's power is in the long run increased. Ingratiation is regarded by Jones as a tactic which is power enhancing or dependence reducing. He suggests that, by making himself attractive, the more dependent person decreases the value of his own sanctioning responses at the same time making it more difficult for the powerful persons to apply the full range of sanctions that were initially part of his repertory.

In the author's view then, there seems to be much promise in looking at both the interaction between power groups within an organization and the various influence strategies or tactics which groups from the "outside" exert in order to assume or maintain power, and the subsequent effects of such practices on organizational structure. This perspective appears to constitute a more dynamic and meaningful interpretation of formal organizational processes. It certainly appears to be more realistic than the rather static "top looking down" perspective mentioned earlier. The next section will consider, in more detail, aspects of the social life of "internal" clients in total institutions, followed by two sections focusing on the interaction between external clients and organizations.

Inmates and "total" institutions

Largely as a consequence of the insightful work of Goffman, attention is being increasingly directed towards the activities of total institutions in controlling and manipulating what society believes are "difficult cases".[65] This section will begin with a brief consideration of the general characteristics thought to be associated with such total institutions as prisons, mental hospitals, and monasteries. Particular attention will then be given to some illustrative recent work pertaining to labeling and self-mortification, and the effects of such processes on the inmates of total insitutions—their subsequent self-concept and social functioning. Finally, an emerging alternative program, which attempts to mediate between the needs of the internal client for possible reintegration into nondeviant roles and the needs and demands of the community for protection will be considered.

Goffman and others suggest that a total institution is characterized by the following features: (1) all aspects of the inmate's life are conducted in the same place and under the same authority; (2) each phase of the inmate's daily activity is carried out in the immediate company of a large number of others—who are treated alike and required to behave in the same way; (3) the activities of the day are tightly scheduled, and the sequence of activities is imposed from the top; (4) all activities are oriented towards the efficient organization of the institution.[66]

Most recent writers on total institutions argue that while an inmate is in such an organization his self-concept undergoes a process of mortification.[67] Such self-mortification is thought to occur regardless of the therapeutic quality of the institution. According to Goffman in *Asylums*, the aspects of the institution's "social atmosphere" that result in mortification are: (1) *barriers* which the total institution places between the inmate and the outside world—the inmate is dispossessed of certain roles that are part of his self; (2) *admission procedures*—here inmates are stripped of many of their personal possessions and their full name. Since these things are associated with one's self, their loss involves a curtailment of the self; (3) *deference requirements*—the inmate must show physical and/or verbal deference to the institution's staff. These acts produce feelings of humiliation and accompanying loss of self-esteem; (4) *verbal and gestural profanations*—the staff or fellow inmates may call an inmate an obscene name, curse him, or as in a convent, publicly point out negative attributes, tease him and talk about him as if he were not there; (5) *contaminative exposure* such as violation of information regarding one's self, physical contamination such as unclean food, interpersonal contamination such as forced social relationships, and the bringing of an outsider into contact with the individual's "significant others"; (6) *disruption of the usual relationship* between the "inmate" and his individual acts, such as "looping" (where the responses of the inmate are taken as the target of the next attack by the staff) and a loss of "personal economy of actions" (where the inmate cannot schedule his activities in an integrated fashion).

Despite manifest goals of treatment and rehabilitation, such organizations espouse underlying latent goals of social control, custody and protection of the wider society. Implicit in much of the literature on total institutions has been the belief that "inmates" improve (or at least ought to improve) as a result of their being in the particular institutions. "Improvement" in each instance is measured by the increase in conformity to certain standards of behaviour defined by the institution as desirable. For example Sykes, in his study of prison life reports that this institution is supposed to make a criminal into a noncriminal either through retribution, deterrence or rehabilitation.[68] Bouyer, while discussing a convent, maintains that this institution is supposedly intended to bring one closer to God.[69] Janowitz states that the army is supposed to increase technical skills and "make a man out of you", while Greenblatt suggests that a mental hospital is supposed to change a person into an adequately functioning human being.[70] Of course it is now quite clear that most social control agencies fail to meet their goals. Several researchers even hold that deviant activities seem to derive support from the very social control agencies designed to suppress them, and that the formal organizations set up within society for guarding against deviance may actually perpetuate the very behaviour that they are supposedly trying to eradicate.

Freidson suggests that in the course of defining and classifying the universe, which they claim needs their services, agencies of social control become responsible for drawing clearer lines than in fact exist in everyday life, or in the processes by which people were originally led into these services.[71] Boundaries are refined and clarified to the extent that the agencies, by assuming responsibility for their control, add elements to the role that may not have existed previously with the result that quite different people are attracted into them.

This is a point to which Scott addresses himself in his discussion of the construction of moral meanings in those agencies which have arisen to "help" the blind.[72] He surveys the rationale of service agencies over time in various societies and concludes that lacking in vision and being blind are not the same as the process of acting blind and exhibiting dependent behavior, both of which he considers are learned roles. In Garfinkle's terms one must divest oneself of the old conception of one who could see sufficiently to "manage", and take on a new identity which reinterprets previous conceptions as shams and redefines a person as truly in need of help.[73]

It is perhaps important to note that the condition itself, is not sufficient to explain the types of service or treatment offered. It is frequently assumed that the definitions advanced by agencies are empirically sound, but when we look closely, and perhaps cross-culturally, this is clearly not the case, since the determination of what is to be stigmatized lies primarily with those in the service agencies who have the power to impose their definitions of the situation. This can be very clearly illustrated by investigating the ways in which agencies for the blind are run in, say, Sweden, where this category are considered "normal", self-sufficient, and are in control of their own helping agencies.[74]

Similar to the type of evidence which Scheff and Goffman consider in mental institutions, is Scott's contention that the labeling of the blind is often applied in an arbitrary manner and that the proportion of those exhibiting the labelled behaviour is often greater on the outside than on the inside. Although it is perhaps difficult to conceptualize various definitions of blindness, Scott emphasizes that there is no direct correspondence between legal definitions, and the ones utilized by laymen in every day life. Another feature—also applicable to the mental patient —is that the closer one is to the point where experts' lines are drawn between normalcy and impairment, the less correspondence between the experts' definitions of these conditions as stigma, and the lay person's subjective experiences and reactions to them. The significance of this is that the largest proportion of those at the borderline of legal blindness lead active, "normal" lives. In sum, therefore, Scott makes it clear that it is bureaucratic necessity that leads to the legal definition of impairments, which consequently seem to transcend their intitial bureaucratic purposes and come to be regarded as empirical truths.

Some of the recent insights of labeling theorists also prove useful in delineating a number of the processes which are thought to characterize total institutions, as well as prove helpful in understanding the maneuvering, manipulation and stigmatizing of "deviants" by agencies of social control.[75]

From the recent work of Lemert, Kitsuse, Erikson and Becker (among others), it would appear that it is not the *forms of behavior* themselves which differentiate deviants from nondeviants, but rather the *response* of conforming members of society, who identify and interpret behavior as deviant.[76] These theorists suggest that deviance is not a property inherent in certain forms of behavior but that it is conferred upon behavior by audiences which directly or indirectly witness them. It is the audience that determines who should be processed as a deviant by formal organizations on the assumption that this processing by officials and public agencies will insure greater conformity in the subsequent behavior of the supposed transgressor.

Given such a process, if Durkheim is correct in his assumption that it is by no means clear that all acts considered deviant in a culture are in fact (or even in principle) harmful to group life, then one is left to wonder whether whole categories of people may be systematically sacrificed and stigmatized, whose system is being maintained and for which segment of society is this process of degradation most beneficial? Generally speaking, the functionality of incarceration is lauded for society as a whole, while there is little concern with the effects of such processes on the stigmatized individuals. Garfinkle has described in detail the ceremonies of degradation which can be found in all societies and discusses their effects on behaviour, and one could argue further that the conditions he lists as prerequisites for successful degradation are most effectively fulfilled in the super-rational, bureaucratic agencies which have arisen to safeguard Western societies from the stigmatized (and the stigmatized from themselves).[77]

Degradation by social control agencies is not, of course, a process which begins only after the client has taken residence within the agency, nor is it one which is necessarily begun after lengthy deliberation on whether the label is applicable to the person in question. One's inmate career—the shift in status from one who has managed his own life to one about whom "something should be done" —may begin through societal reaction in the community and be exacerbated on contact with agencies of social control. What Blumberg asserts for the criminal courts can be shown to hold for mental institutions as well—that once one is "caught" in a system as an accused individual, there is little likelihood of escaping.[78] Blumberg refers to this as "the impoverishment of institutional commitments to people".

An individual, newly categorized as legally blind, may protest that he has always taken adequate care of himself and sees no reason for a change—similarly for elderly people with chronic disabilities. Such protests are attributed by the agency to a failure to grasp the "reality" of the situation. The agency, while redefining reality for the disabled individual, denies him the privilege of face-saving mechanisms. In such a situation, individuals usually find that their protective responses collapse—they can no longer defend themselves in the usual way by employing tactics which distance them from some mortifying situation.

During examining sessions conducted by psychiatrists, for example, it is sometimes not clear whether incorrect responses are due to mental illness or some other factor such as, for example, lack of education. These extraneous alternative factors which may provide plausible counter-explanations, are rarely considered or explored for the obvious reason that they would hinder the ongoing process.[79] Kutner has found that psychiatric certificates were signed with little examination, which was generally made on an assembly line basis and completed in two or three minutes.[80] No case ever took more than ten minutes. Scheff found that in 196 out of 196 cases commitment was recommended even where the actor had answered questions quite correctly and displayed no visible manifestations of derangement.[81]

The rationale for the rapidity by which individuals are committed to total institutions can probably perhaps be found in the medical model, implicit in this model is the ethic that when faced with uncertainty, judging a sick person well is more to be avoided than judging a well person sick.[82] Bolstering this bias towards treatment is the belief that even if a mistake is made, the treatment will not cause undue harm. This view is certainly questionable with regard to commitment to mental hospitals, as the stigma of being an ex-mental patient may do irreparable long-term harm even if the treatment received was somewhat neutral—and the neutrality of treatment has yet to be established.[83] Another factor often overlooked is that most professionals—with an esoteric body of knowledge, autonomy, and a tight-knit professional network—are able to hide errors of judgment in certain ways.[84] Perhaps there is more than a grain of truth in the joke that physicians are able to bury their mistakes.

The mortification process is, of course, not completed in the precommitment phase. The definition of what the individual is now supposed to be is reinforced within the total institution, or by association with it—denial of the label by the individual only serving to further justify its conferment, by constituting further evidence of culpability.[85] As Denzin states, the patient must learn to see the hospital as a legitimate treatment source—evidence of his recovery is rated on the basis of this acceptance.[86] One is rewarded for passive, subservient, docile forms of behavior—behavior, one might add, which is quite unsuitable for adequate functioning *outside* the institution. The need for discipline and the patient's understanding of that need is so great that almost any means which will impress the importance of this upon the inmate is justified. What other explanation can there be for the observations by Dunham and Weinberg that electric shock treatment was performed in front of other patients without explanation of what their own treatment involved.[87]

Such phenomena may be observed in prisons, the armed forces and perhaps even in schools and colleges (although in a more refined form). After all, it is not so long ago that public caning was abolished in secondary schools in Great Britain and debate still continues on whether strapping ought to be allowed. Of course there is a disparity between the public rules as to how officials in bureaucracies ought to behave and their actual behavior in coping with threatening situations. For example, even though formerly disallowed, teachers may still stand a "problem student" in a corner in an attempt to publicly shame him into conformity or to insure that he approximates the teacher's conception of the typical schedule of student progress.

Indeed, the structure of total institutions seems to provide a situation which is conducive to these front and back stage presentations.[88] Moreover, the structure frequently enables lower incumbents to present an acceptable but totally erroneous image to those at higher levels concerning the tasks they are routinely performing. Generally speaking, therefore, the ability of outsiders and perhaps administrators to observe what goes on during everyday encounters with inmates, patients and clients, etc., is always somewhat limited.

Returning to the process of mortification, the inability of many within total institutions to make choices, and the lack of explanations by officials for the arbitrary imposition of rules, poses a profound threat to the inmate's self-image as he finds himself relegated to a state of childhood, being once again weak, helpless, dependent and therefore malleable. Moreover, face-saving skills commonly used in "normal" social interaction are negatively sanctioned or not believed within the total institution. The patient or the prisoner is left to adjust to the fact that his life and self concept are no longer his own. All of his actions within the total institution, as well as the ones he committed while he was a private citizen on the outside are a matter of public record and are open to interpretation, discussion and derision by staff members, and in some situations by fellow inmates.

When one is conforming most to the "normal" patterns of everyday life, one is usually conforming least to an agency's image. When one is conforming most to the "normal" pattern of institutional life, one is conforming least to the image of life on the outside. It should perhaps be emphasized that outside the institution, those who consistently fail to allow others face-saving mechanisms are those considered deviant. Because one's life in a total institution is open to continual and instantaneous reinterpretation by official agents, the labeled person is denied the opportunity to construct what Goffman has termed an "Apologia"—an image he constructs of his life in which he selects, abstracts and distorts items in order to provide himself with a "line" which can be expounded in various situations.[89] This apologia cannot be constructed in a total institution because the inmate is continually reminded that his past was a failure—that he is a sick or harmful individual and that he cannot expect to be treated as an equal. His history is denied and any efforts to retrieve it are distained by those who are responsible for his supervision. By selectively emphasizing specific events in a person's life and perhaps redefining others, the staff are able to make "a tight case" to show how the inmate is presently sick, why it was right to commit him in the first place, and the reasons why he should remain committed.

So far we have been concerned with the hypothesis that while an individual is an "internal" client in a total institution, his self undergoes a process of mortification. While much has been written on the process of institutionalization, prisonization and on such "medical conditions" as hospitalitis and institutional neurosis, there have been few empirical studies of these processes or states. To a large extent this may be a consequence of the difficulty of selecting a suitable before and after time interval: that is, *when to test for self-mortification*. Goffman emphasizes that it is the initial shock period of hospitalization that affects self-mortification and after the "inmate" has been in the institution a while, his self reassembles in a different but acceptable pattern, within the institution. This reassembly supposedly comes about through integration into the inmate subculture. Another difficulty is the *definition of self-mortification*. Although Goffman discusses humiliation and the loss of social identity, he never really connects these concepts explicitly to one of self-mortification.

Karmel, in a recent study of patients in a psychiatric hospital, has attempted to discover if an inmate in a total institution does in fact undergo a process of self-mortification.[90] Using results from a panel sample of fifty patients, Karmel interpreted self-mortification to mean a loss of self-esteem and social identity. The Rosenberg–Guttman scale of self esteem and the Kuhn–McPartland Twenty Statements test were employed. The author concluded that among the sample of patients in her survey in the New Jersey State Hospital at Trenton, no significant self-mortification occurred in patients between the time of their admission and an interval of four weeks following their arrival. There was, in fact, a slight gain in self-esteem and social identity.

Karmel rather surprisingly casts some doubt on the validity of her findings at the end of her paper by pointing out that none of the patients studied were on "back wards". They may have felt that their stay was temporary, that they would be discharged in the near future, and therefore, they may have been willing to tolerate certain features of their environment. Moreover, she feels that since many of the patients believed that the hospital procedures were for their own therapeutic benefit they may have interpreted institutional activity in a positive rather than a negative sense. One cannot help wondering to what extent Karmel was in fact measuring the extent to which the inmates had accommodated to the institutional ideology. 66 percent agreed with the statement "Locked doors help you get well", and 82 percent agreed with the statement "Because I am sick and among other sick people, my belongings were taken away from me for my own good". In the author's view there is still a need for a rigorously designed study of both the *long-term effects* of different kinds of societal labeling and of the process and long-term consequences of self-mortification in various kinds of total institutions.

Reflecting an awareness of the dangers of total institutions, the field of corrections has recently shown increasing concern with finding alternatives to older methods. Many writers have suggested that the difficulties which formerly were attributed to the personal pathology of, for example, criminal and delinquent offenders and mental patients are equally the products of the organizational character of correctional and legal systems. Some suggest that the process of labeling an offender and making him conscious of himself as deviant may evoke the very traits complained of and the offender may be made worse by his institutional experience. All have seriously questioned the adequacy of our total institutional approach to what has been called "treatment" or "rehabilitation". A range of less drastic measures have been proposed, and in some cases implemented with promising results. For offenders who otherwise would have been incarcerated, residential centers having no physical restraints, work furlough programs, daily nonresidential programs, and "half-way houses" have been created. Rather than emphasizing total surveillance and isolation, these alternative programs have taken on a kind of broker's role by attempting to mediate between the needs of the offender for reintegration into nondeviant roles and the needs and demands of the community for protection.

In general, these programs reflect an attempt to develop a new form of institution—termed mediatory—whose major function would be to reverse the process of stigmatization and to develop for the offender, a legitimate route back into a nondelinquent status. In contrast to the total institution, the mediatory institution, would maintain an outward rather than an inward perspective; that is, it would be concerned with examining and resolving problems which are precipitated by the offender's interaction with the community rather than with the artificial environment of a total institution. Sometimes such efforts would require changes in the behavior of the offender, sometimes in the behavior of officials, but most of the time they would require drastic changes in interactional patterns between the two.

Lubeck and Empey recently made a study of the prediction and control of

run-aways at two correctional institutions for delinquent boys in southern California.[91] The first institution was a *mediatory* institution which was located in an
urban community. The second was an isolated and relatively self-sufficient *total*
institution. Subjects were randomly assigned to either institution from a common
population of offenders and run-aways were examined over a thirty-two month
period. The study provides strong support for the view that offender behavior
is very much a result of the character of correctional as well as personal systems.
Not only were different personal characteristics associated with running away in
the mediatory and total institutions, but these characteristics changed as structural
changes occurred within each of the institutions.

Who are served?—some notes on "creaming"

Many studies have uncovered the tendency for client-centered bureaucracies, in
particular, to dissociate themselves in certain ways from those groups whom the
organization was primarily established to assist. For example, the use of referral
to other agencies as a mechanism for closing out contact with the poor has been
noted by Maas who observed that disproportionately more lower occupational-
status families terminate in consultation or referral.[92] Again, the findings from a
study by the Family Service Association of America show that:

> . . . except for the top class, closings at client initiative dropped as social class declined.
> In the upper middle class, nearly six cases in ten took the initiative in terminating in
> contrast to only one in three of the lowest groups. Termination of the relationship
> at the initiative of the employee, while unusual at any level, was more than twice as
> frequent at the lowest level than at any other.[93]

Coleman has compared the selection of applicants for psychiatric treatment
in a clinic and in a family agency.[94] He found no significant differences in the
distribution and severity of psychiatric diagnoses in the two agencies. It is important to note, however, that class V (lowest) patients, regardless of diagnosis,
tended to receive less favorable consideration for continued treatment in the clinic,
and also in family service although to a smaller extent. Again, the FSAA report
cited earlier notes that the average number of interviews decreases as social class
status declines—the drop is from an average of nearly eleven interviews per case
in the higher social classes to less than six for the lowest social class—and shows
that the tendency to select high income people for continuing treatment is not
limited to private agencies. Moreover, it has also been noted that, in public
agencies, the decision to treat or continue in treatment is often discretionary with
treatment personnel.[95]

Although it can be argued that high income groups will always be favored
in a fee-for-service situation, one interesting study was undertaken by the institute
for Juvenile Research of a tax-supported child guidance clinic, available at no
cost to the residents of Illinois, and found, consistant with many other studies,
that while a representative cross-section of the total population applied for service
at this agency, the characteristics of those who actually received treatment are far
from representative.[96] For example while 37 percent of the applicants for service

came from low income groups, only 25 percent were accepted for treatment. In contrast, while 29 percent of the applicants were from a high income group, 47 percent of them were accepted for treatment. On the basis of these data the report concludes that "even though high income level [doesn't] affect intake [it influences] the probability of entering treatment."

In 1958, Hollingshead and Redlich reported relationships between social class, diagnosis and treatment of persons with mental disorders in a community survey in New Haven, Connecticut.[97] In particular, the manner in which patients were treated was linked to class position. While individual psychotherapy was a major treatment in all classes it appeared that the lower the social class the greater the tendency to administer an organic therapy—a shock treatment, lobotomy or drug therapy—even when the agency administering the treatment was held constant. The number of times patients saw their therapists per month as well as the length of the visits, were also significantly different from one class to another, the higher status clients receiving more frequent and longer treatments than those from the lower classes.

It is often held that the "cooling out" of certain clients occurs as a consequence of the differential availability of certain forms of treatment.[98] However, studies of similar agencies treating different social categories have shown that this simply is not so. An interesting example is a study by Siegal and his colleagues who investigated the relationships between social class, psychiatric diagnosis and treatment in three hospitals which had comparable treatment facilities available to patients from different socio-economic levels.[99] Differences in diagnosis, treatment selection and duration of hospitalization were found in all three hospitals. The hospitals which treated higher ratios of patients from the lower socio-economic groups had larger proportions of patients diagnosed as psychotic and employed organic therapies more often (a finding consistent with those of Hollingshead and Redlich). Social class position was also positively related to the length of time a patient spent in these hospitals—the lower the status, the shorter the stay.

Given that some selection process exists, the question then is—why do agencies disengage from certain clients (usually those of lower socio-economic status)? *One* explanation may be found in the fact that most clients are served directly by professionals in organizations. It is not intended to enter the seemingly endless argument over what makes an occupation a profession or what makes one profession "more professional" than another. At the present time, there appears to be little agreement as to the precise definition of a professional, and this is clearly not the place for a review and analysis of the many attempts to clarify the meaning of the term through the use of lists of characteristics.[100]

While such listings may be useful criteria for describing the training and everyday activity of professionals, and comparing one profession with another, each of them, in the author's view, is inadequate as an explanation of either the emergence and· perpetuation of professions or various aspects of professional behavior. It may be, as Becker suggests, that the label "profession" is no more than an everyday usage lending some prestige and general approbation to certain occupations which have more or less "arrived".[101] If an occupational group defines itself as a profession, and manages to receive public acceptance of the term, then to all intents and purposes it can be regarded as a profession. In other words, the notion of a "self-fulfilling prophecy" may more adequately explain the nature and emergence of professions and aspects of professional behavior, than a searching of the numerous descriptive inventories of sociological theorists. Once some occupational group makes a claim to the definition "professional", they may as a consequence of their own and public reaction to this claim appear to become professional in practice.

Accordingly, it may be not so much the match between a particular area of activity and some list of criteria which determines the applicability of the label "professional", but public acceptance or societal reaction to the label. It is quite conceivable that a group which is commonly recognized as "professional" may not meet most or even any of various criteria listed, but still enjoy widespread acceptance of the term. Of course, the ability of an occupational group to gain public acceptance of the label is probably, in large part, fostered by the organizational contexts within which certain occupational groups are located and claims are presented. As mentioned earlier, various organizations have certain experience, resources, and priviledged access to the media which facilitate public acceptance of a claim to professionalism. It may even be in the entrepreneurial interest of certain organizations to promote the label "professional" for certain of its occupational groups. One thinks immediately of airline "cabin attendants", the computer industry's whole range of technicians, analysts, processors and programmers, and the British army's advertisements concerning the "young professionals". Conversely, it may even be in the interests of some formal organizations to discourage the application of the label "professional" to some of its constituent occupational groups. Nursing and social work may be examples of two occupations whose professionalization would constitute a real threat to certain organizations.

By way of summary, therefore, we may say that the term "profession" can be employed to denote any possible group to which the term by being publicly believed, has been successfully applied and sustained.

The *status* of any profession may be a function of the status of its clientele, whether that clientele is defined in terms of age, sex, socio-economic status, ethnicity or other factors. Indeed, because the designation "professional" is perhaps more dependent on societal reaction than on the intrinsic character of tasks or training, we may find certain groups sensitive to association with people or tasks which would question the applicability of the label. The dilemma of social workers, like that of, for example, criminal lawyers or welfare physicians, is that there is little prestige to be derived from serving groups, which in our society are defined as lacking in moral virtue, ambition, self-dependence, etc. Hughes lends support to this interpretation when he suggests that one means of identifying "highly professional" occupational groups is through the clients they serve.[102] Becker has also argued along these lines, suggesting that the typical process of professionalization involves the shedding of "dirty work" in an attempt to devote one's time—and be seen as devoting one's time—to "more professional" activities.[103]

Ideologically, of course, a professional is supposed to serve equally all those in need of his or her skills. The studies already cited, however, show that in many instances this simply is not the case. In the competition for increased prestige, it may be that one way to advance one's claims is to seek a "higher" class clientele, rather than being identified as a lower status servant of the poor. Whether or not an occupational group's claims to professionalism are successful may also be dependent on the relative positions of related occupational groups. In this regard Goode has described this process as a kind of zero sum game—one in which there is only a limited supply of professional kudos—therefore, as one group rises another must decline.[104] Given a limit to the number of groups who can claim whatever elusive advantages professionalism offers, and the reliance on societal reaction, certain professions may have a vested interest in the process which Cloward and Epstein call, "disengagement from the poor".[105]

As certain human service workers and agencies equate "dirty work" with handling undesirable problems and clients, officials may tend to avoid these as obstacles to professionalization or gaining higher professional status. Goffman has similarly described the bearers of "courtesy stigma" as those regarded by others as having a spoiled identity because they are affiliated in some way with the stigmatized.[106] Since this type of stigma is affiliational and not actually physical, it can be postulated that it is relatively easily managed by certain distancing tactics or by deviance disavowal.

A recent study by Walsh and Elling may provide additional support for these interpretations.[107] This research centered on investigations of the orientations and behaviors of three occupational groupings within public health—physicians, nurses, and sanitarians. They found that members of highly striving occupational groups were significantly more negative in their orientation towards the poor and lower-class clients than nonstriving groups within formal organizations.

A *second* possible reasons for the disengagement of the agencies from certain clients may lie in the threat such people pose to service organizations. It has been suggested by Sjoberg, for example, that in order to maintain itself, client-centered bureaucracy tends to neglect those in greatest need of its services—those in fact, whom the organization was primarily established to assist.[108] Certain clients tend to challenge organizational effectiveness by presenting a range of problems which are perceived as less easily resolved. It is thought that a disproportionately large amount of time and effort must be devoted to such clients and problems, even though success cannot be predicted with confidence or, in fact, ever be realized. This organizational achievement ethic therefore prompts bureaucracy to select for "processing" those who are perceived as most amenable to the fulfillment of defined objectives, and to exclude those whose needs pose a threat to organizational effectiveness.

It appears therefore that the criteria for selection by service agencies often tends to favor the advantaged client whose problems may be perceived as less severe or less complex. Thus it is often the case that the most capable school teachers are concentrated in upper-status school districts, while those who may be less well qualified or experienced predominate in lower-class districts.[109]

Similarly, it has been found that lower-class clients in child guidance clinics are generally neglected in favor of middle-class clients who appear to respond better to therapy.[110] In the same way, the Job Corps in the United States is said to bypass men with criminal records, even though they may be in the greatest need of assistance.[111] The process by which local authorities in Great Britain allocate Council houses certainly reflects this bias in favor of people who are not necessarily in the greatest need of public housing. Scott, in a recent study of agencies that service the blind, reports that their programs concentrate on those clients who "enjoy the highest probability of success".[112] He found that, even though the elderly blind account for 56 percent of the blind population, the great majority of these services (67 percent) have programs which are geared to serve the needs of children and employable adults.

A feature then of all these studies, is the evidence for the process of "creaming" —the elimination of those cases which are perceived as likely to jeopardize the realization of certain professional or organizational goals. It is suggested that this creaming, which may take the form of initial, biased selection, removes those very cases which would constitute a real test of organizational effectiveness.

The role of officials in service organizations as mandated labelers is, of course, of primary importance in the creaming process. Generally speaking, if an official "accepts" a client, he is publically declaring that the client is in some need, and publically exposing both himself, and his agency, to the likelihood of being unable to assist them. Moreover, having made such a declaration, the official exposes the organization to the liability that a whole range of related problems, which the client may have not yet declared, may eventually emerge. Such possibilities may be rendered invisible and avoided if bureaucratic regulations can be discretionarily invoked by the official to disqualify the client. There are at least four main *techniques of invisibility* by which certain clients and problems can be effectively concealed, and it is likely that their usage varies both between different social agencies, and between different types of presenting problem.

Firstly, the eligibility requirements for the agency's service can be constructed in such a way that the official can exclude the client on first encounter. This possibility exposes the agency to challenges of callousness or inefficiency. *Secondly*, after accepting a client, an official can prematurely terminate contact while at the same time giving token recognition to some problem. Exposure to criticism from outsiders is probably reduced somewhat, by the use of this technique. *Thirdly*, an official may only recognize a highly segmentalized area of the client's social life as relevant to his agency, and disregard other spheres of activity or problems which are in fact causally related, but probably threatening to the organization. *Fourthly*, and probably the most effective and frequently employed technique of invisibility is for some official to recognize related problems, yet abdicate responsibility by referring the client to another agency. In such a situation the client is more likely to believe that he is receiving some service rather than simply being disengaged, and potential hostility is averted. As a result of this fourth technique, however, certain services (usually publically assisted) become repositories for the disengaged and fail through unmanageable burdens.

Organizations and the poor

We have already referred to the fact that the relationship between those categorized as of low socio-economic status (the poor) and formal organizations has been repeatedly described as one in which there is communication breakdown, misunderstanding, and subsequent alienation. It seems there are two main ways in which this estrangement from organizations can be explained. The *first*, which can be termed "client culpability", lays emphasis on and identifies the knowledge, skills and life-styles that clients lack which, if present, would prevent or minimize any breakdown. The *second* explanation of the general breakdown of the relationship between the poor and organizations locates the source in both the structure of organizations, and aspects of professional behavior. These approaches have already been considered in relation to the creaming activities of officials in organizations. Pursuing the second approach, attention will be directed in this section towards several organizational factors which appear to make it difficult for the poor to make use of certain *types of service*, with the consequence that they often do not receive a number of the benefits to which they are entitled.

One way of introducing the notion of different *types* of services is to employ the classical economic distinction between buyers' and a sellers' market. Given the relative neglect and even disregard of the needs, wishes and demands of potential consumers, by health and welfare professionals and organizations, one is tempted to draw this economic parallel. In *a sellers' market*, demand exceeds supply and it is the seller who is in a position to determine prices, conditions and the extent of services. This is contrasted with a *buyers' market*, in which supply exceeds demand and sellers have to be consumer-oriented, in order to sell to consumers who may perceive no immediate need for a service, or who are able to choose between many similar groups of services being offered. Since health and welfare services appear to operate predominantly in a sellers' market, they tend to be oriented towards the fulfillment of some perceived need (medical or social) often irrespective of the consumer's demand. Generally speaking, most of the health and social welfare "needs" of the poor in particular can be established by reasonably objective criteria, but if this "need" is not translated into "demand" for service, the "sale" has not very much chance of being made. Perhaps planners and administrators could borrow a page from marketing textbooks and seek to determine the extent to which a sellers' or a buyers' market obtains in particular areas of health and social welfare. In particular, attention should be given to the increasing number of "preventive" services, which appear to operate, at present, predominantly in a buyers' market. Obviously in a buyers' market, considerable attention must be paid to techniques for encouraging people to purchase an item and/or to retain loyalty to it.

Two other orientations also provide useful perspectives on the type of service offered, and the behavior of officials in relation to clients. Buyer market services are usually *"client-centered"* and efforts are generally made by officials to encourage them to come and to retain them in service. Often, clients are rewarded in various ways for "buying" the service. For example, in such person-oriented situations, the treatment received is frequently designed to encourage the clients to continued use of that service.

In contrast, seller market services are usually *"object-oriented"* with officials remaining rather formal or impersonal and less interested in the unique characteristics of the client. In such a situation efforts may even be made to turn people away or to deter them from returning in order to regulate a threatening work load. (Some of the techniques employed by officials and agencies to "cool out" certain cases have already been discussed in some detail). These two general orientations (whether person-oriented or object-oriented) may form extremes on a continuum which in effect described *the form in which the service is presented* to potential clients.

A second dimension, which may also shape the type of service delivered, concerns *who takes the initiative* in establishing some relationship with an agency or official. At one extreme a potential client may take the initiative in deciding that he/she has a certain need, identifies it as amenable to ameliorative action, selects a possibly suitable agency, and utilizes it. One may term this type of behavior *self-initiated* action. At the other extreme, some official or agency may take the initiative and decide that some person or group has, or may be in danger of having some need, which could be removed or assisted in some way and acts to help them.[113] One may term this *other-initiated* action.

The types of service which would result from the combination of these two dimensions—*the form of service* (whether person-oriented or object-oriented) and the *initiation of contact* (whether from the client or the service) can perhaps be summarized in the simple diagram presented in figure 1.

Figure 1 Different orientations and types of service

| | | FORM OF SERVICE | |
		Object-oriented	Person-oriented
INITIATION OF CONTACT	Self- or client-initiated	A. e.g. Antenatal clinic Welfare agency	C. e.g. Family doctor
	Other- or service-initiated	B. e.g. Cervical cytology Mass radiography	D. e.g. Health visitor

Given the *absence of a high priority need*, it can be postulated that the rate of utilization for the poor will increase from type A to type D services, in alphabetical order, as presented in the above diagram.

A recent study of the use of a wide range of health and social welfare services by the lower working class in Aberdeen, Scotland, has certainly suggested that a person-oriented service is always preferred, by this group, however the contact is initiated.[114] Through the use of various instruments—attitude profiles, intensive tape recorded interviews and observational work—it was found that A and B type situations were particularly distasteful for the lower working-class sample studied, while C and particularly D type situations, were tolerable and perhaps occasionally even enjoyed. However, although clearly preferring D and C type situations, it appears that people of low socio-economic status are being increasingly directed to A and B type encounters.

Incidentally, not only are there differences in the nature of the agencies encountered by the poor, and treatment orientations experienced, but there are probably related differences in the levels of staff encountered, with important consequences for the treatment received. Encounters by the poor are usually restricted to the "the man at the desk"—often the lowest incumbent who is the most bound by formal bureaucratic constraints. For higher socio-economic categories, contact with "higher ups" is more readily available and even fostered in many formally organized agencies. Note the connotations of such talk as "my broker", "my doctor", "my accountant" and the intention behind the television advertisement depicting a bank manager secreted in one's cupboard at home for instantaneous consultation. A possible consequence of such differential contact may be that the poor have fewer chances of increasing their understanding of organizations. Employing Mannheim's distinction between "substantive" and "functional" knowledge, Janowitz and Delaney, for example, show that those employed at the lower levels of large-scale organizations generally possess a range of social understanding, knowledge, and attitudes (their informational perspective) which is limited to matters experienced directly in performing their specialized jobs—"functional" knowledge.[115] Only at the higher levels of large-scale organizations are there occupational possibilities which permit broader knowledge, attitudes, and understanding—"substantive" knowledge—which involves a more generalized understanding of how the goals of social life may be linked, and how these goals can be achieved.

Overriding all these considerations, however, is the immediacy of need. It is suggested that the presence or absence of such a need will largely determine utilization behavior. For example, while the majority of those in poverty never attend for or receive taxation rebates, one cannot automatically maintain that such a group is underutilizing taxation or internal revenue departments. As is well known most in this social category are either chronically unemployed, or underemployed, and therefore seldom qualify for taxation rebates. In contrast, the same chronically unemployed or underemployed groups will, of economic necessity, utilize such services as the Labor Exchange or the Supplementary Benefits Commission (Great Britain) or welfare departments in the United States. Using a similar argument, if someone breaks a leg or experiences a severe heart attack, this person would most probably utilize an emergency (survival) service, given such an immediate and obvious need to do so. The same individual, however, may or may not perceive the need for either a regular medical check up or immunization.

Some needs, however, are not so universally obvious and immediate. Many are differentially perceived, and may be given varying priority depending on situational and cultural factors. For example, some may perceive a chronic cough as needing attention, while others may consider it a "hazard of living" and not worthy of any medical attention at all. Differential patterns of utilization by the poor may be partially explained in terms of this differential perception of the importance of need, and of taking some ameliorative action.

Associated with this phenomenon, is the appropriateness or "goodness of fit" between services and the values, norms, beliefs and life-styles of the subgroups of society for which they cater. Some needs, perceived or actual, may be recognized as important enough for attention from, say, a social welfare service, and yet the form in which that service is presented may be perceived as so abhorrent or debilitating that it is underutilized. Or, where there exists a choice of services catering for the same need, one service may be preferred above others because of the form in which this particular service is delivered.

Following from this discussion, it is likely that service preference is, to a large extent, a function of the types of agencies and officials one has routine contact with. Generally speaking, the poor have regular contact with A type agencies *out of necessity*, and these typically operate on seller market principles (welfare agencies, emergency rooms). The middle and upper classes in contrast, also experience A type services, but for them such contact is relatively infrequent and when it does occur is *by choice*—banks, insurance and trust companies, building societies, etc., are some examples. The implications of these different experiences with agencies and officials cannot be overemphasized. While all social categories probably have encounters with A and B type services, they may do so for entirely different reasons, and experience quite different treatment from officials. The use of these types of services by the upper and middle classes is largely a matter of choice, with the consequence that they can withdraw if dissatisfied—which is unlikely since these services usually have a buyer market orientation. In contrast, the poor are forced to utilize services out of need, and consequently do not have the freedom to withdraw if dissatisfied—which may be most of the time since the services they routinely encounter operate on seller market principles.

A detailed analysis of tape recorded data, derived from intensive interviews with respondents in the Aberdeen study, revealed that many of those who under-utilized services appeared to be unable to discriminate between the functions of the various health and welfare agencies they were in contact with, particularly if they were, in terms of the preceding typology, organized in an A or B fashion. These data appear to indicate that while being unable to distinguish between services with a predominantly object-orientation, they could distinguish *between* an object—(A and B) and a person orientation (C and D). The following statements illustrate this point:

They're all the same really. Greyfriars (Department of Social Security)—that's just a Government building. Usually Government's awfully official. The hospital is government and the same. Everything's done with red tape in Greyfriars and that, done by the book. Foresterhill (hospital) is more or less the same.
They're all more or less the same. All right but just doing their job and *you've* got to

listen to them. None of them are bothered about you. The National Assistance Board (UAB) or the Employment Exchange. Up at the hospital they're not concerned about you. They just ask you a few questions and you tell them and sign a statement and that's it and you go up and they'll do the same every time you go up. That's just the way they are. Just everything's taken. It's just a habit. They just do everything over and over again in the same way.

A number of the utilizing respondents could discriminate between different types of services as follows:

Oh no, they're different, You know you're not goin' to the Clinic to try and get money, or you're not trying to fight for your house to keep your house, you're going because you're just having a baby. They're no goin' to pry into your affairs. Like the U.A.B. does and the Rent Office. I think you feel more at ease at the clinic. You know the doctor isn't going to jump at you at the least thing.

I think these places are different. Because when you go to the clinic you're goin' there for your health's sake really. If you're going to the Social Security you're goin' cause you have to go, not because you want to go . . . I prefer the doctor's clinic. Because I know the doctor. You go into the doctor's clinic and Miss Watts there and she'll say "Hello, Mrs. Dobbs, How's Alison?" They know you.

These quotations serve to indicate that some of the lower working-class utilizing respondents could discriminate between different agencies, even when a comparable organizational type, and that the basis for this distinction was often the treatment which they felt they received at the hands of certain officials in agencies. It may be therefore, that the organizational differences between certain agencies may be mediated by (and detectable in) the behavior of officials in relation to their clients.

Certainly, the inability to distinguish between the activities and orientations of what appear to be quite different agencies seemed to have at least two deleterious consequences for subsequent utilization behaviour. During the course of field work for the study referred to, the author was struck by the way in which many of the underutilizing respondents had quite detailed knowledge about and negative attitudes towards particular agencies, even though they had never been in contact with these agencies, or the personnel from them. It did seem that many typifications of certain services were not necessarily emergent responses to current situational experiences on the part of the respondent, but were communicated by others who had direct experiences with the service in question. Moreover, many of these negative typifications, while perhaps true for certain services, were apparently transferred and applied to other quite different services. This process was probably assisted by the inability of the underutilizing respondents to discriminate the predominant functions of different services. These "transferred typifications" then came to constitute grounds for underutilizing other services. If a respondent did actually utilize a service, these transferred negative conceptions appeared to act almost as "self-fulfilling typifications"—having defined an agency or official as negative and unhelpfully debilitating, they almost certainly appeared to become so in their consequences.

The other deleterious consequence concerns the effect this may have in constricting one's repertoire of persuasive appeals, as well as in determining the appropriateness of any one appeal for presentation in a particular situation. Logically it would seem that services, which are regarded by clients as indistinguishable, would be likely to call forth the same general appeal strategy, despite possibly quite different situations. The behavior deemed appropriate and effective in, say, a welfare or employment office, most probably will be quite ineffectual in a neighborhood health clinic or outpatient department. By perceiving services as indistinguishable the poor may employ the "wrong" persuasive appeals in the "wrong" context, with the consequence that service to them and the reactions of officials, are measurably affected. This lack of congruence between service and appeal may, consequently, affect the degree of client satisfaction. Most respondents in the Aberdeen study who underutilized services spent a considerable period of time in and around public assistance agencies, consequently developing techniques to present themselves in a particular way and to withold information. During observational field work in a maternity clinic it seemed that these tactics were inappropriately transferred to this organization, calling forth certain unfavorable definitions and responses from the clinic staff.

Certainly it would seem that in many instances, the ability of a client to extract some service from a formal organization or professional has little to do with public entitlement. Rather, it is dependent to a large extent on his or her repertoire of persuasive appeals, and the ability to discriminate service type so as to correctly present them. For many reasons, some of which have been outlined above, such a facility with organizations does not appear readily present for many of the poor.

References and notes

1. See P. Blau, *Bureaucracy in Modern Society*, New York: Random House, 1956; R. Presthus, *The Organizational Society*, New York: Knopf, 1962; W.H. Whyte, *The Organization Man*, New York: Simon and Schuster, 1956.
2. K. Boulding, *The Organizational Revolution*, New York: Harper, 1953.
3. W. Kornhauser, *The Policies of Mass Society*, Glencoe, Ill.: The Free Press, 1959.
4. This is discussed by R.A. Nisbet, *The Quest For Community*, New York: Oxford University Press, 1953.
5. S.M. Lipset, "Trade unions and social structure", *Indust. Relat.*, **1** (Oct 1961), 75–89; C. Argyris, "The fusion of an individual with organization", *Am. Sociol. Rev.*, **19** (June 1954), 267–272.
6. W. Kornhauser, *op. cit.*, see note 3.
7. A.G. Neal and M. Seeman, "Organizations and powerlessness: a test of the mediation hypothesis", *Am. Sociol. Rev.*, **29** (1964), 216–266.
8. J.R. Gusfield, "Mass society and extremist politics", *Am. Sociol. Rev.*, **27** (Feb 1962), 19–30; D. Bell, "America as a mass society: a critique", in *The End of Ideology*, Glencoe, Ill.: The Free Press, 1960, pp. 21–36; S. Greer and P. Orleans, "The mass society and the parapolitical structure", *Am. Sociol. Rev.*, **27** (Oct 1962), 634–46.

9. C.W. Mills, *The Power Elite*, New York: Oxford University Press, 1956, p. 307.

10. For a comprehensive review see L. Feuer, "What is alienation? the career of a concept", reprinted in M. Stein and A. Vidich, *Sociology on Trial*, Englewood Cliffs, N.J.: Prentice-Hall, 1963, pp. 127–147. Also M. Seeman, "On the meaning of alienation", *Am. Sociol. Rev.*, **24** (Dec 1959), 783–91; I. Taviss, "Changes in the form of alienation: The 1900s vs. the 1950s", *Am. Sociol. Rev.*, **37** (Feb 1969), 46–57.

11. E. Josephson and M. Josephson, *Man Alone: Alienation in Modern Society*, New York: Dell, 1962. For two exceptions see M. Aiken and J. Haze, "Organizational alienation: a comparative analysis", *Am. Sociol. Rev.*, **31** (Aug 1966), 497–507; R. Blauner, *Alienation and Freedom: The Factory Worker and His Industry*, Chicago: University of Chicago Press, 1964.

12. C.M. Bonjean and M.D. Grimes, "Bureaucracy and alienation: a dimensional approach", *Soc. Forces*, **48** (March 1970(, 365–373.

13. See, for example, I. Belknap and J. Steinle, *The Community and Its Hospitality*, Syracuse: University Press, 1963; E. Litwak and H. Meyer, "A balance theory of coordination between bureaucratic organizations and community primary groups", *Admin. Sci. Q.*, **11** (June 1966), 33–58.

14. It should perhaps be emphasized that little weight is now given to this perspective in professional sociological literature.

15. The early work of Coser, for example, would be included in this category. R. Coser, "Authority and decision-making in a hospital: a comparative analysis", *Am. Sociol. Rev.*, **23** (Feb 1958), 56–63, "Some social functions of laughter: a study of humor in a hospital setting", *Hum. Relat.*, **12** (1959), 171–182.

16. This perspective is gaining the attention of many scholars, particularly the question of client–agency interaction. A useful set of essays appears in W.R. Rosengren and M. Lefton (Eds), *Organizations and Clients*, Columbus, Ohio: Charles E. Merrill, 1970.

17. In a subsequent section of this chapter ("Inmates and 'Total' Institutions") some of the literature which would be included in this category is discussed.

18. T. Parsons, "Suggestions for a sociological approach to the theory of organizations", in A. Etzioni (Ed.), *Complex Organizations: A Sociological Reader*, New York: Holt Rinehart and Winston, 1961, pp. 39–40; P. Blau and W.R. Scott, *Formal Organizations*, San Francisco: Chandler, 1962, p. 77; C. Perrow, "Hospitals; technology, structure, and goals", in March (Ed.), *Handbook of Organizations*, Chicago: Rand McNally, 1965, pp. 650–677; A. Etzioni, *Modern Organizations*, Englewood Cliffs, N.J.: Prentice-Hall, 1964, p. 94; S.N. Eisenstadt, "Bureaucracy, bureaucratization, and de-bureaucratization", in A. Etzioni (Ed.), *Complex Organizations*, New York: Holt, Rinehart and Winston (2nd ed.), 1969, p. 304; B.G. Glaser, and A.L. Strauss, *Awareness of Dying*, Chicago: Aldine, 1965, p. 284.

19. M. Lefton and W.R. Rosengren, "Organizations and clients: lateral and longitudinal dimensions", *Am. Sociol. Pev.*, **31** (Dec 1966), 802–810; W.R.

Rosengren and M. Lefton, *Hospitals and Patients*, New York: Atherton Press, 1969.

20. See M. Lefton and W.R. Rosengren, *op. cit.*, for a comprehensive listing of illustrative works in this tradition.

21. This tradition corresponds with my "outside looking in" perspective.

22. See for example, P. Selznick, *TVA and the Grass Roots*, Berkeley: University of California Press, 1953; T. Parsons, "Suggestions for a sociological approach to the theory of organizations", *Admin. Sci. Q.*, **1** (June 1956), 63–86.

23. For an excellent collection of papers in this general tradition see E. Rubington and M.S. Weinberg, *Deviance: The Interactionist Perspective*, London: MacMillan, 1968.

24. M. Lefton, "Client characteristics and structural outcomes: toward the specification of linkages", in W.R. Rosengren and M. Lefton (Eds), *Organizations and Clients*, Columbus, Ohio: Charles E. Merrill, 1970, pp. 17–36.

25. For a review of many empirical studies consult M.E.W. Goss, "Organizational goals and quality of medical care: evidence from comparative research on hospitals", *J. Health and Soc. Behav.*, **11** (Dec 1970), 255–269.

26. These "concerns" of course, parallel the present *fashionable* interest in ecology and environmental protection. When this fashion changes, and it will, the manifest claims of certain organizations will also change in order to capitalize on the latest issue.

27. E.A. Krause, "Functions of a bureaucratic ideology: 'Citizen Participation' ", *Soc. Problems*, **16** (1968), 129–143. See also E. Stanton, *Clients Come Last*, Beverly Hills, Calif.: Sage Publications, 1970.

28. D. Bell, *The End of Ideology*, New York: The Free Press, 1960.

29. B.M. Fisher, "Claims and credibility: a discussion of occupational identity and the agent–client relationship", *Soc. Problems*, **16** (1969), 423–433.

30. M.R. Haug and M.B. Sussman, "Professional autonomy and the revolt of the client", *Soc. Problems*, **17** (1969), 153–161.

31. A.M. Carr-Saunders and P.A. Wilson, *The Professions*. Oxford: Clarendon Press, 1933; W.R. Scott, "Professionals in bureaucracies—areas of conflict", in H. Vollmer and D.L. Mills (Eds), *Professionalization*, Englewood Cliffs, N.J.: Prentice-Hall, 1966, pp. 265–275.

32. J. Ben-David, "The professional role of the physician in bureaucratized medicine: a study in role conflict", *Hum. Relat.*, **2** (Aug 1958), 901–911; G.V. Engel, "The effect of bureaucracy on the professional autonomy of the physician", *J. Health Soc. Behav.*, **10** (March 1969), 30–41.

33. C.W. Mills, *White Collar: The American Middle Class*, New York: Oxford University Press, 1951.

34. W. Kornhauser, *Scientists in Industry: Conflicts and Accommodations*, Berkeley: University of California Press, 1962.

35. F.H. Goldner and R.R. Ritti, "Professionalization as career immobility", *Amer. J. Sociol.*, **72** (March 1967), 489–502.

36. R.K. Merton, "Role of the intellectual in public bureaucracy", in *Social Theory and Social Structure*, Glencoe, Ill.: The Free Press, 1957, pp. 207–224.

37. T.S. Szasz, "The psychiatrist as a double agent", *Trans-action*, **4** (Oct 1967), 16–25; A.K. Daniels, "The captive professional: bureaucratic limitations in the practice of military psychiatry", *J. Health Soc. Behav.*, **10** (Dec 1969), 255–265; H. Garfinkel, "Some sociological concepts and methods for psychiatrists", *Psychiat. Res. Reps.* **6** (1956), 181–195.

38. W.W. Burchard, "Role conflicts of military chaplains", *Am. Sociol. Rev.*, **19** (1954), 528–535.

39. B. Barber *et al.*, *Human Experimentation*, New York: Russell Sage Foundation (1973).

40. These factors are briefly discussed in J.B. McKinlay, "Better maternity care for whom . . .?" *Med. Officer*, **70** No. 2 (1968), 273–275; A. Segal, "Workers' perceptions of mentally disabled clients: effect on service delivery", *Soc. Work* (July 1970), 39–46.

41. H.J. Osofsky, "The walls are within: an examination of barriers between middle class physicians and poor patients", in I. Deutsche and E.J. Thompson (Eds), *Among The People*, London: Basic Books, 1968, pp. 239–257.

42. See J.B. McKinlay, "Some approaches and problems in the use of services—an overview", *J. Health Soc. Behav.*, **13** (June 1972), 115–152.

43. A body of pertinent literature is reviewed in H. Gans, *The Urban Villagers*, New York: Free Press, 1962.

44. I.K. Zola, "A social scientists' perspective on the problem of 'unmotivated' clients", *Brandeis University Papers in Social Welfare*, No. 9 (Fall 1965).

45. E. Rubington and M.S. Weinberg, *op. cit.*, see note 23.

46. R.K. Merton, *Social Theory and Social Structure*, Glencoe, Ill., The Free Press, 1957, 421–436; E.M. Lemert, *Social Pathology*, New York: McGraw-Hill, 1951.

47. For a critique of this theory see J.P. Gibbs, "Conceptions of deviant behavior: the old and the new", *Pacific Sociolog. Rev.*, **9** (1966), 9–14.

48. M. Balint, *The Doctor, His Patient, and the Illness*, London: Pitman, 1968. See especially chaps. 3, 16–19.

49. D. Sudnow, "Normal crimes: sociological features of the penal code in a public defender's office", *Soc. Problems.* **12** (Winter 1965), 255–276.

50. T.J. Scheff, "Typification in the diagnostic practice of rehabilitation agencies", in M.B. Sussman (Ed.), *Sociology and Rehabilitation*, American Sociological Association, 1966, pp. 139–147.

51. It is perhaps unfortunate that Scheff employs such terms as "normal" and "valid" which, given his general perspective and argument, appear contradictory.

52. For a sophisticated treatment of typification see J.C. McKinney, *Constructive Typology and Social Theory*, New York: Appleton-Century-Crofts, 1966; J.C. McKinney, "Typification, typologies, and sociological theory", *Soc. Forces*, **48** (Sept 1969), 1–12.

53. T.J. Scheff, "Control over policy by attendants in a mental hospital", *J. Health Hum. Behav.*, **2** (1961), 93–105.

54. G.M. Sykes, "The corruption of authority and rehabilitation", in A. Etzioni (Ed.), *Complex Organizations*, New York: Holt, Rinehart and Winston, 1961, pp. 191–197.

55. J.A. Roth, *Timetables*, New York: Bobbs-Merrill, 1963; also J.A. Roth, "The treatment of tuberculosis as a bargaining process", in A. Rose (Ed.), *Human Behavior and Social Processes*, Boston: Houghton Mifflin, 1962, pp. 575–588.

56. D. Mechanic, "Sources of power of lower participants in complex organizations", *Admin. Sci. Q.*, **7** (1962), 349–364.

57. D. Clemmer, *The Prison Community*, New York: Rinehart, 1958; E.A. Cohen, *Human Behavior in the Concentration Camp*, New York: Norton, 1953; G.M. Sykes, *The Society of Captives*, Princeton, N.J.: Princeton University Press, 1958.

58. R.C. Fox, *Experiment Perilous*, Glencoe, Ill.: The Free Press, 1959; D. Sudnow, *Passing On*, Englewood Cliffs, N.J.: Prentice-Hall, 1967; B.G. Glaser and A.L. Strauss, *Awareness of Dying*, Chicago: Aldine, 1965; *Time For Dying*, Chicago: Aldine, 1968.

59. H.L. Smith, "Two lines of authority: the hospital's dilemma", *The Modern Hospital* (March 1955), Reprinted in E.G. Jaco, *Patients, Physicians and Illness*, New York: The Free Press, 1958, pp. 468–477.

60. T. Parsons, "On the concept of influence", *Public Opin. Q.*, **27** (1963), 37–62.

61. B. Danet, "The language of persuasion in bureaucracy: 'modern' and 'traditional' appeals to the Israel Customs Authorities", *Am. Sociolog. Rev.*, **37** (Oct 1971), 847–859.

62. E. Katz and B. Danet, "Petitions and persuasive appeals: a study of official–client relations", *Am. Sociol. Rev.*, **31** (Dec 1966), 811–822.

63. B. Danet, *op. cit.*, see note 61.

64. E.E. Jones, *Ingratiation*, New York: Appleton-Century-Crofts, 1964.

65. There is an interesting discussion of aspects of this phenomenon in J.A. Roth, "The Right to Quit", Unpublished manuscript, University of California at Davis, 1971.

66. E. Goffman, *Asylums*, New York: Anchor Books, 1961.

67. See A.V. Cicourel, *The Social Organization of Juvenile Justice*, New York: Wiley, 1968.

68. G. Sykes, *Society of Captives*, Princeton, N.J.: Princeton University Press, 1958.

69. F. Bouyer, *The Meaning of Monasticism*, New York: Kennedy, 1958.

70. M. Janowitz, *The Professional Soldier*, New York: Free Press, 1960; M. Greenblatt, *From Custodial to Therapeutic Care*, New York: Russell Sage Foundation, 1955.

71. E. Freidson, "Disability as social deviance", in E. Rubington and M.S. Weinberg (Eds), *Deviance: The Interactionist Perspective*, London: MacMillan 1968, pp. 117–120.

72. R. Scott, "The construction of conceptions of stigma by professional experts", in J. Douglas (Ed.), *Deviance and Respectability*, New York: Basic Books, 1970.

73. H. Garfinkel, "Conditions of successful degradation ceremonies", *Am. J. Sociol.*, **61** (March 1956), 420–424. See also J. Gusfield, "Moral passage: The Symbolic process in public designations of deviance", *Soc. Problems*, **15** (1967), 175–188.

74. Unfortunately there are few studies of intercultural variations in the definition of normalcy. This may be largely attributable to the elusiveness of the concept.

75. See for example, E. Cumming, *Systems of Social Regulation*, New York: Atherton Press, 1968. Also S. Wheeler, (Ed.), *On Record: Forms and Dossiers in American Life*, New York: Russell Sage Foundation, 1969.

76. E. Lemert, *Social Pathology*, New York: McGraw-Hill, 1951; H.S. Becker (Ed.), *The Other Side*, New York: The Free Press, 1964; J.I. Kitsuse, "Societal reaction to deviant behavior: Problems of theory and method", and K.T. Erikson, "Notes on the sociology of deviance", in H.S. Becker (Ed.), *The Other Side*.

77. H. Garfinkel, *op. cit.*, see note 73; see also R.H. Williams, "Scheler's contributions to the sociology of affective action, with special attention to the problem of shame", *Phil. Phenom. Res.*, **2** (March 1942).

78. A. Blumberg, *Criminal Justice*, Chicago: Quadrangle Books, 1967.

79. With regard to mental illness see A.K. Daniels, "Normal mental illness and understandable excuses", *Am. Behav. Sci.*, **14** (Dec 1970), 167–184.

80. B. Kutner, in T.J. Scheff, *Being Mentally Ill*, Chicago: Aldine, 1966.

81. T.J. Scheff, *Being Mentally Ill*, Chicago: Aldine, 1966.

82. T.J. Scheff, "Preferred errors in diagnosis", *Med. Care*, **2** (July–Sept 1964), 166–172.

83. There is still considerable debate over the permanence of labels. See T.J. Scheff and E. Sundstrom, "The stability of deviant behavior over time: a reassessment", *J. Health Soc. Behav.*, **11** (1970), 37–43; H.M. Trice and P.M. Roman, "Delabeling, relabeling and alcoholics Anonymous", Paper to Southern Sociological Society, New Orleans, 1969. R.D. Schwartz and J.H. Skolnick, "Two studies of legal stigma", *Soc. Problems*, **10** (1962), 133–142.

84. See, for example, E. Freidson and B. Rhea, "Processes of control in a company of equals", *Soc. Problems*, **11** (Fall 1963), 120–131; R.L. Coser, "Insulation from observability and types of social conformity", *Am. Sociol. Rev.*, **26** (Feb 1961), 28–39.

85. This phenomenon is vividly described in both K. Kesey, *One Flew Over the Cuckoo's Nest*, New York: Signet, 1962 and more recently, Z. Medvedev and Roy Medvedev, *A Question of Madness*, New York: Alfred A. Knopf, 1971.

86. N. Denzin, "The self-fulfilling prophecy and patient–therapist interaction", in Sptizer and N. Denzin, *The Mental Patient: Studies in the Sociology of Deviance*, New York: McGraw-Hill, 1968.

87. H.W. Dunham and S.K. Weinberg, in C. Perrow, "Hospitals: technology, structure and goals", in J. March (Ed.), *Handbook of Organizations*, Chicago: Rand-McNally, 1965.

88. Goffman's discussion of dramaturgy is, of course, also applicable to organizations. See E. Goffman, *The Presentation of Self in Everyday Life*, New York: Doubleday, 1959.

89. E. Goffman, *Asylums*, New York: Doubleday, 1961.

90. M. Karmel, "Total institution and self-mortification", *J. Health Soc. Behav.*, **10** (June 1969), 134–141.

91. S.G. Lubeck and L.T. Empey, "Mediatory vs. total institution: the case of the runaway", *Soc. Problems*, **16** (1968), 242–260.

92. H.S. Maas, "Sociocultural factors in psychiatric clinic service for children", *Smith College Studies in Soc. Work*, **25** (Feb 1955), 1–90.

93. D.F. Beck, *Patterns in the Use of Family Agency Service*, New York: Family Service Association of America, 1962.

94. J. Coleman, R. Janowicz, S. Fleck and N. Norton, "A comparative study of a psychiatric clinic and a family agency", *Soc. Casework*, **38** (Jan–Feb 1957), 3–8, 74–80.

95. R.A. Cloward and I. Epstein, "Private social welfare's disengagement from the poor: the case of family adjustment agencies", in M.N. Zald (Ed.), *Social Welfare Institutions*, New York: John Wiley, 1965, pp. 623–644.

96. S. Stevens, "An ecological study of child guidance intake, *Smith College Studies in Soc. Work*, **25** (Oct 1954), 73–84.

97. A.B. Hollingshead and F.C. Redlich, *Social Class and Mental Illness*, New York: Wiley, 1958.

98. E. Goffman, "On cooling the mark out: some aspects of adaptation to failure", *Psychiatry*, **15** (1952), 451–463.

99. N.H. Siegal, R.L. Kahn, M. Pollack and M. Fink, "Social class, diagnosis, and treatment in three psychiatric hospitals", *Soc. Problems*, **10** (1962), 191–196.

100. See for example, E. Greenwood, "Attributes of a profession", *Soc. Work*, **2** (July 1957), 44–45; M.L. Cogan, "Toward a definition of profession", *Harv. Educ. Rev.*, **23** (1953), 33–50; W.J. Goode, "Encroachment, charlatanism and the emerging profession: psychology, sociology and medicine", *Am. Sociol. Rev.*, **25** (Dec 1960), 902–914; H. Wilensky, "The professionalization of everyone?" *Am. J. Sociol.*, **70** (Sept 1964), 137–150; E. Freidson, *Profession of Medicine*, New York: Dodd Mead, 1970.

101. H.S. Becker, "The nature of a profession", *Sixty-First Year Book of the National Society for the Study of Education*, Part 2, *Education for the Professions*, Chicago: University of Chicago Press, 1962, pp. 27–46.

102. E.C. Hughes, "Comment to J. Roach", *Am. J. Sociol.*, **71** (July 1965), 75–76; Also relevant is B. Beck, "Welfare as a moral category", *Soc. Problems*, **14** (Winter 1967), 258–77.

103. H.S. Becker, "Some problems of professionalization", *Adult Education*, **6** (Winter 1956), 101–105.

104. W.J. Goode, "The Librarian: from occupation to profession", *Library Q.*, **31** (Oct 1961), 306–320.

105. R.A. Cloward and I. Epstein, *op. cit.*

106. E. Goffman, *Stigma*, Englewood Cliffs, N.J.: Prentice-Hall, 1963.
107. J.L. Walsh and R.H. Elling, "Professionalism and the poor: structural effects and professional behavior", *J. Health Soc. Behav.*, **9** (March 1968), 16–28.
108. G. Sjoberg, R.A. Brymer and B. Farris, "Bureaucracy and the lower class", *Sociol. Soc. Res.*, **50** (1963), 325–337.
109. For an excellent discussion of this see H.S. Becker, "The career of the Chicago public school teacher", *Am. J. Sociol.*, **57** (March 1952), 470–477.
110. R.G. Hunt, O. Gurrslin, J.L. Roach, "Social status and psychiatric service in a child guidance clinic", *Am. Sociol. Rev.*, **23** (Feb 1958), 81–83.
111. A similar problem is detectable in the United States in the advertisements beseeching businessmen not to forget the Vietnam Veteran when hiring.
112. R.A. Scott, *The Making of Blind Men*, New York: Russell Sage Foundation, 1961.
113. See the discussion of internal and external caretakers in H. Gans, *The Urban Villagers*, New York: The Free Press, 1962; R.E. Lindenberg, "Hard to reach: client or case work agency", *Soc. Work*, **3** (Oct 1958), 23–29, J.R. Gibb, "Is help helpful?", *Forum* (Feb 1964), 25–27.
114. J.B. McKinlay, *Some Aspects of Lower Working Class Utilization Behavior*, Doctoral Dissertation, Aberdeen University, Scotland, 1970.
115. M. Janowitz and W. Delaney, "The bureaucrat and the public: a study of informational perspectives", *Admin. Sci. Q.*, **2** (1957–58), 161–162.

NAME INDEX

SUBJECT INDEX

Aberdeen, Scotland, study of health and welfare services, 367–368, 369

Aberdeen, University of, 48, 74, 78

Absenteeism, 160, 161

Academic achievement, 64–65, 75, 79, 83

Academic freedom, 49, 56, 62, 82–83, 328

Accidental offender, 219

Accommodation process, 103, 112, 122–123, 125, 126

Accomplishments, socially constructed, 96

Accountability, professional, 304, 320, 324, 327, 331

Accounting process: and everyday world, 276–279; and organization and bureaucracy, 294–300; organizational structures, 280–294; "sensible" accounts, 271

Actions: legitimization of, 111; self- and other-initiated, 367; union, 171, 174–175, 176–177, 178, 180–181

Activation of commitments, 351

Activities: formal and informal patterns, 295; rule-governed, 279, 281–282, 284, 285, 286, 294

Actors: in bureaucracy, 297; in interaction theory, 220; in processual analysis, 96, 99–103, 106, 109, 114, 117; in systems theory, 94, 95; typifications of, 287. See also Participants

"Ad hoc" practices, 275, 276, 284

Adaptation: of prison, 223; of prisoners, 221, 227, 288–239, 240–241, 253

Adjustment: prisoner's, 229, 242, 243; student's, 70–71

Administration, administrator: and authority, 12, 32; compliance with, 101; hierarchical view, 341, 349; perspectives, 94; prison, 216, 217, 222; as process, 117–120; and professional aims, 314; professionals in, 346; and school teachers, 328; shop-floor, 122–123; systems theory, 94, 95; union, 155; of universities, 45, 53, 60, 61, 62, 63

Admission procedures: total institution, 354; university, 56–59, 75

Adult prisons, 226, 227, 247

"Adventist" sect, 6

Agencies: communication with clients, 347; definitions by, 355–356; diagnostic stereotypes, 348; outside, and organization, 97, 98; and the poor, 367, 368, 369, 370; religious, 6; and social classes of clients, 361, 364–365; of social control, 354–359

ALC (Ill. District, American Lutheran Church), 26, 27, 28, 29, 30–31

Alienation, 236, 339–341, 366

Alliances, 101–102

Altruism, 20, 21, 308, 352, 353

Amana Society, 6–7

America. See United States

American Baptist Convention, 7, 23

American universities, 50, 51, 52, 66, 71, 77, 78, 81

Analogy, use of, 166–167, 168

Anomie, 236, 240

"Apologia," inmate, 359

Appointment: clergy, 20–21; university, 59, 81

Architects, 321, 323, 326; firms, 314, 315

Armies, 2, 355, 358

Association of University Teachers, 62

"Attribute approach," to professions, 305–306

Authority: bureaucracy, and alienation, 340; charismatic, 12; and decision-making, 93; dual structure, 351; employers', 189; extraprofessional, 319, 324, 327–330; of lower participants, 349; of management, 200; organizational, 93; personality type, 248; and power, 160; prison accountable to, 230; of prison staff and administration, 217, 228, 235; of professional, 329, 330; professional resistance to, 303; rational-legal, 12–13, 295; and religious organization, 7, 8, 9, 17, 19, 23–31, 32; for students, 76; traditional, 12; and unions, 157, 172. See also Control; Power

Autonomy: of clergy, 19; denial of, prisoner, 228; managerial, 180, 190; professional, 303–304, 306, 308–313, 315, 320, 326, 331, 345; in religious

512959

em is to b   efore
he las